Basic Legal Writing
for Paralegals

McGraw-Hill Business Careers Paralegal Titles

McGRAW-HILL PARALEGAL TITLES: WHERE EDUCATIONAL SUPPORT GOES BEYOND EXPECTATIONS.

Building a solid foundation for a successful paralegal career is becoming more challenging as the needs of students and instructors continue to grow. The McGraw-Hill paralegal texts offer the solution to this ever-changing environment. Integrated real-world applications in each chapter teach students the practical skills needed for a thriving career in the field. A common vocabulary among all McGraw-Hill titles ensures consistency in learning. Up-to-date coverage of the available technology used in a legal setting and a purposefully designed set of pedagogical features with shared goals across the list provides the systems needed for students to fully grasp the material and apply it in a paralegal setting. With a thorough set of ancillaries and dedicated publisher support, these texts will facilitate active learning in the classroom and give students the skills sets desired by employers.

Introduction to Law & Paralegal Studies
Connie Farrell Scuderi
ISBN: 0073524638
© 2008

Introduction to Law for Paralegals
Deborah Benton
ISBN: 007351179X
© 2008

Basic Legal Research, Second Edition
Edward Nolfi
ISBN: 0073520519
© 2008

Basic Legal Writing, Second Edition
Pamela R. Tepper
ISBN: 0073403032
© 2008

Legal Research and Writing for Paralegals
Neal Bevans
ISBN: 007352462X
© 2008

Contract Law for Paralegals
Linda Spagnola
ISBN: 0073511765
© 2008

Civil Law and Litigation for Paralegals
Neal Bevans
ISBN: 0073524611
© 2008

Wills, Trusts, and Estates for Paralegals
George Kent
ISBN: 0073403067
© 2008

Legal Terminology Explained for Paralegals
Edward Nolfi
ISBN: 0073511846
© 2008

The Law Office Reference Manual
Jo Ann Lee and Marilyn Satterwhite
ISBN: 0073511838
© 2008

The Paralegal Resource Manual
Charles Nemeth
ISBN: 0073403075
© 2008

The Professional Paralegal
Allan Tow
ISBN: 0073403091
© 2009

Ethics for Paralegals
Linda Spagnola
ISBN: 0073376981
© 2009

Family Law for Paralegals
George Kent
ISBN: 0073376973
© 2009

Torts for Paralegals
ISBN: 0073376930
© 2009

Criminal Law for Paralegals
ISBN: 0073376965
© 2009

Real Estate Law for Paralegals
ISBN: 0073376957
© 2009

Law Office Management for Paralegals
ISBN: 0073376949
© 2009

Basic Legal Writing for Paralegals

Second Edition

Pamela R. Tepper

McGraw-Hill
Irwin

Boston   Burr Ridge, IL   Dubuque, IA   Madison, WI   New York   San Francisco   St. Louis
Bangkok   Bogotá   Caracas   Kuala Lumpur   Lisbon   London   Madrid   Mexico City
Milan   Montreal   New Delhi   Santiago   Seoul   Singapore   Sydney   Taipei   Toronto

McGraw-Hill
Irwin

BASIC LEGAL WRITING FOR PARALEGALS

Published by McGraw-Hill/Irwin, a business unit of The McGraw-Hill Companies, Inc., 1221 Avenue of the Americas, New York, NY, 10020. Copyright © 2008 by The McGraw-Hill Companies, Inc. All rights reserved. No part of this publication may be reproduced or distributed in any form or by any means, or stored in a database or retrieval system, without the prior written consent of The McGraw-Hill Companies, Inc., including, but not limited to, in any network or other electronic storage or transmission, or broadcast for distance learning.

Some ancillaries, including electronic and print components, may not be available to customers outside the United States.

This book is printed on acid-free paper.

1 2 3 4 5 6 7 8 9 0 QPD/QPD 0 9 8 7 6

ISBN 978-0-07-340303-8
MHID 0-07-340303-2

Editorial director: *John E. Biernat*
Publisher: *Linda Schreiber*
Associate sponsoring editor: *Natalie J. Ruffatto*
Developmental editor: *Tammy Higham*
Marketing manager: *Keari Bedford*
Marketing specialist: *Megan Gates*
Project manager: *Jim Labeots*
Senior production supervisor: *Carol Bielski*
Lead designer: *Matthew Baldwin*
Lead media project manager: *Cathy L. Tepper*
Cover design: *Studio Montage*
Cover image: *© Getty Images*
Typeface: *10/12 Times Roman*
Compositor: *GTS – New Delhi, India Campus*
Printer: *Quebecor World Dubuque Inc.*

Library of Congress Cataloging-in-Publication Data

Tepper, Pamela R., 1957-
    Basic legal writing for paralegals/Pamela R. Tepper.—2nd ed.
        p. cm. — (McGraw-Hill business careers paralegal titles)
    Rev. ed. of: Basic legal writing/Pamela R. Tepper; contributing author, Herbert
G. Feuerhake. c1992.
    Includes bibliographical references and index.
    ISBN-13: 978-0-07-340303-8 (alk. paper)
    ISBN-10: 0-07-340303-2 (alk. paper)
    1. Legal composition. I. Tepper, Pamela R., 1957-Basic legal writing. II. Title.
KF250.T467 2008
808'.06634—dc22   2006035087

Dedication

To my nephews, Matthew, Drew, and Mason, and my niece, Samantha, who are the "little lights" in my life. Whenever I needed to take a break, you were my entertainment that always made me smile.

About the Author

Pamela R. Tepper is general counsel and Vice President of Legal Affairs at the Gov. Juan F. Luis Hospital, St. Croix, U.S. Virgin Islands. Ms. Tepper worked in the Virgin Islands' Department of Justice as the Deputy Solicitor General, managing government contracts for the Territory and special projects. She has taught paralegal studies at Southeastern Paralegal Institute, Southern Methodist University, and University of Texas, Arlington campus. She continues her teaching at the University of the Virgin Islands where she teaches Legal Research and Writing in the certificate and associates degree programs. *Basic Legal Writing for Paralegals*, second edition, is one of a number of books written by Ms. Tepper, including *Contracts and the Uniform Commercial Code, Texas Legal Research*, and *Basic Legal Research and Writing*. Ms. Tepper graduated from Hamilton College with a B.A. and New England School of Law with a J.D. She is licensed to practice in Texas and the Virgin Islands.

Preface

Legal writing is a skill that can be mastered. By learning the basics of concise and effective legal writing, and appreciating the intangibles of style, the paralegal can develop an ability to render arguments in forceful and lucid prose. The paralegal can aid clients through the clear and unambiguous presentation of their positions, writing with an attribute that even many attorneys lack—*confidence.*

Frank and Ernest

Source: © 2005 Thaves. Reprinted with permission. Newspaper dist. by NEA, Inc.

The philosophy of the second edition of *Basic Legal Writing for Paralegals* has not changed. This book is designed specifically for the paralegal and the tasks performed by the paralegal. It is a comprehensive and accessible approach to basic legal writing. We have attempted to provide a foundation on which to build basic skills in legal writing. The range of communications covered in these pages is wide—from the complexity of an appellate brief to the simplicity of a cover letter. Regardless of the level of complexity, however, effective communication is always important and, for the unwary, often elusive. It has been the goal of this volume to provide the paralegal with the practical tools and, most important, the sense of clarity so necessary to the expression of ideas.

The second edition has a number of new features that enhance the book's approach. Each chapter has case studies entitled "You Be the Judge," which illustrate legal writing issues that have been addressed by the courts. The cases often show the "real-life" problems that arise in the practice of law, such as attorneys ignoring page constraints for briefs, or the effects of missed filing deadlines. The illustrations were chosen to show paralegals the importance of not only reading the rules, but following them. Many of the cases also provide insight into the ethical issues that arise for both attorneys and paralegals. Ethical issues are highlighted in the "Ethics Alert" section in each chapter. Students should pay close attention to this section as it discusses the constraints imposed on their practice. Coupled with the addition of the Ethics Alert is a section entitled "The E-Factor." With all the new developments in the world of technology since the first edition, this section introduces paralegals to the new challenges they will face with e-filings, cellular telephones, and the Internet, to name a few. Each chapter's "E-Factor" section relates a technology issue to the paralegal's areas of practice.

Every chapter has been expanded and new material added. Most chapters contain extensive checklists to guide paralegals in their writing assignments. All chapters have been updated to include the most recent changes in the field, such as the *ALWD Manual* and court procedures.

New exercises are included at the end of each chapter with one comprehensive assignment in the "Portfolio Assignment."

Two new chapters have been added to the second edition of this book. The chapter on legal research has been expanded into two, providing more examples and more in-depth treatment of computer-assisted legal research. This addition is a comprehensive review of legal research prior to beginning the study of legal writing.

The second new chapter added is "Citations in Legal Writing" (Chapter 7). Using citations in legal writing, where to place them in a legal document, and how to use punctuation in cited material are some of the topics discussed in this chapter. Examples of incorporating citations into legal writing are presented throughout the chapter, assisting the paralegal in understanding the mechanics of citing legal authority. When and how to use ellipses and brackets are addressed as well as block quotes and quotations in general. This new chapter is a valuable addition to the second edition of this book. Since the goal of this book is to be practical in approach, practice tips are identified throughout each chapter, adding to the book's usefulness in real-life practice. The practice tips offer many do's and don'ts in the practice of law as well as helpful hints and reminders for the paralegal. In addition to the practice tips, the second edition provides highlighted definitions of new and common words used in the legal profession. These definitions supplement the text of each chapter, introducing the paralegal to the many new words used in the legal profession.

As noted throughout this book, different jurisdictions have specific procedural rules to follow when submitting legal documents. Those rules should always be consulted and should be used to accompany the general writing techniques presented in this book.

ORGANIZATION OF THE TEXT

The text is composed of thirteen chapters and begins where the paralegal with a writing assignment normally begins—with legal research. The remaining eleven chapters focus on the practical aspects of legal writing. The student learns that decisions written by judges are not always models to be emulated; that the centuries-old traditions of the law are both a valued bond and a constraining hindrance to clear writing; that there are audiences to be identified, purposes to be defined, language to be chosen, arguments to be made; that there is a time for the adversarial and a time for the objective; that there are many different types of legal documents, from letters to memoranda to pleadings to briefs; and that legal writing is both fraught with pitfalls and brimming with possibilities.

TEXT DESIGN

The chapter design in the second edition is dramatically different from that of the first edition. Each chapter now begins with chapter objectives, followed by a "Case Fact Pattern" that was created to illustrate the application of legal writing concepts to the practice of law. Any reference to names and places existing in either the past or present is purely coincidental. The list of objectives is a guide to the chapter and provides a focus for understanding the concepts presented in that chapter. The chapters build on one another; therefore, it is important to master the tasks and objectives in each chapter.

Although each chapter discusses the substantive points of legal writing, the second edition provides special features as mentioned above, including "Practice Tips," "You Be the Judge," "Ethics Alert," and "The E-Factor." These sections combine practice, technology, and ethical issues that paralegals will face as they begin practice in real life. A unique section from the first edition remains at the end of each chapter, titled "Practical Considerations." Here helpful pointers and checklists are offered from the paralegal's perspective rather than the attorney's. The "Practical Considerations" section offers insights and suggests pitfalls that will guide the student when confronted with a legal writing assignment.

For convenience and review, each chapter concludes with section summaries and exercises. These summaries and review activities provide an overview of the general points discussed in the chapter and act as a study guide and quick reference. The exercises have been updated and include term mazes to reinforce the new vocabulary identified in the chapter. At the end of each chapter exercise is a comprehensive practical exercise called "Portfolio Assignment." This exercise is designed to use the skills mastered in the chapter and convert them into a practical legal document that paralegals can use as samples of their work as they begin the interview process.

The approach and the design of this text are user-friendly. Key terms are boldfaced and defined in the margins at first use, with a list of these terms appearing at the end of each chapter. Students are encouraged to write in these books, to complete the activities, and to keep this text at home or in the office as a handy reference guide. Also included in the book, promoting its user-friendly approach, are comic strips from many of our favorite illustrators from the daily newspapers. The comic strips provide a backdrop for many of the legal writing concepts discussed in the chapter, including many of the ethical issues that arise in everyday practice.

This book will engage the students and teach them about the world of legal writing in a practical, accessible manner. Hopefully, while the students are learning the concepts, they will have some fun in the process.

Acknowledgments

With any project of this magnitude, there are so many people to thank. I must start with the team at McGraw-Hill: Linda Schreiber, Tammy Higham, James Labeots, and Peter Vanaria. None of this would have been possible without all of you, especially Linda. From our first telephone calls to our meeting in Chicago, this has been a challenging and amazing experience. The vision of the team, its willingness to allow individuality, and the trust to know I could do it, is all you can ask from your publishing team. So, thank you for your suggestions and support throughout the process.

My day-to-day challenges could not have been met without the assistance of my legal assistant, Paula Henderson. She was patient with me when I was "stressing" and was calm and collected, especially when I couldn't get the computer to do what it was supposed to do. Thanks. You know how much I appreciate your support and friendship. And, Julia Beresford, you are my computer "guru" who saved me more times than I can count. What would I have done if you weren't there to help me create some of the graphics and the other "stuff". Thank you.

Thanks to all the "friends" at the hospital in St. Croix who helped me, but particularly, Greg Davila, who helped me collect my comics, and Xaulanda Simmonds-Emmanuel, for all your moral support. Nothing went unnoticed or unappreciated.

My friend and colleague, Pamela Colon, Esq., helped me find interesting examples of legal writing and was a much needed and appreciated "sounding board." I would have been lost without your suggestions and counsel. You are truly a special friend. Whenever I needed anything, you were there to support me, no matter the request. I am indebted to you.

Throughout this process my family has supported and encouraged me. My mom, Irene, and brothers, Marc and Andy, were there when I needed to just talk. But my brother, Marc, went beyond the limits for me. He offered unconditional support, both personally and professionally. Do not think it went unnoticed. You are very important to me. And, the final thank you for my family goes to my nephews, Matthew and Drew Tepper, who introduced me to the world of Internet puzzles and mazes. How would I have completed my mazes without you guys! You both were invaluable to me.

This second edition would not have been possible without the time and invaluable contributions of the reviewers. Thank you, thank you, and thank you to:

Michael W. DeWitt
Capital University
Robert Diotalevi
Florida Gulf Coast University
Janice Hoover
American Institute for Paralegal Studies
Terri Lindfors
Minnesota School of Business
Kathryn L. Myers
Saint Mary-of-the-Woods College

Linda Oliver
Chippewa Valley Technical College
Richard Patete
Keiser College-Sarasota Campus
Diane Tallarita
Leigh Carbon Community College
Chris Whaley
Roane State Community College
Timothy M. Williams
Baker College

The thoughtful suggestions you all made contributed to many of the second edition's new sections and updates. This textbook is a better text because of all of you.

I have saved the best for last. I want to publicly thank Beth Baugh, my editor, at Carlisle Publishing Services. I truly do not know where to begin. You are one of the most amazing, patient, and special human beings I know. Whenever I needed a thoughtful ear, you were there. Whenever I needed guidance and direction, you were there. I do not know how I would have survived the time schedule and the process without you. You were always gracious and never had an unkind word.

This textbook will be a success because of you. I could not have had a better editor than you. There are not enough words in the English language to express my gratitude to you. So, I hope a very heartfelt thank you will do. Thank you, Beth.

A Guided Tour

Want to learn the basics of clear, effective legal writing? The applied, practical approach of *Basic Legal Writing for Paralegals* combines legal concepts and terminology with hands-on applications in legal drafting. It provides students with all the basic tools they need to communicate effectively in the legal field. The pedagogy of the book applies three goals:

Learning Outcomes

- Critical thinking
- Vocabulary building
- Skill development
- Issues analysis
- Writing practices

Relevance of Topics without Sacrificing Theory

- Ethical challenges
- Current law practices
- Technology application

Practical Application

- Real-world exercises
- Portfolio creation
- Team exercises

Chapter Objectives

Introduce the concepts students should understand after reading each chapter as well as provide brief summaries describing the material to be covered.

Chapter 6

Effective and Persuasive Legal Writing

After completing this chapter, you will be able to:
- Inject clarity and precision into your writing.
- Define rhythm, flow, and voice.
- Use similes and metaphors to make a colorful point.
- Avoid ambiguity and redundancy.
- Make subjects and verbs agree.
- the appropriate ton your document.

Case Fact Pattern

Case Fact Pattern

 Hypothetical 6-1

Your supervising attorney has asked that you prepare a draft memorandum in support of a motion he will be filing with the trial court. You perform the necessary research and return to your office, with pages of notes and a small pile of photocopied cases and statutes. You're now confident in your knowledge of punctuation, sentence structure, and paragraphing, but you want to bring more than just grammatical correctness to this memorandum—you want to prepare a document that will persuade the court. Now that you know the rules, you want to learn to evaluate words—to use language effectively to accomplish your purpose.

147

Case Fact Pattern

Illustrates the application of legal writing concepts to the practice of law using a hypothetical case.

Practice Tips

Offer dos and don'ts in the practice of law as well as provide helpful hints and reminders for the paralegals.

Alert
The case-clipping system used by Lexis to monitor legal developments.

PRACTICE TIP

Unless you first see and understand how the law books look and interrelate, on-line research is more difficult. Spend time in your library mastering the research techniques you have learned before you attempt to use computer-assisted legal research.

Alert (formerly known as Eclipse)

Similar to Westclip, the LexisNexis electronic clipping service is now know as **Alert**. This feature allows tracking of pending legislation or regulations, new case law that relates to a particular topic or case of interest, or any area that may be of particular interest. Alert notifies you by e-mail when matters you have queried are updated.

Powerinvoice

Tracking your research by client and time spent on the matter for billing purposes is another feature on Lexis. The system identifies what was researched, who performed the research, how long the research took, and the charges for that research. The online tool shortens client billing as well as monitoring both the paralegal's and attorney's time researching a subject.

The Internet

The Internet provides virtually unlimited opportunities for legal research, although LexisNexis and Westlaw are the most comprehensive.

Many of the federal agencies post rules, regulations, and decisions pertaining to that agency. They also post legal opinions and frequently asked questions with responses from the agency. These sites can be invaluable and time-saving when researching federal matters. Most states and their agencies also have developed extensive websites with invaluable information. Check your state's websites for the extent of their references. By using any Internet search engine, you can easily access these sites.

Accessing some legal research websites on the Internet is free. One of the most comprehensive free websites is www.findlaw.com. This website allows you to find current cases, subscribe to case alerts, and many other valuable legal research resources. A website that provides more commentary and articles on the law is www.law.com. By reviewing the articles, you are alerted to current changes and trends in the law. There are also many law school libraries online and countless websites that may be helpful.

E-Factor

THE E-FACTOR

USING THE INTERNET TO YOUR ADVANTAGE

The electronic age has made it easier to find cases as well as to verify their validity. Because of that, it is inexcusable not to take the time to be thorough in a case briefing assignment. Although the Internet cannot provide the case brief and analysis for you, Lexis and Westlaw have tools that make the process more comprehensive. For example, Westlaw provides a feature that graphs the history of the prior proceedings of a case. Remember our case in Chapter 2, *U.S. v. Booker*. Figure 3.9 illustrates the appellate history of the case.

Lexis provides an appellate history feature as well. Your attorney expects that your case brief will be complete, which includes the updating process.

New cases are decided every day; these case decisions may affect a client's case. Subscribe to case alerts found in many legal websites. Lexis and Westlaw provide case alerts as well. Check the websites of courts in your jurisdiction for new opinions. Don't be left behind. Your firm's opponent surely will not!

Of course, you will need much practice to refine those skills, and you will learn much about the law along the way. Some things that you learn will surprise you—such as the fact that not all judges write with clarity. You will also learn that opinions are written assuming that readers are trained to understand legal concepts and decipher legalese. You must be prepared to overcome these obstacles. Keep your legal dictionary at hand, learn as much as you can about the substantive law, learn where to find the answers to questions that arise, persevere until you understand the problem at hand, and don't be afraid to ask for help.

As you gain experience in case briefing, you will develop your own techniques, or learn techniques preferred by your supervising attorney. For example, in order to conserve space, some firms prefer case briefs that identify the litigants (parties to a lawsuit) as *P* and *D* rather than as plaintiff, defendant, or by the Greek letter (pi) for plaintiff (delta) for

Introduces paralegals to the new challenges they will face with "e-filings," "cellular telephones," and "the Internet" to name a few. Each chapter relates a technology to the paralegal's areas of practice.

Ethics Alert

Raises legitimate ethical questions and situations attorneys and paralegals often face. Ethical issues are highlighted; students should pay close attention to this section as the constraints imposed on their practice are constantly discussed.

Ethics Alert

Know the purpose of your letter. If your intent is to harass, intimidate, or act unethically, the courts may just know how to deal with you and your attorney. In a recent Kansas case, *In re Gershater*, 17 P.3d 929 (Kan. 2001), an attorney was suspended "indefinitely" from the practice of law for sending a letter that "was vicious, offensive, and extremely unprofessional. Her letter employed a number of vile and unprintable epithets referring . . . to the attorneys in the case." *Id.* at 931 Not only did the court admonish the attorney for misrepresenting information in her correspondences but also for engaging in professional misconduct. In its observations regarding this particular attorney's conduct, the court emphatically denounced the behavior as one not befitting members of the bar:

A lawyer should be able to write a letter to an opposing party or a party with an adverse interest and intelligently communicate his or her position without the use of profane,

offensive, or derogatory language. '[A]ttorneys are required to act with common courtesy and civility at all times in their dealings with those concerned with the legal process.' *In re Vincenti*, 114 N.J. 275, 282, 554 A.2d 470 (1989). 'Vilification, intimidation, abuse and threats have no place in the legal arsenal.' *In re Mezzacca*, 67 N.J. 387, 389–90, 340 A.2d 658 (1975). 'An attorney who exhibits the lack of civility, good manners and common courtesy . . . tarnishes the entire image of what the bar stands for.' *In re McAlevy*, 69 N.J. 349, 352, 354 A.2d 289 (1976). *Id.* at 935–36.

Strong language is communicated by the court. Review the case and draw your own conclusions. Was the court justified in its sanctions of the attorney? What acts had the attorney committed for the court to impose an indefinite suspension? What was the court's reasoning and why did it use authority from other jurisdictions?

You Be the Judge

Illustrates legal writing issues that have been addressed by the courts. Students will think critically on the subjects of the chapter and make legal decisions about the hypothetical scenarios presented.

You Be the Judge

 Hypothetical 4-2

Form books can be a great help in drafting and they can also be a downfall. Losing sight of a form book's limitations and usefulness can cause attorneys and paralegals the ire of a court. Take a look at *Clement v. Public Service Electric and Gas Co.*, 198 F.R.D. 634 (D. N.J. 2001), where the use of a form book cost an attorney sanctions and public embarrassment. As the judge in the case pointed out: "[a]ttorneys who merely copy form complaints and file them in this court without conducting independent legal research and examining the facts

giving rise to a potential claim do so at their peril. Lawyers are not automatons. They are trained professionals who are expected to exercise independent judgment." *Id.* at 636. The moral of the story is: watch out for those form books. Copying the boilerplate without any thought or independent legal research can compromise your integrity and reputation. What sanctions did the court impose on the attorney? What are the facts that lead to the attorney's sanctions? Do you believe the judge's disposition was too harsh? Why or why not?

Chapter Summary

Provides a quick review of the key concepts presented in the chapter.

Summary

The legal profession uses correspondence to inform, to advise, and to confirm. Informative letters transmit information; advisory letters are more formal than informative letters and offer legal opinions; and confirmation letters create a permanent record of the oral sharing of information.

The tone of a letter varies with the audience as well as the purpose. Letters to clients should contain concrete answers and be written to the client's level of understanding. They should be drafted so as to avoid unreasonable expectations in the mind of the client. Letters to opposing counsel should be written with caution, since they may be used against your client. Letters to the court should be written with respect. You should generally send copies to opposing counsel, and be aware of the pitfalls of *ex parte* communications.

A letter generally contains the following components: a letterhead; the date on which the letter is sent; identification of the addressee; a brief, descriptive reference line; a salutation opening with "Dear" and followed by a colon; a body containing the message of the letter, which may be short or long, but which should always be written clearly; headers, which identify subsequent pages; and a closing, often "Very truly yours" followed by the signer's name and position. Note that paralegals can *never* sign letters rendering legal advice. Finally, letters show the parties to whom copies have been sent; only your file copy should show those parties to whom blind carbon copies have been sent.

The demand letter is designed to motivate a desired response—often (though not exclusively) the payment of a debt. Demand letters can be in the form of a standard collection letter; a "Fair Debt Collection" letter designed to comply with statutory requirements; a consumer protection letter; or a notice of intention to sue. In drafting a demand letter, you should state your purpose, clarify the action you expect the recipient to take, establish a deadline date, and, under most circumstances, maintain a tone that will keep channels of communication open. In responding to a demand letter, you should review and discuss the situation with your client and identify reasons why you deny the claim. The letter should deny inaccurate factual statements made by the opposition, make your position clear, and, as with a demand letter, keep the channels of communication open.

An opinion letter renders legal advice. In a client opinion letter, work to balance two competing considerations: (1) presenting legal concepts accurately; and (2) presenting them in language the client can understand. Make it clear that your analysis is based upon the facts as you understand them, and make your recommendations clear as well. A third-party opinion letter must

Key Terms

Used throughout the chapters they are defined in the margin and provided as a list at the end of each chapter. A common set of definitions is used consistently across the McGraw-Hill paralegal titles.

descriptive word index
A subject index that provides a researcher with a quick survey of specific key numbers, often from several topics, which apply to a given subject area.

The **descriptive word index** is a subject index that provides a researcher with a quick survey of specific key numbers, often from several topics, which apply to a given subject area. To use the descriptive word index, we would first analyze our legal problem so as to identify terms that serve to define the issues presented. For our landlord/tenant problem, such terms would include *subletting*. Looking in our descriptive word index under "subletting" (see Figure 2.7), we not only find the same key number from the landlord and tenant topic that we found before (that is, key number 80(2)), but also references to key numbers from entirely different topics (see, for example, the reference to key number 16(6) from the topic *Indians*, relating to the subletting of Indian lands). Although these other topics are not relevant to our current landlord/tenant problem, there will be times when the descriptive word index will help you find useful key numbers from less than obvious topics. The descriptive word index also enables you to avoid a line-by-line search through hundreds or even thousands of key number entries in the index of a more obvious topic (for example, rather than searching through the many key numbers in the "landlord and tenant" topic index, we were able to quickly find key number 80(2) by scanning Figure 2.7).

The descriptive word index might be thought of as a master index to all the key numbers contained in all the topics in the digest. Thus it is often an excellent place to start your research.

words and phrases
An index to a digest that construes a judicial term.

The **words and phrases** section of the digest is useful if your research issue turns upon the judicial construction ("construction" in this context is drawn from the verb "construe" and means "interpretation") of a specific word or phrase. The words and phrases are arranged alphabetically, with citations to those cases in which the word or phrase is construed.

Let's use a new example to demonstrate how the words and phrases section works. Suppose an important issue in a case your office is handling in the United States District Court in Pennsylvania turns upon construction of the term *shrink-wrap*. Turning to the words and phrases section of the *Federal Practice Digest, 4th* (see Figure 2.8), you see a listing for the term *shrink-wrap*. Going down the page of cases provided, you'll find that the case of *Peerless Wall and Window Coverings v. Synchronics, Inc.* was a Pennsylvania federal court case decided by the western district. The citation reads "85 F. Supp. 519 affirmed 234 F.3d 1265 and cited in headnote copyr[ight] 107." ("Copyr" is the key system's abbreviation for the topic copyright.) This tells you that the opinion begins on page 519, and under headnote (number 2) "copyr 107" of that opinion, there will be a judicial construction of the term *shrink-wrap*. See Figure 2.9, which reproduces a page from the digest and find the judicial construction.

Review Questions and Exercises

Ask students to apply critical thinking skills to the concepts learned in each chapter. The Review Questions focus on more specific legal topics and promote dialogue among students. The Exercises introduce hypothetical situations, and students will determine the correct answers using their knowledge of topics presented in the chapter. Both sets of questions are found at the end of each chapter.

majority opinion
concur
concurring opinion

Review Questions

1. What is the difference between a case brief and a brief written for a trial or appellate court?
2. What are the components of a printed opinion?
3. Why is star-paging useful?
4. What is the difference between a majority opinion and a dissent?
5. What are the components of a case brief?
6. How do you identify the relevant facts in an opinion?
7. How do you identify the issues presented by a written opinion?
8. How do you locate the procedural history of a case as set forth in the opinion?
9. What is a holding? What is a disposition?
10. What is the reasoning of an opinion?

Exercises

1. Read *Tarasoff v. Regents of the University of California*, 551 P.2d 334 (California 1976) and *Thompson v. County of Alameda*, 614 P.2d 728 (California 1980) and answer the following questions:
   a. What is the holding in Tarasoff? In Thompson?
   b. Are the results different? If so, list the reasoning of each court for reaching its decision.
   c. Can these cases be reconciled?

Portfolio Assignments

Are designed to use the skills mastered in the chapter and convert them into a practical legal document that can be used as samples of work during interviews.

Portfolio Assignment

A new client has retained your law firm. A young widow married a very wealthy elderly gentleman. They were married for nearly two years before he passed away. The husband had adult children who believe that they are entitled to 100% of their father's estate. They want the young widow to get nothing. Your state is a community property state and your attorney believes that the husband intended his widow to share in the estate with his adult children. A recent case in the U.S. Supreme Court involved a similar situation, *Marshall v. Marshall*. You know the Court decided the case in 2006 and your supervising attorney asks you to brief the case and report on it tomorrow.

Locate the case and prepare a detailed case brief. Pay particular attention to the facts and holding of the case. Would it apply to your situation?

Word Searches

At the end of each chapter utilize the key terms and definitions to help students become more familiar using their legal vocabulary.

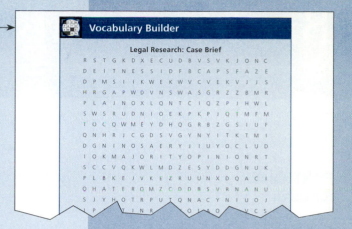

Supplements

Instructor's Resource CD-ROM

An **Instructor's Resource CD-ROM (IRCD)** will be available for instructors. This CD provides a number of instructional tools, including PowerPoint presentations for each chapter in the text, an instructor manual, and an electronic test bank. The instructor manual assists with the creation and implementation of the course by supplying lecture notes, answers to all exercises, page references, additional discussion questions and class activities, a key to using the Power Point presentations, detailed lesson plans, instructor support features, and grading rubrics for assignments. A unique feature, an instructor matrix, is also included which links learning objectives with activities, grading rubrics, and classroom equipment needs. The activities consist of individual and group exercises, research projects, and scenarios with forms to fill out. The electronic test bank will offer a variety of multiple choice, fill-in-the-blank, true/false, and essay questions, with varying levels of difficulty, and page references.

Online Learning Center

The **Online Learning Center (OLC)** is a Web site that follows the text chapter-by-chapter. OLC content is ancillary and supplementary germane to the textbook—as students read the book, they can go online to review material or link to relevant Web sites. Students and instructors can access the Web sites for each of the McGraw-Hill paralegal texts from the main page of the Paralegal Super Site. Each OLC has a similar organization. An Information Center features an overview of the text, background on the author, and the Preface and Table of Contents from the book. Instructors can access the instructor's manual and PowerPoint presentations from the IRCD. Students see the Key Terms list from the text as flashcards, as well as additional quizzes and exercises.

My Portfolio Library is an online appendix with practical examples of the types of documents paralegals will draft and are a guide for future assignments as they begin their assignment—found on the OLC.

The OLC can be delivered multiple ways—professors and students can access the site directly through the textbook Web site, through PageOut, or within a course management system (i.e.,WebCT, Blackboard, TopClass, or eCollege).

PageOut: McGraw-Hill's Course Management System

PageOut is McGraw-Hill's unique point-and-click course Web site tool, enabling you to create a full-featured, professional-quality course Web site without knowing HTML coding. With PageOut you can post your syllabus online, assign McGraw-Hill Online Learning Center or eBook content, add links to important off-site resources, and maintain student results in the online grade book. You can send class announcements, copy your course site to share with colleagues, and upload original files. PageOut is free for every McGraw-Hill/Irwin user and, if you're short on time, we even have a team ready to help you create your site! To learn more, please visit www.pageout.net.

Brief Contents

PART ONE
Research

Chapter 1   The Sources of the Law 2

Chapter 2   Legal Research Finding
             Tools 37

Chapter 3   The Case Brief 70

PART TWO
Legal Writing Basics

Chapter 4   Introduction to Legal
             Writing 103

Chapter 5   The Mechanics of
             Construction 126

Chapter 6   Effective and Persuasive
             Legal Writing 147

Chapter 7   Citations in Legal
             Writing 168

PART THREE
Practical Writing Applications

Chapter 8   The Basics of Legal
             Correspondence 192

Chapter 9   The Internal Office
             Memorandum 224

Chapter 10   The Basics of Pleadings 246

Chapter 11   Discovery 272

PART FOUR
Persuasive Writing

Chapter 12   The Memorandum of Law
             to the Trial Court 295

Chapter 13   The Appellate Brief 317

GLOSSARY 350

INDEX   357

Table of Contents

Dedication   v

About the Author   vi

Preface   vii

Acknowledgments   x

A Guided Tour   xi

PART ONE
RESEARCH

Chapter 1
The Sources of the Law   2

Legal Research in General   3
Precedential Value: Primary Authority versus
Secondary Authority   4
Finding Case Law   6
  Citations   6
  Official Reporters   8
  National Reporter System   8
  United States Supreme Court Decisions   9
  Federal Court Decisions   11
  American Law Reports (A.L.R.)   12
  Other Unofficial Reporters   13
  Looseleaf Services   13
Finding Statutes and Constitutions   16
  Slip Laws and Session Laws   16
  Codes   16
  Annotated Codes   17
  Local Ordinances   17
  Legislative History   17
  Constitutions   17
  Court Rules   17
Finding Administrative Regulations and Decisions   19
  Federal   19
  State and Local   23
The Hierarchy of the Law   23
Secondary Sources   26
  Legal Encyclopedias   26
  Restatements   30
  Treatises and Texts   30
  Law Reviews and Periodicals   30
  Looseleaf Services and Annotations   31
Practical Considerations: The Constraints
of the Internet   33

Summary   33
Key Terms   34
Review Questions   34
Exercises   34
Portfolio Assignment   35
Vocabulary Builder   36

Chapter 2
Legal Research Finding Tools   37

The Digest System   38
  Key Numbers and Digests   38
  Pocket Parts   54
Updating the Law   54
  Shepardizing   54
Online Updating: Shepard's Citations Service and
KeyCite   57
  Shepard's Citations Service   59
  KeyCite   59
Computer-Assisted Legal Research   61
  Lexis and Westlaw   61
Westlaw (www.westlaw.com)   63
Lexis (www.lexis.com)   64
  Case Law Summaries and Headnotes   64
  The Internet   64
Practical Considerations—How to Begin and
When to Stop   66
Summary   67
Key Terms   67
Review Questions   67
Exercises   68
Portfolio Assignment   69
Vocabulary Builder   69

Chapter 3
The Case Brief   70

The Case Brief Distinguished   71
The Components of a Printed Opinion   71
  Star-Paging   71
  Shorthand Case Name   71
  Parallel Citation   72
  Full Name of Case   73
  Docket Number, Court, and Date   73
  Synopsis   73
  West Key Number and Headnote   73
  Attorneys and Judge   73
  Text and Disposition   73

The Components of a Case Brief   89
  Updating the Case   89
  Reading the Case   89
  Identification of the Case   89
  Parties   91
  Issues   92
  Facts   92
  Prior Proceedings   94
  Holding   94
  Reasoning   95
  Disposition   95
Developing the Case Brief   95
Practical Considerations   96
Summary   97
Key Terms   99
Review Questions   99
Exercises   99
Portfolio Assignment   100
Vocabulary Builder   101

PART II
LEGAL WRITING BASICS

Chapter 4
Introduction to Legal Writing   103

Tradition and Trend in Legal Writing   104
Plain English   105
Prewriting Considerations   106
  Identifying the Purpose   106
  Defining and Researching the Issues   107
Constraints on Legal Writing   109
  Time Constraints   109
  Document Length   109
  Format Style   109
Organizing the Legal Document   109
  Outlining   109
  An Alternative to Outlining   114
Types of Documents   114
  Letters   115
  Internal Memoranda   115
  Transactional Documents   115
  A Few Words about Forms   116
  Pleadings   116
  Motions   116
  Briefs   118
  Discovery Documents   119
Post-Writing Considerations: Revising, Editing,
and Proofreading   119
  Revising the Document   119
  Editing the Document   120
  Proofreading the Document   121
Practical Considerations   122
Summary   123
Key Terms   123
Review Questions   123
Exercises   124

Portfolio Assignment   125
Vocabulary Builder   125

Chapter 5
The Mechanics of Construction   126

Punctuation   127
  The Comma   127
  The Semicolon   128
  The Colon   130
  Quotations   130
  Parentheses, Brackets, and the Ellipsis   131
  Hyphens and Dashes   132
  The Period   133
  Question Marks and Exclamation Points   133
  The Apostrophe   133
  Sentence Construction   133
  The Simple Sentence: Subject/Verb/Object   133
  Modifiers: Adjectives and Adverbs   134
  The Complex Sentence: Clauses   134
  The Compound Sentence   134
  *The Run-on Sentence and the Sentence
  Fragment*   135
  Active Voice versus Passive Voice   135
Paragraphing   136
  The Topic Sentence   136
  The Body   137
  The Closing Sentence   138
Transitional Language   138
Basic Grammar and Spelling Reminders:
The Trouble Spots   139
  Common Spelling Mistakes   139
  Capitalize Proper Names and Adjectives   140
  Grammar Hot Spots   140
Practical Considerations   143
Summary   143
Key Terms   144
Review Questions   144
Exercises   144
Portfolio Assignment   145
Vocabulary Builder   146

Chapter 6
Effective and Persuasive Legal Writing   147

Writing Is Reading   148
The Possibilities of Language   148
  Brevity, Clarity, and Precision   148
  Voice   149
  A Word about Tone   151
  Contractions—You Can't Say Can't   152
  Similes and Metaphors   152
Pitfalls in Language   152
  Ambiguity   152
  Misplaced Modifiers   153
  Sexism   154
  Politically Correct Terminology   154
  Clichés, Slang, and Colloquialisms   154

Jargon   155
Redundancy and Verbosity   155
Elegant Variation and the Thesaurus   156
Misused Words   156
Writing Fallacies   157
Write in the Third Person   158
A Word (or Two) about Plagiarism   158
Tell Them!   159
Topic Sentences and Transitions   159
Structured Enumeration   160
Take a Positive and Definitive Approach   160
Logical Development   161
IRAC Method   161
Strongest Argument First   162
Chronological Development   162
Outlining and Subheading   162
Practical Considerations   163
Summary   164
Key Terms   164
Review Questions   165
Exercises   165
Portfolio Assignment   166
Vocabulary Builder   167

Chapter 7
Citations in Legal Writing   168

In the Beginning . . . *The Bluebook*   169
The Young Upstart: *ALWD Citation Manual*   170
The Competition   171
The Other Guides   171
The Basic Citation Form   174
Recent Case Decisions   174
Subsequent History of a Case   174
State Subsequent History Guides   175
Federal Reporters   175
The Federal Reporter   175
The Federal Supplement   175
Federal Rules Decision   176
Federal Appendix: *A New Reporter*   176
Citing Statutes   176
Administrative Rules and Regulations   177
Code of Federal Regulations   177
Federal Register   177
The Constitution and Court Rules   177
Constitutions   177
Court Rules   177
Secondary Sources   178
Restatements   178
Law Reviews   178
Attorney General Opinions   178
A.L.R. Annotations   178
Legal Dictionaries   179
Incorporating Citations into Legal Writing   179
Citations in Sentences   179
A Shortcut: Id. *and* Supra   180
String Citing   181

Signals in Legal Writing   181
Quotations in Legal Writing   182
Practical Considerations   187
Summary   187
Key Terms   188
Review Questions   188
Exercises   188
Portfolio Assignment   190
Vocabulary Builder   190

PART III
PRACTICAL WRITING APPLICATIONS

Chapter 8
The Basics of Legal Correspondence   192

The Function of Legal Correspondence   193
The Informative Letter   193
The Advisory Letter   193
The Confirmation Letter   193
Evaluating the Audience: Tone and Style   194
The Client   194
Opposing Counsel   194
The Court   195
The Components of a Letter   195
The Letterhead   195
The Date   196
The Addressee   196
The Reference Line   197
The Salutation   197
The Body   198
The Header   199
The Closing and Signature Block   199
Referencing Initials   199
Copy and Blind Copy (cc and bcc)   200
Formatting the Letter   201
General Legal Correspondence   201
Transmittal Letters   201
Specialized Legal Correspondence   205
The Demand Letter   205
The Collection Letter   205
The Fair Debt Collection Statutory Letter   206
The Consumer Protection Letter   207
The Letter Notifying of Intention to Litigate   207
Responding to Demand Letters   210
Statutory Letters of Intent to Litigate:
Malpractice Cases   211
New Standards for Requesting Medical
Information   215
The Opinion Letter   216
The Client Opinion Letter   217
The Third-Party Opinion Letter   218
Practical Considerations   220
Summary   221

Key Terms   222
Review Questions   222
Exercises   222
Portfolio Assignment   223
Vocabulary Builder   223

Chapter 9
The Internal Office Memorandum   224

Internal Memoranda: The Basic Types   225
   An Internal Memorandum to Summarize Information   225
   Memorandum to Document Information   227
   Internal Memorandum of Law   227
The Interoffice Memorandum Distinguished   228
Preliminary Considerations   228
The Internal Memorandum of Law   229
   The Heading   229
   The Statement of Issues Presented   230
   Multiple Issues Presented   231
   Short Summary of the Conclusion   231
   Statement of Facts   232
   Discussion and Analysis   233
   The IRAC Method   234
   Conclusion   234
Post-Writing Considerations   237
Practical Considerations   242
Summary   242
Key Terms   243
Review Questions   243
Exercises   243
Portfolio Assignment   244
Vocabulary Builder   245

Chapter 10
The Basics of Pleadings   246

Pleadings in General   247
Types of Pleadings   247
Fact Pleading and Notice Pleading Distinguished   247
The Basic Components of a Pleading   249
   The Caption   249
   Title of the Pleading   250
   Body of a Pleading   250
   Signature   250
The Significance of Rule 11   250
Certificate of Service   250
Filing of Pleadings   251
The Complaint   252
The Caption   252
   Introduction   252
   The Body of the Complaint   252
   The Prayer for Relief   255
   The Signature Block and the Verification   256
   Service of Process   258
   Checklist   259

The Answer   261
   The Components of an Answer   261
   Checklist   262
Additional Pleadings   265
Amending and Supplementing Pleadings   266
   Amended Pleadings   267
   Supplemental Pleadings   267
Practical Considerations   267
Summary   268
Key Terms   269
Review Questions   269
Exercises   270
Portfolio Assignment   271
Vocabulary Builder   271

Chapter 11
Discovery   272

Discovery in General   273
Interrogatories   274
   The Caption   274
   Title   275
   The Introductory Paragraphs   275
   Instructions   275
   Definitions   275
   Interrogatories   275
   Signature Block and Certificate of Service   279
Responses to Interrogatories   279
Requests for Admissions   281
   The Introduction of a Request for Admission   281
   Text of a Request for Admission   281
   Responses to Requests for Admission   282
   Request for Production of Documents and Things   282
   Request for Medical Examination   283
The Deposition   283
   Notice of Intention to Take Oral Deposition   284
   Applicability of a Subpoena   284
   Production of Documents in Conjunction with a Deposition   284
   Deposition Preparation   285
   Digesting a Deposition   285
Discovery Motions   286
   The Motion for Protective Order   286
   The Motion to Compel Discovery   286
   The Motion for Sanctions   287
A Method of Culminating the Case: The Motion for Summary Judgment   288
Practical Considerations   290
Summary   291
Key Terms   291
Review Questions   292
Exercises   292
Portfolio Assignment   293
Vocabulary Builder   293

PART IV
PERSUASIVE WRITING

Chapter 12
The Memorandum of Law to the
Trial Court   295

The Nature and Purpose of the Memorandum of Law to
the Trial Court   296
Types of Trial Memoranda   297
   Memorandum in Regard to a Motion   297
   Memorandum at the Request of a Judge   297
   Unsolicited Memorandum Anticipating
   Legal Issues   298
Getting Ready to Write: The Prewriting
Considerations   298
The Components of a Memorandum of Law
to the Trial Court   298
   The Caption or Heading   299
   Title   299
   Introduction to the Court   299
   Issues or Questions Presented   299
   Statement of Facts   301
   The Argument   305
   Conclusion   307
   Signature Block and Certificate of Service   307
Post-Writing Review   308
Practical Considerations   311
Summary   314
Key Terms   314
Review Questions   314
Exercises   314
Portfolio Assignment   315
Vocabulary Builder   316

Chapter 13
The Appellate Brief   317

A Preliminary Note about Procedural Rules   318
The Appellate Brief Defined   319
   The Parties to the Appellate Brief   319
   The Record   321
   The Standard of Review   322

The Sections of an Appellate Brief   326
   Title or Cover Page   327
   Certificate of Interested Parties or Disclosure
   Statement   328
   Table of Contents   328
   Table of Authorities   328
   Jurisdictional Statement   330
   Statement of the Case   330
   Questions Presented   330
   Statement of Facts   330
   Summary of the Argument   331
   Argument   332
   Conclusion   333
   Signature Block   334
   Certificate of Compliance with Length
   Requirements   334
   Certificate of Service   334
   Appendix   334
The Four Categories of Appellate Briefs   335
   Appellant's Brief   335
   Appellee's Brief   335
   Reply Brief   335
   Amicus Curiac *Brief*   335
Writing the Brief   336
Practical Considerations   338
A Final Word   338
Summary   339
Key Terms   346
Review Questions   347
Exercises   347
Portfolio Assignment   348
Vocabulary Builder   349

GLOSSARY   350

INDEX   357

Part One

Research

CHAPTER 1 The Sources of the Law
CHAPTER 2 Legal Research Finding Tools
CHAPTER 3 The Case Brief

Chapter 1

The Sources of the Law

CHAPTER OBJECTIVES

After completing this chapter, you will be able to:

- Understand a citation.
- Describe the difference between official reporters and unofficial reporters.
- Differentiate between slip laws, session laws, and codes.
- Find the text of an administrative regulation.
- Use secondary sources such as legal encyclopedias and treatises.
- Explain the hierarchy of the law.
- Use the Internet to locate current cases and court rules.

Learning the law is like learning a new language. You will have to learn new words and new concepts, and face new challenges. This chapter introduces you to the "language of the law" and how it developed. You will be introduced to primary and secondary sources of the law, such as cases and encyclopedias. Building on each concept, you will begin the process of learning what the law is and how to "find" it. The process takes time and patience. And once you master the basics, you will approach each concept and assignment like a puzzle whose clues need to be unraveled. Embrace it and attack it like any other task you have studied. The most important point to remember is patience. Rome wasn't built in a day! Now, let's get started.

Case Fact Pattern Hypothetical 1-1

Your attorney was appointed to represent a criminal defendant in federal court. The defendant has his sentencing hearing tomorrow and you read on the CNN website that the U.S. Supreme Court just handed down a decision that may affect the outcome of your attorney's hearing. You hope the case has been posted on the U.S. Supreme Court website so that you can review it. Since you know the name of the case, you check the site to see if the case is available. It is! After reviewing it, you immediately bring the case to your attorney's attention. Can you use the case in the legal brief you are assisting your attorney in preparing for his court case? Does your attorney have to tell the prosecutor about the case?

Welcome to the world of legal research! The field of law is complex, with the American legal system generating over 100,000 published opinions each year, volumes upon volumes of new and existing statutory materials, and thousands of treatises and articles analyzing the evolution and application of the law. No one individual can ever hope to master every element, angle, and detail in the law library. With practice, the process does get easier. So, whenever a new situation arises requiring the application of legal principles, you will be faced once again with that question—What is the law? In this chapter and the chapters that follow in this section, you'll learn how to find answers.

LEGAL RESEARCH IN GENERAL

Congress, the fifty state legislatures, and the thousands of local legislatures all generate legislation in the form of statutes and ordinances. The federal court system, the fifty state court systems, and the local court systems all churn out written opinions. The many executive agencies and departments release regulations and quasi-judicial decisions. Moreover, these activities have been going on for years, decades, centuries! As a result, an enormous quantity of law has been produced and, theoretically, must be sorted through when addressing a legal research problem.

A comprehensive law library, the storehouse for all these materials, is indeed an impressive sight. With rows and rows of uniform volumes, shelves of multivolume treatises and statutory codes, looseleaf binders with up-to-the-minute pronouncements, computers and the Internet, the available resources are vast.

Although the volume of material that might apply to a given research problem is truly staggering, you should not throw up your hands and say "Impossible!" before you even start. Fortunately, there is help. Over the years a logical, thorough, and even ingenious system of research aids has been developed that enables you to focus on the heart of your research problem.

There are a few basic concepts to keep in mind as you begin your study of this system. First, when faced with a specific research project, you need to understand your goal before you start. Are you interested in finding out what the current law is? Are you interested in tracing the development of the law? Do you need to determine precisely what the law was at some specific time when events critical to the resolution of your client's problem occurred? Or are you simply interested in a general understanding of a new area of the law? Your approach will differ depending upon your goal.

Second, you should consciously devise an approach that is both thorough and efficient. It would be unwise to simply plunge in. The complexity of the subject matter and the potential for getting lost and confused in a mass of materials require that you think before you act.

Finally, if you do become stumped or confused, as you inevitably will, get help. Consult with your supervising attorney. Ask another paralegal. Talk to the librarian (law librarians are helpful and often extremely knowledgeable about both research in general and the peculiarities of their specific law library). Don't give up your solo efforts too quickly, but don't waste time floundering, either. Sometimes a brief tip from someone with experience can save you hours of frustration.

As your skills develop, you will begin to understand that mastering legal research is a continuing process in which new ideas and information enable you to refine and perfect your own personal approach. The following sections introduce you to some of the resources available to assist in the process. There are other resources—indeed, whole books have been written on the subject of legal research—but those described herein are the most important. Chapter 2 concludes with a discussion of some practical legal research techniques.

PRECEDENTIAL VALUE: PRIMARY AUTHORITY VERSUS SECONDARY AUTHORITY

stare decisis
Decisions from a court with substantially the same set of facts should be followed by that court and all lower courts under it; the judicial process of adhering to prior case decisions; the doctrine of precedent whereby once a court has decided a specific issue one way in the past, it and other courts in the same jurisdiction are obligated to follow that earlier decision in deciding cases with similar issues in the future.

trial courts
Courts that hear all cases and are courts of general jurisdiction.

appellate courts
The court of appeals that reviews a trial court's record for error.

state supreme court
The final and highest court in many states.

Before we discuss the many available resources, let's consider an important and basic principle that underlies all legal research.

Imagine for a moment an appellate judge sitting in her chambers, having just left the courtroom where opposing sides in an appeal have concluded oral argument. On her desk are the competing briefs, each filled with references to cases, statutes, treatises, and other sources, each presenting a compelling rationale. How does the judge weigh the relative merits of the differing points of view? How does she decide who wins and who loses?

Although every judge has a characteristic style and every case its own peculiar twist, there is in fact a pattern to the manner in which judicial decision making proceeds. That pattern is steeped in legal history and is the doctrine of **stare decisis.** *Stare decisis* means that decisions from a court with substantially the same set of facts should be followed by that court and all lower courts under it. Most of us have a general understanding of the court system, but a quick overview is appropriate before we learn how the principle of *stare decisis* works. You may recall that the courts where most controversies are filed are known as **trial courts.** Trial courts usually have the power to hear all cases and are courts of general jurisdiction. Their names range from district court to common pleas court; and the notable exception, the Supreme Court, which is the trial court in New York.

When a party from the trial court is dissatisfied with the decision of that court, an appeal may be filed. **Appellate courts** review the decisions of trial courts. Often appellate courts consist of panels of three judges who render a decision based upon the existing law of that court. The final and highest court in many states is the **state supreme court.** Most state supreme courts consist of a panel of three to nine justices. Often the state supreme courts are the court of last resort for most litigants unless the case presents a constitutional or federal issue. In those very limited instances, a state court decision may be appealed to the highest court in the United States: the U.S. Supreme Court. Let's see how these legal principles work. Suppose you live in Texas. The civil court system generally appears as in Figure 1.1.

FIGURE 1.1

Texas Civil Court System

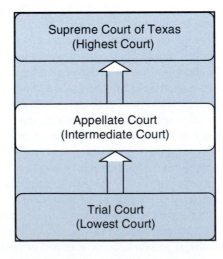

precedential value
The force that a cited authority exerts upon the judge's reasoning.

primary authority
The original text of the sources of law, such as constitutions, court opinions, statutes, and administrative rules and regulations.

mandatory authority
Authority that is binding upon the court considering the issue—a statute or regulation from the relevant jurisdiction that applies directly; a case from a higher court in the same jurisdiction that is directly on point; or a constitutional provision that is applicable and controlling.

persuasive authority
All nonmandatory primary authority.

secondary authority
Authority that analyzes the law such as a treatise, encyclopedia, or law review article.

A decision is handed down by the Dallas Appeals Court. Who must follow that decision? All trial courts under the Dallas Appeals Court and that appeals court. What about a decision from the San Antonio Appeals Court? Does that court have to follow the Dallas Appeals Court? The answer is no. However, if the case is appealed to the Texas Supreme Court, must the San Antonio Appeals Court follow that court's decision? The answer is yes. That is how the doctrine of *stare decisis* works. You will search for cases from the highest applicable court that most closely follow your legal proposition. This search leads you to cases that set the precedent for your research problem.

As a general proposition, decisions are based upon the precedential value of the competing sources cited by the parties. Legal research thus becomes a search for those authorities with the most powerful precedential value. **Precedential value** is the force that a cited authority exerts upon the judge's reasoning. In order to determine the degree of precedential value of a given authority, the judge determines whether it is primary or secondary; if primary, he or she must determine whether it is mandatory or merely persuasive.

Primary authority is composed of the original text of the sources of law—the language of court opinions, the provisions of constitutions, the requirements of statutes, the guidelines of agency regulations. Primary authority is, in effect, the law itself.

Primary authority can be either mandatory or persuasive. **Mandatory authority** is binding upon the court considering the issue—a statute or regulation from the relevant jurisdiction that applies directly; a case from a higher court in the same jurisdiction that is directly on point; or a constitutional provision that is applicable and controlling. It is best to rely upon mandatory authority in your research, because the court is compelled to follow it. If two primary authorities conflict (as where a statute has been passed to counteract a court opinion, or where principles embedded in the applicable constitution render a statute unconstitutional), the court is compelled to follow the mandatory authority.

All nonmandatory primary authority is **persuasive authority.** A case on point, but from a different jurisdiction, or from a lower or equivalent court in the same jurisdiction, would constitute persuasive authority, as would a statute on point but from a different state.

Secondary authority, on the other hand, is a step removed from the original text. It may consist of the comments of an expert expressed in a treatise. It may be found in the pages of a legal encyclopedia, or in articles in a law review, or in analysis set forth in a looseleaf service. It may include the unofficial provisions of a "restatement" of the law. Whatever the source, however, all forms of secondary authority have one thing in common—they are not the law itself, but rather analyses of the law.

Apply these concepts with a simple example. Assume you are writing a brief to be considered by an intermediate appellate court in California. A case on point decided by the California Supreme Court would constitute mandatory authority. If such a case existed and was the only applicable mandatory authority, you might not have to go further in your research. If no such case existed, and no other mandatory authority existed, then a case on point decided by the Nevada Supreme Court would constitute persuasive primary authority—which means that your California intermediate appellate court, although not bound by the Nevada decision, might at least be persuaded by its logic. Finally, in addition to citing primary authorities, you might also want to cite to the principles enunciated in a respected treatise in the applicable field. The treatise, though only a secondary authority, might be held in such esteem by the court that it, too, has substantial persuasive value. Indeed, a secondary authority might be given more persuasive weight by a court than a nonmandatory primary authority.

In the pages that follow, we will be considering numerous different authorities. As you read these pages, and later in your research, you should always keep in mind the concepts of primary and secondary authority. In the context of a specific research project, you should also consider whether a given primary authority is mandatory or merely persuasive.

FINDING CASE LAW

reporters
Hardbound volumes containing judicial decisions.

Judicial opinions, which are often simply referred to as cases, are a primary source of the law and are published in a continuing series of hardbound volumes called **reporters.** Reporters are organized not by topic but chronologically. This poses the problem of how to find those cases relevant to a given research topic without sifting through every case in every volume.

In this section and succeeding sections, we discuss methods of dealing with this obstacle. A logical starting point is the citation concept.

Citations

citation
Information about a legal source directing you to the volume and page in which the legal source appears.

We will begin by focusing on a case decided by the United States Supreme Court, *Miranda v. Arizona*, 384 U.S. 436, 86 S.Ct. 1602, 16 L. Ed. 2d 694 (1966). (You know the case. In almost every episode of television shows like *Law and Order*, people are arrested and read their rights: "You have the right to remain silent . . ."; this is the case that set forth those requirements.) But have you ever wondered where those lists of rights originated, or better yet, how to find the case? You might first ask yourself, "Why all those numbers and letters after the name of the case?" The letters and numbers, together with the name *Miranda v. Arizona*, constitute the citation for the reporter opinion. A **citation** (also called a cite) provides information that directs you to the exact page in the exact volume of each reporter in which the text of this case appears. We will analyze each component of the citation, but first a word about consistency in citation form.

As you can imagine, with the large number of courts in the American system, there are different reporters that publish judicial opinions, each requiring a unique citation. There is also a need for citations associated with statutes, regulations, municipal codes, treatises, law review articles, and other legal publications and materials. In order to minimize inconsistency in practice, standard systems of citation were developed. The leading authority for the rules on citations was *The Bluebook: A Uniform System of Citation*, published in book format by the law reviews of several leading law schools. This citation system became the universal model until 2000 when the *ALWD Citation Manual* was published. *The Bluebook* has been known to be difficult to use and master, resulting in the increasing adoption of the ALWD system. Published by Aspen Publishers, the *ALWD Citation Manual* is easier to use.

PRACTICE TIP

Because *The Bluebook: A Uniform System of Citation* has a bright blue cover, the citation system is known informally as the "bluebook system" or "bluebook format."

Although both systems are recognized, the *ALWD Citation Manual* is becoming the more acceptable alternative. The trend, however, is toward a universal system of citation, erasing the mystery of proper citation once and for all. The *Universal Citation Guide*, published by the American Association of Law Libraries in 1999, offers an alternative form for standardized citation form. Whether this system will become the ultimate "bible" for citation form is anyone's guess. Your attorneys will guide you as to the proper form to use in your jurisdiction. More detail on proper citation format and integrating it into legal writing is addressed in Chapter 7.

Now, let's return to our consideration of the citation for *Miranda v. Arizona*. First, let's take the name of the case. There are literally pages of rules on proper identification of parties in the name portion of the citation. You should check either *The Bluebook* or *ALWD Citation Manual* to review some of the trickier aspects for most cases; however, it is sufficient to remember that the name of a lawsuit (for citation purposes) will contain the last name of the parties to the lawsuit, generally the full name for a business entity (for example, "Widgets, Inc."). The party's names in the case are either underlined or italicized. For example:

Miranda v. Arizona
Miranda v. Arizona

The "v" in the middle stands for "versus." The "v" is always lowercase followed by a period (.) . The "v." is also underlined or italicized as part of the citation.

Now we turn to the remaining components of the citation. We will analyze each group of letters and numbers, one at a time.

First, 384 U.S. 436 represents that the case appears in Volume 384 of the United States Reports at page 436. Reporters are designated as either an official reporter or unofficial reporter as is often determined by the court. The official reporter for the United States Supreme Court is *U.S. Reports*.

Two basic rules can be drawn from the citation 364 U.S. 436. First, volume number always appears before the reporter's abbreviation. Second, the page number always appears after the abbreviation.

The next group of letters and number in our example is "86 S.Ct. 1602." This group refers to another reporter, published by West, called the *Supreme Court Reporter*, which also publishes Supreme Court cases. For citation purposes, it is abbreviated as *S.Ct.* Thus, the case of *Miranda v. Arizona* also appears in Volume 86 of the *Supreme Court Reporter* at page 1602. (Remember our rule: volume number before abbreviation, page number after.)

And the final group of letters and numbers in our example is "16 L. Ed. 2d 694." Like the *Supreme Court Reporter*, this group refers to yet another reporter that publishes United States Supreme Court cases, called *United States Supreme Court Reports, Lawyers' Edition,* published by LexisNexis. It is abbreviated as "L. Ed." and since the case is found in the second series of that reporter, "2d" is added to the citation. Therefore, *Miranda v. Arizona* also appears in Volume 16 of Second Series of *Lawyers' Edition* on page 694. Both the *Supreme Court Reporter* and *Lawyers' Edition* are considered unofficial reporters. You will learn more about the need for and great usefulness of such reporters in succeeding sections of this chapter.

It is important to note that recently there was a major change in legal publishing. For years, the leading legal publishers were West Publishing Company and Lawyers Cooperative Publishing Company. Both companies are now under the umbrella of the Thomson Corporation publishing under the name Thomson West.

The other leading legal publisher is Reed Elsevier, who now owns LexisNexis. You will see some legal publications under the LexisNexis brand that were previously under another publisher. You can use either set of publications; it is simply a matter of preference and availability.

When a case text is found in two or more reporters, the citations for that case are known as **parallel citations** (see Figure 1.2). When parallel citations exist, the official reporter is always listed first. Thus for *Miranda v. Arizona* the official citation, "384 U.S. 436," precedes the parallel citations "86 S.Ct. 1602, 16 L. Ed. 2d 694." We discuss official and unofficial reporters in more detail in later sections.

The final reference in the citation is (1966). This is, as you might have guessed, the year in which *Miranda v. Arizona* was decided. The year of decision, in parentheses, is always included at the end of the citation. Sometimes the name of the court that decided the case will also appear within this final parenthesis. Since some reporters publish decisions from several courts and even several states, it is sometimes impossible to discern the court by simply identifying the reporters; hence, proper citation for a case appearing in such a reporter must include identification of the specific court that decided the case.

PRACTICE TIP

To remember the important pieces of information to retrieve a case, just keep saying to yourself "volume, reporter, page."

parallel citation
A citation of a case text found in two or more reporters.

FIGURE 1.2

Parallel Citations

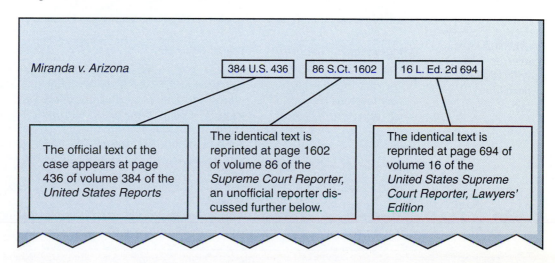

Miranda v. Arizona | 384 U.S. 436 | 86 S.Ct. 1602 | 16 L. Ed. 2d 694

The official text of the case appears at page 436 of volume 384 of the *United States Reports*

The identical text is reprinted at page 1602 of volume 86 of the *Supreme Court Reporter,* an unofficial reporter discussed further below.

The identical text is reprinted at page 694 of volume 16 of the *United States Supreme Court Reporter, Lawyers' Edition*

official reporter
Government publications of court decisions.

PRACTICE TIP

The early U.S. Supreme Court case volumes were published by private individuals (and not the U.S. government) bearing their name. You may see a citation such as *Marbury v. Madison*, 5 U.S. (1 Cranch) 137 (1803). Private reporter names appear for the first ninety volumes of the *U.S. Reports*. Do not cite the private reporter. Use a citation manual for proper citation form.

regional reporters
Reporters that contain the cases of all the states in a particular geographical area.

Citations are the keys that unlock the information in a law library. Your understanding of the citation concept will improve as you work your way through the following sections, and especially as you do your own research. Several citation exercises appear at the end of this chapter.

Official Reporters

An **official reporter** is one sanctioned by the court generating the opinions contained within its pages. The *United States Reports,* for example, is the official reporter for Supreme Court decisions, and is published by the U.S. government. Most of the states have one or more official reporters for the decisions of their various courts. Many of these are published by the respective state governments; for some states, however, the reporter designated as official is one of the unofficial reporters from the National Reporter System (to be discussed further) or some other unofficial reporter.

The citation of a case from a state that has an official reporter will list the official reporter first, generally followed by parallel citations to the National Reporter System. Check your citation manual and find the rule that establishes the appropriate order.

Official reporters are generally less useful than the unofficial reporters. The volumes are often published only long after the opinions are released, and they are generally not indexed well, limiting their usefulness for research purposes.

National Reporter System

By the end of the 1880s, the West Publishing Company of St. Paul, Minnesota (now Thomson West) had developed a reporter system covering the decisions of all the states. Called the National Reporter System, it contained seven **regional reporters** corresponding to geographic areas of the country. This system is still in use today. The seven regional reporters, with their abbreviations for citation purposes, are provided in Table 1.1.

Each of these reporters contains the decisions of the courts of several states. Table 1.2 shows the states currently covered by each reporter. Each regional reporter contains all of the decisions of the highest court, and often many of the decisions of one or more lower courts of these states for the time period covered.

As the number of volumes in each of these regional reporters reached 200 or 300, a second series was initiated, with the numbering starting over again at Volume 1. The second series is designated in a citation by the indicia "2d" appearing after the abbreviation. And now, as volumes in the second series reach 999, a third series, denoted as 3d, exists. Whereas a case in the first series of *Pacific Reporter*, for example, might have the citation "197 P. 32" (meaning the text appears at page 32 of volume 197 of the first series), a case in the second series might have the citation "5 P.2d 17" (meaning the text

TABLE 1.1
Seven Regional Reporters

Northeastern Reporter	N.E.
Atlantic Reporter	A.
Southeastern Reporter	S.E.
Southern Reporter	So.
Northwestern Reporter	N.W.
Southwestern Reporter	S.W.
Pacific Reporter	P.

TABLE 1.2
States Covered in Specific Regional Reporters

Regional Case Reporter	States Covered
Atlantic	Connecticut, Delaware, D.C., Maine, Maryland, New Hampshire, New Jersey, Pennsylvania, Rhode Island, Vermont
Northeastern	Illinois, Indiana, Massachusetts, New York, Ohio
Northwestern	Iowa, Michigan, Minnesota, Nebraska, North Dakota, South Dakota, Wisconsin
Pacific	Alaska, Arizona, California, Colorado, Hawaii, Idaho, Kansas, Montana, Nevada, New Mexico, Oklahoma, Oregon, Utah, Washington, Wyoming
Southeastern	Georgia, North Carolina, South Carolina, Virginia, West Virginia
Southwestern	Arkansas, Kentucky, Missouri, Tennessee, Texas
Southern	Alabama, Florida, Louisiana, Mississippi

advance sheets
Softcover pamphlets containing the most recent cases.

slip opinion
The first format in which a judicial opinion appears.

appears on page 17 of Volume 5 of the second series); and a later case in the third series might have the citation "117 P.3d 365" (meaning the text appears at page 365 of volume 117 of the third series).

Because the number of cases generated by the courts of California and New York is extensive, West established two separate reporters, the *California Reporter* and the *New York Supplement,* to handle the volume of opinions. Although the decisions of the highest courts of these states continue to be published in their respective regional reporters (California's in the *Pacific Reporter*; New York's in the *Northeastern Reporter*), the separate supplementary reporters publish the significant lower court decisions as well. The citation abbreviation for the *California Reporter* is Cal. Rptr., Cal. Rptr. 2d, or Cal. Rptr. 3d; for *New York Supplement* it is N.Y.S. or N.Y.S. 2d.

The National Reporter System remains current not only through the frequent publication of bound volumes, but also by issuance of **advance sheets,** which are softcover pamphlets containing the most recent cases (and paged exactly as they will later appear in the permanent bound volumes). Cases may appear in these advance sheets many months or even more than a year before they appear in an official reporter, making the regional reporters significantly more current, hence more useful, than the official reporters of most states.

Another form of a recently handed court opinion is a slip opinion. A **slip opinion** is the first format in which a judicial opinion appears. It is individually paginated (beginning with page one) and is often simply the typewritten text generated by the court's own clerical staff. In some states, slip opinions are gathered together informally in a binder or folder at the law library or the courthouse. In other states, slip opinions are published, but their high expense and delayed availability make them impractical research tools. The published slip opinion may even appear after the advance sheet version is available. With the advent of the Internet and computer-assisted research such as Westlaw and Lexis/Nexis, case decisions can be retrieved virtually the day they are handed down by the court. Online research will be discussed in more detail in Chapter 2.

Each volume in the National Reporter System contains a table of cases in the front, listing alphabetically by state all those cases whose full text appears in that volume. Each volume also contains subject indexes in the rear of the volume (the subject indexes appear near the front of the advance sheets). The foundation for these indexes is the Key Number System, which is perhaps the single most important element in American legal research. Mastering this system is essential to mastering legal research. In Chapter 2, *Legal Research Finding Tools,* you will learn the details of this system and have a clear understanding of the interrelationship between the sources of the law and finding them in the law library or online.

United States Supreme Court Decisions

The regional reporters of the National Reporter System collect cases from the fifty state court systems and territories. What about the federal courts? Where are federal decisions collected, and how do we go about finding the federal cases we need for our research? Let's start with the Supreme Court.

There are four principal sources of the decisions of the U.S. Supreme Court. You already know the three primary reporters from our discussion of the *Miranda v. Arizona* citation—*United States Reports*, *Supreme Court Reporter*, and *United States Supreme Court Reports, Lawyers' Edition*. These sources comprise bound volumes and advance sheets. There is also an important source published in looseleaf format—*The United States Law Week.*

The *United States Reports* series, as you recall, is the official series, and its publication (even the advance sheets) lags far behind the issuance of opinions, making it less useful than the other sources for research purposes. In addition, *U.S. Reports* also lacks research aids such as effective indexing by topic, available in the other sources. Perhaps the most useful contribution of *U.S. Reports* is its presentation of a syllabus (a relatively detailed summary) of each decision, prepared by the official court reporter. These syllabi, however, appear in the unofficial sources as well. Figure 1.3 shows the syllabus and introductory points of a U.S. Supreme Court slip opinion, *Tory v. Cochran.*

The *Lawyers' Edition* series is a unofficial reporter formerly published by the Lawyers Co-Operative Publishing Company and now part of LexisNexis. These volumes are now in their second series, abbreviated for citation purposes as *L. Ed. 2d.* They are indexed according to a system that categorizes points of law utilizing a case headnote system. This case headnote system is a research "finding tool" and will be addressed in detail in Chapter 2. There are two features of the *Lawyers' Edition* volumes, in addition to their timely publication, that make them useful research tools. First, they often provide summaries of the briefs of the opposing attorneys, which are not found in *U.S. Reports* or the *Supreme Court Reporter*. Second, each volume contains

FIGURE 1.3 A Syllabus of a *U.S. Reports* Case

(Slip Opinion) **OCTOBER TERM, 2004** 1

Syllabus

NOTE: Where it is feasible, a syllabus (headnote) will be released, as is being done in connection with this case, at the time the opinion is issued. The syllabus constitutes no part of the opinion of the Court but has been prepared by the Reporter of Decisions for the convenience of the reader. See *United States* v. *Detroit Timber & Lumber Co.,* 200 U. S. 321, 337.

SUPREME COURT OF THE UNITED STATES

Syllabus

name of case —

TORY ET AL. *v.* COCHRAN

court where case was appealed from —

CERTIORARI TO THE COURT OF APPEAL OF CALIFORNIA, SECOND APPELLATE DISTRICT

docket number and date of decision —

No. 03–1488. Argued March 22, 2005—Decided May 31, 2005

summary of case

Appeals Court action and decision

In a state-law defamation action filed by attorney Johnnie L. Cochran, Jr., a California trial court found that petitioner Tory, assisted by petitioner Craft and others, had, *inter alia,* falsely claimed that Cochran owed him money, picketed Cochran's office with signs containing insults and obscenities, and pursued Cochran while chanting similar threats and insults, in order to coerce Cochran into paying Tory money to desist from such libelous and slanderous activity. Because Tory indicated that he would continue to engage in the activity absent a court order, the court permanently enjoined petitioners and their agents from, among other things, picketing, displaying signs, and making oral statements about Cochran and his firm in any public forum. The California Court of Appeal affirmed, and this Court granted certiorari. After oral argument, Cochran's counsel informed the Court of Cochran's death, moved to substitute Cochran's widow as respondent, and suggested that the case be dismissed as moot. Petitioners agreed to the substitution, but denied that the case was moot.

decision of U.S. Supreme Court —

Held: Cochran's widow is substituted as respondent, but the case is not moot. Despite Cochran's death, the injunction remains in effect. Nothing in its language says to the contrary. Cochran's counsel argues that the injunction is still necessary, valid, and enforceable, and no source of California law says that it automatically became invalid upon Cochran's death. As this Court understands that law, a person cannot definitively know whether an injunction is legally void until a court has ruled that it is. Given this uncertainty, the injunction here continues significantly to restrain petitioners' speech, thus presenting an ongoing federal controversy. Cochran's death, however, makes it unnecessary for this Court to explore petitioners' basic claims. Rather, the Court need only point out that the injunction, as written, has lost its underlying rationale. Since picketing Cochran and his law offices while engaging in injunction-forbidden speech could no longer coerce Cochran to pay for desisting in this activity, the grounds for the injunction are much diminished or have disappeared altogether. Consequently the injunction amounts to an overly broad prior restraint upon speech, lacking plausible justification. Pp. 2–4.

disposition —

Vacated and remanded.

justice who authored opinion —

BREYER, J., delivered the opinion of the Court, in which REHNQUIST, C. J., and STEVENS, O'CONNOR, KENNEDY, SOUTER, and GINSBURG, JJ., joined. THOMAS, J., filed a dissenting opinion, in which SCALIA, J., joined.

justices who dissented from majority opinion —

annotations, which are in-depth articles that analyze selected issues raised in some of the more important cases appearing in that volume, and identify additional relevant cases. You will learn more about annotations in the section on the *American Law Reports* (*A.L.R.*) series.

The *Supreme Court Reporter* (citation abbreviation *S.Ct.*) is a publication of Thomson West, formerly West Publishing Company. It utilizes the key number/digest system seen in the National Reporter System, making it a useful resource for cross-referencing decisions in the state courts and the lower federal courts. As mentioned earlier, this system is the foundation for all legal research and also will be discussed in Chapter 2.

Although both the *Lawyers' Edition* and the *Supreme Court Reporter* issue advance sheets much sooner than does *U.S. Reports*, preparation of headnotes and annotations (and other production realities) still produces a lag time between issuance of the opinions and their appearance in print. To meet the immediate needs of the legal community, *The United States Law Week* publishes full texts of the decisions almost immediately upon their issuance by the Supreme Court. The *U.S. Law Week* publication is a **looseleaf service,** publishing pages with prepunched holes for insertion into looseleaf binders. In addition to the Supreme Court decisions, it contains sections on other recent legal developments. You should cite to *U.S. Law Week* only when the Supreme Court decision has not yet appeared in one of the other advance sheets (citation abbreviation *U.S.L.W.*). The *U.S. Law Week* is published weekly, with special editions when the Supreme Court is releasing substantial volumes of opinions.

There are other sources of Supreme Court decisions, as well. These include other looseleaf services (such as the *U.S. Supreme Court Bulletin*), newspapers (which are never cited as a source for the text of an opinion), and the various online computer services (which we will discuss in Chapter 2).

looseleaf service
A service that publishes recently decided court decisions in looseleaf binders, such as *U.S. Law Week*.

Federal Court Decisions

With the importance attached to decisions of the federal courts in the American legal system, it is odd to note that there is no official government reporter of federal decisions below the level of the Supreme Court. The reporters prepared by West for federal decisions are the *Federal Supplement* (publishing decisions of the United States District Courts and certain other courts since 1932) and the *Federal Reporter* (dating back to 1880 and currently publishing decisions of the appellate circuits; prior to 1932 the *Federal Reporter* published U.S. District Court cases as well). These are the standard sources for federal case law, cited respectively as *F. Supp.* or *F. Supp.2d* and *F., F.2d, or F.3d*. Federal cases prior to 1880 are collected in the West set *Federal Cases*.

When reviewing cases from the federal courts, be alert to the circuit in which your legal problem originates. This issue is important as there are twelve federal circuits and one federal circuit court (in the District of Columbia). Many of the states' federal trial courts are divided into districts. For example, Texas is divided into four districts: northern, southern, eastern, and western. (See Figure 1.4 for a map of the federal circuits and district courts.)

FIGURE 1.4

A Map of the Federal Circuits and District Courts

Source: Map from U.S. Courts, available at: www.uscourts.gov

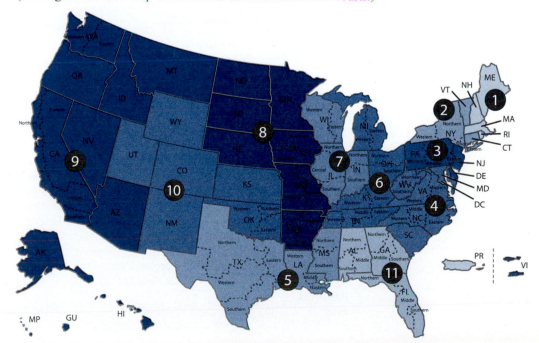

There are also several reporters in the West system that print only those federal decisions relating to a specific topic. For example, *Federal Rules Decisions* is cited as *F.R.D.* and contains decisions relating to the Federal Rules of Civil Procedure (FRCP) and the Federal Rules of Criminal Procedure. *West's Bankruptcy Reporter* (cited as *B.R.*) contains decisions of the federal bankruptcy courts.

All these West reporters utilize the key number/digest system. There are other sources of federal cases as well, including sources related to specific topics and the *A.L.R., Federal* series.

American Law Reports (*A.L.R.*)

The Lawyers Co-Operative Publishing Company produced several series of volumes in addition to the Lawyers' Edition of the *Supreme Court Reports*. In this section we discuss the *American Law Reports* series, referred to as *A.L.R.* and now published by West.

The *A.L.R.* series publishes full texts of only certain state and federal court decisions, which are selected for the level of interest generated by the issues that they address (see Figure 1.5). Each individual case selected is followed by an **annotation,** which provides an in-depth analysis of a specific and important legal issue raised in the accompanying decision, together with an extensive survey of the way the issue is treated in various jurisdictions. Many cases are cited and summarized in these annotations, making them excellent research sources. An example of the first page of such an annotation is found in Figure 1.6 and an interior page is found in Figure 1.7. The *A.L.R.* volumes are now in their sixth series, cited as *A.L.R. 6th.*

A second set of *A.L.R.* volumes is called *A.L.R. Federal*. It is structured identically to the standard *A.L.R.* series, with selected cases (all federal) followed by annotations on the federal issues presented.

annotation
An in-depth analysis of a specific and important legal issue raised in the accompanying decision, together with an extensive survey of the way the issue is treated in various jurisdictions.

FIGURE 1.5   **An Example of an** *A.L.R.* **Case**

Source: From *Annotated Law Reports.* Reprinted with permission from Thomson West.

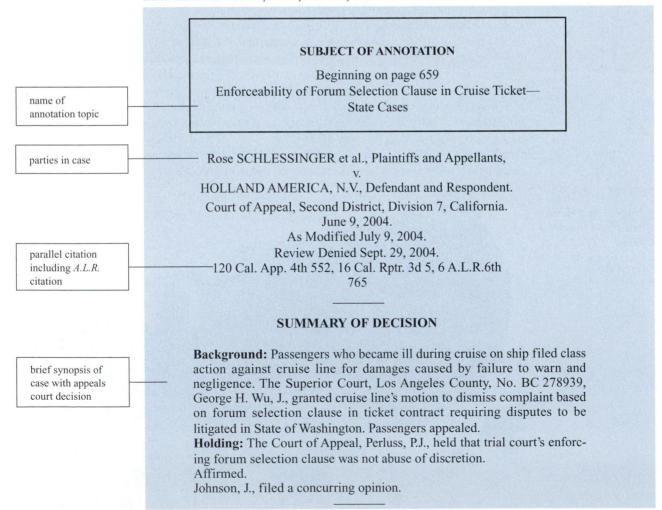

name of annotation topic

parties in case

parallel citation including *A.L.R.* citation

brief synopsis of case with appeals court decision

SUBJECT OF ANNOTATION

Beginning on page 659
Enforceability of Forum Selection Clause in Cruise Ticket—
State Cases

Rose SCHLESSINGER et al., Plaintiffs and Appellants,
v.
HOLLAND AMERICA, N.V., Defendant and Respondent.
Court of Appeal, Second District, Division 7, California.
June 9, 2004.
As Modified July 9, 2004.
Review Denied Sept. 29, 2004.
120 Cal. App. 4th 552, 16 Cal. Rptr. 3d 5, 6 A.L.R.6th
765

SUMMARY OF DECISION

Background: Passengers who became ill during cruise on ship filed class action against cruise line for damages caused by failure to warn and negligence. The Superior Court, Los Angeles County, No. BC 278939, George H. Wu, J., granted cruise line's motion to dismiss complaint based on forum selection clause in ticket contract requiring disputes to be litigated in State of Washington. Passengers appealed.

Holding: The Court of Appeal, Perluss, P.J., held that trial court's enforcing forum selection clause was not abuse of discretion.

Affirmed.

Johnson, J., filed a concurring opinion.

FIGURE 1.6   First Page of *A.L.R.* Annotation

Source: From *Annotated Law Reports.* Reprinted with permission from Thomson West.

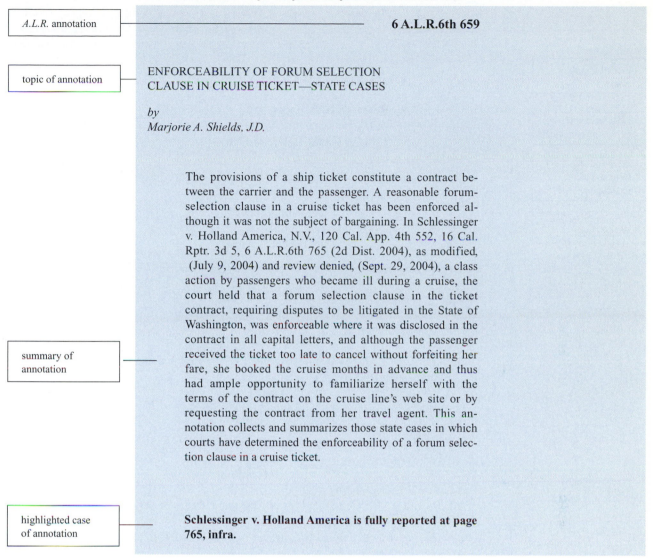

A.L.R. annotation

6 A.L.R.6th 659

topic of annotation

ENFORCEABILITY OF FORUM SELECTION
CLAUSE IN CRUISE TICKET—STATE CASES

by
Marjorie A. Shields, J.D.

summary of
annotation

The provisions of a ship ticket constitute a contract between the carrier and the passenger. A reasonable forum-
selection clause in a cruise ticket has been enforced although it was not the subject of bargaining. In Schlessinger
v. Holland America, N.V., 120 Cal. App. 4th 552, 16 Cal.
Rptr. 3d 5, 6 A.L.R.6th 765 (2d Dist. 2004), as modified,
(July 9, 2004) and review denied, (Sept. 29, 2004), a class
action by passengers who became ill during a cruise, the
court held that a forum selection clause in the ticket
contract, requiring disputes to be litigated in the State of
Washington, was enforceable where it was disclosed in the
contract in all capital letters, and although the passenger
received the ticket too late to cancel without forfeiting her
fare, she booked the cruise months in advance and thus
had ample opportunity to familiarize herself with the
terms of the contract on the cruise line's web site or by
requesting the contract from her travel agent. This annotation collects and summarizes those state cases in which
courts have determined the enforceability of a forum selection clause in a cruise ticket.

highlighted case
of annotation

**Schlessinger v. Holland America is fully reported at page
765, infra.**

There is a digest collecting all the *A.L.R.*, *A.L.R. Federal*, and *Lawyers' Edition* headnotes
arranged alphabetically by topic, called the *A.L.R. Digest.* A much more useful research aid is
the *Index to Annotations*, which indexes all the annotations in *A.L.R. 3d, A.L.R. 4th, A.L.R. 5th,
A.L.R. 6th,* and *A.L.R. Federal*.

Other Unofficial Reporters

Although the West and *A.L.R.* systems are by far the most important unofficial reporters, there are
other unofficial reporters that exist or have existed in the past in various jurisdictions. When doing
research you must make sure that you have accounted for all potential sources of cases, including
other reporter systems. This can be accomplished by conferring with your local legal librarian
or your supervising attorney, by referring to your citation manual, which lists reporters for each
jurisdiction, or by conducting your own thorough library search for potential sources. The latter
method, although more difficult, will provide you with useful exposure to the law library.

Looseleaf Services

Yet another source of case law is found in the looseleaf services, introduced in the discussion
of *U.S. Law Week* in the section on Supreme Court cases. There are a large number of looseleaf
services covering a wide variety of topics. Some of the major publishers are the Bureau of
National Affairs (BNA), Commerce Clearing House (CCH) a Wolters Kluwer business, and

FIGURE 1.7 Interior Page of *A.L.R.* Annotation

Source: From *Annotated Law Reports.* Reprinted with permission from Thomson West.

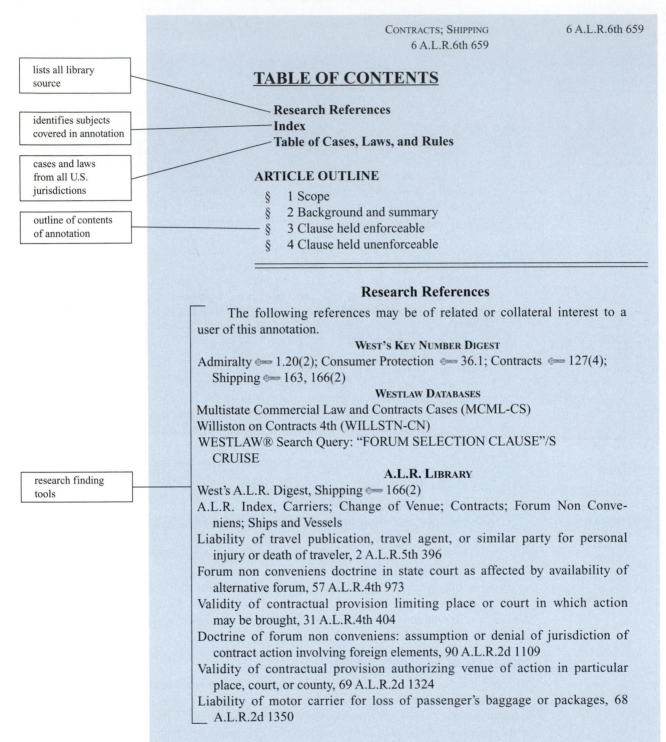

CONTRACTS; SHIPPING   6 A.L.R.6th 659

6 A.L.R.6th 659

TABLE OF CONTENTS

lists all library source ────── **Research References**

identifies subjects covered in annotation ────── **Index**

cases and laws from all U.S. jurisdictions ────── **Table of Cases, Laws, and Rules**

ARTICLE OUTLINE

outline of contents of annotation ──────

§   1 Scope
§   2 Background and summary
§   3 Clause held enforceable
§   4 Clause held unenforceable

Research References

    The following references may be of related or collateral interest to a user of this annotation.

WEST'S KEY NUMBER DIGEST

Admiralty ☞ 1.20(2); Consumer Protection ☞ 36.1; Contracts ☞ 127(4); Shipping ☞ 163, 166(2)

WESTLAW DATABASES

Multistate Commercial Law and Contracts Cases (MCML-CS)

Williston on Contracts 4th (WILLSTN-CN)

WESTLAW® Search Query: "FORUM SELECTION CLAUSE"/S CRUISE

A.L.R. LIBRARY

research finding tools ──────

West's A.L.R. Digest, Shipping ☞ 166(2)

A.L.R. Index, Carriers; Change of Venue; Contracts; Forum Non Conveniens; Ships and Vessels

Liability of travel publication, travel agent, or similar party for personal injury or death of traveler, 2 A.L.R.5th 396

Forum non conveniens doctrine in state court as affected by availability of alternative forum, 57 A.L.R.4th 973

Validity of contractual provision limiting place or court in which action may be brought, 31 A.L.R.4th 404

Doctrine of forum non conveniens: assumption or denial of jurisdiction of contract action involving foreign elements, 90 A.L.R.2d 1109

Validity of contractual provision authorizing venue of action in particular place, court, or county, 69 A.L.R.2d 1324

Liability of motor carrier for loss of passenger's baggage or packages, 68 A.L.R.2d 1350

FIGURE 1.7   Cont.

CONTRACTS; SHIPPING   6 A.L.R.6th 659
6 A.L.R. 6th 659

FORMS
Am. Jur. Legal Forms 2d, Ships and Shipping §§ 233:131, 233:136
Am. Jur. Pleading and Practice Forms, Carriers § 50

LAW REVIEWS AND OTHER PERIODICALS
Dickerson, The Cruise Passenger's Dilemma: Twenty-First Century
   Ships, Nineteenth-Century Rights, 28 Tul.Mar. L.J. 447 (2004)
O'Hara, The Jurisprudence and Politics of Forum-Selection Clauses, 3
   Chi. J. Int'l L. 301 (2002)
Robertson, Recent Developments in Admiralty and Maritime law at the
   National Level and in the Fifth and Eleventh Circuits, 27 Tul. Mar.
   L.J. 495 (2003)

ADDITIONAL REFERENCES
Appellate Materials, Appellants Reply Brief, 2004 WL 1061992
Appellate Materials, Respondent's Brief, 2004 WL 486057
Appellate Materials, Appellants Opening Brief, 2003 WL 23156187

> **KeyCite®:** Cases and other legal materials listed in KeyCite Scope can
> be researched through the KeyCite service on Westlaw®. Use KeyCite
> to check citations for form, parallel references, prior and later his-
> tory, and comprehensive citator information, including citations to
> other decisions and secondary materials.

INDEX

Age of passenger § 3
Background and summary § 2
Bargaining power, lack of § 3
Bold-face notice § 3
Burden on plaintiff contesting forum
   selection clause § 3
Cancellation of reservations § 3, 4
Capital letters § 3
Class action § 3
Contingency fee basis, inability to obtain
   counsel on § 3
Equitable tolling of limitations period
   § 3
False pretenses § 3
Federal law as governing enforceability
   of forum selection clauses § 3, 4
Fine print § 4
Food poisoning § 3

Foreign country, forum in § 3
Foreign registry § 3
Fundamental fairness § 3, 4
Illness § 3
Knowledge of provision § 3, 4
Limitations period, expiration of § 3
Maritime contracts § 3, 4
Negotiating power, lack of § 3
Notice of provision § 3, 4
Opportunity to review contract § 3
Penalty for cancellation § 3, 4
Port charges, assessment and collection
   of § 3
Preemption of field of maritime law by
   federal law § 3, 4
Presumption of validity of forum selec-
   tion clause § 3
Public policy § 3

periodicals

briefs of parties
from subject case

Westlaw
information

areas discussed
in annotation

Aspen Publishers. The specific format of each depends upon the publisher, the nature of the material covered, and the scope of the service.

A few generalizations apply to most looseleaf services. Each usually applies to only one topic; for example, the *Federal Securities Law Reporter* published by CCH relates only to laws regulating securities issuance and transactions. Weekly updates are usually provided in the form of pre-punched supplement or replacement pages to be inserted into the binder in which the service is maintained. Coverage often extends to both state and federal cases relating to the topic, as well as applicable statutes and textual analysis. Looseleaf services are often organized in a complex but extremely effective manner, with numbered paragraphs and topical indexes. For a detailed explanation, refer to the explanatory materials that are included with each service. Often cases are summarized in the text but reprinted in full in companion looseleaf volumes; these companion volumes are organized in a manner similar to reporters, and some looseleaf services ultimately reissue them in permanent bound volumes.

Many of the cases in the looseleaf services are reprinted nowhere else, not even in the reporters of the West system. For this reason, the looseleaf services can be a valuable resource. It is convenient to have textual materials and cases and statutes from many jurisdictions all in one location and with one common system of indexing. Finally, the weekly updates often make the looseleaf services the most current source of information available.

FINDING STATUTES AND CONSTITUTIONS

In addition to finding cases, you will need to locate the text of applicable statutes and constitutions. These sources of law are also organized in a logical fashion.

Slip Laws and Session Laws

The U.S. Congress and the fifty state legislatures pass many bills each year. These bills become statutes with the signature of the president or governor.

slip law
The first format in which a newly signed statute appears.

The first format in which a newly signed statute appears is called a **slip law.** A slip law is an official publication of a single statute or *act* (a group of related statutes). A slip law usually identifies a public act number or other official designation associated with this single statute or act. The federal government and most states issue slip laws, but they are rarely used for research purposes because there are other, more comprehensive formats in which the new statute will shortly appear.

session laws
The second format in which new statutes appear as a compilation of the slip laws.

The second format in which new statutes appear is a compilation called the **session laws.** Session laws are permanent collections of the statutes of one jurisdiction, printed periodically in chronological order of issuance, and with each new edition including only those laws passed since the previous edition. The federal session laws are printed in a series called the *Statutes at Large.* Each of the states has its own version of session laws.

Statutes concerning diverse subjects are generated in each legislative session, with no particular order to their issuance. Session laws are useful for checking recent legislation, but they are often inadequately indexed and difficult to use for comprehensive research.

Codes

codes
Set of volumes that groups statutes by subject matter and is well indexed, in order to make the statutes more accessible for research purposes.

The solution to the problem of research in statutes is provided by the code. A **code** is a set of volumes, issued by order of the legislature, that groups statutes by subject matter and is well indexed, in order to make the statutes more accessible for research purposes. Federal statutes are contained in the *United States Code* (cited as *U.S.C.*); check your library to find the government edition of your state's statutory code.

A code is sometimes deemed the official text of some or all of the statutes it contains. It is important to consider, for a moment, this concept of "official" as it applies to statutes. As a practical matter, if one assumes that each version of a text accurately reproduces the true text, it doesn't matter which is official. On occasion, however, the text of one version may contain an error, creating a situation where different versions of the same statute exist. Under such circumstances it becomes important to know which version—slip or session or code—is deemed by the legislature to be the official version. For the federal government, portions of the *United States Code* have been officially adopted, making the code version official for those portions; for other federal statutes, the official version is found in the *Statutes at Large.* You should check your own jurisdiction to verify which version of its statutes is the official one.

The first group of numbers in a citation to a code is the title, followed by the name of the code, and finally, the section of the statute. Section is identified as §. Two section §§ symbols together indicates more than one section such as 42 U.S.C. §§ 1-10. When you see a statute cited using the words *et seq.*, it means "and what follows." This suggests that the statute is being cited for its general contents and appears as follows: 42 U.S.C. §1 *et seq.*

annotated code
A code that provides, in addition to the text of the codified statutes, such information as cases that have construed the statute; law review articles that have discussed it; the procedural history of the statute (amendments or antecedents); cross-references to superseded codifications; cross-references to related statutes; and other information.

legislative history
The transcripts of the legislative debates leading up to the passage of the bill that became the law or statute.

rules of court
The rules that govern the litigation process in civil and criminal proceedings.

Annotated Codes

The availability of this information makes the **annotated codes** valuable reference tools. All states have at least one annotated code, and in some large states publishers issue competing versions. The principal annotated codes for the federal statutes are the *United States Code Annotated* (*U.S.C.A.*) published by West and the *United States Code Service* (*U.S.C.S.*) published by LexisNexis. A passage from *West's United States Code Annotated* appears in Figure 1.8. Note the corresponding library references, which assist in the research process.

Most state annotated codes are published in hardbound volumes updated with advance sheets and pocket parts. Some are published in looseleaf format. Provision is generally made for publication of some version of the session laws (usually without annotation, but including an index and possibly a table of codified statutes affected), which may appear even before the government's version of the session laws. You should check your law library to learn more about the annotated code in your state. An excerpt from the Texas Codes Annotated appears in Figure 1.9 along with the corresponding section of the pocket part. Notice in Figure 1.9 that the statute has not been amended or repealed.

Local Ordinances

There are far too many local systems in use to make anything but the broadest generalizations about practices regarding the publishing and availability of local ordinances. Many municipalities have a code of ordinances analogous to a statutory code. Municipal codes rarely have case citations, although there is some coverage in the individual state editions of *Shepard's*. Check your local library for more information about the system in your community.

Legislative History

Sometimes the language of a statute may not be entirely clear, and a dispute may arise over its meaning. In such a case the **legislative history** can be consulted. For some bills the legislative history can be extensive. Legislative histories for federal statutes are generally on file at the more comprehensive law libraries; for those pertaining to state statutes, you may have to dig a little deeper. Go to the state library at your state's capital or the legislative archives; check the location of these records for your own state. To obtain the legislative history of an out-of-state statute, you will almost certainly have to contact a library in that state.

Constitutions

The Constitution of the United States is reprinted and annotated in both the *U.S.C.A.* and *U.S.C.S.* It is also printed by the federal government in a separate pamphlet, and can be found as an appendix in a wide variety of sources. The availability of annotation information is as important (perhaps even more important) when researching the Constitution as when researching statutes, in that the impact and accepted meaning of the broad provisions of the Constitution can only be gauged through an analysis of court interpretations. A passage from the text of the U.S. Constitution is shown in Figure 1.10.

The text of state constitutions is likewise found in annotated state codes (and unannotated versions as well). State constitutions vary widely in terms of length and depth of coverage, with some going into great detail about the workings of state government. Access to the cases and cross-references found in the annotations remains important.

There are many other resources relating to the Constitution and state constitutions. However, for most of your purposes as a paralegal, the constitutional texts found in the annotated codes will adequately fulfill your requirements.

Court Rules

Annotated in the U.S.C.A. and U.S.C.S. and reprinted under separate cover are the **rules of court.** The court rules govern the litigation process in civil and criminal proceedings. (Civil law resolves disputes between parties and often involves some type of monetary compensation for the wrongful acts of another party. On the other hand, criminal law involves

FIGURE 1.8 A Passage from *West's United States Code Annotated*

Source: From *West's United States Code Annotated.* Reprinted with permission from Thomson West.

section from U.S. code annotation

§ 154. Regulations for preparation and sale; licenses

The Secretary of Agriculture is hereby authorized to make and promulgate from time to time such rules and regulations as may be necessary to prevent the preparation, sale, barter, exchange, or shipment as aforesaid of any worthless, contaminated, dangerous, or harmful virus, serum, toxin, or analogous product for use in the treatment of domestic animals, or otherwise to carry out this chapter, and to issue, suspend, and revoke licenses for the maintenance of establishments for the preparation of viruses, serums, toxins, and analogous products, for use in the treatment of domestic animals, intended for sale, barter, exchange, or shipment as aforesaid.

(Mar. 4, 1913, c. 145, § 1 [part], 37 Stat. 832; Dec. 23, 1985, Pub.L. 99–198, Title XVII, § 1768(b), 99 Stat. 1654.)

HISTORICAL AND STATUTORY NOTES

Revision Notes and Legislative Reports

statutory history and amendments

1985 Acts. House Report No. 99–271(Parts I and II), Senate Report No. 99–145, and House Conference Report No. 99–447, see 1985 U.S. Code Cong. and Adm. News, p. 1103.

Amendments

1985 Amendments. Pub.L. 99–198, § 1768(b), inserted "or otherwise to carry out this section".

Codifications

Another section 1768 of Pub.L. 99–198 amended section 136y of Title 7, Agriculture.

FEDERAL SENTENCING GUIDELINES

Violations of statutes and regulations dealing with any food, drug, biological product, device, cosmetic, or agricultural product, see § 2N2.1, 18 USCA.

research sources

LIBRARY REFERENCES

Administrative Law

applicable *Code of Federal Regulations*

Licensing and permits for use of biological products, see 9 CFR § 101.1 et seq.

Encyclopedias

secondary source explanation of statute topic

25 Am Jur 2d, Drugs and Controlled Substances § 129.

Forms

10 Federal Procedural Forms L Ed, Foreign Trade and Commerce § 33:1.

FIGURE 1.8 Cont.

secondary source material ⟶

> **21 § 154**   **FOOD AND DRUGS   Ch. 5**
>
> **Law Review and Journal Commentaries**
>   Federal regulation of agricultural biotechnologies. Thomas O. McGarity, U.Mich.J.L.Ref. 1089 (1987).
>
> **Texts and Treatises**
>   Food, Drugs, and Cosmetics, 13 Fed Proc L Ed § 35:491.
>
> **WESTLAW ELECTRONIC RESEARCH**
> See WESTLAW guide following the Explanation pages of this volume.
>
> **Notes of Decisions**
>
> **State regulation and control   1**
> ————————
>
> **1. State regulation and control**
>   Animal and Plant Health Inspection Service's (APHIS) preemption of state laws that "impose requirements which are different from, or in addition to, those imposed by [United States Department of Agriculture (USDA)]" regarding the safe-
>
> ty, efficacy, potency, purity, or labeling of licensed vaccines preempts inconsistent substantive state law "requirement," but not state common law remedies, and thus, common-law claims are not preempted to the extent that they seek relief for alleged violations of the federal substantive standards. Symens v. Smith Kline Beecham Corp., C.A.8 (S.D.) 1998, 152 F.3d 1050.

caselaw on topic ⟶

the wrongful acts committed by an individual against society. Normally, state and federal legislatures define those acts that violate society's standards, imposing a punishment, such as imprisonment, fines, or in extreme cases, death, for violation of those standards.) The rules used to guide the civil process in the federal courts are the Federal Rules of Civil Procedure, and for criminal cases, the Federal Rules of Criminal Procedure. These rules control the court process and are the guide for judges and attorneys in litigating or prosecuting a case.

Other types of court rules are the Rules of Evidence, governing the admission of evidence at a trial, and Rules of Appellate Procedure, governing the parties on an appeal. These rules are often located in either the federal codes or, at the local level, in state codes. The complexity of the rules of court is compounded even further because many courts have their own rules for their individual courts, known as **local rules.** These rules supplement the existing rules of court and also must be consulted when practicing in any court, whether state or federal. The local rules for the district court for the northern district of Indiana are shown in Figure 1.11.

local rules
Individual rules for a particular court that supplement the other rules of court.

FINDING ADMINISTRATIVE REGULATIONS AND DECISIONS

There is a wide variety of federal, state, and municipal agencies that issue regulations. The ability to find these regulations and the administrative decisions construing them is an important element of your skills as a paralegal.

Federal

Federal regulations have been printed for over fifty years in the *Federal Register,* a daily journal of all regulations (as well as proclamations, orders, and notices) issued by federal agencies. The *Federal Register* (cited as *Fed. Reg.*) is analogous to the *Statutes at Large* in that it publishes regulations chronologically, rather than by subject, and thus is unwieldy for comprehensive research. There is an annual compilation of all effective regulations arranged by subject, however, called

FIGURE 1.9 An Excerpt from the Texas Codes Annotated

Source: From *Vernon's* Texas Codes Annotated, Volume 4, 2005. Reprinted with permission from Thomson West.

code section

§ 17.62   **COMPETITION & TRADE PRACTICES**

Title 2

title of code section

§ 17.62. Penalties

penalty section of state

(a) Any person who, with intent to avoid, evade, or prevent compliance, in whole or in part, with Section 17.60 or 17.61 of this subchapter, removes from any place, conceals, withholds, or destroys, mutilates, alters, or by any other means falsifies any documentary material or merchandise or sample of merchandise is guilty of a misdemeanor and on conviction is punishable by a fine of not more than $5,000 or by confinement in the county jail for not more than one year, or both.

(b) If a person fails to comply with a directive of the consumer protection division under Section 17.60 of this subchapter or with a civil investigative demand for documentary material served on him under Section 17.61 of this subchapter, or if satisfactory copying or reproduction of the material cannot be done and the person refuses to surrender the material, the consumer protection division may file in the district court in the county in which the person resides, is found, or transacts business, and serve on the person, a petition for an order of the court for enforcement of Sections 17.60 and 17.61 of this subchapter. If the person transacts business in more than one county, the petition shall be filed in the county in which the person maintains his principal place of business, or in another county agreed on by the parties to the petition.

(c) When a petition is filed in the district court in any county under this section, the court shall have jurisdiction to hear and determine the matter presented and to enter any order required to carry into effect the provisions of Sections 17.60 and 17.61 of this subchapter. Any final order entered is subject to appeal to the Texas Supreme Court. Failure to comply with any final order entered under this section is punishable by contempt.

Added by Acts 1973, 63rd Leg., p. 322, ch. 143, § 1, eff. May 21, 1973.

Historical and Statutory Notes

Prior Laws:

    Acts 1969, 61st Leg., p. 1504, ch. 452, § 1.

    Vernon's Ann.Civ.St. art. 5069–10.08.

Law Review and Journal Commentaries

Taking Texas home equity for a walk, but keeping it on a short leash!, 30 Tex. Tech L.Rev. 197 (1999).

Library References

legal research references

Consumer Protection ☞ 50.

Westlaw Topic No. 92H.

C.J.S. Trade-Marks, Trade-Names, and Unfair Competition §§ 237–238.

6 Texas Pl & Pr Forms, DTPA (Deceptive Trade Practices Act) §§100A:37, 100A:42, 100A:43, 100A:46, 100A:47.

Texts and Treatises

13 Texas Jur 3d, Consum L § 6.

578

FIGURE 1.9   Cont.

case decisions on
the topic

DECEPTIVE TRADE PRACTICES   **§ 17.63**
Ch. 17   **Note 2**
                                        Notes of Decisions

Injunction violations   1   practices, credit bureau was entitled to jury trial
                                             on fact issues relating to whether credit bureau
                                             had knowingly violated the injunction and, if so,
———————   the amount of penalty to be assessed. Credit
1. Injunction violations   Bureau of Laredo, Inc. v. State (Civ. App. 1974)
   In action for civil penalties against credit   515 S.W.2d 706, error granted, affirmed 530
bureau in potential amount of $70,000 for al-   S.W.2d 288.
leged violation of injunction against deceptive

pocket part

statutory reference in
pocket part

no amendments
or changes to
statutory section

COMPETITION & TRADE PRACTICES   **§ 17.63**
Title 2
§ 17.62. Penalties

                                     Research References

ALR Library   Texas Jurisprudence Pleading & Practice Forms
   117 ALR 5th 155, Right to Private Action Under   2d Ed § 100A:34, Penalties.
      State Consumer Protection Act–Preconditions   **Treatises and Practice Aids**
      to Action.   Lange and Leopold, 4 Tex. Prac. Series § 868,
Encyclopedias   Limitation Periods on Actions for Debt.

new research
references

   TX Jur. 3d Consumer & Borrower Protection   Cochran, 27 Tex. Prac. Series § 1.5, Dtpa-Statu-
      Laws § 209, Penalties and Enforcement.   tory Approach-Overview.
Forms
   Texas Jurisprudence Pleading & Practice Forms
      2d Ed § 20:5, Petition-Multiple Grounds for
      Relief-For Disqualification from County Fair.

                                       Notes of Decisions

Federal actions   2   where, in addition to $48,890 in property damages,
                                              insureds' petition sought mental anguish damages,
———————   damages arising from future disease and medical
                                              complications, damages for costs of monitoring,
2. Federal actions   remediating and preventing mold in the future,
   The $75,000 amount in controversy requirement   treble damages and statutory damages under the
for removed diversity case was satisfied in in-   Texas Deceptive Trade Practices Act, treble dam-
sureds' action against homeowners' insurer assert-   ages and statutory damages under the Texas In-
ing breach of contract and other state law claims   surance Code, exemplary damages, and attorneys'

recent cases on
topic

arising from insurer's denial of claim filed after   fees. Lewis v. State Farm Lloyds; S.D.Tex.2002,
insureds discovered toxic mold in their house,   205 F.Supp.2d 706. Removal Of Cases ⟳ 74

FIGURE 1.10   A Passage from the Text of the U.S. Constitution

U.S. Constitution

Amendments to the Constitution of the United States of America

Articles in addition to, and amendment of, the Constitution of the United States of America, proposed by Congress, and ratified by the several states, pursuant to the Fifth Article of the original Constitution

Amendment I

Congress shall make no law respecting an establishment of religion, or prohibiting the free exercise thereof; or abridging the freedom of speech, or of the press; or the right of the people peaceably to assemble, and to petition the Government for a redress of grievances.

Article III.

Section 1.

The judicial Power of the United States, shall be vested in one supreme Court, and in such inferior Courts as the Congress may from time to time ordain and establish. The Judges, both of the supreme and inferior Courts, shall hold their Offices during good Behaviour, and shall, at stated Times, receive for their Services, a Compensation, which shall not be diminished during their Continuance in Office.

Section 2.

The judicial Power shall extend to all Cases, in Law and Equity, arising under this Constitution, the Laws of the United States, and Treaties made, or which shall be made, under their Authority;—to all Cases affecting Ambassadors, other public ministers and Consuls;—to all Cases of admiralty and maritime Jurisdiction;—to Controversies to which the United States shall be a Party;—to Controversies between two or more States;—between a State and Citizens of another State;—between Citizens of different States;—between Citizens of the same State claiming Lands under Grants of different States, and between a State, or the Citizens thereof, and foreign States, Citizens or Subjects.

In all Cases affecting Ambassadors, other public Ministers and Consuls, and those in which a State shall be Party, the supreme Court shall have original Jurisdiction. In all the other Cases before mentioned, the supreme Court shall have appellate Jurisdiction, both as to Law and Fact, with such Exceptions, and under such Regulations as the Congress shall make.

The Trial of all Crimes, except in Cases of Impeachment, shall be by Jury; and such Trial shall be held in the State where the said Crimes shall have been committed; but when not committed within any State, the Trial shall be at such Place or Places as the Congress may by Law have directed.

Section 3.

Treason against the United States, shall consist only in levying War against them, or in adhering to their Enemies, giving them Aid and Comfort. No Person shall be convicted of Treason unless on the Testimony of two Witnesses to the same overt Act, or on Confession in open Court.

The Congress shall have Power to declare the Punishment of Treason, but no Attainder of Treason shall work Corruption of Blood, or Forfeiture except during the Life of the Person attainted.

FIGURE 1.11   Local Rule for the District Court for the Northern District of Indiana

---

L.R. 5.1

General Format of Papers Presented for Filing

(a)   **Form, Style, and Size of Papers.** In order that the files of the clerk's office may be kept under the system commonly known as "flat filing," all papers presented to the clerk for filing shall be flat and unfolded. All filings shall be on white paper of good quality, 8-½" × 11" in size, and shall be plainly typewritten, printed, or prepared by a clearly legible duplication process, and double spaced, except for headings, footnotes and quoted material. The filings shall have no covers or backs and shall be fastened together at the top left corner and at no other place. The filings shall be two-hole punched at the top (the holes shall be 2 3/4" apart and appropriately centered). The title of each pleading must be set out on the first page. Each page shall be numbered consecutively. Any paper presented to the clerk for filing which contains four or more exhibits shall include a separate index identifying and briefly describing each exhibit. The court encourages the use of recycled paper.

(b)   **Signature.** Every pleading, motion, or other paper shall clearly identify the name, complete address, telephone number, facsimile number (where available) and email address (where available) of the *pro se* litigant or attorney. The original of any pleading, motion or other paper that contains a rubber stamp or facsimile signature shall be deemed unsigned for purposes of Fed. R.Civ. P. 11 and 26(g). Affidavits shall require only the signature of the affiant.

(c)   **Number of Copies; Return of File-stamped Copies.** An original and one copy of all pleadings, motions, and other papers shall be submitted for filing unless ordered otherwise. If a party wishes to receive by return mail a file-stamped copy of the pleading, motion, or paper, the party shall include an additional copy to be file-stamped, and a self-addressed envelope of adequate size and with adequate postage.

PRACTICE TIP

Pay close attention to the local rules of courts. Documents that you file may be rejected because you don't follow a local rule. If you and your attorney are practicing in a new court, *always* check the local rules of court for that court's nuances. Doing so could mean the difference between success and failure on a case, or worse, cost you your job.

the *Code of Federal Regulations* (cited and often abbreviated as *C.F.R.*). By checking the current *C.F.R.* and all subsequent issues of the *Federal Register*, you can identify those regulations effective in a given area. Figure 1.12 shows a passage from the *Federal Register;* Figure 1.13 shows a passage from the *C.F.R.*

Administrative agencies also render quasi-judicial decisions. There is no single federal publication that gathers all administrative decisions in one place, as the *C.F.R.* does for federal regulations. Rather, every agency publishes its own decisions. For example, the Equal Employment Opportunity Commission publishes its decisions in a series called *EEOC Decisions* published by Commerce Clearing House. For more specific information, you can contact the relevant agency directly or check the looseleaf services devoted to the relevant topic (these services include regulations and administrative decisions in their coverage).

State and Local

The systems employed by the states and municipalities to compile administrative regulations and decisions vary widely, although many are based loosely on the federal format already described. Some jurisdictions update their publication of regulations fairly frequently, others only occasionally. In many instances you must contact the relevant agency directly in order to identify the current effective regulations. You should learn the system that applies in your state and in any local jurisdiction in which you will be working.

THE HIERARCHY OF THE LAW

This chapter illustrated the types of primary legal source material found in legal research. They are generally constitutions, statutes, cases, court rules, and administrative rules and regulations. Remember, a primary source is the law itself. When researching, is one primary source more authoritative than another? Which one should be used and how?

The U.S. Constitution is the "supreme law" of the land. When you are researching a problem, bear in mind that the U.S. Constitution prevails over all other primary sources of the law.

FIGURE 1.12 Example of *Federal Register*

FEDERAL COMMUNICATIONS COMMISSION

47 CFR Part 76

[MB Docket No. 05–49; FCC 05–187]

Implementation of the Satellite Home Viewer Extension and Reauthorization Act of 2004; Implementation of Section 340 of the Communications Act; Report and Order

AGENCY: Federal Communications Commission.

ACTION: Final rule.

SUMMARY: In this document, the Commission adopts final rules implementing section 202 of the Satellite Home Viewer Extension and Reauthorization Act of 2004 ("SHVERA"), which creates Section 340 of the Communications Act ("Act"), and amends the copyright laws in order to provide satellite carriers with the authority to offer Commission-determined "significantly-viewed" signals of out-of-market broadcast stations to subscribers. This document satisfies the statutory mandate to adopt rules for satellite carriage of significantly viewed signals by December 8, 2005.

DATES: Effective January 26, 2006.

FOR FURTHER INFORMATION CONTACT:
For additional information on this proceeding, contact Evan Baranoff, *Evan.Baranoff@fcc.gov* of the Media Bureau, Policy Division, (202) 418–2120. For additional information concerning the Paperwork Reduction Act information collection requirements contained in this document, contact Cathy Williams, Federal Communications Commission, 445 12th St., SW., Room 1–C823, Washington, DC 20554, or via the Internet to *Cathy.Williams@fcc.gov.*

SUPPLEMENTARY INFORMATION:
This is a summary of the Federal Communications Commission's Report and Order, FCC 05–187, adopted on November 2, 2005 and released on November 3, 2005. The full text of this document is available for public inspection and copying during regular business hours in the FCC Reference Center, Federal Communications Commission, 445 12th Street, SW., CY–A257, Washington, DC 20554. These documents will also be available via ECFS (*http://www.fcc.gov/cgb/ecfs/*). (Documents will be available electronically in ASCII, Word 97, and/or Adobe Acrobat.) The complete text may be purchased from the Commission's copy contractor, Best Copy and Printing, Inc., 445 12th Street,

SW., Room CY–B402, Washington, DC 20554. To request this document in accessible formats (computer diskettes, large print, audio recording, and Braille), send an e-mail to *fcc504@fcc.gov* or call the Commission's Consumer and Governmental Affairs Bureau at (202) 418–0530 (voice), (202) 418–0432 (TTY).

Final Paperwork Reduction Act Analysis

This Report and Order contains modified information collection requirements, which were proposed in the *NPRM*, 70 FR 11314 (March 8, 2005), and are subject to the Paperwork Reduction Act of 1995 ("PRA"), Public Law 104–13, 109 Stat 163 (1995). These information collection requirements were submitted to the Office of Management and Budget (OMB) for review under section 3507(d) of the PRA and approved by OMB on May 25, 2005. In addition, the general public and other Federal agencies were invited to comment on these information collection requirements in the *NPRM*. We further note that pursuant to the Small Business Paperwork Relief Act of 2002, we previously sought specific comment on how the Commission might "further reduce the information collection burden for small business concerns with fewer than 25 employees." We received no comments concerning these information collection requirements. On June 16, 2005, the Commission announced that it had obtained OMB approval for these information collection requirements, encompassed by OMB Control Nos. 3060–0311, 3060–0888, and 3060–0960. This Report and Order adopts the following information collection requirements, as proposed in the *NPRM*.

OMB Control Number: 3060–0311.
OMB Approval Date: 05/25/05.
OMB Expiration Date: 05/31/08.
Title: 47, CFR 76.54, Significantly Viewed Signals; Method to be Followed for Special Showings.
Form Number: Not applicable.
Type of Review: Revision of a currently approved collection.
Respondents: Business or other for-profit entities.
Number of Respondents: 500.
Frequency of Response: On occasion reporting requirement; Third party disclosure requirement.
Estimated Time Per Response: 1–15 hours (average).
Total Annual Burden: 20,610 hours.
Total Annual Costs: $200,000.
Privacy Impact Assessment: No impact(s).
Needs and Uses: 47 CFR 76.54(b) provides for cable operators and

broadcast stations seeking cable carriage of "significantly viewed" signals to use the § 76.7 petition process to demonstrate "significantly viewed" status on a community basis by independent professional audience surveys. The rule changes require satellite carriers or broadcast station seeking satellite carriage of "significantly viewed" signals to use in same petition process now in place for cable operators, as required by 47 CFR 76.5, 76.7 and 76.54 of the FCC's rules.

47 CFR 76.54(c) is used to notify interested parties, including licensees or permittees of television broadcast stations, about independent professional audience surveys that are being conducted by an organization to demonstrate that a particular broadcast station is eligible for significantly viewed status under the Commission's rules. The notifications provide interested parties with an opportunity to review survey methodologies and file objections. The existing notification requirement in § 76.54(c) is retained, however, the rule changes will increase the potential number of parties that would file such notifications.

47 CFR 76.54(d) provides for cable operators and broadcast stations seeking cable carriage of "significantly viewed" signals to use the § 76.7 petition process to demonstrate "significantly viewed" status. The rule changes will expand use of the § 76.7 petition process to include petitions filed by satellite carriers or broadcast stations seeking satellite carriage of "significantly viewed" signals.

47 CFR 76.54(e) and (f) are additions to the rule. These rules will be used to notify television broadcast stations about the retransmission of significantly viewed signals by a satellite carrier into these stations' local market.

OMB Control Number: 3060–0888.
OMB Approval Date: 05/25/05.
OMB Expiration Date: 05/31/08.
Title: Part 76, Multichannel Video and Cable Television Service; Pleading and Complaint Rules; 47 CFR 76.7 Petition Procedures.
Form Number: Not applicable.
Type of Review: Revision of a currently approved collection.
Respondents: Business or other for-profit entities.
Number of Respondents: 500.
Frequency of Response: On occasion reporting requirement; Third party disclosure requirement.
Estimated Time Per Response: 4–60 hours (average).
Total Annual Burden: 16,000 hours.
Total Annual Costs: $200,000.
Privacy Impact Assessment: No impact(s).

FIGURE 1.13   Passage from *Code of Federal Regulations*

SUBCHAPTER E—VIRUSES, SERUMS, TOXINS, AND ANALOGOUS PRODUCTS; ORGANISMS AND VECTORS

PART 101—DEFINITIONS

Sec.
101.1   Applicability.
101.2   Administrative terminology.
101.3   Biological products and related terms.
101.4   Labeling terminology.
101.5   Testing terminology.
101.6   Cell cultures.
101.7   Seed organisms.

AUTHORITY: 21 U.S.C. 151–159; 7 CFR 2.22, 2.80, and 371.4.

SOURCE: 38 FR 8426, Apr. 2, 1973, unless otherwise noted.

§ 101.1   Applicability.

When used in parts 101 through 117 of this subchapter, the meaning of the words and phrases listed shall be as defined in this part.

§ 101.2   Administrative terminology.

The following administrative words and phrases shall mean:

Adjacent herd. Adjacent herds are herds physically contiguous to the herd of origin; there are no herds between an adjacent herd and the herd of origin.

Administrator. The Administrator, Animal and Plant Health Inspection Service, or any person authorized to act for the Administrator.

Animal and Plant Health Inspection Service. The agency in the Department of Agriculture responsible for administering the Virus-Serum-Toxin Act.

Biological products. The *term biological products,* also referred to in this subchapter as biologics, biologicals, or products, shall mean all viruses, serums, toxins (excluding substances that are selectively toxic to microorganisms, e.g., antibiotics), or analogous products at any stage of production, shipment, distribution, or sale, which are intended for use in the treatment of animals and which act primarily through the direct stimulation, supplementation, enhancement, or modulation of the immune system or immune response. The term "biological products" includes but is not limited to vaccines, bacterins, allergens, antibodies, antitoxins, toxoids, immunostimulants, certain cytokines, antigenic or immunizing components of live organisms, and diagnostic components, that are of natural or synthetic origin, or that are derived from synthesizing or altering various substances or components of substances such as microorganisms, genes or genetic sequences, carbohydrates, proteins, antigens, allergens, or antibodies.

(1) A product's intended use shall be determined through an objective standard and not a subjective one, and would be dependent on factors such as representations, claims (either oral or written), packaging, labeling, or appearance.

(2) The term *analogous products* shall include:

(i) Substances, at any stage of production, shipment, distribution; or sale, which are intended for use in the treatment of animals and which are similar in function to biological products in that they act, or are intended to act, through the stimulation, supplementation, enhancement, or modulation of the immune system or immune response; or

(ii) Substances, at any stage of production, shipment, distribution, or sale, which are intended for use in the treatment of animals through the detection or measurement of antigens, antibodies, nucleic acids, or immunity; or

(iii) Substances, at any stage of production, shipment, distribution, or sale, which resemble or are represented as biological products intended for use in the treatment of animals through appearance, packaging, labeling, claims (either oral or written), representations, or through any other means.

(3) The *term treatment* shall mean the prevention, diagnosis, management, or cure of diseases of animals.

Department. The U.S. Department of Agriculture.

Distributor. A person who sells, distributes, or otherwise places in channels of trade, one or more biological

Similarly, state constitutions set out the rights of its citizens. Those rights may not conflict, limit, or decrease the rights granted by the U.S. Constitution, although some state constitutions have extended rights afforded under our Constitution. That is permissible.

The next tier of primary authority is a statute. The Congress of the United States passes legislation subject to signing or veto by the president. Similarly, states have legislatures, which pass legislation signed or vetoed by their respective governors. Any statute passed must not conflict with the U.S. Constitution. And notably, state statutes may not conflict with federal statutes. Federal law preempts state law, which means that states cannot pass laws that conflict with federal law. Think about when you pass through security to board an airplane. The security check is governed by federal law, and as such, states cannot pass laws that interfere or conflict with the process.

Along with statutes, administrative rules and regulations have the full force of law. Although there are no specific constitutional provisions creating administrative agencies, Congress and state legislatures have passed legislation creating individual agencies and defining their powers. The rules and regulations that are ultimately adopted are the law.

Albeit a primary source of the law, case law interprets constitutions, statutes, and administrative rules and regulations. When cases are decided that have far-reaching social and political implications, legislatures may attempt to circumvent a case decision by passing a law that directly overturns that case law. For example, a court finds that burning the American flag is free speech under the First Amendment of the U.S. Constitution. Congress disagrees with that result and passes a statute that makes it illegal to burn the American flag. Now, the law is challenged in court. The U.S. Supreme Court finds that the law violates the U.S. Constitution. If the Court holds that the statute violates the Constitution, then the law is struck down. Therein lies the dichotomy of the law through its hierarchy.

The goal in legal research is to find the best primary sources of the law that apply to your research problem. Unfortunately, the primary sources of the law are not always the most instructive on the subject. Often, it is easier to understand the law or begin your legal research by reviewing a source that presents an overview of a topic. Those sources are the secondary source material defined in the next section.

SECONDARY SOURCES

All the materials we've discussed in this chapter have been primary sources. There are a variety of secondary sources as well—sources a step removed from the primary authority, but valuable for their analytic insights and useful explanations.

Legal Encyclopedias

legal encyclopedia
A multivolume compilation that provides in-depth coverage of every area of the law.

A **legal encyclopedia** is a multivolume compilation that provides in-depth coverage of every area of the law. Such a purpose is difficult to achieve in practice: Legal encyclopedias tend to overgeneralize and are thus rarely cited as authority for a point of law. They should not be disregarded in conducting research, however, since they provide useful general information about a broad range of topics, and can thus be used to obtain background information about an unfamiliar area. They also provide citations to cases, a useful starting point for research. Encyclopedias use footnotes extensively to communicate relevant information. Be sure to review the footnotes when reading a legal encyclopedia.

There are two well-known legal encyclopedias, both now West publications. The first is called *Corpus Juris Secundum* (cited as *C.J.S.*). The *C.J.S.* set references the West Key Number System, so that researchers can often go directly from the encyclopedia review to the appropriate digest volume to find relevant case law quickly. (The key system is discussed in Chapter 2.) Figure 1.14 is an example of a List of Titles in *C.J.S.* with Figure 1.15 referencing a passage from the section on Landlord & Tenant.

The second set, *American Jurisprudence, 2d* (cited as *Am. Jur. 2d*), includes references to *A.L.R.* annotations as well as cases from all reporters. Like *C.J.S.*, *Am. Jur. 2d* is very useful for learning and as a starting place for research but is not looked upon as authoritative. A page from *Am. Jur. 2d* is referenced in Figure 1.16. The subject of the topic is landlord/tenant relations. Compare the *Am. Jur.* and *C.J.S.* texts on the landlord and tenant issue.

Encyclopedias have also been published summarizing the law of some of the larger states, including Texas (*Texas Jurisprudence 2d*), New York (*New York Jurisprudence 2d*), Illinois (*Illinois Law and Practice*), and several others. These encyclopedias have strengths and limitations similar to those of *C.J.S.* and *Am. Jur. 2d*.

FIGURE 1.14   List of Titles in *Corpus Juris Secundum*

Source: From *Corpus Juris Secundum*. Reprinted with permission from Thomson West.

LIST OF TITLES
IN
CORPUS JURIS SECUNDUM

Abandonment
Abatement and Revival
Abduction
Abortion and Birth Control;
  Family Planning
Absentees
Abstracts of Title
Accession
Accord and Satisfaction
Account, Action on
Accountants
Accounting
Account Stated
Acknowledgments
Actions
Adjoining Landowners
Admiralty
Adoption of Persons
Adulteration
Adultery
Adverse Possession
Aeronautics and Aerospace
Affidavits
Affray
Agency
Agriculture
Aliens
Alteration of Instruments
Ambassadors and Consuls
Amicus Curiae
Animals
Annuities
Appeal and Error
Appearances
Apprentices
Arbitration
Architects
Armed Services
Arrest
Arson
Assault and Battery
Assignments
Assistance, Writ of
Associations

Assumpsit, Action of
Asylums and Institutional Care
  Facilities
Attachment
Attorney and Client
Attorney General
Auctions and Auctioneers
Audita Querela
Bail; Release and Detention
  Pending Proceedings
Bailments
Bankruptcy
Banks and Banking
Beneficial Associations
Bigamy and Related Offenses
Bills and Notes; Letters of Credit
Bonds
Boundaries
Breach of Marriage Promise
Breach of the Peace
Bribery
Bridges
Brokers
Building and Loan Associations,
  Savings and Loan Associations,
  and Credit Unions
Burglary
Business Trusts
Canals
Cancellation of Instruments;
  Rescission
Carriers
Cemeteries
Census
Certiorari
Champerty and Maintenance;
  Barratry and Related Matters
Charities
Chemical Dependents
Children Out-of-Wedlock
Citizens
Civil Rights
Clubs
Colleges and Universities

Collision
Commerce
Common Lands
Common Law
Compounding Offenses
Compromise and Settlement
Concealment of Birth or Death
Conflict of Laws
Confusion of Goods
Conspiracy
Constitutional Law
Contempt
Continuances
Contracts
Contribution
Conversion
Convicts
Copyrights and Intellectual
  Property
Coroners and Medical Examiners
Corporations
Costs
Counterfeiting
Counties
Courts
Covenants
Credit Reporting Agencies;
  Consumer Protection
Creditor and Debtor
Criminal Law
Crops
Customs and Usages
Customs Duties
Damages
Dead Bodies
Death
Debt, Action of
Declaratory Judgments
Dedication
Deeds
Depositaries
Depositions
Deposits in Court
Descent and Distribution

FIGURE 1.15   Landlord and Tenant Reference in *Corpus Juris Secundum*

Source: From *Corpus Juris Secundum*. Reprinted with permission from Thomson West.

LANDLORD & TENANT   § 60

privity of contract.[2] However, by merely assigning a lease, the lessee only places the assignee in the same relationship with the lessor as was occupied by the lessee, and nothing else is implied as against the assignor.[3]

Assignee's liability to assignor.

Where an assignee covenants to perform all the covenants in the original lease, he or she is liable to the lessee-assignor in the same manner as the lessee is liable to the original lessor.[4] Where the lessee, after assigning his or her lease, receives a new lease from the landlord to commence on the expiration of the original lease, and the assignee holds over after such expiration, the lessee can recover from the assignee whatever damages are the natural and proximate result of the wrongful trespass of the assignee.[5]

6. *Construction and Operation of Subleases*

§ 59 Generally

A sublease creates a new estate; the construction and operation of a sublease depend generally on the language of the agreement and the circumstances of the case.

Research References

324 Ill. App. 229, 57 N.E.2d 756 (1st Dist. 1944).

Mass.—Maybury Shoe Co. v. Izenstatt, 320 Mass. 397, 69 N.E.2d 666 (1946).

N.J.—Conover v. Solar Oil Co., 14 N.J. Misc. 127, 182 A868 (Sup. Ct. 1936).

[2]Ky.—Entroth Shoe Co. v. Johnson, 260 Ky. 309, 85 S.W.2d 686 (1935).

Minn.—Kostakes v. Daly, 246 Minn. 312, 75 N.W.2d 191 (1956).

[3]Neb.—Beltner v. Carlson, 153 Neb. 797, 46 N.W.2d 153 (1951).

[4]Ariz.—Catalina Groves v. Oliver, 73 Ariz. 38, 236 P.2d 1022 (1951).

Iowa—L. P. Courshon Co. v. Brewer, 215 Iowa 885, 245 N.W. 354 (1932).

[5]Pa.—Taylor v. Kaufhold, 368 Pa. 538, 84 A.2d 347, 32 A.L.R.2d 575 (1951).

[Section 59]

§ 49.

[2]Ark.—Jaber v. Miller, 219 Ark. 59, 239 S.W.2d 760 (1951).

As to distinctions between assignments and subleases, see § 50.

West's Key Number Digest, Landlord and Tenant ☞ 80(1)

While an assignment of a lease transfers an existing estate into new hands,[1] a sublease creates a new estate.[2] When a lease is transferred by a sublease, a new lessor-lessee relationship is created between the original lessee and the sublessee, but the original lessee retains both privity of estate and privity of contract with the original lessor and no legal relationship is created between the lessor and sublessee.[3]

The same rules apply to a sublessor-sublessee relationship as are applicable to a lessor-lessee relationship.[4] However, the construction and operation of a particular sublease depend on all the circumstances of the case and on the language of the agreement construed in accordance with the usual rules of construction.[5]

§ 60 Liability of original tenant to landlord

A subletting does not change the relationship of the landlord and the original tenant, or relieve the tenant of liability on the covenants of the lease, unless this is done by the original lease, or by some other transaction or agreement, such as a surrender and a substitution of tenants.

Research References

[3]Md.—Italian Fisherman, Inc. v. Middlemas, 313 Md. 156, 545 A.2d 1 (1988).

[4]Neb.—Krance v. Faeh, 215 Neb. 242, 338 N.W.2d 55 (1983).

[5]Cal.—Roadside Rest, Inc. v. Lankershim Estate, 76 Cal. App. 2d 525, 173 P.2d 554 (2d Dist. 1946).

Ill.—Sixty-Third & Halsted Realty Co. v. Goldblatt Bros., 342 Ill. App. 389, 96 N.E.2d 838 (1st Dist. 1951), judgment aff'd, 410 Ill. 468, 102 N.E.2d 749 (1951).

Ind.—Bowers v. Sells, 125 Ind. App. 324, 123 N.E.2d 194 (1954).

Mo.—First Trust Co. v. Downs, 230 S.W.2d 770 (Mo. Ct. App. 1950).

Pa.—McRoberts v. Stadelman, 168 Pa. Super. 489, 79 A.2d 119 (1951).

As to the construction and operation of leases, generally, see §§ 412 to 466.

Contract construction rules applicable

The interpretation and construction of a sublease is governed by the principles of interpretation and construction of contracts generally.

Iowa—Fashion Fabrics of Iowa, Inc. v. Retail Investors Corp., 266 N.W.2d 22 (Iowa 1978).

FIGURE 1.16   A Page from *American Jurisprudence*

Source: From *American Jurisprudence*. Reprinted with permission from Thomson West.

---

49 Am Jur 2d	LANDLORD AND TENANT	§ 1158

conveyance to one who is described by a fictitious or assumed name is valid,[18] and accordingly, the reassignment of the term by an assignee although the name of the second assignee is an assumed one, if intended as a bona fide assignment, will be effectual to relieve the assignor of further liability to the lessor, since it effectually destroys the privity of estate.[19]

C. SUBLEASE [§§ 1157–1186]

Research References
ALR Digest: Landlord and Tenant §§ 88 et seq.
ALR Index: Landlord and Tenant
16A Am Jur Pl & Pr Forms (Rev), Landlord and Tenant, Forms 421 et seq.
11 Am Jur Legal Forms 2d, Leases of Real Property §§ 161:1241 et seq.

---

1. In General [§§ 1157–1161]

§ 1157.   Generally

A sublease is a grant by a tenant of an interest in the rented premises less than his or her own, retaining to himself or herself a reversion, and a subtenant is a person who rents all or a portion of leased premises from the lessee for a term less than the original one, leaving a reversionary interest in the first lessee.[20] Where the sublease is for the whole term, it is in law an assignment as between the original lessor and the sublessee, but may be given effect as a contract as between the sublessor and sublessee.[21] An instrument in the form of a sublease is not to be regarded as an assignment so as to transfer the entire interest of the lessee and divest him or her of any reversionary estate or right of re-entry, where the negotiations were for a sublease, the original lessors' consent was to a sublease, the instrument was so designated, the rent was to be paid by the sublessee to the sublessor, the parties were referred to as lessor and lessee, the pleadings referred to the instrument as a sublease, and there were later transactions between the parties with reference to a separate assignment.[22]

§ 1158.   Right to sublet

It is well settled that in the absence of restrictions thereon by the parties,[23] or

18. 23 Am Jur 2d, Deeds §§ 33 et seq.

19. Hartman v Thompson, 104 Md 389, 65 A 117.

20. Jackson v Sims (CA8 Okla) 201 F2d 259; Coles Trading Co. v Spiegel, Inc. (CA9 Ariz) 187 F2d 984, 24 ALR2d 702; Haynes v Eagle-Picher Co. (CA10 Kan) 295 F2d 761, 16 OGR 28, cert den 369 US 828, 7 L Ed 2d 794, 82 S Ct 846; Johnson v Moxley, 216 Ala 466, 113 So 656; Cities Service Oil Co. v Taylor, 242 Ky 157, 45 SW2d 1039, 79 ALR 1374; Marcelle, Inc. v Sol. & S. Marcus Co., 274 Mass 469, 175 NE 83, 74 ALR 1012; Davidson v Minnesota Loan & Trust Co., 158 Minn 411, 197 NW 833, 32 ALR 1418.

Restatement 2d, Property § 95.
Forms: Sublease—Office space. 11A Am Jur Legal Forms 2d §§ 161:1251, 161:1252.
   —Short form. 11A Am Jur Legal Forms 2d §§ 161:1253.

21. Davidson v Minnesota Loan & Trust Co., 158 Minn 411, 197 NW 833, 32 ALR 1418.
As to assignments, see §§ 1076 et seq.

22. Coles Trading Co. v Spiegel, Inc. (CA9 Ariz) 187 F2d 984, 24 ALR2d 702.

23. §§ 1162 et seq.

Restatements

restatement
A recitation of the common law in a particular legal subject.

The uniform laws were drafted with the hope of standardizing state statutes in selected areas of law. The **restatements** were conceived to perform a similar purpose for the common law. In the 1920s a group of distinguished legal experts formed the American Law Institute for the purpose of drafting organized and detailed studies of the common law in certain areas. They feared that the growing complexity and inconsistency of common law would undermine our legal system; their solution was to create a body of law approved by an independent committee of distinguished legal scholars and available to all who wished to cite to it. *Restatements* have been issued in several areas of the law (including contracts, property law, torts, and conflict of laws, among others). Subsequent developments have resulted in the issuance of second editions in several areas, for example, the *Restatement of the Law of Torts, 2d.*

The courts have been receptive to the law as expressed in the *Restatements*, which now carry more authoritative weight than the legal encyclopedias. However, you should keep in mind that the *Restatements*, as a secondary authority, do not overrule existing case precedent in a jurisdiction. They might persuade a court, but they can never mandate a particular result unless adopted by the state.

The text of the restatements may provide useful support if you are attempting to overturn a precedent in your jurisdiction that goes against generally accepted restatement doctrine. In addition to the text, you may also find that the cross-references to cases are useful.

Treatises and Texts

treatise
A scholarly study of one area of the law.

A **treatise** is a scholarly study of one area of the law. Treatises differ from restatements in that they are usually the work of one author or group of authors, rather than the result of a collective effort such as that expended to make the restatements so broadly accepted.

Treatises vary with regard to the force of their persuasiveness. Some, like William Prosser's classic text on tort law, currently published by West as *Prosser and Keeton on the Law of Torts*, 5th ed. (West 1984), is widely recognized as authoritative and often cited by the courts. Others are less widely accepted.

texts
One-volume treatises.

hornbooks
Scholarly texts.

nutshell
A paperback series of the law.

Treatises also vary with regard to depth of treatment. Some are multivolume, some a single volume. A one-volume treatise is commonly referred to as a *text.* West publishes a series of one-volume scholarly **texts** known collectively as **hornbooks** (the Prosser work is part of this series), as well as much less thorough paperback treatments known collectively as the **nutshell** series. Nutshells generally provide good introductions to areas with which you are not familiar, whereas hornbooks fill in many more of the gaps. Neither hornbooks nor nutshells are often cited in legal briefs on disputed points (Prosser being a notable exception), although generally accepted legal principles are sometimes informally categorized as "hornbook law."

Some treatises are multivolume works covering a subject area in extraordinary detail, and some of these have had wide acceptance by the courts over the years (*Wigmore on Evidence* is a good example). Whether or not persuasive when cited to the court, such comprehensive treatises are usually useful for the purpose of learning about an area of law or finding cases on point.

When using a treatise or text, there is one important consideration to keep in mind. You must determine whether the scholarly purpose of the author(s) was to state the law as it *is* or as it *should be.* If the text is presenting the law as it is, it will be valuable as a tool to find primary sources. If the text is presenting the law as it should be, the persuasive value of the conclusions will be affected by their relationships to existing precedent, in conjunction with the logic of the argument presented and the prestige of the author(s).

Law Reviews and Periodicals

law reviews
Periodicals edited by the top students at each law school, featuring scholarly articles by leading authorities and notes on various topics written by the law students themselves.

In addition to multivolume or book-length treatises, there are also legal publications that print articles of interest. **Law reviews** are periodicals edited by the top students at each law school, featuring scholarly articles by leading authorities and notes on various topics written by the law students themselves. A law review usually carries the name of its law school as part of its title (for example, the *Harvard Law Review* or the *University of Pennsylvania Law Review*). Like many other secondary sources, these articles are most valuable as learning tools or sources of citations to relevant primary authorities, and are not often cited in briefs. Nevertheless, an article in a leading law review by a top scholar can have a substantial impact on the profession.

There are also numerous legal periodicals published by bar associations or private publishers. These periodicals vary in quality from scholarly journals to newsletters. Some are useful as research tools for the profession as a whole; others provide limited information to defined segments of the bar.

Looseleaf Services and Annotations

The textual treatment that looseleaf services and annotations provide is a valuable resource. Annotations provide broad analysis and extensive case summaries. The looseleaf services bring together in one topical reporter applicable case texts, statutes, regulations, and independent analysis. A page from a looseleaf service is reproduced in Figure 1.17.

FIGURE 1.17 **A Page from a Looseleaf Service**

Source: From *Immigration Law and Procedure.* Reprinted with permission from Lexis Nexis Matthew Bender.

7–21   SANCTIONS AND DISCRIMINATION   § 7.03[2][b]

§ 7.03   **The Prohibition Against Knowingly Hiring, Referring, or Recruiting An Unauthorized Alien; Employment Authorization, Employment Authorization Document ("EAD")**

[1]—In General

Just as IRCA's underlying purpose is to discourage unauthorized aliens from immigrating by denying them jobs, its primary method of doing so is to prohibit anyone from hiring them or commercially recruiting or referring them, knowing of their unauthorized status. This prohibition is accompanied by the employment verification requirement, designed to uncover whether a job applicant is an unauthorized alien, and backed up by an enforcement system and penalties. A valid verification gives the employer an affirmative defense of good faith which, however, is rebuttable. Particularly as the term "unauthorized alien" is first introduced by IRCA it warrants close study, as does the "knowing" requirement.

[2]—Unauthorized Alien: Concept and Definition

[a]—In General

In recent decades, more and more attention has been given to sub-rosa immigration, by public figures and journalists who have written with alarm or in explanation of the massive penetration of our borders by "wetbacks" or "illegal aliens." However inappropriate these labels, or inadequate such terms as "undocumented" or "deportable aliens," the issue of terminology is now finessed by IRCA which addresses the alien's status solely in terms of this statute's focus, namely, whether the individual is an alien authorized for the given employment. The statute defines the term only "with respect to the employment of an alien at a particular time" as being "not at that time either (A) an alien lawfully admitted for permanent residence, or (B) authorized to be so employed by this chapter or by the Attorney General."[1]

> **PLANNING NOTE**
>
> The immigration agency has suggested the following language for employers who want to ask potential employees about their work authorization: "Are you currently authorized to work for all employers in the United States on a full-time basis, or only for your current employer?"[1.1]

[b]—Prior Law and Impact of IRCA

Prior to the passage of IRCA, it was clear that an employment relationship was not unlawful simply because the employee was in the United States in violation of law. The taking of a job by an already deportable alien was not criminal or otherwise barred by

---

[1] INA § 274A(h)(3), 8 U.S.C. § 1324a(h)(3).

[1.1] Letter from OSC Special Counsel (Jun. 24, 1993), *reprinted in* 70 Interpreter Releases 1303–04 (Oct. 4, 1993).

(Rel.108—4/05 Pub.325)

Ethics Alert

You have just found a great case that may help your attorney win a case. The case was just handed down today by the U.S. Supreme Court and you plan on citing it in the brief you are preparing for tomorrow's hearing. You don't tell your attorney about the case; you just cite it in the brief. Of course you make a copy for yourself and your attorney to review, but not for opposing counsel (who you know is returning from his European holiday today). Can you cite the case in the brief, and what ethical responsibilities, if any, do you have in this circumstance?

The answer is probably "yes" if you provide a copy of the case to all parties and the opposing counsel has an opportunity to review the case. Not only may the court rules guide this hypothetical but also the rules of ethics, more formally known as the Rules of Professional Responsibility. As a paralegal, you may be held to the same ethical standards as attorneys because of the substantive legal work you perform under their supervision. Having a sufficient understanding of the professional conduct expected not only of the attorney, but indirectly of the paralegal, is critical since attorneys *are* responsible for and will be held accountable for the unprofessional misconduct of their staff. Become familiar with the Model Rules of Professional Conduct. Check the American Bar Association (ABA) website, www.abanet.org, for the current professional ethical standards. Additionally, paralegal associations, such as the National Federation of Paralegal Associations and the National Association of Legal Assistants, offer a framework for paralegals and their supervising attorney to follow. Throughout this book, ethical scenarios will be presented to provoke thought, alert you, and provide awareness of some of the ethical issues that are present in the paralegal profession.

THE E-FACTOR

THE COURTS AND THE INTERNET

Most state and federal courts have websites where recently decided cases, court rules, and other important information are posted. These websites provide up-to-date case decisions, which literally can be retrieved within hours of a decision being handed down by a court. Some suggested websites for court and case law information are:

U.S. Supreme Court: The official website for the U.S. Supreme Court is www.supremecourtus.gov. This website provides recent court decisions, slip opinions, and later cases beginning in 1991 and subsequent years. The documents are normally provided in PDF format and identify the procedures for downloading cases and other information. The site also provides the court rules, which are crucial if you are preparing a brief for the U.S. Supreme Court. Other notable sections of the website are the listing of the current docket, briefs of litigants and interested parties in cases, orders, journals, and a host of useful information about the Court.

U.S. Circuit Courts of Appeals: Each of the U.S. Circuit Courts have their own websites, however, the general website for the U.S. Circuit Courts and U.S. Federal Courts is www.uscourts.gov. Connecting to all the federal courts, this website provides access through "courtlinks" to any federal court for which you may need information.

You can directly access the court you need by entering, for example, www.ca3.uscourts.gov if you were interested in finding out information about the Third Circuit Court of Appeals. If you were to visit the website of the Third Circuit, you could access court decisions, the rules of court, including the newly posted amendments to the Third Circuit Local Appellate Rules, brief requirements, orders of the court, and many other important sources of information.

U.S. Federal Courts: As previously mentioned, the U.S. Federal Courts can be accessed by using www.uscourts.gov. Direct links are provided in the website, or simply enter the website of the court for which you are seeking information. If you wanted to access the northern district federal court of Texas, use www.txnd.uscourts.gov or for the southern district federal court of Indiana, use www.insd.uscourts.gov. Indiana also has a website providing information on all the federal courts in Indiana at www.in.gov/judiciary/courts/federal.html. Try one of the search engines, such as Google, Yahoo, or any of the many others to locate information on a federal court.

State Courts: Many state courts post information on websites as well. Larger states such as California and New York may have websites for their many state courts of appeals. Decisions and rules of court are updated daily. Check them!

PRACTICAL CONSIDERATIONS: THE CONSTRAINTS OF THE INTERNET

Not everyone has access to the Internet and electronic resources. Finding up-to-the-minute laws and cases may place others at a disadvantage. Power outages, remote locations, and web unavailability contribute to inaccessibility of electronic resources. Consequently, courts may have rules for presenting cases that have not been published in print format. Review your local rules for guidance on the subject, but always print a hard copy of the electronic resource and either attach it to the legal document your attorney is presenting or prepare sufficient copies for the court and any opposing counsel involved in the case. A court decision may be dispositive of your case, but if you are the only one who can find it or has access to it, the court may prohibit using the case out of fairness to all the parties.

Summary

Before starting a legal research problem, isolate your goal and formulate a plan or approach. Then, if you get lost or confused, get help.

Stare decisis means that decisions from a court with substantially the same set of facts should be followed by that court and all lower courts under it. This principle allows you to search for cases with precedential value. Precedential value is the force that a cited authority exerts upon a judge's reasoning. Primary authority consists of the original text of court opinions, constitutions, statutes, and agency regulations. Mandatory authority is primary authority that a court must follow; persuasive authority need not be followed, although its logic may be persuasive. Secondary authority is a step removed from the original text—not the law itself, but an analysis of the law.

Reporters are series of volumes containing judicial opinions. Opinions can be located by searching for the volume and page number identified in a citation. Proper citation form is established by *The Bluebook* and the *ALWD Citation Manual*. The Key Number System was established by the West Company to index cases appearing in its private reporters, including the regional reporters of the National Reporter System. Annotations are found in the *American Law Reports* volumes; they summarize and provide citations for judicial opinions. Looseleaf services are books with binders in which pages can be easily inserted or replaced, and which often publish case texts. Slip opinions are individually paginated texts of judicial opinions, almost always typewritten, and are usually the first format in which opinions are published.

Slip laws are publications of a single statute or act. Session laws are publications of the statutes of a jurisdiction, printed chronologically as they are enacted, and with each new edition including only those laws passed since the last edition. A code groups statutes by subject matter, and is generally well indexed. Annotated codes provide, in addition to the statutory text, information associated with each statute, including citations to judicial opinions that have construed that statute. A legislative history comprises legislative debates leading up to the enactment or defeat of a proposed statute. The text of constitutions is usually printed as part of a corresponding code or annotated code.

Federal regulations appear in the Federal Register or the Code of Federal Regulations. Federal administrative decisions are available from the agencies rendering the decision or from looseleaf services covering the applicable subject area. The availability and format of state and local regulations and administrative decisions vary widely from state to state and locality to locality.

The "supreme law" of the land is the U.S. Constitution. It prevails over all sources of the law. Statutes are primary sources of the law and may not conflict with the Constitution as well as administrative rules and regulations. Although a primary source of the law, case law interprets the other primary sources of the law.

A legal encyclopedia is a multivolume compilation purporting to provide in-depth coverage of every area of the law. Restatements are drafted by distinguished panels of legal experts for the purpose of developing and encouraging a uniform approach to various areas of common law. A treatise is a scholarly study of one area of the law, differing from a restatement in that it is usually the work of one author or group of authors, rather than a panel of experts.

Texts are one-volume treatises. Law reviews are periodicals edited by law students. Looseleaf services and annotations include secondary discussions of legal topics, as well as texts of cases and statutes.

The Internet provides immediate access to the law and cases. Most courts have websites, which provide case decisions, court rules, and other important information. Use Internet search engines to locate court websites.

Since many people do not have access to the Internet, check court and local rules for usage of recent cases or cases that are only cited electronically. Always print a hard copy of a case for use in court or as an attachment to a brief.

Key Terms

stare decisis
trial courts
appellate courts
state supreme court
precedential value
primary authority
mandatory authority
persuasive authority
secondary authority
reporters
citation
parallel citations
official reporter
regional reporters
advance sheets
slip opinion

looseleaf service
annotation
slip law
session laws
code
annotated codes
legislative history
rules of court
local rules
legal encyclopedia
restatements
treatise
texts
hornbooks
nutshell
law reviews

Review Questions

1. What is a citation?
2. How do official reporters and unofficial reporters differ?
3. What is the National Reporter system? List the regional reporters in that system.
4. What is an annotation?
5. Describe the difference between slip laws, session laws, and codes.
6. Describe the types of legal authority.
7. Identify the hierarchy of the law.
8. Where can the text of administrative regulations be found?
9. What is a legal encyclopedia? What is a treatise?
10. Name two Internet sources where recent court decisions are located.

Exercises

1. Determine whether your state law libraries have the following legal sources and identify the name of each book.
   a. State case reporter
   b. Regional reporter
   c. State digest
   d. State encyclopedia
   e. State statute
2. Locate the cases below and identify the name of the case and the year the case was decided.
   a. 398 N.E.2d 148
   b. 164 A.2d 451
   c. 375 P.2d 245
   d. 97 S.Ct. 2549
   e. 676 F.2d 385
   f. 252 U.S. 416
   g. 597 S.W.2d 134
   h. 298 So.2d 94

    i. 281 N.W.2d 804

    j. 214 Cal. Rptr. 177

3. Identify the abbreviation for the following legal research sources:
   a. *United States Code Annotated*
   b. *California Reporter,* Third Series
   c. *Southern Reporter*
   d. *Federal Rules Decisions*
   e. *Bankruptcy Reporter*

4. Using *The Bluebook* or *ALWD Citation Manual,* prepare the proper citations to the cases identified:
   a. Dreier versus the United States Volume 106 of the Federal Reporter third series page 844 in the ninth circuit in 1997
   b. Thomason versus Sanchez found in Volume 539 of the Federal Reporter Second series on page 955 decided by third circuit in 1976
   c. Federal Rule of Civil Procedure Rule 26

5. Define the following items:
   a. parallel citation _____
   b. mandatory authority _____
   c. *stare decisis* _____
   d. session law _____
   e. treatise _____

6. Identify the reporter in which the following case appears:
   a. 389 F.2d 579 _____
   b. 143 S.W.3d 452 _____
   c. 572 A.2d 501 _____
   d. 87 S.Ct. 339 _____
   e. 476 So.2d 197 _____
   f. 333 F.3d 1082 _____
   g. 148 F.R.D. 553 _____
   h. 518 U.S. 343 _____
   i. 162 N.E. 97 _____
   j. 206 N.Y.S.2d 934 _____

7. Locate 69 Fed. Reg. 28066 (May 18, 2004) and answer the following:
   a. What is the section heading?
   b. What page deals with "Sensitive Security Information"?
   c. What is the date of the publication?

8. Locate 49 U.S.C.A. §44901 and answer the following:
   a. What is the name of the Code Section?
   b. Has this section been amended?
   c. What section of the statute identifies who can supervise the screening of passengers?
   d. What section of the *C.F.R.* does 49 U.S.C.A. section 44901 reference?

9. Continue using 49 U.S.C. §44901 *et seq.* and answer the following questions:
   a. What section of the Code allows for cancellation of a flight if a security threat arises?
   b. Who has the right to cancel the flight?
   c. In 49 U.S.C. §44901 *et seq.,* which section deals with passenger manifests?
   d. Under the passenger manifest section, which are the statutory requirements for the manifest?

Portfolio Assignment

Locate the rules of appellate procedure in the federal circuit where you live. Determine whether there are local rules of that court as well. (Be sure they are current and have not been amended.) Prepare an outline of the brief requirements for filing an Appellant's Brief. Hint: What color is the cover page of the brief? Length of the brief? Size of the paper? Components of the cover page?

Vocabulary Builder

Legal Research: Sources of the Law

```
S  S  K  O  O  B  N  R  O  H  O  F  S  S  P
T  R  E  K  H  P  E  Q  Q  T  T  I  L  L  N
E  U  G  L  H  Q  E  F  R  S  S  H  L  I  F
E  D  W  W  U  F  H  C  R  I  L  W  E  P  T
H  N  V  U  O  R  V  E  C  X  S  C  H  O  N
S  R  E  S  T  A  T  E  M  E  N  T  S  P  E
E  O  L  S  X  R  D  R  S  J  L  P  T  I  D
C  V  J  Q  O  E  E  S  U  U  G  S  U  N  E
N  G  R  P  R  W  I  A  Y  O  E  Y  N  I  C
A  Q  E  A  Z  O  M  P  T  D  C  X  V  O  E
V  R  T  Z  N  Y  J  Y  O  I  Z  V  C  N  R
D  S  X  L  Q  M  Q  C  Z  T  S  E  R  D  P
A  D  A  Q  O  V  G  V  O  F  G  E  W  R  J
P  W  N  O  I  T  A  T  O  N  N  A  S  X  V
S  C  I  T  A  T  I  O  N  S  P  C  Z  Z  B
```

ADVANCE SHEETS	ANNOTATION	CITATIONS
CODES	COURT RULES	HORNBOOKS
NUTSHELLS	PRECEDENT	REPORTERS
RESTATEMENTS	SESSION LAWS	SLIP OPINION
STARE DECISIS	TREATISES	

Chapter 2

Legal Research
Finding Tools

CHAPTER OBJECTIVES

After completing this chapter, you will be able to:

- Explain the Key Number System.
- Use a digest.
- Define the use of a headnote in legal research.
- Shepardize a case or a statute.
- Validate a case on KeyCite or Shepard's Citations Service.
- Understand computer-assisted research.
- State some general principles about how to begin researching, and how to know when to stop.

You now know the different sources of the law, but how do you find them? The world of legal research provides finding tools to help you locate cases, statutes, and other legal sources to support a client's legal position. You will learn how to use digests, which are one of the primary "searching tools" in the law library. In addition to finding the law, you must be sure you are not citing overruled cases; Shepard's Citations and KeyCite provide your validating tools for verifying and updating the law. Miss a step and you might make a big "misstep." By following the process methodically, you will ensure success at all levels of your legal research assignment. Let's see how the process works.

Case Fact Pattern Hypothetical 2-1

Six months ago your firm's client, Mr. Jones, subleased some excess warehouse space to Mr. Smith (a sublease is a lease between a tenant and a subtenant, as opposed to one between the owner-landlord and the original tenant). Under the terms of the sublease, subtenant Smith was to make his payments directly to the landlord. After only two months, however, Smith stopped making his payments, and the landlord has sued Jones for the back rent. Jones has come to your supervising attorney, who has requested from you a memorandum outlining the basic law that applies in this situation, namely: What is the liability of the original tenant when a subtenant fails to pay the landlord?

You should be asking yourself: "Where do I begin? How do I know which law applies?" Therein lies the "million dollar" question.

THE DIGEST SYSTEM

Finding relevant legal sources could be a paralegal's worst nightmare had the digest system not been invented. Imagine your attorney sending you into a library to research a client's legal issues without a systematic, logical approach to the problem. You can't! It is like looking for a needle in a haystack. The digest system is the backbone of the legal research process, allowing you to methodically review topics relevant to your research assignment. Let's learn how the system works.

Key Number System
A detailed system of classification that currently divides the law into more than 400 separate categories or topics.

Key Numbers and Digests

The **Key Number System** employed in the National Reporter System (and most other West publications) is a detailed system of classification that currently divides the law into more than 400 separate categories or topics (see Figure 2.1 for a sample page listing some of these topics).

FIGURE 2.1   Digest Topics

Source: From *South Eastern Digest, 2nd Series.* Reprinted with permission from Thomson West.

DIGEST TOPICS

*See, also, Outline of the Law by Seven Main Divisions of Law
preceding this section.*

*The topic numbers shown below may be used in WESTLAW searches for cases
within the topic and within specified key numbers.*

1	Abandoned and Lost Property	42	Assumpsit, Action of	77	Citizens
2	Abatement and Revival	43	Asylums	78	Civil Rights
		44	Attachment	79	Clerks of Courts
4	Abortion and Birth Control	45	Attorney and Client	80	Clubs
		46	Attorney General	81	Colleges and Universities
5	Absentees	47	Auctions and Auctioneers	82	Collision
6	Abstracts of Title	48	Audita Querela	83	Commerce
7	Accession	48A	Automobiles	83H	Commodity Futures Trading Regulation
8	Accord and Satisfaction	48B	Aviation		
		49	Bail	84	Common Lands
9	Account	50	Bailment	85	Common Law
10	Account, Action on	51	Bankruptcy	88	Compounding Offenses
11	Account Stated	52	Banks and Banking		
11A	Accountants	54	Beneficial Associations	89	Compromise and Settlement
12	Acknowledgment	55	Bigamy	89A	Condominium
13	Action	56	Bills and Notes	90	Confusion of Goods
14	Action on the Case	58	Bonds	91	Conspiracy
15	Adjoining Landowners	59	Boundaries	92	Constitutional Law
15A	Administrative Law and Procedure	60	Bounties	92B	Consumer Credit
		61	Breach of Marriage Promise	92H	Consumer Protection
16	Admiralty	62	Breach of the Peace	93	Contempt
17	Adoption	63	Bribery	95	Contracts
18	Adulteration	64	Bridges	96	Contribution
19	Adultery	65	Brokers	96H	Controlled Substances
20	Adverse Possession	66	Building and Loan Associations	97	Conversion
21	Affidavits	67	Burglary	98	Convicts
23	Agriculture	68	Canals	99	Copyrights and Intellectual Property
24	Aliens	69	Cancellation of Instruments		
25	Alteration of Instruments	70	Carriers	100	Coroners
26	Ambassadors and Consuls	71	Cemeteries	101	Corporations
27	Amicus Curiae	72	Census	102	Costs
28	Animals	73	Certiorari	103	Counterfeiting
29	Annuities	74	Champerty and Maintenance	104	Counties
30	Appeal and Error	75	Charities	105	Court Commissioners
31	Appearance	76	Chattel Mortgages		
33	Arbitration	76A	Chemical Dependents	106	Courts
34	Armed Services	76D	Child Custody	107	Covenant, Action of
35	Arrest	76E	Child Support	108	Covenants
36	Arson	76H	Children Out-of-Wedlock	108A	Credit Reporting Agencies
37	Assault and Battery				
38	Assignments			110	Criminal Law
40	Assistance, Writ of				
41	Associations				

XV

More categories are added as the development of the law requires. Each category is divided into subcategories. There are often hundreds or even thousands of subcategories in a given topic. Each subcategory is assigned a key number.

Each and every case that is to be published in the National Reporter System is analyzed and assigned one or more key numbers based upon the legal principles addressed in the opinion. This analysis and assignment of key numbers has been taking place continuously since the 1880s.

Key numbers are listed near the beginning of an opinion, each followed by a brief paragraph setting forth the corresponding legal principle drawn from the case. A key-numbered paragraph is called a **headnote**. Headnotes are numbered consecutively, and corresponding reference numbers are inserted into the text of the case, indicating the precise location from which the legal principle in the headnote is drawn. Figure 2.2 shows pages from a typical National Reporter System case, *Young v. District of Columbia*, 752 A.2d 138 (D.C. 2000), and identifies various elements of key numbering.

headnote
A key-numbered paragraph; an editorial feature in unofficial reporters that summarizes a single legal point or issue in the court opinion.

FIGURE 2.2   **Pages from a Typical National Reporter System Case**
Source: From *Atlantic Reporter, 2nd Series.* Reprinted with permission from Thomson West.

138   D.C.   **752 ATLANTIC REPORTER, 2d SERIES**

reporter
parties
headnote
court

Willie D. YOUNG, Appellant,

v.

DISTRICT OF COLUMBIA, Appellee.

No. 97–CV–1354.

District of Columbia Court of Appeals.

Argued Dec. 15, 1998.
Decided May 25, 2000.

summary

Ousted apartment occupant brought action against District of Columbia, alleging wrongful eviction, negligence, and deprivation of constitutional rights under § 1983 in connection with incident in which police officers allegedly assisted occupant's alleged sublessor in evicting him. The Superior Court, Frederick H. Weisberg, J., granted summary judgment for District. Occupant appealed. The Court of Appeals, Wagner, C.J., held that: (1) material disputed issue of fact on wrongful eviction claim precluded summary judgment; (2) expert testimony on standard of care was required with respect to claim for negligent training and supervision; (3) occupant did not have viable § 1983 claim against District.

key
topic
disposition

Affirmed in part and reversed in part.

topic
key
headnote

1.   Landlord and Tenant ⬤⟲ 275
Landlord may not use self-help to evict tenant; legislatively created remedies for reacquiring possession of real property are exclusive.

2.   Landlord and Tenant ⬤⟲ 131.1
Tenant has a right not to have his or her possession interfered with except by lawful process, and violation of that right gives rise to a cause of action in tort. D.C.Code 1981, §§ 45–2503(15, 36), 45–2551.

3.   Landlord and Tenant ⬤⟲ 80(2)
Where tenant subleases property, tenant has a responsibility to see that subtenant vacates premises in order to surrender them to landlord without further liability.

4.   Landlord and Tenant ⬤⟲ 80(2)
If subtenant holds over, it is effectively a holding over by tenant, and landlord can hold tenant liable for damages for holdover period.

5.   Landlord and Tenant ⬤⟲ 80(1)
Tenant continues a relationship with property as long as subtenant remains.

6.   Landlord and Tenant ⬤⟲ 80(2)
Landlord can consent to continued occupancy of subtenant and create a new tenancy with subtenant, and thereby relieve tenant from further responsibility to pay rent for premises.

7.   Landlord and Tenant ⬤⟲ 275
Assuming that apartment occupant was tenant's subtenant, tenant could not evict him except through court process. D.C.Code 1981, §§ 45–2503(15, 36), 45–2551.

8.   Landlord and Tenant ⬤⟲ 76(1)
Restrictions in original lease against subletting do not affect, as between lessee and sublessee, the validity of sublease.

9.   Adverse Possession ⬤⟲ 13
Landlord and Tenant ⬤⟲ 5(1), 7
Landlord-tenant relationship does not arise by mere occupancy of premises; absent an express or implied contractual agreement, with both privity of estate and privity of contract, the occupier is in adverse possession as a "squatter."
See publication Words and Phrases for other judicial constructions and definitions.

10.   Landlord and Tenant ⬤⟲ 7
Whether landlord-tenant relationship exists depends upon circumstances surrounding use and occupancy of property.

11.   Landlord and Tenant ⬤⟲ 5(2), 7
Factors for consideration in determination of whether a landlord-tenant relationship exists include lease agreement,

FIGURE 2.2 Cont.

142 D.C.   **752 ATLANTIC REPORTER, 2d SERIES**

the trial court granted summary judgment for the District on Young's remaining constitutional claims. The court also concluded that the District could not be held liable under a respondeat superior theory for Young's remaining constitutional claims.

II.

keys 1 and 2 cited in this section

[1, 2] Young argues on appeal that the trial court erred in concluding that he was not lawfully in possession as Bibbs' subtenant. Therefore, he contends, Bibbs could not evict him without court process, and the District is jointly and severally liable with Bibbs for assisting in his wrongful eviction. It is well settled in this jurisdiction that a landlord may not use self-help to evict a tenant and that "the legislatively created remedies for reacquiring possession [of real property] are exclusive." *Mendes v. Johnson,* 389 A.2d 781, 787 (D.C.1978). "A tenant has a right not to have his or her possession interfered with except by lawful process, and violation of that right gives rise to a cause of action in tort." *Id.* The District acknowledges that Young's wrongful eviction claim may go forward if Young was Bibbs' tenant at the time of the eviction. The District contends, however, that the undisputed facts show that Young was not Bibbs' tenant, but an invitee or roomer who became a trespasser by refusing to leave at the request of the lawful tenant who had surrendered possession to the landlord. Young counters that Bibbs had no right to surrender possession to his landlord without his consent or by first evicting Young through court process, since he was a tenant.

keys 3 through 7 cited in this section

[3–7] Where a tenant subleases property, the tenant has a responsibility to see that the subtenant vacates the premises in order to surrender them to the landlord without further liability. *See Sanchez v. Eleven Fourteen, Inc.,* 623 A.2d 1179, 1181

(D.C.1993). If a subtenant holds over, it is effectively a holding over by the tenant and the landlord can hold the tenant liable for damages for the holdover period. *Id.* The tenant continues a relationship with the property as long as the subtenant remains. *Id.* Of course, a landlord can consent to the continued occupancy of the subtenant and create a new tenancy with the subtenant, and thereby relieve the tenant from further responsibility to pay rent for the premises. *See Comedy v. Vito,* 492 A.2d 276, 279 (D.C.1985). However, the landlord here specifically declined Young's request that he be substituted on the lease, and elected to hold Bibbs responsible for the property. Contrary to the trial court's ruling, Bibbs had not effectively relinquished possession when Young was ousted. Assuming that Young was Bibbs' tenant, Bibbs could not evict him except through court process. See *Mendes, supra,* 389 A.2d at 787. We consider whether there was a landlord-tenant relationship between Bibbs and Young which required court process in order for Bibbs to evict Young.

[8] It is undisputed that Bibbs and Young had no written agreement establishing a subtenancy. However, certain tenancies may arise by oral agreement of the parties. Where real property is rented by the month without a written agreement, by statute, the estate created "shall be deemed [an] estate[ ] at sufferance." See D.C.Code § 45–220; *see also Comedy, supra,* 492 A.2d at 279; *Cavalier Apartments Corp. v. McMullen,* 153 A.2d 642 (D.C.1959); *Miller v. Plumley,* 77 A.2d 173 (D.C.1950). "[S]uch a tenancy requires payment of rent or 'hireings' or a 'rate per month' to accompany the estate." *Smith v. Town Ctr. Management Corp.,* 329 A.2d 779, 780 (D.C.1974) (citing D.C.Code 1973, § 45–820).[5] This statute itself does not prohibit the creation of a tenancy at sufferance in a subtenant.[6]

---

5. The definitions of a tenancy at sufferance in D.C.Code § 45–820 is the same in material respects to the definition in D.C.Code § 45–220.

6. There may be a contractual prohibition to subletting, as there was here. However, "restrictions contained in the original lease against subletting do not affect, as between

FIGURE 2.2   Cont.

> **YOUNG v. DISTRICT OF COLUMBIA**   D.C.   **143**
> Cite as 752 A.2d 138 (D.C. 2000)
>
> [9-14] The question is whether the undisputed facts showed that Young was not a tenant, as the trial court concluded. "A landlord-tenant relationship does not arise by mere occupancy of the premises; absent an express or implied contractual agreement, with both privity of estate and privity of contract, the occupier is in adverse possession as a 'squatter.'" *Nicholas v. Howard,* 459 A.2d 1039, 1040 (D.C.1983). Whether a landlord-tenant relationship exists depends upon the circumstances surrounding the use and occupancy of the property. *See Anderson v. William J. Davis, Inc.,* 553 A.2d 648, 649 (D.C.1989). Factors for consideration in that determination include a lease agreement, the payment of rent and other conditions of occupancy between the parties. *Id.*[7] While it is undisputed that there was no written lease agreement, other material facts surrounding the nature of the relationship between Bibbs and Young are in dispute which bear upon the issue. According to Bibbs, he simply allowed Young to be a guest in his apartment temporarily while Young was unemployed and homeless, and Young occasionally made token contributions to the household. Such an occupancy arrangement would not give rise to a tenancy. *See*
>
> *Jackson v. United States,* 357 A.2d 409, 410 (D.C.1976) (Where a defendant occupied an apartment rent-free without formal consideration, there was no tenancy at sufferance). Young, however, in a verified response to interrogatories, states that he had an agreement with Bibbs to pay him half the rent ($200) for the premises, which he paid. This disputed issue of fact is material because if Young, in fact, had an oral agreement to occupy the apartment in exchange for regular monthly rental payments as Bibbs' subtenant, a tenancy at sufferance would arise, requiring court process for termination. See D.C.Code §§ 45–1404, –16–1501; *see also Mendes, supra,* 389 A.2d at 787. At least as between Bibbs and Young, assuming a sublessor-sublessee relationship, Young would be entitled to the protections afforded tenants under the Housing Act.[8] The Rental Housing Act of 1985 (Housing Act), which enlarged the protections afforded tenants without leases from sudden evictions, extends to subtenants.[9] *See Anderson, supra,* 553 A.2d at 648. The Act itself includes a subtenant within the definition of "tenant." D.C.Code § 45–2503(36). Similarly, a sublessor is included within the definition of "housing provider."[10] That
>
> the lessee and the sublessee, the validity of the sublease." 49 AM. JUR.2d *Landlord and Tenant* § 1162 (1993). *See also* FREEDMAN ON LEASES § 7304d (4th ed.1997).
>
> 7.   In *Anderson, supra,* the issue under consideration was whether two men who occupied an apartment in partial compensation for performing services in the building were tenants. *Anderson,* 553 A.2d at 648–49. In concluding that the men were not tenants, the court considered that "[t]hey did not pay rent, did not have a lease, and were allowed to occupy the employer-landowner's apartment only as an incident to the services they provided." *Id.* at 649. Therefore, the court determined that they were not entitled to a thirty days' notice to quit as required by D.C.Code § 45–1404.
>
> 8.   For disposition of this appeal, we need not address the rights of Bibbs' landlord as against any subtenant. *See Sanchez, supra*
>
> 623 A.2d at 1181; *Haje's, Inc. v. Wire,* 56 A.2d 158, 159 (D.C.1947).
>
> 9.   "This court has 'ruled on several occasions that rent control statutes [such as the 1985 [Housing] Act] prevail over provisions adopted earlier that govern evictions, to the extent that the provisions conflict.'" *Anderson, supra,* 553 A.2d at 649 (quoting *Habib v. Thurston,* 517 A.2d 1, 5 n. 3 (D.C. 1985)).
>
> 10.   D.C.Code § 45–2503(15) and (36) provide respectively that:
> "Housing provider" means a landlord, an owner, lessor, sublessor, assignee, or their agent, or any other person receiving or entitled to receive rents or benefits for the use or occupancy of any rental unit within a housing accommodation within the District. "Tenant" includes a tenant, subtenant, lessee, sublessee, or other person entitled to the possession, occupancy, or the benefits of any rental unit owned by another person.

digest
A collection of all the headnotes from an associated series of volumes, arranged alphabetically by topic and by key number.

The key numbers form the basis of the **digest** system. A digest is a collection of all the headnotes from an associated series of volumes, arranged alphabetically by topic and by key number. For example, the most recent digest associated with the *Pacific Reporter* includes all the headnotes from all the cases beginning with those from volume 585 of the second series and continuing to the present. (Important note: If you want to search through older cases as well, you have to check through other digests covering earlier periods; a thorough search is not complete until all time periods covering all cases have been checked.) Figure 2.3 shows a partial index page

FIGURE 2.3 **A Partial Index Page**

Source: From *Atlantic Digest, 2nd Series.* Reprinted with permission from Thomson West.

20A Atl D 2d—5   **LANDLORD & TENANT**

III. LANDLORD'S TITLE AND REVERSION.—Continued.

    (B) ESTOPPEL OF TENANT.—Continued.

        ⚷ 62. Leases and agreements as ground of estoppel.—Continued.

            (3). Tenant in possession at time relation arose.

            (4). Tenant holding over.

      63. Operation of estoppel against tenant.

            (1). In general.

            (2). Actions in which estoppel is effective.

            (3). Necessity of surrendering possession to discharge ground of estoppel.

            (4). Sufficiency of surrender.

            (5). Denial of title as to part of property.

            (6). Time as to which estoppel is effective.

      64. Persons estopped.

      65. As to whom tenant estopped.

      66. Adverse possession of tenant.

            (1). In general.

            (2). Necessity of surrender of premises by tenant or repudiation of tenancy and notice.

            (3). Character of tenant's possession.

      67. Purchase of tax title.

      68. Attornment to third person.

      69. Effect of eviction by landlord.

IV. TERMS FOR YEARS.

    (A) NATURE AND EXTENT.

        ⚷ 70. Nature of estate for years.

      71. Commencement of term.

      72. Duration of term.

      73. Monthly tenancies.

    (B) ASSIGNMENT AND SUBLETTING.

        ⚷ 74. Assignability and agreements to assign leases and contracts.

      75. Right of lessee or tenant to assign or sublet in general.

            (1). In general.

            (2). Statutory prohibition.

            (3). Consent of lessor.

      76. Covenants, conditions, and restrictions as to assignment or subletting.

            (1). In general.

            (2). What constitutes breach of covenant.

            (3). Consent of lessor, or waiver of condition.

            (4). Evidence of consent.

            (5). Questions for jury.

      77. Parol assignments and sublettings.

      78. Requisites and validity of written instrument.

            (1). In general.

            (2). Delivery of assignment.

            (3). Necessity of record.

      79. Construction and operation of assignments in general.

            (1). In general.

            (2). Rights and liabilities of assignee.

topic & key from *Young v. Dist. of Colombia*

from headnote # 8

from the topic "Landlord and Tenant," which includes the key number associated with headnote 8 from *Young v. District of Columbia*. Figure 2.4 shows the digest page on which the full text of this headnote appears.

FIGURE 2.4 Digest Page

Source: From *Atlantic Digest, 2nd Series*. Reprinted with permission from Thomson West.

☞ **76(1)**   **LANDLORD & TENANT**   20A Atl D 2d—142

For later cases see same Topic and Key Number in Pocket Part

headnote # 8

D.C. 2000. Restrictions in original lease against subletting do not affect, as between lessee and sublessee, the validity of sublease.

  Young v. District of Columbia, 752 A.2d 138.

D.C. 1984. Option clause in lease granting tenant option to lease balance of eighth floor unambiguously entitled tenant to expand demised premises and to utilize all or any part of those premises for any purpose permitted by remaining provisions of lease, and subleasing clause qualified tenant's right to sublet only by requiring landlord's specific consent which was not to be unreasonably withheld; thus, nothing in lease prohibited tenant from exercising option and subleasing entire balance of eighth floor at profit.

  1010 Potomac Associates v. Grocery Manufacturers of America, Inc., 485 A.2d 199.

D.C.Mun.App. 1955. A covenant against subletting is for the benefit of the lessor.

  Goody's, Inc. v. Stern's Equipment Co., 110 A.2d 311.

D.C.Mun.App. 1952. A covenant against subletting is for benefit of lessor because it is regarded as for his interest to determine who shall be a tenant of his property.

  Friedman v. Thomas J. Fisher & Co., 88 A.2d 321, 31 A.L.R.2d 827.

D.C.Mun.App. 1950. Forfeitures of a lease for conditions broken and restrictions upon the right to assign are both looked upon with disfavor.

  Burrows Motor Co. v. Davis, 76 A.2d 163.

D.C.Mun.App. 1946. The Emergency Rent Act does not give a tenant by sufferance power to sublet contrary to landlord's expressed will, but landlord's right in that respect, and even an express restriction against subletting in a written lease, may be waived by landlord by accepting rent in advance with knowledge of the subletting. D.C.Code 1940, §§ 45–820, 45–1605(b)(1).

  Thompson v. Gray, 50 A.2d 594.

D.C.Mun.App. 1944. A covenant in a lease against assigning or subletting without landlord's consent is for benefit of landlord because it is regarded as for his interest to determine who shall be his tenant. D.C.Code 1940, § 45–820.

  Keroes v. Westchester Apartments, 36 A.2d 263.

D.C.Mun.App. 1943. A tenant may not create new tenancy by removing from leased property and placing it completely in charge of sublessees in violation of terms of lease, as Emergency Rent Act protects only actual ten-ants, not mere middlemen. D.C.Code 1940, § 45–1601.

  Hall v. Henry J. Robb, Inc., 32 A.2d 707.

Md. 1990. Contractual restrictions on alienability of leasehold interests are permitted.

  Julian v. Christopher, 575 A.2d 735, 320 Md. 1.

  If clause in lease is susceptible of two interpretations, public policy favors interpretation least restrictive of right to alienate freely.

  Julian v. Christopher, 575 A.2d 735, 320 Md. 1.

Md. 1965. Although landlords agreed that tenants should have right to transfer alcoholic beverage license to any one acquiring all of assets of business should landlords decline to exercise their option to purchase such assets at price offered by prospective purchaser, landlords had right to refuse to assent to removal of one of licensees and substitution of others in absence of provision in lease authorizing such.

  Katz v. Williams, 211 A.2d 723, 239 Md. 355.

N.H. 1961. An unequivocal and unqualified restriction against assignment in a lease, freely entered into between the parties, is valid.

  Segre v. Ring, 170 A.2d 265, 103 N.H. 278

N.J.Super.A.D. 1976. As a general rule, a restriction against lease transfers contained in an express provision in the lease is viewed as a condition subsequent; therefore, the lessee may transfer despite the restriction, and the transfer is effective until avoided by the lessor.

  Xerox Corp. v. Listmark Computer Systems, 361 A.2d 81, 142 N.J.Super. 232.

N.J.Super.A.D. 1954. Covenant in lease against assignment or subletting is personal to lessor and is made for his benefit, and only he or his successors in interest may avail themselves of it.

  Stark v. National Research & Design Corp., 110 A.2d 143, 33 N.J.Super. 315.

N.J.Super.A.D. 1952. Assignment of lease without complying with lease requirement that previous written consent of landlord for assignment be endorsed thereon was invalid.

  K. & J. Markets v. Martin Packing Corp., 90 A.2d 507, 20 N.J.Super. 515.

  Where lease provided that tenant could assign the lease to corporation and that consent for such purpose was given by landlord upon proof of sale of tenant's assets to corporation, assignment by tenant to corporation without knowledge of landlord and without any proof of sale or assets to corporation having been submitted to landlord was invalid and corporation

Digests are an excellent place to begin many research projects. By identifying relevant topics and key numbers and then searching through the corresponding headnotes, you will be able to locate citations for cases that appear to be analogous to the issues posed by your research problem. You can then use the citation included with the headnote to review in detail the published opinion as it appears in the reporter. Since our previous example, using *Young v. District of Columbia*, started with a case and worked backward to show you how the case, key number, headnote, and digest topic all fit together, let's take one more example, using the same case cited, but based upon the landlord/tenant problem from the Case Fact Pattern to this chapter, to see how a typical research session might proceed.

We begin by isolating an appropriate topic. Look through the list of topics found in Figure 2.5. Do you see any topics that might prove useful to our research problem? You should have found

FIGURE 2.5   Digest Topics

Source: From *Atlantic Digest, 2nd Series.* Reprinted with permission from Thomson West.

DIGEST TOPICS

114	Customs Duties	165	Extortion and Threats	213	Innkeepers
115	Damages			216	Inspection
116	Dead Bodies	166	Extradition and Detainers	217	Insurance
117	Death			218	Insurrection and Sedition
117G	Debt, Action of	167	Factors		
117T	Debtor and Creditor	168	False Imprisonment	219	Interest
118A	Declaratory Judgment	169	False Personation	220	Internal Revenue
		170	False Pretenses	221	International Law
119	Dedication	170A	Federal Civil Procedure	222	Interpleader
120	Deeds			223	Intoxicating Liquors
122A	Deposits and Escrows	170B	Federal Courts	224	Joint Adventures
		171	Fences	225	Joint-Stock Companies and Business Trusts
123	Deposits in Court	172	Ferries		
124	Descent and Distribution	174	Fines		
		175	Fires	226	Joint Tenancy
125	Detectives	176	Fish	227	Judges
126	Detinue	177	Fixtures	228	Judgment
129	Disorderly Conduct	178	Food	229	Judicial Sales
130	Disorderly House	179	Forcible Entry and Detainer	230	Jury
131	District and Prosecuting Attorneys			231	Justices of the Peace
		180	Forfeitures	232	Kidnapping
		181	Forgery	232A	Labor Relations
132	District of Columbia	183	Franchises	233	Landlord and Tenant
133	Disturbance of Public Assemblage	184	Fraud		
		185	Frauds, Statute of	234	Larceny
		186	Fraudulent Conveyances	235	Levees and Flood Control
134	Divorce				
135	Domicile	187	Game	236	Lewdness
135H	Double Jeopardy	188	Gaming	237	Libel and Slander
136	Dower and Curtesy	189	Garnishment	238	Licenses
137	Drains	190	Gas	239	Liens
138	Drugs and Narcotics	191	Gifts	240	Life Estates
141	Easements	192	Good Will	241	Limitation of Actions
142	Ejectment	193	Grand Jury	242	Lis Pendens
143	Election of Remedies	195	Guaranty	245	Logs and Logging
		196	Guardian and Ward	246	Lost Instruments
144	Elections	197	Habeas Corpus	247	Lotteries
145	Electricity	198	Hawkers and Peddlers	248	Malicious Mischief
146	Embezzlement			249	Malicious Prosecution
148	Eminent Domain	199	Health and Environment		
148A	Employers' Liability			250	Mandamus
149	Entry, Writ of	200	Highways	251	Manufactures
150	Equity	201	Holidays	252	Maritime Liens
151	Escape	202	Homestead	253	Marriage
152	Escheat	203	Homicide	255	Master and Servant
154	Estates in Property	204	Hospitals	256	Mayhem
156	Estoppel	205	Husband and Wife	257	Mechanics' Liens
157	Evidence	205H	Implied and Constructive Contracts	257A	Mental Health
158	Exceptions, Bill of			258A	Military Justice
159	Exchange of Property	206	Improvements	259	Militia
		207	Incest	260	Mines and Minerals
160	Exchanges	208	Indemnity	265	Monopolies
161	Execution	209	Indians	266	Mortgages
162	Executors and Administrators	210	Indictment and Information	267	Motions
				268	Municipal Corporations
163	Exemptions	211	Infants		
164	Explosives	212	Injunction		

XVI

disest topic

the topic *Landlord and Tenant*. The next step is to locate that topic in the digest and look at the topic index, which appears at the beginning of the topic. Searching through the key numbers listed in the index, we find one, key number 80(2) (Figure 2.6), that relates to our Case Fact Pattern problem (which, as you recall, concerns the liability of the original tenant to the landlord).

FIGURE 2.6   Key Number

Source: From *Atlantic Digest, 2nd Series*. Reprinted with permission from Thomson West.

LANDLORD & TENANT   32C S E D 2d—6

IV.   **TERMS FOR YEARS.**—Continued.
   (B) ASSIGNMENT AND SUBLETTING.—Continued.
      79.   Construction and operation of assignments in general.—Continued.
         (3). Rights and liabilities of assignor.
         (4). Assignment as security.
         (5). Construction as question for jury.
      80.   Construction and operation of subleases.
         (1). In general.
         (2). Liability of original tenant to landlord.
         (3). Rights and liabilities of subtenants.
         (4). Liability of original lessee to sublessee.
      80.5. Evidence of assignment or subletting.

key number

   (C) MORTGAGE.
      81.   Mortgages of leaseholds.
         (1). In general.
         (2). Rights of mortgagee.
         (3). Rights of purchaser at foreclosure sale.
         (4). Recording and filing.

   (D) EXTENSIONS AND RENEWALS.
      81.5. Nature of right in general.
      82.   Provisions for extension of term.
      83.   Covenants for renewal in general.
         (1). In general.
         (2). Conditions precedent to right to renewal.
         (3). Security for renewal.
         (4). Forfeiture of right to renewal.
         (5). Actions for breach of agreement.
      84.   Persons entitled to renewal.
      84.1. _____ In general.
      85.   _____ Assignees or undertenants.
      85.5. Persons bound by agreements to renew.
      86.   Option to renew and election.
         (1). In general.
         (2). Notice of election.
         (3). Waiver of notice.
         (4). Proceedings to fix amount of rent.
      87.   Number of renewals.
      88.   Renewal leases.
         (1). In general.
         (2). Covenants and conditions.
         (3). Evidence of renewal.
      89.   Extension or renewal by indorsement on lease.
      89.5. Implied contracts to extend or renew in general.
      90.   Extension or renewal by holding over.
         (1). In general.
         (2). Conditions in general.
         (3). Term.
         (4). What constitutes holding over so as to create new tenancy.

The next step is to look under key 80(2) for headnotes. If we find a relevant headnote, we can use the citation provided with the headnote to locate and read the full text of the case as it appears in the reporter. See if you can use this method to locate some relevant cases in the digest of your own jurisdiction.

The topics, key numbers, and headnotes are the most important segment of a digest, but there are other useful sections as well. These include the descriptive word index, the words and phrases section, the table of cases, and, in some earlier instances, the plaintiff/defendant table. You should note that not every digest has all of these additional sections.

descriptive word index
A subject index that provides a researcher with a quick survey of specific key numbers, often from several topics, which apply to a given subject area.

The **descriptive word index** is a subject index that provides a researcher with a quick survey of specific key numbers, often from several topics, which apply to a given subject area. To use the descriptive word index, we would first analyze our legal problem so as to identify terms that serve to define the issues presented. For our landlord/tenant problem, such terms would include *subletting*. Looking in our descriptive word index under "subletting" (see Figure 2.7), we not only find the same key number from the landlord and tenant topic that we found before (that is, key number 80(2)), but also references to key numbers from entirely different topics (see, for example, the reference to key number 16(6) from the topic *Indians*, relating to the subletting of Indian lands). Although these other topics are not relevant to our current landlord/tenant problem, there will be times when the descriptive word index will help you find useful key numbers from less than obvious topics. The descriptive word index also enables you to avoid a line-by-line search through hundreds or even thousands of key number entries in the index of a more obvious topic (for example, rather than searching through the many key numbers in the "landlord and tenant" topic index, we were able to quickly find key number 80(2) by scanning Figure 2.7).

The descriptive word index might be thought of as a master index to all the key numbers contained in all the topics in the digest. Thus it is often an excellent place to start your research.

words and phrases
An index to a digest that construes a judicial term.

The **words and phrases** section of the digest is useful if your research issue turns upon the judicial construction ("construction" in this context is drawn from the verb "construe" and means "interpretation") of a specific word or phrase. The words and phrases are arranged alphabetically, with citations to those cases in which the word or phrase is construed.

Let's use a new example to demonstrate how the words and phrases section works. Suppose an important issue in a case your office is handling in the United States District Court in Pennsylvania turns upon construction of the term *shrink-wrap*. Turning to the words and phrases section of the *Federal Practice Digest, 4th* (see Figure 2.8), you see a listing for the term *shrink-wrap*. Going down the page of cases provided, you'll find that the case of *Peerless Wall and Window Coverings v. Synchronics, Inc.* was a Pennsylvania federal court case decided by the western district. The citation reads "85 F. Supp. 519 affirmed 234 F.3d 1265 and cited in headnote copyr[ight] 107." ("Copyr" is the key system's abbreviation for the topic copyright.) This tells you that the opinion begins on page 519, and under headnote (number 2) "copyr 107" of that opinion, there will be a judicial construction of the term *shrink-wrap*. See Figure 2.9, which reproduces a page from the case, and find the judicial construction.

In addition to the words and phrases digest section, West also publishes a multivolume set called *Words and Phrases* that includes words and phrases from all jurisdictions for all time periods, and which provides not only citations but also headnotes for each word or phrase.

table of cases
Lists of all the cases whose text appears in the associated volumes.

The **table of cases** section of a digest lists all the cases whose text appears in the associated volumes. The cases are listed alphabetically by name of the plaintiff. See Figure 2.10, which shows *Peerless Wall and Window Coverings, Inc. v. Synchronics, Inc.* as it appears in the table of cases in *West's Federal Practice Digest, 4th*.

If you know the name of a case but not the citation, the table of cases will provide you with this information, enabling you to locate the text of the opinion. In addition to the National Reporter citation, you will find the official citation and the procedural history of the case (that is, whether it has been affirmed or reversed on appeal), as well as a list of the key numbers assigned to that case. Locate these elements in Figure 2.10.

defendant/plaintiff table
List of the cases alphabetically by the defendant first or a table of cases listing the name of the case both ways.

Sometimes you only know the name of the defendant in a case. Some digests have a **defendant/plaintiff table** listing the cases alphabetically by the defendant first or a table of cases listing the name of the case both ways. The defendant/plaintiff table contains parallel citations, but not procedural history or key numbers; of course, if you want this information for a case you've found in this table, simply look it up in the table of cases (now that you've learned the plaintiff's name). Figure 2.11 shows the listing for *Peerless Wall and Window Coverings, Inc. v. Synchronics, Inc.* as it appears in the table of cases from the defendant's name.

FIGURE 2.7   Descriptive Word Index

Source: From *Atlantic Digest, 2nd Series*. Reprinted with permission from Thomson West.

STUDENTS   37B Atl D 2d–116

References are to Digest Topics and Key Numbers

STUDENTS

BANKRUPTCY,
Automatic stay, loans and transcripts, **Bankr** ☞ **2403**
Injunction against proceedings, loans and transcripts, **Bankr** ☞ **2372**
Loans. See heading **BANKRUPTCY, STUDENT loans.**

COLLEGES. See heading **COLLEGES AND UNIVERSITIES, STUDENTS.**

SCHOOLS. See heading **SCHOOLS AND SCHOOL DISTRICTS,** generally.

UNEMPLOYMENT compensation. See heading **UNEMPLOYMENT COMPENSATION** STUDENTS, duty to find work.

SUA SPONTE

See heading **COURT'S OWN MOTION,** generally.

SUBAGENTS

See heading **AGENCY, SUBAGENTS.**

SUBCONTRACTORS

INDEMNITY. See heading **INDEMNITY, CONTRACTORS.**

INDEPENDENT contractors. See heading **INDEPENDENT CONTRACTORS,** generally.

MAILS, carriage of, **Postal** ☞ **21(2)**

MECHANICS' liens. See heading **MECHANICS' LIENS, SUBCONTRACTORS.**

PUBLIC contracts, **Pub Contr** ☞ **17**

STATES,
Rights and remedies,
Contracts, **States** ☞ **108.5**

UNITED States, **Pub Contr** ☞ **17, 24**

WORKERS' compensation,
Effect of compensation acts as to other remedies, **Work Comp** ☞ **2166, 2167**
Employees covered, **Work Comp** ☞ **334-361**
Evidence,
Sufficiency, **Work Comp** ☞ **1461**
Persons liable as third persons, **Work Comp** ☞ **2165-2167**
Public officers as employees, **Work Comp** ☞ **389**

SUBDIVISIONS

INCOME tax-federal,
Capital gains and losses, **Int Rev** ☞ **3251**

SUBDIVISIONS—Cont'd

MECHANICS' liens, error in name of subdivision in claim or statement, **Mech Liens** ☞ **136(4)**

MUNICIPAL corporations, **Mun Corp** ☞ **40, 43**

MUNICIPAL employees and officials, Apportionment, **Mun Corp** ☞ **127**

TOWNS, **Towns** ☞ **4**

ZONING approval. See heading **ZONING, SUBDIVISION approval.**

SUBJACENT SUPPORT

MINING, injuries to surface, **Mines** ☞ **122**

SUBJECT OF STATUTE

SINGLE-SUBJECT requirement. See heading **SINGLE-SUBJECT REQUIREMENT,** generally.

TITLES of laws. See heading **TITLES OF LAWS,** generally.

SUBLEASES

See heading **SUBLETTING,** generally.

SUBLETTING

BREACH of covenant or restriction, **Land & Ten** ☞ **104**

CONSENT, **Land & Ten** ☞ **75(3), 76(3, 4)**

CONSTRUCTION,
Sublease, **Land & Ten** ☞ **80**

CONTRACTS. See heading **SUBCONTRACTORS,** generally.

COOPERATIVE apartments, **Land & Ten** ☞ **360**

COVENANTS,
Generally, **Land & Ten** ☞ **76**
Breach, **Land & Ten** ☞ **104**

DISTINCT from assignments, **Land & Ten** ☞ **79(1)**

EVICTION,
Subtenants, **Land & Ten** ☞ **177.5**

EVIDENCE, **Land & Ten** ☞ **80.5**

INDIAN lands, **Indians** ☞ **16(6)**

INJURIES,
Subtenants, **Land & Ten** ☞ **164(5)**

LEASED premises, **Land & Ten** ☞ **74-81**

LEASES,
Conditions, **Land & Ten** ☞ **76**

topic

FIGURE 2.7   Cont.

References are to Digest Topics and Key Numbers

SUBLETTING—Cont'd
LEASES—Cont'd

Consent,
  Assignment or subletting, **Land & Ten**
    ☞ **75(3), 76(3, 4)**

Construction,
  Subleases, **Land & Ten** ☞ **80**
  Privity, **Land & Ten** ☞ **43**

> relevant topic and key

LIABILITIES and rights,
  Subtenant, **Land & Ten** ☞ **80(3)**

LIMITATIONS, **Land & Ten** ☞ **76**

MOBILE home parks, **Land & Ten** ☞ **373**

ORIGINAL tenants,
  Liability to landlord, **Land & Ten** ☞ **80(2)**
  Liability to subtenants, **Land & Ten**
    ☞ **80(4)**

PAROL agreements, **Land & Ten** ☞ **77**

RECOVERY of possession,
  Suspension,
    Remedies,
      Unauthorized subletting, **Land & Ten**
        ☞ **278.9(1)**

RENT,
  Liability, **Land & Ten** ☞ **209**
  Liens,
    Subtenant property, **Land & Ten**
      ☞ **246(4)**

REPAIRS,
  Subtenant rights, **Land & Ten** ☞ **150(4), 152(8)**

RESTRICTIVE covenants and conditions,
  Land & Ten ☞ **76**

STATUTES, **Land & Ten** ☞ **75(2)**

SUSPENSION of rights,
  Reentry and possession recovery,
    Subtenants,
      Regulations, **Land & Ten** ☞ **278.4(6)**
      Unauthorized subletting, **Land & Ten**
        ☞ **278.9(1)**

TERMINATION,
  Lease, **Land & Ten** ☞ **104**

TRAILER parks or camps, **Land & Ten**
  ☞ **373**

UNDER tenants,
  Right to renewal, **Land & Ten** ☞ **85**

USE of premises,
  Subtenants, **Land & Ten** ☞ **134(2, 4)**

WAIVER,
  Generally, **Land & Ten** ☞ **75(3)**

SUBLETTING—Cont'd
WAIVER—Cont'd

Assignments,
  Leases, **Land & Ten** ☞ **75(3), 76(3)**
  Covenants, conditions or restrictions, **Land & Ten** ☞ **76(3)**

SUBMERGED LANDS

ACTIONS and proceedings,
  Navigable waters, lands under,
    Boundaries, determination of, **Nav Wat**
      ☞ **36(6)**
    Division, **Nav Wat** ☞ **36(6)**
    Partition, **Nav Wat** ☞ **36(6)**
    Recovery of submerged lands, **Nav Wat**
      ☞ **36(7)**
    Trespass, **Nav Wat** ☞ **36(5)**
  Nonnavigable waters, lands under,
    Lakes and ponds, **Waters** ☞ **114**
    Water courses, **Waters** ☞ **98**

BOUNDARIES, lands under navigable
  waters, determination of, **Nav Wat**
    ☞ **36(6)**

CONSTRUCTION of grants of lands under
  navigable waters, **Nav Wat** ☞ **37(4)**

CONVEYANCES. See subheading GRANTS
  under this heading.

COUNTIES, grants of lands under navigable
  waters to, **Nav Wat** ☞ **37(8)**

DIVISION of lands under navigable waters,
  Nav Wat ☞ **36(6)**

DREDGING and filling, **Nav Wat** ☞ **38**

EQUAL footing doctrine, **Nav Wat** ☞ **36(1)**

FLATS,
  Navigable waters, **Nav Wat** ☞ **36(2)**
  Nonnavigable water courses, **Waters** ☞ **92**

FORFEITURE of grant of land under
  navigable waters, **Nav Wat** ☞ **37(5)**

GRANTS,
  Navigable waters, lands under,
    Generally, **Nav Wat** ☞ **37**
    Construction, **Nav Wat** ☞ **37(4)**
    Counties, grants to, **Nav Wat** ☞ **37(8)**
    Forfeiture, **Nav Wat** ☞ **37(5)**
    Grantees, **Nav Wat** ☞ **37(3, 4)**
    Leases, **Nav Wat** ☞ **37(6)**
    Municipal corporations, grants to, **Nav Wat** ☞ **37(8)**
    Power to grant, **Nav Wat** ☞ **37(2)**
    Riparian lands, **Nav Wat** ☞ **37(7)**
    Towns, grants to, **Nav Wat** ☞ **37(8)**

FIGURE 2.8   Words and Phrases Section

Source: From *West's Federal Practice Digest, 4th.* Used with permission from Thomson West.

113 F P D 4th—149   **SIGNATORY OPERATOR**

Marasco, 227 F.Supp.2d 322, affirmed in part, reversed in part 318 F.3d 497, on remand 2004 WL 633276.—Arrest 68(4).

SHRINK-WRAP

W.D.Pa. 2000. "Shrink-wrap" software licenses, which the customer impliedly assents to by, for example, opening the envelope enclosing the software distribution media, are generally valid and enforceable.—Peerless Wall and Window Coverings, Inc. v. Synchronics, Inc., 85 F.Supp.2d 519, affirmed 234 F.3d 1265.—Copyr 107.

[case →]

[topic & key →]

SHTAR ISKA

Bkrtcy.S.D.N.Y. 2000. "Heter iska" is a type of joint venture designed to avoid Jewish law's prohibition against charging interest, pursuant to which the moneys advanced are treated as a contribution to the venture, and the venturer who advances the funds, that is, the lender, is entitled to an accounting, in lieu of which the parties execute a "shtar iska" which obligates the other venturer, that is, the borrower, to pay a fixed monthly return corresponding to the interest payments called for under the promissory note, and requires the lender to waive any further profits.— In re Venture Mortg Fund, L.P., 245 B.R. 460, subsequently affirmed 282 F.3d 185.—Usury 38.

SICKNESS

C.A.8 (Ark.) 2004. Under Arkansas law, as predicted by Court of Appeals, disabling loss of vision that insured orthopedic surgeon sustained as result of complications from eye surgery constituted "accidental bodily injury" within meaning of disability insurance policies, for which insured was entitled to lifetime benefits, and not "sickness," for which benefits were only payable until age 65; insured's vision loss was not expected, proceeded from unidentified cause, and occurred only by chance.—Kolb v. Paul Revere Life Ins. Co., 355 F.3d 1132.—Insurance 2544(1), 2545(2), 2569.

C.D.Cal. 2002. Neither party's experts, in widow's action against insurer asserting breach of contract claim and seeking declaratory relief arising from insurer's denial of claim under accidental death policy, could testify about whether high-altitude pulmonary edema (HAPE), of which widow's husband died, was a "sickness" within meaning of policy's clause excluding coverage for loss resulting from or caused by physical or mental sickness; the definition of "sickness," not set out in the policy, and the application of that definition to HAPE, were legal, rather than factual, questions, and had to be determined by the Court.—Paulissen v. U.S. Life Ins. Co. in City of New York, 205 F.Supp.2d 1120.—Evid 506, 518.

C.D.Cal. 2002. Although "sickness," "disease," and "illness" have broad, generic definitions, the definitions are narrowly construed in the context of insurance policies.—Paulissen v.

U.S. Life Ins. Co. in City of New York, 205 F.Supp.2d 1120.—Insurance 2589(1).

C.D.Cal. 2002. Mountain climber's high-altitude pulmonary edema (HAPE) was not, under California law, a "sickness" for purpose of accidental death policy's sickness exclusion; his HAPE was not a disorder of a somewhat established or settled character, and did not arise from some organic cause, but rather, arose from exposure to high altitudes, and his symptoms would likely have been completely relieved, without medical intervention, if he had reached a lower elevation more quickly.—Paulissen v. U.S. Life Ins. Co. in City of New York, 205 F.Supp.2d 1120.—Insurance 2589(1).

SICKNESS OR DISEASE

E.D.Mich. 2004. Insured's gallstones constituted "sickness or disease," for purposes of exclusion in accidental death and dismemberment policy precluding recovery for loss resulting from sickness or disease; gallstone developed through internal organic functioning of body, and was present in insured's body for almost two years.— Miller v. Hartford Life Ins. Co., 348 F.Supp.2d 815.—Insurance 2589(1).

SIGNALING

N.D.Ga. 2002. In the antitrust context, "signaling" means either that a competitor is inviting all to make a traditional price-fixing agreement, or that there already exists such an agreement and it is being carried out through indirect communications. Sherman Act, § 1, as amended, 15 U.S.C.A. § 1.—Holiday Wholesale Grocery Co. v. Philip Morris Inc., 231 F.Supp.2d 1253, affirmed Williamson Oil Co., Inc. v. Philip Morris USA, 346 F.3d 1287.—Monop 17(1.12).

SIGNAL PICKETING

C.D.Cal. 2003. As used in labor law context; "signal picketing" generally refers to union activity designed to induce employees to strike, not activity designed to inspire consumer boycott.— Kohn v. Southwest Regional Council of Carpenters, 289 F.Supp.2d 1155—Labor & Emp 1379, 1412.

SIGNATORY OPERATOR

U.S. 2002. A "signatory operator" responsible for annual premiums under the Coal Industry Retiree Health Benefit Act is a coal operator that signed any National Bituminous Coal Wage Agreement or any other agreement requiring contributions to the 1950 or 1974 Benefit Plans negotiated between a mine workers' union and various coal operators. 26 U.S.C.A. § 9701(c)(1).— Barnhart v. Sigmon Coal Co., Inc., 122 S.Ct. 941, 534 U.S. 438, 197 A.L.R. Fed. 689, 151 L.Ed.2d 908.—Labor & Emp 529.

FIGURE 2.9   A Judicial Construction of *Shrink-Wrap*

Source: From *Federal Supplement, 2nd Series.* Used with permission from Thomson West.

topic

PEERLESS WALL AND WINDOW COVERINGS, INC., Plaintiff,

v.

SYNCHRONICS, INC., a Tennessee Corporation, Defendant.

No. CIV. A. 98–1084.

United States District Court,
W.D. Pennsylvania.

Feb. 25, 2000.

Licensee of cash register software which was not year 2000 (Y2K) compliant sued licensor, alleging breach of contract, express and implied warranties, fraud and negligent misrepresentation. Licensor moved for summary judgment. The District Court, D. Brooks Smith, J., held that: (1) possibility of recovering punitive damages satisfied amount in controversy requirement for diversity jurisdiction purposes; (2) implied warranties of merchantability and fitness were disclaimed; (3) 90-day express warranty covered only media containing software, not software itself; (4) integration clause in license precluded fraud claims based on sales literature; (5) under Tennessee law as interpreted by federal court, licensor had duty to disclose that software was not Y2K compliant; (6) fraud claims failed due to lack of showing of reliance; (7) economic loss doctrine precluded recovery for negligent misrepresentation; and (8) nominal damages showing precluded summary judgment based on absence of damages.

Summary judgment for licensor.

1. Federal Courts ☞ 337

Possibility of punitive damages, in putative class action suit by buyer of computer software seeking free upgrade to Y2K compliant software, satisfied amount in controversy requirement for diversity jurisdiction, despite upgrade cost of only $1,500 to $2,000.

2. Copyrights and Intellectual Property ☞ 107

relevant topic and key

"Shrink-wrap" software licenses, which the customer impliedly assents to by, for example, opening the envelope enclosing the software distribution media, are generally valid and enforceable.

 See publication Words and Phrases for other judicial constructions and definitions.

3. Copyrights and Intellectual Property ☞ 107

All implied warranties of merchantability and fitness were disclaimed in software license agreement, through disclaimer statement prominently displayed on outside of software container, and by licensee's having signed and returned software registration form including recitation that licensee had read and agreed to software license terms.

4. Copyrights and Intellectual Property ☞ 107

Provision of license agreement covering cash register software, extended express 90-day warranty that software-diskettes and user manual would be free from defects in materials and workmanship read in conjunction with provision that entire risk of performance of software was with licensee, created express warranty of software media, rather than software itself.

5. Evidence ☞ 400(6)

Broad integration clause contained in software license agreement precluded claim that sales literature for software created warranty more extensive than warranty provided in license.

6. Copyrights and Intellectual Property ☞ 107

Statement in sales literature for cash register software, that user would remain up to date, did not commit provider to offer free upgrade to make software Y2K compliant; reference was to ability of software to keep current records of user's business transactions.

7. Evidence ☞ 400(3)

Presence of integration clause in computer software license precluded resort to parol evidence to elaborate upon statement in license making it effective for "useful life" of software.

8. Contracts ☞ 94(4)

Under Pennsylvania law, "fraud in the execution" applies to situations in which parties agree to include certain terms in an agreement, but the terms are not included.

 See publication Words and Phrases for other judicial constructions and definitions.

9. Fraud ☞ 3

Under Pennsylvania law, "fraud in the inducement" involves allegations of repre-

FIGURE 2.9 Cont.

the existence of every element essential to its case. *Id.* Such evidence must be significantly probative and more than "merely colorable." *Armbruster v. Unisys Corp.,* 32 F.3d 768, 777 (3d Cir.1994).

Once the moving party has satisfied its burden, the nonmoving party is required by Fed.R.Civ.P. 56(e) to establish that there remains a genuine issue of material fact. *Clark v. Clabaugh,* 20 F.3d 1290, 1294 (3d Cir.1994). The nonmovant "may not rest upon mere allegation or denials of [its] pleadings, but must set forth specific facts showing that there is a genuine issue for trial." *Anderson v. Liberty Lobby, Inc.,* 477 U.S. 242, 256, 106 S.Ct. 2505, 91 L.Ed.2d 202 (1986). A fact is material if it "might affect the outcome of the suit under the governing law[,]" *id.* at 248, 106 S.Ct. 2505,[9] and is genuine "if the evidence is such that a reasonable jury could return a verdict for the nonmoving party." *Id.* at 248, 257, 106 S.Ct. 2505.

In determining whether a nonmovant has established the existence of a genuine issue of material fact requiring a jury trial, the evidence of the nonmovant must "be believed and all justifiable inferences are to be drawn in [its] favor." *Id.* at 255, 106 S.Ct. 2505. Whether an inference is justifiable, however, depends on the evidence adduced. *Matsushita Elec. Indus. Co. v. Zenith Radio Corp.,* 475 U.S. 574, 595–96, 106 S.Ct. 1348, 89 L.Ed.2d 538 (1986). An inference based upon speculation or conjecture does not create a material factual dispute sufficient to defeat summary judgment. *Robertson v. Allied Signal, Inc.,* 914 F.2d 360, 382 n. 12 (3d Cir.1990). Likewise, "simply show[ing] that there is some metaphysical doubt as to the material facts" does not establish a genuine issue for trial. *Matsushita,* 475 U.S. at 586, 106 S.Ct. 1348.

III.

A. WARRANTY

[2] As stated *supra,* the software plaintiff acquired was distributed pursuant to a license agreement printed on the diskette envelopes and in the user manuals. The recent weight of authority is that "shrink-wrap" licenses which the customer impliedly assents to by, for example, opening the envelope enclosing the software distribution media, are generally valid and enforceable. *See Hill v. Gateway 2000, Inc.,* 105 F.3d 1147, 1150 (7th Cir.1997) (Easterbrook, J.); *ProCD, Inc. v. Zeidenberg,* 86 F.3d 1447, 1452 (7th Cir.1996) (Easterbrook, J.); *M.A. Mortenson Co. v. Timberline Software Corp.,* 93 Wash.App. 819, 970 P.2d 803, 809–811, *review granted,* 138 Wash.2d 1001, 984 P.2d 1033 (1999); *Paragon Networks Int'l v. Macola, Inc.,* No. 9–99–2, 1999 WL 280385, *4 (Ohio App.Ct. Apr. 28, 1999) (unpublished). *But cf. Step–Saver Data Sys., Inc. v. Wyse Technology,* 939 F.2d 91, 95–106 (3d Cir. 1991) (analyzing enforceability of license under U.C.C. § 2–207 as a "battle of the forms" problem and finding license unenforceable because of prior conduct and manifested expectations of the parties).[10] As Judge Easterbrook insightfully opined:

> Vendors can put the entire terms of a contract on the outside of a box only by using microscopic type, removing other information that buyers might find more useful (such as what the software does, and on which computers it works), or both. . . . Notice on the outside, terms on the inside, and a right to return the software for a refund if the terms are unacceptable . . . may be a means of doing business valuable to buyers and sellers alike. . . . Transactions in which the exchange of money precedes the communication of detailed terms are

---

9. The parties agree that Tennessee law applies in the case *sub judice,* but disagree whether it differs in any material respect from that of Pennsylvania. I will treat the two bodies of law as interchangeable (especially

with respect to the contract claims under the U.C.C.) unless the difference is significant.

10. Neither party contends that *Step–Saver* is controlling here.

FIGURE 2.10   Table of Cases

Source: From *West's Federal Practice Digest, 4th.* Used with permission from Thomson West.

PEEPER   103 F P D 4th—424

References are to Digest Topics and Key Numbers

Peeper's Sunglasses and Accessories, Inc. peepers; American Eyewear, Inc. v., NDTex, 106 FSupp2d 895.—Const Law 305(5); Fed Cts 76.10; Trademarks 1560.

Peeples v. Bradshaw, CA6 (Ohio), 110 FedAppx 590.—Fed Civ Proc 2734.

Peeples v. Coastal Office Products, Inc., CA4 (Md), 64 FedAppx 860.—Labor & Emp 358.

Peeples v. Coastal Office Products, Inc., DMd, 203 FSupp2d 432, aff 64 FedAppx 860.—Civil R 1018, 1019(2); 1218(6), 1225(1), 1243, 1244, 1252, 1431, 1516, 1540, 1541; Labor & Emp 355.

Peeples; U.S. v., CA11 (Fla), 23 F3d 370.—Sent & Pun 652, 664(6).

Peeples v. Wright Inv. Properties, Inc., MDGa, 36 FSupp2d 1378, aff 204 F3d 1122, reh and sug for reh den 209 F3d 726, cert den 120 SCt 2662, 530 US 1231, 147 LEd2d 276.—Civil R 1217, 1218(4).

Peer; U.S. v., CA4 (SC), 102 FedAppx 777.—Crim Law 1023(11).

Peer; U.S. v., CA10 (Utah), 119 FedAppx 216.—Crim Law 1073.

Peer; Venegas-Hernandez v., DPuerto Rico, 283 FSupp2d 491.—Contracts 147(2), 152, Copyr 33, 47, 47.5; Judgm 540, 584, 713(1), 828.15(2), 828.16(2), 828.16(4).

Peer Bearing Co. v. U.S., CIT, 182 FSupp2d 1285, opinion after remand 2002 WL 1285134, aff 78 FedAppx 718.—Admin Law 416.1; Const Law 318(1); Cust Dut 21.5(1), 21.5(3), 21.5(5), 84(6); Statut 219(1), 219(2), 219(6.1).

Peer Bearing Co.-Changshan v. U.S., CIT, 298 FSupp2d 1328.—Admin Law 330; Cust Dut 21.5(1), 21.5(3), 21.5(5); Statut 217.4, 219(1).

Peer Chain Co. v. U.S., CIT, 316 FSupp2d 1357.—Const Law 286; Cust Dut 21.5(5), 81.

Peer Intern. Corp. v. Latin American Music Corp., DPuerto Rico, 161 FSupp2d 38.—Can of Inst 1; Contracts 316(1); Copyr 33, 44, 46, 47, 47.5, 48, 49, 50.16, 52, 66, 67.2, 75.5, 76, 83(1), 83(3.5), 88.

Peer Intern. Corp.; Venegas Hernandez v., DPuerto Rico, 270 FSupp2d 207.—Copyr 33, 44, 51, 103, 104; Hus & W 249(2.1); Judgm 540, 562, 564(1), 585(1), 668(1), 828.6, 828.20(2).

Peerless Importers, Inc. v. Wine, Liquor & Distillery Workers Union Local One, CA2 (NY), 903 F2d 924.—Labor & Emp 1546(1), 1549(4), 1579.

Peerless Importers, Inc. v. Wine, Liquor & Distillery Workers Union Local One, SDNY, 712 FSupp 346, rev 903 F2d 924.—Labor & Emp 1549(19), 1549(21).

Peerless Ins. Co.; M. Fortunoff of Westbury Corp. v., EDNY, 260 FSupp2d 524.—Insurance 2888, 2889; Statut 184, 190, 208, 212.1, 212.5, 223.5(0.5), 230.

Peerless Ins. Co. v. U.S., EDVa, 674 FSupp 1202.—U S 74.1.

Peerless Motor Car Corp.; Wood v., CCA6 (Ohio), 75 F2d 554.—Pat 16.22, 233.1.

Peerless Plating Co., In re, BkrtcyWDMich, 70 BR 943.—Bankr 2830.5, 2876.5.

Peerless Systems, Corp. Securities Litigation, In re, SDCal, 182 FSupp2d 982.—Fed Civ Proc 1832; Sec Reg 60.15, 60.18, 60.27(6), 60.28(10.1), 60.45(1), 60.51, 60.53.

relevant case ── **Peerless Wall and Window Coverings, Inc. v. Synchronics, Inc.,** WDPa, 85 FSupp2d 519, aff 234 F3d 1265.—Contracts 94(4); Copyr 107, Evid 400(3), 400(6), 434(8); Fed Cts 337; Fraud 3, 11(1), 17, 20, 25, 32, 36.

Peer Morton; Ulysses I & Co., Inc. v., CA2 (NY), 11 FedAppx 14, cert den 122 SCt 458, 534 US 992, 151

LEd2d 376.—Civil R 1351(1), 1401; Courts 509; Fed Cts 1142.

Peer Review Systems, Inc.; Whitley v., CA8 (Minn), 221 F3d 1053.—Civil R 1118, 1122, 1137, 1536, 1545; Fed Civ Proc 2497.1; Fed Cts 776.

Peery v. Brakke, CA8 (SD), 826 F2d 740.—Civil R 1448; Judgm 828.7.

Peery; U.S. v., CA8 (Neb), 977 F2d 1230, cert den 113 SCt 1354, 507 US 946, 122 LEd2d 734.—Sent & Pun 765.

Pees; U.S. v., DColo, 645 FSupp 697.—Controlled Subs 6, 9.

Peet; Emmons, Estate of v., DMe, 950 FSupp 15.—Health 699, 703(2); Sent & Pun 1436, 1595.

Peete; U.S. v., CA6 (Tenn), 919 F2d 1168.—Jury 33(5.15); Sent & Pun 1963, 1972(2).

Peets v. U.S., SDNY, 55 FSupp2d 275.—Crim Law 1437, 1438, 1439, 1440(3).

Peffer; Alexander v., CA8 (Neb), 993 F2d 1348.—Civil R 1040, 1304.

Peffley v. Durakool, Inc., NDInd, 669 FSupp 1453.—Civil R 1505(3), 1505(6), 1555; Labor & Emp 806, 1320(14), 1518, 1549(19); Libel 1.

Peffley v. Hermaseal Co., NDInd, 669 FSupp 1453. See Peffley v. Durakool, Inc.

Pegan; Randall v., WDNY, 765 FSupp 793.—Civil R 1457(1), 1457(3).

Pegasus Broadcasting of San Juan, Inc. v. N.L.R.B., CA1, 82 F3d 511.—Labor & Emp 1490(3), 1811, 1860, 1866.

Pegasus Communications of Puerto Rico; Delgado Graulau v., DPuerto Rico, 130 FSupp2d 320.—Admin Law 501; Civil R 1122, 1123, 1168, 1171, 1197, 1505(3), 1505(7), 1711; Fed Civ Proc 2497.1; Lim of Act 95(15), 105(1), 195(3).

Pegasus Gold Corp., In re, CA9 (Nev), 394 F3d 1189.—Bankr 2043(3), 2679, 3570, 3765, 3768, 3782, Fed Civ Proc 776; Fed Cts 14.1, 266.1, 267, 269, 272.

Pegasus Gold Corp., In re, DNev, 296 BR 227, aff in part, rev in part 394 F3d 1189.—Bankr 2043(3), 2056, 2679, 3568(1), 3570, 3782, 3786; Estop 68(2); Judgm 651, 668(1), 713(1), 715(1), 720, 724.

Pegasus Gold Corp., In re, BkrtcyDNev, 275 BR 902, aff 296 BR 227, aff in part, rev in part 394 F3d 1189.—Bankr 2041.1, 2041.5, 2042, 2043(3), 2047, 2056, 2102, 2679, 3568(1), 3570; Const Law 43(1); Fed Cts 5, 14.1, 18, 23, 265, 266.1, 267.

Pegasus Helicopters, Inc. v. United Technologies Corp., CA10 (Colo), 35 F3d 507.—Prod Liab 17.1; Sales 260, 261(6).

Pegasus Petroleum Corp.; Mobil Oil Corp. v., CA2 (NY), 818 F2d 254.—Trademarks 1058, 1081, 1096(3), 1101, 1104, 1111, 1466, 1610, 1630, 1800.

Pegasus Satellite Television, Inc v. DirecTV, Inc., CDCal, 318 FSupp2d 968.—Cons Prot 40; Contracts 187(1); Decl Judgm 301; Fed Civ Proc 103.2, 103.3, 928, 2559; Fed Cts 5, 12.1, 13, 31, 33, 34; Tel 1286; Trade Reg 862.1, 864.

Pegasystems, Inc.; Gelfer v., DMass, 96 FSupp2d 10.—Sec Reg 35.15, 60.45(1).

Pegg v. General Motors Corp., DKan, 785 FSupp 901, on reconsideration 1992 WL 123768.—Civil R 1168, 1204; Labor & Emp 36, 438, 638, 686, 863(1).

Pegg v. U.S., CA11 (Fla), 253 F3d 1274, reh and reh den 273 F3d 395, cert den 122 SCt 1435, 535 US 970, 152 LEd2d 380.—Crim Law 641.5(0.5), 641.13(5), 1517.

Pegg; U.S. v., MDFla, 49 FSupp2d 1322, aff 253 F3d 1274, reh and reh den 273 F3d 395, cert den 122 SC 1435, 535 US 970, 152 LEd2d 380.—Crim Law 1429(2), 1437, 1438, 1451.

For Later Case History Information, see KeyCite on WESTLAW

FIGURE 2.11 Defendant/Plaintiff Table

Source: From *West's Federal Practice Digest, 4th.* Used with permission from Thomson West.

SYMANTEC

103C F P D 4th—392

References are to Digest Topics and Key Numbers

141, appeal after remand 29 F3d 630, cert den 115 SCt 638, 513 US 1044; 130 LEd2d 544.—Fed Civ Proc 2493; Fed Cts 947; Trademarks 1428(2).

Symantec Corp, v. CD Micro, Inc., DOr, 286 FSupp2d 1278.—Copyr 87(3.1); Trademarks 1566, 1653, 1656(3), 1658.

Symantec Corp. v. CD Micro, Inc., DOr, 286 FSupp2d 1265.—Copyr 38.5, 48, 51, 75, 77, 80, 83(3.5); Equity 67; Trademarks 1116, 1208, 1299, 1421, 1435, 1565.

Symantec Corp.; Hilgraeve Corp. v., CAFed, 265 F3d 1336, reh and reh den, cert den 122 SCt 1206, 535 US 906, 152 LEd2d 144, on remand 212 FRD 345.—Fed Cts 763.1, 766; Pat 101(2), 206, 211(1), 226.6, 234, 259(1), 312(2), 314(5), 323.2(2), 323.2(3), 324.5, 328(2).

Symantec Corp.; Hilgraeve Corp. v., EDMich, 90 FSupp2d 850, vac 265 F3d 1336, reh and reh den, cert den 122 SCt 1206, 535 US 906, 152 LEd2d 144, on remand 212 FRD 345.—Judgm 634; Pat 101(2), 159, 162, 165(3), 167(1), 167(1.1), 168(2.1), 226.6, 229, 230, 237, 314(5), 327(13), 328(2).

Symantec Corp.; Hilgraeve Corp. v., EDMich, 212 FRD 345.—Fed Cts 13; Pat 310.11.

Symantec Corp.; Hilgraeve, Inc. v., EDMich; 272 FSupp2d 613.—Pat 259(1), 312(1.1), 312(8), 319(1), 323.2(3), 328(2).

Symantec Corp.; Hilgraeve, Inc. v., EDMich, 271 FSupp2d 964.—Pat 16(2), 59, 101(6), 112.5, 226.6, 323.2(3), 323.2(4), 324.60, 328(2).

Symbiotics, L.L.C. v. F.E.R.C., CA10, 110 FedAppx 76.—Electricity 8.4.

Symbol Technologies, Inc.; Datastrip (IOM) Ltd. v., CAFed, 15 FedAppx 843.—Pat 101(2), 235(2).

Symbol Technologies, Inc. v. Lemelson Medical, CA-Fed (Nev), 277 F3d 1361, reh en bane den, cert den Lemelson Medical, Education & Research Foundation v. Symbol Technologies, 123 SCt 113, 537 US 825; 154 LEd2d 36.—Courts 96(5), 96(7); Fed Cts 766; Pat 289(2.1), 328(2).

Symbol Technologies, Inc. v. Lemelson Medical, Educ. & Research Foundation, Ltd. Partnership, DNev, 301 FSupp2d 1147.—Pat 62(3), 66(1.14), 72(1), 97, 99, 110, 159, 160, 161, 165(1), 165(2), 165(3), 167(1), 167(1.1), 168(2.1), 235(2), 289(2.1), 289(4), 325.11(2.1), 328(2).

Symbol Technologies, Inc. v. Metrologic Instruments, Inc., CA2 (NY), 84 FedAppx 112.—Fed Cts 599.

Symbol Technologies, Inc.; Morrissey v., EDNY, 910 FSupp 117.—Civil R 1176, 1537, 1549.

Symbol Technologies, Inc. v. Opticon, Inc., CAFed (NY), 935 F2d 1569, reh den.—Pat 312(1.1), 312(1.2).

Symbol Technologies, Inc., Oye on Behalf of, v. Swartz, EDNY, 762 FSupp 510. See Symbol Technologies Securities Litigation, In re.

Symbol Technologies Securities Litigation, In re, EDNY, 762 FSupp 510.—Trusts 30.5(1).

Syme; U.S. v., CA3 (Del); 276 F3d 131, cert den 123 SCt 619, 537 US 1050, 154 LEd2d 525.—Crim Law 469, 469.1, 881(1), 1030(1), 1032(5), 1038.1(1), 1042, 1043(3), 1144.15, 1167(2), 1167(4), 1172.1(2), 1172.1(3), 1181.5(3.1); Double J 93; Ind & Inf 55, 159(2); Jury 34(1); Postal 35(2); Sent & Pun 2187; Tel 1014(2); U S 121.

Symens v. SmithKline Beecham Corp., CA8 (SD), 152 F3d 1050, appeal after remand 7 FedAppx 534.—Health 107, 322; Prod Liab 46.4.

Symens v. Smithkline Beecham Corp., DSD, 19 FSupp2d 1062, rev in part 152 F3d 1050, appeal after remand 7 FedAppx 534.—Prod Liab 46.4.

Symeonidis v. Paxton Capital Group, Inc., DMd, 220 FSupp2d 478.—Fraud 4; Labor & Emp 256(5), 759, 771, 777, 778, 782, 852.

Symington v. Daisy Mfg. Co., Inc., DND, 360 FSupp2d 1027.—Evid 513(1), 539, 555.2, 555.7; Fed Civ Proc 2515, 2536.1, 2538, 2539, 2545; 2554.

Symington v. Great Western Trucking Co., Inc., SDIowa, 668 FSupp 1278.—Indem 13.1(2.1).

Symington; Parks College v., CA9 (Ariz), 51 F3d 1480. See Parks School of Business, Inc. v. Symington.

Symington; Parks School of Business; Inc. v., CA9 (Ariz), 51 F3d 1480.—Civil R 1027, 1326(4), 1326(5), 1326(6), 1326(7), 1395(1), 1395(2), 1482, 1484.

Symmetricom, Inc.; Shuster, v., CA9 (Cal), 35 FedAppx 705.—Fed Civ Proc 2511; Sec Reg 60.27(1), 60.45(1).

Symms Fruit Ranch, Inc; Chao v., CA9, 242 F3d 894.—Admin Law 413, Labor & Emp 2605, 2611(3); Statut 219(1), 219(6.1).

Symonds; U.S v., CA8 (Iowa), 260 F3d 934.—Consp 51; Crim Law 1158(1); Sent & Pun 66, 94.

Symons; Gould v., EDMich, 275 FSupp2d 843.—Civil R 1376(1), 1376(2), 1376(4).

Symons Corp.; EFCO Corp. v., CA8(Iowa), 219 F3d 734.—Damag 15; Evid 508, 555.2; 555.9; Fed Civ Proc 2339; Fed Cts 415, 715, 763.1, 776, 798, 801, 823, 825.1, 826; Interest 39(2.10), 39(2.20); Torts 215, 241; Trade Reg 870(1), 984, 991, 1002, 1007, 1009.

Symons Corp.; Watson v., NDIll, 121 FRD 351.—Fed Civ Proc 2651.1.

Symorex, Inc v. Siemens Industrial Automation, ED-Mich, 151 FSupp2d 844, vac.—Damag 2, 67; Fed Civ Proc 2774(1), 2828; Interest 22(1), 31, 39(2.6), 39(2.20), 49.

Syms Corp.; Lawrence v., EDMich, 969 FSupp 1014.—Civil R 1118, 1138, 1158, 1159, 1204, 1744.

Syms Corp.; Levine v., NDOhio, 982 FSupp 492.—Civil R 1201, 1203.

Synagro-WWT, Inc v. Rush Tp., Penn., MDPa, 204 FSupp2d 827.—Commerce 13.5, 56; Const Law 48(4.1), 48(6), 115, 154(1), 211(2), 250.5, 251.3, 278.1; Environ Law 346(1); Fed Civ Proc 948, 1788.6; Fed Cts 41, 43, 46; Mines 92.8; Mun Corp 53, 592(1), 621, 956(1), 957(0.5); States 18.3; Tax 2121.

Synagro-WWT, Inc. v. Rush Tp., Pennsylvania, MDPa, 299 FSupp2d 410.—Environ Law 352, 653; Mines 92.8, Mun Corp 111(4), 121, 592(1); Statut 64(1).

Synanon Church v. U.S., CADC, 820 F2d 421, 261 USAppDC 13.—Judgm 828.16(1), 828.21(3).

Synaptic Pharmaceuticals Corp. v. MDS Panlabs, Inc., DNJ, 265 FSupp2d 452.—Pat 165(5), 226, 226.6, 234, 237, 257, 258, 259(1), 259(3), 323.2(3), 328(2); Statut 190, 217.4

Synar v. U S., DDC, 670 FSupp 410.—U S 147(11.1).

Synbiotics Corp. v. Heska Corp., SDCal, 137 FSupp2d 1198.—Fed Civ Proc 2544; Pat 52, 57.1, 65, 67.1, 69, 70, 72(1), 165(4), 328(2).

Synchronics, Inc.; Peerless Wall and Window Coverings, Inc. v., WDPa, 85 FSupp2d 519, aff 234 F3d 1265.—Contracts 94(4); Copyr 107; Evid 400(3), 400(6), 434(8); Fed Cts 337; Fraud 3, 11(1), 17, 20, 25, 32, 36.

Synchro-Start Products, Inc.; E.E.O.C. v., NDIll, 29 FSupp2d 911.—Civil R 1118, 1140, 1147, 1536.

Syncor ERISA Litigation, In re, CDCal, 351 FSupp2d 970.—Courts 89; Fed Civ Proc 636, 1832, 1835; Labor & Emp 459, 473, 475, 478, 491(2), 646.

Syncor Erisa Litigation, In re, CDCal, 227 FRD 338.—Fed Civ Proc 172, 184.5.

Syncor Intern. Corp. v. Shalala, CADC, 127 F3d 90, 326 USAppDC 422.—Health 322.

Syncor Intern. Corp. Securities Litigation, In re, CDCal, 327 FSupp2d 1149.—Evid 1, 48; Fed Civ Proc

For Later Case History Information, see KeyCite on WESTLAW

relevant case

You Be the Judge

Hypothetical 2-2

Research done by attorneys and paralegals must be thorough and complete. Searching digests for headnotes and key numbers is important to the legal research process. Failure to perform these routine tasks can have devastating effects on a client's case. In *Stephens v. Kemp*, 602 F. Supp. 960 (M.D. Ga. 1984), the court admonished a law firm for its poor research in a *habeas corpus* case. Review the case. What message did the court send to the attorneys in the case? Were the actions of the court warranted? Was the result in the case harsh? Why or why not? Once again, this case shows the importance of proper and complete legal research.

PRACTICE TIP

When preparing a brief, a memorandum of law, or any other legal document, limit the use of secondary authority, especially encyclopedias. Never cite a finding tool as your authority for a legal point.

pocket parts
Annual supplements to digests.

This discussion has focused on the digests in the West system, which are of preeminent importance in legal research. There are also digests for many official reporters, the *American Law Reports (A.L.R.)* system, and other unofficial reporters. You should check your jurisdiction for other official or unofficial digests.

Remember, digests and other finding tools are exactly that—finding tools. They are considered nonauthoritative resources and should not be used or quoted in a legal document. Only cite primary and secondary authority when preparing a formal legal document.

Pocket Parts

The purpose of a multivolume digest—facilitating research—requires that it reference the most recent cases. Each volume, however, is manufactured to last for years. It would be prohibitively expensive to purchase new hardbound volumes every year, so how do these sets stay current?

The answer is through the use of **pocket parts.** Pocket parts are annual (or sometimes more frequent) supplements. Each pocket part corresponds to one volume of the digest set, and is fitted into a pocket inside the back cover of the book. The pocket part contains all the recent headnotes that would have appeared in the main volume had they been available when it went to press. These headnotes are organized in the pocket part as they would have been in the main volume—in the West system, for example, by topic and key number.

In addition to annual pocket parts, digests can be supplemented at more frequent intervals by individual paperbound volumes that collect all the material subsequent to the most recent set of pocket parts. In this manner, the content of the digest set is kept current.

Pocket parts are used in many legal publications besides digests, including the *American Law Reports* series, state and federal statutory sets, legal encyclopedias, and even some treatises.

When doing legal research, it is absolutely essential that you check for pocket parts! If you haven't assured yourself that you've checked all pocket parts and all paperbound volumes updating pocket parts, then you haven't finished your research. You may even have missed the most recent case on the subject! Get in the habit of checking each resource you use to verify that you've utilized its latest update—be it a pocket part, a paperbound volume, or some other form of update.

UPDATING THE LAW

Now that you have learned about the many sources of the law in Chapter 1, and the ways of finding the law that relate to your particular research subject, you may be wondering, How can I be sure a case I found hasn't been overruled? This is, in fact, a very important consideration. Just because a case appears as a published opinion in a reporter doesn't mean the principles established in the case are still "good law" (that is to say, still valid precedents). The opinion may have been reversed on appeal, or a later decision by a higher court in a different case may have resolved the same legal issue in a different way, overruling the earlier decision. The solution to this concern is an amazing series of volumes known as *Shepard's Citations*. The Shepard's system is so useful that verifying the precedential value of a case is now referred to as "**Shepardizing.**"

Shepardizing
Using Shepard's verification and updating system for cases, statutes, and other legal resources.

Shepardizing

The Shepard's system updates every case ever printed in every commonly used reporter. Think about that for a second. Let's say that you found a 1965 case from your jurisdiction that covers our landlord/tenant problem. Without Shepard's, you'd have to search through the text of every subsequent case to see if your 1965 case had been overturned. But with Shepard's, the task is greatly simplified. The Shepard's system lists every reference ever made to your case!

The easiest way to demonstrate the system is by example. Remember our landlord/tenant case, *Young v. District of Columbia*? Let's Shepardize it. We won't do a full search, because by the time this book gets to print the search will already be incomplete. But you'll understand the basic principles even through our partial search.

Figure 2.12 is a page from *Shepard's Atlantic Reporter Citations*. Highlighted are the notations for "752," "A.2d," and "138," which correspond to the citation for our case. We've located the correct Shepard's set, found the reference to volume 752 of the second series, and found the reference to page 138 of that volume. Turning to the entry under the 138 notation, we find a citation to another case, 829 A.2d 515. Figure 2.13 is page 515 from volume 829 of the second series of the *Atlantic Reporter*. Sure enough, there is a reference to our case!

This reference didn't overturn our case. However, suppose a higher court had overturned our case? What then?

The Shepard's system would place a small *o* in the margin by the entry, which stands for *overruled*. The Shepard's system employs a whole series of marginal abbreviations (listed in Figure 2.14), which summarize the direct procedural history and subsequent treatment of the case. The absence of a marginal abbreviation next to the referenced case is an indication that, although the case was cited, it was not cited for any of the significant reasons requiring marginal notation. Our case has an "f" next to it, which means that the court citing the case followed our case. This reference is positive treatment and is the type of case you may want to review. Scan the page reprinted in Figure 2.12 and find as many marginal notations as you can; then use Figure 2.14 to find out what each one means.

You might be saying to yourself, Why bother with the marginal notations? Why not just look up every case in which your case is cited? After all, for *Young v. District of Columbia* there was only one case to look up. For the answer to this question, we suggest you try Shepardizing *Miranda v. Arizona*.

The level of specificity provided in the entries goes even further. For cases with several headnotes, the entry will often identify by the use of a small numeral (see the entries for pages 49 and 194 in Figure 2.12) the headnote to which the referenced citation refers.

The Shepard's system has other uses in addition to verifying precedential value. It can help you find parallel citations, for example, and other cases that are similar in content to the case being Shepardized.

There are Shepard's sets for most reporters, as well as for statutes, law review articles, and other publications. Although the basic system is easy to master, you should spend some time looking over the actual sets in your law library. The high volume of opinions generated by the court system has required many Shepard's sets to adopt a multivolume format that can be somewhat confusing. You must be sure you have Shepardized your case in all necessary volumes. All the information you need to assure yourself of this is printed right on the covers or bindings of the applicable Shepard's volumes, so mistakes can only be the result of sloppiness. Take your time and be thorough—Shepardizing is an important task, often performed by paralegals. In fact, it is inexcusable for attorneys and paralegals not to Shepardize all cited legal references. For some, the omission may be tantamount to legal malpractice. Regardless of the type of legal authority, *always, always* Shepardize. Table 2.1 provides a Shepardizing checklist.

You Be the Judge

Hypothetical 2-3

Shepardizing and validating your research should become a natural part of your research process. Not only do your supervising attorneys expect it, but the courts do as well. By Shepardizing, you will know how other courts view the case you want to cite, and this may alert you to problems with the reasoning in the case. Review *Glassalum Engineering Corp. v. 392208 Ontario Ltd.*, 487 So. 87 (Fla. App. 3 Dist. 1986). In this case, the attorney failed to Shepardize and cited a case that had been questioned; the attorney was ostracized by the judge in the case. Judge Pearson observed: "We remind the bar that, as this case dramatically shows, cases must be Shepardized and that when Shepardizing, counsel must mind the p's and q's." *Id.* at 88. What did the court mean by stating that the attorneys must mind their p's and q's? Had the attorneys in the case Shepardized their cases, would the result in the case be different?

FIGURE 2.12   A Page from *Shepard's Atlantic Reporter*

Source: From *Shepard's Atlantic Reporter Citations.* Used with permission from Lexis Nexis.

volume of case

page where case begins

name of case

case followed

headnote reference

Vol. 752		ATLANTIC REPORTER, 2d SERIES			
—38—	—38—	778A2d⁷140	—83—	2004DelCh LX	Cir. DC
Kirby v Town	Huminski v	786A2d⁵525	Stanley v Stan-	[36	f 227FS2d62
of Bridgewater	Factory Point	f 786A2d⁹1174	ley	2004DelCh LX	—166—
2000	Nat'l Bank	f 786A2d¹⁰1174	2000	[82	In re Kristy Y
(170Vt662)	2000	f 786A2d¹⁰1256	(58CtA327)	f 2004DelCh LX	2000
—38—	(170Vt663)	789A2d507	—85—	[86	(2000ME98)
In re T.S.	—38—	789A2d¹¹508	Gonzalez v	2004DelCh LX	f 838A2d⁴1167
2000	In re C.W.	792A2d⁹117	Commissioner	[94	f 838A2d⁶1167
(170Vt662)	2000	792A2d¹⁰117	of Correction	2004DelCh LX	—170—
—38—	(170Vt663)	792A2d⁸124	2000	[116	State v Quirior
In re Estate of	s 749A2d1142	~ 792A2d130	(58CtA371)	f 2004DelCh LX	2000
Cote	s 752A2d489	j 794A2d1113	Cert den	[193	(2000ME103)
2000	—38—	796A2d¹⁰496	759A2d1024	806A2d153	755A2d1058
(170Vt662)	State v Mar-	804A2d¹³959	cc 537A2d460	d 806A2d155	—176—
—38—	tocci	804A2d¹⁴959	—86—	j 806A2d158	Tarbuck v
In re Persis	2000	812A2d⁹191	State v St.	860A2d319	Jaekel
Corp.	(170Vt663)	812A2d¹⁰191	Pierre	Cir. 3	2000
2000	—38—	812A2d⁴192	2000	f 276BRW4354	(2000ME105)
(170Vt662)	Fenoff v Web-	812A2d⁵192	(58CtA284)	276BRW3355	760A2d629
—38—	ster	816A2d⁴715	Cert den	—115—	812A2d259
Atchinson v	2000	816A2d²716	759A2d508	HFTP Invs.,	—183—
DET	(170Vt663)	816A2d⁸716	779A2d786	L.L.C. v	Kosalka v
2000	—39—	d 816A2d¹⁴716	806A2d¹⁵76	ARIAD	Town of
(170Vt662)	In re Madden	f 822A2d⁵370	f 844A2d248	Pharms., Inc.	Georgetown
—38—	2000	822A2d⁸370	—93—	1999	2000
Estate of Tooley	(170Vt663)	827A2d⁹758	State v Nunes	2000DelCh LX	(2000ME106)
v Robinson	—39—	840A2d44	2000	[25	770A2d648
Springs Corp.	North Field Sav.	f 842A2d586	(58CtA296)	f 2001DelCh LX	780A2d301
2000	Bank v Sch-	846A2d944	De 762A2d906	[40	786A2d619
(170Vt663)	midf	Minn	772A2d¹⁵644	f 752A2d552	790A2d³600
—38—	2000	641NW904	796A2d¹⁶1141	—126—	797A2d30
In re Madden	(170Vt663)	—59—	826A2d231	In re Fuqua	832A2d770
2000	—40—	State v Russell	841A2d1230	Indus.	Cir. 1
(170Vt663)	State v Henry	2000	854A2d36	1999	2003USDist
—38—	2000	(58CtA275)	—101—	s 1999DelCh	[LX1778
In re Tucker	(253Ct354)	797A2d⁹539	In re Christo-	[LX190	—188—
2000	757A2d¹73	829A2d452	pher L.	s 2002DelCh	State v Kelly
(170Vt663)	760A2d98	f 841A2d741	2000	[LX52	2000
—38—	760A2d¹²110	851A2d376	(58CtA380)	2001DelCh LX	(2000ME107)
Havill v	767A2d775	851A2d390	f 857A2d970	[11	760A2d1064
Woodstock	767A2d¹¹781	—65—	—102—	2002DelCh LX	f 772A2d862
Soapstone Co.	769A2d703	Fenton v Con-	Decorso v.	[21	Cir. 1
2000	772A2d²565	necticut Hosp.	Watchtower	802A2d³291	2003USDist
(170Vt663)	772A2d³565	Ass'n Workers'	Bible & Tract	—138—	[LX5377
—38—	773A2d337	Compensation	Soc'y v	Young v Dis-	Wash
Havill v	775A2d361	Trust	Watchtower	trict of Colum-	~ 29P3d758
Woodstock	787A2d¹²585	2000	Bible & Tract	bia	—194—
Soapstone Co.	792A2d¹²898	(58CtA45)	Soc'y of N.Y.	2000	Largay v
2000	f 804A2d⁶800	Cert den	2000	829A2d512	Largay
(170Vt663)	820A2d⁷1048	759A2d504	(46CS386)	f 829A2d515	2000
—38—	857A2d873	782A2d¹²1285	—112—	856A2d1109	(2000ME108)
In re Green Mt.	Mass	820A2d⁹290	Fike v Ruger	—147—	778A2d⁵360
Power Corp.	f 733NE151	—77—	2000	Flocco v State	778A2d⁷360
2000	—49—	Pender v	s 754A2d254	Farm Mut.	j 778A2d363
(170Vt663)	State v	Matranga	f 2002DelCh LX	Auto. Ins. Co.	791A2d⁶109
—38—	Andrews	2000	[31	2000	791A2d⁷110
In re Towne	2000	(58CtA19)	f 2002DelCh LX	cc 520US681	807A2d⁶626
2000	(253Ct497)	759A2d¹⁴1039	[118	cc 137LE945	817A2d⁶870
(170Vt663)	s 729A2d232	759A2d¹⁵1039	2002De1Ch LX	cc 117SC1636	818A2d²1009
s 749A2d1142	s 733A2d234	759A2d¹⁶1039	[136	cc 161F3d528	818A2d²1031
	767A2d715	783A2d¹²1243	2003DelCh LX	cc 990FS657	821A2d⁹19
	e 767A2d716	800A2d559	[59	755A2d³1050	827A2d¹822
		806A2d¹¹579		779A2d¹³270	832A2d²763
					832A2d⁵764

FIGURE 2.13   **A Citation to Another D.C.-Referenced Case**
Source: From *Shepard's Atlantic Reporter Citations.* Used with permission from Lexis Nexis.

page cited in Shepard's

WILSON v. HART   D.C. **515**

Cite as 829 A.2d 511 (D.C. 2003)

See, e.g., Hogue v. Hopper, supra (arbitrator's determination that Hogue had failed the show error in tax return entitling him to added partnership payout collaterally estoppel claim of such error in action against accountant).[7] Thus, to the extent that appellants' suit in Superior Court against Hart and the District depends upon the establishment of a direct landlord-tenant relationship, we agree with the trial court that collateral estoppel operates to preclude recovery.[8]

Shepardized case cited in opinion

[8]   The analysis, however, cannot stop there. In *Young v. District of Columbia, supra,* we held that even where a master lease prohibits the lessee from subleasing or transferring possession of the premises, an unauthorized sublessee has a sufficient interest in the property to prohibit the use of self-help for an eviction, at least by the sublessor.[9] Such a sublessor-sublessee relationship gives rise to a sufficient tenancy to require court process to remove an occupant from the premises. Where there is a genuine issue of material fact as to whether there was a subtenancy, summary judgment is inappropriate as the potential

subtenants may have had a right of action arising out of their removal by self-help. *Id.*

Here, appellants and Hart are in sharp dispute as to exactly what transpired in connection with appellants' occupancy of the property and the role of Bey. The hearing examiner apparently considered it sufficient for purposes of the agency proceeding to determine that no direct landlord-tenant relationship existed between appellants and Hart. However this may be in the context of agency relief, *Young* establishes that wrongful eviction may lie in the case of a sublessee. It is true that in the complaint and an affidavit to support the opposition to summary judgment, appellants asserted that their "agreement to rent the subject premises was with Mr. Hart directly and not with Mr. Bey." But in the opposition itself, appellants listed as material matters in dispute "whether plaintiffs entered into a lease agreement with Bey to lease the premises" and "whether the hearing examiner determined in his final decision that no subtenancy was created between plaintiffs and

7. *Clay v. Faison 583* A.2d 1388 (D.C.1990), relied on by appellants, does not dictate otherwise. There the prior dismissal was determined to be one based on a lack of jurisdiction since the action should have been brought in another division of the court (as contrasted with the alternate ground of failure to state a claim, rather more akin to the ruling of the hearing examiner here).

8. The fact that an issue determination is made in connection with a different underlying claim does not preclude collateral estoppel effect. *Johnson v. Capital City Mortgage Corp.,* 723 A.2d 852, 857 (D.C.1999) (citing Carr v. Rose, supra, 701 A.2d at 1076.)

9. *Young* was an application of the rule in this jurisdiction that a landlord may not use self-help to evict a tenant, first established in *Mendes v. Johnson,* 389 A.2d 781 (D.C.1978) (en banc). In *Young,* the self-help eviction was brought about by the sublessor at the landlord's insistence, even though the master

lease had terminated, since the sublessor had the responsibility to see that the sublessee vacated the premises in order to surrender them to the landlord. 752 A.2d at 142. We expressly left open the question as to the master lessor's eviction rights directly against the sublessee. 752 A.2d at 143 n. 8. In the absence of any clear factual determination as to the precise status of appellants' occupancy of the property, we do not address that issue here nor the issue whether a wrongful eviction or breach of quiet enjoyment action may lie even if appellants' occupancy constituted something less than some sort of tenancy. See *Harkins v. WIN Corp.,* 771 A.2d 1025, 1027, *modified and rehearing denied,* 777 A.2d 800 (D.C.2001) (protection against self-help evictions generally not available to roomer or lodger); *Bown v. Hamilton,* 601 A.2d 1074, 1077 (D.C.1992) (quiet enjoyment is a covenant implied in leases).

ONLINE UPDATING: SHEPARD'S CITATIONS SERVICE AND KEYCITE

The Internet has not only opened the door to retrieving cases the day they are decided but also to updating and validating your research. The leading online services are Westlaw and LexisNexis (discussed later in the chapter). Both services provide quick updates and validation of your legal research, ensuring reliable coverage of your chosen cases.

FIGURE 2.14 Marginal Abbreviations from Shepard's Cases

Source: From *Shepard's Southwestern Citations.* Used with permission from Lexis Nexis.

CASES ANALYSIS—ABBREVIATIONS

History of Case

a	(affirmed)	Same case affirmed on appeal.
cc	(connected case)	Different case from case cited but arising out of same subject matter or intimately connected therewith.
D	(dismissed)	Appeal from or review of same case dismissed.
De	(denied)	Review or rehearing denied.
Gr	(granted)	Review or rehearing granted.
m	(modified)	Same case modified on appeal.
r	(reversed)	Same case reversed on appeal.
ReG	(reh granted)	The citing order grants rehearing or reconsideration in the case you are *Shepardizing.*
ReD	(reh denied)	The citing order denies rehearing or reconsideration in the case you are *Shepardizing.*
s	(same case)	Same case as case cited.
S	(superseded)	Substitution for former opinion.
v	(vacated)	Same case vacated.
W	(withdrawn)	Same case withdrawn.
US	cert gran	Certiorari granted by U. S. Supreme Court.
US	cert den	Certiorari denied by U. S. Supreme Court.
US	cert dis	Certiorari dismissed by U. S. Supreme Court.
US	reh den	Rehearing denied by U. S. Supreme Court.
US	reh dis	Rehearing dismissed by U. S. Supreme Court.
US	app pndg	Appeal pending before the U. S. Supreme Court.

Treatment of Case

c	(criticised)	Soundness of decision or reasoning in cited case criticised for reasons given.
ca	(conflicting authorities)	Among conflicting authorities as noted in cited case.
d	(distinguished)	Case at bar different either in law or fact from case cited for reasons given.
e	(explained)	Statement of import of decision in cited case. Not merely a restatement of the facts.
f	(followed)	Cited as controlling.
h	(harmonized)	Apparent inconsistency explained and shown not to exist.
j	(dissenting)	Citation in dissenting opinion.
L	(limited)	Refusal to extend decision of cited case beyond precise issues involved.
~	(concurring)	Citation in a concurring opinion.
o	(overruled)	Ruling in cited case expressly overruled.
op	(overruled in part)	Ruling in cited case overruled partially or on other grounds or with other qualifications.
p	(parallel)	Citing case substantially alike or on all fours with cited case in its law or facts.
q	(questioned)	Soundness of decision or reasoning in cited case questioned.
su	(superseded)	Superseded by statute as stated in cited case.

TABLE 2.1
Shepardizing
Checklist

- Locate the appropriate set of *Shepard's Citations* in the library. (The *Citations* are usually located near the set of reporters of the case you are Shepardizing.)
- Always be sure you are in the correct *Shepard's Citations*. Read the front covers of the volumes and check the time period the volume covers.
- Using your case citation from the case you want to Shepardize, isolate the volume number first in the book. The volume number will appear at the top of the page, or sometimes, within the page itself. (If there is a volume change on that page, it will clearly appear on the page and say "vol. or volume.")
- Find the corresponding page identified in bold.
- Review the citations in the listed column to determine if an "o" (overruled) is in the margin. Continue reviewing the column for other margin references that may be important to your case analysis. (If you forget what the margin references mean, check the front pages of the volume. It has the explanations of all the margin notes and abbreviations.)
- Check *all* paperbound supplements. These supplements have the most recent updates. Do not miss any. (Cautionary Note: If your case does not appear in one of the softbound supplements, *do not panic*. It simply means your case has not been recently cited by a court.)

Shepard's Citations Service

Shepard's Citations Service online essentially follows the concept of the *Shepard's Citations* in print. However, new features have been added to make the process easier and more comprehensive. You can Shepardize a LexisNexis headnote, which assists in finding relevant research topics faster. Pinpointing cited online references that are relevant can be achieved by using the FOCUS system. The most significant online tool of Shepard's is the Shepard's Signal. LexisNexis created a "pop-up signal legend" that identifies the type of comments that courts made about your cited case. If your case received negative treatment by a court, it is signaled by a yellow triangular flag or red stop-sign flag, indicating that the case may have been overruled. Figure 2.15 shows the signal legend for Shepard's LexisNexis.

KeyCite
The Westlaw case updating and validation system, which is similar to Shepard's Citations Service.

KeyCite

Similar to Shepard's Citations Service on LexisNexis, KeyCite is the citation research and validation system used on Westlaw. KeyCite uses different signals for the treatment of cases than Shepard's, but principally the process is the same. Using "status flags," information is critiqued alerting you to the past and present treatment of a case. For an explanation of the KeyCite status flag system, review Figure 2.16. Watch out for a red triangular flag, which indicates the case is no longer valid law, or a yellow triangular flag, which indicates the case has had some negative comments by courts. If a flag does not appear next to your case, it suggests that no indirect or direct history exists about that case. Therefore, it is safe to use the case. Another feature of KeyCite is a "star system," which indicates the depth of discussion of your case in a particular case. Has your case been explained, discussed, cited, or merely mentioned? This system highlights the importance another court may have placed on your case, narrowing your focus on cases that cited your case. See Figure 2.17 for further illustration of the "star system." Many of the general features found on Shepard's Citations Service are found on KeyCite. Both systems provide the critical case validation step in the legal research process.

To illustrate the Shepard's Citations Service and KeyCite system, let's review *United States v. Booker*, 543 U.S. 220, 125 S.Ct. 738, 160 L. Ed. 2d 621 (2005). Notice in Figures 2.18 and 2.19 a page from both Shepard's Citations Service and KeyCite. The pages indicate the treatment of the *Booker* case. When the case is Shepardized, a number of signals appear with cautionary references in both services. Over 600 cases distinguished *Booker* and received negative comment by the United States Supreme Court. Review the prior history of the case and observe that the case was reviewed by the Supreme Court a number of times until a final decision was rendered in 2005. Thus, the importance of Shepardizing cannot be understated, and Shepardizing must be mastered for complete, accurate, and valid citing of the law.

FIGURE 2.15   **The Signal Legend for Shepard's Citations Service**

Source: From *Shepard's Citations Service.* Used with permission from Lexis Nexis.

Editorial Analysis

The *Shepard's*® results screen lists the citations for cases that cite your case. Each citation is preceded I following indicators:

Positive treatment	Includes the following editorial analyses:

- Affirmed
- Explained
- Followed

Negative treatment	Includes the following editorial analyses:

- Distinguished
- Overruled
- Criticized
- Questioned
- Limited
- Reversed
- Modified

Neutral treatment	Includes the following editorial analyses:

- Connected case at
- Related proceeding at

Cited by	**Cited by** indicates that the editorial staff at *Shepard's*® added no editorial analysis. **Cited by** precedes cases that acknowledge your case as precedent and may cite your case as an authority, but do not expressly revisit your case's reasoning or ruling.

The **Cited by** citing reference does not appear when you click the **Any** link.

See Custom Restrictions for more information on restricting your display to certain editorial analyses.

Shepard's Signal

    Warning   Strong negative treatment indicated. Includes:

- Overruled by
- Superseded by
- Revoked
- Obsolete
- Rescinded

    Questioned   Strong negative treatment indicated. Includes:

- Questioned by

    Caution   Possible negative treatment indicated. Includes:

- Limited
- Criticized by
- Clarified
- Modified
- Corrected

⬥   Positive   Positive treatment indicated. Includes:

- Followed
- Affirmed
- Approved

Ⓐ   Citing References with Analysis   Other cases cited the case and assigned some analysis that is not considered positive or negative Includes:

- Appeal denied by
- Writ of certiorari denied

Ⓘ   Citation Information   References have not applied any analysis to the citation. For example the case was cited by law reviews, ALR® Annotations, or in other case law not warranting an analysis. Example: Cited By

FIGURE 2.16   KeyCite Flag System

Source: From Thomson West website. Used with permission from Thomson West.

KeyCite® Symbols

See at a glance the status of a case or statute.

 A red flag warns that a case or administrative decision is no longer good law for at least one of the points it contains or that a statute or regulation was amended, repealed, superseded, or held unconstitutional or preempted.

 A yellow flag warns that a case or administrative decision has some negative history, but hasn't been reversed or overruled, or that a statute or regulation was renumbered or transferred, had its validity called into doubt, or is affected by pending legislation.

H A blue H indicates that the case or administrative decision has some history.

C A green C indicates that the case or administrative decision has citing references but no direct or negative indirect history, or that a statute or regulation has citing references.

FIGURE 2.17   KeyCite Starring System

Source: From Thomson West website. Used with permission from Thomson West.

KeyCite® Symbols

Depth-of-treatment stars tell you how much the citing case discusses the cited case.

 EXAMINED - Contains an extended discussion of the cited case, usually more than a printed page of text.

 DISCUSSED - Contains a substantial discussion of the cited case, usually more than a paragraph.

 CITED - some discussion of the cited case, usually less than a paragraph.

 MENTIONED - Contains a brief reference to the cited case, usually in a string citation.

 A quotation mark in a citation indicates that the citing case directly quotes the cited case or administrative decision.

COMPUTER-ASSISTED LEGAL RESEARCH

The technological explosion that has made this the information age has made available significant new tools for legal research. These tools—computers, online data services—have not replaced the traditional primary and secondary sources, but rather have broadened their accessibility and deepened their usefulness.

Lexis and Westlaw

The two foremost computer-based legal research systems are Lexis and Westlaw. Each contains the full text of an enormous number of documents, from case opinions to statutes to law review articles. Cases on Westlaw also have the West key numbers and headnotes. Like other online data systems, Westlaw and Lexis require that you have access to a computer. By linking into these systems you obtain the ability to research in four ways:

- First, by allowing a researcher to obtain the text of a specific known document. For example, suppose you need to look at a specific statute from another state, or a case from a reporter not contained in your firm's library. Enter the appropriate information into Lexis or Westlaw, and in a short time the full text will appear on your screen.

FIGURE 2.18 A Page from Shepard's Citations Service for *U.S. v. Booker*

Source: From Shepard's Citations Services off Shepard's Auto-Cite. Reproduced by permission of LexisNexis. Further reproduction of any kind is strictly prohibited.

Home | Sources | How Do I? | Site Map | What's New | Help

Citation: 543 U.S. 220

Restrictions: Jurisdictions: **U.S. Supreme Court**

Analysis: **Distinguished**

FOCUS™ [   ]   [Search Within Results]

[Prin]

(KWIC / Full)   *Shepards*® **- 15 Citing References**

All Negative | All Positive | Any Custom | Restrictions | Unrestricted

543 U.S. 220

Single: **Caution -** Possible negative treatment

Citation: **543 U.S. 220**

Restrictions: Jurisdictions: **U.S. Supreme Court**

Analysis: **Distinguished**

United States v. Booker, 543 U.S. 220, 125 S. Ct. 738, 160 L. Ed. 2d 621, 2005 U.S. LEXIS 628, 73 U.S.L.W 18 Fla. L. Weekly Fed. S 70

PRIOR HISTORY (14 citing references) Hide Prior History

1. United States v. Booker, 2003 U.S. Dist. LEXIS 24609 (W.D. Wis. Sept. 5, 2003)

2. **Subsequent appeal at, Remanded by:**
    United States v. Booker, 375 F.3d 508, 2004 U.S. App. LEXIS 14223 (7th Cir. Wis. 2004)

3. **Later proceeding at:**
    United States v. Booker, 542 U.S. 955, 125 S. Ct. 5, 159 L. Ed. 2d 837, 2004 U.S. LEXIS 4783, 73 U.S.L.W. 3074 (2004)

4. **Writ of certiorari granted, Motion granted by:**
    United States v. Booker, 542 U.S. 956, 125 S. Ct. 11, 159 L. Ed. 2d 838, 2004 U.S. LEXIS 4788, 73 U.S.L.W. 3074 (2004)

5. **Writ of certiorari granted, Motion granted by:**
    United States v. Fanfan, 542 U.S. 956, 125 S. Ct. 12, 159 L. Ed. 2d 838, 2004 U.S. LEXIS 4789, 73 U.S.L.W. 3074 (2004)

6. **Criticized in:**
    United States v. Hammoud, 381 F.3d 316, 2004 U.S. App. LEXIS 19036, 65 Fed. R. Evid. Serv. (CBC) 338 (4th Cir. N.C. 2004)

7. **Motion granted by, Motion denied by:**
    United States v. Booker, 542 U.S. 963, 125 S. Ct. 25, 159 L. Ed. 2d 854, 2004 U.S. LEXIS 4989, 73 U.S.L.W. 3204 (2004)

    Affirmed by, Remanded by (CITATION YOU ENTERED):
    United States v. Booker, 543 U.S. 220, 125 S. Ct. 738, 160 L. Ed. 2d 621, 2005 U.S. LEXIS 628, 73 U.S.L.W. 4056, 18 Fla. L. Weekly Fed. S 70 (2005)

FIGURE 2.19 A Page from KeyCite for *U.S. v. Booker*

Source: From Thomson West website. Used with permission from Thomson West.

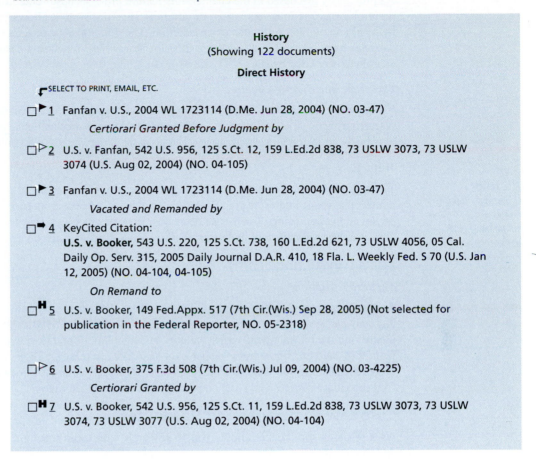

History
(Showing 122 documents)

Direct History

⌐SELECT TO PRINT, EMAIL, ETC.

☐▶1 Fanfan v. U.S., 2004 WL 1723114 (D.Me. Jun 28, 2004) (NO. 03-47)

  Certiorari Granted Before Judgment by

☐▷2 U.S. v. Fanfan, 542 U.S. 956, 125 S.Ct. 12, 159 L.Ed.2d 838, 73 USLW 3073, 73 USLW 3074 (U.S. Aug 02, 2004) (NO. 04-105)

☐▶3 Fanfan v. U.S., 2004 WL 1723114 (D.Me. Jun 28, 2004) (NO. 03-47)

  Vacated and Remanded by

☐➡4 KeyCited Citation:
  U.S. v. Booker, 543 U.S. 220, 125 S.Ct. 738, 160 L.Ed.2d 621, 73 USLW 4056, 05 Cal. Daily Op. Serv. 315, 2005 Daily Journal D.A.R. 410, 18 Fla. L. Weekly Fed. S 70 (U.S. Jan 12, 2005) (NO. 04-104, 04-105)

  On Remand to

☐ᴴ5 U.S. v. Booker, 149 Fed.Appx. 517 (7th Cir.(Wis.) Sep 28, 2005) (Not selected for publication in the Federal Reporter, NO. 05-2318)

☐▷6 U.S. v. Booker, 375 F.3d 508 (7th Cir.(Wis.) Jul 09, 2004) (NO. 03-4225)

  Certiorari Granted by

☐ᴴ7 U.S. v. Booker, 542 U.S. 956, 125 S.Ct. 11, 159 L.Ed.2d 838, 73 USLW 3073, 73 USLW 3074, 73 USLW 3077 (U.S. Aug 02, 2004) (NO. 04-104)

- Second, by performing research in the normal sense (online digests or indexes can be reviewed to find applicable materials).

database
A collection of information used in computer systems to provide access to related fields of interest.

- Third, by searching selected **databases** for key terms or phrases. For example, you could search all the cases from California that use the phrase "strict liability." In addition, because some legal concepts are too complicated to compress to a single word or term, these systems allow you to search for groups of words or terms based upon their proximity—for example, a search for the terms "strict liability" and "ultrahazardous substance" when they appear in the same sentence. Stringing together key terms and words to form a **query** is a skill that takes time and practice to refine.

query
A string of key terms or words used in a computer search.

- Fourth, by some combination of these first three methods. For example, using Westlaw you might want to obtain headnotes under a specific key number (the traditional research method) that contain a specified query term (the third method listed).

Lexis and Westlaw each have unique features for researching. Let's highlight some of those features.

Westlaw (www.westlaw.com)

Westlaw Reporter Images

Accessing the National Reporter system is right at your fingertips. You can now print exact electronic photocopies of cases that appear in the West National Reporter System. This feature contains the exact paging, page breaks, headnotes, key number, digest topics, and other features as they appear in the case. No more guessing.

KeyCite

As previously discussed in the chapter, this feature provides up-to-date information on the treatment of a case, statute, regulation, or administrative decision. It allows you to search for cases by headnote number reference or jurisdiction. The direct history of a case, such as whether the case has been overruled, is red-flagged by the status flag. Whether a case has been extensively examined is notated by stars ****. KeyCite is similar to *Shepard's Citations* on Lexis.

Case Law and Statute Locator

Virtually any case, statute, or administrative decision regulation can be located on Westlaw. You can research using a variety of methods, such as using relevant words and phrases, key number digests, or even by popular name. Anything you can do in the library, you can do online with practice.

Westclip

Westclip
An electronic clipping service used on Westlaw that monitors legal developments.

Through **Westclip,** an electronic clipping service, you can monitor new legal developments in matters that are of interest to you. By setting up a query, you can arrange to have alerts sent to your e-mail address advising of new case decisions, laws, or other legal developments on that subject. Clips can be a valuable tool in delivering the most up-to-date status on a variety of issues.

Lexis (www.lexis.com)

Shepard's Citations

As discussed earlier in the chapter, Lexis provides your exclusive link to *Shepard's Citations.* Not only can you validate your research, but you can also use *Shepard's* as a research method by identifying the relevant cited cases, statutes, and annotations and reviewing their content. A new feature of *Shepard's* now links LexisNexis headnotes to relevant cases, making research more comprehensive. If you want to find cases that "followed" your case, locate recent decisions, or find secondary sources, *Shepard's* on Lexis is an available alternative.

Case Law Summaries and Headnotes

As a research tool, Lexis allows you to research your topic through their headnote system. Although different from the West system, the LexisNexis system provides coordinate topic notations and numbers to easily find cases and other relevant information as you research the topic.

Alert (formerly known as Eclipse)

Alert
The case-clipping system used by Lexis to monitor legal developments.

Similar to Westclip, the LexisNexis electronic clipping service is now know as **Alert.** This feature allows tracking of pending legislation or regulations, new case law that relates to a particular topic or case of interest, or any area that may be of particular interest. Alert notifies you by e-mail when matters you have queried are updated.

Powerinvoice

Tracking your research by client and time spent on the matter for billing purposes is another feature on Lexis. The system identifies what was researched, who performed the research, how long the research took, and the charges for that research. The online tool shortens client billing as well as monitoring both the paralegal's and attorney's time researching a subject.

PRACTICE TIP

Unless you first see and understand how the law books look and interrelate, online research is more difficult. Spend time in your library mastering the research techniques you have learned before you attempt to use computer-assisted legal research.

The Internet

The Internet provides virtually unlimited opportunities for legal research, although LexisNexis and Westlaw are the most comprehensive.

Many of the federal agencies post rules, regulations, and decisions pertaining to that agency. They also post legal opinions and frequently asked questions with responses from the agency. These sites can be invaluable and time-saving when researching federal matters. Most states and their agencies also have developed extensive websites with invaluable information. Check your state's websites for the extent of their references. By using any Internet search engine, you can easily access these sites.

Accessing some legal research websites on the Internet is free. One of the most comprehensive free websites is www.findlaw.com. This website allows you to find current cases, subscribe to case alerts, and many other valuable legal research resources. A website that provides more commentary and articles on the law is www.law.com. By reviewing the articles, you are alerted to current changes and trends in the law. There also are many law school libraries online and countless websites that may be helpful.

THE E-FACTOR

RESEARCHING ON THE INTERNET

Traditional research skills used in digests, such as finding words and phrases that apply to a legal problem, do not always work with Lexis and Westlaw. The predominant method for researching on the Internet follow natural language or Boolean logic. Boolean logic centers on the relationship among search terms—how words connect. The Boolean main connectors are "and," "or," and "not." Depending on the connector chosen, your search will reveal, or not reveal, the results of your query. Let's focus on the main connectors.

The "and" connector: The "and" connector locates concepts that are connected in a document. Since you are searching for two related concepts, an "and" search results in fewer documents. For example, let's assume you are searching for information on the concept of whether attorney's fees includes paralegals. Your search could be:

attorney fees and paralegal

The result of the search would be that the document contains both words. If a document does not have both words, it would not show in the search; hence, a more limited search gives a narrower result.

The "or" connector: Unlike the "and" connector, the "or" connector's results are broader. The "or" connector provides you with synonymous terms and is helpful when similar terms are used in your legal research problem. Synonymous terms would be attorney or lawyer or counsel. Any term could be in your document. Continuing with our example with the "or" connector the search is:

attorney fees or paralegal

The results of this search would contain documents with either the words attorney's fees or paralegal. Sometimes the "or" search may be too general, producing too many docu-ments that prove unhelpful. Now let's try a combination of the "and" and "or" connectors.

attorney fees and paralegal or legal assistant

With a combination of the connectors, your search results in documents that contain the words "attorney fees" and either "paralegal" or "legal assistant," resulting in more choices.

The "not" connector: Using a "not" connector excludes documents from your search. You need to be careful when using the "not" connector, because information you may want may be excluded.

attorney fees and paralegal not legal assistant

This search would result in documents that contain the information on paralegals and attorney fees but not documents that use the words "legal assistant." With this result, you may miss important cases on the subject.

Natural language: A natural language search uses conversational language and words. The words we speak or write are the words used in a natural search. With a natural language search you could search a phrase in quotations such as a famous quote from a U.S. Supreme Court Justice: "I know it when I see it." The resulting search would produce all cases that have cited that expression. Or, try a legal concept such as "confidential and proprietary information" and see what happens. The possibilities are endless.

Both Lexis and Westlaw provide guides in using their legal research systems. Read the guides. They are helpful and will assist you in focusing your search for the best result. Remember, legal research, whether through traditional books or the Internet, takes time to master. Whether you use a natural-language search or a Boolean-style search, don't get frustrated. The more you use the skills you are learning, the better you will become at the task.

TANK McNAMARA   *BY JEFF MILLAR & BILL HINDS*

Lexis and Westlaw have simplified such tasks as cite-checking and updating cases, Shepardizing, and providing instant access to enormous volumes of legal source material. By learning these systems and practicing the art of querying, you will add to your marketability as a paralegal.

PRACTICAL CONSIDERATIONS—HOW TO BEGIN AND WHEN TO STOP

To a great extent one learns how to do legal research by doing it. There is no easy substitute for the benefits of hours of trial and error, nor is there a painless path to satisfying revelation. There are, however, two areas that are fundamental—how to begin your research and when to stop. We'll leave the middle to you.

As we said at the outset of these chapters on legal research, you must isolate your goal and prepare a plan, or risk being overwhelmed by literally millions of pages of materials in the sources we have identified. A legal encyclopedia is a good place to start; it provides a broad overview of the subject area, and might cite to a useful annotation or a case from your jurisdiction. The next stop is probably the index to the relevant annotated statutory code, to see whether a statute governs or affects the issues at hand. If there is a relevant statute, both the text of the statute and the supplemental information provided (case citations, legislative history, references to periodicals) may prove helpful. Next, go to the digest. Using the descriptive word index, the words and phrases section, and the topic indexes, search for relevant case law. Finally, look for secondary sources. There may be law review articles, restatement provisions, or treatises that can contribute breadth and depth to your analysis.

Now assume that you've been researching for some time. You've checked a wide variety of sources, read and photocopied a number of cases, statutes, and secondary sources, taken pages of notes, and found that there is so much material available that you could "go on forever." How do you know when to stop?

There is no easy answer to this question. A definitive reference in a mandatory authority, once adequately Shepardized, may supply all the information you need. A less tidy research session

Ethics Alert

Your attorney has asked you to prepare a memorandum of law supporting the Motion for Summary Judgment he filed on behalf of his friend, George Smithey. Smithey hates going through security at airports and constantly showing his identification to every person he meets. He thinks it violates his right to travel and his right to privacy. And anyway, he's not going to do anything to anyone while he is traveling. He is tired of all the harassment and just wants to put some sanity in the system. Who are those TSA people anyway? The case was filed in California and your attorney wants you to research the issue and discuss the status of the law with you. While researching, you run across a case that was handed down a few months ago, *Gilmore v. Gonzales*. It was decided by the United States Court of Appeals for the Ninth Circuit and you believe that case is on point. Should you tell your attorney about the case? Does your attorney need to cite the case in his supporting brief? Is there an obligation to tell the court of the case?

These are all important questions to ask yourself. Attorneys and paralegals have ethical obligations and are guided by the ABA Model Code and ABA Model Rules on Ethical Responsibility. Typical ethical responsibilities that confront a paralegal are similar to the hypothetical fact pattern that is posed, especially when the case is contrary to the client's interest. However, this case must be disclosed to your attorney regardless of the effect on the case. The attorney has an ethical and legal obligation to report the case if it is "controlling" law in the jurisdiction. When citing the case in your memorandum, you or your attorney may show how the case can be distinguished or criticized for its result. Perhaps the facts are different. What is important is: Do not hide the case from your attorney. You are doing your job by revealing the case to your supervising attorney. Let your attorney decide how to handle the situation. If you do not disclose the case, you run the risk of having the court impose sanctions on your attorney or yourself, which may include monetary or disciplinary action.

may be finished when newly explored avenues yield references to the same cases, statutes, and secondary sources. If you have looked in several competing sources (for example, a West digest and an *A.L.R.* annotation) and turned up the same references, your research is probably adequate.

Finding the same references over and over does not guarantee that you are finished; with legal research, like most things in life, absolute certainty is elusive. A thorough search of the most useful references must maximize your coverage within the constraints of the client's problem (you cannot spend $5,000 of research time on a $1,000 case); it is reasonable cause to believe that you've found the essential sources.

Once you have completed your legal research, you must review your cases and organize your thoughts to prepare the letter, memorandum of law, or brief you were assigned. The remainder of the text will guide you through that process.

Summary

The digest system is the foundation for finding the law. The system comprises the Key Number System. The Key Number System was established by the West Company (now Thomson West) to index cases appearing in its unofficial reporters, including the regional reporters of the National Reporter System. Digests collect headnotes, which are points of law drawn from a case and categorized under one or more applicable key numbers, and organize them consecutively by topic and key number. Pocket parts are used to update bound volumes.

Updating and validating the law is important in legal research. Sheppardizing is a unique method by which researchers can determine whether a case has been overruled or cited by other courts. Shepard's is now online at www.lexis.com. The counterpart to Shepard's Citations is KeyCite used by Westlaw. This system also reviews the treatment and history of a case as does Shepard's. KeyCite uses a flag system to alert you as to the treatment of a case.

Lexis and Westlaw are computer-based legal research systems. A query is a string of key terms or words used in a computer search. Both Lexis and Westlaw provide search mechanisms to find cases, statutes, or any other legal document you may need for your research.

A good place to begin legal research is with a legal encyclopedia, followed by a search in the relevant statutory codes, digests, reporters, and secondary sources. When different research techniques and sources begin to turn up references to the same cases and statutes, that may be an indication that your research is complete.

Key Terms

Key Number System	Sheppardizing
headnote	KeyCite
digest	database
descriptive word index	query
words and phrases	Lexis
table of cases	Westlaw
defendant/plaintiff table	Westclip
pocket parts	Alert

Review Questions

1. Describe the digest system.
2. What is the significance of a case headnote?
3. What is the Key Number System?
4. What is a digest?
5. What does "Sheppardizing" mean?
6. What are the methods for updating the law?

7. Distinguish the differences between Shepard's Citations Service and KeyCite.
8. Identify the advantages of using either Westlaw or Lexis.
9. What is a query?
10. How should you begin a research project, and once you've begun, how do you know when to stop?

Exercises

1. Find the case for 104 S.Ct. 615, 78 L. Ed. 2d 443 and answer the following questions:
   a. What is the name of the case?
   b. What date was the case decided?
   c. Which reporter contains headnotes with topics and keys?

2. Find the case of *Parker v. Twentieth Century-Fox Film Corp.* All you know is that the case originated in California.
   a. What is the citation of the case?
   b. What year was the case decided?

3. Find the parallel citations to the listed cases.
   a. 340 U.S.135
   b. 8 Cal.Reptr.3d 480
   c. 462 S.E.2d 74
   d. 647 N.Y.S.2d 729
   e. 9 L.Ed.2d 265
   f. 91 L.Ed.2d 265

4. Shepardize *Chapa v. Garcia*, 848 S.W.2d 667 (Texas 1992), and answer the following questions:
   a. Has the case been followed? If yes, how many times?
   b. Has any other state cited this case? If yes, what state?
   c. How many times has headnote 1 been cited?
   d. How many times has headnote 3 been cited?

5. Shepardize *Gulf Landings Assoc. v. Hershberger*, 845 So.2d 344, and answer the following questions:
   a. Has the case been distinguished? If yes, cite the case.
   b. Has the case been criticized? If yes, how many cases criticized the decision?
   c. Identify the cases that followed the decision.

6. Shepardize *Nawrock v. Macomb Country Rd. Community*, 615 N.W.2d 702, and answer the following:
   a. What state decided the case?
   b. What, if any, other states cited the case?
   c. Was the case cited in a dissenting opinion? If so, how many times?
   d. Has the opinion been cited in a concurring opinion? If yes, identify the case citation.

7. Find *Russell v. Texas*, 727 S.W.2d 573 (Tx.Ct.App. 1987). Answer the following questions:
   a. Was the case appealed in the U.S. Supreme Court? If yes, what occurred?
   b. What other states cited the case?
   c. Was the case cited in an *A.L.R.* annotation? If so, identify the annotation.

8. Using *Federal Practice Digest, 4th Ed.,* find a case that defines "legal assistant" and answer the following questions:
   a. What is the name of the case?
   b. What is the citation for the case?
   c. From which state does the case originate?
   d. What year was the case decided?
   e. How did the case define "legal assistant"?

Portfolio Assignment

Joe Valentine, an avid baseball card collector, went to purchase a Nolan Ryan rookie card at Sports Card World in Arlington, Texas. After browsing a while, he found what he was looking for, the Nolan Ryan card. A young clerk approached him asking Mr. Valentine if he could be of assistance. Mr. Valentine pointed to the Ryan card. The clerk quickly looked at the price and said that the card was $100.00. Valentine was surprised at the low price as he was prepared to go up to $900.00. Wasting no time, Valentine wrote Sports Card World a check and basked in his find. A day later, Mr. Valentine received a telephone call from the owner of Sports Card World. The owner was very upset that the clerk had misread the price and the real price was $1,100.00 for the Nolan Ryan rookie card, not $100.00. The store owner stated he would refund Valentine's $100.00 and apologized. Mr. Valentine refused the refund and stated they had a contract. Sports Card World sues Mr. Valentine. Your attorney needs some research on the issues involved. Complete the following tasks:

a. Write down words and phrases that may apply to the fact pattern above.

b. Identify the specific procedure you would undertake to accomplish this legal research.

Vocabulary Builder

Legal Research: Finding the Law

```
S  G  C  O  H  H  J  Y  W  S  S  M  K  V  K
T  I  N  R  R  G  O  E  P  E  T  Z  E  E  Y
R  C  X  I  R  B  S  H  T  I  F  D  Y  Y  K
A  L  D  E  Z  T  V  O  N  R  K  N  C  R  V
P  D  B  A  L  I  N  S  S  K  U  N  I  E  Q
T  R  L  A  T  D  D  E  R  M  L  W  T  U  X
E  Z  W  M  A  A  F  R  B  W  L  D  E  Q  D
K  Q  V  E  J  R  B  E  A  T  S  E  G  I  D
C  Q  H  A  L  U  R  A  V  P  C  Z  W  R  X
O  K  Z  A  U  S  G  J  S  N  E  U  A  W  S
P  H  N  V  Y  A  Q  X  R  E  T  H  W  I  J
X  P  I  S  C  I  T  A  T  O  R  S  S  T  Z
D  V  T  G  O  K  M  K  F  K  B  J  U  I  E
S  E  S  A  R  H  P  D  N  A  S  D  R  O  W
M  I  K  E  O  P  P  B  D  M  D  Y  H  Z  A
```

CITATORS	**DATABASE**	**DIGEST**
HEADNOTES	**KEYCITE**	**KEY NUMBER SYSTEM**
LEXIS	**POCKET PARTS**	**QUERY**
SHEPARDIZING	**WESTLAW**	**WORDS AND PHRASES**

Chapter 3

The Case Brief

CHAPTER OBJECTIVES

After completing this chapter, you will be able to:

• Distinguish between a case brief and a trial or appellate brief.

• Describe the components of a printed opinion.

• Explain the usefulness of star-paging.

• Differentiate between a majority opinion and a dissent.

• Describe the components of a case brief.

• Identify the relevant facts in an opinion.

• State the issues presented by a written opinion.

• Trace the procedural history of a case as set forth in the opinion.

• Identify the holding of the court and the disposition of the case.

• Analyze and summarize the reasoning behind an opinion.

We all know how to read. Right! But, learning how to read the law requires "new" reading skills. You must learn the difference between the court's holding (rule of the case) and its reasoning (the legal resources used to support the holding). And you must learn how to summarize cases succinctly, providing the key points and highlights. Determining what's important and what's not is a skill learned over time. You will begin the process of case briefing in this chapter, building on the skills from the previous chapters.

Case Fact Pattern Hypothetical 3-1

Your supervising attorney has an upcoming court hearing on a sensitive matter. She was retained by a family on a medical malpractice case. The case had to be filed before April 20 or the statute of limitations would expire. On April 18, a complaint and summons were sent by Federal Express to San Diego for filing with a check for the filing fee. The filing fee submitted was $3.00 less than required and the clerk refused to file the documents. No one in your office found out until April 25, five days after the statute of limitations had run out. Now, your attorney has filed a motion with the court to deem the documents filed on April 19. One of her partners has brought to her attention a relevant case, *Duran v. St. Luke's Hospital*, 114 Cal. App. 4th 457, 8 Cal. Rptr. 1 (Cal. App. 1 Dist. 2003). You have been provided with a copy of the case (see Figure 3.2) and asked by your supervising attorney to highlight the important points for her review. She wants the opinion crystallized into a straightforward summary.

THE CASE BRIEF DISTINGUISHED

The word *brief* has two separate and distinct connotations in legal practice. First, it can refer to a document filed with a court to present the legal argument of one party in a lawsuit, citing as many cases, statutes, and other sources of law as are deemed necessary to support the argument. Such a brief is usually further identified by including the level of the court in which the brief is filed: if in the trial court, it is a *trial brief;* if an appellate court, it is an *appellate brief.* These briefs do not provide an objective discussion of the law, but rather a one-sided argument intended to persuade the court of the validity of the party's position. We discuss such briefs in some detail in later chapters.

case brief
An objective summary of the important points of a single case; a summary of a court opinion.

The word *brief* also appears in the term *case brief.* A **case brief** is an objective summary of the important points of a single case. If properly prepared, it will provide the reader with a concise abstract of the reasoning of the opinion, as well as important collateral information such as case name, citation, and identity of the parties. The key word is *objective*—the case brief should accurately reflect the meaning of the case, whether that meaning is helpful to your client or harmful.

star-paging
A practice that enables the reader to identify the page breaks in one reporter by reviewing the decision as reprinted in another reporter.

As you might have guessed, the case brief is not a document prepared for the eyes of the court, nor is it shared with opposing parties. It is an internal document, designed to help attorneys develop an objective understanding of the impact of existing case law on the viability of their client's position. Only when such an understanding is reached can persuasive strategies be developed.

THE COMPONENTS OF A PRINTED OPINION

PRACTICE TIP

Sometimes star-paging can be challenging to follow, especially in a long case. The easiest way to assure yourself that you are citing the correct page for your reference is to always start at the top of the case and pinpoint the next star-paging symbol. Keep repeating that exercise and you will always have accurate official paging. Also note, the headnotes and paragraph summaries are from the unofficial publishers. (They are your legal research tools.) Therefore, the gap between the first star-paging symbol and the second may be extensive. That is simply material that was not contained in the official reporter.

As you have learned, reporters are collections of printed opinions, or cases. A case brief is a summary of one of these cases. In order to understand the method of briefing a case, then, it is necessary to learn about the components of a printed opinion. You are already familiar with some of these components from the previous chapter.

Figure 3.1 reprints a full page from volume 8 of the *California Reporter 3d* (which, as you recall, is the West publication for additional California decisions beyond those already appearing in the *Pacific Reporter*). The page shown (page 1) is the first page of our subject case, *Duran v. St. Luke's Hospital,* and it contains a wealth of information.

Let's start with the left side of the top line, identified as *A* in Figure 3.1 notation "114 Cal. App. 4th 459" is a reference to a page from the official reporter, the *California Appellate Reports,* where *Duran v. St. Luke's Hospital* also appears. Unofficial reporters often provide information as to the pagination in the official reporter.

Star-Paging

Pagination as it appears in the official reporter is reflected in an unofficial reporter through the use of **star-paging.** The symbol used to identify star paging is an upside down "T" with the page noted at the bottom. It looks like this: "⊥". Star-paging is a practice that enables us to identify the page breaks in one reporter by reviewing the decision as reprinted in another reporter. The star-paging notations identified as *B* in Figure 3.1 identify the page breaks for pages 458 and 459 as they appear in the *California Appellate Reports.* By utilizing these star-paging notations when writing a brief, the drafter can reference the page and volume of important language as it appears in both West's *California Reporter* and the official *California Appellate Reports,* even though she only has the *California Reporter* at hand. Star-paging is often (but not always) found in unofficial reporters; it is never found in official reporters, and thus constitutes an additional reason why unofficial reporters can be superior to official reporters as research tools.

Shorthand Case Name

We next turn to the section we have labeled *C* in Figure 3.1. This is the shorthand form of the case name, with an instruction as to the appropriate citation. These instructions do not always conform to the rules set down in *The Bluebook* or *ALWD Manual;* where there is a discrepancy, you should follow the appropriate citation manual (for example, the reference to "1 Dist." goes beyond the *Bluebook* requirements, but is cited in the *ALWD Manual Appendix.* Check with your attorney for which form to use.). In any event, this citation will appear on alternate pages.

FIGURE 3.1 From the *California Reporter*

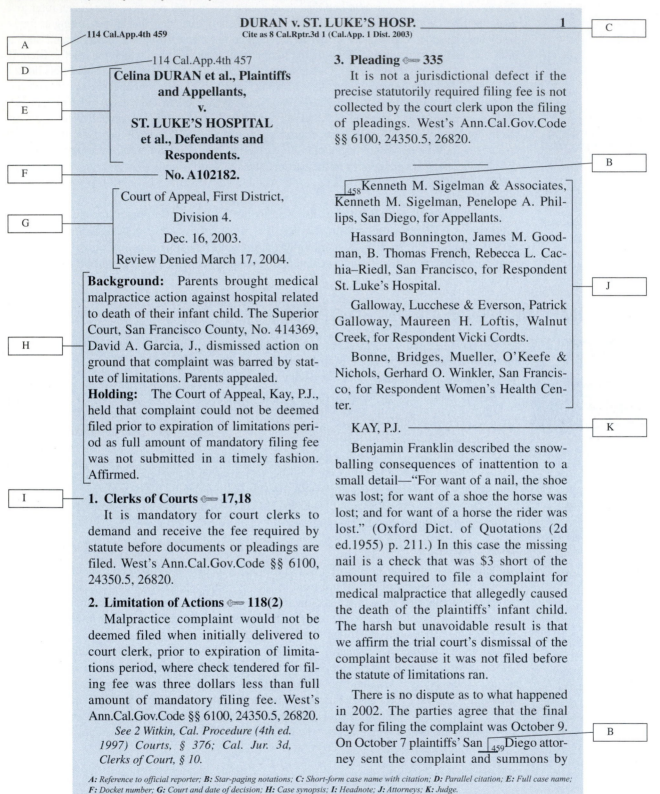

A: Reference to official reporter; B: Star-paging notations; C: Short-form case name with citation; D: Parallel citation; E: Full case name; F: Docket number; G: Court and date of decision; H: Case synopsis; I: Headnote; J: Attorneys; K: Judge.

Parallel Citation

The *D* label shows the correct parallel citation for the case in *California Appellate Reports,* "114 Cal. App. 4th 457." Just as a reminder, this means that the case begins on page 457 of volume 114 of the fourth series of that reporter.

Full Name of Case

E is the full name of the case, identifying all the parties and their roles (that is, plaintiff or defendant; appellant or respondent). The full name, together with the docket number, court, and date of the decision, is called the **caption** (labels *E*, *F*, and *G* combined). Notice the names of the parties. The name of the Plaintiff is Celina Duran. The name Duran is in capital letters. That signals to the reader of the opinion that only the last name of the plaintiff Duran is used in the citation of the case. Likewise, the name of the Defendant Hospital is all in capital letters. Use the entire name of the hospital when citing the case. The case guides you on how to cite the name of the case. However, consult your citation manual for the proper form. In label *C* of Figure 3.1, "Hospital" is abbreviated as "Hosp." Under both *The Bluebook* and the *ALWD Manual*, a listing of permissible abbreviations is noted. Review a citator manual for the correct use of any abbreviation in a case name.

Docket Number, Court, and Date

The *F* identifies the docket number of the case. A **docket number** is assigned by the court to the case for its own administrative purposes. If you visited the appropriate courthouse and asked to see the file for this case, you would need to provide the docket number so that they could locate it in their files.

The *G* label provides the full name of the court that rendered the opinion, and the date of rendering. In this case the Court of Appeal, First District, Division 4 handed down its decision on December 16, 2003. The date that follows tells us that the case was appealed further to the California Supreme Court. That court denied review of the case on March 17, 2004.

Synopsis

Item *H* is called the **synopsis** of the case. It is an extremely short summary, prepared not by the court but by the publisher. It identifies the issue, the procedural history, and the ruling of the court in the instant case ("instant" is used in legal documents to mean *present* or *current;* this instant case is *Duran v. St. Luke's Hospital*). The synopsis is in a sense a preview; since it is an unofficial editorial addition, it should never be formally cited, but only informally reviewed.

Sometimes a synopsis is prepared by the official reporter of decisions. Such an "official" synopsis is called a **syllabus,** as you learned in Chapter 1's discussion of *United States Reports* (where each U.S. Supreme Court case is given a syllabus). Although "official," a syllabus is not part of the court's opinion and, like the synopsis, should never be formally relied upon or cited.

West Key Number and Headnote

I identifies the West key number and headnote. You may recall that a case headnote is a paragraph summary of a point of law contained within the case. This case contains three headnotes, referencing the points of law discussed within the case. Notice each is numbered individually and is referenced within the case. These headnotes can be used to locate other cases that may be relevant to your research. As with the synopsis, the case headnote is used as a quick reference and is not cited as legal authority.

Attorneys and Judge

J identifies the attorney for the parties. (There apparently were other parties to this case, although the case does not discuss their role in the appeal. It is not unusual to have multiple parties in a case.) *K* identifies the judge who wrote the opinion of the court, Justice P.J. Kay.

Text and Disposition

The name of the judge who wrote the opinion is followed by the text of his or her opinion. The text or body of the decision contains the detailed reasoning by which the court reached its result. That result, which appears at the end of the opinion and is often simply a word or two telling the reader who won the lawsuit, is called the court's **disposition.** (For full text and disposition, see Figure 3.2.)

The text of an opinion generally sets forth the facts of the case and the procedural history. It then analyzes the issues presented and, citing precedent and drawing upon applicable legal principles and logic, reaches a conclusion. The text is the heart of a case; it is from the text that analogies can be drawn to pending controversies.

FIGURE 3.2 The Court's Disposition

Source: From the *California Reporter*. Reprinted with permission from Thomson West.

DURAN v. ST. LUKE'S HOSP. 1

114 Cal.App.4th 459   Cite as 8 Cal.Rptr.3d 1 (Cal.App. 1 Dist. 2003)

114 Cal.App.4th 457

**Celina DURAN et al., Plaintiffs
and Appellants,**

v.

**ST. LUKE'S HOSPITAL
et al., Defendants and
Respondents.**

No. A102182.

Court of Appeal, First District,

Division 4.

Dec. 16, 2003.

Review Denied March 17, 2004.

Background: Parents brought medical malpractice action against hospital related to death of their infant child. The Superior Court, San Francisco County, No. 414369, David A. Garcia, J., dismissed action on ground that complaint was barred by statute of limitations. Parents appealed.

Holding: The Court of Appeal, Kay, P.J., held that complaint could not be deemed filed prior to expiration of limitations period as full amount of mandatory filing fee was not submitted in a timely fashion. Affirmed.

1. Clerks of Courts ⟸ 17,18

It is mandatory for court clerks to demand and receive the fee required by statute before documents or pleadings are filed. West's Ann.Cal.Gov.Code §§ 6100, 24350.5, 26820.

2. Limitation of Actions ⟸ 118(2)

Malpractice complaint would not be deemed filed when initially delivered to court clerk, prior to expiration of limitations period, where check tendered for filing fee was three dollars less than full amount of mandatory filing fee. West's Ann.Cal.Gov.Code §§ 6100, 24350.5, 26820.

See 2 Witkin, Cal. Procedure (4th ed. 1997) Courts, § 376; Cal. Jur. 3d, Clerks of Court, § 10.

3. Pleading ⟸ 335

It is not a jurisdictional defect if the precise statutorily required filing fee is not collected by the court clerk upon the filing of pleadings. West's Ann.Cal.Gov.Code §§ 6100, 24350.5, 26820.

———

⌐458Kenneth M. Sigelman & Associates, Kenneth M. Sigelman, Penelope A. Phillips, San Diego, for Appellants.

Hassard Bonnington, James M. Goodman, B. Thomas French, Rebecca L. Cachia–Riedl, San Francisco, for Respondent St. Luke's Hospital.

Galloway, Lucchese & Everson, Patrick Galloway, Maureen H. Loftis, Walnut Creek, for Respondent Vicki Cordts.

Bonne, Bridges, Mueller, O'Keefe & Nichols, Gerhard O. Winkler, San Francisco, for Respondent Women's Health Center.

KAY, P.J.

Benjamin Franklin described the snowballing consequences of inattention to a small detail—"For want of a nail, the shoe was lost; for want of a shoe the horse was lost; and for want of a horse the rider was lost." (Oxford Dict. of Quotations (2d ed.1955) p. 211.) In this case the missing nail is a check that was $3 short of the amount required to file a complaint for medical malpractice that allegedly caused the death of the plaintiffs' infant child. The harsh but unavoidable result is that we affirm the trial court's dismissal of the complaint because it was not filed before the statute of limitations ran.

There is no dispute as to what happened in 2002. The parties agree that the final day for filing the complaint was October 9. On October 7 plaintiffs' San ⌐459Diego attorney sent the complaint and summons by

Facts

FIGURE 3.2 Cont.

2   **8 CALIFORNIA REPORTER, 3d SERIES**

[facts]

Federal Express to the filing clerk of the San Francisco Superior Court. Also sent was a check for $203. On October 8 the clerk received the complaint but did not file it because the filing fee was $206, $3 more than the amount of the check. By the time plaintiffs' attorney learned of the situation and tendered the correct filing fee, the statute of limitations had expired. Plaintiffs filed a petition for "an Order *Nunc Pro Tunc* declaring that the Complaint . . . shall be deemed filed on October 8. . . ." On November 4 the trial court granted the petition but expressly made its order "subject to a motion to strike by defendants." Defendants duly filed motions to strike, as well as general demurrers, all based on the ground that the limitation period had run. The trial court, although "very sympathetic" to plaintiffs' situation, which it described as "a horror story. . . . [¶] . . . [N]onpayment of . . . that $3 is very very minimal," nevertheless believed the authorities cited by defendants required it to grant the motions. A

[prior proceedings]

judgment of dismissal was entered in due course, from which plaintiffs perfected this timely appeal.

The parties approach the problem from different directions. Plaintiffs claim to have the support of our Supreme Court and the Ninth Circuit for analyzing this situation from the perspective of the party attempting to file a document. Plaintiffs also view the amount of the filing fee as governed by local court rules, which do not require the strict compliance demanded of state court rules. Finally, they argue that their complaint "should have been deemed filed on the date initially presented to the clerk for filing, because the $3 discrepancy in the filing fee is an insubstantial defect" and because dismissal solely by reason of discrepancy is "unreasonably drastic." Even though the amount of the filing fee may have a local component, defendants see the issue as one of state law, maintain-

ing that the clerk had the ministerial duty to reject the complaint for filing. What the clerk did was not only statutorily mandated, it was also jurisdictional.

A number of provisions in the Government Code address the topic of court filing fees. Section 6100 states that "Officers . . . of a . . . judicial district[ ] shall not perform any official service unless upon the payment of the fees prescribed by law for the performance of the services. . . ." Section 24350.5 states that "County officers shall . . . demand the payment of all fees in civil cases, in advance." Section 26820 directs that "The county clerk shall charge and collect the fees fixed in this article . . . for service performed by the clerk. . . ."

[1, 2] An unbroken line of decisions by our Supreme Court holds that it is mandatory for court clerks to demand and receive the fee required by statute before documents or pleadings are filed. (*I.X.L. Lime Co. v. Superior Court* (1904) 143 Cal. 170, 173, 76 P. 973 ["Where a fee is required by the law to [460] be prepaid for any official service," payment of the fee is "a condition precedent to the performance of the service"]; *Davis & Son v. Hurgren & Anderson* (1899) 125 Cal. 48, 50–51, 57 P. 684 [clerk refused to file new trial motion submitted without statutory fee; "the mere fact that the clerk received it . . . did not constitute a filing; it was not his duty to file it without the fee; he did not file it; and he could not have been compelled to file it"]; *Boyd v. Burrel* (1882) 60 Cal. 280, 283, 1882 WL 1723 ["The law gave to the Clerk the right to refuse to perform any particular service except upon the condition that his fees therefor should be paid in advance. Plaintiffs and appellants cannot claim that he performed an official act, by legal construction, which he in fact refused to perform, having the legal right so to

[star-paging symbol]

[beginning of courts reasoning]

FIGURE 3.2 Cont.

DURAN v. ST. LUKE'S HOSP.   **3**

114 Cal.App.4th 461   Cite as 8 Cal.Rptr.3d 1 (Cal.App. 1 Dist. 2003)

refuse"]; *Tregambo v. Comanche M. and M. Co.* (1881) 57 Cal. 501, 506, 1881 WL 1687 ["When the demurrers were placed in the custody of the clerk, he had a legal right to refuse to file them, unless the fees for that service were paid to him"].) As one Court of Appeal summarized: "[The Government Code statutes] make it clear that the Legislature has mandatorily required that filing fees in civil actions must be paid in advance. Not only do they declare that they shall be so paid and that the clerk shall so collect them before he shall perform any official act, that is to say, receive for filing and file any document for the filing of which the payment of a fee is required, but the Legislature has also provided, by way of interpretation of its own language, that the word 'shall is mandatory.'. . . Under the plain code provisions it must be held that the clerk properly refused to perform the official service of filing the notice until he received the fees therefor." (*Kientz v. Harris* (1953) 117 Cal.App.2d 787, 790, 257 P.2d 41.) As Division Five of this District has noted, it is "[i]mplicit . . . that the filing fee must be paid in full before the clerk can accept the pleading for filing." (*Mirvis v. Crowder* (1995) 32 Cal.App.4th 1684, 1686–1687, 38 Cal.Rptr.2d 644.)

[3] But while it is mandatory for the court clerks to demand and receive statutorily required filing fees, it is not, as defendants maintain, a jurisdictional defect if the precise fee is not collected. Thus, if the clerk misadvises an out-of-state party as to the amount of the required fee, payment of the incorrectly quoted amount may be deemed sufficient for the filing. (See *Rappleyea v. Campbell* (1994) 8 Cal.4th 975, 35 Cal.Rptr.2d 669, 884 P.2d 126.) If a clerk advises an attorney that a pleading submitted with a check for less than the correct fee will be filed, with the attorney to pay the balance of the fee, the pleading will be deemed filed when submitted. (See *Mirvis v. Crowder, supra*, 32 Cal.App.4th 1684, 1687–1688, 38 Cal.Rptr.2d 644.) Or, if a clerk does file without receiving the fee, the filing is nevertheless valid. (*Tregambo v. Comanche M. and M. Co., supra*, 57 Cal. 501, 506; *Bauer v. Merigan* (1962) 206 Cal.App.2d 769, 771, 24 Cal.Rptr. 203; *Foley v. Foley* (1956) 147 Cal.App.2d 76, 77–78, 304 P.2d 719.) Finally, if the clerk files a pleading accompanied by a check subsequently not honored for insufficient funds, the |461 filing remains valid if the fee is paid within 20 days. (Code Civ. Proc., § 411.20.) None of these exceptions, however, are available to plaintiffs.

It is true, as plaintiffs argue, that in one instance the California Supreme Court did state that in evaluating the timeliness of a petition for a writ of review "it is the filer's actions that are scrutinized" (*United Farm Workers of America v. Agricultural Labor Relations Bd.* (1985) 37 Cal.3d 912, 918, 210 Cal.Rptr. 453, 694 P.2d 138), but the context is clearly distinguishable because the court was considering a statute (i.e., Lab.Code, § 1160.8) that did not require a filing fee, and the issue was not the commencement, but the continuation of litigation already under way. The remainder of the California authorities cited by plaintiffs for the proposition that insubstantial or technical defects of form do not disqualify a submitted pleading from being filed are likewise inapposite because they too do not involve the issue of failure to pay a filing fee. *Carlson v. Department of Fish & Game* (1998) 68 Cal.App.4th 1268, 80 Cal.Rptr.2d 601 involved a complaint returned without filing because it was not accompanied by a "certificate of assignment" as required by local rule; in *Rojas v. Cutsforth* (1998) 67 Cal.App.4th 774, 79 Cal.Rptr.2d 292, the complaint was returned because a "declaration for court assignment" required by local rule was not

FIGURE 3.2   Cont.

signed by the attorney and the summons had the address of the wrong branch of the court; while in *Litzmann v. Workmen's Comp.App. Bd.* (1968) 266 Cal. App.2d 203, 71 Cal.Rptr. 731, the Court of Appeal clerk refused to file a petition for a writ of review because it was not prepared in "the proper form" and on "proper size sheets." Lastly, the Ninth Circuit decision does not aid plaintiffs because there the pleading submitted for filing was accompanied by a check for *more* than the required filing fee. (*Cintron v. Union Pacific R. Co.* (9th Cir.1987) 813 F.2d 917.) In any event, no scrutiny of plaintiffs' actions can ignore the fact that the full amount of the mandatory filing fee was not submitted in a timely fashion.

Plaintiffs' state-rule-versus-local-rule argument is based on *Carlson v. Department of Fish & Game, supra,* 68 Cal.App.4th 1268, 1270, 80 Cal.Rptr.2d 601, where the Court of Appeal stated that a trial court "may not condition the filing of a complaint on local rule requirements." We are not dealing here with conflicting court rules but with state statutes of unambiguous language and meaning, which make the payment of fees the condition precedent to the filing of court documents or pleadings. (E.g., *I.X.L. Lime Co. v. Superior Court, supra,* 143 Cal. 170, 173, 76 P. 973; *Boyd v. Burrel, supra,* 60 Cal. 280, 283; *Kientz v. Harris, supra,* 117 Cal. App.2d 787, 790, 257 P.2d 41.) As for their argument that upon receipt of a pleading by the clerk the pleading will be deemed filed, it is based upon this sentence from United Farm Workers of *America v. Agricultural Labor Relations Bd., supra,* 37 Cal.3d 912, 918, 210 Cal. Rptr. 453, 694 P.2d 138: "[W]e conclude that 'filing' for purposes of compliance with the time limits of Labor Code section 1160.8 means what it does in all other contexts: actual delivery of the petition to the ₄₆₂clerk at his place of business during

holding

office hours." We have already noted that this decision is clearly distinguishable because it addresses a different statutory filing where no filing fee is required. In a situation where a fee is required, the substance of plaintiffs' argument was long ago rejected by our Supreme Court (*Davis & Son v. Hurgren & Anderson, supra,* 125 Cal. 48, 51, 57 P. 684 ["the mere fact that the clerk received it . . . did not constitute a filing"]), and is contrary to the clear import of the authorities quoted above that are applicable to the situation presented here.

The judgment of dismissal is affirmed. ── *court's disposition*

We concur: SEPULVEDA and RIVERA, JJ.

The NATIONAL TAX–LIMITATION COMMITTEE et al., Plaintiffs and Appellants,

v.

Arnold SCHWARZENEGGER, as Governor, etc., Defendant and Respondent.

No. C043583.

Court of Appeal, Third District.

Dec. 4, 2003.

Review Denied March 17, 2004.*

Background: Interested parties commenced mandamus proceeding to compel the Governor to proclaim an end to state of emergency concerning electricity shortages under the California Emergency Services Act. The Superior Court of Sacramento County, No. 02CS01567, Gail D. Ohanesian, J., sustained the Governor's de-

---

* The Supreme Court ordered that the opinion be not officially published. (See California Rules of Court—Rules 976 and 977).

docket number
The number assigned by the court to the case for its own administrative purposes.

synopsis
A short paragraph summary prepared by the publisher in unofficial reporters that identifies the issue, the procedural history, and the ruling of the court in the instant case.

syllabus
A short paragraph summary in the official reporter identifying issue, procedural history, and ruling of the court; an editorial feature in unofficial reporters that summarizes the court's decision.

disposition
Appears at the end of the opinion and tells the reader how the court handled the lower court decision.

affirmed
Disposition in which the appellate court agrees with the trial court.

reversed
Disposition in which the appellate court disagrees with the trial court.

remanded
Disposition in which the appellate court sends the case back to the lower court for further action.

vacated
Disposition in which an appellate court voids the decision of the lower court.

per curiam decision
A decision that reflects agreement of all the judges on the correct disposition of the case.

en banc decisions
Decisions by the court as a whole because of their legal significance.

majority opinion
An opinion where more than half of the justices agree with the decision. This opinion is precedent.

concur
To agree with the majority opinion.

In *Duran v. St. Luke's Hospital,* the court carefully analyzes the history of the law on this issue and is quite clear that the law on this matter in California is very settled. The court spends a considerable amount of time carefully reviewing the case law from all angles, distinguishing facts of previous cases before it reaches its conclusion, because, as the court painfully opines, "the harsh but unavoidable result" in the case is that the case was not timely filed, resulting in its dismissal.

Turning to the end of the opinion, you will see the disposition. The disposition identifies whether the appellate court agreed or disagreed with the lower court's decision. Words such as "affirmed" and "reversed" signal how the appellate court treated the lower court decision. A case is **affirmed** when the appellate court agrees with the lower court's decision. By affirming the court's decision, the appellate court is giving its "stamp of approval" to the lower court. The decision of the lower court was affirmed, meaning that the appellate court agreed with the trial court. If the appellate court had disagreed, the decision of the lower court would have been **reversed.** Since an appellate court has the authority to change the decision of the lower court, the court must follow the directive of the appellate court whether they are in agreement with the decision or not. Sometimes an appellate court agrees with some parts of an appealed decision but disagrees with other parts, resulting in a disposition in which the decision is "affirmed in part and reversed in part." See Figure 3.3 for excerpts of differing opinions of justices in the same case, *U.S. v. Leahy.* Sometimes the disposition requires that the case be sent back to the lower court for further consideration, as would have been the case if the appellate court had reversed the trial court in *Duran.* Such decision has been reversed and **remanded.** When a case is remanded to the lower court, the appellate court instructs the lower court to change its decision, reform it, or have a new hearing.

Sometimes an appellate court simply voids the decision of the lower court. The disposition under these circumstances uses the term **vacated.**

Most appellate cases are decided by a panel of several judges. If all the judges agree on the correct disposition of the case, the decision is rendered *per curiam.* (This phrase means "the court as one body.") No particular judge is designated to write the opinion of the court. *Per curiam* opinions are used when the principles of law are so firmly established as not to warrant further explanation or in areas of the law where the court does not seek to draw particular attention to the case. See Figure 3.4 for an example of a *per curiam* opinion. Notice the disposition in the case—reversed and remanded.

On the other hand, a court may render a decision **en banc.** This type of decision refers to a case where the entire court participates in the decision rather than a select panel. Usually courts decide cases en banc because of the legal significance of the case. The case, *U.S. v. Leahy,* was decided en banc by the Third Circuit Court of Appeals. (See Figure 3.5.)

Occasionally the judges on the panel disagree about the proper disposition. In such a case the majority rules, hence the majority judges issue the binding decision of the court, written as a **majority opinion.** A judge who agrees with the majority opinion is said to **concur.** A judge who agrees with the ultimate result but wishes to apply different reasoning from that in the majority opinion can file a **concurring opinion,** which sets forth the alternative reasoning (in *Duran,* Justice Sepulveda and Justice Rivera concurred; since they wrote no separate opinion, they presumably agreed with the reasoning of Justice Kay's opinion).

If a judge disagrees with the result reached by the majority, he or she is said to **dissent.** An opinion outlining the reasons for the dissent often critiques the majority and concurring opinions, and is known as a **dissenting opinion.** Figure 3.6 is the full opinion from the slip opinion excerpt in Chapter 1, *Tory v. Cochran.* In that opinion, both majority and dissenting opinions were written. Review the case to understand the reasoning behind the majority opinion and the counterview point of the dissenting justices.

It is possible that an individual judge agrees with part of the majority decision and disagrees with part. He or she is then said to "concur in part and dissent in part," and this judge, too, can set forth his or her reasoning in a separate opinion.

Some decisions, particularly those of the U.S. Supreme Court, may have several written opinions with various coalitions of judges concurring and dissenting on different points. It sometimes requires a fair amount of analysis to unravel the meaning of the court's disposition in such a case. In any event, a written opinion always identifies which judges concurred and which dissented. (See Figure 3.3.)

Although most of this analysis relates to appellate opinions, trial court opinion can also be published in reporters. If a trial court opinion relates to a decision on a pending motion, the

FIGURE 3.3   Excerpts from *U.S. v. Leahy*

Source: From the Third Circuit Court of Appeals website: www.ca3uscourts.gov

SLOVITER, <u>Circuit Judge</u>, <u>concurring</u>.

I approve and join Parts I. and II. of the majority opinion. I join in the judgment of Parts III. and IV. While I believe that Judge McKee's dissent has much to commend it, in the last analysis, I join the majority because the majority opinion persuades me that restitution is not a punishment governed by the Sixth Amendment.

FISHER, <u>Circuit Judge</u>, with whom Judge BARRY joins, <u>concurring in part in the judgment</u>.

I approve and join in Parts I, II, and III of the majority opinion. I concur only in the judgment as to Part IV. I would base our holding that the imposition of restitution did not violate the Sixth Amendment right to a jury trial solely on the conclusion that restitution is not the type of criminal penalty to which the right to a jury trial attaches. As the majority opinion correctly notes, "orders of restitution have little in common with the prison sentences challenged by the defendants in <u>Jones</u>, <u>Apprendi</u>, <u>Blakely</u> and <u>Booker</u>." Maj. Op. at 19. The issue of restitution was not before the United States Supreme Court in any of those decisions, and the Supreme Court gave no indication in those decisions that the right to a jury trial applies to any form of criminal penalty other than imprisonment. Accordingly, I would not reach – and do not join – the majority's conclusion that restitution orders do not constitute an increase in punishment beyond the "statutory maximum" for the offense.

McKEE, <u>Circuit Judge</u>. <u>Concurring in part and dissenting in part</u> with Judges RENDELL, AMBRO, SMITH, and BECKER joining.

Given the Supreme Court's holding in *Libretti v. United States,* 516 U.S. 29 (1995), I agree that a judicial determination of the amount of forfeiture when imposing a criminal sentence does not violate the Sixth Amendment right to a jury trial. Although I find it difficult to reconcile *Libretti* with the Court's subsequent decisions in *Blakely v. Washington,* 542 U.S. 296 (2004), and *United States v. Booker,* 125 S. Ct. 738 (2005), any tension between *Libretti* and those cases must be resolved by the Supreme Court, as the majority explains. *See* Maj. Op. at 9 (citing *United States v. Ordaz,* 398 F.3d 236, 241 (3d Cir. 2005)). I therefore join Section II of the majority opinion. However, for the reasons set forth below, I do not agree that a judge can determine the amount of restitution under either the Mandatory Victims Restitution Act ("MVRA"), 18 U.S.C. § 3663A, or the Victim Witness Protection Act ("VWPA"), 18 U.S.C. § 3663, without violating the Sixth Amendment. Accordingly, I respectfully dissent from Section IV of the majority opinion (captioned, "Restitution and *Booker*").

FIGURE 3.4 A *Per Curiam* Opinion

Source: From the U.S. Supreme Court website: www.supremecourtus.gov

court opinion *per curiam*

Cite as: 546 U. S. _____ (2005)   1

Per Curiam

SUPREME COURT OF THE UNITED STATES

ANTHONY KANE, WARDEN v. JOE GARCIA ESPITIA

ON PETITION FOR WRIT OF CERTIORARI TO THE UNITED STATES COURT OF APPEALS FOR THE NINTH CIRCUIT

No. 04–1538. Decided October 31, 2005

PER CURIAM.

Respondent Garcia Espitia, a criminal defendant who chose to proceed *pro se,* was convicted in California state court of carjacking and other offenses. He had received no law library access while in jail before trial—despite his repeated requests and court orders to the contrary—and only about four hours of access during trial, just before closing arguments. (Of course, he had declined, as was his right, to be represented by a lawyer with unlimited access to legal materials.) The California courts rejected his argument that his restricted library access violated his Sixth Amendment rights. Once his sentence became final, he petitioned in Federal District Court for a writ of habeas corpus under 28 U. S. C. §2254. The District Court denied relief, but the Court of Appeals for the Ninth Circuit reversed, holding that "the lack of any pretrial access to lawbooks violated Espitia's constitutional right to represent himself as established by the Supreme Court in *Faretta* [v. *California,* 422 U. S. 806 (1975)]." *Garcia Espitia v. Ortiz,* 113 Fed. Appx. 802, 804 (2004). The warden's petition for certiorari and respondent's motion for leave to proceed *in forma pauperis* are granted, the judgment below reversed, and the case remanded.

A necessary condition for federal habeas relief here is that the state court's decision be "contrary to, or involv[e] an unreasonable application of, clearly established Federal law, as determined by the Supreme Court of the United States." 28 U. S. C. §2254(d)(1). Neither the opinion below, nor any of the appellate cases it relies on, identifies

FIGURE 3.4   Cont.

a source in our case law for the law library access right other than *Faretta*. See 113 Fed. Appx., at 804 (relying on *Bribiesca v. Galaza,* 215 F. 3d 1015, 1020 (CA9 2000) (quoting *Milton v. Morris,* 767 F. 2d 1443, 1446 (CA9 1985)); *ibid.* ("*Faretta* controls this case").

The federal appellate courts have split on whether *Faretta,* which establishes a Sixth Amendment right to self-representation, implies a right of the *pro se* defendant to have access to a law library. Compare *Milton, supra,* with *United States* v. *Smith,* 907 F. 2d 42, 45 (CA6 1990) ("[B]y knowingly and intelligently waiving his right to counsel, the appellant also relinquished his access to a law library"); *United States ex rel. George v. Lane,* 718 F. 2d 226, 231 (CA7 1983) (similar). That question cannot be resolved here, however, as it is clear that *Faretta* does not, as §2254(d)(1) requires, "clearly establis[h]" the law library access right. In fact, *Faretta* says nothing about any specific legal aid that the State owes a *pro se* criminal defendant. The *Bribiesca* court and the court below therefore erred in holding, based on *Faretta,* that a violation of a law library access right is a basis for federal habeas relief.

The judgment below is reversed, and the case is remanded for further proceedings consistent with this opinion.

It is so ordered.

FIGURE 3.5   *U.S. v. Leahy* **En Banc Opinion**

Source: From the Third Circuit Court of Appeals website: www.ca3uscourts.gov

OPINION OF THE COURT

FUENTES, <u>Circuit Judge</u>.

en banc decision of court

We ordered rehearing <u>en banc</u> in three separate appeals to determine whether the District Courts' orders of restitution and forfeiture violated defendants' Sixth Amendment right to trial by jury.

1. Background

In <u>United States v. Paul J. Leahy</u>, No. 03-4490, following trial, a jury found defendant Dantone, Inc. ("Dantone"), and its two senior managers, defendants Paul Leahy and Timothy Smith, guilty of engaging in, and aiding and abetting, bank fraud in violation of 18 U.S.C. § 1344.[1] Defendants' convictions stemmed from their defrauding various banks out of profits derived from Dantone's auctioning of 311 repossessed and after-lease cars on behalf of the banks. At sentencing, the District Court imposed prison sentences upon Leahy and Smith and entered orders of forfeiture in the sum of $418,657 and restitution in the sum of $408,970, jointly and

---

[1]This case was tried together with <u>United States v. Dantone, Inc.</u>, No. 03-4560, and <u>United States v. Timothy Smith</u>, No. 03-4542.

FIGURE 3.5   Cont.

severally, against all three defendants. Dantone, Leahy and Smith appeal both their convictions and the orders of forfeiture and restitution.[2]

In <u>United States v. Kennard Gregg</u>, No. 04-2912, after being arrested and charged for twice attempting to sell counterfeit money to a government informant, defendant Gregg pled guilty to two counts of dealing in counterfeit obligations in violation of 18 U.S.C. § 473. Gregg was sentenced to six months in prison and three years of supervised release, and ordered to pay restitution to the federal government in the amount of $350. He appeals only the restitution order.

In <u>United States v. James C. Fallon</u>, No. 03-4184, a jury convicted defendant Fallon of one count of wire fraud in violation of 18 U.S.C. § 1341, and three counts of mail fraud in violation of 18 U.S.C. § 1343 in connection with marketing his company's Derma Peel skin treatment without FDA approval. Fallon was sentenced to 12 months in prison and ordered to pay restitution in the amount of $55,235. Fallon appeals both his conviction and the District Court's restitution order.

In these appeals, all five of the defendants – Dantone, Leahy, Smith, Gregg and Fallon – challenge their respective restitution orders on Sixth Amendment grounds, arguing that, in accordance with <u>United States v. Booker</u>. 125 S. Ct. 738 (2005), the facts underlying the orders should have been submitted to a jury and established by proof beyond a reasonable doubt. Additionally, on the same grounds, Dantone, Leahy and Smith challenge their orders of forfeiture. We called for rehearing <u>en banc</u> to consider three sentencing <u>issues</u>:

> rationale for en banc hearing

> issues before court

1. Whether the decision of the Supreme Court in <u>Booker</u> applies to forefeiture;

2. Whether orders of restitution are a criminal penalty;

3. Whether <u>Booker</u> applies to orders of restitution under the Victim and Witness Protection Act (the

---

[2]Defendants' appeal of their criminal convictions in this case, as well as in <u>United States v. Fallon</u>, <u>infra</u> will be addressed in separate opinions.

concurring opinion
An opinion in which a judge who agrees with the ultimate result wishes to apply different reasoning from that in the majority opinion.

dissent
Opinion in which a judge disagrees with the result reached by the majority.

dissenting opinion
An opinion outlining the reasons for the dissent, which often critiques the majority and any concurring opinions.

disposition will either "grant" or "deny" the motion. If the opinion is a final decision after trial, the disposition will indicate that judgment was entered for either plaintiff or defendant.

In analyzing the disposition and the text, you should keep in mind the concepts of **holding, reasoning,** and *dictum* (plural *dicta*). The court's holding is that aspect of the decision which directly affects the outcome of the case; it is composed of the reasoning necessary to reach the disposition. The reasoning or rationale sets forth the legal principles the court relied upon to reach its decision or holding. Here, the court cites the constitution, a statute, a case opinion, or a rule or regulation to support its decision. The reasoning, in effect, is the court's legal justification for "how" and "why" it reached its conclusion. *Dicta,* on the other hand, are statements made by the court that are beyond what is necessary to reach the disposition. For example, if a court suggests that a different result might have been reached if certain facts had been different, such a statement is *dictum* (as you read *Duran,* you will see an example of *dictum*). The difference between holding and *dictum* is important: a holding carries the precedential force of *stare decisis,* whereas *dictum* serves as a nonbinding comment having no future effect on a court.

Frank and Ernest

© 2005 Thaves. Reprinted with permission. Newspaper dist. by NEA, Inc.

FIGURE 3.6   Opinion from *Tory v. Cochran*

Source: From the U.S. Supreme Court website: www.supremecourtus.gov

SUPREME COURT OF THE UNITED STATES

No. 03–1488

ULYSSES TORY, ET AL., PETITIONERS *v.* JOHNNIE L. COCHRAN, JR.

ON WRIT OF CERTIORARI TO THE COURT OF APPEAL OF CALIFORNIA, SECOND APPELLATE DISTRICT

[May 31, 2005]

majority opinion written by Justice Breyer

JUSTICE BREYER delivered the opinion of the Court.

Johnnie Cochran brought a state-law defamation action against petitioner Ulysses Tory. The state trial court determined that Tory (with the help of petitioner Ruth Craft and others) had engaged in unlawful defamatory activity. It found, for example, that Tory, while claiming falsely that Cochran owed him money, had complained to the local bar association, had written Cochran threatening letters demanding $10 million, had picketed Cochran's office holding up signs containing various insults and obscenities; and, with a group of associates, had pursued Cochran while chanting similar threats and insults. App. 38, 40–41. The court concluded that Tory's claim that Cochran owed him money was without foundation, that Tory engaged in a continuous pattern of libelous and slanderous activity, and that Tory had used false and defamatory speech to "coerce" Cochran into paying "amounts of money to which Tory was not entitled" as a "tribute" or a "premium" for "desisting" from this libelous and slanderous activity. *Id.,* at 39, 42–43.

After noting that Tory had indicated that he would

FIGURE 3.6 Cont.

2   TORY *v.* COCHRAN

Opinion of the Court

continue to engage in this activity in the absence of a court order, the Superior Court issued a permanent injunction. The injunction, among other things, prohibited Tory, Craft, and their "agents" or "representatives" from "picketing," from "displaying signs, placards or other written or printed material," and from "orally uttering statements" about Johnnie L. Cochran, Jr., and about Cochran's law firm in "any public forum." *Id.,* at 34.

Tory and Craft appealed. The California Court of Appeal affirmed. Tory and Craft then filed a petition for a writ of certiorari, raising the following question:

> "Whether a permanent injunction as a remedy in a defamation action, preventing all future speech about an admitted public figure, violates the First Amendment." Pet. for Cert. i.

We granted the petition. 542 U. S. _____ (2004).

After oral argument, Cochran's counsel informed the Court of Johnnie Cochran's recent death. Counsel also moved to substitute Johnnie Cochran's widow, Sylvia Dale Mason Cochran, as respondent, and suggested that we dismiss the case as moot. Tory and Craft filed a response agreeing to the substitution of Ms. Cochran. But they denied that the case was moot.

We agree with Tory and Craft that the case is not moot. Despite Johnnie Cochran's death, the injunction remains in effect. Nothing in its language says to the contrary. Cochran's counsel tells us that California law does not recognize a "cause of action for an injury to the memory of a deceased person's reputation," see *Kelly v. Johnson Pub. Co.,* 160 Cal. App. 2d 718, 325 P. 2d 659 (1958), which circumstance, counsel believes, "moots" a *"portion"* of the injunction (the portion "personal to Cochran"). Respondent's Suggestion of Death, etc., 4 (emphasis added). But counsel adds that "[t]he [i]njunction continues to be necessary, valid and enforceable." *Id.,* at 9. The parties have

FIGURE 3.6   Cont.

Cite as: 544 U.S. _____ (2005)   3

Opinion of the Court

not identified, nor have we found, any source of California law that says the injunction here *automatically* becomes invalid upon Cochran's death, not even the portion personal to Cochran. Counsel also points to the "value of" Cochran's "law practice" and adds that his widow has an interest in enforcing the injunction. *Id.,* at 11–12. And, as we understand California law, a person cannot definitively know whether an injunction is legally void until a court has ruled that it is. See *Mason v. United States Fidelity & Guaranty Co.,* 60 Cal. App. 2d 587, 591, 141 P. 2d 475, 477–478 (1943) ("[W]here the party served believes" a court order "invalid he should take the proper steps to have it dissolved"); *People v. Gonzalez,* 12 Cal. 4th 804, 818, 910 P. 2d 1366, 1375 (1996) ("[A] person subject to a court's injunction may elect whether to challenge the constitutional validity of the injunction when it is issued, or to reserve that claim until a violation of the injunction is charged as a contempt of court"). Given the uncertainty of California law, we take it as a given that the injunction here continues significantly to restrain petitioners' speech, presenting an ongoing federal controversy. See, *e.g., Dombrowski v. Pfister, 380* U. S. 479, 486–487 (1965); *NAACP* v. *Button,* 371 U. S. 415, 432–433 (1963). Consequently, we need not, and we do not, dismiss this case as moot. Cf. *Firefighters v. Stotts,* 467 U. S. 561, 569 (1984) (case not moot in part because it appears from "terms" of the injunction that it is "still in force" and "unless set aside must be complied with").

At the same time, Johnnie Cochran's death makes it unnecessary, indeed unwarranted, for us to explore petitioners' basic claims, namely (1) that the First Amendment forbids the issuance of a permanent injunction in a defamation case, at least when the plaintiff is a public figure, and (2) that the injunction (considered prior to Cochran's death) was not properly tailored and consequently violated the First Amendment. See Brief for

FIGURE 3.6 Cont.

4   TORY *v.* COCHRAN

Opinion of the Court

Petitioners ii, iii. Rather, we need only point out that the injunction, as written, has now lost its underlying rationale. Since picketing Cochran and his law offices while engaging in injunction-forbidden speech could no longer achieve the objectives that the trial court had in mind (*i.e.,* coercing Cochran to pay a "tribute" for desisting in this activity), the grounds for the injunction are much diminished, if they have not disappeared altogether. Consequently the injunction, as written, now amounts to an overly broad prior restraint upon speech, lacking plausible justification. See *Nebraska Press Assn.* v. *Stuart,* 427 U. S. 539, 559 (1976) ("[P]rior restraints on speech and publication are the most serious and the least tolerable infringement on First Amendment rights"); *Pittsburgh Press Co.* v. *Pittsburgh Comm'n on Human Relations,* 413 U. S. 376, 390 (1973) (a prior restraint should not "swee[p]" any "more broadly than necessary"). As such, the Constitution forbids it. See *Carroll* v. *President and Comm'rs of Princess Anne,* 393 U. S. 175, 183–184 (1968) (An "order" issued in "the area of First Amendment rights" must be "precis[e]" and narrowly "tailored" to achieve the "pin-pointed objective" of the "needs of the case"); see also *Board of Airport Comm'rs of Los Angeles v. Jews for Jesus, Inc.,* 482 U. S. 569, 575, 577 (1987) (regulation prohibiting "all 'First Amendment activities'" substantially overbroad).

disposition

We consequently grant the motion to substitute Sylvia Dale Mason Cochran for Johnnie Cochran as respondent. We vacate the judgment of the California Court of Appeal, and we remand the case for proceedings not inconsistent with this opinion. If, as the Cochran supplemental brief suggests, injunctive relief may still be warranted, any appropriate party remains free to ask for such relief. We express no view on the constitutional validity of any such new relief, tailored to these changed circumstances, should it be entered.

It is so ordered.

FIGURE 3.6   Cont.

Cite as: 544 U.S. _____ (2005)   1

THOMAS, J., dissenting

SUPREME COURT OF THE UNITED STATES

────────

No. 03–1488

────────

ULYSSES TORY, ET AL., PETITIONERS *v.* JOHNNIE L. COCHRAN, JR.

ON WRIT OF CERTIORARI TO THE COURT OF APPEAL OF CALIFORNIA, SECOND APPELLATE DISTRICT

[May 31, 2005]

dissenting opinion joined by Justice Scalia ————————

JUSTICE THOMAS, with whom JUSTICE SCALIA joins, dissenting.

I would dismiss the writ of certiorari as improvidently granted. We granted the writ, as the Court notes, to decide

> "[w]hether a permanent injunction as a remedy in a defamation action, preventing all future speech about an admitted public figure, violates the First Amendment." Pet. for Cert. i; *ante,* at 2.

Whether or not Johnnie Cochran's death moots this case, it certainly renders the case an inappropriate vehicle for resolving the question presented. The Court recognizes this, *ante,* at 3, but nevertheless vacates the judgment below, *ante,* at 4. It does so only after deciding, as it must to exercise jurisdiction, that in light of the uncertainty in California law, the case is not moot. *Ante, at* 2–3; *ASARCO Inc.* v. *Kadish,* 490 U. S. 605, 621, n. 1 (1989) (when a case coming from a state court becomes moot, this Court "lack[s] jurisdiction and thus also the power to disturb the state court's judgment"); see also *City News & Novelty, Inc.* v. *Waukesha,* 531 U. S. 278, 283–284 (2001).

In deciding the threshold mootness issue, a complicated problem in its own right, the Court strains to reach the validity of the injunction after Cochran's death. Whether

FIGURE 3.6 Cont.

2   TORY *v.* COCHRAN

THOMAS, J., dissenting

the injunction remains valid in these changed circumstances is neither the reason we took this case nor an important question, but merely a matter of case-specific error correction. Petitioners remain free to seek relief on both constitutional and state-law grounds in the California courts. And, if the injunction is invalid, they need not obey it: California does not recognize the "collateral bar" rule, and thus permits collateral challenges to injunctions in contempt proceedings. *People* v. *Gonzalez,* 12 Cal. 4th 804, 818, 910 P. 2d 1366, 1375 (1996) (a person subject to an injunction may challenge "the constitutional validity of the injunction when it is issued, or . . . reserve that claim until a violation of the injunction is charged as a contempt of court"). The California courts can resolve the matter and, given the new state of affairs, might very well adjudge the case moot or the injunction invalid on state-law grounds rather than the constitutional grounds the Court rushes to embrace. As a prudential matter, the better course is to avoid passing unnecessarily on the constitutional question. See *Ashwander* v. *TVA,* 297 U. S. 288, 345–348 (1936) (Brandeis, J., concurring).

The Court purports to save petitioners the uncertainty of possible enforcement of the injunction, and thereby to prevent any chill on their First Amendment rights, by vacating the decision below. But what the Court gives with the left hand it takes with the right, for it only invites further litigation by pronouncing that "injunctive relief may still be warranted," conceding that "any appropriate party remains free to ask for such relief," and "express[ing] no view on the constitutional validity of any such new relief." *Ante,* at 4. What the Court means by "any appropriate party" is unclear. Perhaps the Court means Sylvia Dale Mason Cochran, Cochran's widow, who has taken his place in this suit. Or perhaps it means the Cochran firm, which has never been a party to this case, but may now (if "appropriate") intervene and attempt to

FIGURE 3.6 Cont.

> Cite as: 544 U.S. _____ (2005)   3
>
> THOMAS, J., dissenting
>
> enjoin the defamation of a now-deceased third party. The Court's decision invites the doubts it seeks to avoid. Its decision is unnecessary and potentially self-defeating. The more prudent course is to dismiss the writ as improvidently granted. I respectfully dissent.

THE COMPONENTS OF A CASE BRIEF

holding
That aspect of the decision which directly affects the outcome of the case; it is composed of the reasoning necessary and sufficient to reach the disposition.

reasoning
The court's rationale that sets forth the legal principles the court relied upon in reaching its decision.

dictum
A statement made by the court that is beyond what is necessary to reach the final decision.

PRACTICE TIP

Always attach a copy of the citator page to each case brief. Your attorney(s) will always want to know whether the case is still good law. Let them have the opportunity to review the case for themselves, especially if something in the citator page warrants further investigation. This practice will exhibit your thoroughness and show your professionalism.

Rather than simply recite and define the components of a case brief, in this section we take you step by step through the preparation of a comprehensive case brief for *Duran v. St. Luke's Hospital* (the finished product appears as Figure 3.9 at the end of this chapter).

Updating the Case

Before you begin any case brief, you must verify that the case or cases you are briefing are still good law. You wouldn't want to spend your time briefing a case only to learn that it is "overruled." A good practice is to update all your cases either through Shepardizing or KeyCite before you begin reading or briefing your case. In Figure 3.7 are pages from Shepard's Citations Service and KeyCite, the online legal research services. Review both pages and you will observe that both citators indicate that the *Duran* case has not been overruled. (Refer back to Chapter 2 for definitions of the signals.) In fact, there do not appear to be any warning signals from either source. Do notice that each citator service does provide additional research sources, which may be of assistance if you were to research the issue further. In fact, using the facts from the Case Fact Pattern at the beginning of the chapter, you may be able to locate important new sources on the issue presented that may be helpful to the client's position. The usefulness of the citator services cannot be overstated.

Reading the Case

Updating of the case is complete, and now you must begin the process of case briefing. You cannot brief a case until you understand it, and you cannot understand it until you read it. Furthermore, when you read it, you should read the entire case, from start to finish. This might seem obvious, and indeed it should be, but it is a basic rule too often honored in the breach. Resist the temptation to skim, to rely on the editor's synopsis, to rely on the headnotes, or to search for the disposition without reading the court's underlying reasoning. There are problems ahead for those who think that they don't have the time to read the whole case or can get everything they need from the first and last page. Indeed, as we discuss, in *Duran,* you will see excellent examples of the sorts of peculiarities a close reading can reveal.

Remember also that one reading is rarely enough for anyone, and certainly not enough for a beginning paralegal. At a minimum, you should read the case once to develop a general understanding of the obvious points and a second time to pick out the more subtle points. You should probably read it a third time to verify the points you found in the first two readings, then constantly refer back for specifics as you prepare your case brief. Before proceeding with this chapter, read *Duran v. St. Luke's Hospital* with care. Now, read it again!

Identification of the Case

The first component of a case brief is, of course, to identify the case. This is done in our case brief both at the top of the page and in the citation section:

Case Brief — Duran v. St. Luke's Hospital
Citation:
Duran v. St. Luke's Hospital, 114 Cal.App.4th 457, 8 Cal.Rptr.3d 1 (Cal.App. 1 Dist. 2003)

FIGURE 3.7   KeyCite and Shepard's for *Duran v. St. Luke's Hospital*

Source: Copyright © 2006 West, Carswell, Sweet & Maxwell Asia and Thomson Legal & Regulatory Limited. Used with permission of Thomson West. From Shepard's Citations Service. Reprinted with permission from LexisNexis.

KEYCITE

HDuran v. St. Luke's Hosp., 114 Cal.App.4th 457, 8 Cal.Rptr.3d 1, 03 Cal. Daily Op. Serv. 10,868, 2003 Daily Journal D.A.R. 13,671 (Cal. App. 1 Dist., Dec 16, 2003) (NO. A102182)

Citing References
Positive Cases (U.S.A.)
★★★   Discussed

▶ 1   Smith v. Las Virgenes Unified School Dist., 2005 WL 1774970, *3+ (Cal.App. 2 Dist. 2005)

★★   Cited

C   2   Liang v. San Francisco Residential Rent Stabilization and Arbitration Bd., 21 Cal.Rptr.3d 715, 718 (Cal.App. 1 Dist. 2004)

Secondary Sources (U.S.A.)

C   3   Tolling of statute of limitations where process is not served before expiration of limitation period, as affected by statutes defining commencement of action, or expressly relating to interruption of running of limitations, 27 A.L.R.2d 236, §236+ (1953)

4   1 California Affirmative Defenses 2d s 25:6, s 25:6. Commencement of action stopping statute (2006)

5   Rutter, Cal. Practice Guide: Civ. Pro. Before Trial CH. 1-H, H. Filing Fee Considerations (2005)

6   Rutter, Cal. Practice Guide: Civil Trials & Evidence Ch. 18-B, B. Motion For New Trial (2005)

7   2 Witkin Cal. Proc. 4th Jurisdiction s 104, Statutory Condition Precedent.

8   4 Witkin Cal. Proc. 4th Pleading s 14, In General.

9   CA Jur. 3d Clerks of Court s 10, s 10. Right to demand fees in advance (2005)

10   Cal. Civ. Prac. Probate & Trust Proceedings s 1:22, s 1:22. Payable from estate (2005)

FIGURE 3.7   **Cont.**

SHEPARD'S CITATIONS SERVICE

Signal: ⬥ Positive treatment is indicated
Trail: Unrestricted

Duran v. St. Luke's Hospital, 114 Cal. App. 4th 457, 8 Cal. Rptr. 3d 1, 2003 Cal. App. LEXIS 1861, 2003 Cal. Daily Op. Service 10868, 2003 D.A.R. 13671 (Cal. App. 1st Dist. 2003)

SHEPARD'S SUMMARY ⬥ **Hide Summary**

Unrestricted *Shepard's* **Summary**

⬥ **No negative subsequent appellate history.**

Citing References:

Citing Decisions: Citing decisions with no analysis assigned (2)

Other Sources: Statutes (3), Treatises (10)

LexisNexis Headnotes: HN6 (2)

Show full text of headnotes

PRIOR HISTORY (0 citing references) ⬥ **Hide Prior History**

► **(CITATION YOU ENTERED):**
Duran v. St. Luke's Hospital, 114 Cal. App. 4th 457, 8 Cal. Rptr. 3d 1, 2003 Cal. App. LEXIS 1861, 2003 Cal. Daily Op. Service 10868, 2003 D.A.R. 13671 (Cal. App. 1st Dist. 2003)

SUBSEQUENT APPELLATE HISTORY (1 citing reference) ⬥ **Hide Subsequent Appellate History**

↲ Select for Delivery
1. **Review denied by:**
Duran v. St. Luke's Hospital, 2004 Cal. LEXIS 2260 (Cal. Mar. 17, 2004)

CITING DECISIONS (2 citing decisions)

CALIFORNIA COURTS OF APPEAL

2. **Cited by:**
Liang v. San Francisco Residential Rent Stabilization & Arbitration Bd., 124 Cal. App. 4th 775, 21 Cal. Rptr. 3d 715, 2004 Cal. App. LEXIS 2060, 2004 Cal. Daily Op. Service 10683, 2004 D.A.R. 14462 (Cal. App. 1st Dist. 2004) LexisNexis Headnotes HN6

124 Cal. App. 4th 775 p.777
21 Cal. Rptr. 3d 715 p.718

PRACTICE TIP

Invest in a law dictionary. Many of the legal terms in a case are new and unfamiliar. You will need a dictionary by your side, at least in the beginning, until you have mastered basic legal language.

Parties

The parties section of our case brief will reveal the peculiarities we referred to earlier. It is not entirely clear from this decision just who the parties are:

Parties:
Celina Duran (plaintiff/appellant); presumably, the father in the case (plaintiff/appellant) and also referred to as the parents and plaintiffs in the case; St. Luke's Hospital (defendant/respondent); Vicki Cordts (defendant/respondent); Women's Health Center (defendant/respondent). [Note: The identities of the respondents are not entirely clear. The caption of the case identifies only the one plaintiff listed here, Celina Duran, *et al.,* and no one else. The opinion refers to the "plaintiffs," presumably "the parents." The case also identifies three different defendants (St. Luke's Hospital, Vicki Cordts, and Women's Health Center) as "respondents." Presumably, all the defendants/respondents had the same interests and therefore, the court did not distinguish the parties separately. From the case, it is even difficult to know who Defendant Vicki Cordts is (perhaps the filing clerk of the court in this case). The confusion does not appear to have an impact on the decision of the case.]

issue
Point of law or fact on which an appeal is based.

facts
Significant objective information in a case.

Order Nunc Pro Tunc
An entry made by a court of an event that previously happened and made to have the effect of the former date.

General Demurrer
A responsive pleading filed by a party attacking the legal sufficiency of a complaint.

The identities of the plaintiffs are clear, although not the name of the father. Both in the caption of the case and in the text, the plaintiffs are identified as the parents, although of whom is unknown unless the case synopsis is reviewed. (This case was a medical malpractice action filed by plaintiffs due to the death of their infant child.) It is also clear that these two plaintiffs are also the appellants.

It is not clear, however, exactly who are defendants. First look at the caption of the case. It would seem from the caption that St. Luke's Hospital is the defendant/appellant. However, the caption refers to defendants and uses the term *et al.;* the only hint is in the section listing the attorneys and who they represent at the beginning of the case. Consequently, there appear to be three named defendants in this case.

As it turns out, these discrepancies do not have any impact on the court's decision. Nevertheless, two lessons should be taken. First, as we emphasize at great length in later chapters, it is extremely important to express yourself clearly in every legal document you draft. The ambiguity in this decision could have been eliminated had the court used more care in draftsmanship. Second, you have to read with great attention to detail. A discrepancy like this can give you an opening to distinguish a case cited by your opponent; conversely, it could be used by your opponent to discredit a case cited by you. You must analyze opinions with great care.

In any event, since the discrepancies did not affect the court's decision, the case brief deals with the problem by identifying the "parents" as a group and the hospital and other defendants as a group as well. All the "defendants" are also the respondents; that is to say, they are responding to the appeal brought by the parents ("plaintiffs-appellants").

Issues

The **issue** in the appeal is that point or points, if more than one issue is appealed, on which the appeal was based. Our case brief identifies the issue as follows:

> **Issue:**
> 1. Could a complaint be deemed filed prior to the expiration of the statute of limitations if the mandatory filing fee was not submitted in a timely basis?

The derivation of these issues is straightforward. The plaintiffs assert that the trial court was wrong in finding that the complaint was not filed when it was received prior to the running of the statute of limitations even though the filing fee was $3.00 short. The court must address and decide this issue. Many judges make it easy to find the issue in a case. They often state "the issue before us is . . ." or "we are asked to decide . . .". Pay close attention to the language in the case as it will be helpful in formulating the issue.

One quick and easy method of drafting the issues section is to determine the holding, then turn the holding into a question. This method is not recommended, however, because it requires working backward.

You will often observe an issue couched in terms such as "whether," "does," "to the extent that. . .," and other forms of a question. Crafting an issue can be an art, especially in an appellate brief. This concept will be discussed in greater detail in the chapters addressing the legal memoranda and appellate briefs.

Facts

The **facts** that should be included in a case brief are those which are necessary to gain a full and accurate understanding of the impact of the court's decision. Our case brief reads as follows:

> **Facts:**
> The facts in this case are undisputed. The Plaintiffs, parents in this case, hired a San Diego attorney to file a malpractice complaint against St. Luke's Hospital and others. The last day to file a complaint was October 9. The Attorney sent by Federal Express on October 7 a complaint and summons to the filing clerk of the San Francisco Superior Court. Enclosed with the documents was a check for $203.00 for the filing fee. Although the documents were received on October 8, the clerk did not file the complaint because the filing fee was $206.00. The submitted check was $3.00 short. By the time Plaintiffs' attorney learned of the situation and tendered the correct filing fee, it was too late. The statute of limitations had expired. Plaintiffs filed a Petition of ***"Order Nunc Pro Tunc"*** declaring that the complaint "shall be deemed filed on October 8." The petition was granted subject to a Motion to Strike by the Defendants. Defendants filed the Motion to Strike and ***General Demurrer,*** which was granted by the Court. The case was dismissed. Plaintiffs appealed.

FIGURE 3.8   Diagram of Prior Proceedings of *U.S. v. Booker*

Source: From Westlaw. Used with permission from Thomson West.

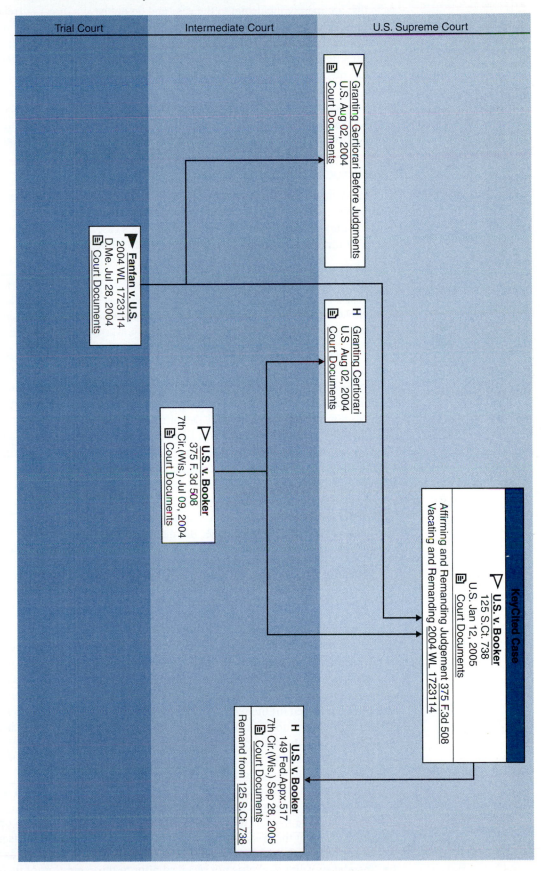

relevant fact
A fact that is significant to a case and its holding.

material fact
A fact that is essential to the case and its holding.

immaterial fact
A fact that is unimportant to the case and its holding.

PRACTICE TIP

Only examine and cite the facts relevant to the litigation about which the court is asked to decide. Do not confuse those facts with a court's discussion of the facts in a precedent-setting case.

prior proceedings
The previous procedural history of a case.

The key facts in this decision are clearly stated by the court as "undisputed." Most cases are not so easy. Often, you will have to extrapolate from the case the "key" facts and disregard those facts that are merely incidental to the case and do not have a direct correlation to the result. For example, the court spends a few paragraphs discussing the arguments of the plaintiffs. These points are not important to the result of the case and are absent from the case brief. Important facts affecting the decision of the court are considered to be **relevant** and **material.** Material facts are pivotal in the court's weighing of their relevance to the case. If the fact was omitted, what effect would it have on the outcome? Is the fact essential to the court's conclusion? If a fact is unimportant, it is considered **immaterial** or incidental; if unnecessary to understand the court's decision, it is considered irrelevant. The concepts of relevancy and materiality are not entirely distinct; there is a certain amount of overlap in meaning and usage.

Prior Proceedings

In order to understand the meaning of an opinion, the reader must first understand the procedural history of the case. Often the procedural setting is a crucial consideration in evaluating the extent to which the opinion can be applied to your client's case. The **prior proceedings** section of our case brief for *Duran v. St. Luke's Hospital* reads as follows:

> **Prior proceedings:**
> Plaintiffs filed an action for medical malpractice case against St. Luke's Hospital, and other Defendants. Plaintiffs filed a petition for an Order Nunc Pro Tunc. Defendants filed a Motion to Strike and General Demurrer based upon the expiration of the Statute of Limitations. A judgment of dismissal was filed by the trial court. Plaintiffs appealed the dismissal of the complaint.

Thus the plaintiffs originally brought suit against the hospital and two other defendants. Based upon the fact that the statute of limitations had run out, the plaintiffs filed a "technical" procedural petition asking the court to accept the filing of the complaint as timely and allowing the plaintiffs to proceed with their lawsuit against the defendants. The defendants responded by filing a Motion to Strike and General Demurrer, stating that the court, as a matter of law, had to dismiss the case because the statute of limitations expired prior to the filing of the complaint. The court agreed and dismissed the case. The plaintiffs filed an appeal with the appeal court.

All prior proceedings are not as straightforward as the *Duran* case. Review *U.S. v. Booker* in Chapter 2 and see how complex prior proceedings can be; also review the diagram in Figure 3.8.

Holding

The holding of a case is, of course, the most important element. The holding establishes the precedent—the rule of law in the case. The holding section of our case brief reads as follows:

> **Holding:**
> Under the circumstances present in this case, a complaint could not be deemed filed prior to the expiration of the statute of limitations since the mandatory filing fee was not received timely.

The wording of this section must be precise. You must carefully read the case and extract the meaning of the court's ruling, being careful neither to overextend nor underestimate the scope.

Let's look more closely at the language we've chosen, so that you can get a sense of the necessary precision. The first phrase, "Under the circumstances present in this case," should set off an alarm in the reader. By drawing attention to the specific circumstances present, the drafter of the case brief has tipped off the reader that the court has rendered a decision in which the facts were taken into consideration in reaching its result. In other words, given a different factual setting, the application of the same general legal principle might nevertheless result in a different holding. For example, in *Duran,* if no filing fee had been required or the statute had "discretionary" language such as the word "may," the result might have different.

What does it mean when a court qualifies its decision by limiting it to the specific facts of the case before it? It means that future parties who seek to use the case to support their argument must show how the facts of their case are analogous. It also presents an opportunity for a party seeking to discredit the precedential value of the case to distinguish it based upon the facts.

The wording of the next portion of our holding section is important as well. It indicates that the "mandatory filing fee" was not received prior to the expiration of the statute of limitations. Had the fee not been mandatory, the result might have been different.

You Be the Judge

Hypothetical 3-2

A case for disciplinary action against an attorney is serious. *In Re Fletcher*, 424 F.3d 783 (8th Cir. 2005), involves an attorney who violated numerous codes of conduct. This case was reviewed by a number of courts; all ultimately found that the attorney's conduct constituted malpractice. Read the case and learn the importance of understanding the lower and appellate review process. What actions did the attorney commit that warranted the disciplinary action? What was the appeals court disposition in the case? Identify the court's reasoning in the case. What were the pivotal facts resulting in the courts holding?

Because the holding resulted in harsh consequences, the court spent considerable time reviewing the history of "filing fees" and the various circumstances in which they were not a condition precedent to the filing of a case. Unfortunately for the plaintiffs, the facts in their case did not present an exception for the court.

Reasoning

In the **reasoning** section of our case brief, we analyze the rationale behind the court's holding:

> **Reasoning:**
> The case law is well settled in this area of law. The California Supreme Court dating back to the late 1800's consistently held that it is mandatory for court clerks to require a fee prior to accepting documents for filing when the statute requires a fee. Such a fee is a condition precedent to filing the legal document. The statutory language is mandatory and thus a clerk must collect the fees before filing a document for which a fee is required. The Court reviewed the history of the law in this matter and indicated that the law was well settled and undisputed.
>
> The Court highlighted a number of cases cited by the Plaintiffs that attempt to distinguish the facts of this case, but the Court concluded that none of them applied nor did they change the inevitable result that the filing fee must be submitted prior to the filing of legal documents. Thus, the statute of limitations barred Plaintiffs from filing their complaint because of the untimely filing of the mandatory fees. The appellate court adopted the reasoning of the trial court.
>
> There is *dictum* which discusses state versus local filing fees. But the Court quickly dismisses this argument since the state statute language is clear in its requirement of a mandatory filing fee.

The first paragraph clearly states the court's position on the issue. The law in California is well established and the court's reasoning makes this abundantly clear throughout its decision. Analyzing the statutes and case law, the court is balanced in its approach, especially given the inevitable result for the plaintiffs. Notice that the court addresses each argument of both the plaintiffs and defendants, methodically applying the case precedents to each.

The second paragraph of the reasoning section analyzes the appellants' attempt to distinguish a number of cases to no avail. In the court's four pages, it painstakingly reviews the case law, ultimately arriving at the same conclusion as the trial court—dismissal.

The final lines of the reasoning section allude to the court's dictum. Here, the dictum refers to the plaintiffs' unsuccessful attempt at distinguishing state and local rules of court and are quickly dismissed by the court.

Disposition

The purpose of the disposition section of the case brief is to alert the reader to the outcome of the case. The key to drafting it is to be concise. In *Duran,* where the appellate court found that the trial court was correct in dismissing the complaint, the disposition can be relayed in one word: "Affirmed." For a more complex disposition, see Figure 3.6, *Tory v. Cochran.* Review the last paragraph of the majority opinion.

DEVELOPING THE CASE BRIEF

Case briefs are a specialized form of note taking. As you become more familiar with the format and language of a case, your note taking will become more precise and developed. There are no hard and fast rules for case briefing; some attorneys prefer more detail—a long form brief;

others prefer a condensed version that identifies the facts, issue, holding, and reasoning—the short form. Whatever form your brief takes, long or short, there are some common practical tips that can be established from the process. Try this:

- Identify the case brief components on a sheet of paper.
- Read the case and take notes by filling in the designated sections, that is, facts, reasoning. That is your rough first draft.
- Review your notes. Read the case again. See if you agree with your original notes or need to add or change some of your notes.
- Begin transforming your notes into sentences for each section identified in the brief.
- Review your draft.
- Read the case one more time.
- Review and edit the case brief for comprehensiveness and clarity.
- Add in a section at the end of the brief entitled "Comments or Notes." Here, you can write down your impressions of the case, such as "case on point," "facts distinguishable," " court applied this type of analysis, when our case requires . . . ," "case favors opposing position," "good alternative view," or "bad case, not on point." Use this section to jog your memory when you meet with your supervising attorney to discuss the case briefs.

Remember, briefs can be as long or as short as you need. Practice and time constraints may establish your needs. And most importantly, it does get easier with practice.

PRACTICAL CONSIDERATIONS

There you have it—a complete and concise case brief for *Duran v. St. Luke's Hospital*. Having followed the step-by-step logic behind that case brief, you have now gained the raw skills necessary to unravel the law that lurks within the thousands, indeed millions, of opinions that fill every law library.

 Ethics Alert

The *Duran* case was chosen for a very specific reason. It illustrates the importance of your and your supervising attorney's professional responsibility. You should have been thinking while reading the case that "it could have been me." Probably what happened in the case is that the attorney knew the statute of limitations was about to run. He had his legal secretary or paralegal contact the court to find out how much the filing fees were, and either the clerk gave them the wrong amount or maybe the individual who prepared the check for the filing fees typed the wrong amount. No matter what occurred, the result was that the complaint was not filed in time. The plaintiffs lost their opportunity to sue for the death of their infant child and, very possibly, the attorney in the case committed malpractice. Malpractice is improper or harmful conduct committed by a professional in the representation of a client. There is no question that the attorney is responsible for the conduct of his subordinates whether he or she committed the act, but the real question is whether a paralegal can be held responsible as well. The answer is probably "yes."

Courts have found paralegals and non-lawyers responsible for malpractice. Review *Busch v. Flangas, 837 P.2d 438* (Nev. 1992), which is a case that held a non-lawyer responsible. Your jurisdiction may have a different view. Regardless of the case law, situations such as the one in the *Duran* case could cost you your job. Could the result in the *Duran* case been avoided? Possibly. Had someone contacted the court clerk to make sure the complaint had been filed properly, the situation might have been avoided. Checking that the Federal Express package reached its destination may not be enough. Had the attorney learned of the error, a new check could have been submitted by the deadline, a service could have been contacted to submit a new check, an affiliated law firm could have been contacted to submit a new check, or someone from the San Diego law firm could have flown to San Francisco to file the documents with a new check. Follow-up could have avoided the result. You should learn from this case to never take things for granted; always follow up, especially when the situation is critical.

THE E-FACTOR

USING THE INTERNET TO YOUR ADVANTAGE

The electronic age has made it easier to find cases as well as to verify their validity. Because of that, it is inexcusable not to take the time to be thorough in a case briefing assignment. Although the Internet cannot provide the case brief and analysis for you, Lexis and Westlaw have tools that make the process more comprehensive. For example, Westlaw provides a feature that graphs the history of the prior proceedings of a case. Remember our case in Chapter 2, *U.S. v. Booker*. Figure 3.9 illustrates the appellate history of the case.

Lexis provides an appellate history feature as well. Your attorney expects that your case brief will be complete, which includes the updating process.

New cases are decided every day; these case decisions may affect a client's case. Subscribe to case alerts found in many legal websites. Lexis and Westlaw provide case alerts as well. Check the websites of courts in your jurisdiction for new opinions. Don't be left behind. Your firm's opponent surely will not!

Of course, you will need much practice to refine those skills, and you will learn much about the law along the way. Some things that you learn will surprise you—such as the fact that not all judges write with clarity. You will also learn that opinions are written assuming that readers are trained to understand legal concepts and decipher legalese. You must be prepared to overcome these obstacles. Keep your legal dictionary at hand, learn as much as you can about the substantive law, learn where to find the answers to questions that arise, persevere until you understand the problem at hand, and don't be afraid to ask for help.

As you gain experience in case briefing, you will develop your own techniques, or learn techniques preferred by your supervising attorney. For example, in order to conserve space, some firms prefer case briefs that identify the litigants (parties to a lawsuit) as *P* and *D* rather than as plaintiff and defendant, or sometimes by the Greek letters π (pi) for plaintiff and δ (delta) for defendant. Another shorthand notation is the letter *K* for contract. No one technique is preferable; but whatever format or style you choose, remember that your brief must be thorough, accurate, and understandable to those who need to read and rely upon it.

Finally, in preparing a case brief you should always keep in mind the goal of the attorney for whom you are working. For some cases an extensive and detailed analysis will be necessary; for other cases, little more will be needed than a brief statement of the facts and holding. Some case briefs are thus long and formalized; others short. You and your supervising attorney are a team, and to function well as a team you must coordinate your goals.

These first three chapters have provided you with an introduction to the American legal system, the challenge of legal research, and basic case analysis. Now it's time to turn to the task of legal writing.

Summary

A case brief is an objective summary of the important points of a case. This is different from a trial brief or appellate brief, each of which is drafted not to be objective, but rather to persuade.

The typical printed opinion appearing in a reporter contains several characteristic components. Star-paging enables the reader to identify page references from other reporters. The shorthand case name identifies the case at the top of the page. The parallel citation provides references to other reporters in which the case text appears. The full name of the case identifies all the parties and their position in the litigation (for example, plaintiff or defendant). The docket number is assigned to the case by the court for administrative purposes, and is usually included along with the date the decision was rendered and the full name of the court. The synopsis is an extremely short summary of the case prepared not by the court, but by the publisher of the reporter. A syllabus is a summary prepared by the court. Key numbers and headnotes are included, as well as the attorneys and judges involved in the matter and, of course, the text and disposition of the case. Decisions can be affirmed or reversed or subject to some other disposition. There can be majority opinions, dissenting opinions, and concurring opinions. The holding of a court is that aspect of the decision which directly affects the outcome of the case; *dictum* is a statement made by the court that goes beyond what is necessary to reach the disposition.

FIGURE 3.9   Sample Case Brief.

Case Brief— Duran v. St. Luke's Hospital

Citation:

Duran v. St. Luke's Hospital, 114 Cal.App.4th 459, 8 Cal.Rptr.3d 1 (Cal. App. 1 Dist. 2003)

Parties:

Celina Duran (plaintiff/appellant); presumably, the father in the case (plaintiff/appellant) and also referred to as the parents and plaintiffs in the case; St. Luke's Hospital (defendant/respondent); Vicki Cordts (defendant/respondent); Women's Health Center (defendant/respondent).

Issue:

1. Could a complaint be deemed filed prior to the expiration of the statute of limitations if the mandatory filing fee was not submitted in a timely basis?

Facts:

The facts in this case are undisputed. The Plaintiffs, parents in this case, hired a San Diego attorney to file a malpractice complaint against St. Luke's Hospital and others. The last day to file a complaint was October 9. The Attorney sent by Federal Express on October 7 a complaint and summons to the filing clerk of the San Francisco Superior Court. Enclosed with the documents was a check for $203.00 for the filing fee. Although the documents were received on October 8, the clerk did not file the complaint because the filing fee was $206.00. The submitted check was $3.00 short. By the time Plaintiffs' attorney learned of the situation and tendered the correct filing fee, it was too late. The statute of limitations had expired. Plaintiffs filed a Petition of **"Order Nunc Pro Tunc."** declaring that the complaint "shall be deemed filed on October 8." The petition was granted subject to a Motion to Strike by the Defendants. Defendants filed the Motion to Strike and General Demurrer which was granted by the Court. The case was dismissed. Plaintiffs appealed.

Prior proceedings:

Plaintiffs filed an action for medical malpractice case against St. Luke's Hospital, and other Defendants. Plaintiffs filed a petition for an Order Nunc Pro Tunc. Defendants filed a Motion to Strike and General Demurrer based upon the expiration of the Statute of Limitations. A judgment of dismissal was filed by the trial court. Plaintiffs appealed the dismissal of the complaint.

Holding:

Under the circumstances present in this case, a complaint could not be deemed filed prior to the expiration of the statute of limitations since the mandatory filing fee was not received timely.

Reasoning:

The case law is well settled in this area of law. The California Supreme Court dating back to the late 1800's consistently held that is mandatory for court clerks to require a fee prior to accepting documents for filing when the statute requires a fee. Such a fee is a condition precedent to filing the legal document. The statutory language is mandatory and thus a clerk must collect the fees before filing a document for which a fee is required. The Court reviewed the history of the law in this matter and indicated that the law was well settled and undisputed.

The Court highlighted a number of cases cited by the Plaintiffs that attempt to distinguish the facts of this case, but the Court concluded that none of them applied nor did they change the inevitable result that the filing fee must be submitted prior to the filing of legal documents. Thus, the statute of limitations barred Plaintiffs from filing their complaint because of the untimely filing of the mandatory fees. The appellate court adopted the reasoning of the trial court.

There is *dictum* which discusses state versus local filing fees. But the Court quickly dismisses this argument since the state statute language is clear in its requirement of a mandatory filing fee.

Disposition:
Affirmed.

When preparing a case brief, you must first read the relevant case, then follow several steps to produce a document with several components. First, identify the case. Second, describe the parties. Third, identify the issues that were before the court for decision. Fourth, set out the relevant facts. Fifth, trace the procedural history of the case. Sixth, identify the holding of the court, taking great care to reflect accurately the precise parameters of the court's decision. Seventh, analyze the court's reasoning, again taking great care to restate and summarize the court's rationale. Eighth, alert the reader to the outcome of the case with a concise, shorthand statement of the court's disposition.

In drafting case briefs, you must overcome obstacles such as poorly drafted or highly technical judicial opinions. Over time you will develop your own style or learn the characteristic style preferred by your firm. Always keep in mind the goal that you and your supervising attorney are attempting to accomplish with the drafting of the case brief. This goal will influence length, formality, and general content.

Key Terms

case brief
star-paging
caption
docket number
synopsis
syllabus
disposition
affirmed
reversed
remanded
vacated
per curiam decision
en banc decision
majority opinion
concur
concurring opinion

dissent
dissenting opinion
holding
reasoning
dictum
issue
facts
Order Nunc Pro Tunc
General Demurrer
relevant fact
material fact
immaterial fact
prior proceedings

Review Questions

1. What is the difference between a case brief and a brief written for a trial or appellate court?
2. What are the components of a printed opinion?
3. Why is star-paging useful?
4. What is the difference between a majority opinion and a dissent?
5. What are the components of a case brief?
6. How do you identify the relevant facts in an opinion?
7. How do you identify the issues presented by a written opinion?
8. How do you locate the procedural history of a case as set forth in the opinion?
9. What is a holding? What is a disposition?
10. What is the reasoning of an opinion?

Exercises

1. Read *Tarasoff v. Regents of the University of California,* 551 P.2d 334 (California 1976) and *Thompson v. County of Alameda,* 614 P.2d 728 (California 1980) and answer the following questions:
   a. What is the holding in Tarasoff? In Thompson?
   b. Are the results different? If so, list the reasoning of each court for reaching its decision.
   c. Can these cases be reconciled?

2. In your law library, find *Trump v. Chicago Tribune,* 616 F. Supp. 1434 (S.D.N.Y. 1985) and perform the following tasks:
   a. Name the parties to the case.
   b. Identify the court and the case reporter.
   c. List the West topics and keys in the case.
   d. Identify the objectives of the parties.
   e. List the prior proceedings.

3. Locate *White v. Samsung,* 971 F.2d 1395 (9th Cir. 1992), and answer the following questions:
   a. What is the holding?
   b. What are the prior proceedings?
   c. What is the court's reasoning behind its holding?

4. Your attorney has asked you to brief *Elvis Presley Enterprises v. Capece,* 141 F.3d 188 (5th Cir. 1998). Prepare the case brief.

5. Define the following terms:
   a. *per curiam*
   b. holding
   c. reasoning
   d. disposition
   e. caption
   f. appellant

6. Check the U.S. Supreme Court website, www.supremecourtus.gov, and determine whether any new cases have been reported in the last six months. Choose one case and prepare a case brief. Hint: Check recent slip opinions.

7. Determine the Federal Court of Appeals in your jurisdiction. Search on the website and locate a criminal case that was decided in the last year. Brief one of the cases and answer the following questions:
   a. Identify the parties to the case.
   b. Who is the appellant? The appellee?
   c. What is the holding and disposition in the case?

8. Brief *Clay v. U.S.,* 537 U.S. 522 (2003) and answer the following questions:
   a. What are the parallel citations for the case?
   b. Who wrote the opinion for the court?
   c. Identify the number of the headnotes with their associated topic and keys.
   d. What is the disposition of the case?

9. Brief *Wright v. Sport Supply Group, Inc.,* 137 S.W.3d 289 (Tex. App.- Beaumont, 2004).

 ## Portfolio Assignment

A new client has retained your law firm. A young widow married a very wealthy elderly gentleman. They were married for nearly two years before he passed away. The husband had adult children who believe that they are entitled to 100% of their father's estate. They want the young widow to get nothing. Your state is a community property state and your attorney believes that the husband intended his widow to share in the estate with his adult children. A recent case in the U.S. Supreme Court involved a similar situation, *Marshall v. Marshall.* You know the Court decided the case in 2006 and your supervising attorney asks you to brief the case and report on it tomorrow.

Locate the case and prepare a detailed case brief. Pay particular attention to the facts and holding of the case. Would it apply to your situation?

Vocabulary Builder

Legal Research: Case Brief

```
R S T G K D X E C U D B V S V K J O N C
D E I T N E S S I D F B C A P S F A Z E
D P M S I I K W E K W V C V E K V J J S
H R G A P W D V N S W A S G R Z Z B M R
P L A J N O X L Q N T C I Q Z P J H W L
S W S R U D N I O E K P K P J Q T M F M
T O C Q W M E Y D H Q G R B Z G S I U F
Q N H R J C G D S V G Y N Y I T K T M I
D G N I N O S A E R Y J I U Y O C L U D
I O K M A J O R I T Y O P I N I O N R T
S C C V Q K W L M D Z E S Y D D G N U K
P L B K E J V K E Z R U U N X D Q A C I
O H A T E R Q M Z C D D B S V R N A N U
S J Y H O T R P U T Q N A C Y N I U O J
I P J A T I N R Q W V O L A O D D V C S
T I D G F B I U I C W E L P T X K T I E
I Q C F M A N I M E D B Y T R P T C F E
O R A I M O J W Y B R K S I L D M E A A
N X X L R E V E R S E D W O K R N U M B
V S M A K C H Y R F K R M N T I J C X D
```

AFFIRMED	**CAPTION**	**CONCUR**
DICTUM	**DISPOSITION**	**DISSENT**
DOCKET NUMBER	**HOLDING**	**MAJORITY OPINION**
PER CURIAM	**REASONING**	**REMANDED**
REVERSED	**SYLLABUS**	**SYNOPSIS**
VACATED		

Part Two

Legal Writing Basics

CHAPTER 4 Introduction to Legal Writing

CHAPTER 5 The Mechanics of Construction

CHAPTER 6 Effective and Persuasive Legal Writing

CHAPTER 7 Citations in Legal Writing

Chapter 4

Introduction to Legal Writing

CHAPTER OBJECTIVES

After completing this chapter, you will be able to:

- Define "legalese."

- Describe a "term of art."

- List basic techniques for good legal writing.

- Identify the audience for a legal document.

- Describe the difference between an "objective" purpose and an "adversarial" purpose.

- Apply the IRAC method for defining and researching a legal issue.

- Balance time constraints.

- Organize a legal document.

- List several different types of legal documents.

- Identify two different types of pleadings.

We all think legal writing should be filled with complicated words that no one understands and all the legal "gobbledygook." In reality, the opposite is true. The art of writing is communicating complicated subjects and words in a simple, understandable manner. Throw away all those notions you have from movies and television. Wipe the slate clean and focus on the concept that simpler is better. Use "plain English" whenever possible to convey your message regardless of the type of assignment. Less is more; precision and clarity rule the written page. But none of this is accomplished unless you have an organized plan of attack for the assignment. The journey of how to write legalese simply begins now.

Case Fact Pattern Hypothetical 4-1

On Monday morning you receive a telephone call from a friend who is buying a used car. The language of the contracts, credit agreements, warranties, and disclaimers has left him in a panic—it's too complicated to understand! He wants to make an appointment to have your supervising attorney review and explain the various provisions before he purchases the car. Since your friend is buying a used car, he especially wants to know what it means to buy a car "As Is" and "Without Warranties."

Your supervising attorney suggests you obtain copies of the contracts prior to the meeting for her review. After the meeting, the attorney asks you to prepare a draft of a letter to your friend and new client, explaining the issues in everyday language. Simplifying complicated legal documents is a task you will perform as a paralegal.

TRADITION AND TREND IN LEGAL WRITING

Most people have the same reaction as the friend in our Case Fact Pattern to legal documents—panic. They consider legal writing to be complicated, cumbersome, and incomprehensible. Although some legal writers do, in fact, allow their writing to deteriorate, most are reasonably competent. Why, then, is the image of legal writing so negative?

clarity
Clear and understandable style of communication.

One answer, oddly enough, is the importance of precision. As with all writing, good legal writing requires **clarity,** *conciseness, accuracy,* and *simplicity*—but above all else, it must be **precise.** It is essential that every person interpreting a document take the same meaning from the words chosen. This leads to an unwritten rule of law—namely, that once a given usage is agreed to have a given meaning, it should ever after be the accepted method of conveying that meaning. Any change from that usage necessarily implies that an alteration of that meaning is intended.

precise
Accuracy of written communication.

This unwritten rule has led to a reliance on archaic legal language. Terms that originated hundreds of years ago and which sound odd in the context of our modern language are still used in legal documents because their meaning is accepted. Legal **jargon,** often referred to as **legalese,** is characterized by the frequent use of Latin, French, and Old English terms unfamiliar to most present-day vocabularies. You have already seen such Latin terms as *in re* and *ex parte* as they are used in case names (*ex parte* also has another meaning, as we will note). Other terms commonly used include *res ipsa loquitor* (a Latin term from tort law meaning "the thing speaks for itself"), *voir dire* (a French term for the questioning of a potential juror for evidence of prejudice or unfitness), and *writ* (an Old English term for an order of a court, or the first written notice of a lawsuit). These are just a sampling. Other examples of legalese are listed in Table 4.1, but a complete list would be enormous.

jargon
Legalese.

legalese
Language that is characterized by the frequent use of Latin, French, and Old English terms unfamiliar to most present-day vocabularies in legal writing.

Legalese is also characterized by usages rarely seen elsewhere. Such phrases as "Hereof fail not but by these presents make due and proper return," or "Comes now James Jones, Plaintiff in the above-styled and numbered cause, who does by these presents make due complaint," are examples of archaic sentence structure seen in legal documents. Such words as *aforementioned* or *hereinafter,* seldom used in everyday language, clutter legal sentences. These practices are often a holdover from centuries of Anglo-Saxon jurisprudence.

Wordiness is another characteristic of legalese. Lawyers often use a phrase with a combination of synonymous, hence redundant, words. Such phrases as *cease and desist, null and void,* and *give, devise, and bequeath* date back to a time when two or three similar words were used to ensure clarity. Documents had to be interpreted correctly by people of different nationalities, in an era when language lacked the consistency of modern times. Although historically there may have been distinctions between the words used, current legal practice has for the most part erased them and rendered such phrases redundant.

Tradition has been a powerful force in the law, as you might expect from a system in which the concepts of precedent and *stare decisis* play so important a role. Things are done a certain way because that is how they have always been done; certain language is used because it has always been used. Thus, not only for the reason of precision, but also because of institutional custom and perhaps even out of sentiment, the legal profession has clung to traditional language at the expense of broader understanding. Therefore language that is clear to a trained lawyer or paralegal is unclear to the average citizen, leading to the negative image of "legalese."

More often than not, legalese is used from habit rather than necessity. The objective of precision can be better achieved by rigorous and exacting use of modern language than by reliance on anachronistic formulas. As Richard Wydick observes in his book *Plain English for Lawyers, 4th Edition* (Durham, NC: Carolina Academic Press, 1998):

> We use eight words to say what could be said in two. We use arcane phrases to express commonplace ideas. Seeking to be precise, we become redundant. Seeking to explain, we become verbose. Our sentences twist on, phrase within clause within clause, glazing the eyes and numbing the minds of our readers.

plain English
The style of legal writing that uses straightforward, clear, precise language and is generally devoid of legal jargon.

The modern trend in legal writing is to emphasize broader comprehensibility. Whenever possible, **plain English** should be used. Long, complicated sentences should be the exception, not the rule. Archaic terms and phrases should be replaced by equivalent modern language. When one word is sufficient, avoid redundant combinations.

TABLE 4.1
Examples of Legalese

Table 4.1 provides examples of legal jargon with the corresponding definitions in plain English. One of the challenges of legal writing is to exercise good judgment in deciding whether to employ legal terminology (which may have value for its precision or its standing as a term of art) or plain English.

Legalese	Translation
a fortiori	for a stronger reason
certiorari	discretionary request to the U.S. Supreme Court or other appellate court for review of a case
demurrer	request by defendant for a dismissal of a cause of action
duces tecum	to bring with you; a form of writ or request
ex parte	1. concerning the application of; 2. independent contact with an official, usually the judge, without the presence of the opposing side
inter alia	among other things
laches	principle of equity in which the passage of time prohibits pursuit of a cause of action
remittitur	judicial review and revision of an excessive judgment
res ipsa loquitor	the thing speaks for itself; in tort law, a doctrine that allows a finding of negligence without proof thereof
sua sponte	by the judge's own motion
tort	civil wrongdoing to another person
voir dire	to speak the truth; in practice refers to the examination of prospective jurors
writ	an order of the court, or the first pleading filed in a lawsuit

PLAIN ENGLISH

PRACTICE TIP

Do not use the word "said" as an adjective. Replace it with the word "the." It is straightforward and clear.

terms of art
Words that are commonly used in the legal profession and have an accepted meaning.

Of course, the survival of some legalese is inevitable, and even justifiable. Just as it is easier for doctors to use certain medical terminology, so it is easier for lawyers to use certain shorthand **terms of art** despite their obscurity to the general public. For example, the concise term *voir dire* mentioned previously requires a lengthy explanation in plain English, as does the alternate meaning of *ex parte* (contact with an official of the court in the absence of the opposing party). You must, however, use good judgment when evaluating the desirability of using legalese, and more often than not, there is a better alternative in plain English.

Legal writing needs to be demystified. Many people are under the impression that legal documents must be complicated, and that quality is related to complexity. This is simply not so. Indeed, the best expression of an idea is often the simplest composition that accurately conveys the intended meaning. The use of archaic legal terms and phrases should be minimized and plain English used instead. In the next few chapters we focus on techniques that

- employ short, succinct sentences;
- minimize legalese;
- avoid redundancy;
- emphasize simple language in simple form (subject-verb-object) using accepted rules of grammar; and
- remind us that writing is reading—and good writing will only develop when we reread what we have written.

Frank and Ernest

Source: © 1996 Thaves. Reprinted with permission. Newspaper dist. by NEA, Inc.

PREWRITING CONSIDERATIONS

audience
The person or persons to whom a legal document is directed, such as a client or the court.

PRACTICE TIP

Understanding the assignment is important. As a new paralegal, you may be hesitant to ask questions or ask for clarification. Don't be! If the assignment is unclear to you, let your supervising attorney know. Asking questions in the beginning saves time and avoids the wrong direction in an assignment.

Now you know why legal language often causes people to panic. You know that eliminating excess legalese can help to reduce that panic. You have learned that some legalese remains useful. You have also learned that certain rules that apply to all forms of writing, such as the superiority of short sentences and simple words, apply to legal writing as well. Before you refine your knowledge of legal writing techniques, however, you must address four preliminary considerations: identifying your **audience;** identifying your purpose; defining and researching the issues presented; and evaluating time constraints.

Lawyers prepare a wide range of writings for a diverse group of recipients. Some will be read by highly trained judges; others by less sophisticated clients. Before beginning a writing task, a lawyer or paralegal must determine

- the person to whom the document is directed;
- the level of legal expertise of that person or persons; and
- the degree of that person or persons' familiarity with the subject.

There may be particular problems in a given situation, for example, language barriers or physical or mental disability. As a paralegal, you have to learn how to overcome potential obstacles.

Don't make assumptions when determining the audience. For example, you might think that the audience for a demand letter is easy to identify: the person upon whom your client is making demand, or in other words, the person to whom the letter is addressed. Such an assumption could lead to a critical error if your demand letter must meet statutory requirements in order to be effective. Consider a demand letter to be sent to a physician accused of malpractice. There may be a statute that outlines specific requirements for you to put the physician "on notice" of the claim. In such a case, the demand letter is drafted for two audiences—the physician who is being notified, of course, and, equally important, the court that may eventually have to determine whether the requirements have been met. The court will not appear in the salutation, nor even, quite possibly, in the letter itself—yet the judge who may someday evaluate the letter is a crucial segment of the audience who must be considered.

Identifying the Purpose

objective documents
Documents that convey information and avoid bias.

adversarial documents
Documents that are argumentative, drafted to emphasize the strong points of your client's position and the weaknesses of the opposing party's.

In order to draft any effective writing, you must identify your purpose. Do you want to update a client on the status of a lawsuit? Do you want to convince a court that your client's position should prevail in a pending motion? Are you summarizing a deposition transcript? Depending on your purpose, your approach to the task will differ markedly. It is therefore critical that you identify this purpose before you begin drafting.

The purpose of most legal documents falls into one of two broad categories—**objective** or **adversarial.** Objective documents accurately convey information and avoid bias. A letter to your client estimating his chances for success would be an objective document, as would an interoffice memo summarizing the current state of the law that applies to a given set of facts. Adversarial documents, on the other hand, are argumentative, drafted to emphasize the strong points of

TABLE 4.2
Strategies for
Different Writing
Purposes

Purpose	Strategy
To inform	1. Identify audience
	2. Determine extent of audience's knowledge
	3. Research relevant information
	4. Determine what you desire to communicate
To persuade	1. Identify audience
	2. Determine relevant information
	3. Research relevant information
	4. Emphasize positive information and present in most favorable light
	5. Convince audience that your position is the better position
To discover information	1. Identify audience
	2. Determine information you need
	3. Research relevant sources
	4. Determine information that audience may possess
	5. Elicit information that is important without revealing your position
To prepare legal documents	1. Identify audience
	2. Determine legal requirements
	3. Elicit client's needs

your client's position and the weaknesses of the opposing party's. They are *not* objective; they are *not* designed to balance both sides. A demand letter written to your client's opponent or a brief submitted to persuade an appellate court are examples of adversarial documents.

Some documents have both objective and adversarial elements. For example, when drafting a contract proposal you will be seeking to reflect accurately the agreement of the parties (an objective purpose), while at the same time construing all ambiguous aspects of the agreement in your client's favor (an adversarial purpose).

By determining your purpose, you establish a focus that will enable you to accomplish your objective in every document you draft. In Table 4.2 we identify some strategies for accomplishing different purposes.

Defining and Researching the Issues

Once you've identified your audience and determined your purpose, are you ready to begin writing? The answer is no. Before you begin writing, you must define the issues presented and conduct the research necessary to address these issues.

For some documents, this last prewriting consideration may be easy. If, for example, you are simply updating a client on recent developments in a case, the issue is identical to the purpose (informing the client), and the research may be as simple as reviewing the file or even relating from memory.

In much legal writing, however, you will have to analyze the issues implied by your purpose and address them so as to accomplish your objective. A commonly used technique is the **IRAC method:**

- Identify the *issue* involved.
- Determine the relevant *rule of law*.
- *Apply* the rule of law to the facts of your matter.
- Reach a *conclusion*.

Taking the first letter of the four key items yields the mnemonic (memorizing) device *IRAC*. Let's take a closer look at each of these items.

The Issue

issue
The legal problem presented.

The **issue** is the legal problem presented. Identifying the issue is crucial to effectively preparing your assignment. If the precise legal problem is not identified, how can the problem be solved? Craft your issues so that the reader does not have to guess the subject of the legal document. The following are two issues from the set of facts in our Case Fact Pattern:

1. Can a buyer of a car change the terms in a contract?
2. When a buyer purchases a car "As Is" and "Without Warranties," what is the legal significance of the language in the contract?

Obviously, the second example is crafted more precisely. The language in the issue tells the reader what the subject of the legal discussion is. There is no guessing. The key to drafting the issue precisely is detail and specificity.

For example, the issue in our Case Fact Pattern problem is the meaning of the documents, specifically the "As Is" and "Without Warranties" provisions involved in the purchase of a used car. Through your supervising attorney, you have to inform your friend of several things—what the documents mean, whether they meet all legal requirements, and whether he has any option to negotiate their content.

The Rule of Law

rule of law
Sources of law that control the issue.

Having determined the issue, you must research the law to identify relevant statutes, regulations, cases, and constitutional provisions. Those sources that apply constitute the **rule of law** controlling the issue. For example, taking our Case Fact Pattern situation, a statute might require certain portions of the contract to be written in plain English or in oversized or boldfaced typeface, or a case might have held that certain financing disclosures are required.

Applying the Law to the Facts

The rule of law is an abstract concept that must be analyzed in the context of the particular facts of your client's matter. Applying the law to the facts enables you to address the issue in a manner meaningful to your client. Suppose, for example, that your research on our Case Fact Pattern problem has shown that a car dealership must identify "As Is" and "Without Warranties" language in conspicuous type, such as boldface, capital letters, or underlined, for the provisions in a sales contract to be enforceable. After you apply this rule of law to the facts of your specific matter, the letter to your friend might read in part as follows:

> *The dealership in an "As Is" purchase is required to inform all prospective purchasers of their rights, to have the "As Is" and "Without Warranties" language conspicuous to draw attention to this provision, and to have the prospective buyer initial the relevant provisions of the contract. Your initials, however, do not appear next to those provisions, nor is the "As Is" language conspicuous as required by the law.*

The letter thus takes the rule (which requires initialing and conspicuous language) and applies it to the facts (your friend did not initial his contract and the language was not conspicuous).

The Conclusion

conclusion
Summation of your analysis.

The result of your analysis is your **conclusion.** Carrying forward the Case Fact Pattern example to this final step, your letter to your friend might conclude

> *The dealership has failed to comply with the requirement that you initial provisions that explain your rights under an "As Is" purchase; nor is the language stating that the purchase is "As Is" and "Without Warranties" conspicuous. This is an important requirement of state law, and the contract is therefore rendered voidable at your discretion.*

The conclusion is the summation of the analysis. It answers the questions raised by the issues.

CONSTRAINTS ON LEGAL WRITING

Often legal documents have certain limitations. Those constraints may be as simple as time; length of the document; or, format of the document. Pay close attention to these issues when preparing your legal documents.

Time Constraints

Deadlines are a fact of life in legal practice. Virtually every document filed with a court is governed by a time requirement. In addition, practical considerations often create unofficial deadlines (a client may need certain legal questions answered immediately to gain an edge on his competitors). Finally, as a paralegal you will be expected to complete tasks within the time assigned by your supervising attorney.

An important prewriting consideration is thus to evaluate the time available and allocate your efforts accordingly. A brief due in 48 hours will be prepared in a fashion and on a schedule quite different from one due in four weeks. You must learn to budget your time without affecting the quality of your writing—which can be accomplished by organizing efficiently and taking advantage of all available resources (for example, if an old case involved similar issues, you might use the research from that file as a starting point).

Document Length

Document length may be dictated by your supervising attorney or the court. Rather than read a thesis on a topic, your attorney may limit your assignment to three pages. Often attorneys are pressed for time and need a concise review of a subject. Here economy of word choice is essential. Similarly, courts limit the length of briefs as well. Local rules and appellate rules of court may dictate the length of a brief. Review the rules of court when preparing a court document. Compare the document requirements of the U.S. Supreme Court and the U.S. Court of Appeals for the First Circuit in Figure 4.1 (page 110).

Format Style

Your attorney may have a particular way to present certain legal documents, such as a letter or memorandum of law. For example, the attorney may want the date of the correspondence centered; others may want the date justified with the contents of the document. Check with your attorney for their style preferences. Ask for samples of previous documents. Likewise, courts have format requirements. These requirements may be the difference between a court accepting or rejecting a document. Some courts only want twenty-five lines to a page or require a certain size of paper. Do not take any court format requirements for granted; familiarize yourself with the courts in your jurisdiction. If you are working on an assignment in a court with which you have not had experience, get a copy of their rules.

ORGANIZING THE LEGAL DOCUMENT

Organizing the document might be considered your final prewriting consideration, but it is better to think of it as the first consideration in the writing stage itself. Your plan of organization provides the blueprint by which your document will be crafted.

Outlining

outline
The skeleton of a legal argument, advancing from the general to the specific.

The best method of organizing a legal document is by outlining. An **outline** is the skeleton of a legal argument, advancing from the general to the specific. You have no doubt prepared outlines in other contexts in the past. A legal outline differs from these other outlines in content but not concept. It is intended to help you to critically examine your approach, leading to a document that flows logically to a conclusion that accomplishes your purpose. An outline will assist you in

- focusing on logical development;
- preventing critical omissions; and
- evaluating how well you accomplish your purpose.

FIGURE 4.1 Document Requirements of the U.S. Supreme Court and First Circuit Court of Appeals

Rules of the Supreme Court of the United States
Adopted March 14, 2005
Effective May 2, 2005

Rule 33. Document Preparation: Booklet Format; 8½- by 11-Inch Paper Format

- 1. *Booklet Format:*

(a) Except for a document expressly permitted by these Rules to be submitted on 8½- by 11-inch paper, see, e. g., Rules 21, 22, and 39, every document filed with the Court shall be prepared using using a standard typesetting process (e. g., hot metal, photocomposition, or computer typesetting) to produce text printed in typographic (as opposed to typewriter) characters. The process used must produce a clear, black image on white paper. The text must be reproduced with a clarity that equals or exceeds the output of a laser printer.

(b) The text of every booklet-format document, including any appendix thereto, shall be typeset in Roman 11-point or larger type with 2-point or more leading between lines. The typeface should be similar to that used in current volumes of the United States Reports. Increasing the amount of text by using condensed or thinner typefaces, or by reducing the space between letters, is strictly prohibited. Type size and face shall be consistent throughout. Quotations in excess of 50 words shall be indented. The typeface of footnotes shall be 9-point or larger with 2-point or more leading between lines. The text of the document must appear on both sides of the page.

(c) Every booklet-format document shall be produced on paper that is opaque, unglazed, 6 1/8 by 9 1/4 inches in size, and not less than 60 pounds in weight, and shall have margins of at least three fourths of an inch on all sides. The text field, including footnotes, should be approximately 4 1/8 by 7 1/8 inches. The document shall be bound firmly in at least two places along the left margin (saddle stitch or perfect binding preferred) so as to permit easy opening, and no part of the text should be obscured by the binding. Spiral, plastic, metal, and string bindings may not be used. Copies of patent documents, except opinions, may be duplicated in such size as is necessary in a separate appendix.

(d) Every booklet-format document shall comply with the page limits shown on the chart in subparagraph 1(g) of this Rule. The page limits do not include the pages containing the questions presented, the list of parties and corporate affiliates of the filing party, the table of contents, the table of cited authorities, or any appendix. Verbatim quotations required under Rule 14.1(f), if set out in the text of a brief rather than in the appendix, are also excluded. For good cause, the Court or a Justice may grant leave to file a document in excess of the page limits, but application for such leave is not favored. An application to exceed page limits shall comply with Rule 22 and must be received by the Clerk at least 15 days before the filing date of the document in question, except in the most extraordinary circumstances.

(e) Every booklet-format document shall have a suitable cover consisting of 65-pound weight paper in the color indicated on the chart in subparagraph 1(g) of this Rule. If a separate appendix to any document is filed, the color of its cover shall be the same as that of the cover of the document it supports. The Clerk will furnish a color chart upon request. Counsel shall ensure that there is adequate contrast between the printing and the color of the cover. A document filed by the United States, or by any other federal party represented by the Solicitor General, shall have a gray cover. A joint appendix, answer to a bill of complaint, motion for leave to intervene, and any other document not listed in subparagraph 1(g) of this Rule shall have a tan cover.

FIGURE 4.1   Cont.

(f) Forty copies of a booklet-format document shall be filed.

(g) Page limits and cover colors for booklet-format documents are as follows:

Type of Document	Page Limits	Color of Cover
i. Petition for a Writ of Certiorari (Rule 14); Motion for Leave to file a Bill of Complaint and Brief in Support (Rule 17.3); Jurisdictional Statement (Rule 18.3); Petition for an Extraordinary Writ (Rule 20.2)	30	white
ii. Brief in Opposition (Rule 15.3); Brief in Opposition to Motion for Leave to file an Original Action (Rule 17.5); Motion to Dismiss or Affirm (Rule 18.6); Brief in Opposition to Mandamus or Prohibition (Rule 20.3 (b)); Response to a Petition for Habeas Corpus (Rule 20.4)	30	orange
iii. Reply to Brief in Opposition (Rules 15.6 and 17.5); Brief Opposing a Motion to Dismiss or Affirm (Rule 18.8)	10	tan
iv. Supplemental Brief (Rules 15.8, 17, 18.10, and 25.5)	10	tan
v. Brief on the Merits by Petitioner or Appellant (Rule 24); Exceptions by Plaintiff to Report of Special Master (Rule 17)	50	light blue
vi. Brief on the Merits by Respondent or Appellee (Rule 24.2); Brief on the Merits for Respondent or Appellee Supporting Petitioner or Appellant (Rule 12.6); Exceptions by Party Other than Plaintiff to Report of Special Master (Rule 17)	50	light red
vii. Reply Brief on the Merits (Rule 24.4)	20	yellow
viii. Reply to Plaintiff's Exceptions to Report of Special Master (Rule 17)	50	orange
ix. Reply to Exceptions by Party Other Than Plaintiff to Report of Special Master (Rule 17)	50	yellow
x. Brief for an *Amicus Curiae* at the Petition Stage (Rule 37.2)	20	cream
xi. Brief for an *Amicus Curiae* in Support of the Plaintiff, Petitioner, or Appellant, or in Support of Neither Party, on the Merits, or in an Original Action at the Exceptions Stage (Rule 37.3)	30	light green
xii. Brief for an *Amicus Curiae* in Support of the Defendant, Respondent, or Appellee, on the Merits or in an Original Action at the Exceptions Stage (Rule 37.3)	30	dark green
xiii. Petition for Rehearing (Rule 44)	10	tan

FIGURE 4.1 Cont.

- *2. 8½- by 11-Inch Paper Format:*

  - (a) The text of every document, including any appendix thereto, expressly permitted by these Rules to be presented to the Court on 8½- by 11-inch paper shall appear double spaced, except for indented quotations, which shall be single spaced, on opaque, unglazed, white paper. The document shall be stapled or bound at the upper left hand corner. Copies, if required, shall be produced on the same type of paper and shall be legible. The original of any such document (except a motion to dismiss or affirm under Rule 18.6) shall be signed by the party proceeding pro se or by counsel of record who must be a member of the Bar of this Court or an attorney appointed under the Criminal Justice Act of 1964, see 18 U. S. C. §3006A(d)(6), or under any other applicable federal statute. Subparagraph 1(g) of this Rule does not apply to documents prepared under this paragraph.

  - (b) Page limits for documents presented on 8½- by 11-inch paper are: 40 pages for a petition for a writ of certiorari, jurisdictional statement, petition for an extraordinary writ, brief in opposition, or motion to dismiss or affirm; and 15 pages for a reply to a brief in opposition, brief opposing a motion to dismiss or affirm, supplemental brief, or petition for rehearing. The page exclusions specified in subparagraph 1(d) of this Rule apply.

Federal Rules of Appellate Procedure

First Circuit Local Rules

Rule 32. Form of Briefs, Appendices, and Other Papers

(a) Form of a Brief.

  (1) **Reproduction.**

   (A) A brief may be reproduced by any process that yields a clear black image on light paper. The paper must be opaque and unglazed. Only one side of the paper may be used.

   (B) Text must be reproduced with a clarity that equals or exceeds the output of a laser printer.

   (C) Photographs, illustrations, and tables may be reproduced by any method that results in a good copy of the original; a glossy finish is acceptable if the original is glossy.

  (2) **Cover.** Except for filings by unrepresented parties, the cover of the appellant's brief must be blue; the appellee's, red; an intervenor's or amicus curiae's, green; any reply brief, gray; and any supplemental brief, tan. The front cover of a brief must contain:

   (A) the number of the case centered at the top;

   (B) the name of the court;

   (C) the title of the case (see Rule 12(a));

   (D) the nature of the proceeding (e.g., Appeal, Petition for Review) and the name of the court, agency, or board below;

FIGURE 4.1   Cont.

(E)   the title of the brief, identifying the party or parties for whom the brief is filed; and

(F)   the name, office address, and telephone number of counsel representing the party for whom the brief is filed.

(3)   **Binding.** The brief must be bound in any manner that is secure, does not obscure the text, and permits the brief to lie reasonably flat when open.

(4)   **Paper Size, Line Spacing, and Margins.** The brief must be on 8 ½ by 11 inch paper. The text must be double-spaced, but quotations more than two lines long may be indented and single-spaced. Headings and footnotes may be single-spaced. Margins must be at least one inch on all four sides. Page numbers may be placed in the margins, but no text may appear there.

(5)   **Typeface.** Either a proportionally spaced or a monospaced face may be used.

(A)   A proportionally spaced face must include serifs, but sans-serif type may be used in headings
and captions. A proportionally spaced face must be 14-point or larger.

(B)   A monospaced face may not contain more than 10½ characters per inch.

(6)   **Type Styles.** A brief must be set in a plain, roman style, although italics or boldface may be used for emphasis. Case names must be italicized or underlined.

(7)   **Length.**

(A)   **Page limitation.** A principal brief may not exceed 30 pages, or a reply brief 15 pages, unless it complies with Rule 32(a)(7)(B) and (C).

(B)   **Type-volume limitation.**

(i)   A principal brief is acceptable if:
- it contains no more than 14,000 words; or
- it uses a monospaced face and contains no more than 1,300 lines of text.

(ii)   A reply brief is acceptable if it contains no more than half of the type volume specified in Rule 32(a)(7)(B)(i).

(iii)   Headings, footnotes, and quotations count toward the word and line limitations. The corporate disclosure statement, table of contents, table of citations, statement with respect to oral argument, any addendum containing statutes, rules or regulations, and any certificates of counsel do not count toward the limitation.

(C)   **Certificate of compliance.**

(i)   A brief submitted under Rules 28.1(e)(2) or 32(a)(7)(B) must include a certificate by the attorney, or an unrepresented party, that the brief complies with the type-volume limitation. The person preparing the certificate may rely on the word or line count of the word-processing system used to prepare the brief. The certificate must state either:
- the number of words in the brief; or
- the number of lines of monospaced type in the brief.

(ii)   Form 6 in the Appendix of Forms is a suggested form of a certificate of compliance. Use of Form 6 must be regarded as sufficient to meet the requirements of Rules 28.1(e)(3) and 32(a)(7)(C)(i).

FIGURE 4.1   Cont.

> **(b) Form of an Appendix.** An appendix must comply with Rule 32(a)(1), (2), (3), and (4), with the following exceptions:
>
> (1) The cover of a separately bound appendix must be white.
>
> (2) An appendix may include a legible photocopy of any document found in the record or of a printed judicial or agency decision.
>
> (3) When necessary to facilitate inclusion of odd-sized documents such as technical drawings, an appendix may be a size other than 8 ½ by 11 inches, and need not lie reasonably flat when opened.
>
> **(c) Form of Other Papers.**
>
> (1) **Motion.** The form of a motion is governed by Rule 27(d).
>
> (2) **Other Papers.** Any other paper, including a petition for panel rehearing and a petition for hearing or rehearing en banc, and any response to such a petition, must be reproduced in the manner prescribed by Rule 32(a), with the following exceptions:
>
> (A) A cover is not necessary if the caption and signature page of the paper together contain the information required by Rule 32(a)(2). If a cover is used, it must be white.
>
> (B) Rule 32(a)(7) does not apply.
>
> **(d) Signature.** Every brief, motion, or other paper filed with the court must be signed by the party filing the paper or, if the party is represented, by one of the party's attorneys.
>
> **(e) Local Variation.** Every court of appeals must accept documents that comply with the form requirements of this rule. By local rule or order in a particular case a court of appeals may accept documents that do not meet all of the form requirements of this rule.

An outline may use a sentence format or a shorthand topic format. When using a topic format, be sure you include enough information to enable you to remember why you included each topic. Unless you are comfortable or familiar with a particular subject area, the fuller sentence format is preferable. An accepted format for an outline is illustrated in Figure 4.2.

An Alternative to Outlining

An alternative to a written outline is to separate your raw research into categories. This can be accomplished by using file cards or by grouping photocopies of related cases and statutes (for cases and statutes that overlap issues, place a separate copy in each group, or remind yourself with a Post-it note). By ordering the cards or groups of photocopies in a logical sequence, you create in effect an unwritten outline—you have made decisions about organization and development. This method is somewhat unorthodox, but as you gain experience it may be a practical timesaver.

Remember, the purpose of an outline is to help you. If a formal outline does not work for you, don't use it. Find a method of organizing your document that works for you. Some individuals are more visual and may use graphs to organize their work. The point of outlining is to get organized and focused. No matter the form, traditional or not, take the time to think about your assignment and prepare a logical, organized plan before you begin to write.

PRACTICE TIP

Do not begin to write until you know what you want to say. Sit down and write; do not procrastinate. Above all, avoid distractions: no telephones, television, or people!

TYPES OF DOCUMENTS

There are many different types of legal documents, which we discuss in later chapters. Let's consider a few right now.

FIGURE 4.2   Example of an Outline

I.   [General Topic]

   a. [Issue]

      1. [Rule of law]

      2. [Application of law to the facts]

      3. [Conclusion]

   b.

      1.

      2.

      3.

II. Requirements of Financing Documents

   a. Disclosure of repossession procedure in event of nonpayment

      1. Purchaser must initial the relevant sections.

      2. Our client did not initial the documents.

      3. Conclusion: the contract is voidable at our client's discretion.

   b.

      1.

      2.

      3.

III. Conclusion

Letters

Correspondence is essential in virtually every legal matter. Letters to the client, to opposing counsel, to the court, to witnesses, to government agencies—the list is endless. Demand letters, opinion letters, retainer letters, settlement letters, update letters advising of case status or court date—some are objective, some adversarial, all important. Chapter 8 identifies different types of legal correspondences in greater detail. However, an example of a common letter to a client is illustrated in Figure 4.3.

Internal Memoranda

internal memoranda
An objective document that presents all aspects of the legal issues involved in the matter.

An interoffice memorandum explains the law so as to inform and educate the attorneys. As mentioned, this memo is an objective writing that relates both good news and bad about the law as it applies to the client's case, and it can be used as a basis for strategy, as basic research for a brief, or as background when drafting pleadings or other documents. Chapter 9 focuses on this type of legal document.

Transactional Documents

transactional documents
Documents that define property rights and performance obligations.

Many documents have, as a result of their language and content, legal effects beyond the mere transmission of information. Executed contracts, leases, wills, and deeds are examples of **transactional documents** that lawyers and paralegals draft. Such documents serve to define property rights and performance obligations, and slight alterations in meaning can have great impact on the parties involved. Without minimizing the importance of precision in every document drafted, it is safe to say that you should be doubly attentive to accuracy in transactional documents, especially if drafted to protect or support a client's legal position. Figure 4.4 is a simple employment contract. Notice the termination language in paragraph 6. Clearly the language is drafted in favor of the employer.

FIGURE 4.3 Example of a Letter to a Client

(Letterhead)

December 27, 2006

Clerk of the Court
552 Main St.
Anywhere, U.S.A 00555

Re: Smith v. ABC Corporation,
    Case No. 2006-7472

Dear Ms. Anderson:

I am enclosing an original and five copies of the answer in the above referenced matter. Please file stamp the copies and return them in the self-addressed stamped envelope provided with the filing.

By copy of this letter, I am notifying opposing counsel of the filing of this document.

I appreciate your assistance in this matter.

Sincerely,

Drew Emmanuel

cc: Eric Charles, Esq.

forms
Documents that set forth standardized language and are used as a drafting guide.

boilerplate
Standard language in a form.

pleadings
Documents filed with the court in a pending lawsuit that define the issues to be decided by the court at trial; the complaint, answer to complaint, and reply.

PRACTICE TIP

Form books can be dangerous. They are invaluable as a guide for the unfamiliar; however, they are wrought with tortuous language most practitioners refuse to eliminate. Always be aware of their positive values and their pitfalls.

A Few Words about Forms

Many types of legal documents, particularly operative documents, incorporate **forms.** Forms are documents that set forth standard language that is the accepted format for accomplishing a given purpose. Recourse to a form is a decision to be made by your supervising attorney, although he or she may delegate some discretion to you.

The language in forms may be cumbersome and confusing, with excessive use of legalese and archaic construction. Forms are valuable, however, based upon their widespread acceptance. This is the paradox of precision—that a document confusing on its face due to peculiar language is actually precise as a result of years, even centuries, of accepted meaning.

There are forms for deeds, for wills, and for leases: indeed, there are multivolume sets of forms covering an enormous range of legal transactions. Most forms provide standard language with blank spaces where specific information from your case can be inserted; others provide the standard language with examples of information from other transactions, which must then be modified to fit your specific situations. The standard language in these forms, often referred to as **boilerplate,** should not be changed unless you are instructed to do so by your supervising attorney. An example of a legal form is the promissory note found in Figure 4.5.

Pleadings

Pleadings are documents filed with the court in a pending lawsuit that define the issues to be decided by the court at trial. The claims, counterclaims, defenses, and special defenses of the parties constitute the pleadings. The document that initiates a lawsuit is the **complaint,** filed by the plaintiff. The defendant responds to the complaint with an **answer,** replying to the claims of the plaintiff. There can be other pleadings as well. Pleadings are adversarial documents, drafted to place your client's position in the best light, and they must be prepared in the format prescribed by the court's rules of procedure. Chapter 10 addresses the various types of pleadings.

Motions

A **motion** requests that the court take an action. It can be filed by either the plaintiff or the defendant in a lawsuit. A defendant might file a "motion to strike," asking the court to rule out

FIGURE 4.4 Simple Employment Contract

EMPLOYMENT AGREEMENT

This **EMPLOYMENT AGREEMENT** ("Agreement") is entered into as of this __ day of ____, 2006 by and between the **Law Firm** (the "Law Firm") and Maria Henderson (the "Employee").

WITNESSETH

NOW THEREFORE, the Law Firm and the Employee, intending to be legally bound, agree as follows:

1. Scope of Services

The Employee shall assume the responsibilities and carry out the functions that are specifically outlined in the Job Description for an Executive Assistant for the law firm, which is attached to and incorporated by this reference as a part of this Agreement.

2. Compensation

Salary: The Employee shall be treated as a regular employee and not as an independent contractor. Therefore, the Employee shall be paid on a bi-weekly basis at $19.23 an hour on an annual salary of $40,000. The Employee hereby consents and the Law Firm agrees to deduct applicable local and federal income related taxes specifically including FICA withholding.

3. Employment Standards

The Employee agrees to maintain the standards of conduct and performance consistent with an Executive Assistant in the Law Firm and consistent with its Personnel Policies and Procedures.

4. Fringe Benefits

In addition, the Law Firm agrees to provide to the Employee a package of fringe benefits. The fringe benefits package will include, but not necessarily limited to, medical insurance, workers' compensation, annual leave, sick leave, holidays and retirement benefits and any other benefits provided by the Law Firm's personnel policies.

5. Effective Date

This Agreement is effective for one (1) year as of December 15, 2006 and will continue until December 14, 2007. The parties may extend this contract for a period of six (6) months upon mutual agreement.

6. Termination

The Law Firm may terminate the Employee with or without cause. Further, the assignment of the Employee will be terminated immediately by the Law Firm if it is determined that Employee is incapable of performing the duties of the position, commits acts of professional negligence, is absent from the position without the Law Firm's permission during regular business hours, is insubordinate, engages in substance abuse, violates the Law Firm's express rules or regulations, engages in other unprofessional conduct or breach or neglect of duty, or is repeatedly absent or tardy without good reason and after receiving a written warning. The employee will be on probation for six (6) months in accordance with the Law Firm's policy.

7. Notice

Any notice required to be given by the terms of this Agreement shall be deemed to have been given when sent by certified mail, postage prepaid, express mail, or personally delivered, addressed to the parties involved. Prior to signing this Agreement, Employee will provide the Law Firm with a mailing address, which shall be updated annually or when Employee has a change of address.

FIGURE 4.4 Cont.

8. Governing Law

This Agreement shall be governed by the laws of the state of Texas and jurisdiction is exclusive in Dallas County. The parties agree that venue is proper in Dallas County, Texas.

9. Waivers and Amendments

No waiver, modification, or amendment of any term, condition, or provision of this Contract shall be valid unless made in writing, signed by the parties or their duly authorized representatives, and specifying with particularity the nature and extent of such waiver, modification, or amendment. Any such waiver, modification, or amendment in any instance or instances shall in no event be construed to be a general waiver, modification, or amendment to any of the terms, conditions, or provisions of this contract.

10. Entire Agreement

This constitutes the entire Agreement between the parties and all prior understandings are merged herein.

IN WITNESS WHEREOF, the undersigned have executed this Agreement.

_____   _____   _____   _____
Employee   Date   Law Firm   Date

complaint
Document that states the allegations and the legal basis of the plaintiff's claims.

answer
Document that is the defendant's response to the plaintiff's complaint.

motion
A procedural request or application presented by the attorney in court.

brief
A formal written argument presented to the court.

part of the plaintiff's claim on the grounds that it fails to state a claim supported by the applicable rules of law. Either party might file a "motion *in limine*," seeking a preliminary ruling on an issue of evidence. Or either party might file a "motion for summary judgment," arguing that there are no disputed questions of fact and that the matter can be decided based on an application of the law to the undisputed facts. This motion is common is a civil lawsuit. Indeed, the number of different motions is high, limited only by the imaginations of counsel. Motions are always adversarial documents, drafted to favor your client's position. Figure 4.6 (page 120) is an example of a Motion to Dismiss.

Briefs

A **brief** is a formal written argument presented to the court, usually countered by a brief written by the opposing party. Note the important difference between a case brief, which you studied in detail in Chapter 2 (an objective document) and the formal brief presented to a court, which is adversarial. A brief filed with the trial court is called a *trial brief;* if filed with an appellate court it is called an *appellate brief.* A close relative of the brief is the *memorandum of law to the court,* which performs exactly the same function as a brief, but is usually filed in support of a less significant motion. The difference between a formal brief and a memorandum of law to the court is more semantic than real. Both types of briefs are discussed in later chapters.

You Be the Judge

Hypothetical 4-2

Form books can be a great help in drafting and they can also be a downfall. Losing sight of a form book's limitations and usefulness can cause attorneys and paralegals the ire of a court. Take a look at *Clement v. Public Service Electric and Gas Co.,* 198 F.R.D. 634 (D. N.J. 2001), where the use of a form book cost an attorney sanctions and public embarrassment. As the judge in the case pointed out: "[a]ttorneys who merely copy form complaints and file them in this court without conducting independent legal research and examining the facts giving rise to a potential claim do so at their peril. Lawyers are not automatons. They are trained professionals who are expected to exercise independent judgment." *Id.* at 636. The moral of the story is: watch out for those form books. Copying the boilerplate without any thought or independent legal research can compromise your integrity and reputation. What sanctions did the court impose on the attorney? What are the facts that lead to the attorney's sanctions? Do you believe the judge's disposition was too harsh? Why or why not?

FIGURE 4.5   Sample of a Promissory Note Form

PROMISSORY NOTE

$ 50,000.00 in Dallas, Texas A.D. 200___.

For value received Andrew Mason promises to pay to Paul Johnson on order, the sum of $50,000.00 dollars, with interest from date at the rate of ten per cent per annum (10%), both principal and interest payable at the offices of Paul Johnson or a place so designated by the parties.

This note payable in 48 monthly installments of one thousand and forty two dollars ($1,042.00).

All past due principal and interest on this note shall bear interest at the maximum rate permissible under the law.

It is understood and agreed that the failure to pay this note, or any installment as above promised, or any interest hereon, when due, shall at the option of the holder of said note, mature the full amount of said note, and it shall at once become due and payable.

And it is hereby especially agreed that if this note is placed in the hands of an attorney for collection, or collected by suit, or in probate or bankruptcy proceedings, Mason agrees to pay a reasonable amount additional on the principal and interest then due thereon as attorneys' fees.

Address: _____

Phone: _____

_____

Signature of Maker

discovery
Process in which the opposing parties obtain information about the case from each other; the process of investigation and collection of evidence by litigants.

interrogatories
Discovery tool in the form of a series of written questions that are answered by the party in writing.

Discovery Documents

The procedural rules governing lawsuits have liberal provisions that allow for **discovery,** when the opposing parties obtain information in the hands of the other party. Requests for documents or for responses to written questions (called **interrogatories**) are important adversarial documents that enable litigants to learn as much as possible about their opponent's case before trial. Although response to discovery requests must be honestly provided (hence they are objective), in fact an adversarial element often creeps into these responses, which can lead to time-consuming disputes in court. More information on drafting discovery documents is found in Chapter 11.

POST-WRITING CONSIDERATIONS: REVISING, EDITING, AND PROOFREADING

PRACTICE TIP

To review a document effectively, print it from the computer. Looking at the hard copy adds a different perspective from the computer screen.

Good legal writing requires revising, editing, and proofreading. Do not think that one draft of a document is sufficient. Often, two and three drafts are still not enough. Legal writing demands precision and clarity, which does not happen in one try. Prepare yourself to draft, redraft, and revise that draft.

Revising the Document

Revising is rewriting. To revise a legal document does not mean changing a word or two. When revision is necessary, entire sections may be deleted or even moved to a different section of the document. Attack a revision with purpose—to make the document better. Ask yourself:

- Have I effectively communicated the purpose of the document?
- Is the document in the correct format?
- Who is my audience?
- Is the document understandable?

FIGURE 4.6 Motion to Dismiss

**IN THE DISTRICT COURT OF THE NEW JERSEY
DIVISION OF CAMDEN**

Harry Archer,	)	
	)	
Plaintiff,	)	
v.	)	Civil No. 06 CV 0000
	)	
Franklin Brandson,	)	
	)	
Defendant.	)	
_____	)	

MOTION TO DISMISS FOR LACK OF PERSONAL JURISDICTION

COMES NOW Defendant, Franklin Brandson, by and through his undersigned attorney, Samantha Daily, Esq., and, pursuant to Rule 12(b)(2) and (3) moves this Honorable Court for the entry of an Order Dismissing this matter With Prejudice, for lack of personal jurisdiction. In support of the Motion Defendant incorporates by reference his Memorandum of Law In Support of Motion to Dismiss filed simultaneously herewith.

WHEREFORE, Defendant Franklin Brandson, asks this Honorable Court for the entry of an Order dismissing this matter with prejudice; and, for attorney's fees, expenses, costs and other relief deemed just by this Court.

Law Offices of Samantha Daily LLC
Attorney for Defendant

DATED:

By:_____
Samantha Daily, Esquire

CERTIFICATE OF SERVICE

I HEREBY CERTIFY that on this _____ day of June, 2006, a true and correct copy of the foregoing **MOTION TO DISMISS FOR LACK OF PERSONAL JURISDICTION** was caused by me to be served HAND DELIVERY upon: Ethan Donaldsen, Esq., Donaldsen, Anderson and Barone, 500 Oak Avenue, Anytown, Pa. 00000.

_____

- Have I addressed all the issues?
- Are the rules of court followed?

These are some of the questions to consider when revising a document. Once a revision is complete, sometimes "fresh eyes" may add a new or different perspective. Ask a colleague to review the document.

Editing the Document

Editing is very different from revising a document. Editing focuses on the more technical aspects of writing, such as grammar, sentence structure, and punctuation. Also, while you edit, review for substantive accuracy of the assignment. During the editing process, you want to make sure the document is understandable. If preparing a brief, check that the headings are presented the same; for example, are they all underlined, in bold, or italics?

FIGURE 4.7
Common
Proofreading Marks

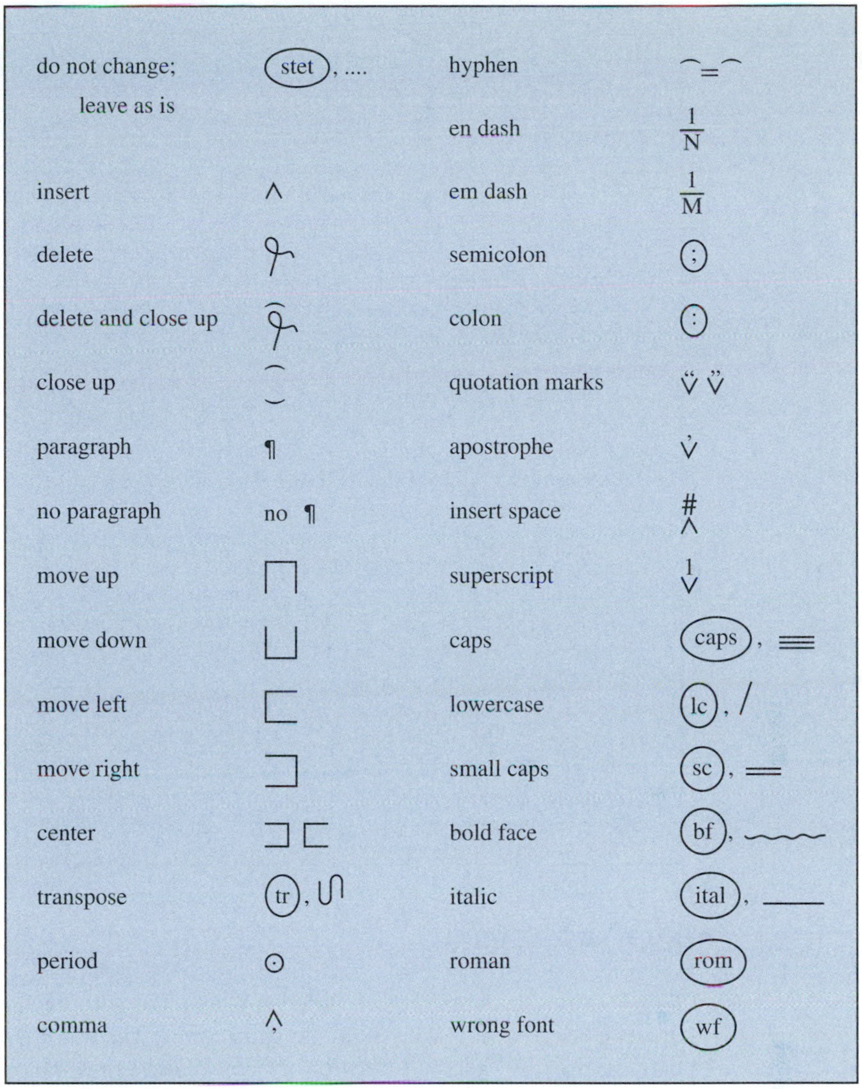

do not change; leave as is	(stet) , ...	hyphen	⌢=⌢
		en dash	$\frac{1}{N}$
insert	∧	em dash	$\frac{1}{M}$
delete	ℒ	semicolon	⊙
delete and close up	ℒ̂	colon	⊙
close up	⌒	quotation marks	�v̈ v̈
paragraph	¶	apostrophe	v̇
no paragraph	no ¶	insert space	#
move up	⊓	superscript	$\frac{1}{v}$
move down	⊔	caps	(caps) , ≡
move left	⊏	lowercase	(lc) , /
move right	⊐	small caps	(sc) , =
center	⊐⊏	bold face	(bf) , ～
transpose	(tr) , ∽	italic	(ital) , ____
period	⊙	roman	(rom)
comma	∧	wrong font	(wf)

PRACTICE TIP

Whether you or someone else is correcting the document, draw attention to the needed corrections by placing a "✓" at the end of each line requiring correction. This practice reinforces the need for a correction on that line and makes the error stand out. Using a red pen helps the correction stand out as well.

When editing, do just that—edit! Strike unnecessary language; correct citations; read for clarity. Certain marks are used for editing and proofreading. Figure 4.7 shows some of the more common marks.

Proofreading the Document

One of the most embarrassing moments for any attorney or paralegal is to find a typographical error in a finished and *submitted* document. Often that shows the level of care devoted to the document. And more importantly, typos look bad and reflect on an individual's attention to detail and professionalism. Documents replete with typos give the wrong impression to your attorney, a client, and a judge. Consequently, one of the most critical stages of writing is proofreading your work. Be sure all words are spelled correctly. Check for mistyping such as inadvertently repeating words or phrases that were not intended, extra spaces, and transposed words or letters. Have someone else proofread your work. New and fresh eyes offer a different perspective. Spending so much time preparing a document clouds our objectivity. After reading a document so many times, the tendency is to miss errors no matter how obvious.

Everyone has their own way to proofread, but one common thread to proofing a document is to read slowly. Do not proofread as though you are reading a novel or the newspaper. You cannot proofread effectively by skimming a document. Proofreading requires deliberate, slow review. Sometimes reading the document aloud is another method of proofreading. It forces you to focus on each word. Whatever your method, proofreading is essential to all legal writing. The quality of your document is a reflection on you and your office. Make a professional statement about your work. What you write and how you write it matters.

Ethics Alert

Writing counts. How you communicate counts. If you produce a substandard product, it is a reflection on you, your supervising attorney, and on your firm. Judges pay close attention to the written documents submitted to their courts. Although as a paralegal you may not be directly responsible for the legal documents submitted, the case law is growing on the subject of attorneys and "poor legal writing." Courts are now holding that poor legal writing is a direct reflection on one's competency. The rules of professional responsibility for lawyers, Canon 6 of the Model Code, require that a "lawyer should represent the client competently." Although competency is a standard that we are striving to achieve, it is often undefined. As U.S. Supreme Court Justice Potter Stewart in a case involving the pornography standard stated, "I know it when I see it." *Jacobellis v. Ohio,* 378 U.S. 184, 197 (1964). That has essentially become the standard for judging competency in legal writing. A recent judge in the United States District Court for the District of New Jersey sanctioned and admonished a repeat offender for filing sloppy, incomprehensible legal documents. In expressing his disgust with the attorney, Judge Orlofsky observed that "[a]ttorneys may not, consistent with their professional obligations, substitute the 'cut and paste' function of their word processor for the research, contemplation, and draftsmanship that are the necessary elements of responsible legal representation." He further said that an attorney cannot substitute "mouse clicks" for legal judgments. *Mendez v. Draham,* 182 F. Supp. 2d 430,431 (D.N.J. 2002). This attorney had been admonished three times in eighteen months, and one of his sanctions was to take a class on professional responsibility. As a paralegal you must decide the level of your competency and not be pushed into areas for which you are not competent. Too often attorneys rely, quite heavily, on their paralegals to do their work. Do not get caught in that trap. You should strive for the highest of standards, but you are not the attorney. You did not attend law school or take the bar exam. Paralegals are easy scapegoats. Be mindful that competent and quality representation is the attorney's ethical obligation—that includes competent legal writing as well.

PRACTICAL CONSIDERATIONS

Legal writing is an extremely varied subject area, with documents ranging from an informal client letter to a full-scale Supreme Court brief. There is room for both great eloquence and extreme brevity. There is a time for objectivity and a time for partisanship. There is a role for legalese and a role for plain English. Perhaps most important of all, there is a need for precision—a need to communicate ideas in a concise and unambiguous fashion.

A few practical considerations are universal. First, do all necessary background research. This includes the prewriting considerations outlined, as well as checking for technical requirements such as court rules on format.

Second, always make your purpose clear by the use of a straightforward introduction. Readers do not enjoy guessing. Assuming too much about the expectations or knowledge of your audience can result in a document that confuses rather than enlightens.

Third, fully explain your position. Satisfy yourself that your points progress logically. Guide the reader through the subject matter. Avoid arriving at conclusions before exhausting your analysis.

THE E-FACTOR: SPELL CHECK

Typographical and spelling errors are a thing of the past. With today's use of spell check in most word processing programs, these types of errors are inexcusable. Programs such as Microsoft Word and Corel WordPerfect highlight the misspelled words, and even offer the correct spelling. Prior to submitting any document for review by your attorney, complete a spell check. This habit is important to acquire. No attorney wants to read a document replete with misspelled words.

Be careful when using spell check programs. Spell check only checks for spelling errors; if a word is mistyped but is still a "proper" word, spell check will not identify the error. For example, if you typed the word "no" but meant "not," spell check will not catch this error. Therefore, spell check is not a substitute for proofreading. It is, however, a mechanism that adds to the final completeness and quality of your legal document.

Fourth, prepare a conclusion that concisely ties together the entire document. Again, be straightforward. As the introduction made your intent clear, so your conclusion should make the achievement of that purpose clear.

Finally, reread! Writing is nothing more than creating documents to be read. It is impossible to gauge how another person will read a document unless you yourself read it. By rereading you can see where your document succeeds and fails, then revise it into a precise, flowing finished product.

Summary

Because of the long-standing and wide acceptance of the meaning of the words of which they are composed, legalese and anachronistic usages persist in legal writing. Although some terms of art remain useful, good legal writing is generally characterized by short, succinct sentences, a minimum of legalese, avoidance of redundancy, emphasis on simple language in simple form, and a recognition of the importance of rereading what you've written.

Prewriting considerations include identifying the audience and recognition that the sophistication of the audience will affect the nature of the language used; identification of the purpose, which will generally be either objective or adversarial; and a commitment to properly defining and researching the issues presented. A good method of analyzing the issues is the IRAC method, in which you identify the *issue* involved, determine the relevant *rule of law, apply* the rule of law to the facts of your matter, and reach a *conclusion*. The final prewriting step is to take into account the time constraints associated with your writing project.

Legal documents are often organized with the help of an outline, which is the framework of the proposed content, advancing from the general to the specific. An alternative to outlining is to group your raw research into categories, either by using file cards or by physically gathering related materials.

There are many different types of legal documents, including letters, internal memoranda, operative documents, forms, pleadings, motions, briefs, and discovery documents.

Revising, editing, and proofreading documents is essential to the legal writing process. Revising often requires complete rewriting of portions of the assignment, whereas editing focuses on the mechanics of punctuation, and structure. Proofreading is a refining technique that checks for typographical and spelling errors.

Writing is an extremely varied subject area. Keep in mind the following considerations: Do all necessary background research; make your purpose clear with a straightforward introduction; fully explain your position; prepare a concise conclusion that ties your argument together; and finally, reread what you've written to ensure that you've accomplished your purpose.

Key Terms

clarity	outline
precise	internal memoranda
jargon	transactional documents
legalese	forms
plain English	boilerplate
terms of art	pleadings
audience	complaint
objective documents	answer
adversarial documents	motion
IRAC method	brief
issue	discovery
rule of law	interrogatories
conclusion	

Review Questions

1. What is legalese?
2. What is a term of art?
3. What are some of the basic techniques associated with good legal writing?
4. What is the audience of a legal document?

5. What is the difference between an objective purpose and an adversarial purpose?

6. What is the IRAC method?

7. How can a paralegal effectively balance time constraints?

8. How does a writer go about organizing a legal document?

9. Name several different types of legal documents.

10. What are the three constraints of legal writing?

Exercises

1. Review the promissory note in Figure 4.2
   a. Determine the purpose of the document and the audience.
   b. Edit out all the legalese and unnecessary words.

2. Obtain a copy of your state's appellate brief requirements and identify all the constraints and legal requirements for filing a brief with your state.

3. Proofread and correct the following paragraph:

   In view of the finding that that respondents conduct did no involve a corrupt motive or morale turpitude ande that his disabilityis remedible, we fund it desireable that and effort be made to remedyt he disability.

4. The following is a passage from a recent court decision. Rewrite the paragraph in plain English.

   Finally, Wife points to an oblique reference at the very end of the hearing on the expungement motion in which the court appears to have observed that Husband had the power to expunge the lis pendiens in his own hands, simply by posting a bond for what Wife thought was the amount below market for which the Balboa house was being sold. *Gale v. Superior Court,* 19 Cal.Rptr.3d 554,561 (Cal.App. 4 Dist. 2004).

5. Review *In Re Shepperson,* 674 A.2d 1273 (Vt. 1996), and respond to the following questions:
   a. Draft the issue in the case.
   b. What ethical issues are discussed in the case?
   c. What is the reasoning in the case?

6. The following is an excerpt from a legal document. Review the paragraph and redraft it.

   Records shall be uniformly destroyed on a manner determined by the Officer upon the expiration of the retention period. However, prior to the destruction of any records, the Officer shall institute a program of notification whereby the destruction schedule can be interrupted for cause by someone in a position of authority, including the Officer interrupt the destruction process.

7. The following is a provision in a state statute. Rewrite the section so that it is clear and in plain English.

   A food shall be deemed to be adulterated:
   (1) a. If it bears or contains any poisionous or deleterious substance which may render it injurious to health; but in case the substance is not an added substance the food shall not be considered adulterated under this paragraph if the quantity of such substance in such food does not ordinarily render it injurious to health. *Coffer v. Standard Brands, Inc.,*30 N.C.App. 134, 226 S.E.2d 534 (1976).

8. The following letter is submitted to you for review by another paralegal. Revise, edit, and proofread it.

   Dear Mr. Martin:

   Pleas take notice that on the date of July 15, the warranty of fitness given by you in our Agreemento f July 10 for the purchase and sale of then (10) DVD players was breeched by you and your Company-that with in fifteen (159)days of recieving goods, severn (7 customers have brought back them DVD players because they are fefective.

   Unless you remedy thes problems within 10 (10) DAYS of reciept of this Letter, I will tak the appropriate legal acton.

   Very truely yours,

Portfolio Assignment

Your attorney has a Summary Judgment hearing next week and needs you to research the standards for that motion. He needs the leading cases on the matter by Friday. Copy and brief the cases on the matter. Draft an outline for the brief your supervising attorney will prepare for the hearing. (Use the techniques learned in the previous chapters.)

Vocabulary Builder

Introduction to Legal Writing

```
X  E  K  Y  C  C  N  L  R  D  E  B  I  H  V  N  I  L  Z  P
Y  N  S  K  T  O  P  U  L  T  N  T  M  S  V  D  K  M  I  M
F  X  B  O  G  I  L  S  A  O  I  H  X  I  S  Q  V  I  H  A
Z  B  U  R  P  E  R  L  V  H  L  K  D  L  T  U  O  W  J  I
G  R  A  L  O  R  P  A  Y  I  T  Y  N  G  H  V  E  F  O  W
D  J  G  F  C  R  U  F  L  Z  U  C  H  N  D  W  N  C  C  J
H  C  L  F  E  R  K  P  V  C  O  E  S  E  L  A  G  E  L  E
V  A  L  L  S  N  T  X  E  R  C  O  S  N  Y  U  H  P  O  V
W  C  I  U  E  R  U  D  X  V  K  Y  X  I  G  R  K  R  B  R
E  O  X  U  T  C  E  L  X  Q  I  K  Q  A  A  N  C  E  N  N
B  T  E  R  M  S  O  F  A  R  T  T  U  L  J  R  H  C  Y  T
J  B  C  Y  D  X  N  N  C  M  S  S  C  P  X  A  J  I  J  L
O  W  T  R  T  U  O  U  C  X  Y  P  N  E  U  L  X  S  B  M
D  S  K  J  Z  E  E  O  U  L  S  C  E  C  J  U  L  I  R  P
F  O  R  M  S  H  Y  C  O  V  U  D  E  M  B  B  S  O  I  W
M  E  J  C  P  M  P  H  N  R  M  S  J  B  T  L  O  N  E  H
J  W  H  K  D  M  X  K  C  Z  N  J  I  V  E  Z  C  S  F  L
N  S  I  T  N  J  U  G  T  O  O  Y  R  O  G  R  O  F  L  R
Y  L  F  I  F  Z  P  K  U  D  X  P  C  T  N  L  V  Y  W  I
T  V  I  Q  U  E  O  C  D  U  S  T  Z  I  F  I  K  V  Y  U
```

BOILERPLATE	**BRIEF**	**CLARITY**
CONCLUSION	**FORMS**	**ISSUE**
JARGON	**LEGALESE**	**OBJECTIVE PURPOSE**

Chapter 5

The Mechanics of Construction

After completing this chapter, you will be able to:

- Set apart a parenthetical phrase.

- Employ commas to provide clarity.

- Identify two methods of combining the clauses of a compound sentence.

- Inject certainty into a series with semicolons.

- Format a block quotation.

- Avoid common spelling and grammar mistakes.

- Learn to distinguish between active and passive voice.

- Distinguish simple, complex, and compound sentences.

- Eliminate sentence fragments and run-ons.

- Draft a paragraph with a topic sentence, a body, and transitional language.

Recall your grammar school days when you thought you learned all you needed to know about the topic of spelling, grammar, and punctuation. Well, it's back! You cannot be an effective legal writer and communicator unless you know and understand the rules of grammar and punctuation. Hopefully, this chapter will be a review of the lessons of the past, but with a twist. The rules of grammar and punctuation in this chapter focus on the nuances used in legal writing, although the basics will be addressed as well. Mastering the basics will provide the foundation for your legal writing. Pay close attention to the practice tips provided and the examples. As painful as spelling, grammar, and punctuation are to learn, a poorly presented document reflects on your standards. So, impress your supervising attorney with your level of professionalism.

Case Fact Pattern

Hypothetical 5-1

You have attended a deposition with your supervising attorney, taking notes on the questions posed and testimony given. Your notes reflect the rapid-fire context—scribbled sentence fragments, abbreviations, and jottings to jog your memory.

Afterward your supervising attorney informs you that, since that transcript is not expected for three weeks, she would like a summary of the deposition. She asks that you translate your notes into a written memorandum.

As you sit at your desk with your notes, you begin to ponder the basic principles of writing—words as the bricks of which a sentence is built, rules as the mortar by which it is held together. Words and rules—language and grammar—provide the foundation from which good writing ascends.

B.C.   Johnny Hart

Source: By permission of John L. Hart FLP and Creators Syndicate, Inc.

PUNCTUATION

We affect the meaning of spoken language all the time—with the tone of our voice, by hesitating or speeding up, with facial expressions, hand movements, and the subtleties of body language. All these techniques are physical—and thus unavailable to writers. The writer must learn to re-create in the mind of the reader the impressions left by these embellishments. One way to accomplish this is by the artful use of punctuation. Let's consider some of its more significant aspects.

The Comma

comma
Punctuation used to re-create verbal pauses.

Commas re-create verbal pauses. They separate distinct concepts and eliminate confusion, enabling the writer to establish a rhythm and maintain clarity. Commas often travel in pairs. They surround and set off phrases, as with the parenthetical phrase in Example 5.1.

Example 5.1 Use of Commas

The plaintiff, who performed every act required of her by the terms of the contract, is seeking damages from the defendant.

parenthetical phrase
A phrase that supplements or adds information to a complete thought.

The phrase set apart between commas could have been placed within parentheses, hence the term **parenthetical phrase.** Parenthetical phrases are often placed between commas, although it is not mandatory, as Example 5.2 shows.

Example 5.2 Use of Commas in Parenthetical Phrase

Between commas:
The plaintiff, James Jones, is assisting in the investigation of his case.
Without commas:
The plaintiff James Jones is assisting in the investigation of his case.

Where the parenthetical is short, as with "James Jones," the choice of which to use is largely a matter of personal style. You seek a document that "flows" (more about flow in the next chapter) and must decide whether the commas advance fluidity or impede it. If the parenthetical is long, as in Example 5.1, it should be set off by commas. Remember that you may use two commas to set off a parenthetical, or none, but never use just one. Example 5.3 shows two incorrect uses of commas.

Example 5.3 Incorrect Use of Commas in Parenthetical Phrase

Incorrect:
The plaintiff, who performed every act required of her by the terms of the contract is seeking damages from the defendant.
   The plaintiff who performed every act required of her by the terms of the contract, is seeking damages from the defendant.

How can you tell if a phrase is a parenthetical? One way is by reading the sentence without the phrase. If the sentence remains logical and grammatically correct, the phrase is likely a parenthetical. Parenthetical phrases supplement, or add information to, a thought that is already complete. Try reading the sentence in Example 5.1 without the parenthetical phrase—it is less informative, but grammatical and logically complete.

If phrase is **restrictive** (specifying or restricting the element that it modifies), it is *not* parenthetical, and should not be set apart by commas, as Example 5.4 shows.

restrictive phrase
A phrase that specifies or restricts the application of something.

Example 5.4 Use of Commas in Restrictive Phrase

Correct:
Bankers who violate these statutes should go to jail.
Incorrect:
Bankers, who violate these statutes, should go to jail.

In the correct example, the phrase "who violate these statutes" specifies *which* bankers; it cannot be removed without changing the fundamental meaning of the sentence. The incorrect sentence creates the impression that *all* bankers violate the statutes (try reading it without the phrase).

We have noted that commas often travel in pairs. There are, of course, entirely proper sentences in which you will find only a single comma. A parenthetical, for example, may appear at the beginning of a sentence, as in Example 5.5.

Example 5.5 Parenthetical Phrase at Beginning of Sentence

Having performed every act required of him by the terms of the contract, the plaintiff is seeking damages from the defendant.

A single comma is also seen where a conjunction such as *but* or *and* joins two complete thoughts, as in Example 5.6.

Example 5.6 Use of Commas with Conjunction

The deposition transcript is lengthy, and its contents are fascinating.
or
Her eyesight is failing, but she heard the impact.

A common error in comma usage occurs when dealing with a series. There should be a comma after all but the last item in the series, as shown in Example 5.7.

Example 5.7 Use of Commas in Series

Correct:
The judge, jury, and prosecutor listened intently as defense counsel examined the witness.
Incorrect:
The judge, jury and prosecutor listened intently as defense counsel examined the witness.

This rule, however, does not necessarily apply to law firm names, something which, as a paralegal, you will be dealing with regularly, as in Example 5.8.

Example 5.8 Use of Commas in Law Firm Names

Correct:
Able, Baker & Charlie
Incorrect:
Able, Baker, & Charlie

PRACTICE TIP

Do not place a comma outside of a closing quotation mark. "A comma belongs inside the quotation mark," she said.

There are many other specific rules governing the use of commas, some of the more important of which are set forth in Table 5.1. Once you have determined the message you intend, the comma can be a powerful means of avoiding confusion. As a paralegal drafting documents, you should be using commas to maximize clarity first, fluidity second.

The Semicolon

semicolon
A form of punctuation used to indicate a break in thought, though of a different sort than that indicated by a comma.

The **semicolon** is a close cousin of the comma. It is used to indicate a break in thought, though of a different sort than that indicated by a comma. Rather than merely separating two thoughts, a semicolon also suggests a relationship between the two—making it a useful tool for an attorney or paralegal trying to make a point.

TABLE 5.1
Some Examples of
Comma Usage

Use Comma To:	Example:
Set apart transitional language	Indeed, the statute is applicable and controlling.
Set apart quotes	The defendant stated, "I'm innocent."
Indicate an omission	The defendant went to Florida; his brother, to New Jersey; and his wife, to Florida.
Clarify a date or number	1,000,000 January 1, 2006
Set apart "yes" and "no"	Is the statute controlling? No, it is not.

compound sentence
A sentence in which the clauses could stand separately, each ending with a period.

Semicolons are often used to join the components of a **compound sentence.** A compound sentence is one in which the clauses could stand separately, each ending with a period. In addition to using a semicolon or a period, a third method of expressing such a compound is with a comma and a conjunction, as we saw in Example 5.6. In Example 5.9 we express the first sentence from Example 5.6 in these three different ways.

Example 5.9 Punctuation of Compound Sentences

With semicolon:
The deposition transcript is lengthy; its contents are fascinating.
As two sentences:
The deposition transcript is lengthy. Its contents are fascinating.
With conjunction and comma:
The deposition transcript is lengthy, and its contents are fascinating.

In this instance the original choice, with comma and conjunction, is probably the best choice, because the writer probably intended to imply no relationship between the two clauses (*i.e.*, the length of the deposition is not what made it fascinating). Consider, however, the sentence in Example 5.10.

Example 5.10 Strategic Use of Semicolon

The defendant's blood alcohol level was twice the legal limit; his driving was erratic and led to the accident.

The use of the semicolon in this sentence implies the close relationship between the defendant's blood alcohol level and the erratic driving and subsequent accident. Although the two-sentence or comma-conjunction methods would convey the same information, the semicolon method conveys it with more force and is preferable.

A semicolon can also be useful in distinguishing separate elements in a series, particularly when commas are used in describing each individual element, as in Example 5.11.

Example 5.11 Use of Semicolon to Distinguish Separate Elements

Correct:
The witness identified defendant Jones, the butler; defendant Smith, the cook; and defendant Brown, the gardener.
Incorrect:
The witness identified defendant Jones, the butler, defendant Smith, the cook, and defendant Brown, the gardener.

The incorrect example would be correct if the witness had identified five separate people: (1) defendant Jones, (2) the butler, (3) defendant Smith, (4) the cook, and (5) defendant Brown (who was the gardener). However, if three witnesses were identified, the first sentence is clear and the second is confusing and misleading. Indeed, even if the second example were intended because there were five witnesses, it would still be preferable to separate all five by semicolons, so that confusion created by the lack of parallelism among the elements—some identified by name, some by occupation—would be eliminated.

The Colon

Colons have several purposes. They follow the salutation in a letter, are used in expressions of time (for example: 10:48 p.m.), and can lead into a specified list.

Example 5.12 Colons Preceding a List

The statutory protection has three prerequisites: adequate notice, sufficient documentation, and a completed application.

Colons can also perform a function similar to a semicolon or period: joining together related phrases, as in this sentence. In general, a colon signifies a closer relationship than does a semicolon or a comma. Explanatory clauses are often preceded by a colon (for example, in Example 5.20 a colon could substitute for the dash). Colons commonly introduce a block quote or a short quotation, such as in Example 5.13 in the next section.

Quotations

The use of quoted materials adds support to memoranda, briefs, letters, and any other legal writing in which the writer is trying to build an argument. Failing to follow the rules with regard to quotation marks, however, may distract the reader and detract from the force of your position.

When using a quote, should you include it in the body of the document or set it aside as a **block quote**? Although the context, and your ear for rhythm, will often dictate the better choice, a good rule of thumb is that any quote longer than 50 words (generally about three to five lines) should be set apart. This 50-word rule is incorporated into *A Uniform System of Citation* (*The Bluebook*) for briefs and other court documents.

If the block quote format is chosen, the quoted passage is indented and single-spaced. Quotation marks are omitted at the beginning and end, but interior quotation marks should be kept. The citation appears on the line immediately following, at the original left margin. An example is shown in Example 5.13.

Example 5.13 Block Quote

It has been said that the case of *Swift v. Tyson* is based upon a fallacy:
[t]he fallacy underlying the rule declared in *Swift v. Tyson* is made clear by Mr. Justice Holmes. The doctrine rests upon the assumption that there is "a transcendental body of law outside of any particular state but obligatory within it ...," [and] that federal courts have the power to use their judgment as to what the rules of common law are ...
Erie Railroad v. Tompkins, 304 U.S. 64, 58 S.Ct. 817, 82 L.Ed. 1188 (1938), quoting from Holmes's dissent in *Black and White Taxicab and Transfer Co. v. Brown and Yellow Taxicab and Transfer Co.*, 276 U.S. 518, 533, 48 S.Ct. 404, 72 L.Ed. 681 (1928).

Note the use of brackets and ellipses (which we discuss further), as well as the use of a period to conclude the citation. Also note that the quote within the quote uses standard double quotation marks, since the outside quotation marks are omitted. If outside quotation marks are included, as when a quoted passage appears in the body of the text rather than in a separate block, the interior quotation marks would be single.

Example 5.14 Interior Quotation

The witness stated, "I heard the defendant shout, 'I didn't mean to kill her!' "

In addition to the standard purpose of attributing words to a specific source, quotation marks can also be used to indicate irony or sarcasm, or to identify or set apart a word or passage.

Example 5.15 Use of Quotation Marks to Indicate Purpose

Irony:
Defendant argues that plaintiff benefited from defendant's partial performance of the obligations of the contract, but this "benefit" is hardly what was intended by the contract or anticipated by the plaintiff.

TABLE 5.2
Concluding
Punctuation

Quotation Mark	Placement of Quotation Mark
The period:	A quotation mark appears *after* a period.
The comma:	A quotation mark appears *after* a comma.
The question mark:	A quotation mark appears *after* a question mark.
The semicolon:	A quotation mark appears *before* a semicolon.
The colon:	A quotation mark appears *before* a colon.

<u>**Sarcasm:**</u>
The alleged "witness" was not even present at the scene of the accident.
<u>**To identify:**</u>
In this contract the word "deliver" means to place in the plaintiff's hands, not send to him in the mail.

Using quotation marks to identify a word or phrase is common and acceptable. Using them for an ironic or sarcastic purpose is generally inappropriate in documents filed with a court, and under any circumstances should be done only after careful reflection.

A common source of confusion with regard to quotation marks is whether concluding punctuation goes inside the final quotation mark, or outside. Table 5.2 lists the rules for different punctuation marks.

Parentheses, Brackets, and the Ellipsis

Clarity often demands grouping or special identification of text. This can be accomplished with punctuation: **parentheses** ( ) and brackets unite cohesive passages, **brackets** [ ] indicate changes or additions, and an **ellipsis** (…) indicates the elimination of text from an extended quote.

Parentheses are an alternative to the commas we used in Example 5.1, as shown in Example 5.16.

Example 5.16 Use of Parentheses

The plaintiff (who performed every act required of her by the terms of the contract) is seeking damages from the defendant.

The two examples, 5.1 and 5.16, are identical except that in 5.16 we've replaced the commas with parentheses. Since both are grammatically correct, how do you choose between parentheses and commas? In general, the closer the relationship between the parenthetical clause and the main sentence, the stronger the tendency is to favor the commas. If the relationship is slight, parentheses are the better choice. The relationship in Examples 5.1 and 5.16 probably justifies commas (it is the plaintiff's performance that entitles her to damages), whereas the sentence in Example 5.17 is better expressed with parentheses.

Example 5.17 Use of Parentheses

The plaintiff (who is eighty-five years old) is seeking damages from the defendant.

The choice is, in these instances, simply a matter of degree. When choosing a particular sentence construction, it is often wise to consider balance and variety in your document as a whole. The need for balance and variety or for parallel construction (discussed further in Chapter 6) will often dictate your choice where it would otherwise be a toss-up.

Some confusion may arise over using parentheses with other punctuation marks. As a general rule, you should leave in ending punctuation *within* the parentheses; with regard to the remainder of the sentence, punctuate it exactly as you would if the material contained within the parentheses were missing (this means the final punctuation mark should be outside the final parentheses, as you see at the end of this sentence).

In Example 5.13 we saw the word *and* in brackets. What do brackets signify? Generally speaking, brackets appearing in a quote identify some departure from the original text—in Example 5.13 the addition of "and" to the original text makes the quote grammatical without changing the meaning. Brackets are also often used to change capitalization in a quoted passage to conform to the sentence in which it appears, as in Example 5.18.

parentheses
A form of punctuation that unites cohesive passages.

brackets
A form of punctuation that indicates changes or additions.

ellipsis
A form of punctuation that indicates the elimination of text from an extended quote.

Example 5.18 Use of Brackets to Identify Departure from Text

The court noted that "[t]he fallacy underlying the rule in *Swift v. Tyson* is made clear by Mr. Justice Holmes."

Compare this to the block quote in Example 5.13, and note how the bracketed lower-case *t* here incorporates the quote into the flow of the sentence.

Brackets have other uses as well. They may be used as parentheses within parentheses, and are used to enclose the word *sic,* a Latin term used to signify an error of spelling or usage in a quoted passage. For example, in *Kentucky Bar Association v. Brown*, 14 S.W.3d 916, 917 (Ky. 2000), the judge used [sic] because the attorney, Brown, misspelled the word "mandamus."

> *Brown "does admit that the Court of Appeals would have been better served if he had styled his brief as a 'Writ of Mandamous [sic].'"*

In addition, brackets can be used to insert editorial comments or explanations into quoted materials, as in Example 5.19.

Example 5.19 Use of Brackets to Insert Editorial Comment

The language of the will states, "Any member of the Jones family [there are four surviving members] alive at the time of my death shall be entitled to $1,000 from my estate."

Another mark used to specially identify text is the ellipsis. Unlike brackets and parentheses, however, an ellipsis indicates the *omission* of text. It is formed by three dots (periods), as we saw in Example 5.13. Punctuation that precedes or follows the omitted text may be included or excluded, depending on the needs of the sentence (the comma, for example, was retained after the ellipsis in Example 5.13). A few simple rules govern the use of the ellipsis. First, there should be a space before the first dot, between each dot, and after the last dot. Second, when the words omitted follow a complete sentence, the sentence should end with the actual period, followed by the three spaced ellipsis points. Finally, when omitting a paragraph or more, the use of a line of dots is sometimes suggested (each spaced several spaces apart), although the three-dot device at the end of the last passage before the omission is also acceptable.

The ellipsis can be a valuable writing tool. Quotes are not always perfectly attuned to the context of your document. By judicious use of the ellipsis, you can eliminate extraneous passages and take your reader right to the heart of the matter. The judge in *re Marriage of Jackson,* 136 Cal. App. 4th 980, 39 Cal. Rptr. 3d 365 (Cal. App. 2d Dist. 2006) used the ellipse to focus on a portion of a statute cited in his opinion.

> *[I]t seems well settled . . . that when a statute authorizes prescribed procedure, and the court acts contrary to the authority conferred, it has exceeded its jurisdiction . . . .*

(Note: Use brackets when the omission of the quote is at the beginning.)

Hyphens and Dashes

Hyphens are used to draw together two or more words to form a single idea—"up-to-date" is an example. As language evolves, accepted usage for such combinations often changes, and there is not always a consensus on proper form (for example: closeup/close-up; byproduct/by-product). In addition, although there are some standard rules (for example: hyphenate fractions such as one-half), they often have exceptions (don't hyphenate fractions when used as nouns, as in, "She wrote one half of the brief"). Perhaps it is best to forget the general rules about hyphens and, when in doubt, look it up in a dictionary. Hyphens are also used to divide words at the end of a line. The division must come between syllables, and it is wise to use a dictionary if the division is not obvious.

Dashes are longer than hyphens and are used for limited purposes. They can substitute for parentheses or parenthetical commas—as in this sentence—and can also be used to separate the segments of a two-part sentence, as in Example 5.20.

Example 5.20 Use of Dashes to Separate Two-Part Sentence

His testimony was useless—biased, inconsistent, and obviously false.

Dashes are often used to indicate the word *to* when used with page numbers, dates, or other numerical references ("Earl Warren was Chief Justice from 1953–1969").

PRACTICE TIP

Add a period to an ellipse if the quote ends a sentence. (. . . .)

PRACTICE TIP

Periods are regularly used in abbreviations such as Ltd., Inc., or LLC. (Note that an additional period does not follow an abbreviation at the end of a sentence.)

hyphen
A form of punctuation used to draw together two or more words to form a single idea.

dash
A punctuation mark longer than a hyphen, which is used for limited purposes, such as separating the segments of a two-part sentence.

The Period

The most common form of punctuation is the period. A period, of course, is used at the end of a sentence. A period is also used at the end of a list. For instance:

The constraints in writing are
1. time;
2. length of document; and
3. format.

Question Marks and Exclamation Points

Question marks are used in the ordinary manner in legal writing, with one caveat (warning): since the purpose of advocacy is to persuade, there is little place for rhetorical questions, hence little use for question marks in briefs or other documents filed with a court, other than formally stating the questions to be addressed.

   Likewise, the **exclamation point** carries with it an air of informality that has little, if any, place in formal legal writing. Even if you find a certain fact extraordinary, it is better simply to state the fact than to emphasize it with an exclamation point.

The Apostrophe

Apostrophes arise primarily in two situations—contractions and possessives. As a general rule, contractions should be avoided in legal writing. "Cannot" is better than "can't"; "would not" than "wouldn't"; "it is" than "it's." (Incidentally, it is unforgivable to confuse "it's" with "its"—the former is always a contraction of "it is," the latter always a possessive, as in "Its deadline is next week.")

   Possessives are, of course, unavoidable. The general rule is to form a possessive for a singular noun by adding an apostrophe and an *s*. For a plural noun, you can usually simply add an apostrophe. The rule is the same for proper names. Although there are exceptions (*e.g.*, men's, children's), in general you should follow this rule even when the result might seem odd.

Example 5.21 Use of Apostrophe in Possessives

Justice Stevens' opinion was lengthy.

Sentence Construction

A sentence uses words, punctuation, and rules of grammar to convey an idea. It is in the sentence that your writing begins to take form. Sentences should carry the reader through your document with a minimum of confusion. Let's turn now to the basics of sentence construction, and then focus on a few things to watch out for.

The Simple Sentence: Subject/Verb/Object

Every sentence has a subject and a verb (also called a *predicate*). On occasion the subject is physically absent but implicit from the context; such usages, although acceptable in literature, have no place in legal writing. The simplest sentence structure is subject/verb.

Example 5.22 Subject/Verb Sentence Structure

The plaintiff won.

The subject in the sentence in Example 5.22 is *The plaintiff* and the verb is *won*. Most sentences also contain an object that identifies the "receiver" of the subject's action.

Example 5.23 Simple Sentence

The plaintiff won the trial.

The object in this sentence—which tells what the plaintiff won—is *the trial*. This sentence format—subject/verb/object—is the most effective means of conveying ideas, and is known as the **simple sentence.** The further your writing departs from this level of simplicity, the weaker it may become.

exclamation point
A form of punctuation used to highlight something extraordinary.

apostrophe
A form of punctuation used to create a contraction or a possessive noun.

simple sentence
A sentence that has a simple format—subject/verb/object.

modifiers
Adjectives and adverbs.

Modifiers: Adjectives and Adverbs

The simple sentence may leave the reader asking questions. What kind of trial was it? How did the plaintiff win? To answer these questions, a writer can use **modifiers**—adjectives and adverbs—to add information. Adjectives modify nouns; adverbs modify other adverbs; and adverbs modify verbs, as in Example 5.24.

Example 5.24 Use of Modifiers

The plaintiff easily won the lengthy trial.

In Example 5.24, "easily" is an adverb describing how the trial was won, and "lengthy" is an adjective describing the trial itself.

Beginning writers often make the mistake of equating lengthy descriptions with good writing. They may think that the more adverbs and adjectives they use, the better their writing will be. This is a false assumption. It is possible to create clear images in the mind of the reader and evoke powerful responses using nothing more than subjects and verbs. Indeed, more often than not, modifiers confuse rather than clarify. The sentence in Example 5.24 may lead the reader to wonder—"lengthy" compared to what? "Easily" as opposed to what? Although it is unfair to evaluate a sentence out of context (perhaps "length" and "ease" are essential to the writer's point), in general you should minimize the use of modifiers.

The Complex Sentence: Clauses

complex sentence
A sentence that contains a subordinate clause or clauses in addition to the main clause.

Although the simple subject/verb/object format is generally best, there are often circumstances that justify a departure. The addition of a subordinate clause or clauses creates a **complex sentence,** as in Example 5.25.

Example 5.25 Complex Sentence

The plaintiff, who had spent a fortune in legal fees, won the trial.

subordinate clause
A clause that cannot stand on its own as a complete sentence.

independent clause
A clause that can stand on its own as a complete sentence.

In this sentence the phrase "who had spent a fortune in legal fees" is a **subordinate** (dependent) **clause** describing the subject of the sentence, and the rest of the sentence forms an **independent clause** that could stand on its own (*i.e.*, without the subordinate clause) as a complete sentence.

Variety in sentence structure tends to create a more readable document, and the use of clauses to combine ideas contained in a succession of simple sentences can improve your writing. Avoid the appearance of a choppy sentence by varying the sentence length. Your goal is to make your point in the simplest manner possible without becoming boring. Complex sentences give readers variety and interest.

The Compound Sentence

Compound sentences have two or more clauses, each of which is independent and could stand alone as a complete sentence. The clauses of a compound sentence are joined by either semi-colons or conjunctions and commas to form a new sentence containing closely related ideas.

Example 5.26 Compound Sentences

Comma and conjunction:
The plaintiff won the trial, and her triumph was the result of hard work by her attorney.

Semicolon:
The plaintiff won the trial; her triumph was the result of hard work by her attorney.

In a compound sentence, the semicolon is not generally followed by a coordinate conjunction such as *and* or *but,* but can be followed by certain subordinate conjunctions such as *however* or *although.* A comma, on the other hand, can never be used to separate independent clauses without a conjunction.

Example 5.27 Separating Independent Clauses

Correct:
The defendant lost the trial; however, since he was thorough in his preparation and argued with eloquence, he should have no regrets.

The defendant lost the trial, but since he was thorough in his preparation and argued with eloquence, he should have no regrets.

Incorrect:
The defendant lost the trial; but since he was thorough in his preparation and argued with eloquence, he should have no regrets.

The defendant lost the trial, since he was thorough in his preparation and argued with eloquence, he should have no regrets.

Compound sentences, together with simple and complex sentences, lend welcome variety to your writing.

The Run-on Sentence and the Sentence Fragment

Run-on sentences have too many clauses for one grammatical sentence, because the independent clauses are not joined by a coordinating conjunction. **Sentence fragments** have too few clauses. This is not the same as saying that run-ons are too long and fragments too short. A sentence can be too long or short stylistically, but grammatically correct. Run-ons and fragments are grammatically incorrect.

Example 5.28 Run-ons and Fragments

Run-on Sentence (incorrect):
The plaintiff won the trial was long.

Correct:
The plaintiff won. The trial was long.
The plaintiff won and the trial was long.

Sentence Fragment (incorrect):
Testifying in great detail about the contract.

Correct:
The defendant is testifying in great detail about the contract.
The defendant was on the stand for two hours, testifying in great detail about the contract.

The run-on was eliminated by separating it into two sentences, or, alternatively, one grammatical sentence restructured to include two ideas. The fragment was corrected by identifying the subject who performed the action of "testifying." The second correct version is slightly more informative than the first. When choosing among alternative corrections, make sure the result is either a simple, complex, or compound sentence that expresses what the original, incorrect version intended.

Run-ons and fragments are indefensible in legal writing, where clarity is critically important. There is no excuse for allowing errors of sentence construction to muddle your point and confuse the reader.

Active Voice versus Passive Voice

In sentences, the subject and verb relate. One aspect of that relationship is known as "voice." One important element of voice is the active/passive voice. In **active voice,** the subject of the sentence performs the action; in **passive voice,** the subject of the sentence is the object of the action.

Example 5.29 Active versus Passive

Active:
The defendant violated the law.

Passive:
The law was violated by the defendant.

In the first example, the subject ("defendant") performed the action ("violated"), and the grammatical object ("the law") is also the object of the action. In the second example, "the law" remains the object of the action that the sentence describes, but grammatically it has taken the role of the subject.

---

run-on sentence
A sentence that contains two independent clauses that are not joined by a conjunction.

sentence fragment
A group of words that lacks necessary grammatical information, such as a verb, that would make it a complete sentence.

PRACTICE TIP

Watch your sentence length. The longer the sentence, the more likely the sentence is difficult to understand or grammatically incorrect. If a sentence runs more than three typed lines, it may be too long, a run-on, a fragment, or simply confusing. Try to create two sentences or eliminate unnecessary words.

active voice
A verb form in which the subject of the sentence performs the action.

passive voice
A verb form in which the subject of the sentence is the object of the action.

Active voice is generally preferable to passive voice. Novice legal writers sometimes adopt passive voice, since it sounds formal, but this usually weakens the power of their words. It is generally better to describe the action than the result. Dull writing can often be enlivened by rewriting passive passages in the active voice.

Passive construction should not be entirely abandoned, however. If the point of the sentence focuses on the object, passive construction may be preferred. In Example 5.30, the active example would be preferable if the writer were discussing the habits of pedestrians, whereas the passive example would be preferable if the writer were discussing the difficulty of enforcing certain laws.

Example 5.30 Active/Passive Preference

Active voice:
Pedestrians have repeatedly violated the jaywalking law, with no enforcement action taken.

Passive voice:
The jaywalking law has been repeatedly violated by pedestrians, with no enforcement action taken.

PARAGRAPHING

topic sentence
The first sentence of the paragraph, which introduces an idea.

body
The portion of a paragraph that contains the material that you claim supports the contention raised in the topic sentence.

transitional function
Moving the reader though the material they are reading in an orderly progression.

A paragraph is more than just a group of sentences—it is a group of related sentences. A paragraph uses sentences to convey an idea, which is introduced in the **topic sentence,** usually the first sentence of the paragraph. Having introduced the idea, the paragraph develops it in the **body.** Then, having developed the idea, the paragraph performs a **transitional function** that facilitates orderly progression through the entire document. Let's look at each of these individual areas—topic sentence, body, and transition.

The Topic Sentence

The topic sentence of a paragraph is necessary because, quite simply, a paragraph must have a topic. Each sentence in a paragraph must be tied to that topic and must advance it in some way. Sentences must avoid digressions, and even "essential" digressions should be tied somehow to the purpose of the paragraph. Otherwise, the digression belongs in a paragraph of its own.

That being said, let us consider the topic sentence. It generally appears at the beginning of a paragraph and, particularly in legal writing, typically states a proposition, which is then supported in the remainder of the paragraph.

Example 5.31 Topic Sentence at Beginning of Paragraph

<u>The defendant's conduct with regard to the accident constituted negligence and possibly recklessness.</u> She was driving at a speed far beyond the speed limit. She was wearing neither glasses nor contact lenses, though her driver's license requires that she do so. She was weaving from lane to lane as a result of intoxication. Each of these offenses was a violation of her duty to drive with care, and therefore constitutes negligence. Taken together, they represent a blatant disregard for the rights of others that rises to the level of recklessness. In short, she was a threat to any driver unfortunate enough—as was plaintiff—to be on the same road.

The topic sentence in Example 5.31 is underlined, and summarizes the argument to come. The sentences that follow support the point established by the topic sentence, culminating in the final two sentences, which repeat the point dramatically.

Topic sentences do not always appear as the first sentence in a paragraph. Sometimes they don't even appear at all—they may be implicit. But the writer who omits the topic sentence is asking a favor of the reader—to store the information provided, sentence by sentence, until the purpose is revealed and the information can be logically fitted into the overall argument. This requires patience on the part of the reader, which constitutes a risk on the part of the writer—a risk that the reader will lose interest before the purpose has been made plain. It may be a risk worth taking—the drama or tension created may add to the overall impact—but it remains a risk nonetheless. In Example 5.32 we see a paragraph with topic sentence at the end.

Example 5.32 Topic Sentence at End of Paragraph

The defendant was driving at a speed far beyond the speed limit. He was wearing neither glasses nor contact lenses, though his driver's license requires that he do so. He was weaving from lane to lane as a result of intoxication. <u>In short, his conduct at the time of the accident constituted negligence and possibly recklessness: he was a threat to any driver unfortunate enough, as was plaintiff, to be on the same road.</u>

The patience required of the reader, and the problems this might pose, should be immediately apparent. In general, then, place your topic sentences at the beginning of each paragraph—and when you depart from this structure, do so with care.

The Body

The body of the paragraph contains the material that you claim supports the contention raised in the topic sentence. In Example 5.31, for example, the sentences describing the defendant's excessive speed, failure to wear corrective lenses, and lane-weaving as a result of intoxication all support the assertion of the topic sentence that defendant was negligent and possibly reckless.

Paragraph development in legal writing often uses basic principles of argumentation. Having stated a proposition in the topic sentence, the writer endeavors to defend or support it in the succeeding sentences using one of several techniques. The proposition can be compared to similar situations; it can be contrasted with, or distinguished from, different situations; it can be explained or illustrated by a straightforward definition or example; it can be demonstrated logically, reasoning from basic principles; or it can be arrived at by some combination of these techniques, or related variants. Whatever technique you use, remember to tie your argument to the topic sentence. In Example 5.31, we show a topic sentence with various alternative follow-ups.

That there is relationship and overlap between and among these techniques is evident. The last two alternatives (explaining and reasoning), for example, are obviously closely related.

You should note that it is possible to use more than one technique in the same paragraph. For example, it is easy to imagine a paragraph that both compares analogous cases and distinguishes dissimilar cases, combining the methods of the first two alternatives.

Example 5.33 Topic Sentence with Follow-Up

<u>Topic sentence:</u>
The defendant is not legally responsible for the injuries suffered by the plaintiff, who fell in defendant's store.

<u>Compare and analogize:</u>
Like the storekeeper in the case of *Jones v. Smith* (who was found to have used due care), she had placed large warning signs in prominent positions.

<u>Contrast and distinguish:</u>
Unlike the negligent storekeeper in *Brown v. Blue*, who allowed his employees to leave a freshly washed floor unattended and unidentified, the defendant stationed a clerk by the wet floor to warn customers, and provided a large sign that read "Caution: Wet Floor!"

You Be the Judge Hypothetical 5-2

Grammar plays an important role in writing. There is no argument about that point. Imagine a pleading that is so grammatically offensive that the court orders the attorney to review grammar in a well-known writing textbook. As far-fetched as that may seem, that is exactly what the judge ordered in *Politico v. Promus Hotels, Inc.*, 184 F.R.D. 184 (E.D.N.Y. 1999). Clarity is an important component in writing, which the court recognized. As the court observed, when pleadings are unclear and verbose, it "places an unjustified burden on the court and the party who must respond to it because they are forced to select the relevant material from a mass of verbiage." *Id.* at 233. Was the judge's order appropriate? What is the standard for drafting a pleading? Identify the court's reasoning in reaching its decision.

Explain or illustrate:
Legal responsibility requires a showing of negligence, and negligence requires the existence of a duty owed to the injured party. Because plaintiff was a burglar trespassing on the premises after hours, no duty was owed.

Reason or demonstrate through logic:
Only the owner of the premises can be held liable under the facts as proven by plaintiff. Defendant herself was not the owner of the premises in question; the building was owned by a corporation. Therefore defendant cannot be held responsible for the injuries suffered by the plaintiff.

The Closing Sentence

closing sentence
A sentence at the end of a paragraph that summarizes the topic.

Along with the topic sentence and body, a paragraph should conclude with a **closing sentence.** This sentence summarizes the topic discussed in the body. Often that sentence is your transition into your next paragraph. Example 5.34 provides an example of a closing sentence.

Example 5.34 A Closing Sentence

Mr. Goodwynn underwent surgery approximately three months after the automobile collision. The surgery left Mr. Goodwynn with over 300 stitches in and around his eye and forehead area that were removed over a six-month period. He was also left with a significant vision impairment. The nature of his injuries has adversely affected his earning capacity as his profession prior to his injuries was a data entry specialist. Due to the requirements of this type of work, he will never be able to engage in that profession again. Consequently, because of the nature of his injuries, a significant portion of Mr. Goodwynn's damages are economic in nature.

A cautionary note about the closing sentence is in order. All paragraphs do not require a closing sentence. Sometimes a group of paragraphs build to a conclusion, or the closing sentence may be implied. When you review and edit your work, you must decide whether you have communicated your point effectively.

TRANSITIONAL LANGUAGE

Transitional language provides signals to readers about the material they are reading. It reassures readers that there is a relationship between the writer's various points, and it serves to clarify that relationship. It is important, particularly in legal writing, that the reader follow, step-by-step, the progression of the argument. You can accomplish this by, quite simply, telling the reader what the argument is, as we discuss further in Chapter 6. It is this "telling" function that transitional language performs.

Example 5.35 Transitional Language

Next, we will consider the cases that are distinguishable.
Since the cases all support the plaintiff's position, the conclusion is inevitable.
For example, the plaintiff in *Jones v. Smith* was held liable on facts similar to those in the instant matter.

The transitional language used—*next, since,* and *for example*—ties each sentence to other sentences in the writing, signaling the reader that there is a connection. See Table 5.3 for other examples of transitional language.

The transitional function can also be performed by using parallel construction or repetition, as in Example 5.36.

TABLE 5.3
Transitional Words and Phrases

Passing of Time	Contrast or Opinion	Introduction	Summary/ Conclusion	Addition
meanwhile	however	initially	therefore	furthermore
still	notwithstanding	to begin	accordingly	moreover
since	on the contrary	in order that (to)	hence	similarly
ultimately	in contrast	primarily	consequently	additionally
presently	although	first	in conclusion	in addition to
nevertheless		finally		

Example 5.36 Parallel Construction or Repetition

The corporate statutes do not apply because *the business is not a corporation;* the partnership statutes do not apply because it is not a partnership; and the public utility statutes do not apply because it is not a public utility.

   The business is not a corporation because stock has never been sold nor corporate filings completed.

In the first paragraph, the parallel construction using the phrase *do not apply* ties the paragraph together; in the second paragraph, the phrase *The business is not a corporation* repeats a phrase taken from the first paragraph, providing the reader with an implicit indication that the sentences to come will explain the proposition first stated in the first paragraph. Repetition and parallel construction are in many instances (as here) virtually identical concepts. We consider them further in the next chapter.

BASIC GRAMMAR AND SPELLING REMINDERS: THE TROUBLE SPOTS

Let's face it; most of us cringe when the subject of grammar or spelling comes up. We remember with distain our school days when we sat through those painful lectures on "*i* before *e* except after *c*." Or, when we had to diagram a sentence—nightmares. We hoped that the subject would never rear its ugly head again. But, whether we like it or not, how we write and how we present our work product does matter. So, this section will be a "quick and dirty" review on grammar and spelling.

Common Spelling Mistakes

Plurals

The general rule in forming the plural of a word is to add an "s." When a word ends in "y," normally you change the "y" to "i" and add "es." Examples are "carry" to "carries"; "modify" to "modifies"; and "robbery" to "robberies."

   Watch out for words ending in an "f" or "fe," such as life, strife, or shelf. Change the "f" or "fe" to a "v" or "ve." Therefore, the plurals are lives, strives, and shelves. But not all follow that rule: the plural of belief is beliefs. When in doubt check a dictionary.

   Many legal words present difficulties in transitioning from singular to plural. Who can remember if "memorandum" is singular or plural? These confounding problems often derive from Latin or Greek. The best advice is to learn the correct form by memorization or a dictionary. Some common words you will use are provided in Table 5.4, but these are only some examples of the singular to plural form you will encounter.

Do You Speak English?

A common divide between the British and Americans is not only the way we say things, but how we spell words as well. How do you spell "judgment" or "judgement"? It depends on where you

TABLE 5.4
Irregular Plural Forms of Commonly Used Terms

Singular	Plural	Incorrect No matter what you think!
memorandum	memoranda	memorandums
appendix	appendices	appendixes
index	indices	indexes
syllabus	syllabi	syllabuses
referendum	referenda	referendums

TABLE 5.5
Variations in Spelling

Common Spelling	Variation
canceled	cancelled
criticize	criticise
acknowledgment	acknowledgement
paid	payed
traveled	travelled
color	colour

You Be the Judge

Hypothetical 5-3

In *Henderson v. State*, 445 So.2d 1364 (Miss. 1984), the grammar in an indictment was pivotal to its legal sufficiency. Note that the judge in the case referred to the indictment as "grammatically atrocious." *Id.* at 1368. And, the judge in the case began the opinion with the words "[t]he case presents the question whether the rules of English grammar are part of the positive law of this state." *Id.* at 1365. The court castigated the prosecuting attorneys by citing William Shakespeare's *Macbeth*:

"It cannot be gainsaid that all the perfumes of Arabia would not eviscerate the grammatical stench emanating from this indictment." *Id.* at 1367, note 1. That sentence catches your attention! Brief the facts and reasoning of the case. What was the court's holding and disposition in the case? Was the result in the case fair? Did the court find in favor of the plaintiff or defendant? Were the grammar errors in the indictment important to the holding? What is the basis of your response?

live. Pay close attention to some words that may "appear" correctly spelled but have an acceptable variation. Table 5.5 provides an example of variations in spelling.

Names

Spelling a client or judge's name correctly seems like a basic courtesy. Nothing is more offensive or annoying to a client than to spell their name incorrectly. Take the extra time to verify the correct spelling of your client, a business, or a judge in a case. There is no louder cry of sloppiness or unprofessionalism when something as simple as the spelling of someone's name is incorrect.

Capitalize Proper Names and Adjectives

There are some basic rules about when to capitalize a title. Capitalize a title when referring to a specific person or thing, for example, President Bill Clinton, Speaker of the House Dennis Hastert or Governor Edward Rendell. If referring to the subject generally, do not capitalize the word. For example:

1. The presidents of five major corporations participated in the symposium on global warming.
2. Most federal agencies, such as Federal Trade Commission and Securities and Exchange Commission, perform their regulatory functions through enforcement.
3. Congress passed a number of acts, which included the Fair Labor Standards Act.

Notice that in examples 2 and 3, the words "federal" and "acts" are used generally and are not capitalized.

The bigger question in legal writing is whether to capitalize words such as plaintiff, defendant, court, appellant, and appellee. Rather than offer a definitive rule on the subject, the suggestion is to be consistent. If you capitalize the word "Plaintiff" in a legal document, continue capitalizing the word throughout the document. Check with your supervising attorney for their preference.

Grammar Hot Spots

Too often grammar plays a secondary role to getting the work done. Either we are rushed to complete an assignment or, even worse, we simply do not know the proper rules to follow. The end result, regardless of the reason, is poor execution of the basic rules of grammar. This text is not designed to rehash what you should already have learned; rather, this text will highlight common trouble spots encountered while preparing a legal document.

Subject and Verb Agreement

Nothing confuses the reader or undermines a sentence more quickly than failure to use the proper verb form. The verb must always agree with its subject. Consider, for example, the compound subject.

Example 5.37 Subject/Verb Agreement

Incorrect:
The traffic and weather was terrible on the day of the accident.

Correct:
The traffic and weather were terrible on the day of the accident.

Although both traffic and weather are singular, the subject of the sentence is "traffic *and* weather," which has two elements and hence requires a plural verb ("were").

Phrases introduced by certain subordinate conjunctions are not considered part of the subject, despite their obvious relation to the subject, and thus are not taken into consideration when determining verb form.

Example 5.38 Phrases Introduced by Subordinate Conjunctions

<u>Correct:</u>
The judge, as well as plaintiff's counsel, was stunned by the verdict.

<u>Incorrect:</u>
The judge, as well as plaintiff's counsel, were stunned by the verdict.

The subject is "judge" and the verb is "was"; "plaintiff's counsel" is not considered to be part of the subject.

A descriptive prepositional phrase that itself contains a noun can be misleading. Be sure that the verb form agrees with the subject, not the descriptive phrase's noun.

Example 5.39 Prepositional Phrases with Nouns

<u>Incorrect:</u>
The lineup of defendants were a sorry sight.

<u>Correct:</u>
The lineup of defendants was a sorry sight.

The first example is incorrect because the verb was made to agree with the noun "defendants," although that noun is not the subject of the sentence. In the correct example, the verb agrees with the true subject, "lineup." The noun "defendants" is part of the prepositional phrase "of defendants," which merely describes the lineup.

A question often arises with regard to verb usage when the subject is "jury." Is a jury a group of individuals, requiring a plural verb, or a single entity, requiring a singular verb? The answer is, it depends: when a jury is acting in unison, use the singular; when acting individually, use the plural.

Example 5.40 Verb Usage with "Jury"

<u>Correct use of singular:</u>
The jury was unanimous in its verdict of acquittal.

<u>Correct use of plural:</u>
The jury were hopelessly divided on the issue of defendant's negligence.

The second example is accepted usage, despite the strange sound. It might be better to use the following clearer version.

Example 5.41 Correct Use of Plural

The jurors were hopelessly divided on the issue of defendant's negligence.

Pronouns

indefinite pronoun
A pronoun that does not specify its object.

Singular pronouns, such as he, she, and it, use singular verbs. Similarly, plural pronouns, such as them, we, or us, use plural verbs. An **indefinite pronoun** does not refer to a definite person or thing. More often than not, an indefinite pronoun refers to a single indefinite person or thing and uses a singular form of a verb.

> *Everyone waits patiently for the verdict. (singular)*
> *He waits patiently for the verdict. (singular)*
> *They wait patiently for the verdict. (plural)*
> *Each person waits patiently for the verdict. (singular)*
> *All of the individuals wait patiently for the verdict. (plural)*

Some examples of indefinite and definite pronouns are:

Indefinite Pronouns	Definite Pronouns
all	I
anybody	them
either	his
everybody	her
neither	it
someone	their

Prepositions

You have heard the statement time and time again: Never end a sentence with a proposition. Well, that may be the statement, but is it truly the rule? No. Grammar rules do permit ending a sentence with a preposition. The problem is that most do not believe the truth and continue to follow the myth. Even though it is not grammatically incorrect to end a sentence with a preposition, the better, and more acceptable, practice is to restructure a sentence that ends in a preposition. Therefore, forget the grammarians and the great World War II leader, Winston Churchill, who used those prepositions at the end of a sentence, and follow the crowd: Don't end a sentence with a preposition.

Rewriting the sentence is often a simple solution. Sometimes coupling the preposition with the words "that" or "with" or "which" and moving the proposition before a phrase may solve the problem. Let's examine the following:

> *This style of writing is the kind I am accustomed to. (with preposition)*
> *-or-*
> *This style of writing is the kind to which I am accustomed. (without preposition)*
>
> *That speech is just the manner of conduct that the First Amendment protects against. (with preposition)*
> *-or-*
> *That speech is just the manner of conduct against which the First Amendment protects. (without preposition)*

Ethics Alert

The quality of the documents paralegals and attorneys produce is the benchmark of competency in the legal profession. Once a document is circulated in the public domain, it is judged by its sentence structure, word choice, and grammar. Words that do not say what you mean or reflect the client's position can raise the ire of a judge. *In Re Hawkins*, 502 N.W.2d 770 (Minn. 1993), conveys a court's concern over the effect of an attorney's representation in a case. The court observed

> Hawkins' contention that because there has been "no harm," there is "no foul" is unacceptable. Moreover, harm has occurred: . . . administration of the law and the legal profession have been negatively affected by his conduct. Public confidence in the legal system is shaken when lawyers disregard the rules of court and when a lawyer's correspondence and legal documents are so filled with spelling, grammatical, and typographical errors that they are virtually incomprehensible. Id. at 771.

As a paralegal, you may not be disciplined for the quality of a court filing, but the concerns identified by the *Hawkins* court should awaken you to the importance of the work product you create. You may not be an "officer of the court" as an attorney, but your work can and will be judged as a reflection of your supervising attorney. You are an extension of the public confidence and you should be meticulous in the work you produce. Credibility is often all we have, and to lose that creates ineffectiveness. We all know that time constraints and deadlines place undue pressure on us. Cutting corners can lead to mistakes and mistakes can lead to ethical violations, or even worse, the lasting embarrassment a published decision has on an attorney's reputation. In a controversial opinion, a district court judge in Texas wrote these stinging words about the quality of legal writing and credibility of two attorneys: "Take heed and be suitably awed, oh boys and girls—the court was able to state the issue and its resolution in one paragraph . . . despite dozens of pages of gibberish from the parties to the contrary!" *Bradshaw v. Unity Marine Corporation, Inc.*, 147 F. Supp. 2d 668, 672 (S.D. Tex. 2001). Let this be a warning to us all—our reputation and credibility are all we have. Do not compromise them.

E-FACTOR

THE GRAMMAR CHECK

Computers are a wonderful thing. They make our jobs easier and, in many instances, make us look better. One of the many attractions of word processing programs is the grammar check. Similar to the spell check feature, many programs offer grammar suggestions and corrections. The questionable sentence or word is underlined or set off from the rest of the text, alerting the user to the error. You can request an explanation of the error and change it, rework it, or ignore it—your choice. Undoubtedly, if a section of your work is highlighted, it would be imprudent to ignore it. Sometimes the correction is as simple as changing a period to a question mark; other times, an entire sentence or phrase may be highlighted. The prompts offer a detailed explanation of the problem and even suggest a rewritten version or, if a word is improperly used, the correct word choice. Learn to use and rely on this computer program feature to enhance and perfect your work product.

Split Infinitives

Similar to using a preposition at the end of a sentence, splitting infinitives is not improper, but years of indoctrination have drummed the opposite into our heads. A split infinitive occurs when an adverb is placed between the word "to" and the verb. The better practice is to place the adverb after the verb.

Example 5.42 Split Infinitive

Split infinitive:
The better practice is to completely rewrite the sentence.

Corrected:
The better practice is to rewrite the sentence completely.

PRACTICAL CONSIDERATIONS

The use of proper punctuation, sentence structure, and paragraphing techniques enables you to communicate ideas clearly. After mastering these basics you can begin to apply more subtle and complicated techniques.

A first draft often contains inconsistencies that will distract the reader and undercut your arguments. The first step in eliminating these problems is to review your draft for errors in the basics. A slight revision to a basic element often leads to dramatic improvement. By eliminating misleading punctuation, or adding punctuation to clarify, you ensure that your sentences accurately convey your ideas. When you vary sentence structure and eliminate run-ons and fragments, your paragraphs combine these ideas into a coherent argument. Finally, by structuring your paragraphs into logical units with clearly defined transitions, you carry the reader along the path to your conclusion.

Summary

Punctuation embellishes writing and removes ambiguity. Commas can be used to set apart parenthetical phrases; semicolons can join the components of a compound sentence or clarify the elements in a list or series. Quotations add support to memoranda and briefs; parentheses, brackets, and ellipses group or identify special passages of text or omitted text. Hyphens draw words together, whereas dashes separate parenthetical clauses or disparate elements of a two-clause sentence. Colons can introduce quotes or lead into specified lists. Question marks and exclamation points are informal usages, and should be used sparingly in formal or legal writing (although question marks are acceptable for use in "questions presented" sections of memoranda or briefs). Apostrophes indicate contractions (although contractions are generally considered informal and should be avoided in legal writing) and possessives.

Simple sentences contain a subject and verb, and may contain an object and modifiers. Complex sentences contain a subordinate clause, and compound sentences contain at least two clauses that could stand alone as complete grammatical sentences. Simple sentences are preferable, although the need for variety (which prevents writing from becoming monotonous) suggests that complex and compound sentences be used as well. Excessive use of modifiers (adjectives and adverbs) undercuts your writing. A run-on sentence fails to join its component clauses grammatically; a sentence fragment lacks a subject or verb.

A paragraph needs a topic sentence to introduce its subject matter to the reader. The topic sentence is usually at the beginning of the paragraph. The body of the paragraph develops the subject matter introduced by the topic sentence. Transitional language helps guide the reader through the various paragraphs and sections of the document, carrying the reader smoothly from the beginning of the document to the end.

Pay close attention to spelling and grammatical form. In writing, your verbs and subjects should agree; pronouns should refer to a specific subject; and, sentences should not end in a preposition.

The first step in eliminating inconsistencies in a first draft is to review the draft for errors in the basics—punctuation, sentence structure, and paragraphing.

Key Terms

comma	simple sentence
parenthetical phrase	modifiers
restrictive phrase	complex sentence
semicolon	subordinate clause
compound sentence	independent clause
colon	run-on sentence
block quote	sentence fragment
parentheses	active voice
brackets	passive voice
ellipsis	topic sentence
hyphen	body
dash	transitional function
exclamation point	closing sentence
apostrophe	indefinite pronoun

Review Questions

1. What is a parenthetical phrase, and how can it be set apart?
2. Describe one way in which commas can bring clarity into a sentence.
3. How can compound clauses be combined?
4. How do semicolons inject clarity into a series?
5. Briefly describe the format for a block quotation.
6. How are parentheses and brackets used to group passages in a sentence?
7. When should a dash be used to separate segments of a sentence?
8. Describe: a simple sentence; a complex sentence; and a compound sentence.
9. What is a sentence fragment? What is a run-on sentence?
10. Describe the function of a topic sentence; define *body* in the context of paragraph structure; and explain what is meant by *transitional language*.

Exercises

1. Rewrite the following passage:

   The Supreme Court, held that a "subject to legal documentation" provision in a handwritten document executed by parties after they had agreed on material terms of sale did not establish, as a matter of law, that no sales agreement had been reached.

2. Proofread and edit the following paragraph:

   I direct that my just and and legal debts and funeral expenses and all federal and state estate and inheratance taxes imposed upon my estate or any beneficiary therof including the portion of any such tax attributable to the proceeds of policies of insurance on my life or other property not constituting a part of my probate estate, be paid in fall out of my residuary estate as soon as convenient. This direction s not obligatory upon my Executrix and he is specifically given the right or renew and extend, in any form that she deems beast, any debt or charge existing at the time of my death, including any mortgage on my home and similarly my Executrix shall have the right and power to incur indebtedness and to borrow money for the purpose of paying any or all of the aforesaid debts, expenses and taxes.

3. Revise and rewrite the following run-on sentence:

   The law is clear that data in computerized form is discoverable even if paper "hard copies" of the information have been produced, and that the prodoucing party can be required to design a computer program to extract the data from its computerized business records, subject to the Court's discretion as to the allocation of the costs of designing such a computer program.

4. Review the sentences and determine which is correct.

   a. The judge admonished the prosecutor and defense attorney who was distracting the jury from the facts of the case.

      -or-

      The judge admonished the prosecutor and defense attorney who were distracting the jury from the facts of the case.

   b. The judge, who often admonishes attorneys, believes his practice is appropriate.

      -or-

      The judge, who often admonishes attorneys, believe his practice is appropriate.

5. Correct the following passage:

   Patient infommation will not be given to any member of the clergy unless approval and written authorization is obtained from the patient or personnel represenative. Under the privacy rule the hospital only give a one word general discription of the patients condition which will not communicate specific medical inforamtion about the individual patient.

6. Correct the following sentences:
   a. The court state it's position succinctly 'the motion is denied".
   b. Mr. Marshall will be finding his accommodation satisfactory.
   c. The judge jury and prosecutor was completely startled by the defense attorneys speech.
   d. Although its critical to the case the attorney failed to completely give the true facts of the case.

7. Review and revise the following paragraph:

   After reviewing al the pleadings the underlining records the party arguments; pertinent caselaw and statutes and the other recommendations filed byt eh party's, this court remains of the opinion and view point that the decision is null and void eeven though the attorneys of record attempt to argue otherwise. Because this court has not found no case law directly on the point of the subject before this Coourt, the court will find for the Plaintiffs and not the defendant"s in this matter.

8. Edit and revise the following:

   the question is that is facing us with this entire labor crisis iw whether or not this problem will arrest itself (sic; or whether or not in fact lawmakers should now take note and take action to avert this insidious crisis. And I think and I believe that most of us are convincing that in fact something must be done post haste. The one and only singular factor that has not adequately been addressed during these entire crisis is the labor ciris themselves and how do we attempt to properly and adequately education the public.

Portfolio Assignment

Your attorney specializes in employment law and was asked to review a job description that his client South Place Hospital plans to post. Please review the job description and correct, revise, and edit the document.

Job Description
Title: Head Nurse
Salary: To be Determined
Closing: Until Position Filled
Responable for administration and clinical dutys of the Medical Unit.
Inspects area daily for compliance with policies and procedures and documentation patient teaching/education integrity of medical record.
Assured ongoing Performance Imporvement activites within the Unit./
Assisst with the I mplementing of the corrective action when determined necessary.
Monitors and evaluate the quality/appropriateness of patientcare based on CMS and Standards and other licensing agenies.
Responsible to the assigned (assistant vice president) for the Organization, coordination, and direction of the unit on a 24 (twenty four) hour base.
Maintains a safe comfortable and therapeutic environment for patient/families/relatives in accordance herewith Hospitial Standands.
Oversee the delivery of patientcare to both Medical and Other patients: direct and delegates patientcare assignments to nursing staff; based on acuteness of patientcare; staff availiability.
Enhance professional growth, andf development, through participation in educational programs current literature inservice meetings and workshops;
EDUCATIONAL AND EXPERIENCE
BSN or associate degree in nursing. Minimum five year(s) recent clinical experiences with demonstrated leadership skills. Current CPR and State License.
Interested individuals should contact Ms. Santiago, Nurse Recruiter in her Nursing Office at ext. 6783

Vocabulary Builder

Mechanics of Construction

```
A E Y F X F H O E Z U F W W B
B X H P Q C F U T N V M H Y K
R R Y P K A G O O V F N T F W
N N A V O J B L U C A O M X G
S G N C X R O G Q H P N R V E
Z M C Z K C T H K I N F Z J L
P H Y A I E Y S C C Q O M D L
O F F M X P T S O R X Y M T I
K Q E Y H Z E S L P H L L A P
U S M E D N W X B M A K O O S
M S N B T M O D I F I E R S I
Y V M E M Y O H F E T L X W S
J M N E J K G R O V D S U L K
Q C S E S E H T N E R A P Z M
E B U N Q D J A N P D Q H S T
```

APOSTROPHE	BLOCK QUOTE	BRACKETS
ELLIPSIS	HYPHEN	MODIFIERS
PARENTHESES	SEMICOLON	TOPIC SENTENCE

Chapter 6

Effective and Persuasive Legal Writing

After completing this chapter, you will be able to:

- Inject clarity and precision into your writing.

- Define rhythm, flow, and voice.

- Use similes and metaphors to make a colorful point.

- Avoid ambiguity and redundancy.

- Make subjects and verbs agree.

- Use the appropriate tone in your document.

- Compare and contrast periodic sentences and cumulative sentences.

- Differentiate active voice from passive voice, and know when to use each.

- Use structured enumeration to identify the items in a list.

- Develop your arguments logically.

How can you effectively communicate the client's legal position? The answer is through the use of writing techniques such as tone, word choice, and voice, to name a few. Your goal is to communicate your point to the reader, whether you are writing an objective or persuasive document. Don't hide your message in long, complicated sentences or repetitive word combinations. Make your point succinctly and simply and move on. Contrary to what you may think an attorney or judge wants to read, the simple, straightforward approach is preferred. Change the way you think and write, and success is right around the corner. Let's learn some of the "do's" and "don'ts" of legal writing.

Case Fact Pattern Hypothetical 6-1

Your supervising attorney has asked that you prepare a draft memorandum in support of a motion he will be filing with the trial court. You perform the necessary research and return to your office, with pages of notes and a small pile of photocopied cases and statutes. You're now confident in your knowledge of punctuation, sentence structure, and paragraphing, but you want to bring more than just grammatical correctness to this memorandum—you want to prepare a document that will persuade the court. Now that you know the rules, you want to learn to evaluate words—to use language effectively to accomplish your purpose.

WRITING IS READING

A writer strings together words to be read. The audience may be merely the writer him- or herself, as with a diary; one other person, as with a letter; or many thousands, as with a newspaper article or book, but in all cases the words written are intended, ultimately, to be read.

Writing, then, as we noted in Chapter 3, is *reading*.

This might seem simplistic. Of course writing is reading, you're saying to yourself. Everybody knows that—what's the big deal?

The big deal is simply that, although most people understand the connection, they fail to make use of it to improve their writing.

The point might be clearer if stated this way: "Writing is *re*reading." Too many novice writers fail to understand that to create "good writing," they must reread what they've written—placing themselves in the position of the reader—and improve it through revision. Not even the best writers are above the constant need to refine and perfect their drafts.

This person we've referred to before—"the reader"—is the key to the whole writing process. Good writers get inside the reader's head. They analyze the quality of the words they've chosen by analyzing their impact upon the reader. Only after such analysis can they be sure that their point has been successfully conveyed.

editing
To delete, eliminate, or change the text of a legal document.

The process of writing is perhaps best illustrated by a comparison. A sculptor starts with a block of granite, which he then chips and shapes until it matches his vision. A writer must *create* her block of granite, called a first draft. Only then can she go about the business of "chipping and shaping" her writing by rereading, **editing,** and revising to match her vision. Let's investigate this process.

THE POSSIBILITIES OF LANGUAGE

In Chapter 4 we identified words as the bricks of good writing and rules as the mortar, but we confined our discussion to rules. In this section we turn to words to explore the possibilities of language.

Brevity, Clarity, and Precision

brevity
Strong, tight writing.

Brevity leads to strong, tight writing. To be brief is to be forceful. A writer must be stingy with words; he must be efficient and focused.

Brevity, of course, requires work. An old story is illustrative: when asked why she had composed such a long piece, a writer responded, "I didn't have time to make it shorter." (French author Blaise Pascal, Lettres Provinciales, Lettre XIV.) Editing takes time; expressing complex concepts in concise packages requires perseverance.

Brevity does not imply the elimination of detail. The writer need not reduce the argument's scope. Rather, the argument must be stated succinctly. This is demonstrated in Example 6.1.

Example 6.1 Being Brief

<u>Correct:</u>
The defendant's negligence is established by his failure to maintain the subject premises and his failure to warn the plaintiff.

<u>Incorrect:</u>
The defendant's conduct was clearly wrong, in that the careless manner in which he maintained the subject premises, combined with the fact that he failed to issue a warning of any kind, certainly violated the duty that he owed to the plaintiff, and hence this court should find that the defendant was negligent.

The two examples convey the same message; the correct version, however, does so with force and brevity.

clarity
The ability to accurately convey the intended message to the reader.

Clarity is likewise key. Good writing accurately conveys its intended message—no more, no less. Every passage less than clear is a passage over which the reader stumbles, hesitates, or worse, loses interest. The writer must make her message plain.

Example 6.2 Being Clear

<u>Correct:</u>
Only on the second day of the trial did the witness testify about the accident.

On the second day of the trial, the witness testified only about the accident.

Incorrect:
The witness testified about the accident only on the second day of the trial.

The first version is incorrect because it can be interpreted as having the meaning of either of the two correct versions.

precision
Legal writing that clearly and definitely conveys the point of the document.

Closely related to clarity is **precision.** Clarity requires that your writing be open to no more than one interpretation; precision requires that this one interpretation represent the point you seek to convey.

Example 6.3 Being Precise

Correct:
The testimony establishes that the defendant had the unusual habit of walking around his block at 3:00 a.m.

Incorrect:
The testimony establishes that the defendant had the unique habit of walking around his block at 3:00 a.m.

It is unlikely that defendant is the only person ever to demonstrate such a habit (the most common meaning of the word *unique*), and even more unlikely that such a meaning was intended by the writer. Choose your words with care.

Brevity, clarity, and precision are essential characteristics of good writing. By analyzing and editing your writing to assure that it is succinct, clear, and precise, you gain an added benefit—a deeper, clearer understanding of your own argument.

Voice

voice
The sound heard in the mind of the reader, or the impression created by virtue of the words chosen.

Writing **voice,** in general, is a concept that is easy to define but difficult to analyze. It can be defined as the sound heard in the mind of the reader, or the impression created by virtue of the words chosen. Analyzing this sound, the "voice," is challenging because a writer can only "hear" her own mind, not that of the reader.

Defined more loosely, voice is the poetic aspect of prose writing—the flow and rhythm, the tone, the lyrical quality of the words. Such considerations might seem out of place in legal writing, but not if viewed as means rather than ends. The point is not to create a document that reads like a poem; the point is first to determine the tone you seek, then use voice to help achieve such a tone.

flow
A quality within or characteristic of the text that moves the reader easily through the text from point to point.

In the last chapter, we touched upon **flow.** A document flows when the reader moves easily through the text from point to point and from argument to argument. The reader's expectations are fulfilled because the writer has provided the elements that the reader needs to understand the content. Establishing flow is the first element of voice.

How is flow established? By using effective transitions (which we've touched on before and will discuss further) and by employing logical development (which we also discuss further), a writer creates a document that carries the reader along. Rereading is once again the key, followed by editing. Improving flow often requires "cutting and pasting": moving paragraphs around. Having placed raw information in a first draft, the writer sets about the task of logical ordering. It also helps to set aside your writing for a time, *then* reread it—the flaws are often readily apparent, since you are not so immersed in the details of your argument.

rhythm
A pattern of writing conveyed through word choice and word placement in the sentence.

Rhythm is an important element of voice as well. A sentence has, so to speak, peaks and valleys and plateaus. A good writer manipulates the terrain, so that major points sit atop the peaks. Suppose you want to emphasize the believable nature of the testimony of an anxious witness. Consider Example 6.4.

Example 6.4 Rhythm in Voice

Correct:
The witness, though nervous, was credible.

Incorrect:
The witness was credible, though nervous.

The high points in a sentence often come at the beginning and at the end, as in this simple example. In the incorrect version the reader is left with the lingering impression that the nervousness undercut the credibility. In the correct version, the impression left is that, despite the nervousness, the witness was credible.

Analysis of rhythm is not as easy as simply making your strongest points first and last in a sentence or paragraph, however. It requires an analysis of style in general, and style in writing is a concept difficult to pin down. Consider the following two examples, both grammatically correct, but one more effective than the other.

Example 6.5 Rhythm to Increase Impact

Ineffective:
The defendant's car had nonfunctional headlights, as well as a barely audible horn and insufficient brakes.

Effective:
The defendant's car had neither functional headlights, nor an audible horn, nor sufficient brakes.

The effective example conveys the same information, but does so with impact.

Several techniques can be used to increase impact. In Example 6.5, the power of a series that lists three items is apparent. The rhythm inherent in a list of three is more effective than a series of two or four or any other number.

Example 6.6 Rhythm Inherent in Lists

Two-item series:
The defendant's car had neither functional headlights nor an audible horn.

Four-item series:
The defendant's car had neither functional headlights, nor an audible horn, nor sufficient brakes, nor adequate steering.

The list of two is acceptable, although its abrupt ending is a less powerful construction than a list of three. (Note that this analysis is in terms of *rhythm*, not the fact that the sheer evidentiary weight of three items is superior to two.) The list of four simply goes on too long. If it is essential to pass along all the information, the list of four might have been better stated as in Example 6.7.

Example 6.7 Four-Item List

Defendant's car had neither functional headlights, nor an audible horn, nor sufficient brakes. Indeed, it even lacked adequate steering.

The four-item sentence has been broken into two sentences, the first of which uses the rhythmic power of three.

The effective example from Example 6.5 also works well because it uses **parallel construction.** Parallel construction means repeating usages to make a point, to suggest either a connection or a contrast. Certain word combinations naturally fall into parallel structures—the "neither/nor" combination, for example, or the "former/latter" combination.

parallel construction
Repeating usages to make a point, to suggest either a connection or a contrast.

Example 6.8 Parallel Construction

The judge addressed the accused juvenile in her chambers, then, separately, the juvenile's parents. To the former, she urged the need for maturity; to the latter, the need for discipline.

Parallel construction in Example 6.8 and in the effective sentence from Example 6.5 requires that grammatical usage be consistent. Compare the two examples in Example 6.9.

Example 6.9 Agreement in Parallel Construction

Correct:
Legal writers should communicate clearly, concisely, and effectively.

Incorrect:
Legal writers should communicate in a clear manner, concisely, and be effective.

In the correct example, all three modifiers are adverbs relating back to and agreeing with the verb *communicate*. In the incorrect example, the relationship and agreement are muddled. Novice writers often shy away from parallel construction, believing that variety is always better than parallelism. Don't make this mistake—parallel construction has impact.

Under other circumstances, however, variety is an important element of good writing. To give just one such example, consider the following: Although simple sentences (subject/verb/object) are often the most powerful, used exclusively they can lead to a monotonous, droning voice that actually drains the power from your words. A mixture of simple, complex, and compound sentences adds texture to the presentation of your thoughts. Thus, whereas variety should be avoided in parallel comparisons, it is desirable in other contexts.

We have noted that the point of establishing voice is not to make your document read like a poem, but rather to achieve the desired tone. But what is the desired tone? In legal writing, you generally seek to evoke a formal, assertive tone. To achieve such a tone, avoid light, familiar language; be straightforward without being ponderous. Your writing should be neither stuffy nor conversational. Stay away from the flip comment; keep your analysis sharp and your language focused.

A Word about Tone

tone
The way the writer communicates a point of view.

Closely related to voice in legal writing is the concept of **tone.** Tone focuses on how the writer communicates a point of view. Is the document conveying a strong message? Is the document conveying information to a client? Is the document addressed to the court? Opposing counsel? Tone is established through word choice and sentence structure. For example, a friendly closing is

> *If additional information is required, please do not hesitate to contact me.*

Compare this to a closing communicating the importance of a matter, which takes on the following tone:

> *Your prompt attention this matter is advised.*

The last example leaves no question in the reader's mind about the tone of the letter or the importance of the matter.

Communicating with colleagues, especially through e-mail, requires attention to tone. Observe the tone in the following e-mail:

> *I received your request to meet regarding the contract issue. The only time I can meet is at 3 p.m. tomorrow. The meeting must start on time since I have a court hearing to prepare for the next day. If you are not there, I will assume you have resolved the matter.*

The tone is matter-of-fact. This tone may or may not offend the reader who requested the meeting.

A better, more diplomatic, approach is

> *I received your request to meet regarding the contract issue. My schedule is tight as I am preparing for a hearing for tomorrow. I do have some time at 3 p.m. if your schedule permits. Otherwise, we can meet after the hearing or early next week. Let me know what works for you.*

The second example responds to the same request but in a less offensive tone. Better word choice conveys the message without angering the reader. The words and phrases you choose set the tone of your document.

Often tone is set by the type of legal document you are drafting. A letter may be friendly or tough; a memorandum may be objective or persuasive, depending on the audience. In a brief to the court, your tone is more formal and persuasive. Choose words and phrases that assert the client's position in a clear, concise manner. However, tone in a formal document should avoid the "first person" reference and personal opinions. Nothing is more annoying to a judge than a "preachy" personalized tone.

Writing in the first person often is expected when writing or e-mailing a client. You want to make personal references, as writing in the third person may be construed as cold or pompous. Writing in the first or third person is discussed later in this chapter. Unless your firm does not want to continue representing a client, use a conversational tone in communications relying on longer sentences rather than short, clipped sentences exhibiting a no-nonsense approach. Of course this approach depends on the message you or your supervising attorney are conveying. You may intentionally choose a tone that is direct and to the point for a reason. The point is: know what you want to say; how you want to say it; and who you are saying it to (or, to whom you are saying it!).

Contractions—You Can't Say Can't

Do not use contractions in formal legal writing. The tone is too informal and familiar. The types of legal documents you will be drafting require precision and professionalism. Contractions do not convey that message. However, in a divorce proceeding a California appellate judge was frustrated at a party's lack of understanding of the appellate process after granting the relief requested. In a footnote, Justice Sills expressed the following toward one of the parties:

> [T]he fact that an appellate court doesn't mention that a litigant didn't raise an argument doesn't mean it wasn't raised, and can't be asserted later if the procedural circumstances warrant. *Gale v. Superior Court,* 122 Cal. App. 4th 1388, 1399 note 7, 19 Cal. Rptr. 3d 554, 561 (Cal. App. 4th Dist. 2004).

Sometimes contractions do make a point and convey a tone.

Similes and Metaphors

simile
A direct comparison of dissimilar objects, for the purpose of emphasizing a common characteristic.

metaphor
A figure of speech that links dissimilar objects, but it is more powerful than a simile in that it equates, rather than compares, the objects.

Similes and metaphors are figures of speech useful to legal writers. A **simile** is a direct comparison of dissimilar objects, for the purpose of emphasizing a common characteristic. A **metaphor** also links dissimilar objects, but it is more powerful than a simile in that it equates, rather than compares, the objects.

Example 6.10 Simile and Metaphor

Simile:
A good simile is like a good after-dinner speech: short and to the point.

Metaphor:
Metaphors are valuable weapons in the legal writer's arsenal.

When using metaphors, be careful of that entertaining but ineffective species, the mixed metaphor.

Example 6.11 Mixed Metaphor

Metaphors are valuable tools in the legal writer's arsenal.
Until soldiers shower their enemies with hammers and screwdrivers, tools are not to be found in an arsenal!

Used selectively, metaphors and similes make a vivid impression in the mind of the reader. Be wary, however, of overuse, which can erode an otherwise effective argument.

PITFALLS IN LANGUAGE

Language presents potential problems, as well as possibilities. When drafting legal documents, there are several pitfalls to avoid.

Ambiguity

ambiguity
Lack of precision and clarity.

Ambiguity exists when a writer has failed in the obligation to provide precision and clarity. In the law, as in perhaps no other subject area, ambiguity can have devastating consequences. At best, ambiguity creates hardships and confusion for the reader; at worst, it can adversely affect your client's essential rights. The legal writer's words must convey her intended message—no more, no less. Consider the following example.

Example 6.12 Pronoun Ambiguity

Neither plaintiff nor defendant knew he had executed the contract without authority.

The sentence in Example 6.12 is ambiguous because the reader is left wondering: Who is "he"? Was it the plaintiff who had executed the contract without authority? Was it the defendant? Did *both* plaintiff and defendant unknowingly execute the contract without authority? Were both plaintiff and defendant unaware that some third party had executed the contract without authority? Because she is left wondering, the reader's inquiry is interrupted and perhaps inhibited. She loses the point of the argument, and she may abandon it altogether. Although the broader context from which this sentence was drawn may clear up some of the confusion, it might have been better stated in one of the following ways.

Example 6.12 provides an example of **pronoun ambiguity.** Pronoun ambiguity results from an unclear indication about the noun to which the pronoun refers back—in Example 6.12, the pronoun "he."

Another form of ambiguity arises when the placement of a modifying clause obscures the object of the modification.

pronoun ambiguity
Lack of clarity that results from an unclear indication about the noun to which a pronoun refers.

Example 6.13 Unambiguous Alternative

Alternative 1:
Neither plaintiff nor defendant knew that plaintiff had executed the contract without authority.

Alternative 2:
Neither plaintiff nor defendant knew that plaintiff's agent had executed the contract without authority.

Alternative 3:
Both plaintiff and defendant were unaware that each had executed the contract without authority.

Example 6.14 Object Ambiguity

The testimony of the accounting expert led to the vindication of the corporation's accounting process as a result of its accuracy.

Was it the testimony that was accurate, or the accounting process? Both, we hope, but you see the problem. The placement of the clause obscures the reference of the pronoun "its." Two alternatives appear in Example 6.15.

Example 6.15 Unambiguous Alternative

The accurate testimony of the accounting expert vindicated the corporation's accounting process.
   -or-
The accounting expert vindicated the corporation's accounting process by testifying to its accuracy.

Misplaced Modifiers

modifiers
Words that describe a subject, verb, or object in a sentence.

Along with pronoun ambiguity, misplaced **modifiers** also cause ambiguity in writing. Modifiers describe a subject, a verb, or an object in a sentence. When a modifier is misplaced, a sentence becomes confusing and may mislead the reader. Keep modifiers close to the word described, as shown in Example 6.16.

Example 6.16 Modifier

Correct:
The witness saw a police officer fire while chasing the gunman.

Incorrect:
Chasing the gunman, the witness saw a police officer fire.
(Who was chasing the gunman? The witness or the police officer? The sentence is confusing.)

Ambiguity is a common problem that is easily avoided by word choice and careful placement of the modifiers in a sentence.

Sexism

Sexist references and gender-based differentiation, which reinforce sexual stereotypes, have no place in legal writing. Consider the question of sexism when choosing pronouns that relate back to occupational nouns. For example, you should not always use the pronoun *he* when referring to a judge, or *she* when referring to a paralegal. One solution to this problem is to use "he or she," although this can be awkward, particularly when used repeatedly. Another alternative is to make a conscious effort to vary or alternate the pronouns used. This latter alternative has been employed in this book.

Another option is to make your original noun plural, enabling you to use a plural (hence gender-neutral) pronoun.

Example 6.17 Relating Back to Occupational Nouns

Gender-specific:
When a judge considers a brief, she reviews form as well as substance.

Gender-neutral:
When judges consider briefs, they review form as well as substance.

The use of plurals eliminates the gender differentiation, but, like the "he or she" construction, can also create an awkward feel to the sentence. You will have to use your judgment about the best means of eliminating sexist references. Some examples are given in Table 6.1.

Politically Correct Terminology

Language references change. We might not refer to a group of individuals in the same way that we would have fifty years ago. An obvious goal in legal writing is precision, but another goal is not to offend your reader. The question is, which term should be used? Is it elderly or senior citizen? Handicapped, disabled, or physically challenged? Gay, lesbian, or homosexual? Black or African American? Hispanic or Latino? Sometimes the law dictates your terminology; however, strive for bias-free language.

Attention should be given when referring to groups. Not all Arabs are Muslim; not all Americans are from the United States (North America includes Canada). When the term "Indian" is used, are you referring to people from India or Native Americans? Be sensitive to inappropriate labels. Do attempt to be culturally sensitive in your writing. And, above all, when in doubt, ask.

Clichés, Slang, and Colloquialisms

clichés
Overused figures of speech.

Clichés are, by definition, overused figures of speech. Legal writing should be crisp and fresh, with points made in clear, logical language that avoids vague references and shopworn phrases. Example 6.18 provides a few of the many clichés to be avoided.

TABLE 6.1
Sexist Terminology and Gender-Neutral Alternatives

Sexist Terminology	Gender-Neutral Terminology
mankind	humanity, human race
man-made	hand-crafted, handmade, fabricated
man-power	work force, personnel
man-to-man	face-to-face
chairman	chair, chairperson, executive, businessperson
workmen's compensation	worker's compensation
policeman	police officer
spokesman	spokesperson

Example 6.18 Clichés

Slow as molasses
Kill two birds with one stone
Birds of a feather
The blind leading the blind

If a seasoned writer were to use a cliché to make a point, she would generally set off the cliché with quotation marks. However, after careful reflection, most such usages, although perhaps seeming clever at first, will be seen to be stylistically weak.

Example 6.19 Setting Off the Cliché

To say that defendants are "birds of a feather" is to commit an injustice to birds.

slang
Informal expressions.

Similarly, **slang** should be avoided. Slang is common to all languages. New forms of expression develop daily and may become acceptable in daily communications. For example, rap, hip-hop, and Ebonics are important culturally and knowing the terminology may help you communicate with a client. A judge may not know that "bling" is jewelry, but this meaning may be relevant in finding out facts in a case. Unless slang describes a client's circumstance, write in appropriate prose. You may need to define the slang, but do not use it in formal writing.

colloquialisms
Informal language used in everyday conversation.

Likewise, **colloquialisms** are informal phrases used in everyday conversation. For example, defendant did not "rip off" the plaintiff; damages are not "30,000 bucks." There is an appropriate phrase for "bucks," such as "dollars." Legal documents can be undermined by sloppy, colloquial usages. Stay away from colloquialisms unless they are part of a quote or critical to your facts.

Jargon

legal jargon
Legalese.

Legal jargon or **legalese** is useful if used in moderation, and if the audience understands it. We discussed some of the problems and benefits of legalese in Chapter 3. To summarize, if you can say it in plain English, say it that way; if your audience is sophisticated legal professionals (as with, for example, an appellate brief), use language that the audience expects and understands, including "terms of art"; and if you feel compelled to use legalese in a document intended for a layman to read (for example, in a letter explaining a technical legal problem to a client), be sure to explain carefully any terms that the average person might not understand.

Redundancy and Verbosity

Just as ambiguity is the result when clarity and precision are disregarded, so are redundancy and verbosity the result when brevity is lost. That is a slightly verbose way of saying: "Get to the point! And don't repeat yourself!"

redundancy
The repeated use of the same point or concept.

Redundancy exists when the writer has made the same point over and over. Say it *once*. Say it *forcefully*, but say it *once*. (Is this paragraph now redundant?) Don't underestimate the intelligence of the reader. You have to use your own judgment in particular instances, but generally speaking, repeated hammering on the same point can offend or bore the reader, and actually weaken an otherwise powerful argument.

verbosity
The use of an excessive number of words, or excessively complicated words, to make a point.

Verbosity is simply the use of an excessive number of words, or excessively complicated words, to make a point. Some novice writers mistake verbosity for impressive analysis; in fact,

You Be the Judge

Hypothetical 6-2

Imagine you are the paralegal on a case where the opposing counsel has filed over 4,000 pages of pleadings. The pleadings fill 18 volumes and require a cart to move them. Does this violate any court rules? The Fifth Circuit Court of Appeals thought so. Read *Gordon v. Green*, 602 F. 2d 743 (5th Cir. 1979). What is the standard for filing a pleading? What was the court's disposition in the case? What message was the court sending by stating "Let Thy Speech Be Short, Comprehending Much In Few Words"? *Id.* at 744.

it seems pompous and often indicates a lack of command of the subject matter. Keep your sentences as short as possible (given the need for variety) and use the simplest words you can: the defendant was "insensitive," not "obtuse"; the departure was "hasty," not "precipitate"; the road was "slippery," not "lubricious."

Elegant Variation and the Thesaurus

Somewhere in our early English classes in high school someone must have said: "Don't use the same word twice in a sentence." That couldn't be more wrong. How many times have you rushed to the thesaurus to find another word similar to the one just used in order to avoid repeating a word in a sentence? The problem is the word chosen from the thesaurus does not mean exactly what the word you just used meant. The meaning of the sentence changed; or worse yet, the word means nothing like the word you tried to replace. More embarrassing is choosing a different word that sounds good, but when asked, you have no idea of the meaning of the word. Let's use a simple example: the word "deposit."

> *Deposit your money in the bank.*

We all understand the meaning of the word in this context. Now, you intend to use the word again in the next sentence, but want to use a different word because you do not want to repeat yourself. Look up deposit in the thesaurus. The entry is:

> *Deposit (submit to a bank) verb*
> *Bank, commit, enter into an account, entrust, invest, keep an account, lay by, present money for safekeeping, put at interest, save.* Legal Thesaurus, *William C. Burton (Macmillan Publishing Co., Inc. 1980).*

Review the preceding above. Do you want to "entrust" your money into the bank? Save? Commit? Account? No, you want to deposit money. No other word makes sense.

Of course, your goal is to write eloquently and with variety. Do not sacrifice variety for inaccuracy and confusion. It is one issue if you have writer's block and you need a slight nudge to get started. Use a thesaurus. If none of the words convey your point accurately, use the word you know. A thesaurus is not a book of synonyms. Use it sparingly.

Misused Words

A major pitfall in legal writing is misused words. You think what you said is accurate, but it is not. This section is a brief overview of some commonly misused words.

- Whether. Many issues in briefs, memoranda, and case briefs begin with the words "whether or not . . . ." This use is redundant. The word whether implies "not" and is used alone. (This may be a tough sell, since most attorneys use the incorrect variation.)

- Shall and may. The word "shall" implies mandatory and "may" implies permissive. Know the result you desire and that will determine the correct word.

- Said (used as an adjective). Replace this word with "this" or "the." Don't use it.

- Affect and effect. "Affect" is a verb, not a noun. It means to influence. "Effect" is either a verb or a noun. As a verb, effect means to bring about a result; as noun, it means immediate result. For example: The judge *affected* the outcome by her comment. The *effect* of the strobe lights was stunning.

- And/or. Avoid this construction. Revise the sentence to convey your point. Using and/or creates ambiguity. For example: The fire was caused by arson and/or negligence of the owner. How was the fire started? It is confusing. Revise the sentence as follows: The fire was caused by arson or negligence of the owner, but not both.

- Etc. Although it is not technically incorrect, do not use the abbreviation for "etcetera" in legal writing.

- The abbreviations *i.e.* and *e.g.* The abbreviation *i.e.* means "that is" or "namely." Limit use of this abbreviation to when you are referring back to what has already been stated. The abbreviation *e.g.* means "for example" and is commonly used in legal writing with citation and case references.

PRACTICE TIP

Try not to misspell or misuse the word *counsel*, which refers to an attorney; *council* is a group of people. (This is an embarrassing error.)

- Pleaded or pled. "Pled" should not be used. "The attorney pleaded (not pled) his case."
- Irregardless. This is not a word. The word is regardless.
- Whose and who's. "Whose" is the possessive pronoun and refers to an object; "who's" is the contraction for "who is." "The court, whose jurisdiction, is plenary has the authority to review the appeal."
- Principal and principle. "Principal" is a noun or an adjective. As a noun, a principal is the head of a school; as an adjective principal means highest authority, importance, or degree. "Principle" is a noun meaning settled rule, doctrine, or legal determination.
- Cite and site. "Site" is a location; cite means "to reference." Most likely, you will use cite rather than site in your work.

There are many more examples of misused words in legal writing. The preceding list is some of the more commonly misused words and is intended as a quick reference guide.

Writing Fallacies

Misconceptions abound in legal writing. Some of those misconceptions are as follows:

- *Do not begin a sentence with "And" or "But."* Why not? There are no grammatical or stylistic reasons to avoid beginning a sentence with "and" or "but." The key here is variation. Do not begin too many sentences with "and" or "but"—that is simple common sense.

PRACTICE TIP

Do not write the number and then spell it out: $ 2,200 (Two Thousand Two Hundred). Avoid the practice and either write the number or spell it out.

- *Always spell out numbers in legal writing.* It depends. Some rules suggest spelling numbers smaller than 10. Others suggest when a number recurs in the text, use numerals. Numbers that begin a sentence are spelled out; larger numbers, such as 10 million, use both numerals and words for clarity; and when referencing a decade, such as the 1960s, do not use an apostrophe—1960's is incorrect.
- *Use variations of the same word for effect.* Doublets and triplets, as they are called, are common in legal writing. Avoid them unless *truly* a term of art. Usually what can be stated in one word is sufficient. Attorneys refer to doublets and triplets from habit, and quite simply, because they think it is right. Why use the phrase "liens and encumbrances" when either word will get the point across? Another infamous use is "due and payable." Avoid doublets and triplets and find the best word for communicating your intent (see Table 6.2).
- *Wills are a common document that uses doublets and triplets.* A sample of the beginning language in a will is: I give, devise, and bequeath to my wife all my right, title, and interest in all my personal and real property. A simpler way would be to say: I give to my wife all my interest in my personal and real property.

TABLE 6.2
Common Doublets and Triplets

Doublets	Triplets
each and every	give, devise, and bequeath
power and authority	promise, agree, and covenant
cease and desist	right, title, and interest
null and void	ready, willing, and able

TABLE 6.3
Commonly Used Complex Words

Complex Word	Simple Substitute
ameliorate	improve
augment	increase
hide	conceal
stop	discontinue
elucidate	explain
indebtedness	debt
kindly	please
reside	live
surmise	guess

- *Choose complex words rather than the simpler equivalent.* Wrong. When writing, choose "use" over "utilize" or "send" over "forward." Communicate in clear terms; there is no need to show off unless, of course, the assignment requires a more formal tone, and even then simpler words convey as much depth as the complex ones. Table 6.3 offers substitutes for commonly used complex words.

Write in the Third Person

Legal documents are drafted toward a particular audience as discussed in Chapter 4. The audience, whether judge, opposing counsel, or client, wants to know the law and how it applies to the case. Simply stated: No one cares what you think. Avoid writing in the first person ("I") or giving your opinion. Statements like "I think," "I believe," or "We submit" are inappropriate in legal writing. Let the law speak and not your personal opinions. Do not distract the reader from the strength of your position by interjecting your feelings.

A Word (or Two) about Plagiarism

You know the concept. Plagiarism is borrowing passages from someone else's work without acknowledging the source. Legal writing uses cases, statutes, and other sources to support a legal position. Although it's cumbersome, always cite your source of law. This practice is commonplace in legal writing. Your supervising attorney and judges expect legal sources to be cited in a legal document. In fact, the absence of cited material raises questions. Review the Ethics Alert section of this chapter for a case where an attorney plagiarized an entire brief from a legal treatise and drew the wrath of the judge. Get in the habit of citing cases and statutes when preparing a memorandum or brief. Chapter 7 will address how to incorporate legal sources into your legal documents. When in doubt, use a source to support your proposition.

You Be the Judge   Hypothetical 6-3

Courts have different views as to what constitutes plagiarism. In drafting documents and preparing briefs, there is often a fine line between what is acceptable and what is not. Review *Frith v. State,* 325 N.E. 2d 186 (Indiana 1975) and *Federal Intermediate Credit v. Kentucky Bar Association,* 540 S.W. 2d 14 (Ken. 1976), and determine whether these cases can be reconciled. Identify the facts of the cases. What facts distinguish *Frith* from *Federal Intermediate Credit*? Did both cases involve plagiarism allegations? How did each court rule?

Source: ©United Feature Syndicate, Inc.

Tell Them!

A writer begins with an advantage: He knows what he wants to say. But this knowledge can turn into a disadvantage. Why? The reason is simple—because the reader doesn't share the same fore-knowledge. The reader doesn't know what the writer wants to say until he says it. And if a writer gets so caught up in the particulars of his argument that he loses touch with this fact, the quality of his writing begins to plummet. He will fail to provide the hints and signals that the reader needs and wants. His message will become obscure.

How do you do away with the obscurity? Often you can cure it by simply telling the reader what you're talking about. Even an excellent writer can become so wrapped up in the details of her argument that she fails to put them in proper perspective. The solution is to step back and review the overall argument for the reader's benefit.

Topic Sentences and Transitions

By rereading an obscure passage, summarizing its importance in your mind, then reintroducing it with the summary, you provide the introduction that the reader needs. In Example 6.20, note the improvement from the addition of a simple sentence that merely states, up front, the intended message.

Example 6.20 Providing an Introduction

Without a lead-in:
In *Jones v. Smith*, the plaintiff claimed that the will was invalid because one of the alleged witnesses had been blind at the time of the will's execution. The court found, however, that the witness had been blind in one eye only. In the present case before the court, the witness in question was blind in both eyes at the time of execution, was partially deaf as well, and hence could not have properly witnessed the testator's signature.

With an informative lead-in:
The case of *Jones v. Smith* is distinguishable, and does not support the plaintiff's contention that the will was properly witnessed. In *Jones v. Smith*, the plaintiff claimed that the will was invalid because one of the alleged witnesses had been blind at the time of the will's execution. The court found, however, that the witness had been blind in one eye only. In the present case before the court, the witness in question was blind in both eyes at the time of execution, was partially deaf as well, and hence could not have properly witnessed the testator's signature.

Simply by telling the reader, at the outset, what will be addressed, the whole passage becomes easier to understand.

This concept of telling the reader what to expect is directly related to the concept of the topic sentence, which we discussed in Chapter 4. Indeed, what we've done in Example 6.20 is nothing more than add a topic sentence. Our approach in this subsection is different from our previous discussion of topic sentences and transitions, however. In the last chapter, we were building a paragraph from the ground up, that is, drafting. In this subsection, think about it from a different perspective—think about it as *troubleshooting*. You've written a document, and you've re-read it, and you know something's wrong. You've corrected all the punctuation and grammatical errors, you've removed the clichés, you've been succinct—and still something's missing. What can it be?

Think back for a moment to our discussion, near Example 5.32, of a paragraph that holds back the topic sentence until the end. We noted that such paragraph structure requires patience on the part of the reader, and creates the risk that the reader will lose interest. Now imagine an entire *document* requiring such patience—it's *inevitable* that the reader will lose interest in such a document. A little of this technique might create useful tension, but a reader should not be kept waiting from beginning to end to find out the writer's point in a brief. Provide topic sentences and transitions to eliminate obscurity—in short, *tell them*!

The problem can exist even within an individual sentence. Some sentences, called **periodic sentences**, force the reader to store information until the end (analogous to the paragraph with topic sentence at the end). Contrast such a periodic sentence with the **cumulative sentences** in Example 6.21.

---

topic sentence
First sentence of a paragraph that introduces an idea.

transition
The writer's ability to move the reader from paragraph to paragraph.

periodic sentence
A sentence that conveys the information at the end of the paragraph.

cumulative sentence
A sentence that conveys the information in a comprehensive manner.

Example 6.21 Periodic and Cumulative Sentences

Periodic sentence:
The treasurer of the corporation, who was elected by unanimous consent of the board of directors, who had been publicly acclaimed by both the corporation's chief executive officer and the local business media, and who in fifteen years of service had never missed a single day of work, has been missing for three weeks, was last seen at the Los Angeles airport, and is believed to have flown to South America with a substantial amount of embezzled funds.

Cumulative sentences:
The treasurer of the corporation is believed to have flown to South America with a substantial amount of embezzled funds. Missing for three weeks, and last seen at the Los Angeles airport, he had never missed a day of work in fifteen years of service. He had been elected by the unanimous consent of the board of directors, and had been publicly acclaimed by both the corporation's chief executive officer and the local business media.

The point is obvious. The periodic example makes the reader work, whereas the cumulative example requires the writer to work harder so that the reader need not.

When "something's missing," improving topic sentences and transitions so as to minimize the work the reader must do will often help cure the problem. But remember, even periodic sentences can have dramatic impact, used sparingly.

Example 6.22 Dramatic Impact of Periodic Sentence

The witness, unruffled in demeanor, untroubled by conscience, and unaffected by the presence of the victim's relatives, testified about her role in the murder.

Like so many other aspects of writing, the final decision on sentence structure is a judgment call. But now you have a foundation on which to base your judgment.

Structured Enumeration

structured enumeration
Identification of each point in a sentence sequentially.

Sequential points are often difficult to follow if not clearly labeled. **Structured enumeration,** which specifically identifies each point, can eliminate the difficulty. Again, the purpose is to tell the reader precisely what is meant.

Example 6.23 Structured Enumeration

Without structured enumeration:
The elements of negligence are all present here. The defendant owed a duty to the plaintiff, and the duty was breached. This breach was the proximate cause of the plaintiff's injury. The plaintiff suffered damage as a result.

With structured enumeration:
The elements of negligence are all present here. First, the defendant owed a duty to the plaintiff. Second, the duty was breached. Third, this breach was the proximate cause of the plaintiff's injury. Fourth, the plaintiff suffered damage as a result.

The structured enumeration makes the paragraph easier to follow and understand. Legal analysis often requires lists of complex factors; structured enumeration helps the reader to comprehend such lists.

Take a Positive and Definitive Approach

Positive statements are almost always more forceful than negative ones.

Example 6.24 Negative/Positive Statements

Negative:
The club did not accept his application.

Positive:
The club rejected his application.

If you are trying to make a point, use the positive approach. If you are trying to de-emphasize a point, use the negative approach. For example, suppose the person whose application was rejected in the preceding example sued the club alleging racial discrimination. The club's counsel might use the following sentence in her statement of facts.

Example 6.25 Muting the Negative

Although plaintiff was not accepted for membership in the club, the club was unbiased in reaching its decision.

This sentence mutes the impact of the rejection, which is the goal of the club's counsel.

You should also be *definitive* when taking a position. There are few words more useless, for example, than "clearly."

Example 6.26 Being Definitive

Correct:
The defendant was negligent.

Incorrect:
The defendant was clearly negligent.

An assumption is built into the incorrect example—an assumption that there are factors to be weighed, and that, based upon these factors, a "clear" conclusion can be reached. Using the word "clearly" in this way actually invites the reader to challenge the main proposition, to weigh the evidence and determine for himself just how "clear" it is that defendant was negligent.

The correct example simply states a proposition: "defendant was negligent." Period. It assumes no analysis; it simply provides the conclusion. This is the best way to present your points—forthrightly, with confidence, and without qualification. Vague, qualifying words such as "quite," "very," and "rather" have no place in legal writing. The road was not "very slippery," it was "slippery"; the defendant is not "unquestionably guilty," she is "guilty."

This is not to say that you should not support your conclusions with analysis. Such analysis is, of course, essential. By all means, point out the testimony that the road was slippery; by all means, point out that the fingerprints left on the gun were the defendant's. Nor is it to say that no one will challenge your conclusions if you state them forthrightly—they surely will. But in stating the propositions upon which your argument rests, don't undercut them by your own word usage. State them conclusively. You want your audience to know something—so *tell them*!

LOGICAL DEVELOPMENT

It takes more than bricks and mortar to build a house; there must be an architect as well. So it is with good writing: There must be central organizing principles within a document, so that the individual components work together to accomplish the overall objective. There must be structure and a plan.

The key to organization is logical development. Logical development is present in writing when each point follows naturally from its predecessor. You have learned that you can use topic sentences, transitions, and structured enumeration to ensure that the reader has a reasonable understanding of where the argument is going. In addition to these techniques, you should also analyze your document on a larger scale, as an organic whole.

Several methods can be used to achieve logical development.

IRAC Method

We discussed the IRAC method in Chapter 3. It involves: (1) identifying the issue; (2) determining the rule of law; (3) applying the rule of law to the facts of your case; and (4) reaching a conclusion. This structure can be applied to a paragraph or to a series of paragraphs constituting a single argument. By using the IRAC format, the development of each individual argument will be logical. If your documents involve multiple arguments, you have to order them according to one of the overriding principles that follow.

Strongest Argument First

Writers often place their strongest argument first. By opening with their strength, they can then build on this foundation. Weaker points may be buttressed by association.

Chronological Development

Sometimes arguments are best ordered chronologically, particularly when they fit in a complex factual context, or when the order of events is crucial to the analysis. For example, in a business dispute over the performance of an electronic component built by defendant and purchased by plaintiff, there may be many letters, test reports, and field results that touch upon the knowledge of the parties and the positions taken and the risks assumed by the parties. The legal arguments may build upon the chronological development. In such a case, chronological assessment is essential, particularly with regard to your statement of facts.

When ordering your arguments chronologically, you must take special care that your strongest argument does not get lost. One possible solution is a preliminary summary that emphasizes your important points, followed by the detailed chronological analysis.

Outlining and Subheading

outlining
A preliminary step in writing that provides a framework for the assignment.

Outlining has already been identified as a preliminary step in writing. By starting with an outline, the writer has a framework within which to work. The outline also provides a shorthand format in which the larger argument can be grasped, and against which the logic of its development can be measured.

subheadings
Subcategories in an outline within a document.

Subheadings are useful both as transition tools (more will be said about this in future chapters) and as a form of outline. By reviewing your subheadings, you can analyze how the elements of your argument fit into the organic whole. If the progression, as seen through the subheads, does not seem logical, then the body of the argument is probably not logically developed.

PRACTICE TIP

Your e-mails, as private and confidential as you may think, are the property of your employer. Think before you hit the "Send" button. Reread all your e-mails for content, tone and, above all, professionalism. Additionally, distinguish between the "Reply" and the "Reply All" button; you may not want all recipients of the e-mail to receive your response.

Ethics Alert

According to a number of case decisions, plagiarism reflects on an individual's level of honesty. Copying material verbatim and claiming it as your own is deceptive. In a recent case, *Iowa Supreme Court Board of Professional Ethics and Conduct v. Lane*, 642 N.W. 2d 296 (Iowa 2002), an attorney's license was suspended for plagiarizing. Lane, an attorney, filed a brief plagiarized from a legal treatise without crediting the true author. The court, incensed by the attorney's conduct, believed that "[t]his plagiarism constituted, among other things, a misrepresentation to the court. An attorney may not engage in conduct involving dishonesty, fraud, deceit, or misrepresentation." *Id.* at 299. This language is strong and representative of how courts view this type of conduct. This type of behavior by attorneys only enhances the public mistrust of the legal profession. Adding further insult to the court, Lane requested attorney's fees for his "work." The court, in its stinging discourse, observed that

[r]*ather, the facts show Lane stole all eighteen pages of his legal argument from a single source. Then to justify his request for attorney fees for the eighty hours it took to "write" the brief, Lane submitted a list of over 200 legal sources to the court. In doing so, Lane attempted to have the court believe he researched and relied on each of these sources in writing the brief. These circumstances only support the conclusion Lane endeavored to deceive the court. Id. at 300.*

Ouch! Obviously, when using legal sources to develop an argument in a brief, memorandum, or legal document, you must credit the source. Although this may seem elementary, attorneys and paralegals, in haste, may omit citing the legal source behind an argument. Don't be the victim of a judge's wrath. Credit all your legal sources or run the risk of a plagiarism charge.

THE E-FACTOR—ELECTRONIC MAIL AND TEXT MESSAGING

Electronic mail (e-mail) and text messaging are common methods of communication. By their nature, e-mail and text messaging are less formal than other written forms of communication. Do not let the informality fool you. Often the way you say something in an e-mail is completely different than the way you would communicate by letter. When e-mailing, you should think about the tone. To whom are you writing? A colleague? A client? Who could read the e-mail? Do not forget the lessons you have already learned when preparing to write. Who is my audience? What is the purpose of the communication? Will this e-mail be read by my supervising attorney or a partner in the law firm?

In the work environment, take a more formal approach to e-mails. Assume the e-mail could be read by a co-worker. What impression is conveyed in the e-mail? Is the tone professional?

The same rules apply to text messaging in the work environment. Assume that your boss will read the text message.

E-mailing and text messaging are representative of the new way business is conducted. Compose your e-mail under the assumption that it is not private. Tone and word choice are important and should be suitable for viewing by anyone.

PRACTICAL CONSIDERATIONS

A novice writes a paragraph. He rereads it. It isn't good. It fails to make the point he wanted to make. The logic doesn't follow from beginning to end. Is he a bad writer?

He might think he is—but he isn't.

He isn't, at least, if he recognized the cardinal rule of writing: almost no one gets it right on the first try.

He isn't a bad writer if he recognizes the weaknesses in his paragraph and then takes out the tools of an editor—a pencil, eraser, scissors, and tape (or their word-processing equivalents)—to begin the task of improving it. Rereading, editing, revising, reworking, shifting paragraphs, substituting words, inserting explanations, deleting redundant elements, eliminating grammatical errors, crossing out, inserting, rereading, rereading, *rereading*—these are the elements that go into good writing.

Nothing you've learned about rules, style, design, and persuasiveness will be of any use if you fail to understand that writing is reading.

Nor is the process easy. "A writer is someone for whom writing is more difficult than it is for other people," said Thomas Mann. Writing is hard work—designed, ironically, to create the appearance of effortlessness—and, in the case of legal writing, to persuade.

Summary

A good writer recognizes that writing is reading and that she must reread what she has written, placing herself in the position of the reader, and improve it through revision.

Good writing requires brevity, clarity, and precision. Include necessary details, but be succinct. Accurately convey your intended message, no more and no less, and make sure the words you have chosen are open to no more than one interpretation. Writing voice is the "sound" that the reader hears in his mind; defined more loosely, it is the poetical or lyrical aspect of writing. Flow is established by combining logical development with a commitment to rereading and editing, so that the reader moves easily from point to point in the finished product. Rhythm in a sentence refers to the varying levels of emphasis of the words—the high points and the low points. Good sentence rhythm can be obtained by employing such techniques as placing the points you wish to emphasize at the beginning or end of a sentence, not hidden in the middle; recognizing the rhythmic power inherent in a series or list of three points; and using parallel construction to emphasize and clarify your points. Similes compare dissimilar objects; metaphors equate them. Both are useful figures of speech that a writer can employ to make a colorful point.

Legal writers must avoid ambiguity. Two things to look out for are pronoun ambiguity and unclear placement of modifying clauses. Sexist references have no place in legal writing, and can be eliminated by using plural forms, by using "he or she," or by alternating male and female pronouns. Misused words are common problems in legal writing. Pay close attention to your word choice in the assignments you prepare. Clichés and slang are overused or excessively informal usages, which are out of place in legal writing. A good writer makes sure verbs agree with their subjects, which requires a careful evaluation of which nouns constitute the subject and which perform some other function in the sentence. Never be redundant, since repetition can undercut, rather than emphasize, your strong points. Don't mistake verbosity for persuasive analysis; it is almost always better to keep your sentences short, your analysis brief, and your words simple.

Obscurity can often be cured simply by telling the reader what you are talking about. Use topic sentences and transitions to make your writing flow easily for the reader. Emphasize the active voice (in which the subject performs the action), but don't eliminate the passive voice entirely. It can be useful where the object of the action is the important point. Structured enumeration enables the reader to follow sequential points easily. Emphasize the strengths of your argument with positive language; deemphasize the weaknesses by stating them in a negative manner. Always be definitive.

Use the IRAC method as a foundation for logical development. State your strongest arguments first, and use chronological development, preliminary outlining, and explanatory subheadings as devices to improve the manner in which your document develops, so that the reader more easily grasps your arguments.

Almost no one gets writing right on the first try. Reread, edit, and revise until you are satisfied that your points have been presented in the best manner possible.

Key Terms

editing	clichés
brevity	slang
clarity	colloquialisms
precision	legal jargon
voice	redundancy
flow	verbosity
rhythm	topic sentence
parallel construction	transition
tone	periodic sentences
simile	cumulative sentences
metaphor	structured enumeration
ambiguity	outlining
pronoun ambiguity	subheadings
modifiers	

Review Questions

1. How can writing be made clear and precise?
2. What do rhythm, flow, and voice mean in the writing context?
3. How are similes and metaphors used?
4. How are ambiguity and redundancy avoided?
5. How are subjects and verbs made to agree?
6. Describe a simple method to eliminate obscurity in your writing.
7. Describe the difference between a periodic sentence and a cumulative sentence.
8. What type of language is inappropriate in a legal document?
9. What is structured enumeration?
10. How can arguments be logically developed?

Exercises

1. Rewrite the following passage from *Cooley v. Board of Wardens* (1851) using proper punctuation and plain English.

   That the power to regulate commerce includes the regulation of navigation, we consider settled. And when we look to the nature of the service performed by pilots, to the relations which that service and its compensations bear to navigation between the several States, and between the ports of the United States and foreign countries, we are brought to the conclusion, that the regulation of the qualifications of pilots, of the modes and times of offering and rendering their services, of the responsibilities which shall rest upon them, of the powers they shall possess, of the compensation they may demand, and of the penalties by which their rights and duties may be enforced, do constitute regulations of navigation, and consequently of commerce, within the just meaning of this clause of the Constitution.

2. Identify the trouble spots in sentence structure in the following passage from *Ranta v. McCarney* (North Dakota, 1986).

   We believe a fair reading of Section 27-1101 and *Christianson* indicate a preference by both the Legislature and our Court of furthering the strong policy consideration underlying the prohibition against the unauthorized practice of law that occurs in this State by barring compensation for any such activities.

3. Rewrite the following passage from *United States v. Nixon* (1974) by simplifying the sentences and word choice.

   [In this case] the traditional contempt avenue to immediate appeal is peculiarly inappropriate due to the unique setting in which the question arises. To require a President of the United States to place himself in the posture of disobeying an order of a court merely to trigger the procedural mechanism for review of the ruling would be unseemly, and would present an unnecessary occasion for constitutional confrontation between two branches of the Government. Similarly, a federal judge should not be placed in the posture of issuing a citation to a President simply in order to invoke the review. The issue whether a President can be cited for contempt could itself engender protracted litigation, and would further delay both review on the merits of his claim of privilege and the ultimate termination of the underlying criminal action for which his evidence is sought. These considerations lead us to conclude that the order of the District Court was an appealable order. The appeal from that order was therefore properly "in" the Court of Appeals, and the case is now properly before this Court on the writ of certiorari before judgment.

4. Revise the following sentences to be gender neutral:

   a. The judge handed down his decision in the case.

   b. When the attorney files his brief with the court, he must file stamp it.

   c. The spokesman for the paralegal association held a regional meeting in Washington, D.C.

   d. The award for fellowship was presented to the policemen's auxiliary foundation.

5. Identify the mistakes in the following paragraph:

I believe that the case completely represents the facts and circumstance that the employee violated the employment agreement. What the noncompete clause held was that the employee couldn't work in the industry for six months. Under the law and the cases at bar, the noncompetition agreement is binding and legal. In conclusion, I recommend completely to pursue all your available legal remedies including filing a lawsuit, request injunctive relief and ask for punitive damages.

6. Replace the following legal phrases with one word in plain English:

a. give, devise, and bequeath

b. each and every

c. indemnify and hold harmless

d. null and void

e. shall and will

7. Correct the following sentences:

a. The Chairman of the Board voted to terminate the contract by and between the contractor and the government of Florida.

b. Finding the legislation unconstitutional, the court ordered the lower court to act accordingly.

c. Don't send the correspondences out of the office until the corrections completely are made.

d. Who's case is that in the conference room scattered all over the table.

e. The messenger delivered the papers, filing the motions and was calling to confirm.

8. A colleague sends you the following e-mail:

The boss wants to have a meeting on the dead baby case.....again! He wants to talk about discovery and prepping for some depo's. When can you meet. I sure hope he doesn't want to meet on a Friday afternoon....I do have a life! So, let me know. Katy

Respond to the e-mail.

Portfolio Assignment

Your supervising attorney has a new client coming in tomorrow. Based upon a brief telephone conversation, she believes the client needs a will. Changes may have occurred in the statute. You receive the following e-mail from the attorney:

Michael,

I have a new client interview tomorrow at 4 p.m. I need you to provide me with an update on the requirements in a will. I think there was a recent change—three witnesses to two. Not sure, but research the legal requirements for wills and e-mail me back by noon tomorrow as to your results. Also, see if there are some updated forms which eliminate some of that awful legalese. Thanks for your help.

Your attorney has asked you to perform three tasks:
- research the legal requirements on wills in your jurisdiction;
- find updated examples of wills
- e-mail the findings back to the attorney.

Prepare the assignment based upon your jurisdiction's law.

Vocabulary Builder

Effective and Persuasive Legal Writing

```
S  G  N  I  D  A  E  H  B  U  S  E  J  U  B
G  F  S  D  L  P  Z  N  B  F  R  D  U  Z  W
L  J  B  K  G  N  Y  R  U  D  O  I  Z  E  I
W  E  T  M  G  B  E  P  Y  U  H  T  X  P  W
Y  U  G  Q  N  V  C  T  N  O  P  I  N  X  L
S  C  O  A  I  P  I  N  N  K  A  N  H  R  J
M  C  N  T  L  S  Z  R  L  Y  T  G  K  V  A
H  S  Y  A  O  E  I  J  S  I  E  B  W  F  B
I  X  I  B  D  D  S  V  C  E  M  Z  C  P  Y
W  F  R  X  D  N  S  E  H  C  I  L  C  R  W
U  E  V  W  E  T  U  Y  C  I  B  N  B  Z  Y
V  O  Z  Y  W  S  K  D  U  O  A  S  C  M  A
T  H  J  E  Z  M  G  C  E  V  R  L  H  N  E
O  U  T  L  I  N  I  N  G  R  X  P  Z  S  K
Q  G  Z  U  N  C  I  H  O  M  U  N  K  U  X
```

BREVITY	**CLICHES**	**EDITING**
LEGALESE	**METAPHORS**	**OUTLINING**
REDUNDANCY	**SEXISM**	**SUBHEADINGS**
VERBOSITY	**VOICE**	

Chapter 7

Citations in Legal Writing

Previous chapters discussed the basics of legal research and writing. Now you are ready to incorporate these concepts into your legal writing. After completing this chapter, you will be able to:

- Understand the differences between *The Bluebook* and *ALWD*.

- Create a proper citation.

- Define a string citation.

- Incorporate citations into legal writing.

- Learn the rules for citing quotations in a legal document.

- Use short form citations.

- Differentiate between the different signals.

- Use *id.* as a short form citation.

- Cite different types of secondary sources properly.

- Verify the accuracy of citations cited in legal documents.

Learning how to research and mastering grammar and punctuation are essential to legal writing. Throughout this text the consequences of poor writing and poor research have been emphasized. You should be wondering how to guard against the mistakes of others. How do I integrate my research into the legal document I prepare? How do I cite a case in a brief? Is there a short form for citing legal authority? How do I cite a quote? All these questions, and more, are answered in this chapter. But before those questions are addressed, some groundwork must be laid, and a foundation set, for understanding the world of legal citations.

Case Fact Pattern

Hypothetical 7-1

A deadline on a trial memorandum approaches. Your supervising attorney has most of the brief written, but just was called out of the office on a personal emergency. He asks you to complete the memorandum since you have worked closely with him on the case. At issue in the case is the interpretation of a statute. Your attorney has asked you to complete the research on the statutory interpretation, write the portion of the memorandum regarding that issue, and cite-check the remaining sections of the memorandum he completed. You only have three days to finish the assignment, which you know will be a challenge. You sit down at your desk, organize your thoughts, prepare a work plan, and begin the assignment.

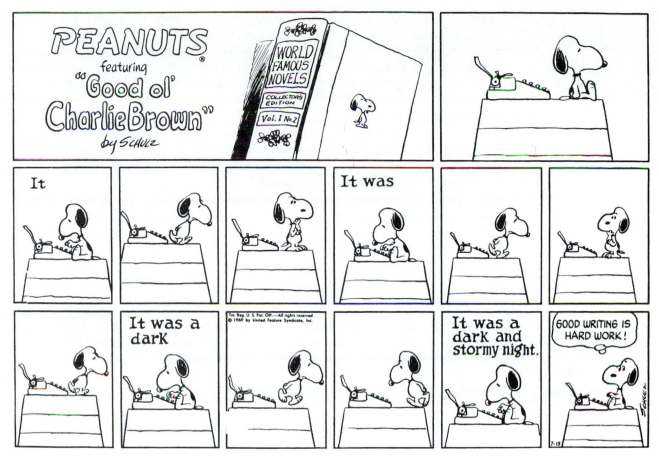

IN THE BEGINNING . . . *THE BLUEBOOK*

Remember we discussed *The Bluebook* in Chapter 1. Since 1926, *The Bluebook, A Uniform System of Citation* (18th ed. 2005) was *the* guide to citation form. It dominated the "world of citation form"—there was no other reference book. Albeit difficult and confusing to use, *The Bluebook* provides the accepted approach to citation form and format.

Every few years, *The Bluebook* publishes a new edition, changing, updating, and refining citation form. Sometimes the changes are helpful; other times not. In the sixteenth edition, the publishers changed the way to cite **signals.** Signals are words that introduce additional references to the legal authority cited. They are set off by words such as *see*, *see also*, and *accord*. Although the changes do not seem earth-shattering to the nonacademic community, in the legal academic community it was a significant change. Unfortunately, the victims of all these "academic" changes are often us—the paralegal and practicing attorney. When using *The Bluebook*, especially for the first time, peruse its sections. The preface is particularly significant as it identifies the changes in that edition. More often than not, the changes will not affect your work, but check to be sure. The *Bluebook* format has changed, for the better, with new user-friendly sections.

The new format is as follows:

signals

Words that introduce additional references to the legal authority cited, such as *see* and or *accord*.

- Quick Reference Guide: The front and back pages of *The Bluebook* provide a "quick reference" guide to citation form in law review footnotes, court documents, and legal memoranda. The back pages are helpful in the practice environment.

- Preface and Introduction: The Preface introduces the changes to that *Bluebook* edition. In the eighteenth edition, the significant change noted is the addition of a section entitled "Bluepages." This section is a practical guide for legal professionals. Another significant addition is the attention to local citation rules. Other changes are always noted in the preface of each edition. The Introduction defines the general content and structure of *The Bluebook*. This section discusses three major parts: the Bluepages, the *Bluebook* system of citation, and the tables to be used with the citation rules.

- Bluepages (new): This section of *The Bluebook* is the newest and is the one you will rely upon in preparing your citations. It is straightforward and geared toward the practicing attorney. The Bluepages section presents a detailed overview and guide for citing all types of legal authority. This section provides examples and discusses all aspects of legal citation. Jurisdiction-specific rules and general style rules of citation are highlighted as well. Take the time to review this section before beginning an assignment.

- Structure and Use of Citation: This section is the heart of *The Bluebook* and provides the rules for citing all legal authority. Printed in the white pages of *The Bluebook*, detailed explanations of the rules of citation and style from the general to the specific are provided. Some of the information is geared toward law review articles; therefore, be sure the form you are using is for the correct legal document.

- Tables: The section on tables is identified by its blue-bordered pages. The nuances of both federal and state jurisdiction citation rules are noted here along with corresponding websites. Also, included in this section are proper citation form for foreign jurisdictions, proper case name abbreviation, and periodical citation form.

- Index: At the end of *The Bluebook* is an extensive index to locate the information contained with *The Bluebook*. The index distinguishes the pages referenced by different colored ink: (1) black ink references instructions; (2) blue ink references examples.

The Bluebook remains the guide for legal citation, but lurching in the wings are challengers to the *Bluebook* rules and form. Publishers of *The Bluebook* never anticipated that the changes to the sixteenth edition would invite a response challenging its dominance.

THE YOUNG UPSTART: *ALWD CITATION MANUAL*

The year was 2000. The twentieth century was coming to a close; Y2K was everyone's fear; and, an academic rebellion began in the legal community regarding citation form—enter the *ALWD Manual: A Professional System of Citation* (3d ed. Aspen Publishers 2006). There are many commentaries hypothesizing what provoked the authors of the *ALWD Manual* to challenge *The Bluebook*. Some suggest the change in citing signals was the culprit; others suggest that the constant, often meritless, changes in form were the trigger. Whatever the reason, the *ALWD Manual* was a "wake-up" call that forced the *Bluebook* publishers to reevaluate their presentation and methodology of citation form. Suffice it to say, the *ALWD Manual* made citation form more accessible. What did *ALWD* accomplish? Simplicity. Directness. Approachability.

For the first time, *ALWD* communicated citation form in a clear, understandable manner. Complaints, from both practitioners and law students, continued because of the *Bluebook*'s difficulty. Tailored for the academician, *The Bluebook* met its challenger—a challenger like no other.

In the past, attempts were made to challenge the *Bluebook*'s authority without much success. (Ever hear of the Maroon book published by the University of Chicago? Probably not. That citation book found only a limited audience.) *ALWD* burst onto the legal market and has never looked back. Now in its third edition, *ALWD* is considered a more practical approach to citation form and a viable competitor for *The Bluebook*. *ALWD* introduces several new concepts:

- It explains citation form in everyday terminology.
- It gives examples of practical usage.
- It illustrates citation formats from all jurisdictions.
- It provides the practitioners' approach to citation form.

ALWD is divided into six parts and appendices, as follows:

- Part 1, Introductory Material: This section presents an overview of how to use the *ALWD Manual* and offers some practical word processing advice. Also provided in the introductory material is the organizational material within each part of the Manual and a note about local citation rules.

- Part 2, Citation Basics: Primarily the "how to" of legal citation, this section discusses typeface, abbreviations, and other technical components of a citation. Format and style components are also highlighted. Among the more significant features of *ALWD* are its Sidebar sections. This section reinforces important points made within the text and is a useful practice tool.

- Part 3, Citing Specific Print Sources: This section is the "guts" of the *ALWD Manual*. Continuing with the Sidebar references, this section also includes Fast Formats, which is a quick reference guide and summary of information contained within the subsection. Another important feature of the manual is its detail to punctuation and spacing within citations. Spaces are set off by a small, solid green triangle " ▲" and small, solid green circles "●" denote the specific citation component. Once again, spend time reviewing this section with its special features.

- Part 4, Electronic Sources: *ALWD* devotes an entire section to online and electronic citation formats. Citing Westlaw and LexisNexis is discussed along with other electronic and Internet sources. The Sidebar and Fast Formats are included as well.

- Part 5, Incorporating Citations into Documents: In this section, *ALWD* provides explanation of how to integrate citations into legal documents. This section presents the fundamentals of citation placement and use, offering helpful hints.

- Part 6, Quotations: Underscoring the importance of quotations, *ALWD* devotes an entire section to them. Considerable time is spent delineating the subtleties of using quotations in legal writing.

- Part 7, Appendices: Extensive coverage of all jurisdictional nuances from court rules to abbreviations is provided in this section. Review your jurisdiction's requirements. The treatment of the federal and state court rules is quite extensive.

- Index: The index references rule numbers, not pages. Common terms are used for easy access to the material within the text.

Review the structure of the *ALWD* before using it. Even though it is more user-friendly, *ALWD* will introduce you to an unfamiliar world and language. Take the time to carefully peruse the sections and pages for a better understanding of its contents.

THE COMPETITION

ALWD teaches citation form, whereas *The Bluebook* assumes a certain level of familiarity with citation form. The end result is that *ALWD* and *The Bluebook* should be used together and are not mutually exclusive. Some jurisdictions have adopted *ALWD;* others remain *Bluebook* loyalists. *ALWD* basically parallels the *Bluebook* form as much as possible unless "real life" practice dictates otherwise. For example, the first edition attempted to change the citation for the Southern Reporter from So. to S. Academic rebellion ensued. The second edition of *ALWD* reverted to the original form. The good news is that the *ALWD Manual*'s apparent wide acceptance forced the *Bluebook* publishers to revisit how they do things. As a result, the *Bluebook* is slowly becoming more accessible and more practice-driven.

The question on your mind should be "which form should I use?" The answer, as always, is "it depends." Your jurisdiction may dictate your format; your supervising attorney may dictate your format. Increasingly the *ALWD* is being taught in law schools and is being adopted by more and more jurisdictions. The *ALWD* website tracks the jurisdiction and law school adoptions. Visit the website at www.alwd.org. Also, visit the *Bluebook* website, www.legalbluebook.com, for helpful information as well. Additionally, there are differences between *The Bluebook* and *ALWD Manual*. Table 7.1 summarizes some of the noted differences.

THE OTHER GUIDES

neutral citation
Uniform citation system that contains the name of the case, year of decision, court (postal code) abbreviation, opinion number, and paragraph pinpoint for references.

There is a real upheaval in the world of citations. As mentioned in Chapter 1, the Universal Citation Guide is yet another citation form. Uniformity is the rule of the day and the American Bar Association (ABA) and American Association of Law Libraries (AALL) are leading the charge. They proposed a universal citation system or **neutral citation** system for adoption. This format departs from both the *Bluebook* and *ALWD* dramatically and is slowly being adopted by some jurisdictions. Approximately ten states, including Maine, Vermont, and Montana, have adopted a neutral citation system. But be careful as adoption by a state court does not signify that the federal courts of the state adopted the neutral citation system as well. For example, the state of Montana adopted a neutral citation system whereas the Montana federal court system uses the *Bluebook* rules.

Characteristics of the universal citation system are as follows:

1. The name of the case

TABLE 7.1
Differences between
The Bluebook and
ALWD Manual

Citation Format Topic	Bluebook	ALWD Manual
United States as a party	Cite as United States (do not abbreviate)	Cite as U.S. (abbreviation accepted)
Use of apostrophes in abbreviation of names	Use apostrophes in name abbreviations: Int'l Gov't	Do not use apostrophes in name abbreviations: Intl Govt
Pinpoint citation	Use only the last two numbers of a reference Pages 100-03	Use either the last two numbers of a referenced number Pages 100-03 or 100-103
Quotations	More than 50 words, single-space and indent.	More than 50 words or more than four lines. single space and indent.
Parallel citations for U.S. Supreme Court	Do not cite parallel citations for U.S. Supreme Court cases	Permits parallel citations for U.S. Supreme Court cases
Information in parentheses for state courts	Provides different information for courts at the appeals level	Provides different information for courts at the appeals level

2. The year of the decision

3. The court abbreviation (The abbreviation for the state is the name as it appears in its postal [U.S. mail] abbreviation. For lower courts, it is the postal abbreviation along with an additional identifier.)

4. A sequentially assigned opinion number

5. A notation of the letter "U," if an opinion is unpublished or unreported

6. A paragraph number to identify quoted material (This rule is a major departure from present practice. Citation rules require the page number of the quoted material only.)

Will the universal citation concept be the rule and not the exception? Only time will tell. Check your jurisdiction to determine whether the universal system is adopted. A citation in the universal (neutral) format is shown in the following example:

> Neutral: *Glidden v. Conley,* 2003 VT 12

(Notice the case pages from *Glidden v. Conley* in Figure 7.1. The paragraphs are individually numbered. This corresponds to the neutral citation system format.)

The same citation in *Bluebook* and *ALWD* format is as follows:

> *Glidden v. Conley,* 2003 VT 12, 820 A.2d 197

And finally, some states have citation and style guides. Texas and California are most notable. They have their own system of citing cases. Many jurisdictions have their own style requirements: Oregon does not place a period after citing their official reporter (Or rather than Or.); Arizona deviates from basic citation form when citing their statutes using West (Publishing); New York cites more specific court information than the *Bluebook* dictates. Check and confirm the citation rules in your jurisdiction; usually these rules are listed in the local rules of court. Most experienced attorneys will know their jurisdictional requirements, but if preparing a legal document for an unfamiliar jurisdiction, do your homework and verify the proper citation form.

The remainder of this chapter will guide you through the process of incorporating citations into your legal writing and erase some of the mystery. Citation format is a learned skill; it is not mastered overnight and takes time to reach a comfort level. Don't get frustrated. Remember, we all began somewhere! Let's start with the basics of legal citation.

FIGURE 7.1   **Pages from a Case with a Neutral Citation System**

Source: From *Atlantic Digest, 2nd Series*. Reprinted with permission from Thomson West.

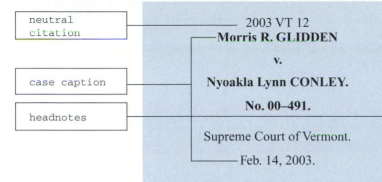

neutral citation

case caption

headnotes

2003 VT 12

Morris R. GLIDDEN

v.

Nyoakla Lynn CONLEY.

No. 00–491.

Supreme Court of Vermont.

Feb. 14, 2003.

Maternal grandmother filed request for visitation. The Windham Family Court, Mary Miles Teachout, J., granted temporary visitation and subsequently denied father's motion for reconsideration of visitation award. Father appealed. The Supreme Court. Skoglund, J., held that: (1) statutory provision governing grandparent visitation was not in violation of a parent's due process rights by not having any absence or consideration to a parent's decision regarding child-grandparent contact, and (2) trial court, in applying statutory provision governing grandparent visitation, impermissibly infringed on father's right to decide what visitation was

in his child's best interests by not giving due deference to father's decision regarding grandparent-child contact, and this violated father's right to due process.

Reversed.

1. Child Custody ⬅➡**921(3)**

An appellate court reviews an order granting visitation to determine whether the court exercised its discretion on grounds that are clearly unreasonable or untenable.

2. Constitutional Law ⬅➡**48(1)**

When considering the constitutionality of a statute, a court begins by presuming that the legislative enactment is constitutional.

3. Constitutional Law ⬅➡**48(1)**

In the absence of clear and irrefragable evidence that a statute infringes the paramount law, a court will not strike down a statute as unconstitutional.

4. Constitutional Law ⬅➡**48(1)**

If a court can construe the statute in a manner that meets constitutional requirements, it will do so unless the statute's plain language precludes it. [text omitted]

paragraph number for neutral citation

headnote

[1–4]. ¶-11. We review an order granting visitation to determine whether the court exercised its discretion on grounds that are clearly unreasonable or untenable. *Cleverly v. Cleverly*, 151 Vt. 351, 355–56, 561 A.2d.99, 102 (1989). When considering the constitutionality of a statute we begin by presuming that the legislative enactment is constitutional. *In re Proceedings Concerning a Neglected Child*, 129 Vt. 234, 240–41, 276 A.2d 14, 18 (1971). In the absence of "clear and irrefragable evidence that [the statute] infringes the paramount law," we will not strike down a statute as unconstitutional. *Id.* Moreover, if we can construe the statute in a manner that meets constitutional requirements, we will do so unless the statute's plain language precludes it. *In re Montpelier & Barre R.R.* 135 Vt. 102, 103–04, 369 A.2d 1379, 1380 (1977). Therefore, we examine Vermont's grandparent visitation statute in the context of the visitation order at issue in this appeal to determine whether the court abused its discretion by applying the statute in a manner that infringes on Glidden's right to raise Amanda without interference by the state.

[5–8] ¶-12. The United States Supreme Court has "long recognized that freedom

of personal choice in matters of marriage and family life is one of the liberties protected by the Due Process Clause of the Fourteenth Amendment." *Cleveland Bd. of Educ. v. LaFleur,* 414 U.S. 632, 639–40, 94 S.Ct. 791, 39 L.Ed.2d 52 (1974). The interest of a parent in the custody, care, and control of his child may be the oldest of the fundamental liberty interests our federal constitution protects. *Troxel,* 530 U.S. at 65, 120 S.Ct. 2054; *In re S.B.L.,* 150 Vt. 294, 303, 553 A.2d 1078, 1084 (1988). The state must generally show a compelling interest "before it encroaches upon the private realm of family life." *In re Proceedings Concerning a Neglected Child,* 130 Vt. 525, 530, 296 A.2d 250, 253 (1972). Indeed, there is a "presumption that fit parents act in the best interests of their children." *Troxel,* 530 U.S. at 68, 120 S.Ct. 2054. "[S]o long as a parent adequately cares for his or her children (i.e., is fit), there will normally, be no reason for the State to inject itself into the private realm of the family to further question the ability of that parent to make the best decisions concerning the rearing of that parent's children." *Id.* at 68–69, 120 S.Ct. 2054. [text omitted]

THE BASIC CITATION FORM

In Chapter 1, a citation to a U.S. Supreme Court case was illustrated. A quick refresher is warranted. A citation consists of the name of the case, the volume where the case is located, the name of the reporter, the page where the case begins, and the date the case was decided. Those are the basics. But, more information is needed to understand proper citation form completely. Let's focus on the technical and practical information of a case citation and build on the example:

> *PGA Tour, Inc. v. Martin*, 532 U.S. 661 (2001)

- Name of the case: The name of the case is either underlined or italicized. After the first name of the case, there is a space, followed by a "v" (standing for versus) with a period. Then add in another space followed by the second named party in the case, followed by a comma.

> *PGA Tour, Inc. v. Martin,*

- Reporter: After the comma in the name, the reporter designation appears. Add a space after the comma, followed by the volume of the reporter, a space, the name of the reporter, a space, and the page number where the case begins:

> *PGA Tour, Inc. v. Martin*, 532 U.S. 661

- Year of the case: The last component is the year the case was decided. After the page where the case begins, there is a space followed by a parenthesis, the year, and a closing parenthesis. There are no spaces when only the year appears in the parenthetical.

> *PGA Tour, Inc. v. Martin*, 532 U.S. 661 (2001)

Cite only to the official reporter unless directed otherwise by a court or your supervising attorney. However, let's add the **parallel citation** for form purposes.

> *PGA Tour, Inc. v. Martin*, 532 U.S. 661, 121 S.Ct. 1879, 149 L. Ed. 2d 904 (2001) When adding the parallel citations, a comma is inserted between the citations, followed by a space, then the parallel citation.

- When a reporter is in its second series or beyond, the series number is placed after the reporter *without* a space followed by the series abbreviation, such as 2d (second series), 3d (third series), or 4th (fourth series).

You must be wondering why so much emphasis is placed on spacing, commas, and periods in the citation. Correct spacing and punctuation are as important to the citation form as in a sentence or paragraph. Although a seemingly small detail, incorrect spacing equals sloppiness. Here's how the citation looks when improperly prepared:

> *PGA Tour, Inc. v. Martin*, 532US661 121SCt1879 149LEd2d904(2001)

The citation looks awful and unprofessional. Take pride in your work product and pay close attention to the details of your citation format.

RECENT CASE DECISIONS

parallel citation
A citation for the same case in a different unofficial reporter.

Although decisions from unofficial reporters are published quickly, the official reporter text lags behind. When the official reporter is unavailable, use blank lines to delineate its absence followed by the name of the official reporter. For example:

> *Metro-Goldwyn-Metro v. Grokster Ltd.*, ___U.S. ___, 125 S.Ct. 2764, 162 L. Ed. 2d 781 (2005)

SUBSEQUENT HISTORY OF A CASE

subsequent history
History of a case on appeal.

Cases proceed through an appellate process. Cases are appealed to a higher court for review; ultimately these cases are accepted or denied review by an appellate court. When a case opinion is issued *after* a previous one, this is known as a **subsequent history.** Include a subsequent history in your case citation. For example:

> *Hale v. Scott*, 252 F. Supp. 2d 728, *aff'd*, 371 F.3d 917 (7th Cir. 2003)

TABLE 7.2
Selected Subsequent
History Notations

affirmed	aff'd
affirmed in part, reversed in part	aff'd in part and rev'd in part
certiorari denied	cert. denied
reversed	rev'd
reversed in part on other grounds	rev'd in part on other grounds
vacated	vacated

writ of *certiorari*
Request for appeal where the court has the discretion to grant or deny it; granting of petition, by the U.S. Supreme court, to review a case.

The exception is a **writ of *certiorari*.** Parties may petition a court of last resort, such as the U.S. Supreme Court, to hear their case. A Petition for Writ of *Certiorari* is filed. The writ of *certiorari* allows the Court the discretion to accept (grant) a case on appeal or reject (deny) it. Citation rules from the *Bluebook* 10.7 and *ALWD* 12 (8)(a) state that a denial of a writ of *certiorari* should be cited in the case history two years or less after the denial of the *certiorari;* or add the history when a case is particularly relevant to your case discussion. Table 7.2 identifies selected subsequent history notations.

The subsequent history is placed after the lower court decision, italicized, and followed by the higher court case citation. An example of two cases with a subsequent history is

> *Cox v. Barber*, 275 Ga. 415, 568 S.E.2d 478, *cert. denied*, 537 U.S. 1109, 123 S.Ct. 851, 154 L. Ed. 2d 780 (2003)
> *Brett v. Jefferson County, Ga.*, 925 F. Supp. 786, *aff'd in part, vacated in part*, 123 F.3d 1429 (11th Cir. 1997)

STATE SUBSEQUENT HISTORY GUIDES

A number of states, such as Texas and California, have separate subsequent history table guides. The subsequent histories are required as part of their citations. In Texas, a case citation with a subsequent history or, as it is more commonly known, a "writ history," is illustrated in the following example:

> *AMR Corp. v. Enlow*, 926 S.W.2d 640 (Tex.App. - Fort Worth 1996, no writ)

Check your jurisdiction to determine the rules for citing a subsequent history of a case.

FEDERAL REPORTERS

**PRACTICE
TIP**

Many attorneys disagree with *The Bluebook* and *ALWD* on when to cite "cert. denied" cases. Most believe a notation of "cert. denied" is important because it indicates the decision of the lower court is final. This point is significant. Check with your supervising attorney on their practice. When in doubt, cite the "cert. denied" subsequent history to be safe.

Recall there are three main federal reporters: the *Federal Reporter, Federal Supplement*, and *Federal Rules Decision*. Citing these reporters is relatively straightforward.

The *Federal Reporter*

The *Federal Reporter* publishes cases from the circuit courts of appeals. (Refer to Figure 1.4 for the U.S. circuit courts of appeals). The reporter citations are: F., F.2d, and F.3d. Along with the name of the case, the reporter, volume, page, and date of the case, include the name of the circuit court of appeals in the parenthetical.

> *Hargis v. Foster*, 312 F.3d 404 (9th Cir. 2002)

The spacing in the parenthetical is:

> (9th Cir. 2002)

There are no spaces between the numbered circuit and the first parentheses. Place a space between the numbered circuit and the abbreviation for the word circuit: Cir. Then add another space followed by the date the case was decided and a closing parenthesis without a space.

The *Federal Supplement*

The *Federal Supplement* publishes cases from the United States District Courts. (Refer to Figure 1.4 in Chapter 1 for the district courts. Presently, the *Federal Supplement* has two series: F. Supp. and F. Supp. 2d. When citing to the *Federal Supplement*, include the district and state of the decision along with the date the case was decided in the parenthetical. The abbreviations of the federal trial courts are as follows:

- N.D.: northern district

- S.D.: southern district

- E.D. : eastern district
- W.D.: western district
- M.D.: middle district
- C.D.: central district
- D.: district (Use this notation for states with only one district court, such as New Jersey, Kansas, and Utah.)

An example of a citation from the *Federal Supplement* is

> Philadelphia Gear Corp. v. Swath Int'l, Ltd., 200 F. Supp.2d 493 (E.D. Pa. 2000)—*Bluebook* form;
> Philadelphia Gear Corp. v. Swath Intl, Ltd, 200 F. Supp.2d 493 (E.D. Pa. 2000)—*ALWD* form.

(Recall there is a difference in the way the respective citation manuals treat abbreviations: *Bluebook* uses apostrophes and periods and the *ALWD Manual* does not.)

In the parenthetical include the district court, the state and date of the decision. Additionally, the order in the parenthetical is

1. parenthesis, no space;
2. district court designation followed by a period and space;
3. the state of the case decision followed by a period and space; and
4. the date of the case decision, no space, followed by a parenthesis.

Federal Rules Decision

Federal Rules Decision publishes cases from the federal district courts on matters involving procedure and evidence. Similar to the *Federal Supplement*, include the district court, state, and date of the decision in the parentheses.

> *Taylor v. Belger Cartage Service, Inc.*, 102 F.R.D. 172 (W.D. Mo. 1984)

Federal Appendix: A New Reporter

A recent addition in 2001 to the federal reporter system is the *Federal Appendix*. This reporter publishes unreported and **unpublished cases** from many jurisdictions. It is cited as Fed. Appx. Be very cautious in using, and even more cautious in citing, this reporter. A number of jurisdictions, such as the fifth and third circuits, forbid citing to unpublished decisions. Mention of this reporter is mainly as an "FYI" (for your information), but do not ever cite to this reporter without alerting your supervising attorney. In fact, many law libraries do not subscribe to this reporter. Consider that a strong warning as to its usefulness. A sample citation to this reporter is

> *Jackson v. Secretary of U.S. Treasury*, 141 Fed. Appx. (2d Cir. 2005) (unpublished)

Notice that the end of the citation adds a parenthetical with the word "unpublished." This notation is required in the citation. Unpublished cases are not selected by a court for publication. They are cases with no new precedential value or cases particular to the parties. When a decision is selected for publication, it is noted on the decision.

CITING STATUTES

As with cases, statutes have official and unofficial publications. Always cite the official version of federal statutes, which is the U.S. Code. Include in the citation the following information:

- The title number, followed by a space
- The statutory code, such as the U.S. Code, followed by a space
- The section sign, which is identified by the section "§" symbol, no space, and the numbered code section, then a space
- The year the code was published in parentheses

For example:

> 42 U.S.C. §1983 (2000)

Do not cite the unofficial codes, such as United States Code Annotated and United States Code Service. If the section you need to cite is unavailable in the official code, cite the unofficial code as follows:

> 42 U.S.C.A. §1983 (West 2005)
> Title, code, section (publisher and date)

Citing state statutes varies. Some states cite to a title and section; others cite to named codes such as California, Texas, and New York.

> Cal. Civ. Pro. Code Ann. § 977 (West 2000)
> Tex. Bus. & Com. Code Ann. § 17.50 (Vernon 2005 Supp.)

Check your jurisdiction for your state's requirements.

ADMINISTRATIVE RULES AND REGULATIONS

Administrative rules and regulations are located in the Code of Federal Regulations (CFR) and the *Federal Register* (Fed. Reg.).

Code of Federal Regulations

Similar to the United States Code, CFR citations include

- the title of the code, followed by a space;
- the Code (CFR) followed by a space;
- the section and chapter of the regulation followed by a space; and
- the date (of the most current edition) in the parenthetical.

An example of a CFR citation is

> 47 C.F.R. §1.333 (2005)

Federal Register

The *Federal Register* contains proposed and final federal rules and regulations, notices, presidential proclamations, and orders. When citing the *Federal Register,* identify the volume number, the *Federal Register,* the page where the material appears, and the date. (Note: The *Federal Register* is printed daily. Indicate the month, day, and year of the cited volume for clarity.) Here is an example:

> 71 Fed. Reg. 17774 (April 7, 2006)

THE CONSTITUTION AND COURT RULES

Constitutions

The U.S. Constitution is cited by identifying the name of the constitution and the article or amendment followed by the specific referenced section. The following is an example of a cite for the U.S. Constitution:

> U.S. Const. art. III, §2
> U.S. Const. amend. V

Do not cite a date at the end of the reference.
State constitutions follow the same format as well. The following is an example of a state constitution citation:

> TEX. CONST. art. I, § 13

Court Rules

Citations for court rules contain the rule (or code abbreviation) and the rule number, for example:

> Fed. R.Civ.P. 56(c)
> Fed. R. Evid. 801

SECONDARY SOURCES

Unless you are dealing with a scholarly source, resist citing to a secondary source. Use secondary sources as a legal research tool and seek the primary source material. However, proper citation form for secondary sources is important. The most cited secondary sources are legal treatises. Other secondary sources are books, restatements, law reviews, attorney general opinions, *A.L.R.* annotations, and legal dictionaries. Cite secondary sources as shown in the following examples.

Legal treatises and books are cited similarly. Include the following:

- Name of the author
- Name of the publication
- The edition of the publication
- Publisher (if following *ALWD* format)
- Date of publication in parentheses

If you are citing a specific page or section, identify the exact location in the book or treatise where the material is located. An example follows:

> John D. Calamari and Joseph M. Perillo, *The Law of Contracts* (5th ed. 2003)
> John D. Calamari and Joseph M. Perillo, *The Law of Contracts* (5th ed. West 2003)

Restatements

The *Restatements* are a compilation of the common law. There is a slight difference between *The Bluebook* and *ALWD*. *ALWD* italicizes the name of the *Restatements*; the *Bluebook* does not.

> *Bluebook:* Restatement (Second) of Contracts § 90 (1981)
> *ALWD: Restatement* (Second) of Contracts § 90 (1981)

Law Reviews

Law review citations include

- name of author of article;
- title of article;
- volume of law review journal;
- name of law review journal;
- page of article in journal; and
- year of journal publication

Robert D. Bills, *Plagiarism in Law Schools: Close Resemblance of the Worst Kind?*, 31 Santa Clara L. Rev. 103 (1990)

Attorney General Opinions

Attorney General opinions are legal opinions issued by an attorney general of a state or the federal government. These opinions represent questions of law usually requested by the different departments or agencies within that state. Opinions are normally state specific and have limited legal authority. An Attorney General Opinion is cited as follows:

> Op. Atty. Gen. Fla. 2006–09 (2006)

A.L.R. Annotations

American Law Reports cites both cases and articles. When citing an *A.L.R.* article identify

- The author's name
- Annotation title
- Volume number
- *A.L.R.* Series
- Page number where article begins
- Date of article

Benjamin J. Vernia, *State and Local Governmental Liability for Injury or Death of Bicyclist Due to Defect for Obstruction in Public Roadway or Sidewalk,* 12 A.L.R. 6th 645 (2006)

Legal Dictionaries

The basic components for citing a legal dictionary are

- name of the dictionary;
- page of the definition;
- edition; and
- year of publication

> *Bluebook: Black's Law Dictionary* 680 (8th ed. 2004)

The *ALWD Manual* adds two more components:

- The name of the editor
- The publisher

> *ALWD: Black's Law Dictionary* 680 (Bryan A. Gardner ed., 8th ed., West 2004).

INCORPORATING CITATIONS INTO LEGAL WRITING

Using citations in legal writing is necessary for paralegals and attorneys. Ordinarily, reference material is tucked away in a footnote or at the end in a bibliography. The way you prepared papers in high school or college is not sufficient in the legal setting. The first request is to throw all those preconceived notions of how to do things out the window. The second request is patience. You will learn the way attorneys prepare a document and understand all those subtleties. The third request is: relax. It seems overwhelming at first, but you *will* master citations and before you know it, your attorney will be asking you how to cite a case. And the final request: read the first three requests again. Everything takes time. Learn one skill at a time and build on those skills. Do not be afraid to look something up in *The Bluebook* or *ALWD Manual.* We all do it.

Citations in Sentences

Let's build on one sentence. The facts surrounding the sentence involve legislative intent. How does a court interpret a statute and determine the legislative intent when the statute is ambiguous? The sentence in your legal document is as follows:

> When interpreting a statute, the court should give effect to the intent of the Legislature as expressed in the statute and begin an interpretation with the statute's language. *Barnhart v. Sigmon Coal Co., Inc.,* 534 U.S. 438 (2002).

The statement requires a legal source to support the legal proposition. You add the case citation directly into the body of the sentence. Notice the case is cited at the end of the statement. When citing a case at the end of a legal proposition, the case citation is an independent sentence, ending with a period. The sentence can be reworded to have the citation introduce the proposition.

You Be the Judge   Hypothetical 7-2

Attorneys cite cases to support their legal positions. There is an obligation to properly cite as well as to verify the authorities cited. When attorneys blatantly ignore the law or fail to make reasonable inquiry as to the status of the law, wasting both the court and opposing counsel's time, courts have something to say. The attorneys in *Smith v. United Transportation Union Local No. 81,* 594 F. Supp. 96 (1984) made the mistake of misleading a district court judge in California, which cost them financially. Review the *Smith* case. What are the facts of the case? What points of law did the attorneys fail to bring to the court's attention? What remedy did the court impose on the attorneys for their misrepresentation of the legal authorities? Undoubtedly, presentation, both oral and written, is essential when appearing before a court.

> In *Barnhart v. Sigmon Coal Co., Inc.,* 534 U.S. 438 (2002), the court observed that when inter-preting a statute the court should give effect to the intent of the Legislature as expressed in the statute and begin an interpretation with the statute's language.

embedded citation
A citation placed within a sentence.

In the second example, the case is part of the sentence and the entire citation is immersed, or as some refer to it, as an **embedded citation** in the sentence. Which form is correct? It is a matter of preference. Both are correct, although the first sentence is less intrusive. Use placement varia-tions to add sentence variety and minimize monotony.

Continuing with the same example, now let's break up the citation in the sentence.

> In *Barnhart v. Sigmon Coal Co., Inc.,* the court observed that when interpreting a statute the court should give effect to the intent of the Legislature as expressed in the statute and begin an interpre-tation with the statute's language. 534 U.S. 438 (2002).

Since the citation is close to the case reference, it is proper form to split the citation in two. The key here is that the sentence should not be too long and there should be close proximity between the name of the case and the citation. Again, notice how the citation is considered a sentence ending with a period.

A Shortcut: *Id.* and *Supra*

id.
The same.

Using the same example from the previous section, let's assume you cite a proposition from the same case in the next sentence. Do you need to repeat the full citation? No. Use the notation *id.* *Id.* means the same. You have just learned your first **short citation form.** A short citation form is used *only* after you have cited your legal authority completely once. There are different variations of short forms for citations. For example:

short citation form
Citation used after the complete citation is used in the legal document.

- *Barnhart,* 534 U.S. at 450. If you cited Barnhart completely once and need to reference it again later in the documents, cite the first name of the case followed by the volume and reporter, then the word "at" followed by the exact page reference to the material in the case. This page reference is known as a pinpoint reference or **pinpoint cite** or **pincite.** Pinpoint citations direct the reader to the exact page where your material appears. This concept will be discussed as well in the section on quotations. Use the first name of the case, unless this causes confusion or is a government, United States; or a state, such as Indiana; or where the notation State or People is used to designate the state. In those instances, use the second name.

pinpoint cite (pincite)
The page reference in a citation that directs the reader to the cited material in a case. Also known as jump site.

- *Barnhart,* 534 U.S. 438. Use this reference if you are referring generally to the case.
- *Barnhart,* at 534 U.S. at 450, 122 S.Ct. at 950, 151 L. Ed. 2d at 920 Use this shorthand refer-ence when parallel citations are required. Some jurisdictions may allow citing to the regional reporter only if a state case is involved. Check with your jurisdiction's local rules.
- *Barnhart v. Sigmon Coal Co., Inc.,* 534 U.S. at 450. A longer version of the first example, but acceptable short form.
- 534 U.S. at 450. If you choose this reference, be sure the original citation is close. This reference forces the reader to search the text for the name of the case.

In review, you must cite a full citation before you resort to a short citation form. Remember what you are trying to accomplish: effectively communicating your supporting legal authority to the reader. Ask yourself, "Will the reader understand where the source of information originated?" "Have I supplied sufficient information for the reader to locate the legal source cited?" Our new example follows:

> In *Barnhart v. Sigmon Coal Co., Inc.,* 534 U.S. 438 (2002), the court observed when interpreting a statute the court should give effect to the intent of the Legislature as expressed in the statute and begin an interpretation with the statute's language. The Court also must determine whether the language is plain and unambiguous. *Id.*

However, you cannot use *id.* if there is an intervening case citation.

Although there is a short form citation when a legal source intervenes between another cited source, *supra* (supra means *above*), this short form should not be used in court documents. Note that *supra* is used in cases by judges when referring to previously cited cases. However, both

supra
Above

the *Bluebook* and *ALWD* advise against using *supra* in formal legal writing, specifically when citing cases, statutes and other legislative related material, constitutions and administrative rules and regulations—the basic primary source material. Whether to use this format is one of those instances where asking your supervising attorney is appropriate. If you use *supra*, use the name of the case, followed by *supra* and the page of your reference. The better approach is a short form citation. For example:

> In *Barnhart v. Sigmon Coal Co., Inc.,* 534 U.S. 438 (2002), the court observed when interpreting a statute the court should give effect to the intent of the Legislature as expressed in the statute and begin an interpretation with the statute's language. The Court also must determine whether the language is plain and unambiguous. *Id.* If the language is plain and unambiguous, the language of the statute is conclusive. *Consumer Product Safety Commission v. GTE Sylvania, Inc.,* 447 U.S. 102 (1980). Therefore, the first step in a statutory construction case is determining the meaning of the language. *Barnhart,* at 450.

String Citing

Suppose more than one case supports your legal point. If you want to communicate to the court that this legal point is well settled, or you want to argue a change in the jurisdiction's position and you need to show all the other jurisdictions that followed the legal position you are presenting, you can use more than one case to illustrate your legal point. This technique is referred to as **string citing.** String citing uses a list of cases to support a legal position. When string citing, separate each case by a semicolon and end the citation string with a period, just like a sentence. Although not improper, string citing is not encouraged. Use the best legal authority which stands for your proposition. Remember, often courts place page limitations on court papers and briefs. Do not waste precious space by restating a point of law by string citing. Say what you have to say and move on! The next example uses string cites to support the legal position from our continuing example:

string citation
List of cases cited in a legal document to illustrate a legal position.

> When interpreting a statute, the court should give effect to the intent of the Legislature as expressed in the statute and begin an interpretation with the statute's language. *Barnhart v. Sigmon Coal Co., Inc.,* 534 U.S. 438 (2002); *Duncan v. Walker,* 533 U.S. 167 (2001); *Reves v. Ernest & Young,* 507 U.S. 170 (1993); *Mallard v. U.S. District Court of Southern District of Iowa,* 490 U.S. 296 (1989).

If you intend to string-cite cases, there is an order of presentation. Use the following as a guide:

- United States Supreme Court: Cases always are cited first in reverse chronological order. That means from the newest to the oldest.
- Federal Circuit Courts of Appeals: These cases are cited next, newest to oldest cases.
- Federal District Court: Cases from this court are cited after the federal circuit court of appeals, newest to oldest cases.
- State cases: The last group to cite in a string cite are state cases. Always cite from the state's highest court, newest to oldest, followed by the next level of state court.

SIGNALS IN LEGAL WRITING

A signal indicates additional information on a subject or particular point cited in the legal document. They can be explanatory, comparative, or informational. Use signals when you are emphasizing a point and not as a method to pepper the legal document with more legal authorities; use signals sparingly but wisely. Signals can have a dramatic effect as they tell the reader you intend to address a significant point. *They are always in italics.* Although there are a number of signals, the most common are as follows:

- *E.g.:* This signal means "for example" and indicates additional authority on the same legal point. This signal represents only some of the legal authorities and is not exhaustive. It is quite common and can be paired with other signals, such as *see* and *generally*.
- *See:* Use *see* when other cases support your legal proposition. This signal indicates that the accompanying cases or authority directly support your statement.

- *See also:* Similar to the signal *see*, but the legal authority, although strong, is not as directly supportive as cases used in with the signal *see*.

- *Compare:* This signal is used for a specific purpose. When you compare legal authorities you may want your reader to understand the distinctions and different results from other jurisdictions.

- *See generally:* Use this signal when you are referencing helpful background information. This signal will assist your reader in gaining a better understanding of the legal proposition you are presenting.

- *Accord:* This signal is used to show support from other jurisdictions of your legal proposition. It also is used when you are quoting a text and to show additional support for your proposition.

Signals are used to begin an independent citation sentence. Use a capital letter if the signal begins your citation sentence. Using our example, an introductory signal is added to the string cite example:

> When interpreting a statute, the court should give effect to the intent of the Legislature as expressed in the statute and begin an interpretation with the statute's language. *Barnhart v. Sigmon Coal Co., Inc.,* 534 U.S. 438 (2002). *See also, Duncan v. Walker,* 533 U.S. 167 (2001); *Reves v. Ernest & Young,* 507 U.S. 170 (1993); *Mallard v. U.S. District Court of Southern District of Iowa,* 490 U.S. 296 (1989).

QUOTATIONS IN LEGAL WRITING

Quotations are commonly used in legal writing. By definition, quotations indicate a reference to a source other than your own and must be attributed to the source or author. Recall the last chapter's discussion on plagiarism; here is your opportunity to guard against plagiarism allegations by learning how to properly identify the material. You may wonder, when do I use a quote, when do I use a general reference, and when are citations or quotations unnecessary? A law review article, *Plagiarism in Law School: Close Resemblance of the Worst Kind?*, sets forth six basic rules to live by:

1. *Cite sources for all direct quotations.* Think of it as copying. You would never consider copying a source without giving credit to the source. No exception exists to this rule.

2. *Cite sources from which language, facts, or ideas have been paraphrased or summarized.* In the examples for using a citation in a sentence, the information was paraphrased, but the court decision was credited for the point of law.

3. *Cite sources for idea(s) or information that could be regarded as common knowledge, but which (a) was not known to the writer before encountering it in a particular source, or (b) the reader might find unfamiliar.* This rule is less definitive, especially given that virtually everything will be a new idea for you in researching the law. If the proposition cited is a general legal point, use a citation. When in doubt, cite a legal source.

4. *Cite sources that add relevant information to the particular topic or argument.* This is the footnote rule. Rather than include explanatory sources in the body of the document, footnote the information. You may also use a parenthetical to introduce the information. The point is to cite a legal source.

5. *Cite sources from and for other kinds of specialized materials.* This rule is limited and focuses on letters and interviews.

6. *Cite sources relied upon for authority to support any legal proposition or rule.* The rule means "when in doubt, use a legal source to support your point." Of course, your work will include many legal sources. It is expected in the legal arena.

Robert D. Bills, *Plagiarism in Law School: Close Resemblance of the Worst Kind?*, 31 Santa Clara L. Rev. 103, 123-30(1990).

These rules are a guide in helping you know when, or when not, to quote or use a legal citation reference in your legal writing.

Returning to the issue of quotations, let's start with two basic rules:

1. Any quote over fifty words is single-spaced and indented into a block, known as a **block quote.** *Do not use quotation marks at the beginning and end of a block quote.* This bears repeating. *Do not use quotation marks at the beginning and end of a block quote.*

2. A quote of 50 words or less is kept within the text and *identified with quotation marks*.

Whether you quote within a paragraph using quotation marks or a block quote, the message is to credit the authority cited.

Let's assume certain facts. A golfer who has a walking disability petitions the PGA Tour to use a golf cart rather than walk the tournament as required by the rules. The golfer, Casey Martin, files a lawsuit based upon the American with Disabilities Act (ADA) in that banning the golf cart violates his rights. The U.S. Supreme Court agreed. Using *PGA Tour, Inc. v. Martin,* 532 U.S. 661 (2001), you will learn how to cite a quote in a legal document. You want to quote verbatim a passage from the case. First, you want to introduce the quote with a lead-in sentence. Do not simply state your quote without any connecting or introductory sentence. Remember in previous chapters we discussed transitions; this area is one of those instances when you should use them. This rule applies to quotations.

PRACTICE TIP

ALWD also permits a quote of four lines or less to be embedded in the paragraph using quotation marks. This alleviates the counting method.

Example 7.1

The U.S. Supreme Court in its *dicta* observed:

> The purpose of the walking rule is therefore not compromised in the slightest by allowing Martin to use a cart. A modification that provides an exception to a peripheral tournament rule without impairing its purpose cannot be said to "fundamentally alter" the tournament. What it can be said to do, on the other hand, is to allow Martin the chance to qualify for, and compete in, the athletic events petitioner offers to those members to enter. That is exactly what the ADA requires.

PGA Tour, Inc. v. Martin, 532 U.S. 661, 690 (2001)

Example 7.2

The U.S. Supreme Court in its *dicta* observed:

> The purpose of the walking rule is therefore not compromised in the slightest by allowing Martin to use a cart. A modification that provides an exception to a peripheral tournament rule without impairing its purpose cannot be said to "fundamentally alter" the tournament. What it can be said to do, on the other hand, is to allow Martin the chance to qualify for, and compete in, the athletic events petitioner offers to those members to enter. That is exactly what the ADA requires. *PGA Tour, Inc. v. Martin,* 532 U.S. 661, 690 (2001)

The citation of the case is at the end of the quote and is placed on a new line and is not placed directly at the end of the quote as a continuation. Many attorneys follow the second approach, which is incorrect.

Quotes can become complex, and *The Bluebook* and *ALWD* guide us in the proper form. A quick reference for common quotation issues is identified as follows.

- When to use an ellipse: Recall from Chapter 5 that an ellipse is used to indicate omitted material. In quoted material, an ellipse is used to show the omission of material. There are rules to follow when using an ellipse at the end of the quoted material as well as the middle of quoted material. If you are omitting material at the end of a quote, end with the ellipse followed by a period. (. . . .)

You Be the Judge

Hypothetical 7-3

Do not use an ellipse to mislead your reader. Be complete and accurate when substituting the ellipse for text. A law firm improperly used a ellipses in an appellate court brief to deliberately mislead a court. The judge, angered by the attorneys dishonesty, sanctioned them in the amount of $71,117.75.

Review *Dube v. Eagle Global Logistics,* 314 F.3d 193 (5th Cir. 2002). Was the court's actions appropriate? What was the reasoning behind the sanctions in the case? What was the court's disposition?

There is always space between the periods. Use an ellipse to indicate omission of material in the middle of quoted material. Do not use an ellipse at the beginning of a quote. The quote from the previous example is modified, deleting parts of the quotation and using an ellipse.

The U.S. Supreme Court in its *dicta* observed:

> The purpose of the walking rule is therefore not compromised in the slightest by allowing Martin to use a cart. A modification that provides an exception to a peripheral tournament rule without impairing its purpose cannot be said to "fundamentally alter" the tournament. What it can be said to do, on the other hand, is to allow Martin the chance to qualify for, and compete in, the athletic events petitioner offers to those members to enter. . . .

PGA Tour, Inc. v. Martin, 532 U.S. 661, 690 (2001)

Using the ellipse signifies to the reader that there is additional information that the writer chose not to include.

- Brackets in a quote: Brackets are used when the letter at the beginning of the quotation changes from lower case to upper case and vice versa. Place the first letter in brackets indicating to your reader that the original material was different. Also use brackets when language at the beginning of a quote is omitted. For example:

The U.S. Supreme Court in its *dicta* observed:

> [t]he walking rule is . . . not compromised in the slightest by allowing Martin to use a cart. A modification that provides an exception to a peripheral tournament rule without impairing its purpose cannot be said to "fundamentally alter" the tournament. What it can be said to do, on the other hand, is to allow Martin the chance to qualify for, and compete in, the athletic events petitioner offers to those members to enter. That is exactly what the ADA requires.

PGA Tour, Inc. v. Martin, 532 U.S. 661, 690 (2001)

- Using [sic]: When there are mistakes in the original text or grammatical errors, use [sic] in the quoted material to indicate that the original was not changed. Recall our example in Chapter 5; where the attorney misspelled mandamus as "mandamous [sic]," the court added [sic] to the reference to indicate the misspelling.

- Punctuation in quotations: Periods and commas are placed inside the quotation marks. This mistake is common in citing quotations embedded in the text and is not as problematic with block quotes. Unless part of the quotation, all other punctuation is placed outside the quotation marks. For example:

> The U.S. Supreme Court observed that "[t]he purpose of the walking rule is therefore not compromised in the slightest by allowing Martin to use a cart." *Id.* at 690.

- Emphasis added and emphasis supplied: The words "emphasis added" may be included at the end of a quote if you, the writer, underscored the importance of a particular word or passage in a quote. The quoted material is usually italicized. If "emphasis added" is used, this notation must be added at the end of the quotation in a parenthetical telling the reader that you, not the original author, added the highlighted importance: (emphasis added) If the quoted material already emphasizes a particular point, do not add "emphasis supplied." In our example, we are emphasizing the following and indicating the change.

The U.S. Supreme Court in its *dicta* observed:

> The purpose of the walking rule is therefore not compromised in the slightest by allowing Martin to use a cart. A modification that provides an exception to a peripheral tournament rule without impairing its purpose cannot be said to *"fundamentally alter"* the tournament. What it can be said to do, on the other hand, is to allow Martin the chance to qualify for, and compete in, the athletic events petitioner offers to those members to enter. *That is exactly what the ADA requires.*

PGA Tour, Inc. v. Martin, 532 U.S. 661, 690 (2001) (emphasis added)

- Quotes within quotes:

1. If there is a quotation within the quote you are citing, keep the quotations in the original if used in a block quote. On the other hand, if the quote is 50 words or less, change the original

Ethics Alert

Misrepresentation

It is unethical to misrepresent a legal authority in a legal document. The rules of professional responsibility require attorneys and those they supervise to cite legal authority that is reflective of the legal position argued. It is one thing to present a novel argument to the court and the court rejects it. It is quite another to mislead a court on the status of existing law. Zealous representation is the standard required of attorneys in representing their clients. However, there is a fine line between zealousness and misrepresentation. Courts exhibit distain when attorneys distort court opinions and misquote. A recent case, *Precision Specialty Metal, Inc. v. United States,* 315 F.3d 1346 (Fed. Cir. 2003), took issue with a brief submitted by an attorney who "omitted directly relevant language from what was represented as precedential authority, which effectively changed the meaning of at least one quotation, and which intentionally or negligently misled the court." *Id.* at 1355. Your duties as a paralegal are not to indulge your attorney's whims but rather to act ethically when presented an assignment regardless of the outcome. In every case, there is a winner and a loser. Your responsibility is to communicate the facts and law accurately by citing the cases, statutes, and other legal authority that supports the client's position. Review the *Precision Specialty Metal* case. What two rules of procedure did the court compare and analyze? What was the basis of the court's sanctions of the attorney? From where did this case originate and what were the facts that led it to the Federal Circuit Court of Appeals?

quotation mark to a single mark and add quotation marks to the entire quotation. An example is from the Barnhart case from our statutory construction example: Cite the quote as follows:

> The Court in *Barnhart* followed well-settled principles of statutory construction. Specifically, the court opined that they will not substitute their judgment for Congress, and stated: This we will not do. "We refrain from concluding here that the differing language in the two subsections has the same meaning in each. We would not presume to ascribe this difference to a simple mistake in draftsmanship." *Id.* at 454.

THE E-FACTOR: CITING CASES FROM ELECTRONIC SOURCES

The Internet is posing unique issues for judges and attorneys. Cases are posted almost the moment they are decided. For those attorneys who do not have access to the Internet, Lexis-Nexis, or Westlaw, the disparity can be great. Can an attorney cite a case from Westlaw or Lexis without it being available in the printed source? The answer is yes, but the electronic source must be provided to both the court and the opposing attorney. Cite electronic cases as follows:

- Case name

- Docket number

- Database identifier (such as WL for Westlaw and Lexis for LexisNexis)

- Court name

- Complete date of the case (include month, date, and year)

- Pinpoint references (with an asterisk preceding the screen or page number)

To cite to Westlaw or Lexis, use the following guide established by the *Bluebook* and *ALWD*:

LEXIS: Irobo v. Martin, No. 16069/03-325D, 2003,___N.Y. Misc.2d___LEXIS 1371 (October 20, 2003)

WESTLAW: Irobo v. Martin, 2003. ___N.Y. Misc.2d ___ 2003 WL 17744 (N.Y.October 20, 2003)

When citing from sources other than Westlaw and Lexis, which have unique database identifiers, add a parenthetical at the end of the citations indicating the source: (VersusLaw) or (Findlaw).

Local court rules guide the use of electronic case law.

Citing to electronic material also poses new problems. An ever-present problem created by the Internet is the access to unpublished cases. They have no precedential value, but attorneys still attempt to use them as persuasive argument. The new reporter, *Federal Appendix,* previously mentioned in this chapter, adds to the dilemma. When a case is labeled as unpublished, do not cite it. Immediately bring the case to your attorney's attention and allow him or her to decide its value.

Depublished cases pose another problem as well. These cases were scheduled for publication but recalled. California has published a procedure for requesting a case be depublished. Figure 7.2 reproduces the California Rule of Court that identifies the procedure to depublish a case. Stay away from depublished cases if your jurisdiction has the same or similar procedure, as they are not binding authority.

FIGURE 7.2 Procedure for Depublishing a Case

Rule 979. Requesting Depublication of Published Opinions

(a) Request

(1) Any person may request the Supreme Court to order that an opinion certified for publication not be published.

(2) The request must not be made as part of a petition for review, but by a separate letter to the Supreme Court not exceeding 10 pages.

(3) The request must concisely state the person's interest and the reason why the opinion should not be published.

(4) The request must be delivered to the Supreme Court within 30 days after the decision is final in the Court of Appeal.

(5) The request must be served on the rendering court and all parties.

(b) Response

(1) Within 10 days after the Supreme Court receives a request under (a), the rendering court or any person may submit a response supporting or opposing the request. A response submitted by anyone other than the rendering court must state the person's interest.

(2) A response must not exceed 10 pages and must be served on the rendering court, all parties, and any person who requested depublication.

(c) Action by Supreme Court

(1) The Supreme Court may order the opinion depublished or deny the request. It must send notice of its action to the rendering court, all parties, and any person who requested depublication.

(2) The Supreme Court may order an opinion depublished on its own motion, notifying the rendering court of its action.

(d) Effect of Supreme Court order to depublish

A Supreme Court order to depublish is not an expression of the court's opinion of the correctness of the result of the decision or of any law stated in the opinion.

Rule 979 repealed and adopted effective January 1, 2005.

Source: 2006 California Rules of Court. Available at: www.courtinfo.ca.gov/rules

2. When a quote is quoting another source, this is signified by referencing the quote in a parenthetical. This often occurs in court cases when a court is quoting a previous case in a newer case. Another example from *Barnhart* illustrates the point:

> The Court in *Barnhart* followed the well settled general principle on statutory construction that when "'Congress includes particular language in one section of a statute but omits it in another section of the same Act, it is generally presumed that Congress acts intentionally and purposely in the disparate inclusion or exclusion.'" *Russello v. United States,* 464 U.S. 16, 23 (1983) (quoting *United States v. Wong Kim Bo,* 472 F.2d 720, 722 C.A.5 1972). *Id.* at 452.

- Pinpoint citations: Always cite the page number where the quotation begins by using a pinpoint citation (pincite) or **jump cite.** This page reference will tell the reader where the cited material is located if they choose to check or reference it. Accuracy is critical when pinpointing your reference. Citing a page reference was discussed in the section on short citation form. There appears to be a difference of opinion when citing multiple pages. *Bluebook* requires citing two digits of the number and when over three or more digits, omitting the repetitive digits, whereas the *ALWD Manual* does not require a minimum amount of digits in the pincite.

jump cite
The page reference in a citation that directs the reader to the cited material in the case. Also called a pinpoint citation or pincite.

Bluebook: Barnhart at 445-06
ALWD: Barnhart at 445-446 or Barnhart at 445-06.
Neither permit Barnhart at 445-6.
Multiple page quotations are separated by a (-) hyphen.

Quotations have a myriad of rules. Learn the basics and never hesitate to consult *The Bluebook* or *ALWD Manual* for further guidance.

PRACTICAL CONSIDERATIONS

Another important factor you must master along with citation form is the process of cite checking. As a paralegal, one of your many assignments will be to verify that the material cited in a brief or memorandum is correct. Is the authority still good law? Is the citation in the proper format? Have the local rules been reviewed? Are the cited authorities accurately reflecting the points referenced in the brief or memorandum? Each question requires skill and attention to detail. Let's review the process for each.

1. **Is the authority still good law?** Any authority cited requires verification. Shepardize or KeyCite the authorities cited to ensure the authority is not overruled or questioned. This task is the minimum requirement for cite checking. Bring to your supervising attorney's attention any problematic authorities.

2. **Is the citation in the proper format?** Verify citation form by using either *The Bluebook* or *ALWD Manual* to determine whether the listed legal sources are cited correctly. Check punctuation as well as form. If the citation identifies a pinpoint reference, check the pincite for accuracy.

3. **Have local rules been reviewed?** Many jurisdictions have local rules that dictate how to cite legal authorities. Sometimes they compliment the *Bluebook* or *ALWD Manual*, but other times they supersede them. Know the requirements in your jurisdiction.

4. **Are the cited authorities accurately reflecting the points referenced in the brief or memorandum?** Read. Retrieve the cases and review them. Verify they say what they are being cited for. Inaccurately citing an authority may have ethical and professional implications. As tedious as the process may be, it is critical to review all the authority.

Learning how to incorporate citations into legal writing is critical to your work as a paralegal. Care in preparing any legal document is essential to being a successful paralegal. Do take the time to master the detail from the placement of a simple period to selection of a pertinent quote. It may appear overwhelming at first, but practice makes perfect!

Summary

Since 1926, *The Bluebook* is the authority for citation form. The *ALWD Manual* is another accepted authority for citation form. *ALWD* has a more user-friendly approach to understanding citation form. Another citation approach is the Universal Citation Guide, formulating a neutral citation format. Each jurisdiction follows different guides; local rules provide guidance on which format to use.

Case citations fall into a basic format. Cite the name of the case, the volume, the reporter, the page where the case begins, and the date of the decision. Unless dictated by citation form, often information about the court is inserted into the parenthetical with the date of the case. Statutes are cited by identifying the title, code, code section, and the date. This basic format is followed for administrative rules and regulations as well. Whether a primary or secondary source, all legal authority cited must be properly identified according to the rules of citation.

Legal authority must be integrated into legal documents. Citations are placed in sentences to direct a reader as to the basis of the authority relied upon. Short form citations may be used after a complete citation is identified in the text. Signals and string citing provide a method of listing additional authorities in a text. Additionally, when used properly, quotations are a vehicle to cite legal authority.

Cite checking is an important responsibility of a paralegal. Cite checking consists of verifying the law, checking proper citation form, including the local rules, and reviewing the case cited for accuracy in the text.

Key Terms

signals	*id.*
neutral citation	short citation form
parallel citation	pinpoint cite (pincite)
subsequent history	supra
writ of *certiorari*	string citation
unpublished case	block quote
embedded citation	jump cite
embedded citation	

Review Questions

1. What is the *Bluebook*? What is *ALWD*?
2. List three differences between the *Bluebook* and *ALWD*.
3. What are the basic elements of a case citation?
4. Identify five legal secondary sources.
5. What is the proper order of citing cases in a string cite?
6. What is a subsequent history?
7. What is the criteria for citing a quotation?
8. What are signals and when are they used in legal writing?
9. What is a pinpoint citation and when it is used in a legal document?
10. List the six rules for when to cite a legal authority.

Exercises

1. Prepare the following legal authorities in proper citation form:
   a. State of Florida versus Robert Thomas. The volume of the case is 532 and the page where the case begins is 774. The case is from the U.S. Supreme Court and was decided in 2001.
   b. *Federal Reporter* case from the third series; the volume is 116 and the first page of the case is 310. The parties are Birchem versus Knights Of Columbus and the year of the case is 1997 from the eighth circuit.
   c. Northwestern Reporter second series. A Nebraska Supreme Court case decided in 1997 and is found in volume 560 and the case begins on Page 157. The parties are the State of Nebraska and Thomas Nissen.
   d. The Plaintiff in the case is John Moore and the Defendant is the Regents Of the University of California. The case is located in three reporters.

   The California Reporter in volume 271 and begins on page 145.
   The California Reports third series in volume 51 and begins on page 120.
   The Pacific Reporter second series in volume 793 and begins on page 479.

   The case was decided in 1990.

2. Identify the signals used in the passage from *Miller v. California*, 413 U.S. 15 (1973):

   This case involves the application of a State's criminal obscenity statute to a situation in which sexually explicit materials have been thrust by aggressive sales action upon unwilling recipients that who had in no way indicated any desire to receive such materials. This Court has recognized that the States have a legitimate interesting prohibiting dissemination or exhibition of obscene material when the mode of dissemination carries with it a significant danger of offending the sensibilities of unwilling recipients or exposure to juveniles.

Stanley v. Georgia, 394 U.S. 557, 567 (1969); *Ginsberg v. New York,* 390 U.S. 629, 637-643 (1968); *Interstate Circuit, Inc., v. Dallas, supra,* at 690, *Redrup v. New York,* 386 U.S. 767, 769 (1967); *Jacobellis v. Ohio,* 378 U.S. 184,185 (1964). *See Rage v. Washington,* 404 U.S. 313, 317 (1972) (BURGER, C.J., concurring); *United States v. Reidel,* 402 U.S. 351, 360-362 (1971) (opinion of Marshall, J.) *(Breard v. Alexandria,* 341 U.S. 622, 644-645 (1951); *Kovacs v. Cooper,* 336 U.S. 77, 88-89 (1949); *Prince v. Massachusetts,* 321 U.S. 158, 169-170 (1944). *Cf. Butler v. Michigan,* 352 U.S. 380, 382-383 (1957); *Public Utilities Comm'n v. Pollak,* 343 U.S. 451, 464-465 (1952).

It is in this context that we are called on to define the standards which must be used to identify obscene material that a State may Regulate without infringing on the First Amendment as applicable to the States through the Fourteenth Amendment.

Provide an explanation of how and why the court used the particular signal to introduce a series of cases.

3. Using the passage from question 2, prepare the citations in *ALWD* format.

4. The passage from question 2 has a number of pinpoint citations; locate the cases after the signal *see* and review them to determine the basis for the U.S. Supreme Court references. Why are there only U.S. Supreme Court cases cited in the passage?

5. Review the following passage from *Duncan v. Walker,* 533 U.S. 167, 171-172, 121 S.Ct. 2120, 2124, 150 L. Ed. 2d 251 (2001), and answer the questions that follow.

We granted certiorari, 531 U.S. 991 (2000), to resolve a conflict between the Second Circuit's decision and the decisions of three other Courts of Appeals. *See Jimenez v. Johnson,* 208 F.3d 488 (C.A.5 1999)(per curiam); *Jones v. Morton,* 195 F.3d 153 (C.A.3 1999). One other Court of Appeals has since adopted the Second Circuit's view. Petrick v. Martin, 236 F.3d 624 (C.A.10 2001). We now reverse.

    a. What does the Court mean when its states: "We granted certiorari"?

    b. What are the signals referenced in the case excerpt?

    c. What do the words *per curiam* indicate about the court opinion?

    d. Correct the citations in the excerpt to *Bluebook* and *ALWD* form.

    e. What did the court signify when it stated: "We now reverse"?

6. Prepare the proper citations for the periodicals listed:

    a. The author is Alex Glashausser and the name of the article is Citation and Representation. The article can be found in the Vanderbilt Law Review Journal in volume 55 and begins on page 59. The article was written in 2002.

    b. The author is Judith D. Fischer and the name of the article is Bareheaded and Barefaced Counsel: Courts React to Unprofessionalism in Lawyers' Papers. The article can be found in the Suffolk University Law Review Journal in volume 31 and begins on page 1. The article was written in 1997.

7. Correct the following citations:

    a. Bruther versus. General Electric Company, 818 Fed. Suppl. 1238 (Southern District of Indiana, 1993).

    b. Lockheed Maring Energy System, Incorporated vs. Slavin, 190 FRD 440 (ED Tennessee: 1999).

    c. Coco Brothers, Inc, vs. Pierce, 741 F2secd. 675 (third circuit 1984).

8. Prepare the short form citation variations as they would appear in the *Bluebook* and *ALWD Manual* for *Carter v. United States*, 530 U.S. 255, 120 S.Ct. 2159, 147 L.E. 2d 203 (2000). The pinpoint reference is page 264 in *U.S. Reports;* 2166 in *Supreme Court Reporter;* 213 in *Lawyers' Edition* 2d.

Portfolio Assignment

A brief is due next week and your supervising attorney requested you review the following section of the brief:

> The second issue befor this Court is the interpretation of the statute. When Interpreting a statute, the words should be given their "ordinary common sense Meaning of the words used." *U.S. v. Alvarez-Sanchez,* 114 S.Ct. 1599, 511 U.S. 350 (1994). See also: *C.I.R. v. Brown,* 85 S.Ct. 1162, 380 U.S. 563 (1965). The Court should not be "guided by a single sentence but rather view the entire statute as to its objects and policy. *Zenith Radio Corp. v. Matushita Elect. Industry Co., Ltd.* 402 F. Supp. 244 (E.D. Pa. 1975), *U.S. v. Manache,* 348 US 528 (1955) Therefore, the Court should only not substitute its judgment for that of the Legislature, particularly when the statute is clear and unambiguous. As the U.S. Supreme stated:
>
> "(I)n determining the scope of a statute, we look first to its language. If the statutory language is unambiguous, in absence of a clearly expressed legislative intent to the contrary, the language must ordinarily be regarded as conclusive." *U.S. v. Turkett,* 452 U.S. 576, 580 (1981); *United States v. Bay,* 736 F. 2d 891 (3rd Cir. 1984); *Negonsott v. Sanuels,* 113 S,Ct. 1119, 507 U.S. 99, 122 L.Ed.2d 457 (1993); *North Dakata v. U.S.* 103 S,Ct. 1095, 450 U.S, 300, 75 L.Ed.2d 77 (1983).
>
> It is clear that the law is well settled in this area. The court's conclusion regarding the language of the statute can be only one outcome; and that outcome must that the statute is clear and unambiguous.

The assignment includes a complete cite check, spelling, and grammar review. Prepare the corrected document for your attorney's review.

Vocabulary Builder

Citations in Legal Writing

```
O  U  V  D  Y  L  R  Q  S  Q  R  X  E  V  U
V  N  X  S  I  G  N  A  L  S  F  B  D  K  I
Q  P  A  T  B  K  N  X  W  G  K  L  K  I  I
A  U  L  R  WZ  M  L  M  C  O  O  G  F  O
L  B  WI  P  B  L  D  I  T  Q  C  J  B  C
B  L  D  N  A  U  P  W  W  M  T  K  U  L  C
K  I  M  G  P  Q  S  X  T  G  V  Q  M  U  L
E  S  A  C  D  E  H  S  I  L  B  U  P  E  D
D  H  N  I  E  X  Q  L  P  C  Z  O  C  B  C
N  E  U  T  R  A  L  C  I  T  A  T  I  O  N
E  D  A  A  S  C  P  U  N  A  A  E  T  O  J
Z  C  L  T  E  O  A  N  C  F  Q  M  E  K  E
F  A  A  I  R  A  R  O  I  T  R  E  C  J  V
T  S  B  O  G  B  N  X  T  U  S  C  P  J  Z
I  E  Y  N  R  O  M  B  E  Z  B  A  P  B  T
```

ALWD MANUAL	**BLOCK QUOTE**	**BLUEBOOK**
CERTIORARI	**DEPUBLISHED CASE**	**JUMPCITE**
NEUTRAL CITATION	**PINCITE**	**SIGNALS**
STRING CITATION	**SUPRA**	**UNPUBLISHED CASES**

Part Three

Practical Writing Applications

CHAPTER 8   The Basics of Legal Correspondence
CHAPTER 9   The Internal Office Memorandum
CHAPTER 10   The Basics of Pleadings
CHAPTER 11   Discovery

Chapter 8

The Basics of Legal Correspondence

After completing this chapter, you will be able to:

- Identify three functions of legal correspondence.
- Prepare appropriate letters for clients, opposing counsel, and the court.
- Identify the components of a letter.
- Format a letter properly.
- Address a letter to the court and other officials properly.
- Distinguish between a demand letter and an opinion letter.
- Prepare a demand letter.
- Understand the importance of statutory requirements for certain types of letters.
- Draft persuasive letters.
- Understand when paralegals can sign letters.

In this chapter and the remaining chapters, you will practice the skills developed in Parts 1 and 2 of this textbook. Writing legal correspondence requires precision and clarity; proper punctuation and grammar; and above all, effective communication. In Chapter 8, we discuss different types of legal correspondence and the strategies behind them.

Case Fact Pattern

Hypothetical 8-1

For over three months your client, Electronics, Inc., has been attempting to collect overdue rent from a difficult tenant. Phone calls to the tenant and several meetings have accomplished nothing. A week ago, an officer of the client firm sought your firm's advice. His initial consultation with your supervising attorney was completed shortly thereafter.

As a result of the consultation, a decision was made to take immediate action. You have just been assigned to draft a letter to the tenant on behalf of the client, demanding payment of an overdue rent.

Preparing basic correspondence, including demand letters, is a task often performed by paralegals.

Source: © Tribune Media Services, Inc. All Rights Reserved. Reprinted with permission.

THE FUNCTION OF LEGAL CORRESPONDENCE

Although letter writing is something of a lost art in social communication, having been replaced by the telephone call and e-mail, in business and legal matters it remains important. Letters form a permanent written record that can be relied upon later to reconstruct events. Used and drafted correctly, they help to prevent misunderstandings, broken agreements, and missed deadlines.

The legal profession relies on letters for three main purposes—to inform, to advise, and to confirm.

The Informative Letter

informative letter
A letter that transmits information.

Letters that transmit information are known as **informative letters,** also called "for your information" or "FYI" letters. Such a letter might be sent to a client to inform him of the progress of a case, the status of billing and payment, or the need for information to prepare a deposition. An informative letter might also be sent to opposing counsel (for example, to provide dates of availability to schedule a deposition or trial), or anyone to whom the attorney or paralegal needs to provide information.

The Advisory Letter

advisory letter
A formal letter that offers legal opinions or demands.

Advisory letters are more formal than informative letters. They offer legal opinions. This might be in the form of an objective analysis of the case at issue, as a detailed letter to a client. Or it might be written in a persuasive style from an advocate's perspective, as when an attorney writes to opposing counsel proposing settlement. Whatever form it takes, an advisory letter is detailed and formal. Research may be involved, and it must be done with the same care as any other research project. There may be statutory requirements to follow or questions of law that must be resolved. If the letter is incomplete or otherwise flawed, the result may harm your client.

Although the advisory letter is certainly informative, its content goes beyond that of an informative letter. The content and style often resemble more sophisticated legal writing, such as an internal memorandum or a brief, and may have statutory requirements. Different types of advisory letters are demand letters, letters notifying of intention to litigate, and opinion letters.

The Confirmation Letter

confirmation letter
A letter designed to create a record or restate the content of the original oral communication.

In the course of a legal matter, information is often shared orally, by telephone or in person. In order to create a permanent record of the passing of such information, a **confirmation letter** is often sent, restating the content of the original oral communication. For example, when an attorney orally advises a client of a court date, a follow-up confirmation letter should be sent immediately. That way, there is no excuse for confusion.

A confirmation letter not only restates orally transmitted information, it also protects the attorney (and the paralegal) from future problems or repercussions. By establishing in writing the date of a court appearance, for example, or the terms of an orally agreed-upon settlement, there is a permanent record, which can be referred to in the event of a disagreement.

EVALUATING THE AUDIENCE: TONE AND STYLE

The tone and style of a letter vary not only with the purpose, but also with the audience. Correspondence with your client, for example, may be less formal than a letter to the court, and less technical than a letter to opposing counsel. A different audience requires a different focus, attention, and style. You create the proper tone by word choice and sentence structure. Depending upon the type of letter you are drafting, your tone may be informal or businesslike. The tone of a letter affects how the reader interprets the letter. Are you communicating to a client? What message do you intend to send? If advice is given on the likelihood of success of a legal claim, the tone is serious and formal. Whereas, if you are communicating a meeting or a court hearing, your tone may be less formal. Think about how you want to be perceived. Do you want to be friends with the client or a member of a professional team? As familiar as you may become with a client or opposing counsel, your tone, informal or formal, should remain, above all else, professional. Therefore, consider your audience and ask yourself:

- What is the purpose of the letter I am drafting?
- To whom is the letter directed?
- Should my tone be informal or formal?
- What result do I want to achieve?

By asking yourself these questions, you will be able to tailor your letter to the given assignment successfully.

The Client

Regular contact with your clients is important, both to keep them informed and to minimize the anxiety they may feel because of their unfamiliarity with the legal system. In corresponding with clients, you should keep in mind several considerations.

First, provide concrete answers. Clients dislike lawyers and paralegals who hedge with vague language. This does not mean that you should misrepresent the state of affairs if it really is indefinite, but rather that you explain the indefinite state with concrete, clear language. If the law in your case is subject to several interpretations, say so clearly and identify the possible interpretations.

Second, write to the client's level of understanding. Avoid legalese or, if you must use it, *explain* it. Don't try to impress the client with your technical vocabulary; write in plain English. To do this is not to patronize or condescend—if a client, even an intelligent and educated client, has no legal training, there is no reason to subject her to difficult jargon.

Third, always be respectful and courteous to your clients. They have hired you because they have a legal problem, and it is probably a difficult time for them. Your compassion and understanding in your legal correspondence and face-to-face contacts can help them cope, whereas a harsh or pompous tone would cause more anxiety and ill will.

Finally, choose your words carefully. In litigation, a result is never certain; in a business deal or real estate transaction, the outcome is often unpredictable; in negotiations, the other party is always an uncontrollable factor. Yet clients are always looking for certainties. They want to be told that everything will be all right. You must make it clear that your opinions are not *guarantees*. Avoid the temptation to act like an all-knowing legal forecaster; be accurate and honest, and communicate the uncertainties.

Opposing Counsel

Opposing counsel is not your friend in the case at hand, even if he is your friend in other contexts. Always remember that information shared with opposing counsel will be available to the opposing client (or might even be brought to the court's attention), and can be used against your client. Thus you must choose carefully what you communicate to opposing counsel. Be courteous in your correspondence with opposing counsel, but be cautious as well.

The Court

Correspondence directed to the court usually comes in one of three forms: either a cover letter accompanying documents to be filed; or a letter requesting a hearing date or other procedural assistance; or a formal letter to a judge stating a legal position.

Cover letters accompanying documents are usually standard form letters. They simply identify the documents and the date of filing. Such letters fulfill the confirmation function of correspondence—they provide a written record establishing that the documents were filed, and when. Copies always should be sent to opposing counsel.

A letter requesting a hearing date or other procedural assistance is similarly straightforward in its text—it simply makes a direct request. Whether a letter is addressed to a judge or **clerk of the court,** opposing counsel receives a copy. The clerk of the court is important to the court process. The clerks are the individuals who manage the day-to-day operations of the court. Often they transmit documents from the court to an attorney, or they may acknowledge the filing of a court order. (Recall the case brief in Chapter 3, which involved the timely filing of a lawsuit.) Cover letters normally are transmitted to the clerk of the court for filing of documents, hearing requests, and any other general business with the court. The clerks of courts are integral to the operations of the court and also offer helpful guidance when needed. Unlike a judge, they can communicate directly with you or your attorney.

A letter to a judge stating a legal position is less commonly seen, usually outside the standard course of a lawsuit, and it involves risks. If such a letter is sent, needless to say a copy must be sent to opposing counsel, and be prepared in a formal manner, as if it were a brief. Be concise, direct, and respectful to judges. Such a communication between one party in a lawsuit and the judge is called an ***ex parte*** communication (recall this term from our discussion of legalese in Chapter 4). Only under *very* limited circumstances is such communication acceptable. The problem with *ex parte* communications is that the other side's opportunity to respond is limited. In any event, no such communication should ever be attempted by you without express authorization from your supervising attorney. (Even then, a fine line is drawn as to the propriety of the communication.)

cover letter
A standard form letter identifying information such as document filings.

clerk of the court
An individual who manages the administrative functions of the court.

ex parte
A communication between one party in a lawsuit and the judge.

THE COMPONENTS OF A LETTER

PRACTICE TIP

Always have a listing of the current clerks of the courts with whom you will deal. Include in the listing the court clerk's name, the court, the address of the court, telephone number, fax, and e-mail, if appropriate.

The format of different types of letters varies, and different firms or attorneys may have different preferences, but the following are generally accepted as the standard components of most letters:

- Letterhead
- Date
- Addressee
- Reference line
- Salutation
- Body
- Headers
- Closing
- Referencing initials
- Copy and blind copy

We consider each of these in turn in the following subsections.

The Letterhead

letterhead
Standard stationery.

Most law firms and businesses have standard stationery, called **letterhead,** with the firm or company name, address, telephone number, and other relevant information. Law firm letterhead often lists, just below the firm name, all the attorneys in the firm.

When writing on behalf of your firm, use letterhead. It shows that you are associated with the firm, making the significance of the letter clear. It may even be relevant for professional liability insurance coverage.

Letterhead is used for the first page of a multiple-page letter. The other pages should be on matching paper, but without the letterhead.

FIGURE 8.1
Address Block

<u>HAND DELIVERED</u>

Ms. Susan Windsor, President
Electronics Company, Inc.
465 Commerce Blvd.
Lincoln, Nebraska 54321
                or
By Fax and U.S. Mail
Ms. Susan Windsor
Chief Operating Officer
Electronics Company, Inc.
465 Commerce Blvd.
Lincoln, Nebraska 54321
                or
Certified Mail, Return Receipt Requested
Ms. Susan Windsor,
Chief Operating Officer
Electronics Company, Inc.
465 Commerce Blvd.
Lincoln, Nebraska 54321

PRACTICE TIP

When sending a letter by certified mail, include the certified mail number in the address block under the certified mail designation. Those green cards could get lost or there may be a question as to actual receipt of a letter. If the certified number of the mailing is located on the letter, the confusion is minimized and your record always will be accurate. Verifying receipt of a letter often becomes an issue if a statutory time frame is involved or in case you need a record that the letter was received. This practice may save you and a case from disaster.

The Date

The date appears below the letterhead. It is important for establishing an accurate chronology in a legal matter. Letters often go through several drafts over a period of several days; make sure the date on the letter matches the date of mailing.

The Addressee

The name of the person to whom the letter is written appears at the top left margin, just below the letterhead. If the letter is sent by other than U.S. mail (for example, by fax or overnight delivery), the method of delivery should be indicated above the address block. Use titles, if applicable (for example, "Dr. William Jones"), and note that all attorneys should be addressed with the suffix "Esquire" or its abbreviation, "Esq." (as in "William Jones, Esq."). Do not use the standard Mr., Mrs., Miss, or Ms. in this context. A typical address block is found in Figure 8.1.

Title of the Addressee

You will correspond with many types of individuals who have different titles. Pay attention to those titles and address them accordingly. The following are examples of the proper method of addressing individuals with whom you may have contact:

- Mr., Mrs., Miss, and Ms.: These are the standard titles used in addressing most individuals. The issue arises whether you address women as Mrs. or Ms; Miss or Ms. When you meet a client, you may want to ask how they want to be addressed. That will set the tone of your communications. Otherwise, use the standard Mrs. or Miss, unless directed otherwise.

- Attorney: Some jurisdictions use "Attorney" as a title. This form is a matter of local preference. It is proper etiquette to use "Esq." after an attorney's name if you are not sure of the local usage.

- Judges: It is customary to address a judge as "Honorable" or "The Honorable." For a federal judge, the address block is

  Honorable Stanley Brotman

  U.S. District Court District of New Jersey

  (Address of the court)

For the Chief Justice of an Appellate Court, the address block is

> *The Honorable Craig Enoch*
>
> *Chief Justice, Texas Supreme Court*
>
> *(Address of the court)*

The address format for other judges follows the same format as the one for a federal court judge.

- Clerk of the Court: You will communicate regularly with the Clerk of the Court. Clerks are addressed as follows:

> *Name*
>
> *Clerk of the Court*
>
> *Name of the Court*
>
> *Address of the Court*

- Political figures: Governors, senators, Congressional representatives, and other government officials have protocols for addressing them. The common protocol for corresponding with an elected official is as follows:

> *Honorable Barbara Boxer*
>
> *United States Senator*
>
> *Address*

Sometimes an elected official dictates the way to address them in a formal correspondence. Investigate the proper protocols for addressing an elected official for the jurisdiction with whom you intend to communicate. Some individuals are sensitive as to how they are addressed. Do not invite the wrath of an elected official because your letter addressed them improperly.

- Clergy: Use the proper title of a religious leader if you are corresponding with them. For example:

> *Reverend Jesse Jackson*
>
> *Name of the Congregation*
>
> *Address*

- Individuals with titles: Generally, titles follow the name of the addressee. Be sure you include a person's title when corresponding with them. Again, you do not want to offend anyone.

Name	*Jonathan A. Potts*
Title	*Chief Executive Officer*
Company	*Medical Supply Company, Inc.*
Address	*Address*

The Reference Line

reference line
A line of text that appears below the address block, and identifies the subject matter of the letter.

The **reference line** appears below the address block, and identifies the subject matter of the letter. It provides a quick (*very* quick) introduction for the reader, and helps your assistant to determine where to file the copy without reading the whole letter.

The detail in the reference line sometimes depends on the stage of the matter. The parties involved are always identified, along with a brief description of the matter. Some firms also include their internal file number and, if a lawsuit has been filed, the docket number is often included as well. If the parties are involved in several matters, or if only one aspect of a complex matter is addressed in the letter, there may be even more detailed identification. Figure 8.2 shows two examples of reference lines, one prior to litigation and the other afterward.

The Salutation

salutation
A greeting that appears below the reference line.

The **salutation** appears below the reference line. It usually begins with the word "Dear," even in formal correspondence. Use "Mr.," "Ms.," "Mrs.," or "Miss," unless you know the person to whom you are writing, and follow the name with a colon, which is more formal than a comma.

FIGURE 8.2
Reference Lines

Prelitigation:
Re: Our Client: Anytime Builders
Our File #99-325
Sale of Aacme Service Company, Inc.

Litigation pending:
Re: Anytime Builders, Inc. v. Aacme Service Company, Inc.
Cause No. 06-00576-X
Our File #99-325

As mentioned in the section entitled "The Addressee," knowing how to address titled individuals is important. The following are guidelines based upon the examples:

- Dear Chief Justice Roberts or Dear Mr. Chief Justice
- Dear Justice Souter
- Dear Judge Brotman
- Dear Governor Rendel
- Dear Congressman Rengal
- Dear Reverend Jackson
- Unless a specific title such as the above, refer to those with business titles as Mr., Mrs., Miss, or Ms.

The Body

body
The text that contains the information you wish to communicate in a letter.

The **body** of a letter contains the information you wish to communicate. It may be as short as one or two sentences (if the purpose, for example, is simply to indicate that you have enclosed documents), or as long as several pages (for an in-depth legal analysis, such as an opinion letter).

As in most effective legal writing, the opening sentence and paragraph of your letters should summarize what you want to say and why. You should make it clear that you are representing the client, unless you have done this already in prior letters. You should use all the writing techniques you've learned—correct sentence structure, parallelism, conciseness, and so on.

Be sure to be complete. Cover all the material you need to communicate, both positive and negative. Avoid a pompous or arrogant tone. In fact, in letters to clients or other friendly parties, you may use a relatively informal tone, although you should be careful that the message is not distorted nor its importance undermined.

When you write an advisory letter, the tone should be formal and authoritative, just as you would write a brief or internal memorandum.

Figure 8.3 shows the body of a letter concerning the resolution of a dispute. In subsequent sections, we discuss the content of other types of letters.

FIGURE 8.3
Body of Confirmation Letter

This letter will confirm our agreement regarding the sale of the Aacme Service Company, Inc., to Anytime Builders, Inc. As a result of our meeting of May 5, 2006, we agreed that Mr. Allen will provide my clients with books and records of the business. Once we have had an opportunity to review the books and records, we will be able to determine whether the sale of the business will be completed.

I have received the weekly installment payment to Mr. Allen in the amount of $1,203.54. As I indicated to you at the meeting, I will be holding all future checks in trust until we can resolve the question of the purchase and sale of the business.

It is my further understanding that some time next week we will meet again to determine whether the business will be sold to my clients, or whether Mr. Allen will reimburse all monies tendered for the purchase of the business to my clients.

I hope we will be able to resolve this matter quickly.

The Header

header
Text that appears at the top left margin of all subsequent pages, and identifies three elements: the person to whom the letter is addressed; the date of the letter; and the page number.

As we stated, letterhead is used only for the first page of multipage letters. However, subsequent pages have identifying information as well, in the form of a **header.** A header appears at the top left margin of all subsequent pages, and identifies three elements: the person to whom the letter is addressed; the date of the letter; and the page number. A practical note: we indicated earlier that the date on the front of the letterhead page should be the date of mailing; this is obviously also true for the date appearing in headers. If the date on your letterhead and headers fails to match the postmark, you will seem disorganized; if different dates appear on the letterhead and headers in the same letter, you will look sloppy and careless. The amount of time it takes to check these details is minor; the impact of an error on your reputation can be great.

The Closing and Signature Block

closing
The concluding message in the letter.

A letter is generally concluded by one or two sentences at the end. A concluding message often contains such courteous statements as, "Please do not hesitate to call if you have any questions." Following the concluding message is the **closing.** In legal correspondence, the typical closing is "Very truly yours," followed by a comma. Note that the *V* in *Very* is capitalized, but the other words are not. There are other proper closing variations that are also acceptable:

- Yours truly or Yours very truly (traditional closing).
- Sincerely (less formal, but does communicate a tone).
- Best wishes or Best regards (very informal). Use this closing in a limited setting and only when informality is appropriate.

Stay away from the extremes: very formal and very informal. These types of closing include the following:

- Respectfully (usually used in a pleading)
- Fondly (do I hear lawsuit?)

Examples of correct and incorrect concluding messages and closings are seen in Figure 8.4. Note that the correct concluding message ends with a period. It is outdated to end the concluding message with a comma leading into the closing, as in the incorrect example.

Most of the letters you prepare will be for the signature of your supervising attorney. Remember that it is improper, and indeed illegal, for a paralegal to give legal advice. If you do sign a letter, identify yourself as a paralegal or legal assistant (see Figure 8.5).

Referencing Initials

At the end of the letter initials appear identifying who wrote the letter, and in many instances, who typed the letter. Placing initials at the end of the letter credits the individual who authored the letter, which is ultimately the individual who is responsible for the contents of the letter.

FIGURE 8.4
Correct and Incorrect Closings of Letters

<u>**Correct closing of letter:**</u>
Thank you for your attention to this matter.

Very truly yours,

Anne Simmonds
General Counsel

<u>**Incorrect closing of letter:**</u>
Thanking you for your attention and courtesies, I remain,

Very truly yours,

Anne Simmonds
General Counsel

FIGURE 8.5
Appropriate Closing by a Paralegal

Very truly yours,

Emily Brady
Legal Assistant or (Paralegal)

               or

Very truly yours,

Emily Brady
Paralegal for Marcus Baker

In limited cases, you may see three sets of initials. This occurs when a partner in a firm signs a letter, an associate prepares the letter and research, and an assistant types the letter. This creates a chain of responsibility. Signify the first set of initials in capital letters followed by a (/) slash and the initials of the preparer of the letter. If there are documents enclosed with the letter, indicate that after the initials of the preparers on a new line. The section will appear as follows:

> *PRT/prh*   *PRT/prh*
>
> *Enclosures*   *Enc. or Encls.*

Copy and Blind Copy (cc and bcc)

cc
Copy.

Copies of correspondence are often sent to parties other than the addressee. The client, for example, is often sent copies of letters to opposing counsel or the court. This fact is denoted at the end of the original letter by the notation **cc** (which technically stands for *carbon copy*). But,

Ethics Alert

The rules of professional responsibility govern what paralegals can and cannot sign. Paralegals cannot render legal advice. Often clients rely heavily on paralegals for guidance simply because they are more accessible than the attorney. Do not get caught in a trap. You may sign letters transmitting information or setting a meeting. That is not to say that you cannot prepare a letter for the attorney's signature. You can. When the letter is signed, it represents that the letter was read and the contents approved. In some instances when an attorney has not read the contents of a letter or document, they attempt to plead ignorance. Courts definitely do not buy that argument. In *Philadelphia Gear Corp. v. Swath International, Ltd.*, 200 F. Supp. 2d 493 (E.D. Pa. 2002), an attorney reviewed an amended pleading, approved it, and had his secretary print it. She printed and filed the wrong amended pleading. Realizing his error, the attorney wrote opposing counsel a letter stating "I am a victim of sophisticated word-processing, self-editing of documents on the system and my own in attention." *Id.* at 495. The attorney did try to remedy the problem, but the opposing counsel wanted attorney's fees for his time. There was a succession of letters where the issue was not resolved, resulting in the court's involvement. The court observed that "[t]here are 'no exceptions to the requirement that all reasonable attorneys will read a document before filing it in court.' Attorneys must always keep in mind that computers are not infallible, nor are secretaries, paralegals, or other lawyers." *Id.* at 496 (citations omitted). Read the case and draw your own conclusions. Do you believe the attorneys acted reasonably in the case? The court? What could have alleviated the problem? What action, if any, did the court take against the attorneys? The moral of the case is read the letter or document before you sign and file it with a court. A more important point is pay attention to what you sign. Do not sign a letter that even remotely appears to render legal advice. Ever heard of the unauthorized practice of law?

carbon copies are no longer used, and *cc* simply stands for copy. After the *cc* come the names of any persons to whom the copy is sent. Thus the original addressee also knows who else has received copies. If enclosures are included, note that as well with the designation after the name "with enclosures."

Under certain circumstances the author of the letter may want to conceal from the original addressee who else has received a copy. The original letter, then, contains no notation about copies (*i.e.*, no *cc*), but your file copy will contain the notation **bcc (blind copy)**, followed by the name of the blind-copy recipient. The blind-copy recipient's copy will also have the *bcc* designation, so that she will know it was a blind copy. Proper use of the *cc* and *bcc* designations requires good communication among the attorney, paralegal, and assistant; it is often wise, for example, to clip a note to the original with an instruction such as "bcc John Doe."

bcc
Blind copy.

FORMATTING THE LETTER

PRACTICE TIP

There are accepted typefaces for legal letters: Times New Roman, Courier, or Arial. Nonstandard typeface styles convey unprofessionalism. Stay with the standards unless otherwise directed by your attorney. Point type of the letter is also standardized. Most letters are typed in 12- or 10-point type for readability.

Many word processing systems have programs to assist in preparing letters: Microsoft Word, Corel WordPerfect, and others. They may provide helpful letter templates with a fixed format. The style of your supervising attorney or law firm may dictate the format of a letter. Some possible formatting options are as follows:

- Block style (blocked or justified in all margins): With this style all the information contained within the letter is blocked or justified on both the left and right margins. A blocked style creates the appearance of clean lines. Paragraphs are designated by double-spacing between paragraphs. Although still considered block style, some attorneys choose to center the date. An example of block style is shown in Figure 8.6.

- Modified block style: As the name implies, parts of the letter are blocked. Usually with a modified block style, the paragraphs are indented (five spaces) with the remaining parts of the letter in a blocked style. Variations of this style include the date being centered and the signature block being centered or indenting the reference clause with the date and signature block centered. Either style is correct. Figure 8.7 is an example of a modified block style.

- Your attorney's preference: This style is probably the one that rules. Many attorneys prefer to block only the left margin, conveying a professional albeit "unstuffy" approach to letter writing. Review existing letters or ask to determine the format to follow.

General Legal Correspondence

Legal correspondence comes in many forms. As a paralegal, you will draft many different types of general correspondences. Earlier we touched briefly on the **transmittal letter,** a type of confirmation letter that accompanies information sent to a designated party. Sometimes documents sent with a transmittal letter must be signed or filed and returned; if that is the case, a return envelope with proper address and postage should be included, and the transmittal letter should contain instructions about what the receiver should do. Two examples of proper transmittal letters are found in Figure 8.6.

transmittal letter
A type of confirmation letter that accompanies information sent to a designated party.

Transmittal Letters

Another type of correspondence is a letter requesting information. Such requests must be specific. By sending such a letter, you not only obtain information, but also create a record that the request was made. Typically the letter will request medical records, employment records, or other investigative materials. Figure 8.7 shows an example of a letter requesting employment records, and Figure 8.8 shows a letter requesting an administrative transcript.

A **retainer letter** is a form of correspondence important in the practice of law, for it sets forth the agreement and relationship between the attorney and the client. Such things as fees and a description of the matter are included. Figure 8.9 provides an example of a general retainer letter.

In an **authorization letter,** the client provides the attorney with official permission to contact employers, doctors, or other individuals who have records that relate in some way to the matter at

retainer letter
A form of correspondence that sets forth the agreement and relationship between the attorney and the client.

authorization letter
A letter the client provides the attorney granting permission to contact employers, doctors, or other individuals who have records that relate to a case.

FIGURE 8.6
Transmittal Letters

(a) Transmittal Letter Forwarding Document to Opposing Counsel (block style)

May 15, 2006

Mr. Jeffrey Smith
Attorney at Law
701 Lawnview Avenue
Dallas, TX 78910

Re: Case No. 2006-432-A
O.K. Binding, Inc. v. Southern Paper Co.

Dear Mr. Smith:

Enclosed is a copy of Plaintiff's First Amended Complaint in the above-referenced matter, which has been filed with the Court this date.

Thank you for your attention to this matter.

Very truly yours,

P. R. Hodge
PRH/sst

cc: Client

(b) Transmittal Letter Forwarding Document to Court and Requesting Return of Document (modified block style)

May 15, 2006

Mary Smith
Clerk of the Court
201st District Court
500 Main St.
Dallas, TX 78910

          Re: No. 2006-432-A
          O.K. Binding, Inc. v. Southern Paper Co.

Dear Ms. Smith:

          I enclose the original and two copies of Plaintiff's First Amended Original Petition. Please file the original with the court's records and return a file stamped copy to this office in the enclosed self-addressed, stamped envelope.

          Thank you for your cooperation in this matter.

                              Very truly yours,

                              Patrick R. Langdon
PRL/sst

hand. The attorney drafts the authorization letter for the client's signature; the client reviews and signs it.

   The list could go on and on. When preparing general legal correspondence, you should keep the following factors in mind:

- Determine the purpose of your letter.
- Identify to whom your letter is directed.

FIGURE 8.7
Letter Requesting Employment Records

June 1, 2006

CERTIFIED MAIL #P117824932
RETURN RECEIPT REQUESTED
Mr. Martin Banks
Director of Human Resources
Medical Supplies Company, Inc.
603 East 21st Street
Houston, TX 77015

      Re: Mrs. Beth Windsor

Dear Mr. Banks:

      Enclosed is an authorization for release of employment records signed by my client. At this time, I would request that you forward to my office copies of all employment records in your possession regarding Mrs. Windsor. Please have this information forward to me by July 3, 2006.

      Thank you for your cooperation in this matter.

            Very truly yours,

            Colleen O. Hayward

COH/bng
cc: Client

- Communicate in plain English.
- If you use legalese or terms of art, explain your meaning unless the audience is trained in legal matters.
- Be specific when requesting information.
- Follow the guidelines we've discussed for demand and opinion letters.
- Be polite and courteous.
- Send copies to the appropriate parties.

FIGURE 8.8
Letter Requesting Administrative Transcript

June 10, 2006

HAND DELIVERED
Office of the City Secretary
City Hall
Minneapolis, MN 75201

Re: Certified Copy of Transcript of Hearings Held on June 3, 2006 before the Urban Rehabilitation Standards Board Property located at 7042 Rocky Road

Dear Board Members:
      I hereby request that a certified transcript of the Urban Rehabilitation Standards Board hearings on June 3, 2006 on the property located at 7042 Rocky Road, Minneapolis, Minnesota, be prepared by the City Secretary of the City of Minneapolis. This transcript is now requested for the purpose of an appeal to the District Court. Please advise when the certified copies of the record will be ready for transmission to the court, and I will have a courier collect them.

      Thank you for your prompt attention to this request.

            Very truly yours,

            Mark O. Walker

MOW/prt
cc: Client

FIGURE 8.9
General Retainer Letter

LETTERHEAD

July 15, 2006

Mr. Cameron Anderson
CPM Management Company
5177 Oaktree Place
Philadelphia, PA 19105

Re: Retainer Letter Agreement

Dear Mr. Anderson:
This letter will confirm the terms of the engagement of the Law Firm effective July 15, 2006 as counsel for the Company ("Clients") in the matter of CPM Management v. HCCD Enterprises.

   a.   Professional Services Fee: The Law Firm will bill for its services at an hourly rate of $300.00 per hour for the services of the partner assigned to this case. The partner will be the attorney primarily responsible for this matter. However, the law firm reserves the right to assign other attorneys and staff to assist the partner. The rates for associate attorneys are $200.00 an hour and $75.00 for paralegals. In addition to this hourly rate, the Clients will be responsible for the costs and expenses incurred by the law firm with regard to its representation of Clients in this matter.

   b.   Costs and Expenses: Law firm will seek reimbursement or request prepayment for all costs incurred and monies expended in connection with this matter. These costs and expenses include, but are not limited to, court costs, transcripts, filing fees, expert witness fees, assessments, investigators, travel expenses, photocopying, telecommunications, computerized research, delivery and courier charges. When substantial or unusual payments to third parties are required, the law firm reserves the right to request an advance of funds to cover these costs or to arrange to have the charge forwarded directly to you for payment.

   c.   Billing: The law firm will charge an initial retainer of $10,000 toward the professional service fee in this matter. The law firm will bill you monthly and that bill will reflect the number of hours worked times the hourly rate, plus the expenses incurred by the law firm in connection with this matter to be charged against the retainer. Your failure to pay any invoice within thirty days of the billing date shall be the basis of the law firm filing with the Court a motion to withdraw from any further representation.

   d.   Appeals: Law firm will represent client in the U.S District Court through the disposition of the matter, inclusive of any interlocutory or other appeals based solely upon the issues in this matter. If Clients desire law firm to continue to represent Clients on appeal to the United States Court of Appeals or the United States Supreme Court, Clients shall enter into a separate retainer agreement and shall pay to the law firm a separate retainer.

If the above is your understanding of our legal representation, please sign the two originals of this letter where indicated and return one of the originals to me for my records.

          Very truly yours,

          David Potter

You Be the Judge

Hypothetical 8-2

Only the attorney can establish the attorney-client relationship, render legal advice, and set fees to the engagement. You may *not* do any of these actions. The rules of professional responsibility for attorneys make this point quite clear. You may interview a client and record information about the interview to pass to your supervising attorney. You may tell a client hourly rates but not set the fee arrangement for the engagement. Case law is well settled on this matter, as is the usage of the respective bar associations around the United States. In a bankruptcy case in Ohio, there was confusion as to the relationship between a nonattorney and a client. Read *In re*

Ferguson, 326 B.R. 419 (Bankr. N.D. Ohio 2005), and think about the message the judge conveyed. In the judge's final remarks he warned: "[r]egulations prohibiting the unauthorized practice of law are intended to protect the public from being advised in legal matters by incompetent, untrained, and potentially unreliable persons over whom the judicial branch of government can exercise little control." *Id.* at 424. What acts did the nonattorney commit? What did the nonattorney ask the court to award, and what was the court's response? Do you agree or disagree with the court's actions? Why?

SPECIALIZED LEGAL CORRESPONDENCE

Attorneys draft different types of correspondences in their practices. Depending on the nature of the case, specialized correspondences may be required on behalf of the client. The most common specialized legal correspondences are demand letters, consumer protection letters, and letters notifying of intention to litigate. These letters require some legal research as they generally have statutory requirements. Requirements for these letters range from setting forth the contents of the letter to specifying the time period in which the letter must be written and received. If you are asked to draft a specialized correspondence, you must

letter bank
A depository for firm letters regarding client cases.

- research the statutory requirements;
- review the client's file for the pertinent facts;
- request examples from **letter banks** or other client files of the type of letter to be drafted;
- check form books for suggested standardized language, if available.

demand letter
A letter requesting action on a legal matter.

The Demand Letter

collection letter
A letter that demands payment of an amount claimed to be owed to a client.

Many disputes are resolved through discussion and negotiation, but some are not. As negotiations stall, a client may need to make demands upon the opposing party. Sometimes clients want to make demands even before negotiations have begun. In your role as a paralegal, you will be drafting **demand letters** on behalf of your firm's clients.

The purpose of a demand letter is to motivate a desired response—often, though not exclusively, the payment of a debt. In the following subsections we discuss several categories of demand letter, as well as some guidelines for preparing a response.

PRACTICE TIP

Most law firms have letter banks. Prior letters on cases are archived and are excellent places to find examples of content and format. If a letter bank is available, ask to review previous files for examples. Do not reinvent the wheel, if possible.

The Collection Letter

A **collection letter** demands payment of an amount claimed to be owed to your client. It is not, however, as simple as a "pay up or else" letter—in practice, the concept is more subtle than that. To prepare an effective collection letter, several considerations should be kept in mind.

First, understand your purpose. Again, this is not as simple as it may seem. Are you seeking immediate payment in full? Are you seeking partial payment? Are you seeking to create a written record of the amount claimed due? Are you trying to satisfy statutory notice requirements? Are you trying to accomplish some combination of these? Are you following up earlier client demands, or is your letter the first demand made upon the opposing party? As you can see, there are many factors to consider.

Second, determine whether there are statutory rules or common-law principles that affect your demand letter. If you fail to satisfy any applicable requirements, not only will your letter be faulty, but you may actually undermine your client's ability to collect.

Third, your letter should set forth your client's version of disputed events, and possibly undisputed events as well. State your claim in a concise, authoritative manner, setting forth the amount of the original debt, the date it was incurred, amounts already paid, interest due, the present amount due, and any other relevant terms. In addition, you should probably include supporting evidence, such as invoices, leases, promissory notes, or relevant correspondence.

Fourth, you should make your demand clear. Do not just demand payment, for example; demand payment by a certain date, called the **deadline date.** Tell the recipient what she can expect if she does not comply by that date, and be prepared to follow through—if your threats are exposed as empty, your credibility is damaged and your future ability to negotiate is undercut.

Finally, if the opposing party is represented by counsel, be sure that you write to the attorney and not to the party. It is a violation of codes of professional responsibility to write directly to a party who you know is represented by a lawyer.

deadline date
A certain date by which a request or demand should be fulfilled.

The Fair Debt Collection Statutory Letter

The federal Fair Debt Collection Practices Act, 15 U.S.C. §§ 1692–1692(o), regulates collection of debts owed by consumers. When preparing a collection letter that must comply with this statute's requirements, you should include the following information:

- The amount of the debt.
- The name of the creditor to whom the debt is owed.
- A statement that you assume the debt to be valid, unless the validity is disputed within 30 days.
- A statement that, if the consumer notifies the attorney in writing within the 30-day period that the debt or any part of it is disputed, verification of the debt will be obtained and sent to the consumer.
- A statement that, upon written request within the 30-day period, the attorney will provide the consumer with the name and address of the original creditor, if different from the current creditor.
- A statement that the attorney is attempting to collect the debt, and that any information received will be used for that purpose.

Unless the federal statute is complied with, your collection letter may be faulty, and your attempt to collect for your client may fail. You should be familiar with this statute and any similar legislation that is applicable in your state or region.

Figure 8.10 shows a collection letter with a slightly aggressive tone. Figure 8.11 shows a more formal collection letter, written to collect a consumer debt in compliance with the federal Fair Debt Collection Practices Act.

FIGURE 8.10

Example of a Minimally Aggressive Collection Letter

May 24, 2006

Mr. Travis Rande
CD'S UNLIMITED
1617 Concord Street
San Diego, CA 90404

Re: Our Client: MOULDE PRODUCTIONS, INC.
Balance Due and Owing: $5,325.87

Dear Mr. Rande:

The law firm of Helman & Jones represents Productions, Inc. in the above-referenced matter. On or about January 4, 2006, Productions, Inc. provided you with production services and air time for a commercial advertisement on the "Music Review" television program. For these services and air time, you agreed to pay Productions, Inc. the total amount of $5,325.87. Presently, there is a balance due and owing of $5,325.87.

In order to alleviate any additional costs and expenses, your prompt attention to this matter is advisable. It is expected that the entire amount will be paid within 30 days. Please contact me to discuss the matter immediately. If we have not received a satisfactory response from you within the time specified above, we will have no alternative but to pursue further action.

Very truly yours,

Jeanne J. Carr

FIGURE 8.11   Collection Letter Prepared in Compliance with the Federal Fair Debt Collection Practices Act

April 28, 2006

CERTIFIED MAIL #P117784262
RETURN RECEIPT REQUESTED
Ms. Linda Starr
Burgers, Etc.
645 Elm Street
Houston, Texas 77204

      Re: Our Client: AAA Equipment
      Amounts Due on Account: $8,847.58

Dear Ms. Starr:

      This law firm has been retained to represent AAA Equipment in the above-referenced matter to effect collection of the amount owed by your company, Burgers, Inc. On or about February 4, 2006, our client provided Burgers, Inc. with restaurant equipment for use in its hamburger business. The cost of the equipment was $9,747.58, for which you paid $1,700 as a down payment, leaving a balance of $8,047.58. As per the contract, the balance was due on or before March 15, 2006. The balance is now past due. If $8,847.58 (constituting the original $8,047.58 plus an additional sum of $800.00 as attorneys' fees) is not received in this office within thirty (30) days from the date of this letter, we will have no alternative but to pursue whatever legal remedies are available to protect our client's interests, including the filing of a lawsuit.

      Pursuant to the Fair Debt Collection Practices Act, 15 U.S.C. §§1692–1692(o), any such action could subject you to additional liability for attorneys' fees and costs of suit.

      If the above amount is not disputed by you within thirty (30) days from the date of this letter, it will be presumed valid. If the debt is disputed, verification of the debt will be provided by my client. Further, any information you provide me will be used in the collection of the debt.

      Please be assured this is not the beginning of a series of collection letters. If we have not received a satisfactory response from you within the time specified above, we will have no alternative than to proceed with litigation. In order to alleviate any additional costs and expenses, your prompt attention to this matter is advised.

            Very truly yours,

            Alex Johnson

The Consumer Protection Letter

Many states have created a statutory method for a consumer to file suit against a business that conducts its affairs in a deceptive or unfair manner. When drafting a demand letter setting forth a claim under such a statute, it is important to mention the statute in your letter, and to comply with all its requirements. As with other demand letters, the facts of your claim should be stated, as well as the amount of the demand; indeed, these things may be prerequisites to making a claim for punitive or other damages under the statute.

The basic requirements for a demand letter under the Texas statute appear in Figure 8.12, and a letter drafted to meet these requirements appears in Figure 8.13. If a statute has been passed in your state, you should obtain a copy and review it.

The Letter Notifying of Intention to Litigate

A special type of demand letter is the letter that places an opposing party or counsel on notice that your client intends to initiate a lawsuit. This may be combined with an ordinary letter demanding payment of an unpaid bill, or may relate to a claim where the amount of damage is not immediately quantifiable, as in a personal injury action or an action seeking an injunction.

Most parties, including insurance companies, like to avoid litigation where possible; your intention to go to court, if perceived as realistic, may spur settlement talks. It may also backfire,

FIGURE 8.12 Texas Deceptive Trade Practices Act Basic Requirements for Demand Letter

Source: Texas Business and Commerce Code; Title 2. Competition and Trade Practices; Chapter 17. Deceptive Trade Practices. From TEXAS STATUTES AND CODES ANNOTATED BY LEXISNEXIS.

17.505. Notice; Inspection

(a) As a prerequisite to filing a suit seeking damages under Subdivision (1) of Subsection (b) of Section 17.50 of this subchapter against any person, a consumer shall give written notice to the person at least 60 days before filing the suit advising the person in reasonable detail of the consumer's specific complaint and the amount of economic damages, damages for mental anguish, and expenses, including attorneys' fees, if any, reasonably incurred by the consumer in asserting the claim against the defendant. During the 60-day period a written request to inspect, in a reasonable manner and at a reasonable time and place, the goods that are the subject of the consumer's action or claim may be presented to the consumer.

(b) If the giving of 60 days' written notice is rendered impracticable by reason of the necessity of filing suit in order to prevent the expiration of the statute of limitations or if the consumer's claim is asserted by way of counterclaim, the notice provided for in Subsection (a) of this section is not required, but the tender provided for by Subsection (d), Section 17.506 of this subchapter may be made within 60 days after service of the suit or counterclaim.

(c) A person against whom a suit is pending who does not receive written notice, as required by Subsection (a), may file a plea in abatement not later than the 30th day after the date the person files an original answer in the court in which the suit is pending. This subsection does not apply if Subsection (b) applies.

(d) The court shall abate the suit if the court, after a hearing, finds that the person is entitled to an abatement because notice was not provided as required by this section. A suit is automatically abated without the order of the court beginning on the 11th day after the date a plea in abatement is filed under Subsection (c) if the plea in abatement:

(1) is verified and alleges that the person against whom the suit is pending did not receive the written notice as required by Subsection (a); and

(2) is not controverted by an affidavit filed by the consumer before the 11th day after the date on which the plea in abatement is filed.

(e) An abatement under Subsection (d) continues until the 60th day after the date that written notice is served in compliance with Subsection (a).

however, creating a hostile reaction that actually scuttles settlement talks. The risk involved is a matter of concern and interest to you, but the decision on how to proceed will be made by your supervising attorney and the client.

When preparing a letter notifying of intention to litigate, you should

- state the facts accurately;
- state the specific damages you claim, even if the amount is only an estimate (as with a personal injury suit);
- state, if the claim is for other than money damages (as, for example, where the proposed lawsuit seeks an injunction to remove toxic waste), the specific relief sought;
- emphasize your good faith and desire to work out the disagreement, if possible; and
- keep the tone courteous, not belligerent; this is more likely to lead to settlement.

These factors are general considerations; in a specific case, they may or may not apply. Consult with your supervising attorney for your strategy, but keep these things in mind. Figure 8.14 is an example of a letter notifying of intention to take a lawsuit to court.

As with other demand letters, an important concern is whether it should be sent under the attorney's name or the client's. If under the attorney's, the recipient may believe that it is too late

FIGURE 8.13
Consumer Demand
Letter

April 25, 2006

Mr. Bryan Henley
Office Manager
SMITHTON CHIROPRACTIC CENTER
1487 Orange Grove Blvd.
Galveston, TX 77553

          Re: Your letter to Deborah Lee Jones dated March 20, 2006

Dear Mr. Henley:

          The undersigned law firm has been retained to represent Ms. Deborah Lee Jones in the matter of her account with Smithton Center. Ms. Jones purchased services from and made use of therapeutic equipment in Smithton Center during the summer of 2006.

          This letter is being sent pursuant to Section 17.50 of the Texas Business and Commerce Code, hereinafter referred to as the Deceptive Trade Practices Act ("DTPA"), which requires that such a letter be sent sixty (60) days prior to the initiating of litigation. The DTPA specifically provides that you may tender a written offer of settlement within this sixty (60) day period of time, and further provides that your offer of settlement must include an agreement to reimburse Ms. Jones for her attorneys' fees incurred to date. To date, Ms. Jones has incurred $1,000 in attorneys' fees.

          After receiving medical treatment rendered by your clinic on August 26, 2005, Ms. Jones experienced severely painful muscle spasms as a direct result of that treatment. Ms. Jones attempted on several occasions to contact your office without success.

          At no time was Ms. Jones informed by your clinic that charges continued to mount even though she no longer subscribed to therapy. Ms. Jones was told that aside from an initial $150.00 charge, she would incur no further cost as a result of her treatment.

          Ms. Jones' specific complaints are as follows:

(i)   you represented that goods and services had sponsorship, approval, characteristics, ingredients, uses, benefits, or qualities which they did not have;

(ii)   you advertised goods and services with no intent to sell them as advertised;

(iii)   you failed to disclose information that you knew at the time of the transaction, and such failure to disclose was intended to induce Ms. Jones into a transaction that she would not otherwise have entered into, in that you represented to Ms. Jones that the services would be rendered at no cost to her after payment of an initial $150.00;

(iv)   you engaged in an unconscionable action or course of action, by taking advantage of the lack of knowledge, ability, experience, or capacity of Ms. Jones to a grossly unfair degree; and

(v)   you charged Ms. Jones for services never rendered.

          As a result of your false, misleading, and deceptive acts and practices and unconscionable conduct, Ms. Jones was deceived into executing a purported agreement you now claim obligates her to pay medical fees of $2,000.00. Not only does she not owe this amount, but she has suffered damages in the amount of at least $325.00 and has incurred attorneys' fees in the amount of $1,000.00, as a result of your wrongful acts. We urge you to make a written offer of settlement pursuant to Section 17.50 of the Texas in the amount of $1,000.00, as a result of your wrongful acts. If settlement cannot be reached within sixty (60) days, please take note that my client has authorized me to initiate a lawsuit on her behalf to seek (1) rescission of any agreements procured by your fraud, and (2) the full measure of allowable damages, which can be three times actual damages, plus attorneys' fees and court costs.

          As an additional cause of action, Ms. Jones has instructed me to initiate a lawsuit based upon your breach of contract, common law fraud, negligent entrustment, and medical malpractice for misdiagnosing her condition and causing her personal injury. Ms. Jones has instructed me to request rescission of any agreements procured by your fraud, and to seek punitive damages based upon the aforementioned fraudulent representations made knowingly by Smithton Center and its agents.

          Very truly yours,

          Peter R. Moore

PRM/prh

FIGURE 8.14
Letter Notifying of
Intention to Litigate

April 28, 2006

CERTIFIED MAIL #P117784262
RETURN RECEIPT REQUESTED
Ms. Carly Ford
AAA Equipment
645 Elm Street
Houston, Texas 77204

     Re: Gourmet Services, Inc.

Dear Ms. Ford:
     Please be advised that the undersigned has been retained by Gourmet Services, Inc. to represent them concerning their dispute with you on the equipment auctioned from the New Orleans Restaurant.
     It is our understanding that you sold equipment owned by Gourmet Services, Inc. without their knowledge or permission. As previously communicated to you in a letter of December 12, 2005 from Gourmet Services, Inc., our client is prepared to settle this matter for the sum of $5,000.12. Demand is hereby made for payment in full of that amount in the form of a cashier's check or money order payable to Gourmet Services, Inc. and sent to me on or before ten (10) days from the date of this letter. Your failure to do so may result in litigation based upon wrongful conversion of the equipment, and other causes of action, which may result in the imposition of court costs, attorneys' fees, and interest. Our client does not desire to pursue this remedy, but is ready to do so if it is made necessary through your failure to comply with this demand.
     Unless you dispute the validity of this debt, or any portion thereof within thirty (30) days after receipt of this letter, the debt will be assumed to be valid. Should you dispute the validity of the debt within thirty (30) days from the date of receipt of this communication, a verification of the debt will be obtained and mailed to you.
     If you have any questions concerning our client's intention or wish to discuss this matter, please contact me.

     Sincerely,

     Donna M. Jackson

DMJ/prh
cc: Client

to settle because the decision to start a lawsuit has already been made. Depending on the circumstances, you may want to send it under the client's name. Consult with your attorney on the proper procedure; and, even if you decide to send it under the client's name, you and your firm should still review (and probably actually draft) the letter.

RESPONDING TO DEMAND LETTERS

When responding to a demand letter, the first step is to review the demand carefully with the client, pointing out the meaning and implications of the offer, and discussing what you believe to be the options for a response. When you begin to draft the response, be careful about reciting details. You should identify your position early, and counter any inaccurate factual claims made by the opposing side. You may want to avoid appearing aggressive, since this may do further harm to what may be a deteriorating situation; again, this is a judgment call.

    One option almost always available is to request further information. This may "buy time" while the opposing party decides how to handle your request.

    If you deny the claim, identify the reasons for your denial. If there are relevant cases or statutes that favor you, you may want to cite them. If there are documents that aid your cause, you

FIGURE 8.15   Response to Notice of Litigation

May 4, 2006

CERTIFIED MAIL #P117784265
RETURN RECEIPT REQUESTED
Ms. Lois J. Jackson
Attorney at Law
2350 Alliance Street
Houston, Texas 77204

      Re: Our Client: AAA Equipment
      Your Client: Gourmet Services, Inc.

Dear Ms. Jackson:
      The undersigned represents AAA Equipment in the above-referenced matter. The matter that you have addressed in your letter dated April 28, 2006 is disputed. I do not know the basis of your claims or the substance of them. Consequently, pursuant to the Fair Debt Collection Statute, we are hereby placing you on notice that we do dispute the validity of any claims that you are alleging in your letter and request further investigation into this alleged debt.
      We appreciate prompt response to this matter.

      Very truly yours,

      Drew Michaels

cc: Client

may want to enclose copies. There may be strategic reasons to avoid such disclosure, however—so check with your supervising attorney first.

The best type of response to a demand letter, in general, is one that makes your position clear, but keeps the door open for negotiation. Be firm, though courteous, in your denial, and try to provide a reason for keeping the dialogue open (for example, the request for further documentation). Remember that sometimes a forceful, aggressive approach may be necessary—for example, to threaten a counterclaim.

Figure 8.15 is a letter designed to maintain channels of communication.

STATUTORY LETTERS OF INTENT TO LITIGATE: MALPRACTICE CASES

Unfortunate as they are, malpractice cases are common in the litigation world. In most states, intent to litigate a medical malpractice issue has specific statutory requirements. For instance, a number of states require that notification is given to the physician or healthcare provider sixty or ninety days prior to filing the case. If this requirement is not fulfilled, the injured party may lose their right to pursue the medical malpractice claim. A defective notice of intent to file a malpractice claim may also affect a party's ability to litigate the claim. Are you seeing a pattern here? If you don't get it right, the client may lose the opportunity to sue. The states of New York and Texas present examples of the strict statutory requirements for notifying the physician, healthcare provider, or both. Notice the word "requirements," as deviation may be another form of malpractice—legal. The requirements for both states are identified in Figure 8.16.

The prerequisites to filing a lawsuit in both states are stringent and that is why the notice letter must conform completely to the statutory requirements.

General considerations when preparing a letter of intent to litigate a medical malpractice claim are

- the date of client's injury;
- the names of the parties involved in the case, *e.g.,* hospital (public or private), physician (hospital staff or private);

FIGURE 8.16 **Statutory Requirements for New York and Texas**

Source: Texas Civil Practice and Remedies Code; Title 4. Liability In Tort; Chapter 74. Medical Liability; Subchapter B. Notice and Pleadings. From TEXAS STATUTES AND CODES ANNOTATED BY LEXISNEXIS. New York General Municipal Law; Article 4. Negligence and Malfeasance of Public Officers; Taxpayers' Remedies. From NEW YORK CONSOLIDATED LAW SERVICE. Copyright (c) 2006 Matthew Bender & Company, Inc., one of the LEXIS Publishing (TM) companies. All rights reserved.

NEW YORK
50-e. Notice of Claim

1. When service required; time for service; upon whom service required.

(a) In any case founded upon tort where a notice of claim is required by law as a condition precedent to the commencement of an action or special proceeding against a public corporation, as defined in the general construction law, or any officer, appointee, or employee thereof, the notice of claim shall comply with and be served in accordance with the provisions of this section within ninety days after the claim arises; except that in wrongful death actions, the ninety days shall run from the appointment of a representative of the decedent's estate.

(b) Service of the notice of claim upon an officer, appointee, or employee of a public corporation shall not be a condition precedent to the commencement of an action or special proceeding against such person. If an action or special proceeding is commenced against such person, but not against the public corporation, service of the notice of claim upon the public corporation shall be required only if the corporation has a statutory obligation to indemnify such person under this chapter or any other provision of law.

2. Form of notice; contents. The notice shall be in writing, sworn to by or on behalf of the claimant, and shall set forth: (1) the name and post office address of each claimant, and of his attorney, if any; (2) the nature of the claim; (3) the time when, the place where, and the manner in which the claim arose; and (4) the items of damage or injuries claimed to have been sustained so far as then practicable but a notice with respect to a claim against a municipal corporation other than a city with a population of one million or more persons shall not state the amount of damages to which the claimant deems himself entitled, provided, however, that the municipal corporation, other than a city with a population of one million or more persons, may at any time request a supplemental claim setting forth the total damages to which the claimant deems himself entitled. A supplemental claim shall be provided by the claimant within fifteen days of the request. In the event the supplemental demand is not served within fifteen days, the court, on motion, may order that it be provided by the claimant.

TEXAS

74.051. Notice

(a) Any person or his authorized agent asserting a health care liability claim shall give written notice of such claim by certified mail, return receipt requested, to each physician or health care provider against whom such claim is being made at least 60 days before the filing of a suit in any court of this state based upon a health care liability claim. The notice must be accompanied by the authorization form for release of protected health information as required under Section 74.052.

(b) In such pleadings as are subsequently filed in any court, each party shall state that it has fully complied with the provisions of this section and Section 74.052 and shall provide such evidence thereof as the judge of the court may require to determine if the provisions of this chapter have been met.

(c) Notice given as provided in this chapter shall toll the applicable statute of limitations to and including a period of 75 days following the giving of the notice, and this tolling shall apply to all parties and potential parties.

(d) All parties shall be entitled to obtain complete and unaltered copies of the patient's medical records from any other party within 45 days from the date of receipt of a written request for such records; provided, however, that the receipt of a medical authorization in the form required by Section 74.052 executed by the claimant herein shall be considered compliance by the claimant with this subsection.

(e) For the purposes of this section, and notwithstanding Chapter 159, Occupations Code, or any other law, a request for the medical records of a deceased person or a person who is incompetent shall be deemed to be valid if accompanied by an authorization in the form required by Section 74.052 signed by a parent, spouse, or adult child of the deceased or incompetent person.

You Be the Judge

Knowing the statutory requirements, or at least performing the legal research to determine them for a particular cause of action, is the difference between success and failure. In *Toledo v. Ordway*, 576 N.Y.S. 2d 886 (A.D. 2d Dept. 1991), the plaintiff failed to comply with the statutory notice requirements in a medical malpractice case; the court barred the action against the physician. That means whether a claim existed is irrelevant since the statute of limitations expired. What are the facts in Toledo? What statute did the court rely upon to reach its result? What were the requirements of the statute? The case provides two important lessons: (1) obtain accurate dates from the client, and (2) review the applicable law prior to drafting a specialized or statutory letter. This case is not unusual and should be viewed as a warning.

- the jurisdiction's statutory requirements; and
- strict compliance with statute's requirements.

Using the Texas statute as our guide, Figure 8.17 is a compliant Notice of Intention to Litigate a Medical Malpractice claim. Included in that figure is a series of letters resulting in the filing of a lawsuit.

FIGURE 8.17   Series of Letters in Medical Malpractice Case

(a) Notice of Claim
February 21, 2006

CERTIFIED MAIL #P117784223
RETURN RECEIPT REQUESTED

Dr. Ned Radcliffe
18015 15th Street, Suite 310
Goodnight, Texas 75020

> Re: Lynn Murray
> Health Care Liability Claim

Dear Dr. Radcliffe:

The undersigned represents Lynn Murray in the above-referenced matter. NOTICE IS HEREBY GIVEN that my client, Lynn Murray, has a "health care liability claim" against you, as the quoted term is defined in Article 4590i, §1.03, Subdivision (a), Paragraph (4) of the Revised Civil Statutes of Texas. This claim is based on the fact that you negligently administered and cared for Ms. Murray upon giving anesthesia on November 12, 2005, in the course of treating her to fill two abscessed teeth. As a result of your negligence, Ms. Murray suffered a sensitivity reaction to the anesthesia, including violent shaking of arms and legs, chattering of teeth, and convulsions.

Due to your negligence, Ms. Murray also contracted a severe skin reaction, triggered by the anesthesia. This condition has caused substantial rashes on her arms and upper body, and could in the future affect her entire body.

As a result of her reaction, Ms. Murray has had to engage the services of medical specialists and undergo and incur expenses for examination and diagnosis of the condition, for psychological consultation and for medication to help her condition, and she will have to continue various treatments, consultations, and medications in the future, and incur expenses.

Prior to your negligence hereinabove referred to, Ms. Murray was twenty-eight (28) years old, in good health, and employed as a representative with MBI Corporation. As a result of your negligence, she has had to miss work at her job and has, therefore, lost wages and will be required in the future to lose further time from her job for an as-yet-undetermined period. As a further result of your negligence, she has suffered severe mental and physical pain and anguish, and in all probability will continue to suffer such mental and physical pain and anguish for the rest of her life, all to her further damage. To date, the amount of damages is $12,587.37, and continues to grow.

YOU ARE FURTHER NOTIFIED that this claim is given pursuant to the provisions of Article 4590i, Section 4.60, Subdivision (a) of the Revised Civil Statutes of Texas, and that, if it is

FIGURE 8.17 Cont.

not settled within sixty (60) days from the date this notice is given, the undersigned will commence an appropriate legal action against you to recover her damages.

Your prompt attention to this matter is advised.

Very truly yours,

Emma M. Costello

(b) Reply from Insurance Carrier

March 10, 2006

Ms. Emma M. Costello
Attorney at Law
6301 Marley Avenue
Anyplace, TX 75311

Re: Lynn Murray vs. Dr. Ned Radcliffe

Dear Ms. Costello:

Your notice letter addressed to Dr. Radcliffe has been referred to us as the professional carrier for the doctor. It is my understanding that Dr. Radcliffe has previously forwarded your client's medical records to you, along with a release executed by your client on December 7, 2005. Thus, not only is there no liability on the part of Dr. Radcliffe, your client has signed a release.

I personally guarantee that if you file a lawsuit with regard to this matter, it will be countered with a lawsuit against your client for breach of contract and a Motion for Sanctions, since the matter is a frivolous claim.

Please address any further correspondence or inquiries to my attention. Do not call or write the doctor with regard to this matter.

Sincerely,

Edward Z. Plant

MEDICAL INSURANCE COVERAGE COMPANY

(c) Response to Insurance Company's Letter

March 18, 2006

Mr. Edward Z. Plant
MEDICAL INSURANCE COVERAGE COMPANY
1601 Ohio Avenue, 5th Floor
Sandy, Illinois 42930

Re: Lynn Murray vs. Dr. Ned Radcliffe

Dear Mr. Plant:

This is in response to your letter dated March 10, 2006. I do not appreciate the statement in your letter regarding the filing of frivolous lawsuits. Perhaps you should investigate the facts of this matter, as well as the law in Texas.

If you are trying to make threats to me regarding any claims Ms. Murray has against Dr. Radcliffe, those threats are so noted. However, let me assure you that I am well aware of the Texas Rules of Procedure. I can further assure you that I intend to pursue this matter, and will shortly be filing a lawsuit.

Let me encourage you, in the future, to investigate and examine the facts of your cases before you begin threats of Motions for Sanction.

If you choose to discuss this matter in a civil and professional manner, I would be happy to do so. Otherwise, you can expect to be hearing from me with a lawsuit.

Your prompt attention to this matter is advised.

Very truly yours,

Emma M. Costello

NEW STANDARDS FOR REQUESTING MEDICAL INFORMATION

In April 2003, new standards for requesting and acquiring patient information became law. The Health Insurance Portability and Accountability Act, "HIPAA" as it is more commonly known, set forth a host of requirements for accessing patient-protected health information (PHI). Not only does this requirement apply in the medical malpractice setting, but it applies to a personal injury lawsuit, an automobile accident, or any other situation where medical records are required. As a paralegal, you may be asked to not only draft the notice letter, but also a letter requesting medical information, which complies with HIPAA. Texas has included an HIPAA authorization as a statutory requirement in a medical malpractice claim. The authorization requesting patient information must be signed by the client, the client's legal representative, or the client's guardian, if a minor. The authorization required under the Texas law is illustrated in Figure 8.18.

This authorization is a good example of the requirements under HIPAA throughout the United States. Since HIPAA is a federal law, it applies to everyone. Use it as a guide for any case involving medical records, but research your own jurisdiction for its requirements.

FIGURE 8.18   **Authorization Form for Release of Medical Information**

Source: Adapted from *Texas Jurisprudence Pleading and Practice Forms* (Thomson West, 2004).

AUTHORIZATION FORM FOR RELEASE OF PROTECTED HEALTH INFORMATION

A. I, Morgan Reilly, hereby authorize Raymond Sullivan, MD and Memorial Hospital to obtain and disclose, within the parameters set out below, the protected health information, described below for the following specific purposes:

1. To facilitate the investigation and evaluation of the health care claim described in the accompanying Notice of Health Care Claim; or

2. Defense of any litigation arising to of the claim made the basis of the accompanying Notice of Health Care Claim.

B. The health information to be obtained, used or disclosed extends to and includes the verbal as well as the written and is specifically described as follows:

1. The health information in the custody of the following physicians or health care providers who have examined, evaluated, or treated Nathan Reilly in connection with the injuries alleged to have been sustained in connection with the claim asserted in the accompanying Notice of Health Care Claim. _____ [*Listing of names and current addresses of all treating physicians or health care providers*]. This authorization shall extend to any additional physicians or health care providers that may in the future evaluate, examine, or treat Nathan Reilly for injuries alleged in connection with the claim made the basis of the attached Notice of Health Care Claim;

2. The health information in the custody of the following physicians or health care providers who have examined, evaluated, or treated Nathan Reilly during a period commencing five years prior to the incident made the basis of the accompanying Notice of Health Care Claim. _____ [*List name and current address of such physicians or health care providers, if applicable.*]

C. Excluded Health Information—The following constitutes a list of physicians or health care providers possessing health care information concerning Nathan Reilly to which this authorization does not apply because I contend that such health care information is not relevant to the damages being claimed or to the physical, mental, or emotional condition of Nathan Reilly arising out of the claim made the basis of the accompanying Notice of Health Care Claim:

FIGURE 8.18 Cont.

_____ [*None/listing of names of each physician or health care provider to whom authorization does not extend, and inclusive dates of examination, evaluation, or treatment to be withheld from disclosure.*]

D. The persons or class of persons to whom the health information of Nathan Reilly will be disclosed or who will make use of said information are:
    1. Any and all physicians or health care providers providing care or treatment to Nathan Reilly;
    2. Any liability insurance entity providing liability insurance coverage or defense to any physician or health care provider to whom Notice of Health Care Claim has been given with regard to the care and treatment of Nathan Reilly;
    3. Any consulting or testifying experts employed by or on behalf of Raymond Sullivan, MD and Memorial Hospital with regard to the matter set out in the Notice of Health Care Claim accompanying this authorization.
    4. Any attorneys, including secretarial, clerical, or paralegal staff, employed by or on behalf of Raymond Sullivan, MD and Memorial Hospital with regard to the matter set out in the Notice of Health Care Claim accompanying this authorization;
    5. Any trier of the law or facts relating to any suit filed seeking damages arising out of the medical care or treatment of Nathan Reilly.

E. This authorization expires on resolution of the claim asserted or at the conclusion of any litigation instituted in connection with the subject matter of the Notice of Health Care Claim accompanying this authorization, whichever occurs sooner.

F. I understand that, without exception, I have the right to revoke this authorization in writing. I further understand the consequences of any such revocation as set out in § 74.052 of the Texas Civil Practice and Remedies Code.

G. I understand that the signing of this authorization is not a condition for continued treatment, payment, enrollment, or eligibility for health plan benefits.

H. I understand that information used or disclosed pursuant to this authorization may be subject to redisclosure by the recipient and may no longer be protected by federal HIPAA privacy regulations.

Dated:_____ [*date*]

_____
Signature of Patient/Representative
Dated:_____ [*date*]

_____
Name of Patient/Representative
Dated:_____ [*date*]

_____ [*Description of Representative's Authority*]

THE OPINION LETTER

opinion letter
A letter that renders legal advice.

An **opinion letter** renders legal advice. Based upon specific facts, and applying information gained through research, it analyzes a legal problem and reaches a conclusion about the resolution of the problem. In the subsections that follow, we first discuss an opinion letter directed to your client, and then address some separate considerations when the opinion letter is directed to a third party.

The Client Opinion Letter

A comprehensive client opinion letter should contain several distinct elements. Let's consider these elements.

Date

The date listed at the top of the letter is important. Your research must be accurate through that date. You cannot be held responsible for changes in the law or new cases or statutes that arise after that date, but you are responsible for all changes in the law *up to* that date.

Introductory Paragraph

disclaimer
A limiting claim or denial.

An introductory paragraph should identify the issue or problem that the letter will address. Included in this paragraph should be a **disclaimer** (limiting claim or denial) indicating that the analysis that follows is based upon the facts as they are set forth in the letter. If a different version of the facts develops, the analysis may change as well. It is important that you emphasize this to protect your firm from liability—and it is important to emphasize to the client the need to provide accurate and complete factual information.

Facts and Background

The next section should set forth the facts and background that have been developed through client conferences and independent investigation. It should again be emphasized that the analysis is based upon these facts. You should take great care in gathering and presenting these facts. Remember that clients' memories may be selective, concentrating on their own strong points and forgetting their weak points. Thus, as with other writing projects, a good client interview is the foundation for a good opinion letter.

Conclusion

A brief statement of your conclusion may precede the analysis. This will help the client, or other reader, to follow the arguments to come. The scope of the conclusion should be indicated here, including any limitations or qualifications.

Analysis

This section is like the discussion section of the internal memorandum. In it you analyze the applicable case law, statutes, and other sources. Both strengths and weaknesses of your client's position should be discussed. Remember that you are balancing two goals here—informing the client, and accurately stating the law. This balance requires that you both (1) accurately present complicated legal concepts, and (2) present them in language the client can understand. Don't misrepresent by oversimplifying; take the time and effort necessary to make the document both accurate and understandable. This may, on occasion, require explaining things twice—once using terms of art or other complicated language, and a second time, describing what these terms and language mean in plain and practical language.

Be sure, again, to identify the limitations upon, and qualifications of, the analysis. Define all terms that might create confusion; identify the extent of your investigation; and indicate any and all assumptions on which the analysis is based.

Recommendation

In reaching her conclusion, an attorney rendering an opinion generally makes a recommendation to the client about the best approach to resolving the problem presented. This is perhaps the most important section of the opinion letter—where the attorney takes a position based upon his research. Again, emphasize that the opinion is based upon the facts as they are known to the attorney. If the attorney needs to qualify her position, or indicate problems, she should do so here as well as in earlier sections. Do not use qualifiers to make your position ambiguous, however—use them to describe precisely what you have concluded to be an ambiguous situation.

Directive

Your last paragraph should be an instruction or directive to the client to contact the attorney after reviewing the letter. This contact is important, because it will enable you, your supervising attorney, and the client to discuss and clarify any questions that the client has regarding the facts, the conclusion, and the recommendations.

FIGURE 8.19 Client Opinion Letter

July 21, 2006

Mr. Neil Crosby
9250 Kingsley Road
Aurora, Colorado 80011

　　　　Re: Evaluation of Insurance Claims

Dear Mr. Crosby:

　　　　You have retained me to review the law regarding the responsibility of insurance companies to provide coverage for preexisting medical conditions.

　　　　I have reviewed the documentation that you have supplied to me. Based on the medical response from Dr. Stills, it appears that you did not have a preexisting condition at the time you applied for medical insurance. The problem is convincing the insurance company of that fact.

　　　　The most logical first step would be to send a letter to the insurance company detailing our position, namely that you did not have a preexisting condition at the time you applied for insurance. However, before a letter is sent, it would be appropriate for us to meet so that I may discuss with you the result of my research on the legal meaning of preexisting condition.

　　　　Briefly, the case law on this issue is unsettled. The courts generally look to the definition of "preexisting condition" in your insurance policy, then apply this to your medical history. There is no generally accepted definition of preexisting condition; it is determined by a judge or jury as a question of fact.

　　　　This means that estimating our chances for success will be difficult. Unfortunately, unless the insurance company willingly agrees with our position, the most logical next step would be to file a lawsuit against the insurance company for failing to pay your claims.

　　　　As we had discussed in our first meeting, this may be quite costly, with the results uncertain. Please call me in the next ten days so we can decide how to pursue this matter: whether to send the letter to the insurance company based on your medicals and my research, or not pursue the matter at all. I look forward to hearing from you.

　　　　Thank you for your attention and courtesies.

　　　　　　　　Very truly yours,

　　　　　　　　Steven N. Young

Remember that, as a paralegal, you can *never* sign an opinion letter—only an attorney can render legal advice. However, you may be drafting these letters for an attorney to review. Figure 8.19 shows an example of a client opinion letter.

The Third-Party Opinion Letter

There are occasions when a third party will require that your client provide a legal opinion, so that he can complete a transaction. For example, a client seeking a mortgage may need to provide the bank with a legal opinion regarding a title question. If you are called upon to draft such a letter, there are several points to remember. First, be sure to identify in the letter the firm's relationship with the client. Second, indicate that, despite this relationship, your opinion is based upon honest and unbiased analysis. Third, use language that restricts the applicability of the opinion, for liability purposes—for example, stating: "This opinion has been prepared for the benefit of First National Bank only, and no other party may rely on the representations contained herein." Fourth, identify the reason for the opinion—for example, "This opinion has been requested by First National Bank in connection with a mortgage sought by my client, William Doe." Fifth, be sure that you clearly identify your opinion or conclusion. This can be done with plain, unequivocal language: "Based on the above, it is our opinion that . . ." or "We hereby render the following opinions based upon the preceding analysis. . . ." Finally, clearly identify who is rendering the opinion. For example, on the signature line, the signer (who, as we have noted, will always be an attorney) should probably sign not on his own behalf, but on behalf of his firm.

FIGURE 8.20
Third Party Opinion Letter

September 18, 2006

Ms. Roberta McMillan, Examiner
Individual Benefit Department
UNITED INSURANCE AGENCY
716 Milton Drive
Richmond, VA 32187

Re: Our Client: Mr. Neil Crosby
Health Coverage Due and Owing Under
Policy number 718465023GB8A dated December 2, 2005

Dear Ms. McMillan:

The undersigned represents Mr. Neil Crosby in the above-referenced matter. You have requested a legal opinion of the law in the state of Texas on preexisting conditions as it relates to my client. A brief synopsis of the facts is necessary.

On December 2, 2005, Mr. Crosby became insured with United Insurance Agency for health insurance with a quarterly premium of $587.60. A copy of the policy is attached hereto as Exhibit A. The policy contained certain contractual obligations, one of which was to pay medical expenses, over and above the noted deductible, for the insured in the event of the occurrence of any health problems. In January 2006, your company failed and refused to pay Mr. Crosby for his health care costs, stating that he had a preexisting condition before the policy was issued and therefore was not covered under your company's policy. A representative contended that Mr. Crosby did not properly and accurately inform your company of his medical history in answers supplied by him on your company's application for insurance. This application, with the responses, is attached hereto as Exhibit B. As noted on the application, Mr. Crosby had not been diagnosed as having any type of disease condition within the five (5) years prior to applying for insurance with United Insurance Agency.

His policy was conditioned upon the information contained within the application being "to the best of my [Mr. Crosby's] knowledge and belief . . . complete and true." Mr. Crosby's information was in fact a truthful representation of his condition.

United Insurance Agency never followed up his application with any type of medical examination by its own physicians. This was a condition that your company would have had to so follow up as a condition precedent to justify any denial of coverage.

The Texas Administrative Code, Section 3.3018 defines preexisting illness as:

> The existence of symptoms which could cause an ordinarily prudent person to seek diagnosis, care, or treatment within a five-year period preceding the effective date of the coverage of the insured person or a condition for which medical advice or treatment was recommended by a physician or received from a physician within a five-year period preceding the effective date of the coverage of the insured person.

My client had no knowledge of any preexisting illness that would preclude coverage as defined in the Texas statute. Further, the law requires knowledge of a preexisting condition, or that the insurer make independent investigation. My client did not have any latent symptoms that were intentionally ignored. Your company had an affirmative duty to investigate independently my client's representation of "good health." Due to your company's failure to investigate my client's health history, my client is not precluded from coverage. Mr. Crosby does fall within the protected class covered under your health insurance application.

United Insurance Agency knew of all medical records pertaining to the medical history of Mr. Crosby, based upon the completed information and history. As a result, you are contractually bound and responsible to pay his health expenses.

Based on my evaluation of the law, it is my opinion that there should be complete reimbursement of all medical expenses of my client from the inception of the policy to the present, as well as the payment of any future medical expenses.

This opinion is based on the present state of the law, as well as the documentation that has been supplied by my client, which included the insurance policy and application. Please contact me at your earliest convenience so that we may discuss this matter.

Thank you for your attention to this matter.

Very truly yours,

Steven N. Young

Ethics Alert

Know the purpose of your letter. If your intent is to harass, intimidate, or act unethically, the courts may just know how to deal with you and your attorney. In a recent Kansas case, *In re Gershater*, 17 P.3d 929 (Kan. 2001), an attorney was suspended "indefinitely" from the practice of law for sending a letter that "was vicious, offensive, and extremely unprofessional. Her letter employed a number of vile and unprintable epithets referring . . . to the attorneys in the case." *Id.* at 931. Not only did the court admonish the attorney for misrepresenting information in her correspondences but also for engaging in professional misconduct. In its observations regarding this particular attorney's conduct, the court emphatically denounced the behavior as one not befitting members of the bar:

A lawyer should be able to write a letter to an opposing party or a party with an adverse interest and intelligently communicate his or her position without the use of profane, offensive, or derogatory language. '[A]ttorneys are required to act with common courtesy and civility at all times in their dealings with those concerned with the legal process.' *In re Vincenti*, 114 N.J. 275, 282, 554 A.2d 470 (1989). 'Vilification, intimidation, abuse and threats have no place in the legal arsenal.' *In re Mezzacca*, 67 N.J. 387,389-90, 340 A.2d 658 (1975). 'An attorney who exhibits the lack of civility, good manners and common courtesy . . . tarnishes the entire image of what the bar stands for.' *In re McAlevy*, 69 N.J. 349, 352, 354 A.2d 289 (1976). *Id.* at 935-36.

Strong language is communicated by the court. Review the case and draw your own conclusions. Was the court justified in its sanctions of the attorney? What acts had the attorney committed for the court to impose an indefinite suspension? What was the court's reasoning and why did it use authority from other jurisdictions?

THE E-FACTOR: FAXING

Faxing is a way of life—instant gratification for the parties. Maybe. Using a fax machine to transit letters can be both a blessing and a curse. You fax the document and it is instantaneously received on the other end. You hope. Of course, you have your confirmation, but the attorney, paralegal, or assistant claims they never received the document. Now you are faced with a "he said," "she said" situation, where the winner probably is the other side, who claims they never received the document. What are you to do? To guard against this situation, do not assume the fax was received unless you contact the receiving party confirming receipt. Write down the name of the person whom you spoke with and the time you made the contact. Some attorneys may request a return confirmation from the receiver of the fax, avoiding any confusion. Faxing also poses confidentiality problems. Suppose the fax is sent to the wrong number or gets in the wrong hands. Of course we all place warnings on the fax that if the fax is incorrectly received, the recipient should contact the sender immediately. The damage is already done. Information in the wrong hands can cause a wealth of problems for you, your attorney, and the client. No one is suggesting not using a fax machine; what is being suggested is to be careful in its use and mindful of the consequences for a missent fax.

Most of these points are designed to define clearly the areas, and the limits, of your firm's liability for the opinion rendered, since in the third-party situation, they may not be immediately clear. Figure 8.20 on preceding page shows an example of a third-party opinion letter.

PRACTICAL CONSIDERATIONS

We end this chapter with one practical consideration: When framing correspondence, keep the ball in *your* court!

What does this mean? It's quite simple, and the best way to demonstrate is by example. Assume that your client has a dispute with a customer to whom he has supplied building materials, but from whom he has received no payment. You take the trouble to write a comprehensive demand letter, setting forth the terms on which you would be willing to settle the matter. The following are two possible closings to your letter (Figure 8.21), or consider the following comments from letters trying to schedule a deposition (Figure 8.22).

The point is this: When you leave the ball in your court, you have control over the situation, and inaction on the part of the other party will not impede your ability to take action. When you pass the ball

FIGURE 8.21   Closings to Your Letter

<u>**Closing 1: Ball in *opponent's* court:**</u>
Please advise as soon as possible if the enclosed terms are acceptable to you.

<u>**Closing 2: Ball in *your* court:**</u>
If we have not heard from you by September 1, 2006, we will assume the terms are unacceptable and immediately institute suit.

FIGURE 8.22   Closings to Your Letter: Scheduling a Deposition

<u>**Comment 1: Ball in *opponent's* court:**</u>
Please advise whether September 1, 2006 is an acceptable date for the deposition of John Doe.

<u>**Comment 2: Ball in *your* court:**</u>
The deposition will be held on September 1, 2006, unless you advise that this date is unacceptable.

to the other side's court, you place yourself in the position of having to wait for acceptance of an offer, or some other matter. Thus, you needlessly handicap your ability to respond to events as you see fit.

So, in drafting correspondence, use language that keeps your side in control of events. Keep the ball in your court!

Summary

The legal profession uses correspondence to inform, to advise, and to confirm. Informative letters transmit information; advisory letters are more formal than informative letters and offer legal opinions; and confirmation letters create a permanent record of the oral sharing of information.

The tone of a letter varies with the audience as well as the purpose. Letters to clients should contain concrete answers and be written to the client's level of understanding. They should be drafted so as to avoid unreasonable expectations in the mind of the client. Letters to opposing counsel should be written with caution, since they may be used against your client. Letters to the court should be written with respect. You should generally send copies to opposing counsel, and be aware of the pitfalls of *ex parte* communications.

A letter generally contains the following components: a letterhead; the date on which the letter is sent; identification of the addressee; a brief, descriptive reference line; a salutation opening with "Dear" and followed by a colon; a body containing the message of the letter, which may be short or long, but which should always be written clearly; headers, which identify subsequent pages; and a closing, often "Very truly yours" followed by the signer's name and position. Note that paralegals can *never* sign letters rendering legal advice. Finally, letters show the parties to whom copies have been sent; only your file copy should show those parties to whom blind carbon copies have been sent.

The demand letter is designed to motivate a desired response—often (though not exclusively) the payment of a debt. Demand letters can be in the form of a standard collection letter; a "Fair Debt Collection" letter designed to comply with statutory requirements; a consumer protection letter; or a notice of intention to sue. In drafting a demand letter, you should state your purpose, clarify the action you expect the recipient to take, establish a deadline date, and, under most circumstances, maintain a tone that will keep channels of communication open. In responding to a demand letter, you should review and discuss the situation with your client and identify reasons why you deny the claim. The letter should deny inaccurate factual statements made by the opposition, make your position clear, and, as with a demand letter, keep the channels of communication open.

An opinion letter renders legal advice. In a client opinion letter, work to balance two competing considerations: (1) presenting legal concepts accurately; and (2) presenting them in language the client can understand. Make it clear that your analysis is based upon the facts as you understand them, and make your recommendations clear as well. A third-party opinion letter must indicate your relationship with the client; the purpose of the letter; any limitations for liability purposes; and a clear statement of the bounds of the opinion.

Transmittal letters accompany information, confirming its nature and the fact that it was sent. Letters requesting information should be specific, and serve two purposes: to obtain information and to create a record that the request was made. A retainer letter sets forth the agreement between attorney and client on fees and services to be rendered. An authorization letter enables the attorney to pursue an investigation for the client's benefit into records maintained by third parties.

An important practical point in drafting legal correspondence is to keep the ball in your court, which means that whenever possible, you should maintain control over subsequent events.

Key Terms

informative letter	cc
advisory letter	bcc
confirmation letter	transmittal letter
cover letter	retainer letter
clerk of the court	authorization letter
ex parte	letter banks
letterhead	demand letters
reference line	collection letter
salutation	deadline date
body	opinion letter
header	disclaimer
closing	

Review Questions

1. Name three functions of legal correspondence.

2. List some characteristics of letters addressed to: clients; opposing counsel; and the court.

3. What are the components of a letter?

4. What are the appropriate methods of addressing a letter to: (a) a judge, (b) a chief executive officer, (c) a governor.

5. How is a reference line prepared?

6. Distinguish between a cc (copy) and a bcc (blind carbon copy).

7. What is the purpose of a demand letter?

8. What is the purpose of a client opinion letter?

9. How does a third-party opinion letter differ from a client opinion letter?

10. List two possible purposes of a letter that requests information, and describe its most important characteristic.

Exercises

1. Your law firm has just been retained to represent a woman who has been injured in an industrial accident. Your attorney has instructed you to request the client's medical history. Draft the letter requesting the information.

2. A client has a claim against an insurance company for nonpayment of medical bills. Draft the representation letter to the insurance company.

3. Prepare a transmittal letter to the court sending the Defendant's Original Answer. (Remember to state that the opposing counsel has been notified of this transmittal.)

4. The issue of universal healthcare coverage is scheduled for a hearing on Capitol Hill. Draft a letter to your Congressional representative requesting a copy of the transcript testimony.

5. Your state Attorney General has issued an opinion on your state's Open Records Act regarding the protection of government employees' personnel records. Draft a letter requesting the opinion.

6. Your attorney interviewed a new client who just bought a new car and it is a lemon. You reviewed the attorney's notes and he has asked you to prepare a consumer protection letter

based upon your jurisdiction's law. The name of the car company is America's Car, Inc., and it is located at 563 Highway Blvd., your city and state.

7. You need to file a Motion to Dismiss in the U.S. District Court for your attorney. She forgot to prepare the transmittal letter to the clerk of the court (in your jurisdiction). Prepare the transmittal letter.

8. Your attorney's best friend, Anthony Scott, has a medical malpractice case against his doctor and the hospital. Your attorney requested you research the statutory requirements for a medical malpractice case in your jurisdiction and provide a sample medical malpractice letter. All you know about the case is that the surgeon left a sponge in George's stomach after the surgery.

Portfolio Assignment

A new client, Apartment Management, Inc., has retained your firm to assist in the collection of an account for past due rent. The tenant was a start-up Internet company, "We Search for You, Inc." Their rent was due on the first day of each month in the amount of $1,250.00. Their lease was for two years and they paid only the first six months of the lease. The lease provided for late fees in the amount of $50.00 per month plus interest. Your attorney has requested you prepare the collection letter on behalf of Apartment Management, Inc. The tenant's mailing address is 712 Broad St., Philadelphia, Pa. 19106. The President of We Search for You, Inc., is Margaret Mattheson. (Hint: You need to research the jurisdictional requirements.)

Vocabulary Builder

Basics of Legal Correspondence

```
C R O Y W D W J G O D S D L F
O J E J R D H N Y A Q E Z A F
N I J T G O I C E M M M A T H
F C U F T S S H M A M S D T R
I J M C O E R I N L I C D I E
R W Z L A E L D V R X T R M N
M F C S T R L R S D O A E S I
A O L T V E B I E X A C S N A
T E E O T P A O M V S J S A T
I L B T O E Z A N B O O E R E
O P E J A Y V R E C N C E T R
N R S A L U T A T I O N D O G
E C N E R E F E R K L P C N C
E V I T A M R O F N I F Y S L
M V Z R Y D C H E A D E R G U
```

ADDRESSEE	**ADVISORY**	**CARBON COPY**
CLOSING	**CONFIRMATION**	**COVER LETTER**
DEMAND LETTER	**HEADER**	**INFORMATIVE**
LETTERHEAD	**REFERENCE**	**RETAINER**
SALUTATION	**TRANSMITTAL**	

Chapter 9

The Internal Office Memorandum

After completing this chapter, you will be able to:

- Identify different types of internal office memoranda.

- Understand the difference between an interoffice memorandum and the memorandum of law to the trial court.

- Prepare a memorandum summarizing a client or witness interview.

- Describe the objective nature of an internal memorandum of law.

- List several purposes of an internal memorandum of law.

- Identify the information that should be included in the heading section of a memorandum of law.

- Explain the importance of the "issues presented" section.

- Identify the purpose of the "short summary of the conclusion" section.

- Prepare an appropriate statement of facts.

- Identify key elements in the "discussion and analysis" section.

Along with legal correspondence, paralegals draft different types of internal office memoranda. In this chapter, you are introduced to your first assignment integrating both your legal research and writing skills.

<table>
<tr>
<td>Case Fact Pattern</td>
<td></td>
<td>Hypothetical 9-1</td>
</tr>
</table>

Your supervising attorney calls you into her office to tell you about a telephone call she just received from the friend of a client. The friend, whose name is Mr. Giles, has briefly described a problem he is experiencing with regard to a power of attorney document. The problem appears to be urgent, so your supervising attorney immediately schedules an appointment with Mr. Giles to discuss his legal problem.

After the meeting, your attorney requests that you prepare an internal memorandum summarizing the facts of, and law relating to, Mr. Giles' problem.

INTERNAL MEMORANDA: THE BASIC TYPES

Internal office memoranda have different purposes and functions. Some memoranda are used to present an objective analysis of a client's legal issues; others summarize meetings, such as a client's initial interview or witness statements; others may document events, such as a memorandum documenting a telephone call. All these situations conclude with a memorandum. You need to know the purpose of your memorandum to determine the type you will be drafting.

An Internal Memorandum to Summarize Information

A client interview is an important aspect in developing a case. Interviews can be a time to gather information, to evaluate a client's case, or to determine whether the attorney has expertise to even handle the matter. If you are either attending an interview or conducting the interview, impressions are important. First, before beginning your investigation into the facts, be sure to identify yourself as a paralegal. You are not someone who is authorized to practice law, and the client should understand this. You are, however, someone whose knowledge of the case is protected under the **attorney/client privilege** (assuming the individual is a client or prospective client; if a nonclient, such as an eyewitness, the privilege does not apply). Privilege is important because it enables the client to speak freely and honestly, without fear of self-incrimination or fear that you could be compelled by subpoena to reveal the information provided. You should also make the client aware that you are trained as a paraprofessional; this should be emphasized to cultivate the client's confidence.

attorney/client privilege
The legal relationship established between attorney and client allowing for free exchange of information without fear of disclosure.

Second, the matter of fees may also arise, particularly if the client is a new or potential client, as in the Case Fact Pattern in this chapter. You should consult your supervising attorney about how to field questions on fee structure. The client is entitled to a precise understanding of this structure, but the responsibility to inform him is ultimately the attorney's.

Finally, you may be asked to prepare documents that will be required during the interview, such as authorization to obtain medical or employment records, and other documents. You should also review any materials already in your firm's file on the matter. If you are aware of any of the details of the client's problem, you should perform some background research to familiarize yourself with the substantive areas of law that seem to be applicable.

During the interview you should be taking comprehensive notes. You will be referring to these notes in the final segment of the interview, when you review the entire account with the client.

After the interview, you should prepare a memorandum summarizing the client's statement in detail. This is not the internal memorandum of law that we discuss in the remainder of this chapter; it is simply a memorandum reviewing the content of the client interview, for the case file. This memorandum should be prepared immediately after the interview, when the details remain fresh in your mind and the references in your notes (including abbreviations and summaries) are still familiar to you. If you wait too long, your own notes may become incomprehensible.

Therefore, one of the tasks you may be asked to undertake is to summarize the facts of an interview or notes from a meeting and present them to your supervising attorney. In a memorandum summarizing facts or notes you should include the following information:

- A standard heading that includes the name of the person to whom the memorandum is directed, the author of the memorandum, the date, and the subject of the memorandum. This information will be discussed in more detail in the next section of this chapter.

- The date and time when the interview or meeting that you are summarizing occurred.

- The objective facts in detail, based upon the interview or meeting.

- Dates that may be critical, such as the date of an automobile accident or filing deadlines.

- A list of assignments that may result from the interview or meeting.

- A summary of any impressions from the interview or meeting.

Often these types of memoranda become an integral part of the file and are an important mechanism for documenting events that occur in a case. Figure 9.1 provides an example of an internal memorandum summarizing information.

FIGURE 9.1   **Example of an Internal Memorandum Summarizing Information**

Memorandum

To: Christine J. Ashton

From: Samantha Daily

Date: July 17, 2006

Re: Interview with Stephen Houseman
     Automobile Accident Dated July 4, 2006

This memorandum summarizes the meeting between Stephen Houseman and myself regarding an automobile accident he was involved in the weekend of July 4th. The facts are as follows:

• On July 4, 2006, Mr. Houseman was driving back from the fireworks around 9 p.m. It was dark, but a clear night. As he approached the intersection at Main St. and First Avenue, a black SUV approached quickly and ran through a red light.

• Mr. Houseman was hit on the passenger side close to the left front bumper area. Also in the car at the time were his wife, in the front seat, and his daughter, who was buckled up in the back seat in a booster chair. His daughter, Maddy, is seven years old. She was sitting behind his wife on the passenger side.

• Because of the sudden impact, everyone in the car was pushed forward. All had seat belts on and the airbags activated. Mrs. Houseman suffered injuries of the face and chest due to the impact and the airbags.

• Mr. Houseman suffered face and neck injuries. He also is having back problems, which he never experienced before the accident. The entire family was taken by ambulance to the Community Hospital, where everyone was treated. The little girl, Maddy, was kept overnight for observation and had some head injuries.

• The driver, a young man, Joey Pearson, who is 21 years old was tested for alcohol at the site. He had an alcohol level of 1.9 at the time. The police officer who came to the scene arrested Joey and his friends.

• Mr. Houseman brought a copy of the police report. It is attached.

• Mr. Houseman wants to retain us to represent him and his family.

• I indicated to him that we need to have him sign a retainer agreement and a medical authorization.

• I also indicated to him that you would need to meet with him as soon as possible to discuss the process and what is anticipated.

• I have scheduled an appointment for you on July 20 to meet with Mr. Houseman. I indicated to him that if he had any additional information, such as medical bills and any insurance information, for himself, his family and the driver, he should bring them with him for your review.

I will prepare a draft retainer agreement and medical authorization for your review. If you need any additional documents prepared, let me know.

Memorandum to Document Information

You just received a telephone call from opposing counsel threatening to cancel a settlement meeting. The attorney was rude, shouting obscenities through the phone. Even you know how important the meeting is for the client, but behavior such as that is inappropriate. Since your attorney is out of the office, you want to document the telephone call and have a record of what happened. You should prepare a memorandum to your attorney detailing the substance of the conversation. In a memorandum that documents an occurrence or event, you should

- prepare a heading similar to the one for the memorandum summarizing information;
- specify the date and time of the occurrence;
- summarize the facts leading to the occurrence;
- present a detailed account of the occurrence;
- identify impressions of the occurrence; and
- identify any required action(s).

An example of an internal memorandum documenting information is illustrated in Figure 9.2.

Internal Memorandum of Law

internal memorandum of law
An internal document that analyzes objectively the legal issues in a client's matter.

The final type of internal memorandum is an **internal memorandum of law** that provides an objective analysis of the issues presented by the client's matter. Although memoranda differ in

FIGURE 9.2   **An Example of an Internal Memorandum Documenting Information**

Memorandum

Date: July 10, 2006

To: Emma Hernandez, Esq.

From: Martha Thompson
    Paralegal

Re: Telephone conversation with Rhys Powell
    (Singleton case)

On June 10, I received a telephone call from Rhys Powell, one of the attorneys in the Singleton matter. He began shouting at me and kept asking where you were. He said it was urgent that he speak with you and wanted to know where you were. I explained to him that you were at a deposition out of town and would not be available until tomorrow afternoon. I did tell him I would contact you and have you call him as soon as you were free. That was not good enough for him. He then started yelling obscenities at me through the telephone, such as "You women, you think you know it all, well you don't. I am not going to participate in any f***** settlement meetings, even if that pansy a** judge ordered it. Who do you all think you are? The bloody police? I am not showing up with my client and if you f***** don't like it, you can kiss my ***." He then hung up on me.

To say that I was shocked at his outburst is an understatement. I know Mr. Powell has been difficult and abusive, but this was even more abusive than in the past. I immediately told Mr. McKinney, senior partner, about the matter and he instructed me to prepare this memorandum detailing the conversation. I then contacted you to relay the conversation as well. Mr. McKinney asked that I prepare an affidavit, since he thinks the firm will be taking this matter to court.

If you need me to prepare anything else, please let me know.

PRACTICE TIP

Many law firms or organizations use the individual's title following their name in the heading. Using one's title is a matter of preference and practice. Ask your supervising attorney or review a sample memorandum to determine the attorney's practice.

completeness, complexity, and the stage of the matter at which they are prepared, the purpose is always the same: to *inform*, to *explain*, and to *evaluate*. Internal memoranda analyze the law as it relates to the client's matter for such purposes as

- deciding whether to take the case;
- determining how to proceed in the case;
- providing a summary of the facts and the law;
- preparing for a hearing; and
- drafting appropriate legal documents.

The key to understanding the internal memorandum of law is in understanding its point of view—objective.

THE INTEROFFICE MEMORANDUM DISTINGUISHED

Unlike a memorandum of law to the trial court, the internal memorandum is not intended to advocate the client's position; it is intended to provide an objective assessment of the client's position. It is thus prepared only for review by the members of your law firm, and perhaps the client's inner circle. In an internal memorandum of law, both sides of the client's matter are analyzed, setting forth the positive and negative aspects of the case. An attorney wants an objective evaluation of the client's case to determine strategy, weaknesses in the case, complete view of the law, and any other legal issues that may be pertinent to the matter. Because all matters often are addressed, this type of memorandum is only used as an in-house tool.

Clearly, this differentiates the internal memorandum from a brief filed with a court, which is written from an advocate's perspective and does not analyze all aspects of the case. In a brief filed with a court, you write to persuade. Your writing style is not objective, but written with a point of view—your client's. The memorandum of law to the trial court is a persuasive document, minimizing the weaker aspects of a client's case. As many cases in our "You Be the Judge" or "Ethics Alert" sections indicate, this is not the time to hide the adverse opinion. It is incumbent upon you and your supervising attorney to advocate your client's position zealously but with candor and integrity. However, the remainder of the chapter is devoted to an objective viewpoint — the internal memorandum.

PRELIMINARY CONSIDERATIONS

Throughout this textbook, the importance of "getting ready" has been emphasized. Now that you are ready to write, don't forget what to do.

Remember, in preparing to begin an assignment, you will complete the following tasks:

- Determine your audience: To whom is the memorandum directed? Will the memorandum be reviewed by your supervising attorney or the client?

- Determine your purpose: Since the internal memorandum is an objective document, your goal is to present both sides of the law—positive and negative.

- Determine your deadline: Are there time constraints on the assignment? Are there statute-of-limitation issues? Was the client promised an evaluation of their case by a particular date? Check out all this information before you begin your assignment. Make sure your deadline is clear.

- Prepare an outline: An outline will help you organize the assignment. Identify the issues of the case and note what needs to be accomplished.

- Begin your legal research: At this stage of the assignment, you will gather your cases, statutes, and other legal resources that apply to the assignment.

- Verify the status of the law: Shepardize or KeyCite your legal resources. You do not want to cite overruled or questionable legal sources.

brief bank
A document depository of briefs prepared by a law firm in previous matters.

- Prepare to write: Determine your format. Does the attorney or law firm have a particular format to follow? Many attorneys or law firms index internal memoranda of law in a **brief bank.** (Recall from Chapter 7 that correspondences are often compiled in one place for future use.) The same is true for internal memoranda of law. Check with your supervising attorney for samples of memoranda to use as a guide in drafting your memorandum. This practice is especially helpful in the beginning when you are just learning how to prepare legal documents or when you begin a new job.

You are now ready to begin to draft, write, rewrite, redraft, and work toward the completed product: the internal memorandum of law.

THE INTERNAL MEMORANDUM OF LAW

The format of the internal memorandum may vary from project to project, from firm to firm, and even from lawyer to lawyer (or department to department) within the same firm, depending on personal style preferences. When preparing a memorandum, you should make sure that you understand the format preferred by your supervising attorney. In general, however, most internal memoranda have the following components:

- Heading
- Statement of issues presented
- Short summary of the conclusion
- Statement of facts
- Discussion and analysis of the law and facts, with citations to applicable authorities
- Conclusion

In the next several subsections we discuss each of these components in turn. As we do so, we make reference to figures drawn from an internal memorandum.

The Heading

heading
A line or more of text that identifies the party for whom the memorandum was prepared; the person by whom it was prepared; the date of preparation; and the subject matter.

The **heading** identifies the party for whom the memorandum was prepared; the person by whom it was prepared; the date of preparation; and the subject matter. The heading for our memorandum appears in Figure 9.3.

Begin by identifying the name of the document: Memorandum of Law. Styles vary according to office or attorney preferences. Check a sample to determine your title. The next part of the heading identifies the person to whom the memorandum is directed. The person for whom the memorandum is prepared is usually the attorney who gave you the assignment, and the person actually preparing the memorandum is usually you. This standard scenario may differ in an individual case, however. For example, an associate attorney may ask you to prepare a draft of a memorandum that he will ultimately submit to a partner under his own name (or with both your names). Make sure you understand this circumstance from the outset.

The next element of a heading is the date. If it takes more than one day to prepare a memorandum, do not identify the date when you started the memorandum, nor all the dates on which you worked on it, but rather the date on which you submit it. You should take care that Shepardizing (or other updating) has been completed through that date.

PRACTICE TIP

The date is significant for two reasons: (1) it determines when the memorandum was completed, and (2) if the memorandum is used at a later time, updating of the law may be required. The date of the memorandum determines the starting point for any updating.

FIGURE 9.3   **Example of Heading**

MEMORANDUM OF LAW

TO: Mark Harrison, Senior Partner

FROM: Gregory Johnson, Paralegal

DATE: June 1, 2006

RE: Giles v. Harris

The validity of a transfer of a joint venture interest with a blank power of attorney.

Finally, the heading must identify the subject matter of the memorandum. This usually involves a brief capsule description of the legal issues presented, and possibly identification of the client as well. Although this information may be well known at the time of preparation both to you and the memorandum's recipient, it helps, for future reference, to label it. Such labeling also greatly assists in indexing when the memorandum is placed in the firm's permanent research files, which many firms maintain to avoid duplicating research.

The Statement of Issues Presented

statement of issues presented
A statement that identifies the legal and factual issues to be discussed in your memorandum.

The **statement of issues presented** or **questions presented** identifies the legal and factual issues to be discussed in your memorandum. In framing these issues, be concise and direct, and number each issue (unless there is only one). Another key component in drafting the issue for the internal memorandum of law is objectivity. Remember your purpose: to present an objective analysis of the facts and the law. Do not use language that appears to persuade. For example:

> Objective issue: Can an individual recover for the pain and suffering of a spouse?

> Persuasive issue: Can an individual injured by a reckless intoxicated driver recover damages for pain and suffering of an incapacitated spouse?

The second statement of the issue has a point of view, whereas the first statement is neutral. Additionally, many attorneys pose their issues beginning with the word "Whether." This construction has been discussed in previous chapters. The question is whether to use the word "whether" in presenting the statement of issues. Using the word "whether" is stylistic and clearly a matter of preference of your supervising attorney. This above issues can be redrafted using the "whether" construction.

> Objective: Whether an individual can recover for the pain and suffering of a spouse. (Notice this construction of the issue ends with a period.)

> Persuasive: Whether an individual injured by a reckless intoxicated driver can recover damages for pain and suffering of an incapacitated spouse.

In determining how to draft your issue, pay attention to word choice. Stay away from emotional language, such as "outrageous," "heinous," or other words that tend to incite a reader. Of course, if the legal standards require the use of expressions such as the "intentional infliction of emotional distress," or "gross negligence," then include them in your issue. Simply remember your audience and your purpose.

You will have an opportunity to test your persuasive drafting skills when you draft the Memorandum of Law to the Trial Court or an Appellate Brief in later chapters.

Figure 9.4 shows an example of appropriate form for a statement of issues presented. Each issue should be no longer than one or two sentences, and should generally be drafted to be answerable with a yes or no response.

Although the statement of issues presented is short, the time needed to prepare it may not be. In order to frame the issues properly, you must understand the facts and the relevant substantive law. Often your research will be well underway before you have adequate understanding even to draft a proper statement of issues presented. This may be true even if the ultimate statement amounts to a single short sentence summarizing a single simple issue. Take care in your analysis.

Often your supervising attorney will provide you with a preliminary statement of the issues that she wants investigated, or which she believes are relevant. If that is the case, then your memorandum should be limited to these points. If, however, your research indicates that other areas are more relevant, or at least worthy of consideration, you should consult with your supervising attorney and determine whether further research is warranted. Be careful not to go far afield from the original assignment without authorization; you may waste valuable time and money. Your supervising attorney should provide you with an understanding of the limits of your research; often, as your working relationship is established, you will develop an intuitive understanding of the requirements of a given project. When in doubt, however, ask.

FIGURE 9.4   **Statement of Issue Presented**

Under Texas law, is the transfer of a joint venture interest with a blank power of attorney valid?

Multiple Issues Presented

The client's problems are not singular in nature, and therefore a memorandum of law may have multiple issues. The best approach when presented with multiple issues in a memorandum is to address each issue separately. Think of them as "mini memos" within one document. Each issue should be identified separately with complete legal analysis before you move on to the next issue. As issues are discussed, they should build on each other. Think about your organization. Move from point A to point B. Be logical in your development. This point is important for the clarity of your memorandum. Outlining is crucial when a memorandum of law involves more than one issue, as this will help you remain organized. An outline of a multiple-issue memorandum is presented in Figure 9.5.

Short Summary of the Conclusion

short summary of the conclusion

A summary that provides the reader with a quick answer to the yes or no questions raised by the issues.

The purpose of the **short summary of the conclusion** is to provide the reader with a quick answer to the yes or no questions raised by the issues. It is always short, but rarely quite as simple in actuality as a mere yes or no. Qualifiers are generally needed to provide a response representative of the analysis and conclusion to follow.

The short summary of the conclusion is useful for two purposes. First, to the attorney too busy to review the memorandum completely, it provides a capsule summary; second, to those who will study the memorandum in detail, it provides a preview of the end result, helping to place the analysis in perspective. An example is found in Figure 9.6.

PRACTICE TIP

Prepare your issue after you have completed your legal research and determined your legally significant facts. The two will be combined to create your issue or issues, if more than one, in your memorandum.

FIGURE 9.5   **An Outline of a Multiple-Issue Internal Memorandum**

Memorandum of Law

Issue I:

    A. Identify the issue.

    B. Present the law for the issue.

    C. Apply the law to the facts of the case.

    D. Conclusion for that issue.

Issue II:

    A. Identify the issue.

    B. Present the law for that issue.

    C. Apply the law to the facts of the case. (If there is any overlap of the facts and issues incorporate them, if appropriate.)

    D. Conclusion for that issue.

Issue III:

Continue general analysis and format. At the end of the memorandum, prepare a general conclusion with recommendations from your legal research.

FIGURE 9.6   Short Summary of the Conclusion

Yes. Since the power of attorney presented was devoid of any terms, it did not contain the necessary elements to be a valid power of attorney. The acts of the agent exercised under a limited power of attorney are not binding on the principal. However, the cases hold that if the principal received any personal benefits from the transaction, the issue of ratification may be sufficient to validate the acts of the agent.

Statement of Facts

statement of facts
A statement that sets forth the significant facts needed to analyze the issues presented in the memorandum of law.

The **statement of facts** sets forth the significant facts obtained in the client interview or provided to you by your supervising attorney, or otherwise present in the client's file. Individual facts are deemed legally significant if they are necessary for an understanding of, or have an impact upon the conclusion drawn regarding, the issues addressed in the memorandum. Although the intended scope and depth of the memorandum is a factor to consider in deciding whether to include specific facts, as a general rule you should lean toward inclusiveness.

Facts should be neither embellished nor downplayed, nor interpreted in the "best light." Rather, they should be objectively and accurately portrayed so that the reader can assess the situation presented. After your review of available materials, you may determine that further investigation is needed for a fair presentation; if so, discuss it with your supervising attorney and proceed if authorized.

A simple, logical, and understandable presentation of the facts is crucial, so that the reader has a clear understanding of the context in which the issues are analyzed and the conclusion reached. Chronological development is often best; sometimes it may be useful to emphasize crucial facts first, and then demonstrate how they fit into the chronological whole. Figure 9.7 illustrates a clear, concise statement of facts.

In presenting your statement of facts for a memorandum of law, you should strive to complete these goals:

PRACTICE TIP

Unless directly dispositive of your results, do not cite legal authority in your conclusion. Legal authority is cited in your discussion section.

- Be objective: Remember the purpose of the document. Do not let your opinions creep into your work.

- Be complete: Do not leave out relevant facts, no matter if they support your client's position or not. State the disputed facts as they may have bearing on your legal analysis.

FIGURE 9.7   Statement of Facts Section

Statement of Facts:
Mr. Giles went to a pre-Thanksgiving party at the home of Mr. Swan. Swan had been his friend and attorney for approximately two years.
At the party, Giles and Swan discussed Giles's desire to purchase a piece of real estate before the end of the year. Giles indicated that he was going out of town for Thanksgiving, and would not be back until January 1. Swan stated that he could close the real estate transaction if Giles would execute a power of attorney. Giles then signed a document entitled "Power of Attorney," which Swan kept. Giles then left the party and departed on his trip.
While Giles was away, Swan was contacted by Giles's partner, Mr. Harris, regarding a joint venture transaction completely unrelated to the real estate transaction. Harris told Swan that Giles was supposed to assume all of Harris's interest in the joint venture before January 1. Swan told Harris he had a power of attorney to close a real estate transaction, but did not know how he could help Harris out. Harris suggested to Swan that he could use the power of attorney to facilitate the transfer of the joint venture interest. Swan hesitated, but Harris indicated that Giles would not receive the tax benefits attendant to the transfer if he did not close the deal before December 31. Swan finally agreed to execute the transfer of the joint venture interest using the power of attorney, and shortly thereafter the deal was completed.
When Giles came back to town, he was furious, and told Swan that he did not want to assume the entire joint venture interest and wanted the transaction voided.

You Be the Judge

Hypothetical 7-2

Substantiating the truthfulness of facts is a responsibility of an attorney. When an attorney knowingly misrepresents facts to a court, a violation of the rules of professional responsibility occurs. Such was the case in Nebraska when an attorney decided to represent his brother in his divorce. In *State Ex. Rel. Bar Association v. Zakrzewski*, 560 N.W.2d 150 (Neb. 1997), an attorney filed an affidavit that contained false claims about the attorney representing his sister-in-law. The issue centered on child abuse allegations of the wife/mother of a child (his nephew), which the attorney stated in his affidavit she was directed to file by her attorney. Because of this directive, the parties were trying to "vilify" and "interfere" with his brother's rights of visitation. *Id.* at 153. The plain facts were that his sister-in-law's attorney never directed her to do anything claimed. In fact, the facts established the opposite conclusion.

The court's investigation showed that the attorney possessed no knowledge to support his assertions in the affidavit antd conducted no investigation to substantiate his claims. *Id.* at 155. Because the attorney's actions were maliciously motivated, and his behavior toward the disciplinary committee investigating the allegations was unprofessional, the court ordered suspension for 18 months. The court believed the conduct so serious that in its reasoning it opined that "[t]he making of false statements by an attorney obviously reflects negatively on both that attorney's ability to practice law and the reputation of the entire bar in general. Such a practice must be deterred by this court." *Id.* at 156. Review the case. Which rule of professional responsibility did the court cite? What are the facts that lead to the suspension of the attorney? What is the court's reasoning in the case?

legally significant facts
Facts that are critical to the analysis of a case.

- Identify legally significant facts: Your legal analysis may turn on a fact in the case. Be sure you include the **legally significant facts** in your Statement of Facts. Certain facts set the tone and background; other facts are so critical to the analysis that they are integral to the case.

- Be clear: The order of presentation of the facts guides the reader. Do not confuse facts with analysis or facts with conclusions. Present a roadmap for the reader to follow that is decisive.

- Be accurate: Do not embellish the facts; do not hide facts; do not create facts. The law directly relates to the facts. If you misstate the facts, you could create a domino effect in which your analysis becomes flawed.

Discussion and Analysis

discussion and analysis
The heart of the memorandum, which presents the legal analysis with supporting citations.

The **discussion and analysis** section is the heart of the memorandum. In this section you will be

- identifying points of law and supporting them with citations;
- quoting from relevant cases, statutes, and other sources; and
- relating your research to the facts of your matter.

Always remember that your purpose is to discuss objectively the strengths and the weaknesses of your case. You must view the issues not only from your client's perspective, but also from that of your opponent. The negative side of your client's position will surface eventually; the internal memorandum prepares your firm to deal with such weaknesses. Discuss both those points that operate to your client's advantage and those likely to be cited against him; identify counterpoints to your own strong arguments and counterpoints to the opponent's. The reader should get a sense of how an objective observer might look at the matter.

As with the statement of facts, and indeed the other components of a memorandum as well, the scope and depth of your discussion will vary with the intended use. In some cases, your assignment will be to prepare an exhaustive survey of the law in a given area, citing all possibly relevant cases and statutes, and perhaps even providing separate copies or abstracts of these primary sources. In other cases, the assignment will be to obtain a quick answer, citing only the most relevant cases. Know your assignment, and hence your goal, from the outset.

Quotations from cases can be as useful in a memorandum as they are in other projects (and they are often incorporated into later briefs), and references to secondary sources can give added support to your arguments. All these possibilities should be discussed with your supervising attorney, and you should be sure that you understand her expectations before you begin.

Discuss the cases, statutes, and other material *favoring* your client first. Describe how they support your argument, and how they may be attacked. Then discuss the materials that go *against* your client's position, stating how they are harmful, and whether and how they can be distinguished.

PRACTICE TIP

Do not state legal conclusions in the statement of facts. Remember "just the facts" stated objectively.

Emphasize primary sources over secondary and mandatory precedents over merely persuasive precedents. If the issues involved are state law issues, emphasize research in state law sources; if federal issues, emphasize federal sources.

You should constantly integrate the law and the facts. Don't do this at the expense of an extended discussion of a complicated legal concept, however; by all means, make the status and meaning of the law clear. But make sure the reader understands throughout the discussion, and particularly at the end, how the law affects the specific facts of the client's matter. A means to communicate this information is by using the IRAC method.

The IRAC Method

In the previous chapters, the IRAC method of legal analysis was discussed. To review, IRAC is the acronym for issue, rule of law, analysis or application of law (to the facts), and conclusion. Although this method appears restrictive, it provides a good guide, especially in the beginning when writing an internal memorandum of law is unfamiliar. Let's review each letter of IRAC:

Issue: The issue is analogous to your topic sentence. This sentence will tell the reader what the paragraph or succeeding paragraphs will discuss. Recall that paragraphs should have a lead-in sentence, a topic sentence, or a transitional sentence. If the issue is your topic sentence, it will identify to the reader the topic that you are to cover. The issue is your starting point in the paragraph or the paragraphs that follow.

Rule of Law: Present your legal research in this part of the analysis. Here is where you cite your relevant cases, statutes, and other legal authority that will ultimately support your analysis. Incorporate your cases into your sentences. Quote your legal authority. Use the information you mastered in Chapter 7 in this section. Remember, you must cite legal authority for a legal proposition. Support a legal statement by a legal source.

Analysis or Application: Together with the facts and law of your case, you must now analyze how the law affects your facts. Does the law support the client's position or the opposing party? Your analysis sets the stage for the conclusion, so be thorough. Do not forget to relate your legal research to the facts; otherwise, the exercise becomes a report on the law. Remember why you are preparing the memorandum—for the client. Unless you incorporate the primary objective, your client's problem, into your analysis, you have not accomplished your goal.

As part of your analysis, you must present the opposing party's position. What will the other side argue? Consider this the "yes, but . . ." section of the analysis. You need to present the counterarguments so that a true picture of the client's problem can be analyzed. You know there are three sides to an argument: my view, your view, and the right view! Therefore, take a broader approach in your analysis and look at all sides of the issue.

Conclusion: The conclusion is the summation sentence of your analysis of the law and facts of the case. This section should be no more than one or two sentences and should succinctly state your conclusions based upon your research for that issue. This section, after reviewing the law and facts, tells the reader the reasons for the possible legal outcome in the case. This section differs from the conclusion section in that "this" conclusion is a sentence that summarizes the paragraphs that preceded it. The conclusion section summarizes the entire memorandum of law and recommends strategies based upon the legal research.

An example of a proper discussion section appears in Figure 9.8. Note how *Bluebook* citation form is used. You should not deviate from proper citation form, regardless of whether it is *Bluebook* or *ALWD*, just because the memorandum is to be used internally, rather than filed with a court. Your text may someday be incorporated into a brief; the more accurate its form and substance, the more valuable the memorandum will be.

Conclusion

conclusion
The summary of research and recommendations.

Although the discussion section forms the heart of your memorandum, the **conclusion** is the culmination. In a paragraph or two, you summarize what your research has shown about the law relating to your client's problem. You may even recommend a course of action, if that was part of your assignment.

Though coming to a conclusion generally means stating your opinion about how the legal issues will be resolved, it does not imply that you should become an advocate when drafting your conclusion. If you have strong reservations about your conclusion, or believe that a court could

FIGURE 9.8
Discussion Section

Discussion:

Before a thorough analysis can be completed, a power of attorney must be defined. Under the law, a power of attorney creates an agency relationship whereby one person, the principal, appoints another person, the agent, to act on the principal's behalf. *Lawler v. Federal Deposit Insurance Corp.,* 538 S.W. 2d 245 (Tex. Civ. App.–Dallas 1976, writ ref'd n.r.e.). The relationship is consensual. *Texas Processed Plastics, Inc. v. Gray Enterprises, Inc.,* 592 S.W. 2d 412 (Tex. Civ. App.–Tyler 1979, no writ); *Green v. Hanon,* 367 S.W. 2d 853 (Tex. Civ. App., Texarkana 1963, no writ). The law specifically defines a power of attorney as "[a]n instrument by which the authority of one person to act in the place and stead of another as attorney in fact is set forth." *Olive-Sternberg Lumber Co. v. Gordon,* 143 S.W. 2d 694 (Tex. Civ. App.–Beaumont 1940, no writ). The document in this case identified neither the principal, nor the agent, nor the extent of the authority of the agent. The document's validity is thus questionable.

However, before the validity of the document is determined, it must be interpreted using the current standards of the law. Under Texas law, certain rules of construction and interpretation must be followed. The rules of construing a document date back as far as 1889, to the leading case of *Gouldy v. Metcalf,* 75 Tex. 455, 12 S.W. 830 (1889). In *Gouldy*, the Texas Supreme Court set out the rules of construction for a power of attorney:

> [w]hen an authority is conferred upon an agent by a formal instrument, as by a power of attorney, there are two rules of construction to be carefully adhered to:
>
> 1. The meaning of general words in the instrument will be restricted by the context, and construed accordingly.
>
> 2. The authority will be construed strictly, so as to exclude the exercise of any power which is not warranted, either by the actual terms used or as a necessary means of executing the authority with effect. *Id.* at 245.

Expanding the guidelines set forth in *Gouldy*, case law establishes that "all powers conferred upon an agent by a formal instrument are to receive a strict interpretation, and the authority is never extended by intendment or construction beyond that which is given in terms, or is necessary for carrying the authority into effect, and the authority must be strictly pursued." *Bean v. Bean,* 79 S.W. 2d 652 (Tex. Civ. App.–Texarkana 1935, writ ref'd); *See, Dockstader v. Brown,* 204 S.W. 2d 352 (Tex. Civ. App.–Fort Worth 1947, writ ref'd n.r.e.).

In applying the rules of construction, for a power of attorney to be valid certain elements must be contained within the document. The necessary elements are the name of the principal, the name of the agent, and the nature and extent of the authority granted. *Sun Appliance and Electric, Inc. v. Klein,* 363 S.W. 2d 293 (Tex. Civ. App.–Eastland 1962, no writ).

The power of attorney in the present matter contained only the signature of the principal, and nothing else. In analyzing the power of attorney under the strict considerations, the essential terms of the power of attorney were missing. As such, it appears that the document does not comply with the legal definition of a power of attorney.

The facts further indicate that the power of attorney was executed for a specific purpose, although not stated. Giles had orally instructed Swan to use the power of attorney to consummate a real estate transaction only. As stated in *Giddings, Neiman-Marcus v. Estes,* 440 S.W. 2d 90 (Tex. Civ. App.–Eastland 1969, no writ):

FIGURE 9.8
Cont.

The authority will be construed strictly, so as to exclude the exercise of any power which is not warranted either by the actual terms used or as a necessary means of executing the authority with effect.

Since no authority was conferred to Swan by the document, he could not have acted on Giles's behalf. Consequently, any acts performed by Swan for Giles under the power of attorney are invalid.

However, the facts reveal that Swan had acted as Giles's attorney on a number of occasions. This fact may give rise to an implication that Swan was acting with apparent authority. This is defined as "such authority as a reasonably prudent man, using diligence and discretion in view of the principal's conduct, would naturally and reasonably suppose the agent to possess." *Great American Casualty Company v. Eichelberger*, 37 S.W. 2d 1050 (Tex. Civ. App.–Waco 1931, writ ref'd). Thus, as the Houston Court of Civil Appeals stated in its dicta:

> [a]n agency may arise with respect to third persons if acts or appearances reasonably lead third persons to believe that an agency in fact has been created. And . . . apparent authority of an agent to bind a principal, by want of ordinary care, clothes the agent with such indicia of authority as to lead a reasonably prudent person to believe that he actually has such authority. *Hall v. Hallamicek*, 669 S.W. 2d 368 (Tex. App.–Houston [14th Dist.] 1984, no writ).

Because of the standard in the *Hall* case, Harris may try to use apparent authority as a means to validate the transfer, as Giles has the burden of proof that Swan did not have the authority to act on Giles's behalf. *Dockstader v. Brown*, 204 S.W. 2d 352 (Tex. Civ. App.–Fort Worth 1947, writ ref'd n.r.e.).

There is a problem with the apparent authority argument, however. Harris knew that the power of attorney was for a specific purpose: to close the real estate transaction. The law is very clear that a third party has a duty to inquire into the scope and fact of the agency and the burden is on the third party to "ascertain at his peril the nature and scope of the authority of such agent." *Lawrie v. Miller*, 2 S.W. 2d 561 (Tex. Civ. App.–Texarkana 1928, no writ); *Eliot Valve Repair v. Valve*, 675 S.W. 2d 555 (Tex. App.–Houston [1st Dist.] 1984, no writ); *Boucher v. City Paint & Supply*, 398 S.W. 2d 352 (Tex. Civ. App.–Tyler 1966, no writ).

The facts of our case indicate that Mr. Harris neither investigated nor examined the extent of Swan's authority. As such, Giles cannot be held responsible for the acts of Swan and their effect.

In analyzing the facts and the law, it is apparent that the document which purports to be a power of attorney is not a valid one; and that Swan did not have the authority to act on Giles's behalf under any circumstance. Consequently, the power of attorney is valueless and any action resulting from the use of the document is void.

Although the case law appears to be in our client's favor, there is an issue that may be raised by the defense which weakens our case substantially. The issue is the principal's ratification of the transaction. Ratification requires that the principal have full and complete knowledge of all material facts pertaining to the transaction prior to any affirmation of the act. *Leonard v. Hare*, 161 Tex. 28, 336 S.W. 2d 619 (1960). For ratification to occur, the principal must retain the benefits and "the critical factor in determining whether a principal has ratified an unauthorized act by his agent is the

FIGURE 9.8
Cont.

principal's knowledge of the transaction and his actions in light of such knowledge." *Land Title Company of Dallas, Inc. v. Stigler,* 609 S.W. 2d 754, 756 (Tex. 1980); *First National Bank in Dallas v. Kinnabrew,* 589 S.W. 2d 137 (Tex. Civ. App.–Tyler 1979, writ ref'd n.r.e.). In the event that it is determined that Giles took benefits from Swan's actions, specifically tax benefits, the transaction may be valid, regardless of whether the initial power of attorney was legally insufficient.

easily justify a different ruling, say so. Once again, you must keep in mind the most important rule of the internal memorandum of law—*objectivity*!

An example of a good conclusion is found in Figure 9.9.

A sample of a complete memorandum of law is provided in Figure 9.10.

POST-WRITING CONSIDERATIONS

Do not forget to practice what you learned in previous chapters. Before you present your internal memorandum of law to your supervising attorney, be sure you have completed the following post-writing exercises:

- Reread your work.
- Redraft your work.
- Proofread for spelling, grammar, and punctuation.
- Cite-check your legal sources for correctness and accuracy.
- Edit.
- Proofread, again.
- Edit one last time.

FIGURE 9.9   Conclusion Section

Conclusion:
Since the power of attorney did not grant specific authority to the agent, the power of attorney is void. Based upon the strict construction doctrine, one cannot construe a grant of authority which is nonexistent. The power of attorney did not contain the name of the agent, the purpose of the agency, or the grant of authority to the agent, and therefore could not confer any powers upon the agent. The acts of the agent were improper and the principal is not legally responsible for the effects of those acts. However, as noted, if the principal received any benefits from the transaction, the acts of the agent may be ratified, which would validate any acts of the agent. This act could make the transaction valid.

FIGURE 9.10
Sample Memorandum of Law

Memorandum

TO: Mark Harrison, Senior Partner

FROM: Gregory Johnson, Paralegal

DATE: June 1, 2006

RE: Giles v. Harris

FIGURE 9.10
Cont.

The validity of a transfer of a joint venture interest with a blank power of attorney.

Issue Presented:

Under Texas law, is the transfer of a joint venture interest with a blank power of attorney valid?

Answer to the Issue:

Yes. Since the power of attorney presented was devoid of any terms, it did not contain the necessary elements to be a valid power of attorney. The acts of the agent exercised under a limited power of attorney are not binding on the principal. However, the cases hold that if the principal received any personal benefits from the transaction, the issue of ratification may be sufficient to validate the acts of the agent.

Statement of Facts:

Mr. Giles went to a pre-Thanksgiving party at the home of Mr. Swan. Swan had been his friend and attorney for approximately two years.

At the party, Giles and Swan discussed Giles's desire to purchase a piece of real estate before the end of the year. Giles indicated that he was going out of town for Thanksgiving, and would not be back until January 1. Swan stated that he could close the real estate transaction if Giles would execute a power of attorney. Giles then signed a document entitled "Power of Attorney," which Swan kept. Giles then left the party and departed on his trip.

While Giles was away, Swan was contacted by Giles's partner, Mr. Harris, regarding a joint venture transaction completely unrelated to the real estate transaction. Harris told Swan that Giles was supposed to assume all of Harris's interest in the joint venture before January 1. Swan told Harris he had a power of attorney to close a real estate transaction, but did not know how he could help Harris out. Harris suggested to Swan that he could use the power of attorney to facilitate the transfer of the joint venture interest. Swan hesitated, but Harris indicated that Giles would not receive the tax benefits attendant to the transfer if he did not close the deal before December 31. Swan finally agreed to execute the transfer of the joint venture interest using the power of attorney, and shortly thereafter the deal was completed.

When Giles came back to town he was furious, and told Swan that he did not want to assume the entire joint venture interest, and wanted the transaction voided.

Discussion:

The basic question to address is can a blank power of attorney be used to transfer a joint venture interest. Before a thorough analysis can be completed, a power of attorney must be defined. Under the law, a power of attorney creates an agency relationship whereby one person, the principal, appoints another person, the agent, to act on the principal's behalf. *Lawler v. Federal Deposit Insurance Corp.*, 538 S.W. 2d 245 (Tex. Civ. App.– Dallas 1976, writ ref'd n.r.e.). The relationship is consensual. *Texas Processed Plastics, Inc. v. Gray Enterprises, Inc.*, 592 S.W. 2d 412 (Tex. Civ. App.–Tyler 1979, no writ); *Green v. Hanon*, 367 S.W. 2d 853 (Tex. Civ. App. Texarkana 1963, no writ). The law specifically defines a power of attorney as "[a]n instrument by which the authority of one person to act in the place and stead of another as attorney in fact is set forth." *Olive-Sternberg Lumber Co. v. Gordon*, 143 S.W. 2d 694 (Tex. Civ. App.–Beaumont 1940, no

FIGURE 9.10
Cont.

writ). The document in this case identified neither the principal, nor the agent, nor the extent of the authority of the agent. The document's validity is thus questionable.

However, before the validity of the document is determined, it must be interpreted using the current standards of the law. Under Texas law, certain rules of construction and interpretation must be followed. The rules of construing a document date back as far as 1889, to the leading case of *Gouldy v. Metcalf*, 75 Tex. 455, 12 S.W. 830 (1889). In *Gouldy*, the Texas Supreme Court set out the rules of construction for a power of attorney:

> [w]hen an authority is conferred upon an agent by a formal instrument, as by a power of attorney, there are two rules of construction to be carefully adhered to:
>
> 1. The meaning of general words in the instrument will be restricted by the context, and construed accordingly.
>
> 2. The authority will be construed strictly, so as to exclude the exercise of any power which is not warranted, either by the actual terms used or as a necessary means of executing the authority with effect. *Id.* at 245.

Expanding the guidelines set forth in *Gouldy*, case law establishes that "all powers conferred upon an agent by a formal instrument are to receive a strict interpretation, and the authority is never extended by intendment or construction beyond that which is given in terms, or is necessary for carrying the authority into effect, and the authority must be strictly pursued." *Bean v. Bean*, 79 S.W. 2d 652 (Tex. Civ. App.–Texarkana 1935, writ ref'd); *See, Dockstader v. Brown*, 204 S.W. 2d 352 (Tex. Civ. App.–Fort Worth 1947, writ ref'd n.r.e.).

In applying the rules of construction, for a power of attorney to be valid certain elements must be contained within the document. The necessary elements are the name of the principal, the name of the agent, and the nature and extent of the authority granted. *Sun Appliance and Electric, Inc. v. Klein*, 363 S.W. 2d 293 (Tex. Civ. App.–Eastland 1962, no writ).

The power of attorney in the present matter contained only the signature of the principal, and nothing else. In analyzing the power of attorney under the strict considerations, the essential terms of the power of attorney were missing. As such, it appears that the document does not comply with the legal definition of a power of attorney.

The facts further indicate that the power of attorney was executed for a specific purpose, although not stated. Giles had orally instructed Swan to use the power of attorney to consummate a real estate transaction only. As stated in *Giddings, Neiman-Marcus v. Estes*, 440 S.W. 2d 90 (Tex. Civ. App.–Eastland 1969, no writ):

> The authority will be construed strictly, so as to exclude the exercise of any power which is not warranted either by the actual terms used or as a necessary means of executing the authority with effect.

Since no authority was conferred to Swan by the document, he could not have acted on Giles's behalf. Consequently, any acts performed by Swan for Giles under the power of attorney are invalid.

FIGURE 9.10
Cont.

However, the facts reveal that Swan had acted as Giles's attorney on a number of occasions. This fact may give rise to an implication that Swan was acting with apparent authority. This is defined as "such authority as a reasonably prudent man, using diligence and discretion in view of the principal's conduct, would naturally and reasonably suppose the agent to possess." *Great American Casualty Company v. Eichelberger*, 37 S.W. 2d 1050 (Tex. Civ. App.–Waco 1931, writ ref'd). Thus, as the Houston Court of Civil Appeals stated in its dicta:

> [a]n agency may arise with respect to third persons if acts or appearances reasonably lead third persons to believe that an agency in fact has been created. And . . . apparent authority of an agent to bind a principal, by want of ordinary care, clothes the agent with such indicia of authority as to lead a reasonably prudent person to believe that he actually has such authority. *Hall v. Hallamicek*, 669 S.W. 2d 368 (Tex. App.–Houston [14th Dist.] 1984, no writ).

Because of the standard in the *Hall* case, Harris may try to use apparent authority as a means to validate the transfer, as Giles has the burden of proof that Swan did not have the authority to act on Giles's behalf. *Dockstader v. Brown*, 204 S.W. 2d 352 (Tex. Civ. App.–Fort Worth 1947, writ ref'd n.r.e.).

There is a problem with the apparent authority argument, however. Harris knew that the power of attorney was for a specific purpose: to close the real estate transaction. The law is very clear that a third party has a duty to inquire into the scope and fact of the agency and the burden is on the third party to "ascertain at his peril the nature and scope of the authority of such agent." *Lawrie v. Miller*, 2 S.W. 2d 561 (Tex. Civ. App.–Texarkana 1928, no writ); *Eliot Valve Repair v. Valve*, 675 S.W. 2d 555 (Tex. App.–Houston [1st Dist.] 1984, no writ); *Boucher v. City Paint & Supply*, 398 S.W. 2d 352 (Tex. Civ. App.–Tyler 1966, no writ).

The facts of our case indicate that Mr. Harris neither investigated nor examined the extent of Swan's authority. As such, Giles cannot be held responsible for the acts of Swan and their effect.

In analyzing the facts and the law, it is apparent that the document which purports to be a power of attorney is not a valid one, and that Swan did not have the authority to act on Giles's behalf under any circumstance. Consequently, the power of attorney is valueless and any action resulting from the use of the document is void.

Although the case law appears to be in our client's favor, there is an issue that may be raised by the defense which weakens our case substantially. The issue is the principal's ratification of the transaction. Ratification requires that the principal have full and complete knowledge of all material facts pertaining to the transaction prior to any affirmation of the act. *Leonard v. Hare*, 161 Tex. 28, 336 S.W. 2d 619 (1960). For ratification to occur the principal must retain the benefits and "the critical factor in determining whether a principal has ratified an unauthorized act by his agent is the principal's knowledge of the transaction and his actions in light of such knowledge." *Land Title Company of Dallas, Inc. v. Stigler*, 609 S.W. 2d 754, 756 (Tex. 1980); *First National Bank in Dallas v. Kinnabrew*, 589 S.W. 2d 137 (Tex. Civ. App.–Tyler 1979, writ ref'd n.r.e.). In the event that it is determined that Giles took benefits from Swan's actions, specifically tax benefits, the transaction may be valid, regardless of whether the initial power of attorney was legally insufficient.

FIGURE 9.10
Cont.

Conclusion:

Since the power of attorney did not grant specific authority to the agent, the power of attorney is void. Based upon the strict construction doctrine, one cannot construe a grant of authority which is nonexistent. The power of attorney did not contain the name of the agent, the purpose of the agency, or the grant of authority to the agent and therefore the document could not confer any powers upon the agent. The acts of the agent were improper, and the principal is not legally responsible for the effects of those acts. However, as noted, if the principal received any benefits from the transaction, the acts of the agent may be ratified, which would validate any acts of the agent. This act could make the transaction valid.

Ethics Alert

Care must be taken when eliciting information from clients, as your attorney may be relying on you to verify the accuracy of the facts presented. Therefore, you have the same duty as an attorney in investigating the validity of facts. If you are interviewing a client, be sure to write down an accurate account of the facts. Do not accept the client's word as the only source of the "truth." Sometimes clients have improper motives for pursuing legal actions and may be unfounded in law. Sometimes their memories are selective or skewed. The rules of professional responsibility require a good-faith basis for a claim. Relying on the client's version of the facts is insufficient.

Remember our attorney from New Jersey in Chapter 4 who filed incomprehensible pleadings *Mendez v. Draham,* 182 F. Supp. 2d 430 (D.N.J. 2002)? Well, he managed to incite the wrath of the court on another occasion as well. In this case, *Carlino v. Gloucester City High School,* 57 F. Supp. 2d 1 (D.N.J. 1999), the court sanctioned Mr. Malat again for not investigating the facts of his case prior to filing a lawsuit. In the case, some students became intoxicated on a class trip and were prohibited from participating in graduation exercises. Mr. Malat filed a lawsuit claiming violations of constitutional rights and other causes of action. The court publicly admonished the attorney for his "flagrant failure to conduct any legal research." *Id.* at 38. The court pointed out that even the most minimal investigation would have showed that the claims of the students were barred by statute. *Id.* at 38. He was fined again and ordered "to attend two continuing legal education courses." *Id.* at 39.

Although this attorney's practice is the exception and not the rule, the message from the court is undeniable: investigate and make reasonable inquiry to determine the validity of the facts in a case. This inquiry involves not only independent verification of the facts but also verification of the law. No matter what the assignment is, diligence on your part is directly linked to your performance and integrity as a professional. Do not squander the confidence your supervising attorney instills in you.

THE E-FACTOR

COMMUNICATING WITH THE CLIENT

Everybody has one; everybody uses them. Cellular telephones. But, should you be using them to discuss sensitive client matters? Cell phones have become a way of life; however, their level of security is questionable. If client matters are overheard by a third party, are those communications still privileged? Many of the bar associations around the country have issued opinions on the issue, and with the different opinions come varying conclusions. Some opinions recognize that cell phones are so common that even if a conversation is intercepted, the privilege continues. Others suggest gaining authorization from the client to communicate by cell phone because of the possible interception or crossing of lines. Whatever your jurisdiction's position on the issue, cell phones are not a safe mode of communication with a client. If a cell phone must be used, keep the conversations brief and delay sensitive matters for a secure telephone. You do not want to test the waters if information is inadvertently released and it gets into the hands of the opposing party. Some courts view the risk as "your risk," and if the information is improperly intercepted, it may be your supervising attorney's burden to show why the information is still protected by attorney/client privilege. Do not place yourself in that situation—limit the circumstances in which you use cell phones with clients.

PRACTICAL CONSIDERATIONS

An internal memorandum will inevitably involve at least some of your own opinions, since you must reach a conclusion based upon your research. It is important, however, that you let neither your opinions nor your conclusion color your analysis—which is to say that you must also include in your memorandum those portions of your research that go against your conclusion. The memorandum is designed to *inform* your supervising attorney, so that he is prepared to advocate on behalf of your client; it should not itself advocate a position.

In drafting your memorandum, remember the many basic rules you've learned in previous chapters. Use punctuation, sentence structure, and paragraphing to make your points clear; write with precision and forcefulness; avoid ambiguity, use logical development, and be sure your writing tells the reader what you want her to know.

Frank and Ernest

Source: © 2005 Thaves. Reprinted with permission. Newspaper dist. by NEA, Inc.

Summary

Prepare all necessary documents ahead of time, and do preliminary background research. Before commencing the initial client interview, be sure to identify yourself as a paralegal. Be prepared to discuss fees. In the interview itself, establish a positive relationship with the client, and proceed in stages to gather the facts. Ask focused questions after the client has told his story, and review the entire fact pattern before he leaves. Then immediately prepare a post-interview memorandum.

The internal memorandum of law is designed to inform, to explain, and to evaluate. It is intended to assist with such things as deciding whether to take a case or determining how to proceed on a case. Its purpose is objective. The heading identifies the parties preparing and receiving the memorandum, the date of submission, and the subject matter covered. The statement of issues presented identifies the legal and factual issues to be discussed. The short summary of the conclusion provides a quick answer to the questions raised by the statement of issues presented. The statement of facts presents an accurate picture of the facts. The discussion and analysis section identifies applicable points of law and supports them with citations to, and quotes from, relevant cases, statutes, and other sources, always relating the research to the facts of the specific matter. The conclusion is the culmination of the research, summarizing the implications of your analysis and possibly including a recommended course of action.

Although an internal memorandum of law necessarily involves some of the writer's own opinions (since she must reach a conclusion), these opinions should not be allowed to color the analysis. The writer must remain objective, including in the text both those references that support her conclusions and those which go against it.

Key Terms

attorney/client privilege
internal memorandum of law
brief bank
heading
statement of issues presented

short summary of the conclusion
statement of facts
legally significant facts
discussion and analysis
conclusion

Review Questions

1. Identify the different types of memoranda.
2. What is the difference between an interoffice memorandum and a memorandum of law to the trial court?
3. What are three prewriting considerations in preparing an interoffice memorandum of law?
4. What does it mean when we describe an internal memorandum of law as "objective"?
5. What are some of the purposes of an internal memorandum of law?
6. List the information that should be included in the heading section of an internal memorandum of law.
7. What is the importance of the "issues presented" section?
8. What is the purpose of the "short summary of the conclusion" section?
9. What factors should be considered in preparing an appropriate "statement of facts"?
10. What are the key elements of the "discussion" section?

Exercises

1. Read *American Heritage Life Insurance Company v. Koch*, 721 S.W. 2d 611 (Tex. App., Tyler 1986, no writ), and draft the issue presented.
2. Draft the statement of facts from the memorandum in Figure 9.1.
3. Prepare a memorandum of law on the status of law in your state regarding the comparative negligence statute.
4. A new client interview was completed by your supervising attorney. She wants you to prepare an interoffice memorandum based on the following facts:

    Mr. Hunter is a 45-year-old man who was fired from his job on May 10, 2006. The company claims that he was terminated because of his performance, but Mr. Hunter was never disciplined and does not have any negative evaluations in his personnel file. He believes he was fired because they want to hire a younger person for less money. He believes the company discriminated against him and he wants to file a lawsuit. What are the procedures, if any, that we must follow prior to filing the lawsuit? Do we need to have a determination by the EEOC (Equal Employment Opportunity Commission)? What is the status of the laws and how do they relate to our client?

5. Your office represents Community Hospital. They have just been sued by a visitor who slipped on a wet floor on the second floor. There was a sign posted stating that the floor was wet. What is the hospital's liability to the visitor? Does the liability change if the hospital is a government hospital or private hospital? Prepare the interoffice memorandum of law discussing all issues.
6. Your supervising attorney just discovered some new information on a case and wants to prepare an interoffice memorandum of the status of the law on whether admissions of liability in settlement discussions can later be used at trial against the person who made the statement. (This memorandum will be limited to mainly a discussion on the law.)

7. The now-defunct Enron and WorldCom companies created a new corporate environment. Your attorney was retained by a nonprofit hospital and is concerned about the new standards created under the Sarbanes-Oxley Act. He believes section 404 of the statute is critical in advising his client. The hospital wants to know what is required to comply with Sarbanes-Oxley, even though they know it is not a legal requirement now; because they are a non-profit corporation, they still want guidance on the compliance issue. Prepare an internal memorandum of law on the general requirements of the "best practices standard" under Sarbanes-Oxley.

8. A new client has arrived quite upset. Her husband just emptied all their joint accounts and canceled the credit cards; he has left her penniless. Her husband is a wealthy business-man and he wants revenge. The client says she has been a loyal wife and has not cheated on her husband. They have two minor children who both attend private school. The wife wants to know if she can get immediate spousal support and begin divorce proceedings today. Prepare the memorandum of law on the issues based upon your jurisdiction's requirements.

Portfolio Assignment

Your attorney wants to bill for your services as a paralegal. She believes that you have contributed in a meaningful manner to the case, but does not know the legal standards for billing paralegal services. In the case you prepared numerous memoranda, drafted pleadings and motions, copied cases, and participated in numerous meetings. A hearing on attorney's fees is scheduled for next week. Your assignment from your supervising attorney is

   a. research the law regarding billing a paralegal's services as part of an attorney's fee;
   b. prepare an internal memorandum for your attorney's review.

Vocabulary Builder

Internal Memorandum of Law

```
P  N  Z  M  S  Z  Z  C  G  B  B  F  U  N  U
R  G  V  U  F  M  H  F  V  J  M  I  O  S  H
E  N  F  D  C  O  N  C  L  U  S  I  O  N  Q
C  I  F  N  T  Q  K  Q  R  B  S  I  P  D  Y
E  D  F  A  S  W  U  S  I  S  Y  L  A  N  A
D  A  B  R  H  E  I  O  U  M  C  X  Q  F  W
E  E  U  O  N  K  T  C  T  Y  F  A  T  M  J
N  H  C  M  Q  A  S  U  W  A  U  A  E  L  L
T  J  F  E  P  I  Q  A  T  T  T  B  C  K  C
S  W  H  M  D  H  L  E  H  A  V  I  Z  T  S
Q  I  S  S  U  E  S  O  K  N  T  J  O  C  S
D  O  D  K  S  P  R  B  X  K  S  S  Q  N  R
W  N  E  A  Q  I  P  S  P  V  C  H  X  W  S
B  K  C  S  T  Z  K  Q  P  F  N  C  Z  Z  R
J  G  X  Y  R  G  E  S  X  X  H  N  N  H  U
```

ANALYSIS	AUTHORITY	CASE LAW
CONCLUSION	DISCUSSION	FACTS
HEADING	ISSUES	MEMORANDUM
PRECEDENTS	QUOTATIONS	STATUTES

Chapter 10

The Basics of Pleadings

After completing this chapter, you will be able to:

- Differentiate fact pleading from notice pleading.

- Prepare a caption.

- Identify a certificate of service.

- Explain why preliminary research is important to the proper drafting of a complaint.

- Describe the components of a complaint.

- Identify the benefits and pitfalls of using form books and models to assist in the preparation of pleadings.

- Prepare an answer with affirmative defenses.

- Define the term affirmative defense, and identify several affirmative defenses.

- Explain the difference between a counterclaim and a cross-claim.

- Describe the difference between amended and supplemental pleadings.

Drafting pleadings is a basic litigation skill that is important to master, both as a means of defining the issues in a lawsuit and as a means to develop a deeper understanding of the litigation process. In this chapter, you will learn how to draft pleadings on behalf of both the plaintiff and defendant, coupled with drafting the pleadings, you will learn how to integrate the court rules into the document as well.

Case Fact Pattern Hypothetical 10-1

Your firm's client, Mary Mackey, is 51 years old. After 30 years of continuous employment with XYZ Corporation, and despite a personnel file that contains exceptional performance reviews and no hint of misconduct, she was recently fired with no explanation and for no apparent reason. Based on conversations she has since had with former coworkers, she believes that she was replaced by a 23-year-old woman who came in at a higher salary despite minimal qualifications.

Your supervising attorney believes that Mrs. Mackey's termination constitutes age discrimination. He has written to XYZ Corporation, demanding that Mrs. Mackey be reinstated and that she be reimbursed for the weeks of salary missed since the firing. The corporation has rejected this demand, and refuses to discuss the situation further.

Your supervising attorney has decided that litigation can no longer be avoided. You have been assigned to draft a complaint on behalf of Mrs. Mackey.

PLEADINGS IN GENERAL

pleadings
Formal documents filed with the court that establish the claims and defenses of the parties to the lawsuit; the complaint, answer to complaint, and reply.

When a lawsuit is begun, it is important for the court and the litigants—the competing parties—to identify the issues in dispute. If the issues are unclear, the plaintiff will be unable to prepare for trial; the defendant will be unable to prepare a defense; and the court will be unable to evaluate the competing positions. The problem is solved by the filing of pleadings. **Pleadings** are formal documents filed with the court that establish the claims and defenses of the parties to the lawsuit.

Although pleadings are filed with a court, they are not necessarily drafted with only the court in mind. Pleadings are drafted for two audiences: the court and the parties to the case. Know that your purpose is twofold and think about the message you want to convey. For the court, you want to comply with the legal requirements as well as communicate your client's problem effectively. On the other hand, you need to convey to the opposing party the claims you are pursuing. As discussed in Chapter 5, "tell them" and create a story that leaves the reader wanting to right a wrong or correct an injustice. The pleadings are not objective documents and are drafted from either the plaintiff's or defendant's perspective. Word choice is important; writing in plain English is important; but communicating in a precise, clear fashion is most important. You will use all the tools you have developed in previous chapters to draft pleadings.

TYPES OF PLEADINGS

complaint
The first pleading filed by any party to a lawsuit; the document that states the allegations and the legal basis of the plaintiff's claims.

answer
The defendant's response to the plaintiff's complaint.

counterclaim
A claim made by the defendant against the plaintiff—not a defense, but a new claim for damages, as if the defendant were the plaintiff in a separate suit; a countersuit brought by the defendant against the plaintiff.

cross-claim lawsuit
A lawsuit against a party of the same side; plaintiffs or defendants suing each other (defendant versus defendant or plaintiff versus plaintiff).

There are several different types of pleadings. They are filed in sequence, in a manner specified by procedural rules. Some are filed by a plaintiff, some by a defendant.

The **complaint** is the first pleading filed by any party to a lawsuit. It is the filing of the complaint that actually commences the lawsuit; before the complaint reaches the court, no lawsuit is pending. The complaint tells the defendant who is suing him and why and also identifies the nature and extent of the damages claimed.

The **answer** is filed by the defendant in response to the complaint. It generally denies the plaintiff's claim, sets forth the reasons for the denial, and identifies affirmative defenses that the defendant asserts.

A **counterclaim** or **cross-claim** may also be included in the pleadings in a particular case. A counterclaim is made by the defendant against the plaintiff—not a defense, but a new claim for damages, as if the defendant were the plaintiff in a separate suit. A cross-claim is made in a suit where there are two or more defendants, one of whom also acts like a plaintiff in a separate suit. But rather than making her claim against the plaintiff (as in the counterclaim), she makes it against another defendant. (Think of it as a lawsuit within a lawsuit.)

Figure 10.1 diagrams the different counter suits and the relationship of the parties.

In this chapter we use the complaint and the answer as a backdrop for exploring the drafting of pleadings by the legal writer. We then briefly consider the other types of pleadings. Where procedural rules are mentioned, we often discuss the Federal Rules of Civil Procedure (FRCP), since they are uniform throughout the United States. Remember, however, that our purpose is to teach you how to draft a pleading, as opposed to mastering the rules. Although the two concepts are connected, teaching you to master the rules of civil procedure, whether the FRCP or state rules, is beyond the scope of this book.

We cannot, however, overemphasize the importance of learning the rules. Even when the FRCP are applicable, for example, there will be additional local rules that govern certain technical matters. Failure to follow *all* applicable rules and to file pleadings in the manner and in the order that the rules require can waive (forfeit) your clients' rights and lead to a disastrous result.

FACT PLEADING AND NOTICE PLEADING DISTINGUISHED

fact pleading
A style of pleading that requires that you identify all the facts necessary to allege a valid cause of action.

There are two broad styles of pleading—fact pleading and notice pleading. You should always determine which style is required in the jurisdiction in which your lawsuit is pending.

Fact pleading requires that you identify all the facts necessary to allege a valid cause of action. In other words, the pleading must include, at a minimum, those facts which must be proved in order to win on the claims made.

FIGURE 10.1   Counter Lawsuits between Parties

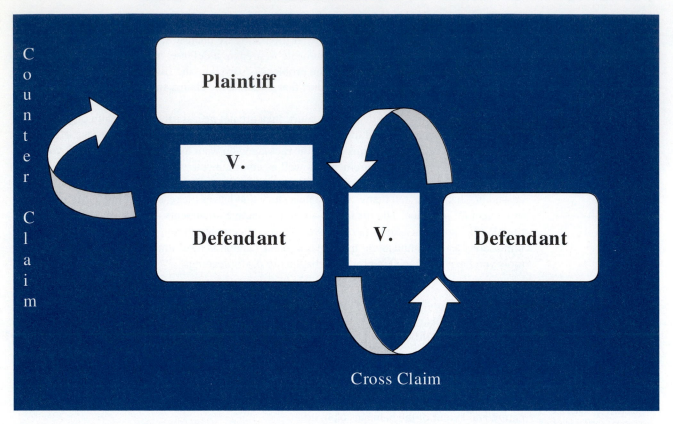

notice pleading
A short and plain statement
of the allegations in a
lawsuit.

Notice pleading, which has been incorporated into the FRCP, requires only a short, plain statement of the grounds on which a party is basing her claim, and a showing of why the party is entitled to relief. The party need not allege all the facts needed to support the claim, but only such facts as are needed to put the opposing party on notice of the claim. The text of FRCP 8(a), which sets out the requirements of notice pleading for a complaint filed in federal court, appears in Figure 10.2.

discovery process
The investigation aspect
of pretrial procedure; the
process of investigation
and collection of evidence
by the litigants.

The rationale behind the less strict requirements of notice pleading is that the facts will be developed by the parties through the **discovery process,** which is the investigation aspect of pretrial procedure (which we discuss further in Chapter 11). Parties often, however, include significant detail in their pleadings anyway, for two reasons: (1) to make their claims clear from the start, and (2) because the jurors can take the pleadings into the jury room, so that the added detail helps to clarify the party's position.

You should note the exceptions to notice pleading in federal court, set forth in FRCP 9. For example, when a plaintiff is alleging a fraud committed by a defendant, Rule 9 requires that the facts surrounding the alleged fraud be stated with "particularity," that is, in detail. This is to protect defendants from unsubstantiated allegations of fraud, which can damage reputations.

FIGURE 10.2   Rule 8(a), General Rules of Pleading

(a) Claims for Relief. A pleading which sets forth a claim for relief, whether an original claim, counterclaim, cross-claim, or third-party claim, shall contain (1) a short and plain statement of the grounds upon which the court's jurisdiction depends, unless the court already has jurisdiction and the claim needs no new grounds of jurisdiction to support it, (2) a short and plain statement of the claim showing that the pleader is entitled to relief, and (3) a demand for judgment for the relief the pleader seeks. Relief in the alternative or of several different types may be demanded.

THE BASIC COMPONENTS OF A PLEADING

All pleadings have the same basic components. Those components are: the caption, title of pleading, body of pleading, prayer for relief, signature block, and certificate of service. Each is discussed in more detail in the remainder of this section.

The Caption

caption
A heading in a case, containing the name of the parties, the court and docket number.

All pleadings filed with the court require a **caption.** The caption goes at the top of the first page of the pleading, and identifies (1) the name of the case; (2) the court in which the case is pending; and (3) the docket number of the case. The caption is identical for all parties in the case, whether plaintiffs or defendants. Captions vary slightly in style and format from one jurisdiction to another, as can be seen from the examples shown in Figure 10.3.

FIGURE 10.3
Variations of Captions

(a)
UNITED STATES DISTRICT COURT FOR THE SOUTHERN
DISTRICT OF CALIFORNIA
Civil Action, File Number_____

MICHAEL BUFFETT, et al.   §
      Plaintiffs   §
           §   ANSWER
vs.   §
           §
CARMEN BROWN, et al.   §
      Defendants   §

(b)
UNITED STATES DISTRICT COURT FOR THE EASTERN
DISTRICT OF NEW JERSEY

XTC CORPORATION, Plaintiff   §
      vs.   §
SMITH, INC., Defendant   §   THIRD-PARTY COMPLAINT
and Third-Party Plaintiff   §
      vs.   §   CIVIL ACTION NO. _____
FRANCOIS BENET, Third-Party   §
Defendant

(c)
UNITED STATES DISTRICT COURT FOR THE NORTHERN
DISTRICT OF ILLINOIS, CHICAGO DIVISION
Civil Action, File Number_____

XTC CORPORTION, Plaintiff   §
      vs.   §
SMITH, INC., Defendant   §   INTERVENER'S ANSWER
FRANCOIS BENET, Intervener   §

(d)   NO. 89-7786-J
XTC CORPORATION,   )   IN THE DISTRICT COURT OF
)
      Plaintiff   )
)
vs.   )   DALLAS COUNTY, TEXAS
)
SMITH, INC.,   )
)
Defendant   )   191st JUDICIAL DISTRICT

Title of the Pleading

It is necessary to identify the type of pleading with a title appearing below the caption. With multiple parties it is often helpful to include enough information in the title to clearly differentiate the pleading from other, potentially similar pleadings (for example, "Defendant Johnson's Answer and Affirmative Defenses").

Body of a Pleading

PRACTICE TIP

As discussed in the context of letters, paralegals cannot sign pleadings as well. Only an attorney can sign a pleading or any document filed with a court. Signing a pleading is considered the unauthorized practice of law.

Consider the body of the pleading the section that conveys the substantive information to the reader. The body of the pleading states the party's problem. With sufficient detail, the party, plaintiff or defendant, sets forth the claims it has against another party in the lawsuit. Using all the skills you learned in previous chapters is critical to drafting a proper pleading. In this section you set out your claims or defenses, your legal theories, and your relief. Be complete yet precise in your presentation. Do not plead facts unless you have a reasonable basis for believing them to be true. As you will see throughout this chapter and the ones that follow, unless you file a pleading or court document in good faith, the court can impose sanctions. Therefore, in the body of a pleading:

- know your purpose;
- understand the law;
- check the court rules; and
- draft with sufficient specificity to communicate your claim or legal issue.

Signature

Someone must sign all pleadings, usually the attorney for the party filing the pleading. The signature constitutes a pledge by the person signing that the contents have been prepared in good faith. If it can be shown that this is not the case, a lawyer can be sanctioned under FRCP 11.

THE SIGNIFICANCE OF RULE 11

PRACTICE TIP

Some jurisdictions require the attorney to sign the certificate of service; others allow the paralegal or executive assistant to sign. Check your jurisdiction for the rule or standard of practice.

Rule 11 of the Federal Rules of Civil Procedure requires a pleading to be filed in good faith and not for purposes of harassment or delay. Pleadings cannot be frivolous or without legal foundation. That is the standard. Throughout this text, case examples are given where attorneys filed groundless, incomprehensible pleadings and were severely sanctioned by a court. Rule 11 is not to be taken lightly. By signing a pleading, the attorney makes certain representations. The representations are as follows:

- The case has a legal basis.
- Legal research was performed to determine the law.
- The facts are verified.
- The pleading is filed in good faith.

When a pleading is filed in violation of Rule 11, an attorney may be sanctioned by the court. Sanctions include the imposition of attorney fees, payment of court costs, dismissal of the lawsuit, disciplinary action, or a combination of them all. Review the text of Rule 11 at www.law .cornell.edu/rules/frcp/.

Courts review Rule 11 claims with great care. It is serious when a Rule 11 claim is raised and even more serious when sanctions are assessed. Be sure all clients' claims are properly verified and researched before a case is filed. The legal ramifications are significant, as experienced by the parties in the following case in "You Be the Judge."

Most states have a Rule 11 equivalent. Review your state's requirements for filing a pleading and the sanctions for violations of the rule.

CERTIFICATE OF SERVICE

Almost every jurisdiction requires some form of certification or guarantee by an attorney (or a party, if the party does not have an attorney) that copies of the pleading have been sent to all

You Be the Judge

Hypothetical 10-2

We now know that good faith is inherent in filing of pleadings. When good faith is ignored, there are legal and financial consequences. In *Taylor v. Belger Cartage Service, Inc.,* 102 F.R.D. 172 (W.D. Mo. 1984), union members filed a lawsuit against the union and employer alleging unfair representation. The court not only considered the circumstances of the filing of a case but "the conduct of the litigation" as well. *Id.* at 175. The standard the court reviewed was "bad faith." The plaintiff's attorney failed to investigate the facts of the case, failed to conduct discovery, and failed to cite the proper legal standards, which could have been discovered through legal research. The court specifically noted in its dicta that "this conclusion is reached reluctantly" that the plaintiff's attorney failed to meet the "liberal threshold standards for initiating litigation." *Id.* at 180. As the court warned: "At the very least, trained attorneys who are licensed by the state owe their clients, the judicial system and the public a duty to analyze problems brought to them in light of easily ascertainable legal standards and to render detached, unemotional, rational advice on whether a wrong recognized by the law has been done. Attorneys should file and pursue on behalf of their clients only those cases which they reasonably believe are well grounded in fact, are warranted by existing law or a good faith argument for the extension, modification or reversal of existing law." *Id.* at 181. Read the *Taylor* case. Was the attorney wrong in pursuing the case? Were the sanctions by the court reasonable? Why? What was the court's reasoning in the case for awarding attorney's fees? Pleadings cannot be filed simply because you "feel" a wrong has been or may have been committed. Facts, real facts, must substantiate the claims prior to filing a pleading with a court.

certificate of service

Verification by attorney that pleadings or court documents were sent to the opposing counsel in a case.

other parties. The certification is called a **certificate of service.** This certification is very important, because unless the other parties are aware that the pleading has been filed, they cannot make appropriate responses in accordance with the applicable rules and deadlines. The certificate of service generally contains basic information such as identified in Figure 10.4.

FILING OF PLEADINGS

When a document is filed with a court, usually with a clerk, a date stamp or file stamp is affixed to the document. That date stamp is critical. It identifies the date, and often the time, the pleading was filed. Not only is this a record of when the court received the document, but it also indicates a timely filing of a pleading, such as a court-ordered deadline or a statute of limitations deadline. (Recall our case brief in Chapter 3. That case centered on the issue of when a document was received and file stamped.) Always verify that a pleading or court document you file is properly date stamped. You never know when a filing date stamp may be an issue. Take the extra time to review court filings for a date stamp. This practice may save you, and a case, in the future.

PRACTICE TIP

When filing court documents, *inspect* the returned, file-stamped documents for proper date stamping. Do not overlook or assume the obvious. People do make mistakes and you do not want to be the victim of someone's inadvertence or sloppiness.

FIGURE 10.4   **Certificate of Service**

Certificate of Service

I, **Mary Attorney,** hereby certify that a copy of the foregoing Motion to Dismiss was mailed, U.S. mail to all counsel of record on this 15th day of June, 2006.

_____

Mary Attorney

or

I certify that a copy of Defendant's Answer was served on Marshall Friedman who is the attorney in charge for Plaintiff, ABC Corporation and whose address is (address of counsel) by certified U.S. mail, return receipt requested on August 26, 2006.

_____

Name of Attorney

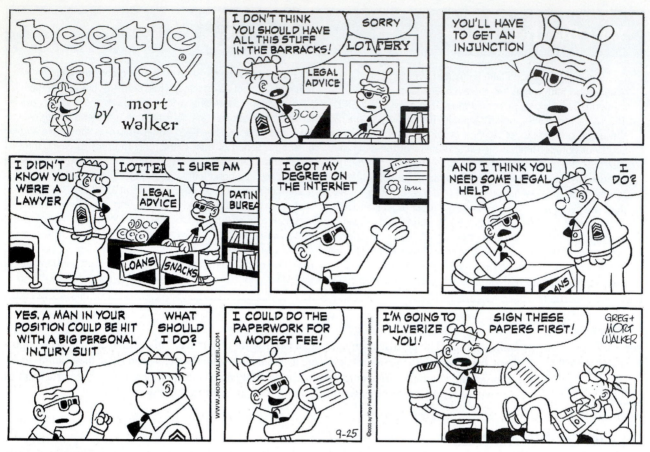

Source: © King Features Syndicate.

THE COMPLAINT

As noted, the complaint is the pleading that commences the lawsuit. In addition to the caption and signature block, a complaint prepared in accordance with the FRCP includes an introduction, an identification of the parties, a statement of the basis for jurisdiction, numbered paragraphs containing the allegations (including damages) and causes of action, and a prayer for relief. It does *not* include an ordinary certificate of service, because a complaint must be served according to its own special rules. Let's take a look at each of these areas.

THE CAPTION

The caption that appears on the complaint includes the same information that appears on every other caption, with the exception of the docket number. The court clerk assigns the docket number after the filing of the complaint; subsequent pleadings will show it, but the complaint cannot show the docket number until the clerk assigns it (more about the sequence of events later). The only time the docket number is left blank is when the initial complaint is filed.

Introduction

Although the trend is to eliminate the introductory paragraph of pleadings, it is still used in many jurisdictions. The introductory paragraph identifies the party filing the pleading and the nature of the pleading. Figure 10.5 shows several examples of introductory paragraphs in a complaint.

The Body of the Complaint

The body of the complaint consists of the identification of the parties, the basis for jurisdiction, and the numbered paragraphs containing the **allegations** and cause of action.

allegations
Facts forming the basis of a party's complaint.

The parties are identified by name and status (*i.e.*, whether an individual, corporation, or some other status), state of citizenship, and street address. These characteristics can be important; their

FIGURE 10.5
Introductory
Paragraphs

Simple, General Clause:

Plaintiff alleges . . .

Comes Now, Plaintiff in the above-styled cause, and complains of Defendant and would show unto the Court as follows:

Single Claim Stated:

Plaintiff for his claim alleges . . .

Plaintiff for its complaint alleges . . .

Claims Made in Separate Counts:

Plaintiff for a first count alleges . . .

Alternate Forms:

The Plaintiff, for his complaint against the Defendant through Michelle Carr, his attorney; alleges . . .

The Plaintiffs bring their complaint against the Defendants and for their claims would respectfully show . . .

significance is discussed in the subsection on "service of process." Figure 10.6 shows examples of paragraphs identifying various parties.

Complaints prepared under the FRCP must also identify the basis for the alleged jurisdiction of the federal court. This usually requires identifying the substantive federal statutes that apply to the facts to form the basis of the jurisdiction, or, if no substantive statute is the basis for the jurisdiction, then the applicable federal jurisdictional statute (usually relating to diversity of citizenship) is cited, with a statement showing that its requirements have been satisfied. Figure 10.7 shows some examples of jurisdictional paragraphs.

Following the identifying and jurisdictional paragraphs are the allegations of the plaintiff. The allegations set forth the claims of the party. Asserted as a group, they form the plaintiff's cause of

FIGURE 10.6 General Paragraphs Identifying the Parties

Natural Persons—Single Parties

Plaintiff is a citizen of the State of Montana, and resides in the City of Billings. Defendant is a citizen of the State of Minnesota and resides in the City of International Falls and may be served with process at (address of Defendant). The matter in controversy, exclusive of interest and costs, exceeds seventy-five thousand dollars ($75,000.00).

Multiple Plaintiffs

Plaintiff, ALBERT CROSS, is a citizen of the State of Rhode Island, Plaintiff, SANDRA CROSS, is a citizen of the State of Rhode Island, and Defendant, CHRISTOPHER VAIL, is a citizen of the State of Rhode Island and may be served with process at (address). The matter in controversy exceeds, exclusive of interest and costs, the sum of one hundred thousand dollars ($100,000.00).

Corporations

Plaintiff is a corporation incorporated under the laws of the State of Delaware, having its principal place of business in the State of New Hampshire, and Defendant is a corporation incorporated under the laws of the State of New Hampshire, having its principal place of business in a State other than the State of New Hampshire. Defendant may be served with process by serving its registered agent at (name of agent and address). The matter in controversy exceeds, exclusive of interest and costs, the sum of fifty thousand dollars ($50,000.00).

FIGURE 10.7   Statutory Jurisdictional Allegations in the Body of Complaint

General Form

The section arises under the Constitution of the United States, Article II, Section 8, and the 14th Amendment to the Constitution of the United States, U.S.C., Title 28 § 1 *et. seq.*

Diversity of Citizenship and Federal Question

The jurisdiction of this Court is based upon diversity of citizenship and Title 15, U.S.C. Sections 1, *et. seq.* The matter in controversy, exclusive of interest and costs, exceeds the sum of seventy-five thousand dollars ($75,000.00).

count
The cause of action in the complaint.

action, which is the particular legal theory upon which plaintiff claims a right to judicial relief, or recovery of damages, against the defendant. The complaint should include all claims that plaintiff has against the defendant that arise from the same facts and circumstances. If there is more than one claim, each separate claim or cause of action is set forth in a separate **count.** Figure 10.8 shows FRCP 8(e) regarding multiple causes of action.

The allegations are the substantive heart of the complaint. It is here that legal writing considerations come into play. The drafter cannot simply state facts and claim damages. Preliminary research must be conducted to determine what elements the law requires the plaintiff to prove. All such elements must then be pleaded, or else plaintiff has "failed to state a claim" on which relief can be granted, leaving himself open to the Motion to Dismiss discussed in this chapter, which is filed by the defendant. Careful drafting often requires that certain specific language be used to comply with statutory or common law requirements; the sufficiency of the complaint depends on it. The extent of detail required varies, of course, depending on whether the jurisdiction requires fact pleading or notice pleading.

Case law is never cited in the complaint, but statutes and regulations relied upon are generally identified. For example, the complaint based on the facts in the Case Fact Pattern to this chapter would identify the federal age-discrimination statute on which the claim is based.

The allegations are contained in consecutively numbered paragraphs. Sometimes the identification of the parties is included in these numbered paragraphs. Each paragraph should be limited to one concise idea or statement. The language used should be accurate but adversarial—telling the plaintiff's story from the plaintiff's perspective, and sympathetic to the plaintiff for the wrong allegedly committed against her. The writer should strike a balance between mundane, unemotional language and excessively expressive language; the reader should be able to visualize events without sensing that they have been exaggerated or embellished.

Often the requirements of a later count require a restatement of allegations already set forth as paragraphs in an earlier count. If this is the case, it is not only acceptable but indeed important to eliminate redundancy by using a phrase such as the one shown in Figure 10.9.

FIGURE 10.8   Guideline for Pleading Multiple Causes of Actions.

8(e) Pleading to be Concise and Direct; Consistency

(1) Each averment of a pleading shall be simple, concise, and direct. No technical forms of pleading or motions are required.

(2) A party may set forth two or more statements of a claim or defense alternately or hypothetically, either in one count or defense or in separate counts or defenses. When two or more statements are made in the alternative and one of them if made independently would be sufficient, the pleading is not made insufficient by the insufficiency of one or more of the alternative statements. A party may also state as many separate claims or defenses as the party has regardless of consistency and whether based on legal, equitable, or maritime grounds. All statements shall be made subject to the obligations set forth in Rule 11.

FIGURE 10.9   Restatement of Allegations

Second Count

1. Paragraphs 1–8 of the First Count are hereby set forth as paragraphs 1–8 of this, the Second Count.

legal remedy
The recovery of money damages in a lawsuit; relief provided by the court to a party to redress a wrong penetrated by another party.

equitable relief
A remedy that is other than money damages, such as refraining from or performing a certain act; nonmonetary remedies fashioned by the court using standards of fairness and justice. Injunction and specific performance are types of equitable relief.

form books
Publications that contain complete or partial sample complaints, with sample factual situations and various alternative methods of stating the legal basis for the cause of action.

models
Copies of actual complaints, obtained from your firm's files, that have a similar factual foundation.

prayer for relief
A summation at the end of a pleading, which sets forth the demands by a party in the lawsuit.

By thus eliminating redundancy, the writer minimizes the risk that the reader will become bored or miss the significant points as a result of wading through repetitions.

The allegations should also identify the damages suffered by the plaintiff. The recovery of damages in the form of money is a **legal remedy.** If such legal damages are sought, you should be as specific as possible. Sometimes this is difficult, as with a personal injury situation where the nature of the damage defies precise evaluation. If the remedy sought is **equitable relief** (which resolves a lawsuit by directing the wrongdoer either to perform a certain act, or to refrain from performing a certain act), the specific nature of the equitable remedy sought should be identified as well.

When you begin drafting complaints, and even when you are more experienced, it is often helpful to refer to form books and models. **Form books** are publications that contain complete or partial sample complaints, with sample factual situations and various alternative methods of stating the legal basis for the cause of action. **Models** are copies of actual complaints, obtained from your firm's files, that have a similar factual foundation. These sources are useful in that they give you a basic framework within which to begin drafting your complaint. In the case of a model, you have an actual complaint that has withstood scrutiny; in the case of a form book, a sample complaint that has withstood editorial scrutiny by a panel of experts. You must be careful, however, when using models and form books. Problems can arise. If the law has changed since the model or form book was prepared, for example, or if you fail to recognize the significance of a twist in your particular factual situation, you may make critical drafting errors. Thus, you should use models and form books to supplement your research, not in place of it.

In general, when drafting the body of the complaint you should keep in mind the many factors we've discussed in previous chapters about effective legal writing—concise sentences, a minimum of legalese, and good punctuation and grammar. Figure 10.10 shows an example of the body of a complaint.

The Prayer for Relief

The **prayer for relief** sets out the specific demands that the plaintiff has against the defendant. It requests judgment in favor of the plaintiff on the causes of action alleged, and identifies the damages (legal and/or equitable) the plaintiff asserts judgment should allow (including interest and attorneys' fees). In essence, the plaintiff is telling the court what he seeks to gain from the lawsuit.

Since the prayer for relief often begins with the phrase "Wherefore, the plaintiff claims . . . ," followed by a statement of the relief sought, it is often called the "wherefore clause." The current trend toward simplifying pleadings has streamlined the language in some jurisdictions, however, eliminating the archaic term "wherefore."

Almost all prayers for relief have a "catch-all" provision, which states that the plaintiff also seeks "such other and further relief as the court may deem proper or appropriate." By using this or a similar catch-all clause, the plaintiff gives the court discretion on the relief it may grant, even allowing it to go beyond the plaintiff's specified requests.

You should note that in some jurisdictions, the prayer for relief is also the location for a jury-trial request. You should also note that some jurisdictions require a prayer for relief at the end of every count, not just at the end of the complaint. Examples of a prayer for relief are shown in Figure 10.11.

FIGURE 10.10
Example of Body of Complaint (Fact Pleading)

TO THE HONORABLE JUDGE OF SAID COURT:

1. Plaintiff Robert Andrews is an individual residing in Travis County, Texas, and is the natural parent of Francis Andrews, the minor Plaintiff. Defendant George Peters is an individual residing in Any Town, Oklahoma, and service of process may be had at 8362 Longhorn Drive, Any Town, Oklahoma. Defendant D.C. Computers, Inc. is a corporation duly formed and existing under the laws of the State of Texas and may be served with process by serving its agent for service, David Clark at 287 South Main, Austin, Texas 75853.

2. On the 4th day of June, 2006, Plaintiff Francis Andrews was a passenger in a vehicle driven by Plaintiff Robert Andrews, which was traveling eastbound in the 8700 block of Elm Street in Austin, Travis County, Texas.

3. Defendant Peters attempted to make a left turn in front of the Andrews' vehicle. As a result, the Andrews vehicle and the vehicle driven by Defendant Peters collided, causing injuries to Plaintiff, Francis Andrews. At the time of the collision, the vehicle driven by Defendant Peters was owned by Defendant D.C. Computers, Inc.

4. As a result of the negligent conduct of Defendant Peters, Plaintiff Francis Andrews suffered the damages and injuries set out hereinafter.

5. Plaintiffs would show that Defendant Peters was guilty of the following acts and omissions of negligence, each of which, separately or concurrently, was a proximate cause of the damages and injuries sustained by the Plaintiff, Francis Andrews:

a) Failure to yield right of way;

b) Failure to keep a proper lookout;

c) Failure to take proper evasive action;

d) Failure to apply brakes.

6. At the time of the collision described above, Defendant Peters was the agent, servant, and employee of Defendant D.C. Computers, Inc. and was acting within the scope of his authority as such agent, servant, and employee.

7. Defendant Peters was incompetent and unfit to safely operate a motor vehicle on the public streets and highways.

8. Defendant D.C. Computers, Inc. knew, or in the exercise of due care should have known, that Defendant Peters was an incompetent and unfit driver and would create an unreasonable risk of danger to persons and property on the public streets and highways of Texas.

9. Plaintiff Francis Andrews was severely injured as a proximate result of the negligent conduct of the Defendants. Plaintiff Francis Andrews has suffered physical pain and mental anguish in the past and in reasonable probability will suffer from such in the future. Plaintiff Francis Andrews has sustained physical impairment and in reasonable probability will sustain such impairment in the future.

10. Plaintiffs have sustained reasonable medical expenses in the amount of $52,000.00 as a result of the Defendants' negligence in the past and in reasonable probability will sustain additional medical expenses in the future.

11. At the time of this collision, Defendant Peters was under the influence of an alcoholic beverage. The conduct of Defendant Peters in driving the vehicle while under the influence of an alcoholic beverage constitutes gross negligence. As a result of such conduct, the Plaintiffs are entitled to recover exemplary damages.

The Signature Block and the Verification

The attorney preparing the complaint must sign it and, as we noted earlier, Rule 11 of the FRCP states that the signature constitutes a written affirmation that she has a good-faith basis for filing it (protecting against frivolous or harassing suits). Usually the attorney's name, address, fax number,

FIGURE 10.11
**Prayer for Relief
Section of Complaint**

WHEREFORE, PREMISES CONSIDERED, Plaintiffs pray that the Defendants be cited to appear and answer herein and further pray that upon final hearing, Plaintiff have final judgment against each Defendant, jointly and severally, for damages in excess of the minimum jurisdictional limits of this Court, for exemplary damages, for prejudgment and post-judgment interest as allowed by law, for costs of court and for such other and further relief, both general and special, at law and in equity, to which the Plaintiffs may show themselves justly entitled.

OR

WHEREFORE:

The Plaintiffs, Robert Andrews and Francis Andrews, demand judgment against the Defendant in the sum of Fifty-Two Thousand Dollars ($52,000.00).

The Plaintiff demands a trial by jury.

OR

The Plaintiffs demand judgment . . .

and telephone number are typed below the signature. Many jurisdictions have attorney identification numbers, called bar card numbers, which are required with all court submissions; check the rules in your jurisdiction for the requirements of a signature block, or review a sample block from a pleading from your law firm or company. Figure 10.12 shows sample signature blocks.

verification
A brief affidavit at the end of the complaint swearing to the truth of the assertions in the pleading.

Some complaints require a brief affidavit, called a **verification,** in which the plaintiff swears to the truth of the contents. This requirement is usually dictated by statute or court rule. By signing the verification, the plaintiff shows that he (1) has read the complaint, (2) understands the contents, and (3) pledges that, to the best of his personal knowledge, the allegations are true. The purpose of the verification is to protect further against false claims. Often the requirement applies where the allegations of the complaint are particularly strong, as where fraud is claimed. Signing

FIGURE 10.12   Sample Signature Block

Respectfully submitted,

_____

Andrea Boxman
Attorney Bar No. or Identification No.
Address
City, State and zip code
Telephone number
Fax number
E-mail address
(Party Representing)

If a law firm

Respectfully submitted,
(Name of Law Firm)

_____

Name of Attorney in Charge of Case or Signing Pleading
Address
Bar No. or Identification
Telephone number
Fax number
E-mail address
(Party Representing)

FIGURE 10.13
Sample Verification Block

STATE OF NEW JERSEY   §
COUNTY OF CUMBERLAND   §

BEFORE the undersigned Notary Public for the State of New Jersey, at large personally appeared, ROBERT ANDREWS, Plaintiff in the above-styled cause, who, being by me first duly sworn, deposes and says that the averments contained in the foregoing Complaint are true and correct.

This the ___ day of August, 2006.

_____

ROBERT ANDREWS

Sworn to and subscribed before me, this ___ day of August, 2006

_____

NOTARY PUBLIC IN AND FOR THE STATE OF NEW JERSEY
My Commission Expires: _____

OR

STATE OF _____
_____ COUNTY

On this day, Cameron Chapman appeared before me, the undersigned notary public. After I administered an oath to him and upon his oath he stated that he read the Complaint and that the facts stated in it are within his personal knowledge and are true and correct.

_____

Cameron Chapman

SWORN TO and SUBSCRIBED before me
Cameron Chapman on _____, 2006.

_____

Notary Public in and for the State
Of _____

an untruthful verification can lead to criminal prosecution, and the possible results should be explained to the plaintiff before he signs. An example of a verification appears as Figure 10.13.

Service of Process

The certificate of service is not needed in a complaint because, since the complaint is the first notice of a lawsuit that a defendant receives, the service requirements are actually much stricter than merely requiring a certificate of service. **Service of process** is the procedure by which a defendant is notified by a **process server** (a person statutorily authorized to serve legal documents such as complaints) that she is being sued. Among the papers that a defendant receives is a summons, ordering her to appear in court at a certain time or suffer the consequences. Service of process is accomplished by delivery of the complaint and **summons;** the procedure has many technical requirements, which vary from one jurisdiction to another. The *status* of the defendants is also significant for the purpose of service of process. Rules of service differ depending on whether the defendant is an individual, a corporation, or of some other status.

In some jurisdictions the complaint is filed with the court, *then* served on the defendants, whereas in other jurisdictions it is served first, then filed. If the complaint is filed before service, the procedure is as follows: (1) original is filed with the court; (2) the clerk assigns a docket number to the case; then (3) copies are returned to the plaintiff for service on the defendants. Make sure you find out and follow the proper sequence in your jurisdiction. In general, you should learn the specific rules of service for all the courts in your area, and always review questions with your supervising attorney.

service of process
The procedure by which a defendant is notified by a process server of a lawsuit.

process server
A person statutorily authorized to serve legal documents such as complaints.

summons
The notice to appear in court, notifying the defendant of the plaintiff's complaint.

Checklist

The full text of a complaint answer appears in Figure 10.14. The following is a checklist for preparation of a complaint:

- Determine the parties who will be sued.
- Identify the court in which suit will be filed, and verify that the court has jurisdiction.
- Research and determine the necessary elements for the causes of action you intend to allege, including the applicable statutes.
- Identify the necessary and useful facts, and determine whether yours is a fact- or notice-pleading jurisdiction.
- Identify the damages suffered and the relief sought.
- Prepare the caption and the introduction.
- Check the applicable procedural rules, form books, and models to determine the proper style of pleading.
- Draft concise, effective statements that establish the cause of action in a light that favors your client.
- Draft the prayer for relief.
- Prepare the summons and determine the proper procedure to complete service of process. Review and edit your draft.

FIGURE 10.14   Complaint

UNITED STATES DISTRICT COURT FOR THE SOUTHERN DISTRICT OF
CALIFORNIA SAN DIEGO DIVISION

Civil Action, File Number _____

MELANIE COLEMAN,	§	
Plaintiff	§	
	§	COMPLAINT
vs.	§	
	§	
PRODUCTS OF AMERICA, INC.	§	
Defendant	§	

Plaintiff alleges:

1. Defendant is a Pennsylvania corporation, doing business in the State of Delaware. The address of its principal place of business is Philadelphia, Pennsylvania.

2. At all times relevant, Defendant was an "employer" as defined by 29 U.S.C. § 640(b) and is thus covered by and subject to the Age Discrimination in Employment Act of 1967 ("ADEA"), 29 U.S.C. § 621 *et seq.* This court has jurisdiction under 29 U.S.C. 640 (b).

3. As of July 15, 2006, Plaintiff was fifty-five years and two months of age and is an individual protected by the ADEA.

4. As of December 1, 2006, Plaintiff was employed by Defendant in the capacity of "project manager."

5. Plaintiff had been employed in various positions by Defendant from approximately October, 1982 until December, 2006.

FIGURE 10.14 Cont.

6. Plaintiff was discharged by Defendant on December 2, 2006.

7. Plaintiff's discharge was because of Plaintiff's age in violation of the ADEA.

8. Defendant's violation of the ADEA was willful.

9. Plaintiff has satisfied all of the procedural and administrative requirements set forth in 29 U.S.C.§ 626.

a. Plaintiff has filed a timely charge with the appropriate state fair employment practice office.

b. Plaintiff has filed a timely charge with the Equal Employment Opportunity Commission.

c. These charges were filed more than sixty (60) days prior to the filing of this action.

10. Proper venue is in this court as the unlawful action occurred within this jurisdiction where Defendant is doing business.

11. Plaintiff has suffered, is now suffering, and will continue to suffer irreparable injury as a result of Defendant's actions.

WHEREFORE, Plaintiff hereby demands a trial by jury and prays for the following legal and equitable remedies:

a. Defendant be ordered to employ and reemploy the Plaintiff to the position from which she was discharged, together with all benefits incident thereto, including but not limited to wages, benefits, training, and seniority.

b. Defendant be required to compensate Plaintiff for the full value of wages and benefits that Plaintiff would have received had it not been for Defendant's unlawful treatment of the Plaintiff, with interest thereon, until the date Plaintiff is offered reemployment into a position substantially equivalent to the one Plaintiff occupied on December 2, 2006.

c. That a final judgment in favor of Plaintiff and against Defendant be entered for liquidated damages in an amount equal to the amount of wages due and owing Plaintiff as provided by 29 U.S.C. §§ 626(b) and 216 (b).

d. That defendant be enjoined from discriminating against Plaintiff in any manner that violates the Age Discrimination in Employment Act.

e. That Plaintiff be awarded against the Defendant the costs and expenses of this litigation and reasonable attorneys' fees.

f. That Plaintiff be granted such other and further legal and equitable relief as the court may deem just and proper.

Respectfully submitted,

KEATCH AND WYNN

By _____

Cynthia Goodman
Attorney for Plaintiff
1801 S. Main St., Suite 104
Any Town, State
Telephone Number
Fax Number
E-mail address
Attorney Identification Number

THE ANSWER

The complaint has been correctly served. Under FRCP 12(a), the defendant must file a response within 20 days of receipt of the complaint; you should always check the rules of your jurisdiction to verify such a deadline.

If the defendant believes that some aspect of the plaintiff's allegations is inadequate, he may file one of the motions described in the next section. If, however, no such motion is filed, then the defendant files his response, called an *answer.*

The Components of an Answer

answer
The defendant's response to the plaintiff's complaint.

An **answer** is the defendant's response to the plaintiff's complaint and comprises several distinct parts. First, it contains a section responding specifically to the plaintiff's numbered paragraphs. It either admits an allegation, denies it, or pleads that the defendant "lacks sufficient knowledge or information to form a belief as to the truth or falsity" of the allegation. This last category would apply to those of the plaintiff's allegations that relate to issues of her own status or conduct, necessarily outside the knowledge of the defendant. Each and every allegation must be addressed and responded to by the defendant; failure to respond can be taken as an admission.

Rule 8 of the FRCP does not allow for a "general denial" disputing all of plaintiff's claims in one generalized statement; rather, each allegation must be identified and responded to. Most jurisdictions follow this rule; Texas and California are two notable exceptions.

general defenses
Specific responses by the defendant to plaintiff's complaint.

Second, **general defenses** are sometimes included in the answer. These are items that, under the FRCP, can also be made by motion; we discuss them further in the section on Additional Pleadings. They cover such things as an assertion that the court lacks jurisdiction, or that the plaintiff has failed to state a claim on which relief can be granted.

affirmative defenses
"Excuses" by the opposing party that do not just simply negate the allegation, but put forth a legal reason to avoid enforcement. These defenses are waived if not pleaded.

The next section of the answer contains the **affirmative defenses,** which are also called **special defenses.** Affirmative defenses are those which go beyond mere denial of the plaintiff's claims; because of a separate affirmative fact, the defendant asserts that a defense exists even if plaintiff's allegations are true. Such defenses are usually waived unless specifically pleaded, which means that the defendant can only introduce evidence to prove an affirmative defense if he has included it in his answer. The affirmative or special defenses that must be included in the pleadings are often identified by statute or rule, as with Rule 8(c) of the FRCP. Examples of affirmative defenses are such issues as contributory negligence, assumption of risk, or statute of limitations. Figure 10.15 is an example of an answer with general and affirmative defenses.

special defenses
Affirmative defenses.

Under some circumstances, the defendant includes a counterclaim after her defenses. A counterclaim may be filed with the answer or separately. It may arise out of the same facts as the complaint or be unrelated. Whatever the context, a counterclaim can be thought of as a separate lawsuit within a lawsuit, in which the defendant sues the plaintiff. The drafting considerations are similar to those for a complaint.

compulsory counterclaim
A counterclaim that is required to be pleaded because the facts relate to the same transaction as that set forth in the original complaint.

There are two types of counterclaims—compulsory and permissive. A **compulsory counterclaim** is one in which the facts relate to the same transaction as that set forth in the original complaint. It is *compulsory* because, if it is not included in the pending lawsuit, it is waived forever (see FRCP 13[a]). The purpose of making this sort of counterclaim compulsory is to conserve judicial resources: The court is able to adjudicate in one trial all claims arising out of the same set of facts, so that repetitive trials can be avoided. A **permissive counterclaim** (also discussed in FRCP 13) arises out of different facts. It may be filed in the pending lawsuit, but if it is not, it may be filed at a later date in a separate lawsuit. That is, no rights are waived by failing to include it. If it is filed as a counterclaim, a plaintiff may move to sever it if its presence serves to cloud or confuse the original issues. Figure 10.16 is an example of a counterclaim in a negligence action.

permissive counterclaim
A counterclaim that is not required to be filed with a complaint because the facts do not arise out of the same set of circumstances as the complaint.

To complicate matters even more, a cross-claim (which we discussed as a type of pleading) can be brought within the original lawsuit. A cross-claim is filed against a co-party, almost always by one defendant against another defendant, and must relate to the cause of action in the

FIGURE 10.15 Answer with General and Affirmative Defenses Alleged

<u>**DEFENDANT'S ORIGINAL ANSWER**</u>

1. Defendant admits the allegations of Paragraph 1 of the complaint.

2. Defendant denies the allegations of Paragraph 2 of the complaint.

3. Defendant denies the allegations of Paragraph 3 of the complaint, but has no knowledge of information sufficient to form a belief regarding the ownership of the vehicle.

4. Defendant denies the allegations of Paragraph 4 of the complaint.

5. Defendant denies the allegations of Paragraph 5 of the complaint.

6. Defendant admits the allegations of Paragraph 6 of the complaint.

7. Defendant denies the allegations of Paragraph 7 of the complaint.

8. Defendant D.C. Computers, Inc. has no knowledge or information sufficient to form a belief regarding the truth of the allegations of Paragraph 8 of the complaint.

9. Defendant D.C. Computers, Inc. has no knowledge or information sufficient to form a belief regarding the truth of the allegations of Paragraph 9 of the complaint.

10. Defendant D.C. Computers, Inc. has no knowledge or information sufficient to form a belief regarding the truth of the allegations of Paragraph 10 of the complaint.

11. Defendant denies the allegations of Paragraph 11 of the complaint.

GENERAL DEFENSES

12. This court lacks personal jurisdiction pursuant to Federal Rule 12(b).

13. Plaintiff has failed to state a claim upon which relief can be granted.

AFFIRMATIVE DEFENSES

14. Plaintiff was contributorially negligent in operating his automobile and is barred from recovery.

15. Plaintiff was traveling at an excessive speed and the alleged accident was unavoidable due to Plaintiff's negligence.

Defendant requests that this matter be dismissed and that Defendant be reimbursed its costs and attorneys' fees expended in the defense of this matter.

main complaint. The circumstances justifying a cross-claim often arise when a plaintiff sues two defendants who themselves have a business relationship—for example, when a person falls down in rented premises, then sues both the owner of the property and the tenant.

Although the terminology we have used applies in all federal jurisdictions, you should take great care in reviewing your state and local rules, because state and local terminology can vary dramatically. In California, for example, what we have just described as a "counterclaim" is referred to as a "cross-complaint."

Checklist

The full text of an answer appears in Figure 10.17. The following is a checklist that you can use in drafting an answer:

— Check the rules to verify the deadline for filing the answer.

— Admit or deny each allegation of the complaint, or allege that you have insufficient information to respond.

FIGURE 10.16   Counterclaim in a Negligence Action

The Defendant, counterclaiming against Plaintiff, says:

1. On September 17, 2006, the Defendant was driving an automobile in a southerly direction on Highway 42 in Cumberland County, New Jersey, and entered the intersection of that highway and Atlantic County Road.

2. At the same time, Plaintiff was driving an automobile in a general easterly direction and entered the intersection after the Defendant was well within the intersection.

3. At about the same time Wesley Whittaker was driving an automobile in a general westerly direction upon the same highway.

4. The automobiles driven by Plaintiff and by Defendant came into contact within the intersection, and in the collision, the Defendant suffered damages to his property and injuries to his person.

5. At and about the time and place of the collision and just prior to it, Plaintiff negligently managed and operated the automobile he was driving. Plaintiff was negligent in the following respects: (a) in carelessly driving at an excessive rate of speed contrary to the statute; (b) in failing to use ordinary care to keep a proper lookout; (c) in failing to use ordinary care to have the automobile he was driving under proper control.

6. As a proximate result of the negligence of Plaintiff, the Defendant suffered the following damage and injuries: Defendant's automobile front end was demolished; the left side of his ribs were broken; he was forced to incur expense for medical treatment and hospitalization; he suffered great pain and suffering, and was prevented from pursuing his business, thus suffering economic loss.

7. Defendant will be partially disabled for a long period and unable to attend his usual occupations, and to his damage in the sum of fifty-five thousand dollars ($55,000.00).

WHEREFORE, the Defendant demands judgment as follows:

(1) Dismissing Plaintiff's complaint;

(2) Against Plaintiff for Defendant's damages in the sum of fifty-five thousand dollars ($55,000.00) together with costs and disbursements; and

(3) For such other and further relief as Defendant is justly entitled.

Respectfully submitted,

_____

Bonnie Maloney
Attorney for Defendant
8201 South Broadway
Any Town, State 40387
(telephone number)
(fax number)
(attorney identification number)

— Check to be sure that every paragraph and allegation of the complaint has been responded to.

— Allege any affirmative or general defenses that apply.

— Set forth any applicable counterclaim or cross-claim.

— Review and edit your draft.

FIGURE 10.17 Answer

UNITED STATES DISTRICT COURT FOR THE SOUTHERN DISTRICT OF
CALIFORNIA SAN DIEGO DIVISION

MELANIE COLEMAN, Plaintiff	§	
	§	
	§	DEFENDANT'S ORIGINAL
vs.	§	ANSWER
	§	
	§	CIVIL ACTION NO. ___
PRODUCTS OF AMERICA, INC., Defendant	§	

1. Defendant admits the allegations contained in paragraph 1 of the complaint.

2. Defendant admits that Plaintiff seeks to bring a cause of action under Title 29 U.S.C. § 640(b), but denies that Plaintiff is entitled to relief.

3. Defendant has no knowledge of information sufficient to form a belief regarding the truth of allegations of paragraph 3 of the complaint.

4. Defendant admits the allegations contained in paragraph 4 of the complaint.

5. Defendant admits the allegations contained in paragraph 5 of the complaint.

6. Defendant admits that Plaintiff was relieved of job responsibilities but denies that Plaintiff was discharged unlawfully under Title 29 U.S.C. § 640(b).

7. Defendant denies the allegations contained in paragraph 7 of the complaint.

8. Defendant denies the allegations contained in paragraph 8 of the complaint.

9. Defendant admits that he received a charge filed by Plaintiff but denies that the charge was filed timely.

10. Defendant denies the allegations contained in paragraph 10 of the complaint.

11. Defendant denies the allegations contained in paragraph 11 of the complaint.

GENERAL DEFENSES

12. Plaintiff has failed to state a claim upon which relief can be granted.

13. Plaintiff's suit is barred by virtue of statute of limitations.

AFFIRMATIVE DEFENSES

14. Plaintiff failed to file the complaint in this court within ninety (90) days following Plaintiff's right to sue notice as required by the statute.

WHEREFORE, Defendant requests that this matter be dismissed and that Defendant be reimbursed its costs and attorneys' fees expended in the defense of this matter.

Respectfully submitted,

_____

Barbara Johnson
Attorney for Defendant
8201 South Broadway
Any City, USA
Telephone number
Fax number
E-mail address
Attorney identification number

ADDITIONAL PLEADINGS

Motion for More Definite Statement
A request by a defendant for additional specificity of plaintiff's complaint.

Motion to Dismiss
A motion that dispenses with the lawsuit because of a legal defense.

In addition to the complaint, answer, counterclaim, and cross-claim, there are also several motions considered to be pleadings. For example, a party who believes that the claims made in the pleadings of another party are unclear can file a **Motion for More Definite Statement.** A party who believes his opponent has "failed to state a claim" for which the court can grant relief can file a **Motion to Dismiss,** which, if granted by the court, dismisses the claim. Other motions may be available with other names, or similar motions with variant names, depending on the rules of your jurisdiction; you should become familiar with the rules that apply in your area.

In the previous section we mentioned general defenses, which can be raised either in the answer, or by a separate motion. Rule 12(b) of the FRCP identifies the following defenses, any one or more of which may be made by motion:

1. Lack of jurisdiction over the subject matter
2. Lack of jurisdiction over the person
3. Improper venue (which is an assertion that plaintiff has filed the complaint in the wrong court)
4. Insufficiency of process (which means the summons or some aspect of the papers served by the process server was not correct)
5. Insufficiency of service of process (which means that the process server did not follow the rules in delivering the lawsuit)
6. Failure to state a claim on which relief can be granted

If a party chooses to assert these defenses in a motion, the motion is called a Motion to Dismiss. It is generally supported by a brief, to which plaintiff responds and on which the court renders a decision. Before making its decision, the court often allows oral argument. An example of a Motion to Dismiss appears as Figure 10.18.

FIGURE 10.18   Rule 12(b) Motion to Dismiss

(CAPTION)

MOTION TO DISMISS

Defendant, RAINEY, INC., moves the court to dismiss Plaintiff's complaint on the following grounds:

1. That there is no actual controversy between the parties under the provisions of Title 42 U.S.C. §2000(e), as Plaintiff is not within the protected class under Title VII of the Civil Rights Act of 1964.

2. The court lacks jurisdiction of the subject matter of the complaint.

3. The complaint fails to state a claim against the Defendant upon which relief can be granted, since Plaintiff is male, thirty-nine (39) years of age, and not subject to protection under 42 U.S.C. §2000(e).

Respectfully submitted.

_____

Katherine Haley
Attorney for Defendant
333 E. Denton Drive
Richardson, Texas 75221
(telephone number)
(fax number)
(e-mail address)
(attorney identification number)

You Be the Judge
Hypothetical 10-3

A defendant filed a Motion to Dismiss in *Ernst Haas Studio v. Palm Press, Inc.* 64 F.3d 110 (2d Cir. 1999). The plaintiff appealed the dismissal of the case. In the case, a photographer claimed copyright to a picture of Albert Einstein that his father had taken. The plaintiff, Ernest Haas Studio, in fact did not have the copyright to the photograph, and as the court determined, never had the copyright. Since the case and ultimately the appeal were frivolous, the Appeals Court ordered sanctions of attorney's fees. Moreover, the court addressed the inadequacy of the appellant's brief by reminding the appellant that the "brief must contain 'the contentions of the appellant on the issues presented, and the reasons therefor, with citation to the authorities, statutes, and parts of the record relied on.' Appellant's brief utterly fails to comply with the mandatory direction. A reasonable reader of the Brief is left without a hint of the legal theory proposed as a basis for reversal. The Brief creates utter confusion . . ." *Id.* at 112. What are the facts of the Ernest Haas Studio case? Why did the court impose monetary sanctions? What is the court's reasoning in the case? What is the court's disposition? We see another plaintiff filing a frivolous baseless pleading. Additionally, the legal theory for the appeal is without merit. The result—sanctions. Once again, the court's message to litigants is: investigate your facts properly and research the law prior to filing a court document, or suffer the "financial" consequences.

As we noted earlier, the complexities of procedural rules are beyond the scope of this discussion. Nevertheless, as you review the six defenses listed, you should keep in mind the following points:

- A defendant in a lawsuit has numerous options available to attack the claims in a complaint, in addition to admission, denial, or claim of insufficient knowledge.

- The six defenses listed constitute a sampling of these options, by no means exhaustive.

- There is great variety between and among jurisdictions as to the manner and timing of the filing of defenses, and the names of the related motions.

- It is necessary to study and master the applicable rules.

- When in doubt, discuss questions and problems with your supervising attorney.

A special kind of response, which we have referred to previously as the Motion for More Definite Statement, is authorized by FRCP 12(e) and merits brief additional mention. The filing of this motion is an assertion by the defendant that more information must be provided by the plaintiff before an intelligent response can be prepared. In some jurisdictions this pleading is called a Request for More Definite Statement, or some similar name. Such a motion or request is often useful to pin down a plaintiff who has made vague allegations, and it can set the stage for the assertion of other defenses.

Strategy lies behind the filing of pleadings. Because they define the issues before the court, and because they are provided to the jury, if the matter is a jury trial great care must be taken to ensure that the issues presented are the issues intended by the parties. The strategist/drafter should always strive to limit the issues, to the extent possible, to those most favorable to her client, and draft them in language sympathetic to her client.

AMENDING AND SUPPLEMENTING PLEADINGS

Although pleadings must be prepared in good faith, and hence should be prepared fully and to the best of the drafter's knowledge and ability, often information arises after filing that a party may wish to add. In addition, a party may be *required* to add information when a Motion for More Definite Statement is granted. A drafter may also have forgotten to include some information. Such additions (or analogous deletions) are made by filing amended or supplemented pleadings.

Amended Pleadings

amended pleading
A pleading that changes, corrects, revises, or deletes information from a prior pleading.

An **amended pleading** changes, corrects, revises, or deletes information from a prior pleading. Information from the original pleading that is not changed remains in force, but information that is superseded is no longer in force. It is critically important to distinguish that which is changed from that which remains as before—your skills of writing with clarity become important in this regard. It is generally best to file an entirely new pleading, identifying it as "amended" in the title (for example, "Amended Complaint") incorporating all the old and new provisions in one place.

If an optional amended pleading (*i.e.*, one not required by the granting of a motion) is not filed within a certain number of days of the original pleading, it generally can be filed thereafter only with the permission of the court. Check the applicable rules to verify such a deadline.

Supplemental Pleadings

supplemental pleading
A pleading that adds to a pleading without deleting prior information.

A **supplemental pleading** adds to a pleading without deleting prior information. The prior pleading remains intact and is read in conjunction with the supplement. A supplemental pleading is usually filed when additional facts become known after the filing of the original pleading, perhaps after information is learned through a deposition or other discovery procedure (discussed in the next chapter). Court permission may also be required prior to the filing of a supplemental pleading.

PRACTICAL CONSIDERATIONS

Pleading is both a science and an art. It is a science in that specific rules must be strictly followed, or the pleading fails on technical grounds. It is an art in that the pleader must use creative skills to plot a strategic course and draft pleadings that assist in reaching the intended destination.

It is difficult to separate the science from the art, and this chapter has talked as much about rules as about writing. Mastering the rules is essential to mastering pleadings, and hence you should take the time to thoroughly review both the Federal Rules of Civil Procedure and the state and local rules applicable in your jurisdiction. We have only touched on these considerations; you should go much further.

Ethics Alert

Throughout this chapter and Chapter 8, *The Basics of Legal Correspondence,* the message is that paralegals cannot sign certain documents that render legal advice. That is clear. Another ethical concept also related to the filing of pleadings is the requirement under the Federal Rules of Civil Procedure, Rule 8, that filed pleadings are not frivolous. What the rule requires is due diligence in investigating the claims upon which the attorney bases a lawsuit. Not only must a claim be investigated, but there must be a "good faith" basis for filing of the pleading. Recall our attorney in the last chapter who represented his brother. His conduct went beyond the duty to investigate; he simply invented the allegations. This type of action is inappropriate for both the attorney and paralegal. In *Yankee Candle Company, Inc. v. Bridgewater Candle Company, LLC,* 140 F. Supp. 2d 111 (D. Mass. 2001), the court awarded over $1 million in legal fees and court costs because of the behavior of the plaintiff, The Yankee Candle Company. The case was disguised as a copyright infringement case, but the court determined that the case was filed primarily to harass and intimidate the defendant, damaging them financially. The court noted that "Yankee's handball conduct in pursuing this litigation provides evidence of an improper motivation: to drain as much profit as possible out of a far smaller competitor." *Id.* at 118. In reviewing the cases, the court examined such components as the plaintiff's conduct and oppressive actions, economic coercion, and groundless arguments. *Id* at 121. Review the case. Were the actions of the court appropriate? Why or why not? How did the court calculate the award of attorney's fees? What fees were included in the calculation? What is the message the court is communicating in its decision? The *Yankee Candle Company* case's message is quite clear. Filing pleadings in a court has legal significance and ethical responsibilities. Courts will not hesitate to sanction a party for inappropriate conduct that constitutes bad faith and harassment.

E-FACTOR

ELECTRONIC FILINGS OF PLEADINGS

Two important issues arise in the electronic age: amending pleadings and filing pleadings. One issue was discussed in the previous chapter regarding amending of pleadings. With computers comes an ease in adding, changing, and deleting information. Usually the information we choose to change in the computer document is changed; the problems occur when a program fails or human error intervenes. In *Philadelphia Gear Corp. v. Swath International,* we examined the case for the proposition "read before you sign." But that case also addressed another issue: human error. In the case, a pleading was supposed to be amended. Something happened. The attorney inadvertently filed the original pleading without the changes. The attorney acknowledged the error but the opposing counsel was not so cooperative. All this could have been averted if the attorney had checked his work. The moral is "what you think you prepared and changed may not be changed at all." Computers are not infallible. Remember to take the extra time to check your work and ensure its correctness.

The other important issue, apart from the word processing function of the computer, is the electronic filing of pleadings and how to address some of its inherent problems.

Many courts offer electronic filing of pleadings. E-filing, as it is known, allows parties to a lawsuit to electronically file court documents instead of filing paper pleadings. With a push of a button on a keyboard, pleadings are filed with courts, eliminating the need to personally serve court papers to the court clerks. Although this is the wave of the future, all courts have not subscribed to e-filings. Obviously, money is an issue forcing many jurisdictions to invest millions of dollars to upgrade their infrastructure to accommodate e-filings. There is debate as to "how" e-filings should be implemented. Concerns over privacy exist; concerns over bad faith and harassing tactics exist. Since the e-filing access is virtually instantaneous, issues arise how to best protect litigants in sensitive situations.

The philosophical debates will continue among attorneys, judges and academicians, but for you, the paralegal, your role is to understand and comply with the protocols of the courts in which you will practice. What are the rules of practice for filing e-pleadings? They vary, of course, among the courts and jurisdictions around the country. What is considered acceptable practice for one court may be taboo for another. Some courts have instituted a Case Management/Electronic Case Files (CF/ECF) system. Others are still in the process of determining how they will implement e-filings and under what conditions they will be permitted. Before you file a pleading electronically, be clear on the procedures for e-filing. Do not place yourself in a compromising situation by violating court rules and having an e-pleading rejected for filing. Not all courts' rules are the same. You have learned this time and time again throughout this textbook. Filings in a state court, and even a county or parish within a state, may differ dramatically; differences exist for filings among the federal district courts as well. Appropriate procedures in the northern district of California, for example, and the southern district of California for the federal courts may differ, and you need to know the difference before you file the pleading. Read your court rules!

But remember that drafting pleadings requires more than merely knowing and following rules, and more than mechanically adapting the facts of your case to the formats suggested in a form book. Pleadings define your case for yourself, the opposition, the court, and (if a jury matter) the jury. But *you* define the pleadings, by careful and effective drafting.

Summary

Pleadings are formal documents filed with the court that establish the claims and defenses of the parties. The complaint is filed by the plaintiff, and commences the lawsuit. The answer is filed by the defendant in response to the complaint. There may also be counterclaims and cross-claims, and motions directed to the content of the pleadings. In filing pleadings, it is critical to know and understand the applicable procedural rules. Fact-pleading jurisdictions require more detail in their pleadings than notice-pleading jurisdictions. The caption, title, signature, and certificate of service are common components of pleadings.

The complaint begins with a caption and an introduction followed by the body of the complaint, with a statement of the jurisdiction of the court (if in federal court), identification of the parties, and numbered paragraphs containing the allegations of the plaintiff. The language of the complaint is adversarial; the story it tells is sympathetic to the plaintiff. Each cause of action is stated in a separate count. Form books and models can be used to supplement the drafter's preliminary research, but should not be used as a substitute for such research. The prayer for relief identifies the remedy sought by the plaintiff. A complaint must be signed, and sometimes verification is required. Rather than a certificate of service, delivery of the complaint is made by the more complicated procedure of service of process.

The answer responds to the allegations of the complaint by admitting them, denying them, or pleading insufficient information to respond. General defenses, affirmative defenses, counterclaims, and cross-claims are also often included. A general defense can be made by motion as well as in the answer; an affirmative defense must be stated in the answer, or is waived. A counterclaim is filed by a defendant against a plaintiff; a cross-claim is filed by one co-party against another, usually by a defendant against another defendant. A compulsory counterclaim must be filed or the claim is waived; a permissive counterclaim can be filed as a counterclaim, or can be filed in the future in a separate lawsuit.

A Motion to Dismiss is a means to assert certain specified defenses, including (in a federal lawsuit) an assertion that the plaintiff has failed to state a claim on which relief can be granted. A Motion for More Definite Statement seeks more information from the other party about the details of their pleading, as a means of pinning down vague allegations; it can set the stage for other defenses.

An amended pleading changes, corrects, revises, or deletes information from a prior pleading. Amendments should be carefully identified to avoid confusion; the best practice is to file an entirely new pleading, labeled as an amended pleading, that includes both the still-accurate parts of the original content and the newly drafted changes. A supplemental pleading adds to a pleading without deleting prior information. Court permission may be required for amended and supplemental pleadings.

Pleading is both a science and an art: science in that rules must be strictly followed; art in that creative skills are required for writing and strategy. Pleadings define your case, but you define the pleadings.

Key Terms

pleadings	prayer for relief
complaint	verification
answer	service of process
counterclaim	process server
cross-claim lawsuit	summons
fact pleading	answer
notice pleading	general defenses
discovery process	affirmative defenses
caption	special defenses
certificate of service	compulsory counterclaim
allegations	permissive counterclaim
count	Motion for More Definite Statement
legal remedy	Motion to Dismiss
equitable relief	amended pleading
form books	supplemental pleading
models	

Review Questions

1. What is the difference between fact pleading and notice pleading?
2. What is a caption?
3. What is a certificate of service?
4. Why is preliminary research important to the proper drafting of a complaint?
5. What is the purpose of FRCP Rule 11?
6. Describe a benefit and a pitfall of using form books and models to assist in the preparation of pleadings.
7. Why can an attorney sign a pleading and a paralegal cannot?
8. What does the term affirmative defense mean? List several affirmative defenses.
9. What is the difference between a counterclaim and a cross-claim?
10. What is the purpose of a Motion to Dismiss?

Exercises

1. Mr. and Mrs. Crandall are from Bangor, Maine, and were traveling cross-country in their new automobile on August 3, 2006. While en route to their destination of Cheyenne, Wyoming, they traveled through Illinois. Harry Hart of New Town, Illinois, was crossing through the town square in New Town and hit the Crandall's car. Mrs. Crandall was thrown against the windshield, and Mr. Crandall hit the steering wheel. Mr. Hart was barely scratched, because his car had airbags, but his car was completely destroyed. The medical and hospital expenses for the Crandalls were $78,000.00, and repairs to their car were $6,000.

   a. Draft a complaint on behalf of the Crandalls, based on the facts above.

   b. Using the facts in Exercise 1, draft the answer of Mr. Hart.

   c. Go to the library and find your state's procedural requirements for complaints, answers, and defenses.

2. Dr. Evan Potter just received a complaint for medical malpractice from a former patient, April Dawson. He performed surgery on her right arm over three years ago and he is now receiving the complaint. The doctor has not heard from April since her surgery. He believes the statute of limitations is two years; but he also thinks that since April never paid her medical bill, she is trying to find a way out of paying him. Dr. Potter has hired your law firm to represent him.

   a. Prepare the Motion to Dismiss for your supervising attorney's review. (Assume for purposes of this exercise that Dr. Potter has been sued in your state's trial court. Determine the appropriate court in which the lawsuit should be filed. Check the rules of court for compliance with any rules, both state and local.)

   b. Assume that April Dawson wants to file an amended complaint. Using the facts from Exercise 2, what are the procedures in your jurisdiction for filing an amended complaint?

   c. Determine the rules in your state and federal courts for filing of e-pleadings.

3. Drew Michelson bought a new computer from Computers R Us, Inc., on September 5, 2006. When he went home to set up the new desktop, there was a dent in the hard drive and a big scratch on the screen. Upset, Drew went back to Computers R Us and told them he wanted his money back. The salesperson told Drew all sales were final, as they were a discount retailer. Drew lives in Chicago, Illinois. Drew paid cash for the computer, so he was stuck with the damaged equipment. Drew decided to sue Computers R Us and wants your law firm to represent him. Prepare the appropriate documents that will be needed to pursue Computers R Us.

4. Arts of the World, Inc., receive the following letter from their lead actress:

   Dear Mr. Weston:

   I realize that there are five weeks left until the show closes, but I cannot continue. Mary Jean Warner is abusive and unprofessional. I cannot work under these conditions. You will have to find a replacement for me. My notice is effective today. I am sorry I could not continue, but Ms. Warner's behavior is causing me emotional distress.

   Sincerely,

   Adele Taylor

   Mr. Weston is furious. He will have to put the understudy on for tonight's show. He wants his lawyers on the telephone now. Ms. Taylor has a contract. The contract states that she is committed to the show until October 31, 2006. She cannot quit the show. He wants to sue Adele. Prepare the questions that you and your supervising attorney would ask Mr. Weston, prior to filing the lawsuit.

Portfolio Assignment

Your firm has been retained to represent Dana Marsh in her suit against A1 Delivery Service, Inc., a New Jersey corporation. On April 20, 2006, A1 delivered Mrs. Marsh's new refrigerator to her house located at 323 Garfield Lane, Haddonfield, New Jersey. While backing out of the driveway, the deliveryman, Herbert Killington, drove over Mrs. Marsh's cat, Buttons. Mrs. Marsh, who is 75 years old, had the cat for 15 years and was quite upset over its death. She wants to sue A1 and collect as much damages as she can. Mrs. Marsh says she still cannot get over how her "poor Buttons" looked and cannot get the blood out of her driveway.

1. Draft the complaint for your supervising attorney's review. Include in your complaint the method of service of process. Check the New Jersey laws for service of process on a corporate defendant.
2. As part of your assignment, draft the answer of A1 Delivery Service, Inc. (A1 is not happy with its employee, Herb; seems as though he was drinking on the job again. A1 wants to file a cross-claim against Herb.)
3. Draft the cross-claim of A1 against Herbert Killington.
4. Draft the answer for Herb. (Herb claims the brakes on his truck were faulty again. He says he couldn't stop the truck when he saw Buttons.)

Vocabulary Builder

Basics of Pleadings

```
C  P  K  V  A  Y  C  N  T  H  I  Q  E  M  S
D  R  R  O  N  G  O  X  S  E  R  V  I  C  E
T  A  O  X  O  I  S  S  Y  I  H  A  I  G  S
H  Y  U  S  T  B  U  W  C  A  L  P  L  B  N
C  E  C  P  S  S  M  O  E  C  K  L  A  N  E
Y  R  A  G  H  C  M  R  R  R  V  E  E  N  F
T  C  W  Z  Q  P  L  E  O  A  M  A  B  N  E
B  H  E  A  L  K  T  A  I  F  H  D  G  F  D
O  Y  S  A  Y  N  D  W  I  E  D  I  F  Y  B
G  W  I  I  U  B  B  H  U  M  W  N  E  E  J
L  N  V  O  Q  I  B  S  V  F  E  G  N  M  H
T  Z  C  F  F  D  T  Y  B  R  A  S  Z  V  B
C  B  W  J  C  U  W  Y  U  N  J  O  C  J  R
F  A  C  T  P  L  E  A  D  I  N  G  I  Q  H
I  H  N  X  F  W  T  N  E  M  D  N  E  M  A
```

AMENDMENT	ANSWER	CAPTION
COMPLAINT	COUNTER CLAIM	CROSS CLAIM
DEFENSES	FACT PLEADING	FORM BOOK

Chapter 11

Discovery

After completing this chapter, you will be able to:

- Explain why a discovery process is needed.

- List some characteristics of a properly drafted interrogatory.

- Explain the importance of instructions and definitions in discovery requests.

- List the different types of discovery.

- Explain what is meant by the "continuing duty to respond."

- Explain the usefulness of a request for admissions.

- Draft requests for production that are sufficiently specific.

- Explain who a "deponent" is.

- Define "subpoena."

- Explain the difference between a Motion for Protective Order and a Motion to Compel Discovery.

After a complaint and answer are filed, the true investigative process begins. Involvement in the discovery process is often an important segment of a paralegal's responsibilities. This chapter focuses on drafting various forms of discovery, including request for interrogatories, request for admissions, and request for production of documents. The most common discovery motions filed by attorneys are highlighted with an emphasis on a Motion for Summary Judgment. Now, let's explore the world of discovery.

Case Fact Pattern

Hypothetical 11-1

A complaint has been prepared and served in the matter of *Ascot v. Wellington Company*. Your firm represents Mr. Ascot. The attorney for Wellington Company has filed an answer, denying the claim.

Your supervising attorney wants to take the deposition of Henry Wellington, president of Wellington Company. Before he does so, however, he wants to do some preliminary investigation to determine the understanding of Wellington Company about the chronology of events. He has asked you to prepare interrogatories, requests for admission, and requests for production of documents and things, all of which are to be answered by Wellington Company.

Discovery is an important aspect of almost every lawsuit. As a paralegal, you will often be involved in preparing and responding to discovery requests.

DISCOVERY IN GENERAL

The "surprise witness" who arrives to testify at the eleventh hour of a trial, turning certain defeat into stunning victory, is a character still seen in television or movie courtrooms, but not in reality. The days of "trial by ambush," where one side or the other held back key information until unleashing it in front of a jury, have been replaced by the era of discovery. Rule changes in FRCP 26(a)(1) now require litigants in federal court to voluntarily disclose information to the other party such as

- the names of individuals who may have discoverable information;
- a copy of, or description of, documents in the possession of the party;
- a computation of, any category of damages; and
- a copy of any insurance agreement, if at issue.

As with any rule, exceptions are listed. The rule should be reviewed to determine whether any of the exceptions apply to the initial disclosure of information. The point is, discovery has changed, and the days of "Perry Mason" are long gone. But, what is discovery and what is its purpose? These questions and the methods of discovery will be examined in this chapter. The focus will be on the "drafting" of discovery.

discovery
The pretrial investigation process authorized and governed by the rules of civil procedure; the process of investigation and collection of evidence by litigants.

Discovery is the pretrial investigation process, authorized and governed by the rules of civil procedure. Discovery rules are broad, so that parties have the ability to pursue information in the hands of other parties to a lawsuit.

To be "discoverable," information must be relevant and not protected by attorney-client privilege. The party requesting the information need not show that it will be admissible at trial, however, but only that it "appears reasonably calculated to lead to the discovery of admissible evidence" (Rule 26[b] of the FRCP; see Figure 11.1). Discovery requests may be directed to other parties, but not to nonparties, except that nonparties are subject to deposition (and related production of documents) if subpoenaed (more about subpoenas later).

In Chapter 8 we discussed the Motion for More Definite Statement. You may now be wondering: If more information about a party's claim is needed, why not simply file that motion? The reason that a distinct and separate discovery process is needed, at least in part, is this: there are limits on the detail that a party can be required to place in her pleadings. Indeed, a court will often deny a Motion for More Definite Statement on the grounds that the detail requested is more appropriately sought through the discovery process, and goes beyond the requirements of even a fact-pleading jurisdiction. Pleadings are intended to be straightforward summaries, not all-inclusive tracts. Furthermore, there may be strategic reasons why one party wishes to learn information about another *without* having it placed in the pleadings. Finally, such forms of discovery as a deposition or a medical examination are of a character entirely different from mere written information—they supply not just words, but also the personal characteristics or condition of the person deposed or examined.

FIGURE 11.1
Rule 26(b)

(b) Discovery Scope and Limits.

Unless otherwise limited by order of the court in accordance with these rules, the scope of discovery is as follows:

(1) In General.

Parties may obtain discovery regarding any matter, not privileged, that is relevant to the claim or defense of any party, including the existence, description, nature, custody, condition, and location of any books, documents, or other tangible things and the identity and location of persons having knowledge of any discoverable matter. For good cause, the court may order discovery of any matter relevant to the subject matter involved in the action. Relevant information need not be admissible at the trial if the discovery appears reasonably calculated to lead to the discovery of admissible evidence. All discovery is subject to the limitations imposed by Rule 26(b)(2)(i), (ii), and (iii).

There are, in fact, five different types of discovery: interrogatories; requests for admission; requests for production of documents and things; requests for medical examination; and depositions. Some aspects are common to all; some unique to each. In the sections that follow, we discuss each form in turn, highlighting format, drafting, and strategy requirements.

INTERROGATORIES

interrogatory
A discovery tool in the form of a series of written questions that are answered by the party in writing, to be answered under oath.

PRACTICE TIP

Many jurisdictions have limitations on the number of interrogatories a party can send. This limitation applies to an interrogatory with subsections. If you draft an interrogatory with four subsections, many jurisdictions consider these four separate answers and therefore four questions. Be very mindful of the requirements in your jurisdiction and carefully review the restrictions and requirements. FRCP 33 limits the responses to 25 including subsections.

instructions and definitions
A section in many forms of discovery requests that defines terms in the document to avoid confusion.

An **interrogatory** is a written question submitted by one party to another, to be answered under oath. Rule 33 of the FRCP sets out the requirements governing the use of interrogatories in the federal courts. Most states have adopted a similar rule; check the rules that apply in your jurisdiction.

By following certain preliminary procedures, you will be able to prepare more effective interrogatories. First, review the case file and pleadings to become thoroughly familiar with the facts and allegations. Identify the information you need to fill in gaps or increase your understanding. Make lists of areas of appropriate inquiry. Next, as with pleadings, you can use form books and models for assistance. Again, be wary of relying on them exclusively. Also consult the rules, and review any questions you have with your supervising attorney. Form books and models will also be helpful in drafting documents associated with the other discovery methods to be discussed.

When you draft your interrogatories, use specific and detailed language that precisely identifies the information you seek. Use short sentences in simple language. Avoid the phrase "and/or," or a large number of colons and semicolons, which can confuse the reader and lead to an unsatisfactory response. Avoid multiple subtopics and sections in the interrogatory, which can also cause confusion. Such subtopics may even be prohibited in some jurisdictions, or each subtopic may be counted as a separate interrogatory in a jurisdiction that limits the total number of interrogatories allowed.

Take care in choosing verb tenses. If an interrogatory is phrased in the present tense, the information received may be different than if worded in the past tense. Who *has* possession of the records of Wellington Company, for example, may be a different party than who *had* those records.

Interrogatories should also be drafted to avoid a response of "yes" or "no." The request should require the respondent to present additional information. If all that is desired is a "yes" or "no" response, another form of discovery, such as the request for admissions, might be the better method.

Certain interrogatories are common to many different types of cases, seeking such information as identification of the person responding to the interrogatories (if the party to whom the request is directed is a corporation or other form of business); the names of witnesses and experts who will testify; and identification of documents that are relevant, such as correspondence or contracts. The format of such questions is often similar, even for different types of cases. Other interrogatories must be tailored to reflect the peculiar circumstances of the particular case at hand.

To add to the precision of individual interrogatories, the drafter often includes **instructions** and **definitions** that precede the interrogatories and define terms to avoid confusion. The drafter can often anticipate and eliminate potential problems by clarifying ambiguous terms with precise definitions. Instructions often serve to eliminate evasive answers, as, for example, an instruction that if a party objects to one subpart of a question, he should still respond to the remaining subparts.

Although you should be sure to check the rules of your jurisdiction for specific guidance in the drafting of interrogatories, the following subsections discuss elements common to all sets of interrogatories.

The Caption

Just as with pleadings, discovery requests, including interrogatories, must be identified by case name, court, and docket number. Although jurisdictions differ on the precise documents that are filed with the court (some courts require notice of filing interrogatories, for example, but not the interrogatories themselves until answers are provided), you should always put the caption of your case at the top of the first page of your interrogatories.

FIGURE 11.2
Introduction

TO: Irene Miller, by and through her attorney of record, Malcolm Anders, 1776 Declaration Drive, Boston, Massachusetts 20185

Title

Also as with pleadings, discovery requests require a title. Again, the value of the title is in its capacity to differentiate documents. Thus, in a case with multiple parties and extensive discovery, it is useful to use a title that identifies the requesting party, the party from whom a response is sought, and whether the request is the first such request or a subsequent, supplemental set. For example, a proper title might be, "Plaintiff Ascot's First Set of Interrogatories to Defendant Wellington Company."

The Introductory Paragraphs

The introduction directs the interrogatories to the party from whom a response is sought, often showing that the request is made through that party's attorney of record. Figure 11.2 illustrates an acceptable introduction.

After the introduction, another introductory paragraph identifies the appropriate state or federal rule that governs the interrogatories. It also identifies the oath requirement, which mandates that the person responding attests to the truth of the responses. Figure 11.3 shows such a paragraph.

Instructions

Following the introduction are the instructions, which, as mentioned, provide guidelines to the party responding. Figure 11.4 shows an example of common instructions found in interrogatories.

Definitions

Following (or sometimes combined with) the instructions is a section defining terms and abbreviations used in the interrogatories. The meanings established in this section eliminate ambiguity, which in turn eliminates the justification for many potential objections. Also eliminated is the need to define terms repeatedly within the interrogatories. Figure 11.5 shows an example of a definition section.

Interrogatories

After the definitions come the interrogatories themselves. They are numbered, and enough space is generally left between interrogatories for the party responding to type in her response. The detail in the questions should be enough to make them clear and precise, and will vary depending on the detail already set forth in the instructions and definitions. For example, if the term "identify" is defined to mean "provide the full name, residence address and phone number, business address and phone number, age, and marital status of," then a proper interrogatory designed to elicit all this information would simply state: "Identify Mr. Wellington." If no such definition is provided, then the information must be requested specifically.

We next discuss interrogatories relating to five areas: background information; specific case information; information about experts consulted; content of the pleadings; and generalized conclusory information.

FIGURE 11.3
Introductory
Paragraph

Defendant in the above-entitled and numbered cause pursuant to Rule 33 of the Federal Rules of Civil Procedure, propounds the attached Interrogatories. You are advised that your answers to such Interrogatories must be answered fully in writing and under oath and served on the undersigned within thirty (30) days from the date of service thereof.

You are further notified that these Interrogatories and your sworn Answers to them may be offered in evidence at the time of trial of the above cause.

FIGURE 11.4
Instructions Section

INSTRUCTIONS

In answering these interrogatories, defendant is required to set out each responsive fact, circumstance, act, omission, or course of conduct, whether or not admissible in evidence at trial, known to defendant, or about which he has or had information, which is or will be the basis for any contentions made by defendant with respect to this lawsuit. If you are unable to answer any Interrogatory completely, so state, and to the extent possible, set forth the reasons for your inability to answer more fully, and state whatever knowledge or information you have concerning the unanswered portion.

These Interrogatories are deemed to have continuing effect to the extent that if, after filing your responses to these interrogatories, you obtain information upon the basis of which you know that a response was incorrect when made, or you know that a response though correct when made is no longer true, you are required to amend your response in accordance with Rule 33 of the Federal Rules of Civil Procedure. In addition, defendant is required to supplement his responses with respect to any question directly addressed to the identity and location of persons having knowledge of discoverable matters, and with respect to the identity of each person expected to be called as an expert witness at trial, the subject matter on which he or she is expected to testify, and the substance of his or her testimony.

Background Information

It is important to develop general background information about the person responding to the interrogatories. If the person is an individual defendant, it will be important to have a current address if a subpoena needs to be served in the future; other information such as past and present employers, educational background, prior medical history, marital status, age, or other general

FIGURE 11.5
Definition Section

DEFINITIONS

The following terms have the meanings stated wherever used in these interrogatories, unless otherwise indicated:

"You" and "your" means Gilda Murray.

"Patient" means Gilda Murray.

"This Defendant" means Dr. Ned Radcliffe.

"Identify" means to state the person's full name, date of birth, marital status and spouse's name, social security number, present or last known residence and business addresses and telephone number, occupation, employer, and business address at the date of the event or transaction referred to, present or last known position and business affiliation, present or last known employer and business address. If a person is identified more than once, only the name need be provided after the first identification.

"Health care provider" means any person involved in the examination, care, or treatment of injuries, illnesses, or other health-related conditions, both physical and mental. This term includes, but is not limited to, physicians, dentists, podiatrists, chiropractors, nurses, therapists, psychologists, counselors, home care attendants, and special education instructors.

"Health care facility" means any organization or institution involved in the examination, care, or treatment of injuries, illnesses, or other health-related conditions, both physical and mental. This term includes, but is not limited to, hospitals, clinics, health maintenance organizations, outpatient facilities, testing facilities, laboratories, nursing homes, and pharmacies from which medications were obtained.

"Person" means, in the plural as in the singular, any natural person, corporation, firm, association, partnership, joint venture, or other form of legal or official entity, as the case may be.
"Document" means any document within the meaning and scope of Federal Rule of Civil Procedure 34 and includes computer records in any format. Document also includes any tangible things as that term is used in Rule 34.

FIGURE 11.6
Interrogatory That
Elicits Background
Information

INTERROGATORY NO. 1: Please state:

a. Your full legal name and any other names by which you have ever been known;

b. Your date and place of birth;

c. Your social security number;

d. Your driver's license number; and

e. Each address where you have lived in the past ten years.

ANSWER:

INTERROGATORY NO. 2:

Please state the name, address, telephone number, and employer of each and every person known to you or your attorneys who has or may have knowledge, directly or indirectly, of any facts relevant to this case. For each such person, state generally the subject matter of the facts which may be known to him or her. NOTE: This interrogatory includes, but is not limited to, any person who may be called by you as a witness at the trial of this cause.

ANSWER:

facts may become significant as well. In addition, if the person responding is an employee of a defendant corporation, it is important to know the person's job title and the scope of the person's knowledge about the events in question, as well as the person's authority to speak on behalf of the corporation. Examples of a background interrogatory appear in Figure 11.6.

Specific Case Information

After requesting background information, the drafter should begin a more focused, customized inquiry. Information specific to the case should be requested about witnesses (names, addresses, and other pertinent facts should be sought), documents (volume, description of contents, and current location should be sought), and any other facts or matters that bear on the outcome. Figure 11.7 shows examples of specific interrogatories.

Information about Experts Consulted

In cases involving technical issues, expert testimony is often crucial. If such issues are present in your case, one or more interrogatories should be included that inquire into the identity and qualifications of the opposition's experts, the nature of their inquiry and intended areas of testimony, and the existence of any written reports. Figure 11.8 illustrates interrogatories drafted to gain information about experts consulted. Note that these interrogatories are submitted to the other *party*, not to the expert; interrogatories, as we noted earlier, can only be served on other parties.

FIGURE 11.7
Examples of
Case-Specific
Interrogatories

6. Identify all employees of Wellington Company with whom Henry Wellington has discussed his meeting of March 15, 2006, with John Ascot.

7. Identify all correspondence in the possession of Wellington Company, including copies of correspondence, which in any way references, describes, or relates to the meeting of March 15, 2006, at which Henry Wellington and John Ascot were present.

8. List the dates of every in-person meeting between Henry Wellington and John Ascot between January 1, 2006 and April 30, 2006.

9. Provide the date and time of day of every phone call between Henry Wellington and John Ascot that occurred between January 1, 2006 and April 30, 2006.

FIGURE 11.8
Interrogatories
Regarding Expert
Witness

INTERROGATORY NO. 3

Please state the following information for each person who may be called by you to testify as an expert witness at the trial of this cause:

a. name, address, telephone number, and employer;

b. the date on which the witness was first contacted in connection with this case;

c. the subject matter on which the expert is expected to testify;

d. the qualifications of the expert to give testimony on that subject;

e. the specific opinions and conclusions of the expert regarding the matters involved in this case, and the factual basis for each;

f. the name, address, and telephone number of each person whose work forms a basis, in whole or in part, of the opinions of the expert.

ANSWER:

INTERROGATORY NO. 4:

Identify each individual with whom you have consulted or your attorneys have consulted as an expert, indicating whether a decision has been reached about whether: (1) said individual(s) may testify in this lawsuit; and (2) written reports were made or requested, in connection with the incidents made the basis of this lawsuit. For each expert listed, please also identify the following:

a. complete educational background of such individual, beginning with the year in which said individual graduated from high school and continuing through completion of the formal education process of such expert;

b. his or her occupation and field of specialization, as well as qualifications to act as an expert;

c. all published writings of the individual expert, listing the titles of any article(s) or book(s), the name(s) of the publication(s), the year(s) of publication(s), volume and page number;

d. for what remuneration Defendant has employed said individual;

e. whether said individual has ever been a witness in any other lawsuit, and, if so, for each lawsuit give the name of the suit, the name of the court, the date of the filing, and the name and address of the other party for whom said individual provided evidence or testimony;

f. all mental impressions and opinions held by the expert relating to the lawsuit in question;

g. all facts known to the expert (regardless of when the factual information was acquired) that relate to or form the basis of the mental impressions and opinions held by the expert; and

h. the complete employment history of such expert for the preceding five (5) years, including the name and address of the employer, and the general nature of the expert's work for such employer.

Content of the Pleadings

Pleadings present factual allegations and legal contentions. It is very important to explore the basis for these allegations and contentions. Interrogatories should be drafted to uncover the facts behind the pleadings.

Consider, for example, a complaint that contains the following paragraph: "The president of Wellington Company, Henry Wellington, forged the signature of John Ascot on the Modification of the contract between the parties." From the perspective of Henry Wellington and Wellington Company, this is a very strong allegation, which must be investigated. Wellington Company should file an interrogatory similar to the following: "State the facts upon which you rely, in paragraph 6 of the complaint, for the allegation that Henry Wellington forged the signature of John Ascot."

Similarly, if a plaintiff states a legal claim that has several prerequisites, the defendant may want to inquire into the facts behind each of the prerequisite elements. However, be careful in this regard—if a plaintiff has failed to allege one or more prerequisite elements, there may be

FIGURE 11.9
Common "Catch-All"
Interrogatory

> **INTERROGATORY NO. 5:**
>
> State any additional information relevant to the subject of this action not previously set out in your answers above.

strategic reasons to avoid inquiry in discovery (it might alert the plaintiff to the deficiency) so that you can later attack the deficiency by a Motion to Dismiss.

Generalized Conclusory Information

It is wise to conclude your interrogatories with generalized questions that inquire broadly into areas that may have been overlooked or omitted. An interrogatory with such a purpose is a "catch-all" designed to prevent a surprise at trial. The trick in drafting such an interrogatory is to devise language that can survive an objection that it is so broad as to constitute an unjustifiable "fishing expedition." An example of a potential concluding interrogatory appears in Figure 11.9.

Signature Block and Certificate of Service

In most jurisdictions the interrogatories are signed by the attorney preparing them, but not by the party she represents (in contrast to the *responses*, which must be signed not only by the attorney but also by the party responding; more about that later). To verify the date that the interrogatories were sent to opposing counsel, a certificate of service is required (see Figure 11.10).

RESPONSES TO INTERROGATORIES

Responses to interrogatories must be prepared within the time established by the applicable procedural rules. Under Rule 33 of the FRCP, the time limit is 30 days. Extensions can be requested by motion; at least in the early stages of the discovery process, the court will probably be lenient about granting such requests, and few opposing counsel will object to reasonable extensions.

PRACTICE TIP

Checking the rules of procedure is important. Do not assume that your current practice conforms to the rules. For example, there are a number of rule changes for discovery effective December 1, 2006. They mainly relate to electronic data. This change will affect you, so always take the extra time to verify the current obligations under the rules of discovery.

FIGURE 11.10 Signature Block and Certificate of Service

> Respectfully submitted,
>
> _____
>
> Andrea Chapman
> Attorney for Defendant
> Address
> Any City, State
> Telephone number
> Fax number
> Bar number or identification
> E-mail address
>
> **CERTIFICATE OF SERVICE**
>
> I certify that a true copy of this Plaintiff's First Set of Written Interrogatories was served on Katherine Haley, Attorney for Defendant, 333 E. Denton Drive, Richardson, Texas 75221, by certified mail, return receipt requested, in accordance with the Federal Rules of Civil Procedure on November 29, 2006.
>
> _____
> Andrea Chapman

FIGURE 11.11
Verification Used
with Interrogatories

THE STATE OF_____   §

                                                    §

COUNTY OF _____   §

NED RADCLIFFE, being duly sworn upon his oath deposes and says: I am the Defendant in the above-entitled action and have read the interrogatories served upon me by the Plaintiff, Gilda Murray; and the foregoing answers to those interrogatories are true according to the best of my knowledge, information, and belief.

_____

NED RADCLIFFE

SUBSCRIBED AND SWORN to before me

this ___ day of December, 2006_____

_____

NOTARY PUBLIC IN AND FOR THE

STATE OF _____

My Commission Expires:_____

verification
Acknowledgment by a
party of the truthfulness of
the information contained
within a document.

**PRACTICE
TIP**

Some jurisdictions do not require discovery requests to be filed with the court. Because of this, the certificate of service is important as a verification of when the opposing party received the discovery document. Deadlines will flow from the date of receipt. Certified mail is a recommended method of transmitting discovery requests.

**supplemental
response**
Additional response to
previously filed discovery
because of newly found
information.

Responses must be signed and verified by the client. The attorney preparing them signs them as well, but the client must attest to their accuracy. Figure 11.11 shows an example of **verification.** The response can be either a presentation of the information requested, or an objection. Objections should be addressed to individual interrogatories; it is not proper to object to *all* the interrogatories, and it remains necessary to provide responses for all those interrogatories not objected to (which is to say that the presence of one or more objectionable interrogatories does not negate the entire set of interrogatories).

As you might expect, wide-ranging requests are often met with objection. Common objections include contentions that: the instructions or definitions are overbroad, or include requirements that go beyond the scope of the rules; the information requested is privileged; the information requested is irrelevant; the request is unduly burdensome; the request is so broad as to be meaningless (an objection often raised to the generalized conclusory interrogatories); or the request is ambiguous or unintelligible.

It is important to identify and comply with time requirements in making objections. If not raised in time, objections may be waived, or dismissed.

It is also important to note that, in the federal courts and many state and local jurisdictions, there is a "continuing duty to respond" to interrogatories. This means that if new information arises *after* responses are filed that would have been included in the original responses had it been known at the time of filing, it must be forwarded to the other side as a **supplemental response.** If such supplement is not made, the court at trial can refuse to allow the presentation of evidence that includes or relates to the undisclosed materials. Such supplementation is often necessary in a case where medical treatment of an injured plaintiff is ongoing—so make sure you have provided copies of all relevant medical materials to the other side before trial.

A party is required to make reasonable good-faith efforts to locate materials and information responsive to a discovery request. Be wary of a client who has a selective memory, or who wishes to avoid the difficulty of complying with a lengthy discovery request. You may wish to file objections claiming the request is unduly burdensome; but if such objections are not sustained, your client must turn over the requested materials or information, however unpleasant and time-consuming the task may be.

In addition to filing objections, a responding party can obstruct the information-gathering efforts of the opposition by filing a Motion for Protective Order. This motion will be discussed further.

FIGURE 11.12
Introductory
Paragraph for
Request for
Admissions

Plaintiffs in the above-entitled action request pursuant to Rule 36 of the Federal Rules of Civil Procedure that Defendant, within thirty (30) days after service of this request, admit for the purpose of this action that the following facts are true:

REQUESTS FOR ADMISSIONS

request for admissions
A document that provides the drafter with the opportunity to conclusively establish selected facts prior to trial.

The **request for admissions,** authorized under Rule 36 of the FRCP, provides the drafter with the opportunity to conclusively establish selected facts prior to trial. A proposition is presented to the opposing party for admission or denial; if admitted, no further evidence need be presented on the point; the trial court accepts it as fact, at least with regard to the party who admitted it. Admissions serve to limit the complexity and expense of trials.

The caption, signature of the preparing attorney, and certificate of service are the same for a request for admissions as for a set of interrogatories. The introductory paragraph and the text of the requests are discussed in the next subsections, followed by a few words about preparing responses.

The Introduction of a Request for Admission

The introductory paragraph of a request for admissions includes an identification of the party to whom the request is directed, the rule providing for the request, and the time period allowed for response. Figure 11.12 shows an example of an appropriate introductory paragraph for a request for admission.

Text of a Request for Admission

The requests themselves consist of statements that are to be admitted or denied by the recipient. The statements are numbered sequentially.

An effective technique for drafting the requests is to move through the case point by point, from general points to those more specific. Alternative versions can appear as different numbered statements, and consecutive questions can feature finely drawn distinctions; the responses to such a pattern of requests can assist the drafter in reaching an understanding about the nuances of the other party's position. An example of this technique is shown in Figure 11.13.

Several different formats are acceptable for requests for admission, three of which appear in Figure 11.14. The most important consideration in drafting requests for production is that they be so straightforward that they avoid an evasive response. The more detail added to the sentence, the greater the tendency to elicit a qualified response. Although the responding party retains some freedom to explain the response (as we discuss further), your goal as a drafter

FIGURE 11.13
Technique for
Drafting Request for
Admissions

Alternative requests for admission:

Admit or deny the following:

1. On June 1, 2006, defendant Jones executed the contract that is attached as Exhibit A.

2. On June 2, 2006, defendant Jones executed the contract that is attached as Exhibit A.

3. On June 3, 2006, defendant Jones executed the contract that is attached as Exhibit A.

Requests for admission with finely drawn distinctions:

1. On March 15, 2006, defendant Jones attended a meeting at which were discussed the terms of a contract with Mr. Smith.

2. On March 15, 2006, defendant Jones and plaintiff Smith attended a meeting at which were discussed the terms of a contract with Mr. Smith.

3. On March 15, 2006, defendant Jones and plaintiff Smith attended a meeting at which they executed the contract that is attached hereto as Exhibit A.

FIGURE 11.14
Formats for Request for Admission

(a) Admit or deny that you requested a refund on March 6, 2006 for the car repairs performed by Defendant.

(b) Do you admit or deny that you requested a refund on March 6, 2006 for the car repairs performed by Defendant?

(c) Do you admit that you requested a refund on March 6, 2006 for the car repairs performed by Defendant?

(d) Admit or deny the following facts:

(1) That you requested a refund on March 6, 2006 for the car repairs performed by Defendant.

PRACTICE TIP

Most law firms have systems to diary when discovery responses are due. Learn the system in your office. If your office does not have a formal diary or "tickle" system, be sure you have a methodology to track when discovery is received and when it is due. Do not leave discovery responses to the last minute as poorly drafted responses can have long-lasting effects on a case.

request for production of documents and things
A type of discovery request requesting the production of relevant documents in a lawsuit.

should be to minimize the responder's ability to hedge, assuring a straightforward admission or denial.

A common use of requests for admission is to establish the authenticity of documents. A copy of a document can be appended to the set of requests, and the requests can ask for an admission or denial that the copy is an exact copy of the original. Figure 11.15 shows an example of a request for admission inquiring into the genuineness of a document.

Responses to Requests for Admission

Requests for admission must be answered with great care because of the impact of an admission. If a request is impossible to respond to with a flat admission or denial, but is not otherwise objectionable, a qualified response is acceptable. A qualified response should not be used for the purpose of evading, however.

Another possible response is a motion for protective order, to be discussed. Be sure to keep in mind the deadline for a response—failure to file a timely response can, as noted, be deemed to be an admission.

Request for Production of Documents and Things

Under Rule 34 of the FRCP, a party can request the other side to produce for inspection documents or objects in its possession. The materials requested need not be specifically identified, nor need they even be known to exist; but the description in the request should be sufficiently specific so that the opposing party can reasonably determine whether a document is responsive. It would not, for example, be acceptable to ask the other side to produce "all relevant documents"; it *would*, however, be acceptable to request "all correspondence between Henry Wellington and John Ascot." The request for production allows for the evaluation and assessment of the physical evidence that is available for presentation at trial.

As with other forms of discovery, the request for production has a caption, title, introductory paragraphs, the requests themselves, the signature of the attorney making the request, and a certificate of service. In preparing requests, the drafter should take care that all relevant documents have been requested; this generally requires a review of the pleadings and facts of the case. In responding, you must take care that all requests not objected to are fully complied with; failure to produce a document requested is grounds for excluding that document, even if otherwise admissible, at trial.

As a practical matter, where documents are requested compliance is usually made by providing a set of copies of the requested documents. Tangible objects may not be able to be copied, requiring you to arrange a convenient time and location for them to be inspected.

An acceptable introductory paragraph for a request for production appears in Figure 11.16. An example of general requests for production of documents and things appears in Figure 11.17.

FIGURE 11.15
Request for Admission Regarding Genuineness of Document

Admit or deny that the document marked "Exhibit A" and attached hereto is a true and genuine copy of the Lease dated June 17, 2006.

FIGURE 11.16
Introductory
Paragraph for Request
for Production

Pursuant to Rule 34 of the Federal Rules of Civil Procedure, Plaintiff requests that Defendants make available for inspection and copying the documents described herein at a time and place to be arranged by counsel, but in no event later than thirty (30) days from the date of service of this request.

If a document is no longer in possession of or subject to the control of Defendant, state when such document was most recently in the possession of defendant or subject to the defendant's control and what disposition was made of it. If documents have been destroyed, please identify when they were destroyed, the person who destroyed the documents, the person who directed that they be destroyed, the reason(s) for such action, and any communications or documents that relate or refer to the destruction of the documents.

This request is continuing in character and requires defendant to provide any supplemental documents if, prior to trial, defendant should obtain any additional or supplemental documents that are responsive to this request.

Request for Medical Examination

request for medical examination
Form of discovery that requests a medical examination of an opposing party in a lawsuit.

Preparing a **request for medical examination** involves issues of litigation strategy almost exclusively, with little emphasis or importance on writing other than to make the request clear and to conform to the rules that establish the right. Because an examination is a substantial invasion of the opposing party's person, it will likely be granted only in cases where the physical or mental condition is an issue, as in a personal injury case.

THE DEPOSITION

deponent
The party or witness who is questioned in a deposition.

In a deposition, a party or witness is placed under oath and questioned by attorneys, and the content of the examination is recorded in a transcript prepared by a certified court reporter. The party or witness who is questioned is referred to as a **deponent.**

There are three types of deposition: the oral deposition; the deposition on written questions; and the video deposition. The nature of each varies somewhat.

oral deposition
A discovery tool in a question-and-answer format in which the attorney verbally questions a party or witness under oath.

The **oral deposition,** in which the witness responds to questions from an attorney, is by far the most common. Depending on the answers to the questions, the attorney generally frames follow-up questions that explore an area in detail.

In the **deposition on written questions,** questions are submitted in advance; only those questions are answered, with no follow-up questions allowed. Often, no attorney is even present; the court reporter swears the witness in and records the responses to the prepackaged questions. This type of deposition has very limited use.

deposition on written questions
A deposition based on written questions submitted in advance to a party; only those questions are answered, with no follow-up questions allowed.

Video depositions are simply videotaped versions of the oral deposition; the videotape serves as an additional method of preserving the testimony, in addition to the transcript. If a witness is going to be unavailable for trial because he is beyond the subpoena power of the court (more about subpoenas later) or is aged or ill, a video deposition is a good means of preserving the immediacy of real testimony for trial.

FIGURE 11.17
General Request
for Production of
Documents

1. All documents pertaining to or reflecting any damages for which you are seeking recovery in this suit.

2. All correspondence, notes, memoranda, recordings, or other documents evidencing or reflecting any communication, conversation, transaction, or dealing between Plaintiff and this Defendant (including Defendant's agents, employees, or representatives), or between the Plaintiff's family and Defendant (including Defendant's agents, employees, and representatives).

3. All documents and tangible things prepared by any person whose work product forms a basis, in whole or in part, of the opinions of the expert witness.

4. The expert's entire file pertaining to this case.

video deposition
Videotaped version of the oral deposition; the videotape serves as an additional method of preserving the testimony, in addition to the transcript.

PRACTICE TIP

Review the law for your jurisdiction on the requirements and parameters of discovery of computerized data. This area of the law is relatively new and continually developing.

There are few limitations on the areas of questioning at a deposition; objections can (and generally should) be stated by the attorneys present, but rulings on the objections are generally reserved until trial, and thus the witness answers despite the objection. A witness can be instructed not to answer by an attorney, but this is usually a dramatic step, evidence of an exceedingly bitter, contentious deposition. When a deposition grows so quarrelsome that excessive objections and instructions not to answer erode the ability of the parties to continue, the parties can file motions to the court to rule on the objections before the deposition proceeds. Courts generally frown on this, however, and costs can be imposed against the party adjudged to have caused the problem.

Depositions are useful means of learning about the demeanor of a party or witness when subjected to questioning. They are also useful as a means of immediate follow-up when answers suggest further lines of inquiry—the follow-up question can be posed on the spot. This distinguishes depositions from interrogatories, which give no opportunity for immediate follow-up. Although subsequent sets of interrogatories can be filed that follow up initial answers, they lack the immediacy of a follow-up question at a deposition. Indeed, interrogatories and requests for production are often most useful as a means of gathering information in preparation for a deposition.

Notice of Intention to Take Oral Deposition

A formal document must be drafted to notify all parties that a deposition is to be taken. This is called a Notice of Intention to Take Oral Deposition (or often simply Notice of Deposition). In addition to a caption, title, and introductory information, the notice identifies the deponent, the location of the deposition, often the rule under which the deposition is authorized, and the fact that it will be taken before a certified court reporter or official authorized to administer oaths. An example of the body of a deposition notice appears in Figure 11.18.

Applicability of a Subpoena

If a *party* is identified as the deponent, the party is required to appear at the time and place identified, unless a Motion for Protective Order is filed (more about such a motion later). This requirement can be enforced because parties are subject to the rules of the court. Plaintiffs have submitted to them voluntarily; defendants have been brought under the control of the court by effective service of process. The deponent need not necessarily be a party, however—she may be merely a witness. A witness has not submitted to nor been brought under the control of the court; a witness might simply refuse or neglect to appear for the deposition.

subpoena
A document that is served upon an individual under authority of the court, and orders the person to appear at a certain place and certain time for a deposition, or suffer the consequences; an order issued by the court clerk directing a person to appear in court.

The solution to this potential problem is the subpoena. A **subpoena** is a document similar to a summons, in that it is served upon an individual under authority of the court, and orders the person to appear at a certain place and certain time, or suffer the consequences. Subpoenas are often used to ensure the presence of a witness at a deposition; the subpoena and deposition notices are served simultaneously. Subpoenas can also be used to compel a witness to testify at a trial.

Production of Documents in Conjunction with a Deposition

duces tecum
A deposition notice requiring the deponent/witness to "bring with him" specified documents or things.

It is possible to combine a request for production of documents with a deposition notice. In this case, the deposition notice contains an additional sentence, referring to the request for production attached to the notice. The Latin term ***duces tecum*** signifies a deposition notice or subpoena requiring the deponent/witness to "bring with him" specified documents or things. Figure 11.19 shows an example of a Notice of Intention to Take Oral Deposition *Duces Tecum*.

FIGURE 11.18
The Body of a Notice of Oral Deposition

TO: Dr. Ned Radcliffe, by and through his attorney of record, Matthew Brockton, Suite 850, 3265 Montclaire Avenue, Waco, Texas 75683

PLEASE TAKE NOTICE that on October 12, 2006, at ten o'clock (10:00) a.m. at the law office of Emma M. Costello, 6301 Marley Avenue, Waco, Texas 75204, Plaintiff, GILDA MURRAY will take the deposition of DR. NED RADCLIFFE. The deposition will be taken on oral examination pursuant to Rule 200 of the Texas Rules of Civil Procedure before an officer authorized to administer oaths, and will continue from day to day until completed.

FIGURE 11.19
Notice of Intention to
Take Oral Deposition
Duces Tecum

TO: Dr. Ned Radcliffe, by and through his attorney of record, Matthew Brockton, Suite 850, 3265 Montclaire Avenue, Waco, Texas 75683

PLEASE TAKE NOTICE that on October 12, 2006, at ten o'clock (10:00) a.m. at the law office of Emma M. Costello, 6301 Marley Avenue, Waco, Texas 75204, Plaintiff, GILDA MURRAY will take the deposition of DR. NED RADCLIFFE. The deposition will be taken on oral examination pursuant to Rule 200 of the Texas Rules of Civil Procedure before an officer authorized to administer oaths, and will continue from day to day until completed.

Please take notice that the deponent identified above will be required to produce at the taking of his deposition all the materials described in Exhibit A attached hereto and incorporated herein. The definitions and instructions included in Exhibit A shall control the production of the materials requested in Exhibit A. (Additional language for a deposition with a *duces tecum* [production of documents request].)

Deposition Preparation

Because a deposition is generally an oral exercise, the need for writing skills to prepare formal documents is minimal. Nevertheless, it is important to apply your organizational skills—outlining, focusing on key factual points, identifying the secondary elements of legal arguments—in order to assist your attorney in her preparation to conduct the deposition, covering all necessary areas of inquiry. Often you may be asked to attend a deposition to take notes and determine the witness's effectiveness. You may be requested to draft an internal memorandum detailing your impressions of the deposition or prepare a summary of the witness's testimony for future use in the case. All the lessons you have perfected thus far will be useful in assisting your supervising attorney to prepare for the case.

For the deposition on written questions (which, as noted, is a format rarely employed), you will of course draft questions ahead of time. The key to drafting such written questions is to keep them short and precise, so as to avoid evasive answers.

Digesting a Deposition

After a deposition is completed, the court reporter who recorded the questions and testimony prepares the **transcript,** which is a written account of the entire proceeding. The transcript of a deposition can run to many hundreds of pages or more, and a complex case can require many depositions. It is often helpful for the attorneys handling the matter to have a **digest** of the deposition, which is a summary of the testimony indexed with references to the corresponding page numbers of the deposition. (This type of digest is not to be confused with the digest we discussed in Chapter 1, which contains research topics and headnotes from reported judicial opinions.) There is no standard method of digesting a deposition; if you are given such an assignment, you should strive to be accurate, using the writing techniques we have discussed to avoid ambiguity, and you should ask your supervising attorney the appropriate format and degree of detail desired. Digest summaries may be as detailed as a page-line summary of the information, chronological summary, or more general, such as a topical summary. The keys to any deposition summary are as follows:

transcript
A written account of the deposition proceeding.

digest
A summary of the testimony indexed with references to the corresponding page numbers of the deposition.

- Organization: Identify in the deposition where the information appears, either by page or line and page.
- Clarity: Make sure that the information is conveyed in a clear, precise manner.
- Legal issues: Some cases demand more detail than others. Investigate the type of deposition you will be summarizing.
- Attorney preference: Determine the style your attorney prefers. The style may also be dictated by the complexity of the case. Should information be paraphrased or quoted verbatim? Should you summarize in complete sentences or bullet phrases? Ask your attorney for guidance.
- Deadline date: Determine when the summary is due.

DISCOVERY MOTIONS

Motion for Protective Order
A motion filed by a party upon whom a discovery request has been made to protect the disclosure of information.

Motion to Compel Discovery
A motion filed by a party seeking to force compliance with a discovery request.

Motion for Sanctions
A motion filed by any party to counter alleged violations by another party in the case.

In previous sections we have touched upon some factors to consider in responding to discovery requests. Although these factors, coupled with the desire to protect your client, give you some flexibility in drafting responses to discovery requests, the good-faith requirement that governs discovery responses implies a duty to provide all reasonable information requested. Nevertheless, parties often try to evade in the discovery process by making indefensible requests, failing to respond to reasonable requests, or otherwise abusing the process. This may lead to the filing of motions designed to resolve disputed issues. The three principal motions seen in discovery practice are the **Motion for Protective Order,** filed by a party upon whom a discovery request has been made; the **Motion to Compel Discovery,** filed by a party seeking to force compliance with a discovery request; and the **Motion for Sanctions,** filed by any party to counter alleged violations by another. Each of these motions generally includes attachments consisting of the discovery requests objected to or sought to be enforced; check the rules for format and special requirements. Each is discussed in the subsections that follow.

The Motion for Protective Order

When the party upon whom a discovery request has been filed contends that the request oversteps the bounds of the rules, she can file a Motion for Protective Order. Such a motion argues that the information sought is irrelevant or privileged, or that the request is unduly burdensome or overly broad or ambiguous. It may argue that a deposition is inappropriate at the location suggested. Whatever the argument, the purpose is to obstruct the other side. Figure 11.20 shows an example of a Motion for Protective Order opposing certain interrogatories and a request for production of documents.

The Motion to Compel Discovery

The Motion to Compel Discovery is the reverse of the Motion for Protective Order—it seeks not to obstruct discovery, but to force it.

Simply because a party chooses not to disclose information, or has objected to its disclosure, does not mean it isn't discoverable. The party seeking the information must notify the court of the failure to respond, and the need to have the court rule on the dispute. This can be done through a Motion to Compel Discovery, which identifies the information sought, notes that it is relevant, unprivileged, and not otherwise subject to protection, and argues that it should be supplied. Such a motion can also be supported by a brief. A Motion to Compel Discovery is often filed in response to a Motion for Protective Order, or sometimes simply as a means of prodding a party who has allowed the deadline for discovery response to pass without having filed the response. An example of a typical Motion to Compel Discovery is found in Figure 11.21.

FIGURE 11.20
Motion for Protective Order

(Caption of the Case)

Defendant, Dr. Ned Radcliffe, in the above-entitled and numbered cause, files this his Motion for Protective Order, and in support of this Motion would show unto the Honorable Court as follows:

1. On or about September 17, 2006, Plaintiff issued upon this Defendant Plaintiff's First Set of Written Interrogatories and Request for Production of Documents. In responding to the discovery requests, this Defendant objected to Interrogatory Nos. 4, 11, 13, and 15 and Request for Production Nos. 1, 2, and 4, as well as making general objections. The objections are attached hereto and incorporated herein as Exhibit A.

WHEREFORE, Defendant hereby requests that upon final hearing and trial hereof, that the Court enter an Order sustaining his objections to the discovery requests of the Plaintiff, and for such other and further relief, in law or in equity, to which this Defendant may show himself to be justly entitled.

(Signature block)

FIGURE 11.21
Motion to Compel
Discovery

(Caption of the Case)

Defendant by her attorney and moves the Court as follows:

1. On October 14, 2006, Defendant, after commencement of the above-entitled action, served on the Plaintiff in this cause ten interrogatories in writing pursuant to Rule 33 of the Federal Rules of Civil Procedure, which interrogatories are attached hereto.

2. Plaintiff answered Interrogatories 1, 2, 3, 4, 5, and 10, but did not answer such interrogatories under oath as required by Rule 33 of the Federal Rules of Civil Procedure.

3. Plaintiff failed to answer Interrogatories 6, 7, 8, and 9.

Defendant moves that this Court enter an order directing and requiring Plaintiff to answer all of said interrogatories under oath.

Defendant further moves the Court for an order awarding Defendant the reasonable expenses, including attorneys' fees incurred in this motion.

(Signature block)

The Motion for Sanctions

A Motion for Sanctions is filed when there have been attempts to force cooperation, but based upon alleged deliberate inaction or gross indifference of one party, discovery has been stalled. Failure to appear at a duly noticed deposition, without making an objection or indicating the intention not to attend, would be an example of behavior that might justify a Motion for Sanctions, since time and resources were wasted (a court reporter had to be paid to attend) with no justification. Another example would be a failure to follow the order of the court on a Motion to Compel Discovery. The granting of a Motion for Sanctions often includes an award of attorney's fees and expenses incurred in its preparation.

Sometimes, if the circumstances justify, a party files a Motion for Sanctions at the same time as a Motion for Protective Order or a Motion to Compel Discovery. Sanctions are an extreme remedy, however, and Motions for Sanctions should be filed only after a cautious review of the facts.

You Be the Judge

Hypothetical 11-2

Judges will examine an attorney's motive for filing a motion, when a simple telephone call would have addressed the problem. In *United States v. Kouri-Perez*, 8 F. Supp. 2d 133 (D. Puerto Rico 1998), an attorney wanted to change the place of a deposition. Instead of simply calling the opposing counsel, the attorney filed a motion to modify the location of a foreign deposition. The court determined that the motion was filed in bad faith and politically motivated. The attorney attacked the prosecutor's ancestry; she apparently was the granddaughter of a Dominican Republic dictator. The prosecutor did not even know her grandfather and had grown up in the United States. The court found the attorney's behavior was willful and vexatious. Taking all the legal standards into account, the court observed that "[i]n imposing sanctions, we are mindful that we should not impose them 'to chill an attorney's enthusiasm, creativity, or zealous advocacy.' Contrary to what was argued at the hearing, however, the issue is not about 'style' but about content. Simply stated, the allegations in the motion went far beyond the bounds of zealous advocacy. This court has asserted, 'there is a point beyond which zeal becomes vexation, the 'novel' approach to a legal issue converts to frivolity . . . .'" *Id.* at 140 (citations omitted). Examine the case and draw your own conclusions. What are the facts of the case? Why were sanctions imposed on the attorney? What is the reasoning of the court in this case? Rules dictate behavior. Most jurisdictions have rules requiring communication before motions, costing time and money, are filed. Familiarize yourself with the federal and local rules in your jurisdiction regarding discovery disputes.

A METHOD OF CULMINATING THE CASE: THE MOTION FOR SUMMARY JUDGMENT

At some point either during discovery or after it is completed, an attorney may recognize that there are no factual issues in dispute and the case can be decided as a matter of law through a motion. That motion is a Motion for Summary Judgment. Either party may file a Motion for Summary Judgment. The standard in a Motion for Summary Judgement is that one party asserts (1) that there is "no genuine issue of material fact," and (2) that it is entitled to judgment in its favor "as a matter of law" (see Rule 56 of the FRCP). If granted by the court, the case ends. To explain these concepts fully, a brief discussion is in order.

There are two aspects to every legal controversy—the *facts* and the controlling *law*. When a lawsuit is filed, the parties involved are in essence saying to the court, "We will each present our version of the facts and our interpretation of the law; you decide who is right." The presentation of evidence in the form of documents, exhibits, and witness testimony is designed to enable the trier-of-fact (the jury or the judge; more about this later) to weigh the competing positions and determine whose version of the facts is accurate. Once the facts have been established by the trier-of-fact, the judge applies the controlling law and renders a decision.

Sometimes there is no dispute as to the facts, or at least one party *asserts* that there is no significant and genuine controversy over important facts. If the court finds this assertion to be true, no trial is necessary. The only matter left for the court is to apply the controlling law to these facts. When one party files a Motion for Summary Judgment, the other party can contest it by asserting (1) that there *is* a genuine factual dispute that needs to be decided by the court, or (2) that, although there is no factual dispute, the court should nevertheless find against the moving party based on the controlling law. In a Summary Judgment motion, no witnesses appear. A determination is made based upon the pleadings, discovery, affidavits submitted, and other documentary "paper" information submitted by the parties. Sometimes both parties file Motions for Summary Judgment simultaneously, agreeing to stipulate as to the facts. Then the only things necessary to resolve the lawsuit are for the parties to file trial memoranda stating their competing legal arguments, and for the court to decide the contested legal issues.

Motions for Summary Judgment are not readily granted by courts. Where the nonfiling party contends that there *are* contested issues and can show even a slight amount of evidence (physical evidence or deposition testimony) that supports its version of the facts, a court will not grant the motion but will, rather, allow the factual issues to be decided after the full presentation of evidence at trial.

The Motion for Summary Judgment should include a brief statement of the basis for the motion, and you should attach all documentary evidence and deposition passages that support your position. A brief in support of the motion, arguing that there is no contested factual issue and developing the filing party's legal position, is generally filed as well (and sometimes the attachments are appended to this brief rather than to the motion). This brief is styled as a memorandum to the trial court, which is discussed in the next chapter. Unlike the interoffice memorandum, a brief in support of a Motion for Summary Judgment is persuasive.

FIGURE 11.22

Summary Judgment: Body of Motion and Order

Body of Motion for Summary Judgment

1. Plaintiff's Complaint has been filed and served on Defendant VICTRONIC, INC. Defendant has appeared and answered herein. Plaintiff's action is based upon a lease agreement.
2. The pleadings on file herein, together with all the pretrial discovery documents on file herein, the official records of the Court, and the Affidavits of Victor Brennan and Amelia Johnson, attached hereto, all show that there is no genuine issue to any material fact and that the Defendant, as moving party herein, is entitled to judgment in its favor as a matter of law.
3. Defendant asks the Court that, on hearing of this Motion, judgment be entered against Plaintiff.
4. If the Court grants this Motion for Summary Judgment, Defendant requests that immediately after hearing of the Motion, the Court shall award Defendant its attorney fees and costs of suit.

LUANN   *BY GREG EVANS*

Source: LUANN © GEC Inc./Dist. by United Feature Syndicate, Inc.

Rule 56 of the FRCP, quoted previously, governs the procedure for Motions for Summary Judgment filed in federal court. You should check your local jurisdiction for its requirements. The body of a Motion for Summary Judgment is shown in Figure 11.22.

Ethics Alert

Throughout the chapters of this book, the different tasks that paralegals perform were discussed. What are the standards for billing paralegal services, and what are the ethical obligations of paralegals regarding those services performed? By definition, attorney's fees imply fees for services performed by a licensed attorney. In 1989, the U.S. Supreme Court in *Missouri v. Jenkins,* 491 U.S. 274 (1989), recognized that included in that definition are fees for paralegal services. The basis for the fees, however, must not be secretarial in nature, such as copying. But, attorneys can charge and recover as part of their fees the services performed by a paralegal. Justice Brennan stated that "our starting point is the self-evident proposition that the 'reasonable attorney's fee' provided for . . . should compensate the work of paralegals, as well as that of attorneys." *Id.* at 285. Many state courts have reviewed the issue and there is a consistent theme: If a paralegal is included under the definition of attorney's fees, the work must be substantive and not clerical. (Recall our case in Chapter 10 where over $1 million was awarded for attorney's fees. The court in that case exempted those paralegal fees that were not substantive in nature.) Five years later, the Supreme Court of Oklahoma not only included paralegal fees in the definition of attorney's fees, but also defined the tasks paralegals could perform. In *Taylor v. Chubb Group of Insurance Companies,* 874 P.2d 806 (Okla. 1994), the court listed the tasks legal assistants and paralegals can perform as "interview clients, draft pleadings and other documents, carry out legal research, both conventional and computer aided, research public documents, prepare discovery requests and responses, schedule depositions and prepare notices and subpoenas, summarize depositions and other discovery responses, coordinate and manage document production, locate and interview witnesses, organize pleadings, trial exhibits and other documents, prepare trial notebooks, prepare for attendance of witnesses at trial, and assist lawyers at trial." *Id.* at 809. But paralegals cannot directly share in the fees earned by an attorney; this is known as fee splitting. The rationale behind this rule is that compensation of a paralegal cannot be directly linked to the work he produces. Moreover, fee splitting with a paralegal, a nonlawyer, may also be in violation of the rules against sharing fees with a nonlawyer. This concept also applies to nonlawyer referrals. Review your jurisdiction's rules of ethics for the type of compensation paralegals are allowed to receive for the work they provide.

E-FACTOR

CYBERSPACE DISCOVERY AND COMPUTERS

Discovery has expanded considerably with computer technology; and with the expansion come burdens as well. It is now the **black letter law** that computerized data is discoverable, subject to relevancy. The Federal Rules on discovery, specifically Rule 34, clearly include electronic data, and the burden of producing the information, in whatever form, remains with the responding party. This responsibility extends to computerized data even if it is available in hard copy. But those are the simple issues. The complexity and challenges facing today's litigants regarding electronic data discovery are sometimes mind-boggling. Imagine, not just paper files of records, but megabytes of information that hold hundreds of thousands of pages. Discoverable electronic data includes voice mail, e-mail, data files, program files, back-up files, and any other electronic generated data that a litigant argues is relevant. It seems as vast and endless as cyberspace.

Many questions arise as to the preservation of both paper and electronic data. Must all data be preserved? Are there limitations? If litigation is anticipated, courts may place a duty to preserve that data. How far that goes depends on the litigants' cooperation. Courts attempt the least invasive method, hoping that the threat of sanctions is a deterrent to willful destruction of data. Cases have shown that willful disregard for courts can be costly.

A mechanism that can be used to facilitate discovery is FRCP Rule 26(f), which requires parties to discuss discovery issues among themselves and make good-faith efforts to work out discovery issues, especially those involving electronic data. For paralegals in the litigation arena, this discovery issue percolates at the top of "contentious" and "burdensome." Follow the trends in your jurisdiction for handling discovery requests for electronic data. Read the case law in your jurisdiction and others for the parameters set by courts. Those cases could be a helpful guide. And finally, communicate with the client, who may be subject to an electronic discovery request. The process is invasive, and discussing the process and what to expect may make everyone's experience palatable.

black letter law
The strict meaning of the law as it is written, without concern or interpretation of the reasoning behind its creation.

PRACTICAL CONSIDERATIONS

The role of paralegals in discovery is often an important one. Complex cases may involve hundreds or thousands of documents, which must be tracked, reviewed, evaluated, disclosed, requested, and catalogued. Numerous depositions may be needed; numerous areas inquired into with interrogatories; multiple medical examinations may be necessary, and lengthy medical records may require interpretation. Much time-consuming work is involved—work that can be tedious, but that requires a sharp and trained mind nevertheless. By refining your skills at organizing the discovery process, you can heighten your value as an essential member of your firm's litigation team.

The following is a checklist of items to keep in mind when formulating discovery requests and responses:

— Review the rules of procedure to determine the applicable bounds of discovery.

— Make a point of identifying and remaining alert to all applicable deadlines. Review your client's file and make notes about the areas of the case in which discovery is desirable or necessary.

— Prepare discovery requests that are detailed and specific.

— Draft requests that will survive the opposition's efforts to object.

— Organize materials so that confusion is minimized and access maximized.

— Coordinate with your supervising attorney at every step.

— Analyze your client's position and determine whether objections to discovery requests are in order.

— Evaluate discovery responses to determine whether they are in compliance with the requirements of the rules and fully responsive to the corresponding requests. Evaluate both responses that you receive from the other side and responses that you prepare.

— If the discovery process breaks down, prepare all necessary motions.

Summary

Discovery is the pretrial investigatory process authorized and governed by the rules of civil procedure. To be discoverable, information requested must be reasonably calculated to lead to the discovery of admissible evidence. Discovery requests may be directed to parties but not to nonparties, except that it is acceptable to take the deposition of a nonparty.

An interrogatory is a written question submitted by one party to another to be answered under oath. Interrogatories should be specific and precise. Definitions and instructions can be included to reduce ambiguity. Titles should be sufficiently specific as to distinguish one set of interrogatories from another, particularly in cases with multiple parties on either side. Basic background information can be sought with interrogatories, as well as specific information about the case at hand, information about experts consulted, and information about the content of the pleadings. The truth of the responses must be attested to by the signature of the party on whose behalf the responses are filed. Objections to interrogatories can be justified on several grounds, including a contention that the information sought is privileged or that the request is overbroad. There is a continuing duty to respond to interrogatories, which means that a supplemental response must be filed if new information is uncovered.

The request for admissions allows the filing party to conclusively establish contested issues prior to trial. This serves to limit the complexity and expense of the ensuing trial. A common use of requests for admission is to authenticate documents. Requests should be drafted to minimize the potential for a qualified response; responses should be made with great care due to the impact of an admission.

A request for production of documents and things enables one party to inspect the physical and documentary evidence of the other party. The responding party must be reasonably able to determine whether a given document or thing is responsive.

The request for medical examination should be drafted clearly and in conformity with the rules. The issues associated with such a request are largely issues of litigation strategy, not legal writing.

In a deposition, the deponent (who can be a party or a witness) provides testimony that is transcribed by a court reporter. The deposition can be taken in response to oral or written questions, and can also be videotaped. The opportunity for follow-up questions makes the oral deposition a useful form of discovery. A notice of intention to take deposition must be filed by the party seeking to take the deposition; if the intended deponent is a witness rather than a party, a subpoena can be served to ensure the witness's attendance. A document request can be combined with a deposition notice. Lengthy deposition transcripts can be summarized in a deposition digest.

A Motion for Protective Order can be filed by a party in opposition to a discovery request that it believes oversteps the acceptable bounds of the discovery rules. The Motion to Compel Discovery is filed by a party seeking to force compliance with a discovery request. A Motion for Sanctions can be filed by a party who believes that the opposing party's discovery conduct is particularly uncooperative or unlawful.

Complex cases often involve an extended and complex discovery process. Paralegals can heighten their value by using organizational skills to assist in the workings of that process.

Key Terms

discovery
interrogatory
instructions and definitions
verification
supplemental response
request for admissions
request for production of documents
   and things
request for medical examination
deponent
oral deposition

deposition on written questions
video depositions
subpoena
duces tecum
transcript
digest
Motion for Protective Order
Motion to Compel Discovery
Motion for Sanctions
black letter law

Review Questions

1. Why is the discovery process needed?

2. What are some of the characteristics of a properly drafted interrogatory?

3. Why are instructions and definitions important to include with discovery requests?

4. What are appropriate areas of inquiry about the opposition's consultation with experts?

5. What is meant by the continuing duty to respond?

6. How is a request for admissions useful?

7. How can requests for production be made sufficiently specific to avoid objection?

8. Who is a deponent?

9. What is a Motion for Summary Judgment?

10. What is the difference between a Motion for Protective Order and a Motion to Compel Discovery?

Exercises

1. Based on the facts of Figure 10–13 in Chapter 10, draft seven interrogatories, five requests for admission, and five requests for production of documents.

2. Draft a Motion for Protective Order, based on the fact that the information sought in the request for production of documents is overly broad and unduly burdensome.

3. Check your state rules of procedure and compare and contrast your rules for interrogatories, admissions, and production of documents. Determine the differences or similarities to the Federal Rules in your jurisdiction's discovery requirements.

4. Andrew Goddard is James Lewiston's landlord. James signed a one-year lease from January 14, 2006 to January 13, 2007 for an apartment located at 674 Brandy Lane, Dallas, Texas. He stopped paying rent nine months into the lease and the landlord sued for the back rent. Prepare the Motion for Summary Judgment in the case.

5. Peter Hall was a patient at County Hospital, Any Town, Florida on October 7, 2006. He was scheduled for surgery to have his gallbladder removed. During the surgery he went into cardiac arrest and died in the operating room. The medical records indicate that Mr. Hall was healthy and he should not have arrested on the operating table. Through the grapevine, Mrs. Hall, Peter's widow, found out that the new anesthesiologist did not properly operate the anesthesia machine during the surgery, possibly causing the cardiac arrest. Prepare the discovery in the case to County Hospital.

6. Amanda Bennington signed a confidentiality agreement when she began working at Pharma, Inc. The agreement contained a noncompetition provision that stated that Amanda could not work as a salesperson for a pharmaceutical company for one year in the states of California, Washington, Oregon, Arizona, and New Mexico. Amanda lives in California and cannot move to any other state. Her family lives there. She believes the noncompete agreement is unconscionable and against public policy. Amanda left Pharma, Inc., and became employed with World Drug Company. Pharma sued Amanda for breach of the confidentiality agreement. Draft the interrogatories and production of documents for Pharma, Inc.

7. Denise Bailey went to the hair stylist to have her hair colored. Color Cuts, Inc., employed William Tonbridge as a stylist. He has worked for Color Cuts for approximately 6 months. When applying the color, Denise's scalp began to tingle. She told William and he said that it was normal. While she was waiting for the color to set, her scalp began to burn. William quickly washed the color out, but it was too late. Denise's scalp was badly burned. She went to the emergency room when they determined she had second degree burns on her scalp. Most of her hair fell out. She had to wear scarves until her scalp was less sensitive. Denise sued Color Cuts and William. Draft the interrogatories and request for admissions in the case.

8. The defendant's counsel, David Fredericks, has made a request for production of documents in *Software Corporation v. Data Information Systems Inc.* He has requested all electronic documents, including but not limited to, invoices, accounting records, e-mails, letters, and memoranda from 1990 to present between Software Corporation and Data Information Systems. This request is overly broad and burdensome.

a. Prepare the Motion for Protective Order for your client Software Corporation.
b. Data Information Systems has filed a Motion for Sanctions against Software Corporation for filing the Motion for Protective Order. Prepare the response to the Motion for Sanctions.

Portfolio Assignment

Mrs. Marsh wants to proceed with discovery in her case against A1 Delivery Service, Inc., and Herbert Killington. Using the facts from the Portfolio Assignment in Chapter 10, prepare the following discovery:

a. Draft interrogatories to A1 Delivery Service and Herbert Killington.
b. Draft request for admissions for A1 and Herbert Killington.
c. The request for production of documents for A1.
d. The Notice of Depositions for A1 and Herbert Killington.

Mrs. Marsh wants a Motion for Summary Judgment filed against the parties. Prepare the motion with supporting affidavits.

Remember to use models and form books to prepare your discovery. Also, research the status of the law on the liability of an employer for the negligence of an employee. Does the employer have any legal defenses to the lawsuit?

Vocabulary Builder

Discovery

```
F  J  C  Z  M  D  I  S  C  O  V  E  R  Y  W
T  Y  W  G  D  U  U  H  V  U  Z  L  L  Z  S
P  R  Y  U  S  E  C  Z  R  X  Z  C  L  M  D
I  Q  A  R  N  B  F  E  B  L  P  V  X  R  E
R  E  D  R  O  E  V  I  T  C  E  T  O  R  P
C  A  M  P  I  T  W  N  N  S  P  U  S  R  O
S  B  I  V  T  S  A  G  Z  I  E  L  X  A  N
N  T  S  C  C  I  A  G  C  X  T  C  S  I  E
A  R  S  P  U  M  U  N  O  F  I  I  U  J  N
R  C  I  R  R  B  D  G  C  R  D  J  O  D  T
T  O  O  F  T  P  A  W  T  T  R  B  U  N  K
A  X  N  I  S  P  A  L  Q  H  I  E  R  S  S
I  Y  S  A  N  E  O  P  B  U  S  O  T  T  P
P  V  E  R  I  F  I  C  A  T  I  O  N  N  O
N  O  I  T  I  S  O  P  E  D  P  C  F  S  I
```

ADMISSIONS	DEFINITIONS	DEPONENT
DEPOSITION	DISCOVERY	DUCES TECUM
INSTRUCTIONS	INTERROGATORY	PROTECTIVE ORDER
SANCTIONS	SUBPOENA	TRANSCRIPT
VERIFICATION		

Part Four

Persuasive Writing

CHAPTER 12 The Memorandum of Law to the Trial Court
CHAPTER 13 The Appellate Brief

Chapter 12

The Memorandum of Law to the Trial Court

After you have completed this chapter, you will be able to:

- Identify the two audiences for a trial memorandum.

- Explain how to prepare a trial memorandum so as to assist the trial judge.

- Draft your trial memorandum so as to minimize the impact of the attack of opposing counsel.

- Describe the characteristics of a trial memorandum in regard to a motion.

- Identify the reasons why a judge might request a trial memorandum.

- Explain the potential importance of an unsolicited trial memorandum that anticipates issues.

- Understand the importance of the caption and the title of a trial memorandum.

- Explain the perspective from which the "issues presented" section is drafted.

- List four objectives of a statement of facts.

- Describe the difference between the discussion section of an internal memorandum and the argument section of a trial memorandum.

The memorandum of law to the trial court is an important document in the litigation process, commonly seen and often instrumental in defining the scope and nature of the trial and its outcome. In your role as a paralegal, you will likely be called upon to participate in the preparation of such memoranda. This chapter focuses on the components and the skills needed to draft the memorandum of law to the trial court.

Case Fact Pattern Hypothetical 12-1

Your firm's client, Dr. Williams, has been served with a subpoena *duces tecum,* commanding her to testify at a deposition and to produce all medical records of an identified patient. Neither Dr. Williams nor her patient wishes to disclose these records.

The doctor has consulted with your supervising attorney, and a decision has been made to file a motion for protective order asserting the existence of a patient/physician privilege. Since the law on this point in your state is not entirely clear, a supporting memorandum that argues in favor of the motion must be prepared. You have been assigned the task of drafting this memorandum.

The Wizard of Id   Brant Parker and Johnny Hart

Source: By permission of John L. Hart FLP, and Creators Syndicate, Inc.

THE NATURE AND PURPOSE OF THE MEMORANDUM OF LAW TO THE TRIAL COURT

memorandum of law to the trial court
An adversarial document filed with the trial court and written to persuade the trial court of a party's position on a disputed point of law.

The **memorandum of law to the trial court** (which we will refer to as a *trial memorandum*) is an adversarial document filed with the trial court and written to persuade the trial court that one party's position on a disputed point of law is superior to the opposing party's position. It may be written in support of or in opposition to a motion; it may be written at the request of a judge to assist her in rendering a decision; or it may be an unsolicited memorandum filed at trial in order to persuade the judge on anticipated legal questions. Whatever the reason, the content should be one-sided, or *partisan*.

We have already used two names, trial memorandum and memorandum of law to the trial court, for this. There are still other names that refer to the same type of document: memorandum of points and authorities, memorandum in opposition to motion, brief in support of motion, trial brief in opposition to motion, and others. These titles all refer to the same basic document—an adversarial document setting forth legal arguments to the trial court. The title depends upon the jurisdiction, and even on individual attorneys and judges. Different courts and individuals have different styles. It is important to remember that, regardless of the name applied, the factors to take into account are essentially the same.

One potential area of confusion should, however, be cleared up at the outset. In some areas, the term *trial brief* refers to the materials that an attorney prepares, not for filing with the court, but rather to assist him with the conduct of the trial—such things as witness lists, summaries of pleadings, an outline of his opening statement, copies of important cases, possible jury instructions, and so on. Such preparatory materials will be called a *trial notebook*, to distinguish it from a trial brief. Thus, we consider a trial brief to be the same as a trial memorandum.

Although some trial courts have specific requirements for the format of a trial memorandum, in general these requirements are less formal than those for an appellate brief (which we discuss in Chapter 13). You should learn your jurisdiction's requirements for a trial memorandum.

It is important to take into consideration the audience for the trial memorandum. Although your client may read your trial memorandum, and should certainly be consulted about the factual background, she is *not* part of the audience for whom the trial memorandum is written. The audience is composed of two segments—the judge, whom you must convince, and the opposing counsel, whom you must refute and whose attack your arguments must survive. Let's take a moment and consider these two audiences.

First, the judge. Unlike appellate judges, who sit in judgment only on appeals, trial judges handle varied responsibilities, from overseeing courtroom personnel, to deciding motions, to conducting trials. Often their schedules are busy, and time is short. Whereas an appellate judge may have the time and the responsibility to read and research enough to render appropriate decisions (which have broad impact), a trial judge generally only needs to know how the higher courts have dealt with the issues presented, or analogous situations. This is not to say that trial judges are not thoughtful, or do not take their responsibilities seriously; they are and they do. It is simply a warning that a trial memorandum needs to get to the point. Tell the judge what you want, why you want it, and why you are legally entitled to it, as concisely as you can. If you must make a complicated argument, by all means make it—but if it can be done more simply, it is a mistake to write a lengthy explanation. Keep your memoranda short, concise, and direct.

Opposing counsel are the second audience. Unlike judges, who will give your arguments a fair reading, opposing counsel are the enemy. They scour your arguments looking for logical holes and unjustified analytical leaps, in an effort to refute your arguments and prove that your client's position is not supported by law. You must, therefore, write *accurately*. Do not overstate your arguments, and never misstate or misrepresent the law. If you are honest in your interpretations (partisan, yes, but nevertheless honest), and if you Shepardize with care, your arguments should survive the attack of opposing counsel. Indeed, by recognizing the threat posed by opposing counsel, you may well be saved from making the type of borderline argument that, if read and rejected by a judge, might tend to poison your other, more logical arguments in the eyes of the court.

TYPES OF TRIAL MEMORANDA

memorandum in regard to a motion
A persuasive memorandum supporting the points and authorities in a motion.

memorandum at the request of a judge
A persuasive memorandum of legal points requested by the trial court judge.

unsolicited memorandum anticipating legal issues
A memorandum of law prepared by one of the parties to the case in support of an anticipated legal issue.

All legal memoranda argue a point of law in an adversarial manner. Each of the three broad categories we identified earlier, however—a **memorandum in regard to a motion,** a **memorandum at the request of a judge,** and an **unsolicited memorandum anticipating legal issues**—presents its own unique considerations for the drafter. Let's take a look at each.

Memorandum in Regard to a Motion

Many issues arise in the course of a lawsuit—issues about the content of the pleadings, the propriety of discovery requests, the sufficiency of responses, the right of a party to file amendments, and on and on. Such issues must be resolved before the case is ready for trial. Sometimes they are resolved by mutual agreement of the parties, but often they are not. When agreement is not possible, a motion is generally made to the court in which one party requests that the court resolve the dispute in its favor, so that the case can move to trial. The motion itself generally identifies the nature of the dispute and the order or relief that the filing party seeks, but generally does *not* contain any legal analysis or arguments. These analyses and arguments are reserved for the trial memoranda filed in regard to the motion.

The trial memorandum of the party that filed the motion is drafted, of course, in support of it, whereas the opposing party files a trial memorandum in opposition. For example, in conjunction with the motion for protective order filed on behalf of Dr. Williams from our Case Fact Pattern problem, a supporting trial memorandum would discuss the issues of physician/patient privilege that are posed by the motion and argue that they justify withholding the information requested; a trial memorandum in opposition, arguing for disclosure, would be filed by the party that requested the deposition. The issues discussed in the two memoranda are limited to the issues raised by the motion.

During the course of a lawsuit, there may be several motions pending and, hence, several trial memoranda in regard to these motions. Each should have a title that identifies the party filing it and the motion to which it relates. We discuss format further in the following subsections. Perhaps one of the most common motions where a memorandum of law in support of the Motion is prepared is the Motion for Summary Judgment. (See Figure 11.22 in Chapter 11.) A typical Brief in Support of a Motion for Summary Judgment is exhibited at the end of this chapter.

Memorandum at the Request of a Judge

Contested issues continually arise during the course of a lawsuit, both during the pretrial stage and during the trial itself. During oral argument on a motion, for example, the judge may raise a point that the parties had not anticipated or addressed in their trial memoranda. Or an objection to the introduction of a piece of evidence at trial may present a novel legal problem that neither the judge nor the parties have ever considered. Under such circumstances the judge, rather than ruling immediately on the issue at hand, may request that the parties submit trial memoranda setting forth their positions on the disputed issue before he makes his decision.

The response of the attorneys is the memorandum at the request of the judge. This memorandum will be adversarial, like a memorandum in regard to a motion, and will be limited to the issue that the judge raised. It is designed to provide the judge with guidance on the issue presented, in the form of legal support for the position favoring your client. Your goal is to predispose the judge to your client's position, and downplay the opponent's position. The memorandum should be direct and concise, particularly at trial, where time is short.

The judge may even request an additional memorandum on a given point *after* the trial is completed, but *before* her decision is rendered. Again, you will be emphasizing the superiority of your client's position on the issue raised.

Unsolicited Memorandum Anticipating Legal Issues

By the conclusion of a trial, the legal issues that control the trial's outcome are clear. It is often useful to prepare a trial memorandum that identifies these issues, then argue in favor of a resolution that benefits your client. By clarifying the issues and identifying your strongest arguments at the conclusion of trial and for the benefit of the judge, you can establish a foundation on which the judge can render a decision in which your client prevails.

An unsolicited trial memorandum should be straightforward, identifying the issues at the outset and presenting arguments that are clear and direct. You should highlight the issues that are most important to you, and include every issue that you believe has bearing on the result. In other words, if you are going to file an unsolicited memorandum, you should be thorough; prepare it correctly. If, for strategic reasons, you want to emphasize only a particular aspect of the contested issues, then make that absolutely clear. Otherwise, you may leave the impression that you are conceding on the points left unaddressed. An example of a situation where an unsolicited memorandum may occur is when the attorney wants to include paralegal fees as part of an attorney's fees in a case. To ensure proper consideration of the issue, the attorney may file a brief in support of this request. (Recall your portfolio assignment in Chapter 9. The interoffice memorandum could easily be converted into a Memorandum of Law to the Trial Court in Support of Inclusion of Paralegal Fees as Part of an Award for Attorney's Fees.)

GETTING READY TO WRITE: THE PREWRITING CONSIDERATIONS

Don't forget what you have learned in previous chapters. Incorporate all your prewriting skills to begin composing a concise, persuasive trial memorandum. Remember to

- get organized;
- outline;
- research the law;
- validate the law through Shepard's or KeyCite;
- determine your audience;
- choose appropriate words for a persuasive document;
- check all court rules: state and local or federal and local;
- review requirements for specific judges;
- reference attachments or evidence in brief as required;
- check your time constraints; and
- ask your supervising attorney any questions needed for clarification.

Regardless of the assignment, you must always perform the basic preparatory work. If you skip a step, you may risk having a brief rejected, information stricken, or worse yet, having the opposing counsel identify improperly cited authority, embarrassing both yourself and your supervising attorney. So, don't get complacent—always stick to your game plan. Prepare, prepare, prepare.

THE COMPONENTS OF A MEMORANDUM OF LAW TO THE TRIAL COURT

The format of trial memoranda varies from jurisdiction to jurisdiction, and from judge to judge. The following comments are offered as a general frame of reference; you should check the rules applicable in your jurisdiction for more specific guidance. Note that some courts lean toward a more formal presentation of memorandum of law or brief than others. Many courts have page

You Be the Judge

Hypothetical 12-2

Often the court and not the rules of procedure set limitations on briefs and memoranda of law. The judge in *Insulated Panel Company v. The Industrial Commission*, 318 Ill.App.3d 100, 743 N.E.2d 1038 (Ill. 2001), set page limitations on trial briefs. On appeal, one of the issues was whether the judge abused his discretion by limiting the briefs to 10 pages and "considering only the first 10 pages of respondent's" 50-page brief. *Id.* at 1040. The court reviewed the arguments of counsel and held that the "court has the inherent power to control its own docket, and the ruling limiting briefs to 10 pages was not an abuse of discretion." *Id.* at 1040. The case represents the importance of complying with court rules and court orders. They are indistinguishable. Read the case. Identify the facts and issues on appeal. What was the court's reasoning in the case? What is the rule of law for the case?

limitations similar to those identified in the appellate rules of procedure. Pay attention to the trial court's requirements. Some judges refuse to accept the brief or simply stop reading. An example of trial court brief requirements is identified in Figure 12.1, which is an excerpt for Local Civil Rule 7.1 Affidavits and Briefs in the United States District Court for the Northern District of Illinois.

The Caption or Heading

As with pleadings and discovery requests, trial memoranda must have captions identifying the court, parties, and docket number. The title of the pleading may be included as well. Figure 12.2 shows two alternative captions.

Title

If the title of the pleading is not included in the caption, it must appear below it. As mentioned earlier, the title should be specific enough to identify the party filing it and, if in regard to a motion, the title of the motion. If not in regard to a motion, it should identify the context—for example, "Plaintiff's Memorandum Regarding Admissibility of Plaintiff's Psychotherapy Records" or "Plaintiff's Trial Brief" (if an unsolicited summary of the issues after trial).

Introduction to the Court

A formal introductory section is still required in some jurisdictions, although others, such as California, have done away with the requirement. The introduction seen in Figure 12.3 illustrates the formal tone associated with a document filed with a court. For example, the opening phrase, "To the Honorable Judge…," is a means of showing respect to the court. The trend today, however, is toward the elimination of such introductions.

issues or questions presented
A section that identifies the legal issues presented in the memorandum of law to the trial court.

Issues or Questions Presented

Although similar to the analogous section of an internal memorandum, the **issues or questions presented** section of a trial memorandum should be slanted toward your client's position. The issues should be stated accurately, but the outcome you seek should be implied in the questions.

FIGURE 12.1   **Excerpt for Local Civil Rule 7.1 Affidavits and Briefs in the United States District Court for the Northern District of Illinois**

Neither a brief in support of or in opposition to any motion nor objections to a report and recommendation or order of a magistrate judge or special master shall exceed 15 pages without prior approval of the court. Briefs that exceed the 15-page limit must have a table of contents with the pages noted and a table of cases. Any brief or objection that does not comply with this rule shall be subject to being stricken by the court.

FIGURE 12.2
Examples of Caption Setups

PRACTICE TIP

Do not overlook the rules of procedure of your jurisdiction as well as the local rules. Sometimes the rules for motions and briefs are tailored to a particular judge's court requirements. For example, in the United States District Court for the Western District of Wisconsin, two district court judges have completely different requirements for filing a Motion for Summary Judgment. The requirements are so specific that the judge indicates that a fact must be identified in a numbered paragraph followed by the supporting evidentiary reference, such as an interrogatory response, request for admission, page of deposition testimony, or an affidavit. Pay close attention to all the rules of court, especially the local rules. Check the websites of the courts for updates and changes to the rules. Failure to follow the rules of a court or local rule may result in the pleading, motion, or brief being stricken from filing or the record.

(a)   IN THE DISTRICT COURT OF DALLAS COUNTY, TEXAS

101st JUDICIAL DISTRICT

STEPHEN GILES, Plaintiff	§ § §	
	§	
vs.	§	No. 12344
	§	
GEORGE HARRIS, Defendant	§ § §	

OR

(b)   IN THE UNITED STATES DISTRICT COURT FOR

THE NORTHERN DISTRICT OF TEXAS

STEPHEN GILES, Plaintiff	§ § §	
	§	
vs.	§	CIVIL ACTION NO. 2006-12387
	§	
GEORGE HARRIS, Defendant	§ §	

Plaintiff's Memorandum in Support of Motion for Summary Judgment

Several styles for this section are commonly seen. The issue can be stated commencing with the word "Whether," followed by a statement of your client's position. The issue can also be drafted as a positive statement, or as an ordinary question. Figure 12.4 shows three numbered alternative formats for stating the issue presented; the (A) section of each alternative is drafted from a plaintiff's perspective, and the (B) section from the defendant's perspective. The best method of drafting the issue may be dictated by the court or your supervising attorney's pref-

FIGURE 12.3   Introduction to the Court

(1)
TO THE HONORABLE JUDGE OF SAID COURT:

COMES NOW, STEPHEN GILES, Plaintiff, and files this Memorandum of Law to the Trial Court in Support of Plaintiff's Motion for Summary Judgment and would show unto the Court as follows:

—or—

(2)
Plaintiff STEPHEN GILES submits this Memorandum of Law in Support of this Motion for Summary Judgment in this matter:

FIGURE 12.4

Forms of the Issues Presented Section

After the introduction of a party, you may want to use a shorthand reference. Long names often lend themselves toward using this technique. Refer to the full name first, such as the United States Government, and then in a parenthetical state your shorthand reference: (hereinafter referred to as "the Government"). You can use this technique for all parties or long names that may be repeated throughout a document, such as Community Memorial Hospital (hereinafter referred to as "Hospital"). Use this technique in pleadings and discovery documents as well.

statement of facts
A section that sets forth the pertinent facts that are the subject of the memorandum of law.

Alternative 1

(A)

Issue Presented. Whether there exists a genuine issue of material fact when a blank power of attorney is used by an agent who was not authorized to act on behalf of Plaintiff, the principal.

(B)

Issue Presented. Whether an issue of fact exists if Plaintiff accepts tax benefits ratifying the actions of an agent where a blank power of attorney was used.

Alternative 2

(A)

Issue Presented. No issues of fact exist in a transaction where an unauthorized agent used a blank power of attorney to act on behalf of the Plaintiff, the principal.

(B)

Issue Presented. No issue of fact exists in a transaction where an agent using a blank power of attorney attempts to create a valid transaction through ratification by the principal.

Alternative 3

(A)

Issue Presented. Are there issues of material fact in a transaction where an agent using a blank power of attorney creates an agency relationship to validly act on behalf of the Plaintiff, the principal?

(B)

Issue Presented. Are there issues of material fact when the principal ratifies the unauthorized acts of his agent?

---

erence. This situation is one where not only checking court rules is appropriate but reviewing models from other cases as well.

Statement of Facts

The trial memorandum, like the internal memorandum, contains a **statement of facts** that relates the factual context of the issue posed. The critical difference between the facts as stated in an internal memorandum and those stated in a trial memorandum, however, is in the point of view of the drafter. In the internal memorandum (which is drafted to be objective), the facts are set out in straightforward fashion. In a trial memorandum, the facts should be set out accurately, but drafted so as to favor your client's position.

Facts should be presented chronologically. You seek to develop sympathy for your client's position, using descriptive words and emotional facts to predispose the court toward accepting your client's position. You have four objectives in drafting a statement of facts:

1. Introduce your client's case to the court.

2. Provide an accurate presentation of the events.

3. Minimize those facts which favor your opponent.

4. Paint a memorable picture of your client's position.

Although you are writing from your client's perspective, do not misstate, misrepresent, or ignore key facts that are detrimental to your case. A misrepresentation of damaging facts will be pointed out to the court by the opposition; ignoring them allows the other side an unchallenged opportunity to emphasize their importance. Rather, identify them, attempt to minimize their importance in your statement of facts, and then, in your argument section, show why you contend that they are unimportant.

Courts and judges may determine the format of the statement of facts. Two judges in the same district offered different requirements for preparing the statement of facts in a Motion and Brief for a Summary Judgment. Judge Crabb offered the following requirements repro-duced in Figure 12.5.

The requirements of Judge Shabaz were decidedly different. And yes, both judges were from the same district court in Wisconsin. Compare the statement of facts from Judge Shabaz in Figure 12.6 with that of Judge Crabb.

Figure 12.7 shows a statement of facts written from the plaintiff's perspective.

FIGURE 12.5
Summary Judgment Requirements of Judge Crabb

HELPFUL TIPS FOR FILING
A SUMMARY JUDGMENT MOTION
IN CASES ASSIGNED TO JUDGE BARBARA B. CRABB

Please read the attached directions carefully – doing so will save your time and the court's.

REMEMBER:
1. All facts necessary to sustain a party's position on a motion for summary judgment must be explicitly proposed as findings of fact. This includes facts establishing jurisdiction. (Think of your proposed findings of fact as telling a story to someone who knows nothing of the controversy.)
2. The court will not search the record for factual evidence. Even if there is evidence in the record to support your position on summary judgment, if you do not propose a finding of fact with the proper citation, the court will not consider that evidence when deciding the motion.
3. A fact properly proposed by one side will be accepted by the court as undisputed unless the other side properly responds to the proposed fact and establishes that it is in dispute.
4. Your brief is the place to make your legal argument, not to restate the facts. When you finish it, check it over with a fine-tooth comb to be sure you haven't relied upon or assumed any facts in making your legal argument that you failed to include in the separate document setting out your proposed findings of fact.
5. A chart listing the documents to be filed by the deadlines set by the court for briefing motions for summary judgment or cross-motions for summary judgment is printed on the reverse side of this tip sheet.

IN THE UNITED STATES DISTRICT COURT
FOR THE WESTERN DISTRICT OF WISCONSIN

PROCEDURE TO BE FOLLOWED ON MOTIONS FOR SUMMARY JUDGMENT

I. MOTION FOR SUMMARY JUDGMENT

A. Contents:

1. A motion, together with such materials permitted by Rule 56(e) as the movant may elect to serve and file; and

2. In a separate document, a statement of proposed findings of fact or a stipulation of fact between or among the parties to the action, or both; and

3. Evidentiary materials (see I.C.); and

4. A supporting brief.

B. Rules Regarding Proposed Findings of Fact:

1. Each fact should be proposed in a separate, numbered paragraph.

2. Each factual proposition must be followed by a reference to evidence supporting the proposed fact. For example,

"1. Plaintiff Smith bought six Holstein calves on July 11, 2001. Harold Smith Affidavit, Jan. 6, 2002, p.1, ¶ 3."

3. The statement of proposed findings of fact shall include ALL factual propositions the moving party considers necessary for judgment in the party's

FIGURE 12.5
Cont.

favor. For example, the proposed findings shall include factual statements relating to jurisdiction, the identity of the parties, the dispute, and the context of the dispute.

  4. The court will not consider facts contained only in a brief.

C. Evidence

  1. As noted in I.B. above, each proposed finding must be supported by admissible evidence. The court will not search the record for evidence. To support a proposed fact, you may use:

  a. Depositions. Give the name of the witness, the date of the deposition, and page of the transcript of cited deposition testimony;

  b. Answers to Interrogatories. State the number of the interrogatory and the party answering it;

  c. Admissions made pursuant to Fed. R. Civ. P. 36. (State the number of the requested admission and the identity of the parties to whom it was directed); or

  d. Other Admissions. The identity of the document, the number of the page, and paragraph of the document in which that admission is made.

  e. Affidavits. The page and paragraph number, the name of the affiant, and the date of the affidavit. (Affidavits must be made by persons who have first-hand knowledge and must show that the person making the affidavit is in a position to testify about those facts.)

  f. Documentary evidence that is shown to be true and correct, either by an affidavit or by stipulation of the parties. (State exhibit number, page and paragraph.)

[text omitted]

Source: Guides and Procedures for the U.S. District Court for the Western District of Wisconsin, available at www.wiwd.uscourts.gov/rules/guidproc/html

FIGURE 12.6
Summary Judgment Requirements of Judge Shabaz

IN THE UNITED STATES DISTRICT COURT
FOR THE WESTERN DISTRICT OF WISCONSIN

PROCEDURE TO BE FOLLOWED ON MOTIONS FOR SUMMARY JUDGMENT

I. A motion for summary judgment made pursuant to Rule 56 of the Federal Rules of Civil procedure shall be served and filed in the following form:
  A. The motion itself together with such materials permitted by Rule 56(e) as the movant may elect to serve and file; and
  B. Either (1) <u>a stipulation of facts</u> between or among all the parties to the action, or (2) <u>a statement of the findings of fact proposed by movant</u>, or (3) <u>a combination of (1) and (2)</u>.
    1. Whether a movant elects a stipulation or a statement of proposed findings, or both, it is movant's obligation to present no more and no less than the set of factual propositions which movant considers necessary to judgment in movant's favor, and as to which movant considers there is no genuine issue.
    2. Such factual propositions shall be set forth in numbered paragraphs, the contents of each of which shall limited as far as practicable to the statement of single factual proposition.
    3. At the close of each numbered paragraph shall be set forth one or more references to the PLEADINGS, DEPOSITION TRANSCRIPTS, ANSWERS TO INTERROGATORIES, ADMISSIONS on file or AFFIDAVITS supporting movant's contention there is no genuine issue as to that factual proposition.

FIGURE 12.6
Cont.

4. References to the record shall include:

  a. in the case of pleading, the numbered paragraph of that pleading;

  b. in the case of a deposition transcript, the name of the witness and the page of the transcript;

  c. in the case of an answer to an interrogatory, the number of that interrogatory and the identity of the party to whom it was directed;

  d. in the case of an admission in response to, or resulting from a failure to respond to, a request for admission made pursuant to Rule 36, Federal Rules of Civil Procedure, the number of the requested admission and the identity of the party to whom it was directed;

  e. in the case of an admission on file which is not in response to, or resulting from a failure to respond to, a request for admission made pursuant to Rule 36, the form such admission takes and the page or paragraph of the document in which that admission is made. Admissions made solely for the purpose of the motion for summary judgment should be so designated.

C. A statement of the conclusions of law proposed by movant, in numbered paragraphs.

D. A motion for summary judgement in the form required by I., above, shall be served and filed together with a <u>supporting brief</u>.

[text omitted]

Source: Guides and Procedures for the U.S. District Court for the Western District of Wisconsin, available at www.wiwd.uscourts.gov/rules/guidproc/html

FIGURE 12.7
Statement of Facts

The facts in the case are undisputed. Mr. Giles went to a holiday party on November 20, at the home of Mr. Swan, a business associate. Mr. Swan had been Mr. Giles' friend and attorney for some time. Giles was going out of town for Thanksgiving and would not be back until the first of the new year. Giles wanted to purchase a piece of real estate before the end of the year, but was going out of town. The only business discussion that evening concerned the real estate transaction.

Swan suggested that Giles could execute a power of attorney, with Swan as Giles' representative. The gentlemen went into Swan's study and Giles signed a document entitled "Power of Attorney." Neither man filled in any information in the document. Swan's name did not appear anywhere on the document. Swan kept the Power of Attorney in his top desk drawer. Giles went on his trip.

While Giles was on his trip, one of his partners, Mr. Harris, contacted Swan regarding a joint venture transaction completely unrelated to the real estate transaction. Giles and Harris had been discussing dissolving the joint venture, with Giles acquiring Harris' interest. Swan knew nothing about this transaction.

Harris stated to Swan that Giles was supposed to assume all Harris' interest in the joint venture before January 1. Harris inquired whether Swan could help him. Swan told Harris that he had a power of attorney to close a real estate transaction, but did not know how he could help Harris out.

Harris asked Swan to use the power of attorney to transfer the joint venture interest. Harris told Swan this would save his friend some money. Swan continued to tell Harris that he only had authority to close a real estate transaction. Harris, however, was able to persuade Swan to execute the transfer of the joint venture interest, using the power of attorney on December 29.

When Giles came back to town, Swan informed him of the transfer from Harris and told him that he had used the power of attorney. Giles was enraged and told Swan he had no authority to transfer the interest. Giles wanted the transaction rescinded.

The Argument

argument
A section of the memorandum of law that presents your client's legal position.

The **argument** of a legal memorandum presents your client's position; it is the heart of the memorandum. You present the results of your research in an adversarial form intended to persuade the court of the superiority of your client's contentions. The partisan purpose and slant of the argument section differentiate it from the discussion section of an internal memorandum, where the legal analysis is objective, not adversarial. In the trial memorandum, your purpose is to have your position prevail.

Effective writing techniques are essential for this section. Outline for logical organization. Be definitive. Write to convince, not simply to inform. Use language that is positive and forceful. Make the court believe that your position is correct.

Move from general points to those more specific, applying the law to the facts and using the IRAC model as your guide. A method of guiding the judge through your brief when multiple issues are involved is by using **point headings** and **subheadings.** They act as an outline of the memorandum of law. A point heading identifies the argument in a section of the brief. A subheading presents subpoints of the point heading. Like the issue, they are drafted with a persuasive slant. The practice of using point headings helps the judge in two ways: First, by highlighting your arguments in a precise form. And second, judges who do not have lots of extra time can scan the brief and focus on the pinpoint and subheadings in the brief. Using these headings streamlines your brief and organizes the argument.

point headings
Headings that outline and identify the argument in the section.

subheadings
Headings that identify the subpoints in an argument section.

Therefore, in your brief emphasize your strong points and facts; de-emphasize and attack the opposition's strong points and facts. Most of all, avoid obscurity—tell the court your position clearly and effectively. But do not misstate or mislead the court. When a point is not favorable, distinguish it, but do not lose credibility by ignoring adverse authority. Integrity in your presentation goes along way in gaining the confidence of the court. An example of an argument section is provided in Figure 12.8.

Another reason to clearly and effectively state your legal position is that the issues raised in the trial court may determine the issues on appeal. In most circumstances, the issues argued at the trial court level are the same legal issues on appeal. If issues are not raised in the pleadings and briefs before the trial court, there is no record identifying those issues existed. Appellate courts frown upon attorneys attempting to use an appeal as the first time to raise issues that should have been raised at the trial court. Often the result is either dismissal of the appeal or refusal to hear the "new" issue on appeal. Consequently, you and your supervising attorney should take care in addressing all the issues at the trial court level or face having them forever waived at the appellate level. That means you should be thinking strategically from the moment the complaint and answer are filed in a case. Every document in a trial level case has legal significance. Thus the information and evidence used at the trial court are the building blocks that set the foundation for the record on appeal.

You Be the Judge Hypothetical 12-3

In *Independent Towers of Washington v. State of Washington*, 350 F.3d 925 (9th Cir. 2003), the judge ripped into the attorneys for their poorly written brief as well as their failure to articulate well-defined legal arguments. The court refused to search through the briefs to find the arguments. The judge's stinging comments regarding Independent Towers of Washington's (ITOW) brief were: "[w]hen reading ITOW's brief, one wonders if ITOW, in its own version of the 'spaghetti approach,' has heaved the entire contents of a pot against the wall in hopes that something would stick. We decline, however, to sort through the noodles in search of ITOW's claim." *Id.* at 929. The court continued its comments by citing a Seventh Circuit case "in its now familiar maxim, 'judges are not like pigs, hunting for truffles buried in briefs.'" *Id.* at 929 citing *United States v. Dunkel*, 927 F.2d 955, 956 (7th Cir. 1991). The court continued its comments by observing, "[t]he art of advocacy is not one of mystery. Our adversarial system relies on the advocates to inform the discussion and raise the issues to the court. Particularly on appeal, we have held firm against considering arguments that are not briefed. But the term 'briefed' in the appellate context does not mean opaque nor is it an exercise in issue spotting. However much we may importune lawyers to be brief and get to the point, we have never suggested that they skip the substance of their argument in order to do so." *Id.* at 929-30. Review the case. What was the court's disposition in the case? Were all the issues raised by the attorneys decided on appeal? What was the court's reasoning in the case? Be sure all issues are articulated not only at the trial level but in the appellate brief as well.

FIGURE 12.8
Argument Section

PRACTICE TIP

Since subheadings follow the rules of outlining, you must use more than one subheading within a point heading. Otherwise, limit yourself to one general point heading for each argument section within the memorandum of law. The point heading is typed in capital letters with the subheadings in regular type. Present your strongest arguments and points first. By doing this, you set the tone of your brief. Guide the judge logically and methodically through the argument.

This case presents a unique question of law which is what is the authority granted a principal by an agent when the power of attorney is blank. The answer is none. Any acts performed by a principal with a blank power of attorney are void. It is clear that a power of attorney must set forth the authority and the name of the principal and agent. The document before this court does neither.

The law on this matter is well settled in Texas and dates back to the 1880s. To determine the validity of the power of attorney and the extent of the authority granted, certain rules of construction and interpretation must be addressed. The leading case of *Gouldy v. Metcalf,* 75 Tex. 455, 12 S.W. 830 (1889), sets out the rules of construction for a power of attorney, which are:

> [w]hen an authority is conferred upon an agent by a formal instrument, as by a power of attorney, there are two rules of construction to be carefully adhered to:
>
> 1. The meaning of general words in the instrument will be restricted by the context, and construed accordingly.
> 2. The authority will be construed strictly, so as to exclude the exercise of any power which is not warranted, either by the actual terms used or as a necessary means of executing the authority with effect.
> *Id.* at 458.

Expanding the guidelines set forth in *Gouldy,* case law establishes that "all powers conferred upon an agent by a formal instrument are to receive a strict interpretation, and the authority is never extended by intendment or construction beyond that which is given in terms, or is necessary for carrying the authority into effect, and the authority must be strictly pursued." *Bean v. Bean,* 79 S.W. 2d 652 (Tex. Civ. App.– Texarkana 1935, writ ref'd); *Dockstader v. Brown,* 204 S.W. 2d 352 (Tex. Civ. App.– Fort Worth 1947, writ ref'd n.r.e.).

Giles and Swan had a specific conversation about Swan closing a real estate transaction. No mention of a joint venture ever took place. Swan did not have the authority to use the power of attorney for the joint venture transfer. As stated in *Giddings, Neiman-Marcus v. Estes,* 440 S.W. 2d 90 (Tex. Civ. App.–Eastland 1969, no writ), "[t]he authority will be construed strictly, so as to exclude the exercise of any power which is not warranted either by the actual terms used or as a necessary means of effecting the authority with effect." Since no authority was conferred on Swan by the document, he could not have acted on Giles' behalf. Consequently, any acts performed by Swan for Giles under the power of attorney are invalid, especially ones (like the joint venture transfer) not anticipated.

Swan told Harris that the power of attorney was for a specific purpose, which was to close the real estate transaction. The law is clear that a third party has a duty to inquire into the scope and fact of the agency, and the burden is on the third party to "ascertain at his peril the nature and scope of the authority of such agent." *Lawrie v. Miller,* 2. S.W. 2d 561 (Tex. Civ. App.–Texarkana 1928, no writ). *See also, Eliot Valve Repair v. Valve,* 675 S.W. 2d 555 (Tex. App.–Houston [1st Dist.] 1984, no writ); *Boucher v. City Paint & Supply,* 398 S.W. 2d 352 (Tex. Civ. App.–Tyler 1966, no writ). It was Harris' responsibility to investigate the extent of Swan's authority. Harris indeed knew the purpose of the power of attorney, but chose to coerce Swan to sign the document under the guise of "friendship." Any acts resulting from Harris' coercion and Swan's misuse of his authority cannot be imputed to Giles, and thus cannot be his responsibility.

The document that Harris is relying upon to effectuate the transfer of the joint venture interest is useless and invalid. The power of attorney does not comply with the requirements for a valid power of attorney, and Swan's actions violated Giles' instructions and interests.

The standard for a summary judgment is that there are no genuine issues of material fact and the moving party is entited to judgment as a matter of law. *Lear Siegler, Inc. v. Perez,* 819 S.W. 2d 470 (Tex. 1991). The facts are undisputed. The power of attorney is blank. It did not, nor could not, confer authority to anyone much less Swan. The law is clear on this point and the court must find for Giles.

FIGURE 12.9
Conclusion and
Requested Relief

Since the purported power of attorney from Giles to Swan did not contain specific authority granted to the agent, the power of attorney is void. Based upon the strict construction doctrine, one cannot construe a grant of authority that is nonexistent. The power of attorney contained neither the name of the agent, the purpose of the agency, nor the authority of the agent; therefore, it could not confer any powers upon the agent. Swan's acts were improper, and Giles is not legally responsible for the effects of those acts. Giles requests that the Motion for Summary Judgment be granted upon the court's finding, as a matter of law, that the transfer of the joint venture interest was invalid and the power of attorney void.

Conclusion

The conclusion section is a summary of the legal position taken in the trial memorandum. It informs the court of the finding and relief sought. Although a one-sentence conclusion requesting relief is sometimes acceptable, particularly for a short trial memorandum, a better approach summarizes the entire argument, crystallizing the legal contentions. Figure 12.9 shows a conclusion that summarizes the argument, and identifies the relief requested.

Signature Block and Certificate of Service

As with all other documents filed with a court, the trial memorandum must be signed by the responsible attorney. As we have noted before, you as a paralegal are not authorized to sign a court document on behalf of a client. The name of the attorney and firm name, address, telephone number, fax, and sometimes a state bar identification number are among the items to be included in a signature block. Figure 12.10 shows an example of an acceptable signature block.

If a brief or pleading is filed electronically, the courts have rules for the signature block. A typical example of a rule for filing an electronic document and signature is shown in Figure 12.11 from the United States District Court for the District of New Jersey. This rule provides for multiple as well as nonattorney signatures.

Likewise, a certificate of service attesting to the fact that copies of the trial memorandum have been sent to other attorneys of record (or parties) must be included. The method of service—ordinary mail, certified mail, hand delivery, or other accepted means—is identified. A simple statement certifying delivery is adequate for the purposes of the certificate; remember, if service ever comes into question, proof will become important. Hence the certified mail option (with a return receipt proving delivery) is better than, say, ordinary mail. Check the rules and practices of your jurisdiction to determine applicable rules and requirements. A typical certificate of service is seen in Figure 12.12.

Since many courts are requiring that documents are filed electronically, the certificate of service must conform to the court's requirements. Review Figure 12.13 for the requirements in the District Court for the Northern District of Ohio.

FIGURE 12.10
Signature Block

Respectfully submitted,

_____
Nicholas Barron
State Bar #12344567
1234 Main Street, #10030
Dallas, Texas 75202
(214) 555-1212
Attorney for Plaintiff

FIGURE 12.11

Example of a Rule for Filing an Electronic Document and Signature

14. Signatures.

(a) **Attorney Signatures.** The user login and password required to submit documents to the Electronic Filing System serve as the Filing User's signature on all electronic documents filed with the court. They serve as the signature for purposes of Federal Rules of Civil Procedure 11, all other Federal Rules of Civil Procedure, Federal Rules of Criminal Procedure, and the Local Rules of this court, and any other purpose for which a signature is required in connection with proceedings before the court.

An electronically filed document, or a document submitted on disk or CD-ROM, and in compliance with Local Civil Rules 10.1 and 11.1, must include a signature line with "s/," as shown below.

<u>s/ Jennifer Doe</u>

No Filing User or other person may knowingly permit or cause to permit a Filing User's password to be used by anyone other than an authorized agent of the Filing User.

(b) **Multiple Signatures.** A document requiring signatures of more than one party must be filed electronically either by: (1) submitting a scanned document containing all necessary signatures; or (2) in any other manner approved by the court.

(c) **Non-Attorney Signatures.** A document requiring the signature of a non-attorney must be filed electronically by: (1) submitting a scanned document containing all necessary signatures; or (2) in any other manner approved by the court.

15. Retention Requirements.

A document that is electronically filed and requires an original signature other than that of the Filing User must be maintained in paper form by the ECF Filing User and/or the firm representing the party on whose behalf the document was filed until one year after all periods for appeals expire. On request of the court, the ECF Filing User or law firm must provide the original document.

Source: United States District Court for the District of New Jersey.

POST-WRITING REVIEW

As with the prewriting considerations that were discussed earlier in the chapter, the post-writing considerations must be performed as well. Never forget the lessons learned in presenting a final polished document. Your post-writing review should include

- checking for punctuation, spelling, and grammatical errors;
- paying attention to transition and topic sentences;
- reviewing citations for correct format;
- checking that quotations are properly cited;
- incorporating the facts with the law;
- editing the document for conciseness and precision;
- reviewing the redraft and re-editing the document;
- revising the final draft;

FIGURE 12.12

Certificate of Service

<u>CERTIFICATE OF SERVICE</u>

I certify that a true copy of the Memorandum of Law in Support of Plaintiff's Motion for Summary Judgment was served on Jane Smith, Attorney for Defendant, at 111 Main Street, Suite 123, Ft. Worth, Texas, by certified mail, return receipt requested, in accordance with the Texas Rules of Civil Procedure on May 12, 2006.

_____

Nicholas Barron

Source: United States District Court for the District of New Jersey.

FIGURE 12.13   **Certificate of Service Requirements for Northern District of Ohio**

Source: United States District Court Northern District of Ohio, available at www.ohnd.uscourts.gov/Clerk_s_Office/Local_Rules/Civil_Rules-06_05_06.pdf

The following is a suggested certificate of service for electronic filing:

Certificate of Service

I hereby certify that on [date], a copy of foregoing [name of document] was filed electronically. Notice of this filing will be sent by operation of the Court's electronic filing system to all parties indicated on the electronic filing receipt. All other parties will be served by regular U.S. mail. Parties may access this filing through the Court's system.

> s/ [Name of Password Registrant]
> Name of Password Registrant
> Address
> City, State, Zip Code
> Phone: (xxx) xxx-xxxx
> Fax: (xxx) xxx-xxxx
> E-mail: xxx@xxx.xxx
> [attorney bar number, if applicable]

It is the responsibility of the filing party to ensure that all other parties are properly served. Fed. R. Civ. P. 5(b)(3) notes that service by electronic means is not effective if the party making service learns that the attempted service did not reach the person to be served. If a party requiring service is not listed on the electronic filing receipt as having been sent an electronic notice of the filing, the filing party must serve that party by other appropriate means.

- complying with court rules for preparing briefs and submitting attachments;
- checking length, font size, and margins of brief; and
- filing deadlines with court.

PRACTICE TIP

Remember from Chapters 1 and 7 that many courts dictate the correct form for citations. Do not assume a court follows *Bluebook* or *ALWD*. Remember that a number of jurisdictions have adopted the universal citation format. Citation form should conform to the local rules of the court in which you intend to file your brief.

Ethics Alert

Throughout this text, you have been consistently reminded of the prohibition of signing pleadings and certain types of letters. Electronic filings present some unique ethical issues that were never considered in the past. The United States Court for the Eastern District of Michigan has a section on their website that discusses electronic case filing. In the section there is a Frequently Asked Questions section that poses some interesting ethical issues for attorneys and paralegals. The question posed was: "Can an attorney authorize someone in the attorney's office (such as a paralegal) to use the attorney's login name and password to file documents in CM/ECF?"(case management/electronic case filing). The answer from the court's website was: "Yes, but access should be limited and controlled since whatever is filed under that login and password is deemed to have the attorney's signature on it." A follow-up question was: "Can any member of the public register to e-file documents with the court?"

The response was "No. Only eligible attorneys can register to e-file."

Interesting ethical issues are posed by electronic filings of documents. The assumption for e-filings is that the attorney read the document, filed the document, and is responsible for its content. Recall some of our cases where these issues were addressed. The ultimate responsibility was the attorney's. Since e-filing is a relatively new practice, rules are being developed and the case law is sparse on the issue. As problems arise, the rules behind e-filings will be refined. The advice to you is to pay close attention to the rules of the courts in which you practice; read the case law as it develops on e-filings; and never forget as a paralegal you *do* have restrictions as to what you can and cannot do. Do not allow attorneys to compromise your integrity or ethics. Most bar associations have ethics hotlines for sensitive questions, or you can check with courts' written protocols to determine the parameters of practice.

THE E-FACTOR

FILING YOUR BRIEF ELECTRONICALLY

Electronic filing of briefs presents unique issues for the paralegal and attorney. Many courts have limitations on the size of the electronic file. If your brief and supporting documents exceed the megabytes requirement, then the document must be filed manually. With the manual filing is often a Notice of Manual Filing. Most courts provide an example of this document. Figure 12.14 is sample Notice of Manual Filing. The courts make it quite clear that a document filed manually does not excuse untimely filing of the entire submission. Since e-filing is becoming mandatory in most federal courts, stay current on your jurisdiction's requirements.

---

redacted
Eliminated from a legal document due to privacy and security matters.

Another e-filing issue requiring attention is privacy. As so many individuals have been victims of identity theft, personal information about parties to a case should be **redacted,** when possible. Redacted is the fancy way of saying "take out." Balancing the public's rights to know against the privacy and security of litigants is a fine line. Courts warn attorneys not to include sensitive information in documents filed with the court. Courts suggest to redact "personal data identifiers" such as

1. Social Security numbers;
2. financial account numbers;
3. dates of birth

FIGURE 12.14
Sample Notice of Manual Filing

Appendix C

UNITED STATES DISTRICT COURT
NORTHERN DISTRICT OF OHIO

	)	
	)	
Plaintiff	)	Case No.
	)	
v.	)	Judge
	)	
Defendant	)	Notice of Manual Filing
	)	
	)	

Please take notice that [Plaintiff/Defendant, Name of Party] has manually filed the following document or thing

[Title of Document or Thing]

This document has not been filed electronically because

the document or thing cannot be converted to an electronic format; the electronic file size of the document exceeds 1.5 megabytes (about 15 scanned pages). [Plaintiff/Defendant] is excused from filing this document or thing by court order.

The document or thing has been manually served on all parties.

Respectfully submitted,
s/ [Name of Password Registrant]
Name of Password Registrant
Address
City, State, Zip Code
Phone: (xxx) xxx-xxxx
Fax: (xxx) xxx-xxxx
E-mail: xxx@xxx.xxx
[attorney bar number, if applicable]

Source: United States District Court Northern District of Ohio, available at http://www.ohnd.uscourts.gov/Clerk_s_Office/Local_Rules/Civil_Rules06_05_06.pdf

4. names of minor children; and

5. (in criminal cases only) home addresses.

(See United States District Court Northern District of Ohio Electronic Filing Policies and Procedures Manual, January 1, 2006.)

Although e-filing has many attributes, such as 24-hour, 7-day-a-week filing capabilities, reduced use of paper clutter in court files, and instantaneous access to court documents, the technical glitches we all experience are not eliminated. There are help desks and trainings for use of the "new" e-filing systems. Understanding the process and how that process interacts with the rules of court will take time for those just introduced to the world of law and legalese. Do not get frustrated. Ask questions, review the court websites, and get trained. E-filings are here to stay, so learn the process and rules.

PRACTICAL CONSIDERATIONS

A trial memorandum is an important document in the litigation process, because if properly drafted it can resolve issues in your favor and begin to turn the lawsuit toward your client. Furthermore, since the amount at issue in many cases will not justify the expense of an extended appeals process, prevailing at the trial level is often the guarantee of prevailing once and for all.

An example of a completed trial memorandum appears as Figure 12.15. In general, you should keep in mind the following points when preparing a trial memorandum:

- Check for local jurisdictional requirements about format or content.
- Identify your purpose.
- Always draft from your client's perspective.
- Present the law honestly and accurately, but with a partisan slant.
- Identify all significant facts, and present them in a manner that minimizes the opposition's strong points and paints a memorable picture of your client's position.
- Write convincingly, using effective and persuasive writing techniques.
- Be clear, precise, and concise.
- Tell the judge what result and relief you seek.

FIGURE 12.15
Memorandum of Law to the Trial Court

IN THE DISTRICT COURT OF DALLAS COUNTY, TEXAS
101st JUDICIAL DISTRICT

STEPHEN GILES	§	
	§	
Plaintiff	§	
	§	
vs.	§	No. 12344
	§	
GEORGE HARRIS	§	
	§	
Defendant	§	

MEMORANDUM OF LAW IN SUPPORT OF PLAINTIFF'S MOTION FOR SUMMARY JUDGMENT

TO THE HONORABLE JUDGE OF SAID COURT:

STEPHEN GILES, Plaintiff files this Memorandum of Law to the Trial Court in Support of Plaintiff's Motion for Summary Judgment and would show unto the Court as follows:

Issue Presented

No issues of fact exist in a transaction where an unauthorized agent used a blank power of attorney to act on behalf of the Plaintiff, the principal.

FIGURE 12.15
Cont.

Statement of Facts

The facts in the case are undisputed. Mr. Giles went to a holiday party on November 20, at the home of Mr. Swan, a business associate. Mr. Swan had been Mr. Giles' friend and attorney for some time. Giles was going out of town for Thanksgiving and would not be back until the first of the new year. Giles wanted to purchase a piece of real estate before the end of the year, but was going out of town. The only business discussion that evening concerned the real estate transaction.

Swan suggested that Giles could execute a power of attorney, with Swan as Giles' representative. The gentlemen went into Swan's study and Giles signed a document entitled "Power of Attorney." Neither man filled in any information in the document. Swan's name did not appear anywhere on the document. Swan kept the Power of Attorney in his top desk drawer. Giles went on his trip.

While Giles was on his trip, one of his partners, Mr. Harris, contacted Swan regarding a joint venture transaction completely unrelated to the real estate transaction. Giles and Harris had been discussing dissolving the joint venture, with Giles acquiring Harris' interest. Swan knew nothing about this transaction.

Harris stated to Swan that Giles was supposed to assume all Harris' interest in the joint venture before January 1. Harris inquired whether Swan could help him. Swan told Harris that he had a power of attorney to close a real estate transaction, but did not know how he could help Harris out.

Harris asked Swan to use the power of attorney to transfer the joint venture interest. Harris told Swan this would save his friend some money. Swan continued to tell Harris that he only had authority to close a real estate transaction. Harris, however, was able to persuade Swan to execute the transfer of the joint venture interest, using the power of attorney on December 29.

When Giles came back to town, Swan informed him of the transfer from Harris and told him that he had used the power of attorney. Giles was enraged and told Swan he had no authority to transfer the interest. Giles wanted the transaction rescinded.

Argument

This case presents a unique question of law which is what is the authority granted a principal by an agent when the power of attorney is blank. The answer is none. Any acts performed by a principal with a blank power of attorney are void. It is clear that a power of attorney must set forth the authority and the name of the principal and agent. The document before this court does neither.

The law on this matter is well settled in Texas and dates back to the 1880s. To determine the validity of the power of attorney and the extent of the authority granted, certain rules of construction and interpretation must be addressed. The leading case of *Gouldy v. Metcalf*, 75 Tex. 455, 12 S.W. 830 (1889), sets out the rules of construction for a power of attorney, which are:

> [w]hen an authority is conferred upon an agent by a formal instrument, as by a power of attorney, there are two rules of construction to be carefully adhered to:
>
> 1. The meaning of general words in the instrument will be restricted by the context, and construed accordingly.
> 2. The authority will be construed strictly, so as to exclude the exercise of any power which is not warranted, either by the actual terms used or as a necessary means of executing the authority with effect.
> *Id*. at 458.

Expanding the guidelines set forth in *Gouldy*, case law establishes that "all powers conferred upon an agent by a formal instrument are to receive a strict interpretation, and the authority is never extended by intendment or construction beyond that which is given in terms, or is necessary for carrying the authority into effect, and the authority must be strictly pursued." *Bean v. Bean*, 79 S.W. 2d 652 (Tex. Civ. App.–Texarkana 1935, writ ref'd); *Dockstader v. Brown*, 204 S.W. 2d 352 (Tex. Civ. App.–Fort Worth 1947, writ ref'd n.r.e.).

FIGURE 12.15
Cont.

Giles and Swan had a specific conversation about Swan closing a real estate transaction. No mention of a joint venture ever took place. Swan did not have the authority to use the power of attorney for the joint venture transfer. As stated in *Giddings, Neiman-Marcus v. Estes*, 440 S.W. 2d 90 (Tex. Civ. App.–Eastland 1969, no writ), "[t]he authority will be construed strictly, so as to exclude the exercise of any power which is not warranted either by the actual terms used or as a necessary means of effecting the authority with effect." Since no authority was conferred on Swan by the document, he could not have acted on Giles' behalf. Consequently, any acts performed by Swan for Giles under the power of attorney are invalid, especially ones (like the joint venture transfer) not anticipated.

Swan told Harris that the power of attorney was for a specific purpose, which was to close the real estate transaction. The law is clear that a third party has a duty to inquire into the scope and fact of the agency, and the burden is on the third party to "ascertain at his peril the nature and scope of the authority of such agent." *Lawrie v. Miller*, 2 S.W. 2d 561 (Tex. Civ. App.–Texarkana 1928, no writ). *See also, Eliot Valve Repair v. Valve*, 675 S.W. 2d 555 (Tex. App.–Houston [1st Dist.] 1984, no writ); *Boucher v. City Paint & Supply*, 398 S.W. 2d 352 (Tex. Civ. App.–Tyler 1966, no writ). It was Harris' responsibility to investigate the extent of Swan's authority. Harris indeed knew the purpose of the power of attorney, but chose to coerce Swan to sign the document under the guise of "friendship." Any acts resulting from Harris' coercion and Swan's misuse of his authority cannot be imputed to Giles, and thus cannot be his responsibility.

The document that Harris is relying upon to effectuate the transfer of the joint venture interest is useless and invalid. The power of attorney does not comply with the requirements for a valid power of attorney, and Swan's actions violated Giles' instructions and interests.

The standard for a summary judgment is that there are no genuine issues of material fact and the moving party is entited to judgment as a matter of law. *Lear Siegler, Inc. v. Perez*, 819 S.W. 2d 470 (Tex. 1991). The facts are undisputed. The power of attorney is blank. It did not, nor could not, confer authority to anyone much less Swan. The law is clear on this point and the court must find for Giles.

<u>Conclusion and Requested Relief</u>

Since the purported power of attorney from Giles to Swan did not contain any specific authority granted to the agent, the power of attorney is void. Based upon the strict construction doctrine, one cannot construe a grant of authority that is nonexistent. The power of attorney contained neither the name of the agent, the purpose of the agency, nor the authority of the agent, and therefore it could not confer any powers upon the agent. Swan's acts were therefore improper, and Giles is not legally responsible for the effects of those acts. Giles requests that the Motion for Summary Judgment be granted upon the court's finding, as a matter of law, that the transfer of the joint venture interest was invalid and the power of attorney void.

Respectfully submitted,

_____

Nicholas Barron
State Bar #12344567
1234 Main Street, #10030
Dallas, Texas 75202
(214) 555-1212
Attorney for Plaintiff

<u>CERTIFICATE OF SERVICE</u>

I certify that a true copy of the Memorandum of Law in Support of Plaintiff's Motion for Summary Judgment was served on Jane Smith, Attorney for Defendant, at 111 Main Street, Suite 123, Fort Worth, Texas, by certified mail, return receipt requested, in accordance with the Texas Rules of Civil Procedure on May 12, 2006.

_____

Nicholas Barron, Esq.

Summary

The memorandum of law to the trial court is an adversarial document written to persuade a trial court on a disputed issue of law. It is also known as a trial memorandum, and other similar names, depending on the jurisdiction. The audience for a trial memorandum consists of the judge, who will read it fairly but must be convinced, and opposing counsel, who will read it looking to attack logical holes and unjustified analytical leaps. Be accurate but partisan in drafting a trial memorandum.

There are three broad categories of trial memoranda: the memorandum in regard to a motion; the memorandum prepared at the request of a judge; and the unsolicited memorandum that anticipates and addresses key legal issues. All are drafted with an adversarial purpose, designed to persuade a judge that a disputed question of law should be resolved in favor of a particular party.

There are several components to a trial memorandum. First come the caption, title, and introduction to the court. Next, in the "issues presented" section, the drafter presents the legal questions raised in a manner that suggests a resolution in favor of the client on whose behalf the drafter is working. Similarly, the statement of facts should state all events accurately, but with a slant toward the position of the client. The argument is the heart of the trial memorandum, presenting the results of the drafter's research in an adversarial argument designed to persuade the court of the superiority of the client's contentions. The conclusion summarizes the argument and identifies the relief sought. It is followed by a signature block and a certificate of service.

A properly drafted trial memorandum is an important part of the litigation process. Indeed, since appeals are often too expensive for clients to pursue, drafting effective trial memoranda can lead to a victory in the trial court that stands once and for all.

Key Terms

memorandum of law to the trial court
memorandum in regard to a motion
memorandum at the request of a judge
unsolicited memorandum anticipating
  legal issues
issues or questions presented

statement of facts
argument
point headings
subheadings
redacted

Review Questions

1. Who are the two audiences for a trial memorandum?
2. How should a trial memorandum be prepared so as to assist a judge?
3. How should a trial memorandum be drafted so as to minimize the impact of the attack of opposing counsel?
4. What are the characteristics of a trial memorandum prepared in regard to a motion?
5. Why might a judge request a trial memorandum?
6. What is the potential importance of an unsolicited trial memorandum that anticipates issues?
7. What is the importance to a trial memorandum of the caption and the title?
8. From what perspective is the "issues presented" section of a trial memorandum prepared?
9. What are the four objectives of a statement of facts?
10. What is the difference between the discussion section of an internal memorandum and the argument section of a trial memorandum?

Exercises

1. Assume that your attorney has been served with a request to produce tax returns in a personal injury case in your jurisdiction. Go to the library and research whether the tax returns are protected information. Then prepare the argument section of the memorandum of law to the trial court, requesting an order that the documents not be produced.

2. Determine for your jurisdiction the format for a memorandum of law to the trial court. Check both the state and federal requirements.

3. Louis Harris is a resident of Florida and files a lawsuit against George Hillary of Miami, Florida, in the U.S. District Court in Miami, Florida, based upon diversity jurisdiction. Mr. Harris claims that on July 31, 2006 Mr. Hillary negligently hit Harris's Airstream trailer, damaging it in the amount of $75,000.00. Mr. Hillary's attorney, Jonathan Lineman, files a Motion to Dismiss based upon lack of diversity jurisdiction. Prepare the Motion to Dismiss and Brief in Support of the Motion.

4. Laura Coleman filed an age and sexual discrimination lawsuit against her employer, Designers Corporation. She claimed in an affidavit that she was over 45 years old and that on May 12, 2006 her supervisor, Carlton Peterson, made sexual advances, which she rejected, and on June 15, 2006, Mr. Petersen kissed Coleman on the cheek. Through investigation, Designers determined that Coleman is really 40 years old. Coleman deliberately lied on her affidavit. Had the attorney performed minimum investigation, Coleman's attorney would have known that the allegation in the affidavit was untruthful. Designer's attorney wants to file a Motion for Sanctions against Coleman. Prepare the Motion for Sanctions and Brief in Support of the Motion.

5. The time has passed for responses to Interrogatories in *Paradise Paving Company v. Discount Wholesalers, Inc.* Prepare the Motion to Compel and Brief on Behalf of Paradise. Assume the case is filed in the U.S. District Court in Rhode Island.

6. Paradise Paving Company (from Exercise 5) notices the President of Discount Wholesalers, Avery Pennington, for a deposition on May 27, 2006. Mr. Pennington is very busy and cannot attend the deposition. The case involves nonpayment for paving services on a parking lot in one of Discount's Providence stores. Prepare the Motion for Protective Order and Brief in Support of the Motion.

7. Community Nursing Home has not paid their utility bill for electricity and water in six months. They now owe $275,000. Revenues have been down at the nursing home. South Carolina Water Power Authority sent Community a demand letter dated August 15, 2006 requesting payment of the outstanding balance signed by the Chief Financial Officer (CFO) Harvey Buckman. Assume the Authority sued the nursing home. Prepare the interrogatories and request for admissions on behalf of the utility company.

8. Using the facts from Exercise 7, prepare the Motion for Summary Judgment, affidavit of Harvey Buckman, CFO, and the Brief in Support of the Motion. (Hint: Determine what you need to prove to support the case, such as the outstanding balance.)

Portfolio Assignment

Using the facts from the Portfolio Assignment, in Chapters 10 and 11, Mrs. Martha Marsh has requested that your office bring this matter to a close. Your supervising attorney has assigned you to complete the following tasks:

1. Prepare a Motion for Summary Judgment and Memorandum of Law in Support of Plaintiff's Motion for Summary Judgment against A1 Delivery Service, Inc., and Herbert Killington.

   Assume that A1 and Herb have received the Motion and must now file a reply as part of this assignment.

2. Prepare the Response to the Motion and Brief in Opposition of to the Summary Judgment. Remember, you must submit evidence to support your motion, such as interrogatory and admission responses. Affidavits are important as well. An opposition must also have evidence as well, such as an Affidavit of Herb Killington or a representative of A1. Get creative.

Vocabulary Builder

Memorandum of Law to the Trial Court

```
G  C  J  G  E  J  I  E  A  D  F  R  Y  A  M
X  L  O  J  N  Q  P  T  E  E  G  D  U  R  Y
H  F  A  N  V  I  T  Y  I  I  R  D  D  G  P
F  D  Y  T  C  O  D  L  W  O  W  N  Z  U  B
P  Y  K  G  R  L  E  A  X  R  A  U  W  M  F
T  S  Q  N  K  R  U  P  E  R  Y  Y  Z  E  Z
X  Y  E  L  F  M  M  S  O  H  L  B  J  N  X
S  Y  J  U  D  G  E  M  I  G  S  O  D  T  K
E  U  S  U  E  P  E  J  N  O  I  T  P  A  C
U  R  G  O  Z  M  S  U  I  C  N  P  V  J  U
S  G  Q  S  L  N  V  Y  B  X  S  N  X  Z  B
S  A  B  A  A  Q  P  I  L  S  S  B  Z  X  X
I  S  I  G  N  A  T  U  R  E  B  L  O  C  K
M  R  C  S  D  V  Z  K  J  T  Y  W  H  F  X
T  A  U  C  J  H  D  U  K  J  X  Y  X  D  T
```

ATTORNEY	**ARGUMENT**	**CAPTION**
CONCLUSION	**HEADING**	**ISSUES**
JUDGE	**RELIEF**	**SIGNATURE BLOCK**
TRIAL MEMORANDUM		

Chapter 13

The Appellate Brief

After completing this chapter, you will be able to:

- Explain the importance of following the appellate rules.

- Explain the function of the appellate brief.

- Identify the components of the record on appeal.

- Differentiate errors of fact from errors of law.

- Describe the jurisdictional statement section of an appellate brief.

- Explain the "road map" function of the table of contents.

- Identify two key points to remember in drafting the statement of facts section.

- Use point headings to divide the body of your brief into distinct segments.

- Draft a persuasive appellate argument.

- Distinguish between an appellant's brief, an appellee's brief, a reply brief, and an *amicus curiae* brief.

Writing an appellate brief is an art. Learning how to frame issues and write with just the right amount of passion and persuasiveness requires time and patience. In appellate brief writing, the record must be mastered, the legal standards researched, and the rules of the court followed to the letter. You will participate in all aspects of the preparation of an appellate brief whether your firm represents the appellant or the appellee. As a paralegal, it is your job to assist your supervising attorney in this process. This final chapter concludes with the last stage of the legal process and incorporates all the skills learned in this textbook. Let's begin the final stage of the process.

Case Fact Pattern Hypothetical 13-1

Closing arguments have concluded in a court trial in which you have been the assisting paralegal, and the judge informs counsel that a decision will be rendered after trial briefs are submitted. Briefs are then filed and both sides nervously await the result.

Within a week the decision arrives in your office mail. The judge has denied the permanent injunction sought by your supervising attorney—in short, your client has lost. The supervising attorney reviews the opinion, determines that there are valid reasons to question the judge's reasoning, consults with the client, and decides that she will file an appeal.

The next morning there is a memorandum on your desk. You have been assigned to assist in the legal research and preparation of the appellate brief.

Source: © King Features Syndicate.

A PRELIMINARY NOTE ABOUT PROCEDURAL RULES

Although this chapter addresses the preparation of the appellate brief, a proper examination of that subject requires that we consider two preliminary steps essential to *all* phases of an appeal, from its initiation through the briefing phase, and even beyond. These preliminary steps relate to the content of the rules of your specific jurisdiction.

Appealing the decision of a trial court is a complicated process. It involves extensive technical requirements. Before the appellate court will review your client's arguments, it must be satisfied that post-trial motions, briefs, and other filings comply with specific, detailed criteria. This is true in every appellate court, state or federal. Figure 13.1 provides a diagram of the appellate process in the federal court system.

appellate rules
Procedures set forth by the appeals court in processing an appeal.

Fortunately, these criteria are spelled out in the **appellate rules** of each jurisdiction. Although there are many broad similarities among the rules of various appellate courts, a word of caution is in order. There are often significant differences in specific formats, filing deadlines, and other particulars. Furthermore, the rules can be strict in their requirements (see Figure 13.2, which reproduces a section of the Federal Circuit requirements of Rule 32). Failure to follow with precision the rules that apply to your jurisdiction can be fatal to your appeal. Never assume anything; check to make sure.

The *first step* in pursuing an appeal, then, is to obtain a copy of the applicable rules of your jurisdiction, and to verify that they are current.

The *second step*, having obtained the current rules, is obvious but commonly disregarded. Simply stated, you must read the rules, and make sure you understand them.

The importance of the two steps cannot be overemphasized for the preparation of the appellate brief as well as every other aspect of an appeal. They are critical. Although the attorney for whom you work is ultimately responsible for compliance with the rules, your value as an assisting paralegal is directly related to your ability to follow the detailed requirements that govern the appeal process.

FIGURE 13.1 Diagram of Appellate Process in the Federal Court System

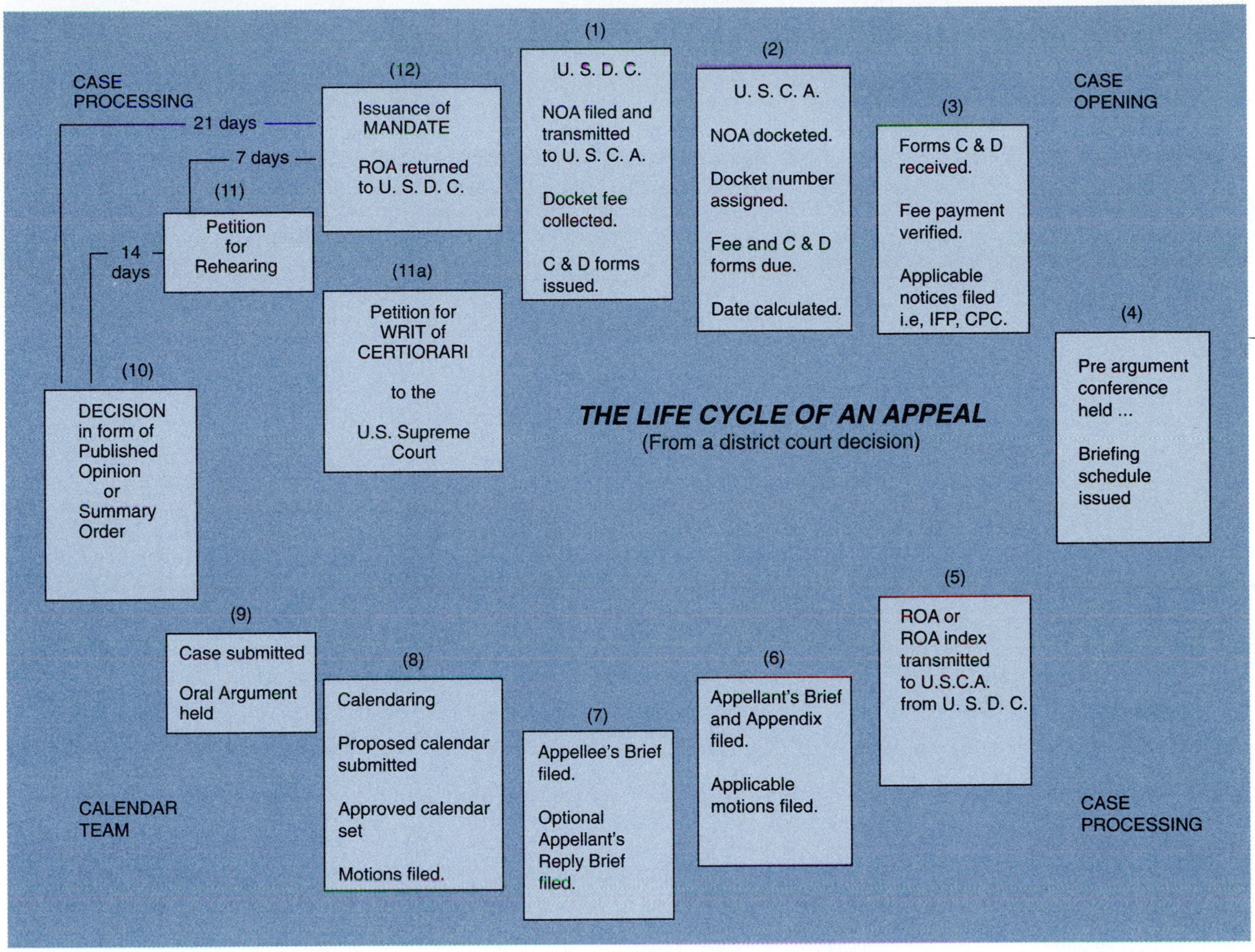

U.S.D.C: United States District Court; U.S.C.A.: United States Court of Appeals; NOA: Notice of Appeal; ROA: Record on Appeal.
Source: United States Court of Appeals for the Seventh Circuit.

What follows is a discussion of those elements of an appellate brief that are in large measure uniform across all jurisdictions. This discussion is intended to provide you with the background and insight necessary to follow your own local rules. Mastering the elements described will prepare you to assist in preparation of an appellate brief. But remember: there is no substitute for a thorough understanding of the precise requirements of the specific appellate court in which your brief will be filed.

Know the rules!

THE APPELLATE BRIEF DEFINED

To understand the purpose of an appellate brief, and thus properly prepare it to achieve your objective, it is necessary to consider the context in which the brief is drafted and the role it plays in the appellate process.

appellate brief
Brief filed in an appeals court.

An **appellate brief** is a legal document filed with an appellate court and drafted so as to persuade that court to decide contested issues in favor of the filing party. The appellate court uses the appellate briefs filed by the parties to gain familiarity with the facts and controlling law of the case. The appellate brief that you and your supervising attorney prepare will not present this information objectively, however, but will argue from your client's viewpoint, with the goal of convincing the court of the validity of your client's position. An example of an appellate brief appears as Figure 13.11 at the end of this chapter.

The Parties to the Appellate Brief

Unless you understand who the parties are in the appellate process, the process is meaningless. Therefore, a quick review of the labels given to the parties in the appellate process is necessary.

FIGURE 13.2
Appellate Brief
Requirements

<u>**Federal Rules of Appellate Procedure**</u>

Rule 32. Form of Briefs, the Appendix, and Other Papers
(a) Form of Briefs and the Appendix. Briefs and appendices may be produced by standard typographic printing or by any duplicating or copying process which produces a clear black image on white paper. Carbon copies of briefs and appendices may not be submitted without permission of the court, except in behalf of parties allowed to proceed in forma pauperis. All printed matter must appear in at least 11 point type on opaque, unglazed paper. Briefs and appendices produced by the standard typographic process shall be bound in volumes having pages 6 1/8 by 9 1/4 inches and type matter 4 1/6 by 7 1/6 inches. Those produced by any other process shall be bound in volumes having pages not exceeding 8 1/2 by 11 inches and type matter not exceeding 6 1/2 by 9 1/2 inches, with double spacing between each line of text. In patent cases the pages of briefs and appendices may be of such size as is necessary to utilize copies of patent documents. Copies of the reporter's transcript and other papers reproduced in a manner authorized by this rule may be inserted in the appendix; such pages may be informally renumbered if necessary.
If briefs are produced by commercial printing or duplicating firms, or, if produced otherwise and the covers to be described are available, the cover of the brief of the appellant should be blue; that of the appellee, red; that of an intervenor or *amicus curiae*, green; that of any reply brief, gray. The cover of the appendix, if separately printed, should be white. The front covers of the briefs and of appendices, if separately printed, shall contain: (1) the name of the court and the number of the case; (2) the title of the case (see Rule 12(a)); (3) the nature of the proceeding in the court (e.g., Appeal; Petition for Review) and the name of the court, agency, or board below; (4) the title of the document (e.g., Brief for Appellant, Appendix); and (5) the names and addresses of counsel representing the party on whose behalf the document is filed.

PRACTICE TIP

The notice of appeal is normally filed with the trial court clerk and not the appellate court unless court rules dictate otherwise.

The Appellant

The appellant is the party who is dissatisfied with the lower court's decision and begins the process by filing a request for appeal or Notice of Appeal. This notice informs the parties and the trial court of the appeal. An example of a Notice of Appeal is presented in Figure 13.3. The notice begins the appellate process. When the Notice of Appeal is properly filed, the succession of deadline dates begins. A missed deadline by an appellant could risk dismissal of the appeal. This point reinforces what was stated earlier in the chapter (page 319): "Know the rules!"

The Appellee

The appellee is the party responding to the appeal. They are satisfied with the decision of the lower court, and for all practical purposes, don't want to be involved. Although critical, the appellee does not drive the process like the appellant. The appellee wants the result of the lower court to be affirmed; remember, they already have a favorable decision.

Petitioner and Respondent

Petitioner
Name designation of the party filing an appeal.

Respondent
Name designation of the party responding to an appeal.

Many appellate courts designate the parties by the terms **Petitioner** and **Respondent.** The Petitioner is the party appealing the lower court's decision, whereas the Respondent is, as the name suggests, responding to the appeal. The rules of the particular appellate court tell you the proper party designation. Review the appellate court rules in your jurisdiction for the proper terms.

After reviewing the arguments set forth in the briefs, the appellate court often allows the parties to elaborate on their positions in oral argument. The attorneys appear before the court and verbally present their competing positions, emphasizing the strong points and clarifying any complex or confusing points. The oral argument stage also enables the appellate judges to directly question the attorneys on specific points that require further explanation.

The appellate court will not always allow oral argument, however. Thus, you must prepare the appellate brief as if it is your only opportunity to present your client's position. Use skill and care; each word must count.

There are two key elements of the context in which the appellate brief is filed: (1) the record and (2) the standard of review.

FIGURE 13.3
Notice of Appeal

Form 1. Notice of Appeal to the United States Court of Appeals for the Federal Circuit from a Judgment or Order of a United States District Court

Name of United States District Court for the_____

Case Number_____

_____, Plaintiff,

v.   **NOTICE OF APPEAL**

_____, Defendant.

Notice is hereby given that _____ (name all parties* taking the appeal) in the above named case hereby appeal to the United States Court of Appeals for the Federal Circuit from the _____ (from the final judgment) ((from an order) (describe the order)) entered in this action on _____, _____ (date).

_____
(Signature of appellant or attorney)

_____
(Address of appellant or attorney)

*See Fed. R. App. P. 3(c) for permissible ways of identifying appellants.

PRACTICE TIP

When a litigant is unrepresented by an attorney, you will see the term *pro se* used. According to *Black's Law Dictionary*, fifth edition, page 1099 (West Publishing Co. 1979), *pro se* means for himself or in his own behalf. Either party may be represented *pro se*. *Pro se* parties are often seen in the criminal setting at the appellate level. *In Fischer v. Cingular Wireless, LLC,* ____ F.3d __ 2006 U.S. App LEXIS 10790, decided May 1, 2006 (7th Cir. 2006), the plaintiff was *pro se* and is identified by the court with that label by stating "Donna Fischer filed a suit Pro se against her former employer, Cingular, charging age and sex discrimination." *Id.* at *1.

record
Documentation of the trial court, including pleadings, physical evidence, transcript, and decision of the trial court.

pleadings
Documents filed in the trial court that set forth the underlying claims of the parties; the complaint, answer to complaint, and reply.

The Record

At trial, having defined the disputed issues in the pleadings, the parties began the presentation of evidence with a blank slate. They could bring to the attention of the court any and all facts that were relevant and material, and were free to cite to any and all legal authorities deemed applicable. With a few technical exceptions, such as failure to disclose information during the discovery stage (which need not concern us here), there were generally no prior restraints on the introduction of evidence, nor was there any limitation on the right to formulate legal arguments.

The situation is quite different on appeal. The parties do not start with a blank slate in an appellate court. *No* new evidence is presented on appeal. The appellate court considers only whether, based upon the evidence and legal arguments already offered in the trial court, the trial court in fact reached the correct conclusion. If a particular piece of evidence or legal argument was not at least offered in the trial court, as a rule it will not be considered by the appellate court.

This brings us to consideration of the **record.** The record is the documentation of the trial, including pleadings; briefs; physical evidence introduced; a transcript of the proceedings, including all witness testimony and judge's rulings on admissibility of evidence and testimony; and the decision of the trial court. It is the record on which the appellate court will rely in evaluating the appeal. A consideration of the individual components of the record is worthwhile.

Pleadings

The **pleadings** appearing in the record include the complaint, which defines the underlying claim; the answer and special defenses, which define the response to the complaint; and all cross-claims and responses thereto. The pleadings establish the bounds of the lawsuit.

Briefs

The briefs filed by the parties in the lower court are often part of the record as well, and can set the stage for the legal arguments addressed in the appellate court.

Discovery

Interrogatories, Request for Admissions, and deposition testimony may be included as part of the record. This information is of particular importance in appeals of Motions for Summary Judgment when the only evidence consists of affidavits, responses to interrogatories, admissions, and deposition testimony.

Physical Evidence

All exhibits admitted into evidence by the trial court, as well as those exhibits offered into evidence but denied admission by the trial court, are part of the record. The issues on appeal often result from the trial court's rulings on admissibility of the physical evidence.

Transcript

transcript
Written account of the proceedings of the trial court.

The **transcript** is a written account of all proceedings in the trial court, including questions and comments of the attorneys; witness testimony; and the judge's rulings and comments. The transcript is usually a stenographic record created by a **court reporter** (who is a court employee certified to record and transcribe court proceedings).

court reporter
Individual who transcribes the court proceedings and certifies their authenticity.

Decision of the Trial Court

The decision of the trial court, and any written opinion of the judge explaining her reasoning, is always a part of the record.

Motion Practice in the Court of Appeals

Unlike the trial courts, motion practice is limited in the court of appeals. There are, however, specific procedures to follow if a motion is filed. The following motions are typical in the court of appeals:

- Motions to Accelerate Appeal. This motion is only used in limited circumstances, such as in an injunction situation where one party may suffer harm if the process is prolonged.
- Motion to Dismiss. Either party may file a Motion to Dismiss. Issues may change; the appeal may be untimely; the court may not have jurisdiction.
- Motion to Supplement the Record. Additional information may be required to be filed. You cannot file additional information without permission of the court.
- Motion to File a Longer Brief. If the brief is anticipated to be longer than the rules permit, a motion requesting permission to file a longer brief is required, or the party risks sanctions being imposed by the court.

PRACTICE TIP

A motion must be filed under particular rules of the court and may have a special color cover sheet to identify it as a motion. Do not risk rejection of a motion for failure to comply with the rules.

The Standard of Review

As stated, the issue on appeal is whether, based on the evidence and legal arguments presented at trial, the trial court decided the case correctly. You and your supervising attorney will be scouring the record to determine whether the lower court made any errors in reaching its conclusion.

You Be the Judge

Hypothetical 13-2

In one case, an appellate court judge refused a motion to file a "fat brief" as he called it. Obviously, the judge was not convinced that the request had merit. In *United States v. Molina-Tarzon*, 285 F.3d 807 (9th Cir. 2002), the attorney represented that he did everything possible to edit his brief to meet the court's page limits. His original brief was 30 pages when the limit was 15 pages. He submitted a 19-page brief with the accompanying motion. The judge chastised the attorney by saying "[c]ounsel's belief that he has exhausted his ability to edit the brief is not a showing of 'diligence and substantial need.' To satisfy the standard, counsel must show that the additional space is justified by something unusual about the issues presented, the record, the applicable case law or some other aspect of the case. Counsel has shown nothing of the sort; nor is it self-evident what this something might be." *Id.* at 808. This case is typical of most judges' disdain for verbose, inarticulate, and often unfounded briefs and motions. Review the case. Why did the judge deny the motion? What are the facts of the case? Were the judge's actions reasonable? Why or why not?

If errors are found and an appeal taken, the appellate court must then evaluate these alleged errors and determine whether reversal of the lower court is justified or, rather, that the lower court be upheld. The guideline that the court applies in evaluating the alleged errors is called the **standard of review.**

There are two types of error to which a standard of review must be applied: errors of fact and errors of law.

Errors of Fact

The parties at trial often present competing versions of the facts. The trial court must sift through the evidence and decide which version of the facts is correct. The party whose version was not accepted by the trial court has the right to appeal the decision, on the ground that the facts as found by the trial court are not supported by the evidence that was admitted—in other words, that there was an **error of fact.** The standard of review by which the appellate court evaluates such an appeal, however, is extremely difficult to satisfy. In general, an appellate court shows great deference to the trial court's judgment with regard to fact finding. Only if the facts found by the court are wholly unsupported by the record can a decision be overturned based on errors of fact. For example, a trial court's factual findings with regard to an injunction application (as in our Case Fact Pattern) will be overturned in most jurisdictions only if the appellate court finds that the trial court's interpretation of the facts constituted an **abuse of discretion,** meaning that it was completely unreasonable and not logically based upon the facts.

Errors of Law

The more common basis of appeal is an **error of law.** Errors of law include procedural errors, in which the trial court allowed the lawsuit to proceed in a manner not authorized by the rules; evidentiary errors, where the court admitted evidence that should have been excluded, or excluded evidence that should have been admitted; and substantive errors, where the court incorrectly interpreted the specific rules of law applicable to the facts of the case. Procedural or evidentiary errors must be shown to have caused harm to the appellant's position for a reversal to be granted (another term for this is that the appellant was "prejudiced" by the error). Otherwise it is considered to be **harmless error,** and the original decision is allowed to stand. Where errors are substantive, the appellate court will generally reverse if its interpretation of the law differs from that of the trial court.

De Novo *Review*

Another standard of review is *de novo.* This word means "a new." When a court reviews an appeal *de novo,* the appeals court reviews the record independent of the trial court's decision. No deference or consideration is given to the trial court's decision. The reviewing appellate court exercises judgment completely separate from the trial court, and makes its own conclusions regarding the facts and law of the case.

Determining the Standard of Review

The question you should ask yourself is, "How do I know which standard of review applies?" The answer is "legal research." Case law, through its many precedents, sets forth the standard of review. The cases often actually say "the standard of review for this action is." You must locate a case that identifies the standard of review for your case and cite that standard and case in your appellate brief. For example, the standard of review for overturning a denial of a temporary injunction is abuse of discretion. The following example is from *Dallas Anesthesiology Associates, P.A. v. Texas Anesthesia Group, P.A.,* 2006 Tex. App. LEXIS 3630, May 1, 2006:

> A. Standard of Review
> Section 51.014(a)(4) of the Texas Civil Practice and Remedies Code permits an interlocutory appeal of a district court's grant or denial of an application for a temporary injunction. TEX. CIV. PRAC. & REM. CODE ANN. § 51.014(a)(4) (Vernon Supp. 2005). The decision to grant or deny an application for a temporary injunction is within the sound discretion of the trial court. *See, e.g., Butnaru v. Ford Motor Co.,* 84 S.W.3d 198, 204, 45 Tex. Sup. Ct. J. 916 (Tex. 2002); *Walling v. Metcalfe,* 863 S.W.2d 56, 57, 37 Tex. Sup. Ct. J. 18 (Tex. 1993) (per curiam); *Wilson N. Jones Mem'l Hosp. v. Huff,* No. 05-03-00596-CV, 2003 Tex. App. LEXIS 8769, 2003 WL 22332387, at *2 (Tex. App.-Dallas, Oct. 14, 2003, pet. [*9] denied) (published, but not

standard of review
Guideline the court applies in evaluating the errors on appeal.

error of fact
Legal standard on appeal alleging the facts accepted by the trial court judge are incorrect.

abuse of discretion
Standard of review on appeal that judge's decision is unreasonable and not logically based upon the facts.

error of law
Standard of review on appeal alleging error of the court in applying the standards of the law.

harmless error
Standard of review that has not caused legal error requiring reversal of the trial court's decision.

de novo
Standard appellate review where the appellate court review the facts and law independent of the trial court's decision.

yet reported in S.W.3d). An appellate court will not reverse a trial court's decision to deny an application for a temporary injunction absent an abuse of discretion. *See, e.g., Butnaru*, 84 S.W.3d at 204; *Walling*, 863 S.W.2d at 58; *Wilson N. Jones Mem'l Hosp.*, 2003 Tex. App. LEXIS 8769, 2003 WL 22332387 at *2.

This excerpt is directly from the case. The case guides you to the standard of review. Similarly, in *Crawford v. Dammann*, 277 Ga. App. 440, 444 626 S.E.2d 632, the standard of review is clearly identified:

> Restrictive covenants on real estate run with the title to the land and are specialized contracts that inure to the benefit of all property owners affected. n2 'The [***7] construction, interpretation and legal effect of [such] a contract . . . is an issue of law' to which the appellate court applies the plain legal error standard of review. n3 Accordingly, we determine de novo whether the trial court correctly ruled that all of the fees at issue were permitted by the Covenants. *Id.* at 444.

And finally, we present a case from a Nebraska Supreme Court showing the same concept. Again, the standard of review is clearly delineated in *Pony Lake School District 30 v. State Committee for the Reorganization of School Districts*, 271 Neb. 173, 179-180, 710 N.W.2d 609 (2006):

> IV. STANDARD OF REVIEW
> [1] An action for injunction sounds in equity. In an appeal of an equity action, an appellate court tries the factual questions de novo on the record and reaches a conclusion independent of [*180] the findings of the trial court. *Denny Wiekhorst Equip. v. Tri-State Outdoor Media*, 269 Neb. 354, 693 N.W.2d 506 (2005).
> [2] The constitutionality of a statute is a question of law, and this court is [***10] obligated to reach a conclusion independent of the decision reached by the trial court. *State v. Diaz*, 266 Neb. 966, 670 N.W.2d 794 (2003).
> [3] Constitutional interpretation is a question of law on which the Nebraska Supreme Court is obligated to reach a conclusion independent of the decision by the trial court. *Hall v. Progress Pig, Inc.*, 259 Neb. 407, 610 N.W.2d 420 (2000).

Format Requirements

Assume that every appeals court has different brief format requirements; in doing this, you will always check the rules of court before proceeding in the appeal. The federal appeals are different from the state appeals; state appeals differ among the fifty-plus jurisdictions in the country. Many appeals courts, both federal and state, have local appellate rules that supplement the primary appellate rules of that jurisdiction. The slightest misstep can jeopardize a case resulting in dismissal—starting to get the "big" picture? Appeals are complex and the rules only add to the complexity. The rules dictate the spacing, the font, the margins, and the paper, to name just a few requirements. And, the judges *do* notice the presentation of your brief. Also, notice the rules even provide instruction on how to assemble the brief, such as the type of binding. Never use staples, paper clips, or other improper fasteners. Do not overlook even the smallest detail. The court will notice. Appellate courts are notorious and particular about following their rules to the letter. Review Figure 13.4, which sets forth the appellate rules for the state of Oregon. Notice the rules detail. Strict compliance is the rule of the day.

FIGURE 13.4
Appellate Court Rules for the State of Oregon

Rule 5.05
SPECIFICATIONS FOR BRIEFS

(1) Briefs, including petitions for review or reconsideration in the Supreme Court, shall be reproduced by any duplicating process that makes a clear, legible, black image; the Administrator will not accept carbon copies, copies on slick paper, or copies darkened by the duplicating process.

(2) (a) No opening, answering, or combined brief shall exceed 50 pages. That limitation does not include the index, excerpt of record, or appendix.

(b) A party's excerpt of record or appendix or combined excerpt of record and appendix shall not exceed 50 pages.

(c) No reply brief shall exceed 15 pages.

(d) Unless the court orders otherwise, no supplemental brief shall exceed five pages.

FIGURE 13.4
Cont.

[text omitted]

(4) All briefs shall conform to these requirements:

(a) Front and back covers shall be paper of at least 65-pound weight. The cover of the brief shall be:
(i) For an opening brief, blue;
(ii) For an answering brief, red;
(iii) For a combined answering and cross-opening brief, violet;
(iv) For a reply or combined reply and answering brief on cross-appeal, or an answering brief to a cross-assignment of error under Rule 5.57, gray;
(v) For the brief of an intervenor, the color of the brief of the party on whose side the intervenor is appearing;
(vi) For the brief of *amicus curiae*, green;
(vii) For a supplemental brief, the same color as the primary brief.
(viii) For a petition for review or reconsideration in the Supreme Court, yellow;
(ix) For a response to a petition for review or reconsideration in the Supreme Court, orange;
(x) For a brief on the merits of a petitioner on review in the Supreme Court, white;
(xi) For a brief on the merits of a respondent on review in the Supreme Court, tan.

(b) The front cover shall set forth the full title of the case, the appropriate party designations as the parties appeared below and as they appear on appeal, the case number assigned below, the case number assigned in the appellate court, designation of the party on whose behalf the brief is filed, the court from which the appeal is taken, the name of the judge thereof, and the names, bar numbers, addresses, and telephone numbers of counsel for the parties and the name, address, and telephone number of a party appearing pro se. The lower right corner of the brief shall state the month and year in which the brief was filed.

(c) Pages and covers shall be a uniform size of 8-1/2 x 11 inches.

(d) Paper for the text of the brief shall be white bond, regular finish without glaze, and at least 20-pound weight with surface suitable for both pen and pencil notation. If both sides of the paper are used for text, the paper shall be sufficiently opaque to prevent the material on one side from showing through on the other.

(e) Printed or used area on a page shall not exceed 6-1/4 x 9-1/2 inches, exclusive of page numbers, with inside margin 1-1/4 inches, outside margin 1 inch, top and bottom margins 3/4 inch.

(f) Briefs shall be legible and capable of being read without difficulty. Briefs may be prepared using either uniformly spaced type (such as produced by typewriters) or proportionally spaced type (such as produced by commercial printers and many computer printers). Uniformly spaced type shall not exceed 10 characters per inch (cpi). If proportionally spaced type is used, it shall not be smaller than 12 point for both the text of the brief and footnotes. Reducing or condensing the typeface in a manner that would increase the number of words in a brief is not permitted. Briefs printed entirely or substantially in uppercase are not acceptable. All briefs shall be double-spaced with double space above and below each paragraph of quotation.

(g) The last page of the brief shall contain the name and signature of the author of the brief, the name of the law firm or firms, if any, representing the party, and the name of the party or parties on whose behalf the brief is filed.

(h) Pages shall be consecutively numbered at the top of the page within 3/8 inch from the top of the page. Pages of the excerpt of record shall be numbered independently of the body of the brief, and each page number shall be preceded by "ER," *e.g.,* ER-1, ER-2, ER-3. Pages of appendices shall be preceded by "App," *e.g.,* App-1, App-2, App-3.

(i) A brief shall be bound in a manner that allows the pages of the brief to lie flat when the brief is open, as provided in this paragraph. Regardless of whether a brief is prepared with text on one or both sides of the pages, the brief may be bound with a plastic comb binding, with the binding to be within 3/8 inch of the left edge of the brief. A brief also

FIGURE 13.4
Cont.

may be bound by stapling if the brief is prepared with text only on one side of each page or if the brief is prepared with text on both sides of the pages and does not exceed 20 pages (10 pieces of paper), excluding the cover but including the index, the excerpt of record and any appendix. A brief bound by stapling shall be secured by a single staple placed as close to the upper left-hand corner as is consistent with securely binding the brief.

(5) The court on its own motion may strike any brief that does not comply with this rule.

[Footnotes omitted]

Source: Oregon Rules of Appellate Procedure, amended January 1, 2005.

THE SECTIONS OF AN APPELLATE BRIEF

Several basic sections to an appellate brief are required by the rules of virtually all appellate courts. Though the precise title of each section, as well as its order of appearance in the finished brief, may differ between jurisdictions, the substantive content is universal. Keeping in mind, then, that you should refer to your own local rules for specific guidance, what follows is a general discussion of the sections:

- Title or Cover Page
- Certificate of Interested Parties
- Table of Contents
- Table of Authorities
- Jurisdictional Statement
- Statement of the Case
- Questions Presented
- Statement of Facts
- Summary of the Argument
- Argument
- Conclusion
- Signature Block
- Certificate of Compliance with Length Requirement
- Certificate of Service
- Appendix

You Be the Judge

Hypothetical 13-3

Another attorney on appeal earned the wrath of a judge for failing to comply with the format and substantive requirements of the rules of that jurisdiction. In *Catellier v. Depco, Inc.,* 696 N.E.2d 75 (Ind. App. 1998), the attorney was sanctioned and had to pay attorney's fees to the other party for his failure to conform to the rules. The court found that the attorney committed bad faith. In its *dicta,* the court found "[p]rocedural bad faith 'is present when a party flagrantly disregards the form and content requirements of the Rules of Appellate Procedure, omits and misstates relevant facts appearing in the record, and files briefs appearing to have been written in a manner calculated to require the maximum expenditure of time both by the opposing party and the reviewing court.' Conduct can be classified as procedural bad faith even if it falls short of being deliberate or by design.'" *Id.* at 79. This case is yet another of an attorney falling short in his professional responsibilities. Review the case. What are the facts of the case? What facts led the court to impose sanctions on the attorney? What rules did the attorney violate?

Title or Cover Page

title page
Cover page of the brief.

The first page of an appellate brief is called the **title page** or the cover page. The title page identifies

- the *court* in which the appeal is pending;
- the *lower court* in which the case originated;
- the *names of the parties* involved in the appeal;
- the *docket number* of the case;
- the name of the *party on whose behalf* the brief is being filed;
- the name of the *attorney* or *law firm* filing the brief; and
- the *date* of filing.

Some courts also require that, if oral argument is desired, it be requested on the title page. If your appeal is pending in such a court, failure to include this request may waive your client's right to demand oral argument at a later stage. This can damage the outcome of the appeal. Part of your responsibility as a paralegal, then, is to know your jurisdiction's rule for requesting oral argument.

When the list of parties involved in an appeal is long, some jurisdictions allow the use of the abbreviation *et al.,* which means "and others," to substitute for a full listing. Again, check your local rules.

A question always arises as to the order in which parties are listed in the appellate caption. In the past, the party making the appeal was generally listed first. This could lead to confusion when a defendant was making the appeal, however, since a case known as *Smith v. Jones* in the trial court (with Smith being the plaintiff and Jones the defendant) would become *Jones v. Smith* in the appellate court. The modern practice is to retain the caption order as it appeared in the lower court and simply identify the parties as appellant or appellee. Of course, you must check your own local rules on this point.

Some courts require that the color of the title page correspond to the status of the filing party. Thus, an appellant might have a light blue title page, an appellee a red title page, and an

FIGURE 13.5
Format of Title Page

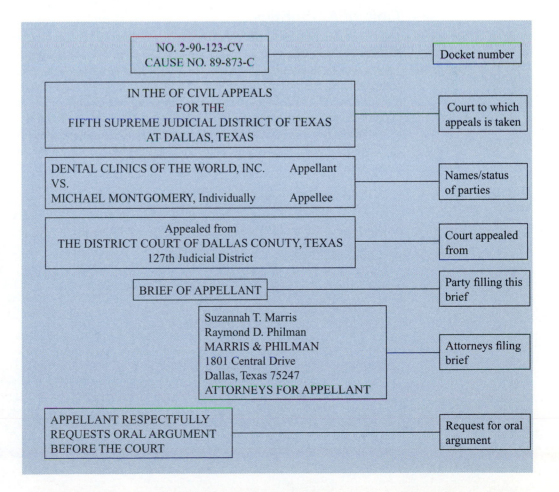

amicus curiae
Brief filed by a nonparty known as a "friend of the court."

amicus curiae (literally, "friend of the court," discussed later in the chapter) a green title page. Jurisdictions are not consistent on this practice, so again you must check.

A title page of an appellant's brief appears in Figure 13.5, with various components identified.

Certificate of Interested Parties or Disclosure Statement

certificate of interested parties
Statement in a brief identifying parties who have an interest in the outcome and financial affiliations.

The **certificate of interested parties** or **disclosure statement** identifies all those parties to the case who have an interest in the outcome. It appears immediately after the title page (see Figure 13.11 at the end of this chapter) and is intended to provide the appellate judge with an opportunity to determine the existence of a conflict between her own financial and personal interests and those of a party to the appeal.

recusal
Voluntary disqualification by a judge due to a conflict of interest or the appearance of one.

If the judge determines that a conflict exists, she will exercise the **recusal** option. A recusal occurs when the judge voluntarily disqualifies herself from further participation in the disposition of the case.

Some jurisdictions do not require the certificate of interested parties. Check your local rules.

Table of Contents

table of contents
Road map of the appellate brief, which includes the section headings and corresponding page numbers in the brief.

Although the **table of contents** exists primarily to identify section headings with corresponding page numbers, it is far more than just an index. It is, rather, a concise outline of your client's contentions, the road map by which the court will follow the path of your argument.

The "road map" objective is achieved through expanded reference to the "argument" section. As will be discussed further, point headings and subpoint headings in the argument section identify, in an orderly and logical fashion, the rationale behind your client's position on appeal. In the table of contents, the complete text of each of these headings is set forth. Thus, simply by referring to the table of contents the court will be able to learn the broad parameters of your argument before exploring the details. Review the table of contents that appears in Figure 13.6.

Although the table of contents is one of the first sections to appear in your brief, it is one of the last sections you will draft. This is because page numbers, and perhaps even the text of the point headings, will not be finalized until you approach completion of the project.

Table of Authorities

table of authorities
Section of the appellate brief that identifies the cases, statutes, constitutional provisions, and all other primary and secondary authority contained within the brief.

The term **table of authorities** refers to the cases, statutes, constitutional provisions, and all other primary and secondary sources that are cited in your brief. Since both the court and opposing parties will be examining these sources in detail, it is useful to have an easily referenced list. Although the requirements for the table of authorities may vary in different jurisdictions, Table 13.1 provides a common format. References appearing in the table of authorities should be drafted in conformity with the rules of *The Bluebook* or *ALWD Manual* unless your appellate court has its own special requirements. The table should also reference every page on which each authority appears in the brief. (See sample appellate brief in Figure 13.11 at the end of this chapter.)

FIGURE 13.6
Table of Contents

Table of Contents

Certificate of Interested Parties
Table of Contents
Table of Authorities
Statement of the Nature of the Case
Questions Presented
Fact Statement
Argument and Authorities

    I.   The trial court abused its discretion by not granting the temporary injunction
    II. Texas prohibits the use of trade secrets and confidential proprietary information when misappropriated by a corporate officer
        A. A trade secret, by definition, may be a compilation, including a customer list
        B. An injunction is an appropriate remedy for misappropriation of trade secrets and for the breach of a fiduciary relationship

Conclusion
Certificate of Service

TABLE 13.1
Table of Authorities

Case opinions	Judicial decisions are listed first and *alphabetically* (some states require cases ranked by court: The U.S. Supreme Court, the U.S. Courts of Appeal, etc.). List each page number where case appears.
Constitutional provisions	Federal constitutional provisions are listed first, with state constitutional provisions to follow. List the provisions in descending numerical order.
Statutory provisions	Federal statutory provisions are listed after constitutional provisions; state statutes follow. As with the constitutional provisions, list in descending numerical order.
Secondary authority	Secondary authorities are listed last, alphabetically by author. Secondary authorities range from legal periodicals to treatises, and include all other sources that are neither case decisions, constitutional provisions, nor statutes.

Along with the table of contents, the table of authorities is one of the last sections prepared. Accuracy in both is important. If inaccurate and sloppy, they will undermine the court's confidence in the credibility of your arguments. Figure 13.7 sets forth the rules in the First Circuit Court of Appeals for citing cases, law review articles, and unpublished cases. Notice the strict requirements of the court.

Preparing these tables is a task often left to paralegals. Great care should be taken.

FIGURE 13.7
Citation Requirements of the First Circuit Court of Appeals

Local Rule 32.2 Citation of State Decisions and Law Review Articles
All citations to State or Commonwealth Courts must include both the official state court citation and the National Reporter System citation when such decisions have been published in both reports; e.g., Coney v. Commonwealth, 364 Mass. 137, 301 N.E.2d 450 (1973). Law review or other articles unpublished at the time a brief or memorandum is filed may not be cited therein, except with permission of the court.

Local Rule 32.3 Citation of Unpublished Opinions
(a) An unpublished opinion of this court may be cited in this court only in the following circumstances:
(1) When the earlier opinion is relevant to establish a fact about the case. An unpublished opinion of this court may be cited to establish a fact about the case before the court (for example, its procedural history) or when the binding or preclusive effect of the opinion, rather than its quality as precedent, is relevant to support a claim of res judicata, collateral estoppel, law of the case, double jeopardy, abuse of the writ, or other similar doctrine.
(2) Other circumstances. Citation of an unpublished opinion of this court is disfavored. Such an opinion may be cited only if (1) the party believes that the opinion persuasively addresses a material issue in the appeal; and (2) there is no published opinion from this court that adequately addresses the issue. The court will consider such opinions for their persuasive value but not as binding precedent.
(3) Procedure. A party must note in its brief or other pleading that the opinion is unpublished, and a copy of the opinion or disposition must be included in an accompanying addendum or appendix.
(4) Definition. Almost all new opinions of this court are published in some form, whether in print or electronic medium. The phrase "unpublished opinion of this court" as used in this subsection and Local Rule 36(c) refers to an opinion (in the case of older opinions) that has not been published in the West Federal Reporter series, e.g., F., F.2d, and F.3d, or (in the case of recent opinions) bears the legend "not for publication" or some comparable phraseology indicating that citation is prohibited or limited.
(b) Unpublished or non-precedential opinions of other courts, as defined or understood by those courts, may be cited in the circumstances set forth in subsection (a)(1) above. Such opinions may also be cited in circumstances analogous to those set forth in subsection (a)(2) above, unless prohibited by the rules of the issuing court. If an unpublished or non-precedential opinion of another court is cited, the party must comply with the procedure set forth in subsection (a)(3) above.

Jurisdictional Statement

The **jurisdictional statement** identifies the legal authority that grants to the appellate court jurisdiction over the appeal. It usually makes reference to the statute establishing the right of appeal. The jurisdiction conferred by such a statute is a prerequisite to the appeal. (See Figure 13.11 at the end of this chapter.)

Statement of the Case

The **statement of the case** sets forth the procedural history of the case. It identifies the lower court or courts in which the case has been heard and the decision of each. It is analogous to the "prior proceedings" section of a case brief. (See Figure 13.11 at the end of this chapter.)

There are several different titles in use for this section besides "statement of the case." Others include "preliminary statement," "nature of the action," or "nature of the case." The case history information is also frequently incorporated into the statement of facts.

Your statement of the case should include the following items:

- A concise statement of the nature of the cause of action (one or two sentences), not to be confused with the detailed statement of facts.

- Whether the appeal is from a court trial, a jury trial, or a hearing.

- The name of the court whose decision is being appealed.

- The name of other courts that have had jurisdiction over the case, and the nature of their disposition.

- The name of the party bringing the appeal.

Questions Presented

In the **questions presented** section of the brief, you provide the appellate court with a convenient, concise statement of the grounds upon which the decision of the trial court is being questioned. For each ground, there should be a separately numbered question.

Although at first glance it might appear that drafting these questions is an objective task, in fact, you should be applying your persuasive skills. The questions should be framed so as to suggest an answer that favors your client. Useful techniques include

- identifying the erroneous ruling of the lower court and suggesting, in question form, the result you seek;

- keeping the questions short, clear, and succinct;

- presenting separate issues in separate questions; and

- identifying the applicable standard of review.

The "questions presented" section is sometimes referred to as "points of error," "issues presented," or "assignments of error." As always, check your local rules.

In Figure 13.8, two questions are set forth that were drafted by opposing sides on the same appeal. Note the manner in which the appellant and appellee have stated the same basic issue in a contrasting, and partisan, fashion.

Statement of Facts

The **statement of facts** is the first of the two major sections of the appellate brief, the other being the argument. In it you set forth the background information and significant facts of your client's case, so that the appellate court has a clear factual framework within which to consider the legal questions presented. (See Figure 13.11 at the end of this chapter.)

FIGURE 13.8

Examples of Contrasting Versions of a "Question Presented"

From the appellant's perspective:
Did the District Court err and abuse its discretion by denying appellant's application for a temporary injunction, since appellant proved a probable right and probable injury and thereby established sufficient grounds to impose an injunction and preserve the status quo?

From the appellee's perspective:
Was the District Court correct in denying plaintiff's request for an injunction?

The statement of facts is not based upon your memory of events in the case, nor is it based upon those facts which you believe you can prove, since there is no opportunity to "prove" facts on appeal. It is based, rather, on the record of the case. If a fact is not contained in the record of the case, then, for the purposes of the appellate court, that fact simply doesn't exist.

There are two key points to remember in drafting your statement of facts:

- Every fact set forth should be followed by a reference in parentheses to that portion of the record in which the fact appears.

- The statement of facts should be drafted in a persuasive fashion, setting forth the facts in a light most favorable to your client, while at the same time remaining accurate, straightforward, and faithful to the record.

The first of these points, making reference to the record, is easy to understand but often difficult to accomplish. The record of a trial court can be bulky. Many trials are lengthy, and the transcript can run to hundreds of pages or more, with a large number of exhibits. Sometimes the exhibits themselves are lengthy and complicated documents, the meaning of which is disputed by the parties.

There is no magic solution to mastering the record. Simply stated, you must study the transcript and exhibits until you develop a full understanding of their content. It is likely that, in your role as a paralegal, you will be responsible for having a good working knowledge of the record. You will be expected to locate references quickly. Your supervising attorney may draft a statement of facts without parenthetical references, and then expect you to provide the missing information.

indexing method
Referencing method of the record to assist in identifying the important pieces of information, such as the transcript excerpts and pleadings, which will be used in the various parts of the appellate brief.

One method that is useful for mastering the record is the **indexing method.** By preparing an index to the transcript—for example, identifying (1) the party testifying, (2) the attorney conducting the examination, (3) the content of the testimony, and (4) the transcript page on which the testimony appears, you will have a useful shorthand reference enabling you to locate specific items quickly. An index can also be used to summarize documentary exhibits.

Indexes are sometimes also called "digests." Although some might say that a "digest" suggests a summary more detailed than an index, the difference is largely semantic, and the purpose of each is identical—namely, to summarize a lengthier document.

Different appellate courts have different rules with regard to referencing the record. For example, references to the transcript might be identified by "(T-78)," meaning "page 78 of the transcript," or a variation such as "(R-78)," meaning "page 78 of the record." You should check your local rules for the appropriate style in your jurisdiction.

Though a tedious task, providing comprehensive parenthetical references is very important to the success of your brief. By identifying all those portions of the record that support your factual claims, you not only provide a useful summary of the record but also establish credibility in the eyes of the court. A thorough and well-referenced statement of facts provides the foundation on which you build your arguments and persuade the appellate court.

The second point requires that your statement of facts be not only honest and accurate but also partisan. Although on the face of it this might seem to be inconsistent, in fact it goes to the essence of persuasive legal writing. In order to set the stage for your legal arguments, you want the court to interpret the facts in a light most favorable to your client. At the same time, you do not want the court to think that you are distorting the record. In order to accomplish these objectives, you should employ several techniques:

- Set forth the facts in chronological order, which is the easiest and most logical to follow.

- Emphasize those facts which support your client's position.

- When negative facts are essential to an accurate presentation, resist the temptation to omit them, since this will erode your credibility in the eyes of the court (you can be sure that the other side will draw such facts to the court's attention anyway). You should address these negative facts in such a way that their impact is minimized.

Summary of the Argument

A concise summary of the argument is required prior to the argument section of the brief. In this section, those arguments presented in the body of the argument are summarized for the court. This section should not be merely a restatement of the issues, but a well-thought-out, accurate

You Be the Judge
Hypothetical 13-4

Proper referencing of the facts in your appellate brief is important. The attorney in *Hurlbert v. Gordon*, 824 P.2d 1238 (Wash. App. 1992), learned the hard way that failure to cite specific references to the record is inexcusable, resulting in sanctions by the appeals court. Apparently, in *Hurlbert*, the record on appeal was voluminous—some 6,000 pages. The rules, like all appellate rules, require reference to the record when establishing facts on appeal. The judge cited the purpose behind the rule and admonished the attorney for forcing the court and opposing counsel to wade through the mass of court pages. As the court warned: "[s]everal references were made to 20- or 50- or 100-page documents rather than to specific pages of the record relating to the particular factual statements made." *Id.* at 1245. Opposing counsel was forced to request permission to file a 95-page responding brief because of the complexity of the issues and lack of references in the case. Because of the attorney's behavior, the judge ordered a fine. Read the case. Identify the facts of the case. What are the ethical issues addressed in the case? What rules of appellate procedure were violated?

account of the legal argument in the brief. This section is your "snapshot" of the brief. Treat this section as if this were the only section the court was going to read. Be precise. Choose your words carefully. Don't restate what you have already stated in the main argument section. This section should be no more than a paragraph or two.

Argument

argument
Section of the brief where the issues are analyzed through citation of legal authorities.

The most important section of the appellate brief is known as the **argument.** In this section you analyze the legal issues raised by the "questions presented" section and interpret the applicable cases and statutes to demonstrate that your client's position should prevail on appeal.

The argument section of an appellate brief is the highest point of persuasive legal writing. Its preparation represents the climax of all your training in written advocacy. The success or failure of your appeal will turn in large measure on your ability to state logically and forcefully, in writing, your client's position. Every stylistic decision has an impact; every substantive choice a consequence; every word an effect.

The argument section comprises two components, the point headings and the body. (See Figure 13.11 at the end of this chapter.)

Point Headings

Recall from Chapter 12 that point headings are brief synopses of the argument to follow, set apart from the body of the brief by underlines or type style. (See Figure 13.11 at the end of this chapter.) They perform both a stylistic function, in that they divide the brief into distinct sections for easier reading, and a substantive function, in that they separate the argument into logical components. They provide concise answers to the questions posed in the "questions presented" section, thus giving the court a preview of the detailed argument, and in general, introduce the complex reasoning to follow.

The level of complexity of the brief determines the number of point headings. Isolate the distinct legal issues presented, and begin the discussion of each separate issue with a new point heading.

If the discussion of a given legal issue is complex, you may need subpoint headings as well. In deciding whether subpoint headings are needed, you must keep in mind that too many subpoint headings may actually confuse the reader. If you decide that subpoint headings are justified, choose a format or type style that clearly distinguishes subpoint headings from point headings, so as to maintain clarity.

The brief in Figure 13.11 at the end of this chapter shows both point headings and subpoint headings. In reviewing this brief, note both the substantive content of the headings and the manner in which capitalization, indenting, spacing, and underlining are used to differentiate headings from the body, and point headings from subpoint headings.

Body

body
Main text of the argument section of the appellate brief.

The **body** of the argument is the section in which the main text is set forth. (See Figure 13.11 at the end of this chapter.) It is here that you inform the court of the detailed arguments that support your client's position.

The sole purpose of the body of the brief is to present the law so as to persuade the court. Although this purpose may appear obvious, many attorneys and paralegals lose sight of this consideration when drafting a brief. The problem arises as a result of the interpretation that the drafter attaches to the term "detailed argument." Appellate courts often see briefs that exhaustively document the issue presented, but fail to persuade. You must keep in mind that your job is not to draft a treatise on the issues raised, but rather to persuade the court to resolve the issues in favor of your client. This requires that you cite essential sources and discuss relevant concepts, hence the word "detailed." It does not require that you cite every source, nor discuss every concept, that might arguably be deemed relevant to your brief. Say what you have to say and move on. A former Judge Ruggero J. Aldisert, Senior United States Circuit Judge of the United States Court of Appeals for the Third Circuit, in his book *Winning on Appeal, Second Edition* (National Institute for Trial Advocacy, 2003) quoted a University of Vermont Professor Robert Huber who taught debate. He explained to his debate students a "schematic N-E-P-C," which means "NAME IT, EXPLAIN IT, PROVE IT, CONCLUDE IT." *Ibid.* at p. 23. These are words to remember and live by when writing an appellate or trial brief. Judges want you to get to the point and tell them what you want. They do not want to scour through your brief trying to figure out the issues and the arguments. Before you begin to write, think about the result you want and how best to achieve that result. Place yourself in the shoes of the judge, who has to read hundreds of briefs over the course of a year. You would want the writer to present the legal argument in as few words as possible.

If the issue presented is not complex (or even in many cases where it *is* complex), it is possible that one or two controlling cases and one or two applicable statutes may adequately define and support your argument. If you address such a context in an excessively complicated manner, you dilute the impact of these essential authorities.

Remember that deciding upon the final content of a brief is often a balancing act between simplifying the issues for ease of understanding on the one hand, and accurately reflecting the state of the law on the other. Your goal is a brief that is easy to understand, thorough, and an accurate and defensible representation of the law—in a word, *persuasive*. In achieving this goal, you should follow the basic rules and techniques of writing that we addressed in previous chapters, including clarity and brevity. In addition, keep in mind the following points:

- Place your strongest point first. Write in a manner that is easily understood. Do not pontificate. Remember keep your reader's interest and attention.

- The court will be relying on precedent, not your personal theories. When the law is on your side, *tell* the court. When it is not, distinguish the precedents by pointing out factual or other differences between their context and that of your appeal. It is almost always advisable to avoid the temptation to improvise theory.

- Where the case law is against you, argue that "justice and fair play" compel the court to find for your client and reverse the precedents. This is the so-called "equitable argument".

- *Never* misrepresent facts or case law to the court.

- A court is often persuaded by "public policy arguments." Whether your case is supported by precedent or not, it is always useful to show the court how a decision in your favor will benefit the public interest.

string citations
List of citations in the brief following a point of law cited.

- **String citations** (long lists of cases that you claim support your point) may actually undercut your argument, if the significance of the most important precedent is diluted. The trend is to cite the one best and most recent case for your point.

Conclusion

conclusion
Short statement at the end of the brief telling the appeals court the relief requested.

The **conclusion** is a brief statement appearing after the "argument" section. It does not summarize your argument, but rather "respectfully submits" that, based upon the logic of your argument, the court must grant the relief you desire. All the sections of your brief lead to the conclusion, which convinces the court to grant the relief requested, *e.g.,* reverse, vacate, or affirm the lower court's decision. In other words, the appellant concludes that the trial court should be reversed, whereas the appellee concludes that it should be upheld.

The key here is to be specific. Do not leave the court to guess at the relief you seek—*tell* the court. (See Figure 13.11 at the end of this chapter.)

Signature Block

signature block
Section of the brief for attorney's signature that includes the name, address, bar card identification, fax, and telephone number.

The **signature block** provides a line for the signature of the attorney who is ultimately responsible for the brief. His name, bar card identification number, address, fax, and telephone number are typed below the signature. The client on whose behalf the brief is filed is also identified and sometimes other information as well. (See Figure 13.11 at the end of this chapter.) Check your local rules for the specific requirements in your jurisdiction.

Certificate of Compliance with Length Requirements

certificate of compliance
Attorney certification at the end of an appellate brief attesting to compliance with the page limitations set forth by that court's rules.

It will come as no surprise that all briefs have page limitations. Now, the federal courts of appeal require a **certificate of compliance** at the end of a brief that attests to the page limits. This requirement is set out in Federal Rules of Appellate Procedure Rule 32(A)(7). The certification tells the court that not only the page limits are met, but also that footnotes were not used to undercut the page limitations. See Figure 13.9 for an example of a Certificate of Compliance. Check state appellate rules for similar requirements.

Certificate of Service

certificate of service
Acknowledgment at the end of the brief that the brief was sent to the opposing counsel in accordance with the rules of the appellate court.

Discussed in previous chapters, the **certificate of service** is an acknowledgment at the end of any court-filed document, including an appellate brief, verifying delivery of the document to all persons entitled to a copy, and identifying the date and type of service. (See Figure 13.11 at the end of this chapter.) Mail delivery is usually sufficient.

Those entitled to service generally include the attorneys in the case, as well as parties who represent themselves without the assistance of an attorney. Sometimes the certification must also verify that a copy was served upon the court.

The certificate of service is attested to by the attorney filing the brief. Your local rules will provide specific guidance.

Appendix

appendix
Contains the supplementary collection of the sources from the trial court.

Appellate briefs often contain an **appendix,** which is a supplementary collection of primary source materials. Most of these materials are taken from the record. In many jurisdictions it is mandatory to include certain portions of the record in the appendix, for example, those pages from the transcript that are referenced in the text of the appellate brief.

The appendix appears as the last section in the brief. In addition to transcript pages, it often contains relevant passages from pleadings, evidentiary exhibits introduced at trial, and the lower court's judgment and opinion.

PRACTICE TIP

Most courts require a "joint appendix." This is often a requirement of the rules of the court. Each of the parties to the appeal must confer regarding the portions of the trial court record that should be included for review by the appellate court. When the appellant refuses to include some portion of the trial court record requested by the appellee, a supplemental appendix may be filed, usually through a motion.

FIGURE 13.9   **Certificate of Compliance with Length Requirements**

SAMPLE CERTIFICATE OF COMPLIANCE REQUIRED BY FRAP 32(A)(7)(C)

If your principal brief exceeds 30 pages of your reply exceeds 15 pages, you must include a certificate of compliance within the brief, immediately preceding the certificate of service. You may use the following certificate:

CERTIFICATE OF COMPLIANCE

I certify that this brief complies with the type-volume limitation set forth in FRAP 32(a)(7)(B). This brief contains ＿＿＿ words.

Or, if you are using a monospaced face, you may instead use the following certificate:

CERTIFICATE OF COMPLIANCE

I certify that this brief complies with the type-volume limitation set forth in FRAP 32(a)(7)(B). This brief uses a monospaced face and contains ＿＿＿ lines of text.

With either certificate, you must fill in the blank line; you may rely on the word or line count of the word-processing system used to prepare the brief.

Source: United States Eleventh Circuit Court of Appeals.

THE FOUR CATEGORIES OF APPELLATE BRIEFS

All appellate briefs share the same basic characteristics outlined. The approach to drafting a specific appellate brief, however, varies somewhat with the procedural status of your client. An appellant, for example, takes a different approach than an appellee, whereas the brief filed by an *amicus curiae* has its own unique emphasis. The stage at which a brief is filed also affects its content, a reply brief being a different creature altogether from an opening brief. It is worthwhile to take a moment and review the differences in emphasis among the four categories of appellate brief: appellant's; appellee's; the reply brief; and that of the *amicus curiae*.

Appellant's Brief

appellant's brief
Brief of the party filing the appeal.

The appellant, as you recall, is the party making the appeal. It is the appellant who asserts that the decision of the trial court must be overturned. Almost without exception, the **appellant's brief** will be filed first. Thus the appellant has the opportunity to set the tone of the appeal and define the issues that will be brought before the appellate court. Although this might appear to be an advantage, any edge inferred is offset by the fact that the appellant is seeking to overturn the judgment of a trial court that has carefully considered the issues and found for the other side. The burden of proving the trial court wrong is on the appellant.

Appellee's Brief

appellee's brief
Brief of the party responding to the appeal.

The **appellee's brief** is filed in response to the appellant's brief. Thus the appellee has the appellant's brief in hand as the response is prepared. This enables the appellee to review and attack the specific arguments made by the appellant. In addition to attacking the arguments of the appellant, the appellee should also set forth independent reasons that demonstrate why the lower court should be upheld.

Reply Brief

reply brief
Short responsive brief of the appellant to the appellee's brief.

The term **reply brief** could be attached to any brief filed by a party in response to an earlier brief filed by an opposing party. The appellee's opening brief is thus technically a reply brief, since it is filed after, and in response to, the appellant's brief. In general, however, the term reply brief refers to a brief filed by the appellant in response to the appellee's opening brief.

The justification for allowing such a reply brief is simple. It would be unfair to deny the appellant an opportunity to respond to the arguments of the appellee, since the appellee had the opportunity to review and attack the arguments set forth in the appellant's first brief. Hence the appellant is authorized to file a reply brief.

When preparing a reply brief, the appellant should resist the temptation to restate arguments already set forth in the first brief. The court will not forget these earlier arguments. Rather, the appellant should concentrate on addressing issues raised for the first time in the appellee's brief. It is similarly inappropriate (although probably prudent) for the appellant to raise points in the reply brief that it failed, through negligence or oversight, to address in the opening brief. If such points are raised in the reply brief, the court may allow the appellee another chance to respond, or disregard the new points entirely.

Amicus Curiae Brief

amicus brief
Brief filed by a nonparty to an appeal who has an interest, whether political, social, or otherwise, in the outcome of the case.

An *amicus curiae* is a person or organization that was not directly involved in the lawsuit between the parties, but which has an interest in the outcome of the appeal and has succeeded in petitioning the court for the right to file a brief on the issues presented. An *amicus* **brief** (as it is often called) may correspond to any of the other three categories of brief, depending on whose interest the *amicus* brief mirrors and what stage the appeal has reached. One difference between the *amicus* brief and others is that the *amicus* brief argues from a public policy viewpoint. This type of brief is most common in the U.S. Supreme Court, where significant legal and public policy issues arise that often change the course of history. Recall *Brown v. Board of Education* (separate is not equal—segregation), *Roe v. Wade* (abortion), *U.S. v. Nixon* (Watergate), and *Bakke v. California Board of Regents* (reverse discrimination), to name a few.

WRITING THE BRIEF

Regardless of whether you are appellant or appellee, the writing process does not change. You must be vigilant in both your preparatory work as well as your concluding review. Practice what you have learned by performing these tasks:

- Analyze the issues on appeal with your supervising attorney; this preliminary step in an appeal is critical to determine whether an appealable issue exists.
- Review the current appellate rules of court and any local appellate rules; check the court's website, if one is available, to determine any recent changes.
- Determine your timetable and time limitations; appellate cases have specific time constraints, such as when to file a Notice of Appeal, the briefs of the parties, and the record. Prepare a graph, diagram, or schematic to help you keep track of the court-imposed deadlines. Check the deadline schedule daily.
- Research the law; identify the standard of review, which is one of the first critical steps in beginning the appeals process. Choose cases that best represent the legal position forwarded on the client's behalf. But do not gloss over adverse authority. Confront it directly, exhibiting integrity to the court.
- Update the law through Shepard's Citators or KeyCite; do not cite overruled cases or cases whose history is highly suspect.
- Determine your audience; remember you are writing to the court and the opposing counsel, but mainly to the court.
- Identify the components for that court's appellate brief; remember that not all appellate courts have the same components. Conform your brief to the requirements of the court.
- Organize your document; prepare an outline to assist you in organizing the sections of the brief, especially the statement of facts and argument and authorities sections.
- Write succinctly; say what you have to say and move on. Craft your issues, statement of facts, and argument in a persuasive tone. An appellate brief is no time to be objective. You do have a point of view. Communicate it. State your strongest arguments first and build on that argument. Use point and subpoint headings for organizing the flow of the brief.
- Redraft and revise your brief; remember, you and your supervising attorney will prepare a number of drafts before everyone is satisfied with the final product.
- Check punctuation, grammar, and spelling; do not rely solely on word processing programs because they will not pick up properly spelled words used incorrectly, such as typing "of" when you mean "or."
- Edit the final draft; recheck for proper citation format and review the final draft for clarity, precision, and accuracy.
- Format the brief; conform the brief to the court's font specifications, and word and page limitations. Be sure you have the correct color cover page and correct size of paper.
- Prepare the Table of Authorities; this section will be one of the last sections you complete since you will not know the authorities cited until the brief is completed. It is a good practice to begin compiling the Table of Authorities as you prepare the brief. Keep a separate tablet to list the legal sources cited in the brief. When the brief is completed, compare the cited authorities with the list. This should ease the preparation of this section. Remember to cite the corresponding page numbers where the case appears in the brief in the Table of Authorities.
- Prepare the Table of Contents; along with the Table of Authorities, this will be one on the last sections prepared in the brief.
- Check your word count; if required, prepare your certificate of compliance.
- Assemble the final product; one last check.
- File your brief with the court; be sure the required copies are prepared, or if e-filing is required, check the rules for verification of filing. Transmit the brief to opposing counsel.

That's it! You have completed your appellate brief and can breathe a sigh of relief. It is on to the next project. (See Figure 13.11 at the end of this chapter for a sample appellate brief.)

Ethics Alert

During the pendency of a case, an attorney and a paralegal are prohibited from contacting a represented person. Simply stated, you cannot directly contact a plaintiff in a case if your office is representing the defendant. Attorneys may use "you" to contact a represented person under the guise that either you do not know any better or you are not the attorney. Both situations are unethical. This anti-contact rule, as it is commonly known, continues through the appellate process as well. Do not have direct conversations or contact with someone you know is represented by an attorney in a matter your firm is handling against that party. In short, you are held to the same standard as an attorney.

If individuals are not represented by an attorney, you may contact them directly. Be careful to ask whether they are represented by an attorney and document that inquiry. You should also identify yourself, your position, whom you represent, and the reason for the contact. Often individuals think you are acting in a friendly manner or twist the conversation to suggest an inappropriate contact. Or, they may attempt to glean legal advice or information from you. Make your position clear and avoid creating any misunderstanding between yourself and the unrepresented party. More importantly, you do not want to give an unrepresented person the impression you are rendering legal advice, partaking in the unauthorized practice of law. Undoubtedly, contacting unrepresented parties poses unique issues, especially when representing themselves *pro se.* Proceed with caution when speaking with unrepresented parties in whatever stage of the proceeding you are in.

There are *very limited* situations when contact is appropriate, but emphasis is on the words "very limited," and you should consult your attorney before making the contact. Communications may be permitted with a public entity or large corporation when the communication with the represented party is unrelated to the litigation between the parties. Often this situation occurs between government agencies. For example, your law firm has a lawsuit against the government in an eminent domain action for which contact is inappropriate, but may contact the government on an unrelated licensing issue. The situation is tricky, and probably the best approach is to not only identify yourself as a paralegal acting on behalf of your law firm, but also disclose to the person the pending litigation. These are difficult areas of the law—think before you speak.

THE E-FACTOR

MANIPULATING THE SYSTEM TO CONFORM TO RULE REQUIREMENTS

Courts are keenly aware that attorneys will manipulate the system to skirt the rules of appellate procedure when it comes to the formatting requirements. In fact the Seventh Circuit Court of Appeals in *DeSilva v. DiLeonardi,* 185 F.3d 815 (7th Cir. 1999), investigated an attorney's certification of the "type-volume limit." In that case, the court discussed the 14,000-word limits for briefs. The attorney certified his brief was 176 words short of that limit—13,824. After review of the contents of the brief, the court was skeptical and performed its own count. The court's count included the main text and the 20 footnotes for a total of 15,056, making the brief over the limit. According to the court, the problem was with the word processing program and as the opinion concludes that the "Appellants' brief was prepared with Microsoft Word 97, and an unfortunate interaction occurred between that software and the terms of Rule 32." *Id.* at 815. The court determined that "Microsoft Word does not offer a way to count words in those footnotes attached to the selected text." *Id.* at 815. Amazing as all this sounds, the court determined that other word processing systems did not have the design problem of Microsoft Word and "flagged" briefs using Microsoft Word. In the final paragraph of the opinion, the court noted that "[w]e will send copies of this opinion to those responsible for such design decisions. In the meantime, we will flag this issue in the court's Practitioner's Guide and in materials distributed to counsel when an appeal is docketed. Law firms should alert their staffs to the issue pending resolution at the software level. Our clerk's office will spot-check briefs that have been prepared on Microsoft Word, are close to the word limit, and contain footnotes." *Id.* at 817. True to their word, the Seventh Circuit Checklist does caution attorneys who use Microsoft Word about the "word counting flaw." See Figure 13.10.

FIGURE 13.10 Seventh Circuit Checklist about Word-Counting Programs

---

<u>**Seventh Circuit Brief Filing Checklist**</u>

13. Fed. R. App. P. 32(a)(7) requires principal briefs not exceed 30 pages unless it contains no more than the greater of 14,000 words or 1,300 lines of text if a monospaced face is used. Reply briefs must contain no more than half of the type volume specified in Rule 32(a)(7)(B)(i). In cross-appeals the appellants' principle [sic] brief - 30 pages or 14,000 words; appellees' combined principle brief/response brief - 35 pages or 16,500 words; appellants' combined reply brief responsive brief - 30 pages or 14,000 words; appellees' reply brief in cross appeal - 15 pages or 7000 words. Fed. R. App. P. 28.1(e). Briefs submitted under the word count sections of the rules require a certificate of compliance that the brief complies with the volume limitations. **NOTE TO USERS OF MICROSOFT WORD** – Be advised that the word counting feature of some early versions of Microsoft Word may not properly count words in footnotes. Counsel must assure [sic] that they count all words in the brief before certifying compliance with Rule 32 or 28.1. *See DeSilva v. DiLeonardi*, 185 F.3d 815 (7th Cir. 1999). Briefs less than 30 pages do not require a certificate of compliance. Fed. R. App. P. 32(a)(7)(C).

The obvious point of all the attention paid to formats, word counts, spacing, margins, and all the other requirements of the Appellate Rules is read those rules. And, read those rules again. Many of the courts have checklists to follow. Use them. Take the process seriously and do not deviate from the process or the rule. Do not try to manipulate the word processing system and attempt to outsmart the system and the court. You may not get caught the first time, but it will, at some point, catch up with you. Remember, the attorney has to sign a certification of compliance with the page limitations. Your attorney is held accountable and could be sanctioned for filing a false certification. If you believe a brief borders on the word limit or some other rule limitation, tell your attorney and either edit the brief or prepare a motion for your supervising attorney to file with the court.

PRACTICAL CONSIDERATIONS

An appellate brief is not prepared in a day. Unlike briefing schedules in the trial court, often characterized by tight deadlines imposed by the trial judge, an appellate briefing schedule is generally established by specific rules that set reasonable minimum time periods.

Thus the most important practical consideration in preparing an appellate brief is twofold: first, you have ample time to polish your brief; second, because of this appellate judges expect a polished product. You must schedule sufficient time to perform the tasks that go into every appellate brief—reviewing the record; researching the issues; writing a draft; editing; finalizing your draft; preparing the tables of contents and authorities, as well as all other supplements; and reviewing the final version to ensure that it is as polished as you can make it. It's easy to delude yourself into thinking, "The brief's not due for four weeks—I'll do other things first." If you fall into this trap, you'll end up with a major headache—a brief due in a week or less, and insufficient time to prepare it correctly.

There is one other important practical consideration. Remember that this chapter is only an *introduction* to writing the appellate brief, and is not the final word. There are as many opinions on appellate advocacy, briefing strategies, and brief writing as there is on trial advocacy. But all good briefs have a few common characteristics—they are thorough, yet concise; accurate, yet partisan; and most of all, they are *persuasive*.

A FINAL WORD

You have acquired the skills to become a top-rate paralegal. But as with all things, unless you practice the skills learned, you get rusty. Keep writing and refining those skills. You are an invaluable contributor to the legal process, and this is only the beginning. Attorneys often forget how accomplished and important you are to the process of successful lawyering. Don't let

Source: © King Features Syndicate.

lawyers overpower you and compromise your integrity. This textbook has combined legal writing and legal ethics for a reason. They are the backbone of our profession. Learn your craft well, but above all else, be professional and ethical in your practice.

Summary

The first step in pursuing an appeal is to obtain a copy of the current appellate rules applicable in your jurisdiction. The second step is to read and understand them.

An appellate brief is a legal document filed with an appellate court and drafted so as to persuade that court to decide contested issues in favor of the filing litigant. An appeal is based on the record, which is the written documentation of the trial. The guideline that the court applies in evaluating an appeal is called the standard of review. There are two types of errors to which a standard of review is applied: errors of fact and errors of law.

There are several basic sections to an appellate brief, which may vary slightly in designation or content from one jurisdiction to the next, but are otherwise always required. The title page identifies the parties and court, and usually also contains the request for oral argument. The certificate of interested parties identifies those parties with a direct interest in the outcome of the case. The table of contents provides section headings with corresponding page numbers, and performs a "road map" function. The table of authorities identifies references cited. The jurisdictional statement identifies the legal authority that grants the appellate court authority over the appeal. The statement of the case sets forth the procedural history of the case. The questions presented section provides a convenient and concise statement of the grounds of the appeal. The statement of facts is based upon the record, and should be both accurate and partisan. The argument is the most important section of an appellate brief, comprised of point headings and the main text or body, and containing the legal and factual positions of the party preparing it. The conclusion identifies the relief sought. A signature block and certificate of service are also included, as well as an appendix containing source materials from the record.

An appellant's brief is filed first, and sets the tone and defines the issues. The appellee's brief is filed in response to the appellant's brief, and both attacks the appellant's arguments and makes its own arguments. The reply brief is filed by the appellant in response to the appellee's brief. An *amicus curiae* brief is filed by a nonparty presenting public policy arguments.

Because of the nature of appellate briefing schedules, you have ample time to prepare an appellate brief. However, this means that judges expect a polished product, so make sure that you leave yourself adequate time to do your best work.

FIGURE 13.11

Sample Appellate Brief

1

No. 2-06-123-CV
CAUSE NO. 05-873-C
IN THE COURT OF CIVIL APPEALS
FOR THE FIFTH SUPREME JUDICIAL DISTRICT OF TEXAS
AT DALLAS, TEXAS

DENTAL CLINICS OF THE WORLD, INC.   Appellant
vs.
MICHAEL MONTGOMERY, Individually   Appellee

Appealed from
THE DISTRICT COURT OF DALLAS COUNTY, TEXAS
127th Judicial District

BRIEF OF APPELLANT

Suzannah T. Marris
Raymond D. Philman
MARRIS & PHILMAN
1801 Central Drive
Dallas, Texas 75247

ATTORNEYS FOR APPELLANT

APPELLANT RESPECTFULLY
REQUESTS ORAL ARGUMENT
BEFORE THE COURT

Refer to the corresponding key numbers to identify each element of this Brief.

❶ — Title or Cover Page	❽ — Statement of Facts
❷ — Certificate of Interested Parties	❾ — Argument
❸ — Table of Contents	❿ — Point Heading
❹ — Table of Authorities	⓫ — Body
❺ — Jurisdictional Statement	⓬ — Conclusion
❻ — Statement of the Case	⓭ — Signature Block
❼ — Questions Presented	⓮ — Certificate of Service

FIGURE 13.11
Cont.

[2]
[3]

CERTIFICATE OF INTERESTED PARTIES

The following are all the interested parties in this Appeal:
1. Dental Clinics of the World, Inc.
2. Michael Montgomery
3. Joseph Dean

Table of Contents

Certificate of Interested Parties .... (i)

Table of Contents .... (ii)

Table of Authorities.. (iii)

Jurisdictional Statement 1

Statement of the Case..1

Question Presented...1

Fact Statement..1

Argument and Authorities
  I. THE TRIAL COURT ABUSED ITS DISCRETION
     BY NOT GRANTING THE TEMPORARY INJUNCTION....................................2
  II. TEXAS PROHIBITS THE USE OF TRADE SECRETS AND
     CONFIDENTIAL PROPRIETARY INFORMATION WHEN
     MISAPPROPRIATED BY A CORPORATE OFFICER 3
       A. A trade secret by definition may be a compilation of
          information, including a customer list..3
       B. An injunction is an appropriate remedy for
          misappropriation of trade secrets and for the breach
          of a fiduciary relationship..6

Conclusion 6

Certificate of Service..7

[4]

Table of Authorities

UNITED STATES SUPREME COURT
E.I. DuPont De Nemours Power Co. v. Masland, 244 U.S. 100 (1917)

TEXAS SUPREME COURT
Butnaru v. Ford Motor Co., 84 S.W. 3d 198 (Tex. 2002)
City of Spring v. Southwestern Bell Telephone Company, 484 S.W. 2d 579
(Tex. 1974)
Hyde Corp. v. Huffines, 158 Tex. 566, 314 S.W. 2d 763 (1958)
International Bankers Life Ins. Co. v. Holloway, 368 S.W. 2d 567 (Tex. 1963)
K & G Oil Tool & Service Co. v. G & G Fishing Tool Service, 158 Tex. 594, 314 S.W.
2d 782 (1958)
Southland Life Insurance Co. v. Egan, 126 Tex. 160, 86 S.W. 2d 722 (1935)
Transport Co. of Texas v. Robertson Transports, 152 Tex. 551, 261 S.W. 2d 549 (1953)

TEXAS COURT OF APPEALS
Green v. Stratoflex, Inc., 596 S.W. 2d 305 (Tex. Civ. App.–Ft. Worth 1980, no writ)
Jeter v. Associated Rack Corp., 607 S.W. 2d 272 (Tex. Civ. App.–Texarkana 1980, writ
ref'd n.r.e.), *cert. denied,* 454 U.S. 965 (1980)
Lamons Metal Gasket Co. v. Traylor, 361 S.W. 2d 211 (Tex. Civ. App.–Houston 1962,
writ ref'd n.r.e.)
Morgan v. City of Humble, 598 S.W. 2d 364 (Tex. Civ. App.–Houston [14th Dist.]
1980, no writ)
Plagge v. Gambino, 570 S.W. 2d 106 (Tex. Civ. App.–Houston [1st Dist.] 1978, no
writ)
Texas Shop Towel, Inc. v. Haine, 246 S.W. 2d 482 (Tex. Civ. App.–San Antonio 1952,
no writ)
Weed Eater v. Dowling, 562 S.W. 2d 898 (Tex. Civ. App.–Houston [1st Dist.] 1978,
writ ref'd n.r.e.)

FIGURE 13.11
Cont.

5

JURISDICTIONAL STATEMENT

This court has jurisdiction of this appeal pursuant to the Texas Constitution Art. 5 § 6 and Tex. Civ. Prac. & Rem. Code Ann. § 51.014 (Vernon 1986).

6

STATEMENT OF THE CASE

This case is an appeal from the denial of a temporary injunction. Dental Clinics of the World, Inc. ("Dental Clinic" or "Appellant") filed suit against Michael Montgomery ("Montgomery" or "Appellee") alleging that Appellee used Appellant's confidential and proprietary information and trade secrets. Montgomery used information that he gained through his employment with Dental Clinic to bid on a servicing contract with Health Care, Inc., Dallas, Texas. The information was Dental Clinic's proprietary, confidential information and trade secrets, which Montgomery acquired and used in violation of his obligations to Dental Clinic. Montegomery also contacted other persons to attempt to establish a business that would compete with Appellant, using Dental Clinic's information. A temporary injunction hearing was held by the 127th Judicial District Court, Dallas, Texas. On June 20, 2005, the Court entered an Order denying the temporary injunction.

7

QUESTION PRESENTED

Did the District Court err and abuse its discretion by denying appellant's application for a temporary injunction, since appellant proved a probable right and probable injury thereby establishing sufficient grounds to impose an injunction and preserve the status quo?

8

FACT STATEMENT

Dental Clinic is a Texas corporation specializing in dental clinic services. It offers personnel and equipment (for example, drills, x-ray machines, and other equipment) to dental clinics in Texas. (Tr. 47)

In 2000, Dental Clinic employed Montgomery as a salesperson. Montgomery became Vice President of the company in 2004. (Tr. 36) While Vice President, Montgomery had many responsibilities, including hiring employees, purchasing equipment, compiling marketing data, selling the company's services, and dealing with customers. (Tr. 38) Throughout his tenure with the company, Montgomery gained confidential knowledge and information, which he would not have gained but for his employment with Dental Clinic. As a service-oriented business, Dental Clinic develops business relationships with its customers. (Tr. 44) Through contracts with its customers, Dental Clinic provides equipment and personnel. The customers are normally small clinics or health centers. (Tr. 45) Dental Clinic installs the equipment and provides the technicians as well. Only three other companies provided a similar service in Texas. (Tr. 31)

To determine whether an area is appropriate for a dental clinic, a sizable amount of research and development takes place. This research and development takes years. (Tr. 51) If competitors obtained this information, thousands of research dollars could be saved, as well as the time spent researching. Having this information would allow a competitor to set up a clinic in an area or forego an area based on Dental Clinic's research.

Dental Clinic treated this information as confidential, proprietary data and trade secrets. This information was kept from employees unless needed in their job functions. (Tr. 55) Montgomery was one of the few employees of Dental Clinic who had access to <u>all</u> Company information. (Tr. 55) This information included, but was not limited to, customer lists, supplier lists, pricing lists, clinics, and manufacturers. As an employee and fiduciary of the Company, Montgomery knew this information was confidential and proprietary. (Tr. 56)

Montgomery worked directly with Dental Clinic's customers. In fact, Montgomery worked with clinic administrators and found out that one of Dental Clinic's customers had received a bid from another company. Montgomery was asked to revise Dental Clinic's prior contract and gave the information to the President of the company. (Tr. 71) The new bid was resubmitted to the clinic with Montgomery's new prices. (Tr. 72) Montgomery gained all this information while employed with the Company and he only could have gained this information because of his employment with Dental Clinic.

On November 17, 2004, Montgomery resigned and terminated his employment with Dental Clinic. (Tr. 95) Not more than one month after he left Dental Clinic, Montgomery formed his own company, Dental Health Care. This company offered the same services as Dental Clinic. (Tr. 98)

FIGURE 13.11
Cont.

8

Montgomery contacted one of Dental Clinic's customers regarding a dental services contract. (Tr. 101) The clinic turned out to be the same clinic Montgomery had revised the pricing for while employed with Dental Clinic. Montgomery did not contact anyone for pricing information. In fact, Montgomery knew his bid would be lower than Dental Clinic's since he had access to the information while employed with Dental Clinic. (Tr. 107) Months later, in January 2005, Dental Clinic was notified that its contract with the clinic would be cancelled and that Montgomery's company would receive the contract. (Tr. 158) Montgomery also contacted other customers of Dental Clinic and attempted to gain their contracts. Clearly, Montgomery knew all Dental Clinic customers, the services performed for them, and the prices charged. This information could only be gained from Montgomery's employment. Dental Clinic sued Montgomery for misappropriation of trade secrets and confidential proprietary information and requested a temporary injunction. This injunction was denied, and the denial has been appealed.

SUMMARY OF THE ARGUMENT

A former Vice President of Dental Clinic misappropriated confidential and proprietary and trade secret information. This information was a compilation of years of work and finanical investment which Montogomery had access to because of his fiduciary relationship with Dental Clinic. While Dental Clinic was negotiating a contract for which Montgomery prepared the financial data, he resigned his employment and began his own business using the confidential and proprietary information he gained through his employment with Dental Clinic. Montgomery's actions caused immediate and irreparable injury for which Dental Clinic requested a temporary injunction to preserve the status quo pending a trial on the merits.

9

ARGUMENT AND AUTHORITIES

10

I. THE TRIAL COURT ABUSED ITS DISCRETION BY NOT GRANTING THE TEMPORARY INJUNCTION.

The trial court refused to grant the temporary injunction in this case and abused its discretion because the facts clearly established the elements of a temporary injunction. Under the Texas Civil Practice and Remedies Code, section 51.014 (a) (4), an interlocutory appeal is proper when a district court grants or denies an application for temporary injunction. TEX.CIV.PRAC.& REM. CODE ANN. section 51.014 (a) (4) (Vernon Supp. 2005) The standard of review for an appeal in a temporary injunction hearing is whether the trial court abused its discretion in granting or denying the temporary injunction. *Butnaru v. Ford Motor Co.*, 84 S.W. 3d 198, 204 (Tex. 2002); *City of Spring v. Southwestern Bell Telephone Company*, 484 S.W. 2d 579 (Tex. 1974). In determining whether the granting or denial of a temporary injunction is proper, this Court must look to the record in the trial court and determine whether the party requesting relief is entitled to preservation of status quo of the subject matter pending trial on the merits. *Green v. Stratoflex, Inc.*, 596 S.W. 2d 305 (Tex. Civ. App.–Ft. Worth 1980, no writ). In evaluating whether the trial court abused its discretion in granting or denying a temporary injunction, this Court must consider whether the trial court erroneously applied the law to undisputed facts, where pleadings and evidence presented a probable right and probable injury. *Southland Life Insurance Co. v. Egan*, 126 Tex. 160, 86 S.W. 2d 722 (1935); *Plagge v. Gambino*, 570 S.W. 2d 106 (Tex. Civ. App.–Houston [1st Dist.] 1978, no writ); *Morgan v. City of Humble*, 598 S.W. 2d 364 (Tex. Civ. App.–Houston [14th Dist.] 1980, no writ).

11

The purpose of the temporary injunction is to preserve the status quo of a matter in controversy until final hearing on the merits of the case. For a temporary injunction to be issued by a trial court, a party need show only a probable right and a probable injury, and is not required to establish that he will finally prevail in the litigation. Therefore, the burden in a temporary injunction hearing is substantially different than it is in a trial on the merits. The movant has to prove there is a probable right to recovery at a trial on merits, but does not have the burden to prove that he would ultimately prevail at a final hearing. *Transport Co. of Texas v. Robertson Transports*, 152 Tex. 551, 261 S.W. 2d 549 (1953).

At the temporary injunction hearing, Dental Clinic proved a probable injury was suffered and Dental Clinic had a probable right to recovery. Montgomery stole information from his employer, Dental Clinic, and, in turn, used the information to injure the company. The misappropriation of this information was wrongful, for which Dental Clinic was entitled to relief in the form of a temporary injunction. The trial court abused its discretion by failing to properly apply the law to the facts. Dental Clinic made a proper showing to meet the standards necessary for issuance of an injunction.

FIGURE 13.11
Cont.

Dental Clinic did have a probable right to recovery and clearly sustained an injury by losing an established contract with one of its customers.

10

II. TEXAS PROHIBITS THE USE OF TRADE SECRETS AND CONFIDENTIAL PROPRIETARY INFORMATION WHEN MISAPPROPRIATED BY A CORPORATE OFFICER.

Montgomery was a Vice President of Dental Clinic. The Supreme Court of Texas has held that corporate officers are fiduciaries of the corporation. *International Bankers Life Ins. Co. v. Holloway*, 368 S.W. 2d 567 (Tex. 1963). Not only do the courts impose a general fiduciary obligation on officers, but additionally, the courts have articulated a specific rule that an employee has a duty *not* to disclose the confidential matters of its employer. *Lamons Metal Gasket Co. v. Traylor*, 361 S.W. 2d 211 (Tex. Civ. App.–Houston 1962, writ ref'd n.r.e.); *Jeter v. Associated Rack Corp.*, 607 S.W. 2d 272 (Tex. Civ. App.–Texarkana 1980, writ ref'd n.r.e.), *cert. denied*, 454 U.S. 965 (1980). Certain information was considered confidential by Dental Clinic. The undisputed testimony of the President shows that Dental Clinic considered customer lists, renewal dates, and pricing as confidential. (Tr. 57-59) Montgomery intentionally disregarded his fiduciary responsibilities to further his own personal endeavors. But for Montgomery's relationship to Dental Clinic, he would not have known the trade secrets and confidential and proprietary information. The law is clear that Texas prohibits the use of confidential information by a former corporate officer, which Montgomery clearly was in this case. *Weed Eater v. Dowling*, 562 S.W. 2d 898 (Tex. Civ. App.–Houston [1st Dist.] 1978, writ ref'd n.r.e.)

A. A TRADE SECRET BY DEFINITION MAY BE A COMPILATION OF INFORMATION, INCLUDING A CUSTOMER LIST.

In defining a trade secret, the Texas Supreme Court has adopted the <u>Restatement of Torts,</u> 2nd § 757, which defines a trade secret as follows:

11

A trade secret may consist of any formula, pattern, device, or *compilation of information which is used in one's business and which gives him an opportunity to obtain an advantage over competitors who do not know or use it.* It may be a formula for a chemical compound, a process of manufacturing, treating, or preserving materials, a pattern for a machine, or other device, or *a list of customers.** * * Trade secret is a process or device for continuous use in the operation of the business. *See, Hyde Corp. v. Huffines*, 158 Tex. 566, 314 S.W. 2d 763, 776 (1958) (emphasis added). <u>The Restatement of Torts</u> § 757 further states that:

One who discloses or uses another's trade secrets, without a privilege to do so, is liable to the other if (a) he discloses the secret by improper means, or (b) his disclosure or <u>use</u> constitutes a breach of confidence reposed in him by the other in disclosing the secret to him. *Hyde Corp.* at 769 (emphasis supplied).

Dental Clinic had developed confidential and proprietary information that it used in its business. This information gave it an advantage over competitors. For years Dental Clinic compiled information. The information included but was not limited to customer lists, contact persons at clinics, pricing information, financial information, and market planning strategies. (Tr. 57) Information had been exclusively developed through Dental Clinic's financial investment and research and was not readily accessible to outsiders of the company without substantial monetary and time investment. This compilation of information is Dental Clinic's trade secrets and proprietary and confidential information, which it uses in the development of its business activities.

It is undisputed Montgomery had access to trade secrets and confidential and proprietary information of Dental Clinic by virtue of his position of confidence and trust with the President, Joseph Dean. As the testimony showed, Dean and Montgomery worked together in the development of Dental Clinic. Montgomery had access to all the information regarding Dental Clinic. The information Montgomery acquired is a valuable asset of Dental Clinic. A temporary injunction is the only remedy that will protect Dental Clinic's investment. A temporary injunction will preserve the status quo pending a trial on the merits. Without the injunction, Dental Clinic will continue to suffer harm and injury.

In the temporary injunction hearing, Montgomery admitted he took information he gained while employed with Dental Clinic to contact other dental clinics. He made offers and submitted proposals to the clinics. (Tr. 88) Specifically, Montgomery contacted Dental Resources of the Southwest, with whom Dental Clinic had been negotiating a renewal of its contract. Montgomery breached his fiduciary relationship with Dental Clinic by using its proprietary and confidential information and trade secrets. When a vice president breaches his fiduciary duty, it is proper under Texas law to grant

FIGURE 13.11
Cont.

a temporary injunction. *Weed Eater v. Dowling*, 562 S.W. 2d 898 (Tex. Civ. App.–Houston [1st Dist.] 1978, writ ref'd n.r.e.). The trial court should have granted the temporary injunction to protect Dental Clinic's proprietary and confidential information and trade secrets. Now, Dental Clinic is left without a viable remedy as it continues to suffer due to its former Vice President's actions.

More importantly, in any analysis of trade secrets and confidential and proprietary information, the Court must evaluate how the information was acquired. Although it may be argued by Montgomery the information was generally available for someone with time and money to accumulate the information, the fact is clear that the data which Montgomery utilized to compete with his former employer came from Dental Cllinic's investment of hundreds of hours and substantial sums of money to accumulate and develop the data. Even if Montgomery could acquire the information that does not mean he is entitled, through a breach of confidence, to gain the "information in usable form and escape the efforts of inspection and analysis." *K & G Oil Tool & Service Co. v. G & G Fishing Tool Service*, 158 Tex. 594, 314 S.W. 2d 782 (1958). The law in Texas imposed equitable measures against an individual who has breached a fiduciary relationship through a temporary injunction. As the court in its dicta in *Weed Eater* recognized,

> [W]here an employee will acquire trade secrets by virtue of his employment, the law permits greater restrictions to be imposed on the employee than in other contracts of employment.
>
> *Confidential business information* is not given protection merely as a reward to its accumulator. The courts condemn employment of improper means to procure trade secrets. *The fact that a trade secret is of such a nature that it can be discovered by experimentation or other fair and lawful means does not deprive its owner of the right to protection from those who would secure possession by unfair means.* (emphasis added). 562 S.W. *Id*. at 901.

Texas law clearly imposes a responsibility on a corporate officer such as Montgomery not to disclose information gained during employment. The responsibility of the corporate fiduciary is implied and is part of a contract of employment.

Although Montgomery would suggest that liability can be imposed only if a written contract existed, this is not the law. In confidential and proprietary information actions, a contract of employment is not necessary to create the right. As *Texas Shop Towel, Inc. v. Haine* points out:

> [a]n owner may protect a trade secret even in the total absence of any contract with his employees, and the agents and employees who learn of the trade secret or secret formula are prohibited from its use. *In the case of a trade secret, a contract does not create the right, for the right exists by reason of the confidence.* It will exist in the total absence of a contract. A contract may be additional evidence of the existence of the trade secret but an owner's rights in his secrets do not depend upon a contract (emphasis added). *Texas Shop Towel* at 485 (Tex. Civ. App.–San Antonio 1952, no writ).

No employment contract is necessary to hold Montgomery legally responsible for his actions. The testimony and the evidence before this Court are undisputed:

- Montgomery received Dental Clinic's confidential, proprietary, and trade secret information in confidence as Dental Clinic's employee
- Montgomery was an officer of Dental Clinic and as such was a fiduciary of the corporation.

In *E.I. DuPont De Nemours Power Co. v. Masland*, 244 U.S. 100 (1917), the Supreme Court of the United States recognized the importance of a fiduciary duty and the consequence of a breach of that duty. The Supreme Court in its dicta made the following observation:

> [w]hether the Plaintiffs have any valuable secret or not, the Defendant knows the facts, whatever they are, through a special confidence that he accepted. The property may be denied, but the confidence cannot be. Therefore, the starting point for the present matter is not property or due process of law, but that the Defendant stood in confidential relations with the Plaintiff, or one of them. These have given place to hostility, and the first thing to be made sure of is that the Defendant shall not fraudulently abuse the trust reposed in him. It is the usual incident of confidential relations. If there is any disadvantage in the fact that he knew the Plaintiff's secrets, he must take the burden with the good. *Id*. at 102.

The U.S. Supreme Court recognized the rights of an employer over fifty years ago. It is a right that continues today. The only remedy Dental Clinic has is a temporary injunction.

B. AN INJUNCTION IS AN APPROPRIATE REMEDY FOR MISAPPROPRIATION OF TRADE SECRETS AND FOR THE BREACH OF A FIDUCIARY RELATIONSHIP.

The evidence is clear that Montgomery acquired trade secrets and confidential and proprie-

11

FIGURE 13.11
Cont.

11

tary information from Dental Clinic while an employee. After his resignation, Montgomery used the trade secrets and confidential and proprietary information of Dental Clinic to his own benefit. Though the information may have been available to a competitor, that availability did not give Montgomery the right to violate his confidential relationship with Dental Clinic. *See generally, Texas Shop Towel, Inc. v. Haine*, 246 S.W. 2d 482 (Tex.Civ.App.-San Antonio 1952, no writ). By not issuing a temporary injunction and preserving the status quo, the trial judge abused his discretion. The facts in this case are undisputed by the evidence and the testimony.

By applying the undisputed facts to the law, Dental Clinic is entitled to a temporary injunction to preserve the status quo. Dental Clinic proved through the testimony and evidence that it had a probable injury, which would result from (1) Montgomery's utilizing information to undercut Dental Clinic's contract bid, and (2) Montgomery's contacting users of Dental Clinic services. Dental Clinic also showed that there was a probable right to recovery since the information was admittedly gained through Montgomery's employment with Dental Clinic. Montgomery admitted that he learned the information that he utilized to prepare the clinic's contract from his employment with Dental Clinic. Therefore, clearly the trial court abused its discretion by not granting the temporary injunction as the court did not properly apply the law to the undisputed facts. In *Weed Eater*, the Houston Court of Appeals recognized that a temporary injunction is a proper remedy when there is a breach of confidence and a misuse of proprietary information and trade secrets. 562 S.W. *Id* at 901. The facts in this case support such a conclusion of probable injury and probable right and the law dictates the issuance of an injunction.

CONCLUSION

12

In a temporary injunction hearing, Dental Clinic had to show only a probable right to recovery and a probable injury and that there was not an adequate remedy at law. In applying the law to the facts, Dental Clinic showed an injury, Montgomery's interference with a business contract, and a right to recovery arising from Montgomery's use of information gained while employed with Dental Clinic. As a matter of law, this information was confidential and proprietary and trade secrets of Dental Clinic. By not granting the temporary injunction, the trial court erred and abused its discretion by misapplying the law to the facts. Dental Clinic requests that this court instruct the trial court to issue and enter a temporary injunction to preserve the status quo in this case until a final trial on the merits can be heard.

Dental Clinic requests this Honorable Court instruct the trial court to issue and enter a temporary injunction against Montgomery to preserve the status quo until a final trial on the merits by ordering Montgomery not to contact any customers or dentists who are customers of Dental Clinic during the pendency of the litigation.

Respectfully submitted,

13

SUZANNAH T. MARRIS
State Bar #18769283
RAYMOND D. PHILMAN
State Bar #27619317
MARRIS & PHILMAN
1801 Central Drive
Dallas, Texas 75247
(214) 512-0927

ATTORNEYS FOR APPELLANT

CERTIFICATE OF SERVICE

14

I certify that a true and correct copy of the foregoing Brief of Appellant has been forwarded to Appellee, by and through their attorney of record, C. J. Coldaway at 617 LBJ Freeway, Dallas, Texas, 76202, by certified mail, return receipt requested, on this _____ day of _____, 2006.

Suzannah T. Marris

Key Terms

appellate rules
appellate brief
Petitioner
Respondent
record

pleadings
transcript
court reporter
standard of review
error of fact

abuse of discretion	indexing method
error of law	argument
harmless error	body
de novo	string citations
title page	conclusion
amicus curiae	signature block
certificate of interested parties	certificate of compliance
recusal	certificate of service
table of contents	appendix
table of authorities	appellant's brief
jurisdictional statement	appellee's brief
statement of the case	reply brief
questions presented	*amicus* brief
statement of facts	

Review Questions

1. Why is it important to follow the applicable appellate rules?
2. What is the function of the appellate brief?
3. What are the components of the record on appeal?
4. Explain the difference between errors of fact and errors of law.
5. What is a jurisdictional statement?
6. What is the "road map" function of the table of contents?
7. What are two key points to remember when drafting the statement of facts?
8. What are point headings?
9. What is the significance of a Certificate of Compliance?
10. Describe the different characteristics of the appellant's brief, the appellee's brief, the reply brief, and the *amicus curiae* brief.

Exercises

1. Check the federal, state, and local appellate court rules for your jurisdiction and answer the following questions:
   a. When must an appeal be filed?
   b. When must the record be filed? The transcript?
   c. How much time does the appellant have to prepare and file the appellant's brief? The appellee?
   d. List the page length, the paper size, color of cover page, and binding requirements.
2. Compare your state rules of appellate procedure and the Federal Rules of Appellate Procedure, and list the differences in the rules.
3. Using the Memorandum of Law in Chapter 12, create the table of authorities based upon the rules of the court in your state's appeals court.
4. Based upon the facts of the Memorandum of Law in Chapter 12, prepare a motion to the state appellate court to file a longer brief.
   a. Determine the rules for filing the motion.
   b. Determine the color of the cover page and the requirements. Prepare the cover page according to the rules of the court.
5. Ms. Liann Wang sought political asylum in the United States because of alleged political persecution by the Government of China. Ms. Wang entered the United States illegally. Because of her illegal entry, the United States government sought removal proceedings against Ms. Wang in case number INS No. A99-000-098. The immigration judge

denied Ms. Wang's petition for asylum because her testimony did not support her claims of political persecution. Ms. Wang requested her removal hearing be reopened. The immigration judge denied the request. Ms. Wang appealed to the Board of Immigration Appeals. The Board of Appeals issued an order denying the request. Ms. Wang appeals the case to the third circuit court of appeals under Local Appellate Rule (LAR) 34.1(a). What is the standard of review to reopen a removal case in an immigration matter? Research the law in the Third Circuit and U.S. Supreme Court. Find the cases with the highest precedential value on the issue.

6. Using the facts in Exercise 5, prepare the cover sheet and title page for appeal to the Third Circuit Court of Appeals. The case number for the Third Circuit Court of Appeals is No. 06-10000. The attorney representing Ms. Wang is Charles Reese, 111 Market St., Philadelphia, Pa. 19103. Oral argument is requested.

7. Historical Preservation Society of America, Inc. seeks a temporary injunction against Demolition R Us, Co. It seems that Demolition has been hired by Property Management Inc. to demolish a historic hotel in downtown Miami, Florida on October 15, 2006. The historic hotel was built in 1912 and is certified as a landmark. Unfortunately, the building was abandoned years ago and Property Management Inc. wants to build a five story parking lot on the site. Property Management owns the land and building. Historical Preservation files a request for temporary restraining order and temporary injunction requesting the demolition cease and the building remain in tact. The judge denies the temporary restraining order and temporary injunction on October 25, 2006. Property Management intends to begin the demolition in 10 days. Historical Preservation files a Notice of Appeal in the trial court in Miami. The appeal is properly perfected and your law firm has been hired to prepare the appellate brief. Determine the proper appeals court to file the appeal. Review the rules of the court.

   a. What motion should be filed with the appeals court in this case?

   b. Prepare the motion (from your response to Exercise 7(a) in the above set of facts).

8. Using the facts from Exercise 7, prepare the following:

   a. standard of review for the case

   b. statement of facts

   c. argument and authorities section

   d. conclusion

   Use your best persuasive writing skills to "save" the historic site. Be creative.

Portfolio Assignment

Continuing with our Mrs. Marsh and "Buttons" facts, Mrs. Marsh was granted a summary judgment against A1 and Herbert Killington. Both parties want to appeal.

1. Choose one of the parties to represent and prepare the appellate brief on behalf of one of the appellants. (Remember the standard of review is for a summary judgment.)

2. Prepare the appellee's brief on behalf of Mrs. Marsh. (Hint: Stay focused on the fact that there are no genuine issues of material fact. If the appellant can create one, the judgment may be overturned.)

Be sure your brief complies with the rules of the jurisdiction. Check to see if the appellate court has any local rules to follow.

Vocabulary Builder

Appellate Brief

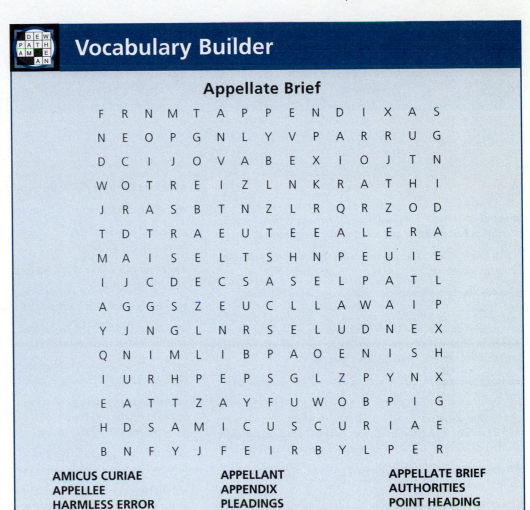

```
F  R  N  M  T  A  P  P  E  N  D  I  X  A  S
N  E  O  P  G  N  L  Y  V  P  A  R  R  U  G
D  C  I  J  O  V  A  B  E  X  I  O  J  T  N
W  O  T  R  E  I  Z  L  N  K  R  A  T  H  I
J  R  A  S  B  T  N  Z  L  R  Q  R  Z  O  D
T  D  T  R  A  E  U  T  E  E  A  L  E  R  A
M  A  I  S  E  L  T  S  H  N  P  E  U  I  E
I  J  C  D  E  C  S  A  S  E  L  P  A  T  L
A  G  G  S  Z  E  U  C  L  L  A  W  A  I  P
Y  J  N  G  L  N  R  S  E  L  U  D  N  E  X
Q  N  I  M  L  I  B  P  A  O  E  N  I  S  H
I  U  R  H  P  E  P  S  G  L  Z  P  Y  N  X
E  A  T  T  Z  A  Y  F  U  W  O  B  P  I  G
H  D  S  A  M  I  C  U  S  C  U  R  I  A  E
B  N  F  Y  J  F  E  I  R  B  Y  L  P  E  R
```

AMICUS CURIAE	APPELLANT	APPELLATE BRIEF
APPELLEE	APPENDIX	AUTHORITIES
HARMLESS ERROR	PLEADINGS	POINT HEADING
RECORD	RECUSAL	REPLY BRIEF
STRING CITATION	TRANSCRIPT	

Glossary

A

abuse of discretion Standard of review on appeal that judge's decision is unreasonable and not logically based upon the facts.

active voice A verb form in which the subject of the sentence performs the action.

advance sheets Softcover pamphlets containing the most recent cases.

adversarial documents Documents that are argumentative, drafted to emphasize the strong points of your client's position and the weaknesses of the opposing party's.

advisory letter A formal letter that offers legal opinions or demands.

affirmative defenses "Excuses" by the opposing party that do not just simply negate the allegation, but put forth a legal reason to avoid enforcement. These defenses are waived if not pleaded.

affirmed Disposition in which the appellate court agrees with the trial court.

Alert The case-clipping system used by Lexis to monitor legal developments.

allegations Facts forming the basis of a party's complaint.

ambiguity Lack of precision and clarity.

amended pleading A pleading that changes, corrects, revises, or deletes information from a prior pleading.

amicus brief Brief filed by a nonparty to an appeal who has an interest, whether political, social, or otherwise, in the outcome of the case.

amicus curiae Brief filed by a nonparty known as a "friend of the court."

annotated code A code that provides, in addition to the text of the codified statutes, such information as cases that have construed the statute; law review articles that have discussed it; the procedural history of the statute (amendments or antecedents); cross-references to superseded codifications; cross-references to related statutes; and other information.

annotation An in-depth analysis of a specific and important legal issue raised in the accompanying decision, together with an extensive survey of the way the issue is treated in various jurisdictions.

answer Document that is the defendant's response to the plaintiff's complaint.

apostrophe A form of punctuation used to create a contraction or a possessive noun.

appellant's brief Brief of the party filing the appeal.

appellate brief Brief filed in an appeals court.

appellate courts The court of appeals that reviews a trial court's record for error.

appellate rules Procedures set forth by the appeals court in processing an appeal.

appellee's brief Brief of the party responding to the appeal.

appendix Contains the supplementary collection of the sources from the trial court.

argument Section of the brief where the issues are analyzed through citation of legal authorities.

attorney/client privilege The legal relationship established between attorney and client allowing for free exchange of information without fear of disclosure.

audience The person or persons to whom a legal document is directed, such as a client or the court.

authorization letter A letter the client provides the attorney granting permission to contact employers, doctors, or other individuals who have records that relate to a case.

B

bcc Blind copy.

black letter law The strict meaning of the law as it is written, without concern or interpretation of the reasoning behind its creation.

block quote A quotation over 50 words that is single-spaced and indented.

body The text that contains the information you wish to communicate in a letter.

body The portion of a paragraph that contains the material that you claim supports the contention raised in the topic sentence.

body Main text of the argument section of the appellate brief.

boilerplate Standard language in a form.

brackets A form of punctuation that indicates changes or additions.

brevity Strong, tight writing

brief A formal written argument presented to the court.

brief bank A document depository of briefs prepared by a law firm in previous matters.

C

caption The full name of the case, together with the docket number, court, and date of the decision.

case brief An objective summary of the important points of a single case; a summary of a court opinion.

cc Copy.

certificate of compliance Attorney certification at the end of an appellate brief attesting to compliance with the page limitations set forth by that court's rules.

certificate of interested parties Statement in a brief identifying parties who have an interest in the outcome and financial affiliations.

certificate of service Verification by attorney that pleadings or court documents were sent to the opposing counsel in a case.

citation Information about a legal source directing you to the volume and page in which the legal source appears.

clarity The ability to accurately convey the intended message to the reader in a clear, precise manner.

clerk of the court An individual who manages the administrative functions of the court.

clichés Overused figures of speech.

closing The concluding message in a letter.

closing sentence A sentence at the end of a paragraph that summarizes the topic.

codes Set of volumes that groups statutes by subject matter and is well indexed, in order to make the statutes more accessible for research purposes.

collection letter A letter that demands payment of an amount claimed to be owed to a client.

colloquialisms Informal language used in everyday conversation.

colon A form of punctuation that joins together phrases or explanatory clauses or introduces a block quote.

comma Punctuation used to re-create verbal pauses.

complaint Document that states the allegations and the legal basis of the plaintiff's claims.

complex sentence A sentence that contains a subordinate clause or clauses in addition to the main clause.

compound sentence A sentence in which the clauses could stand separately, each ending with a period.

compulsory counterclaim A counterclaim that is required to be pleaded because the facts relate to the same transaction as that set forth in the original complaint.

conclusion Summation of your analysis in a memorandum or relief requested in a brief.

concur To agree with the majority opinion.

concurring opinion An opinion in which a judge who agrees with the ultimate result wishes to apply different reasoning from that in the majority opinion.

confirmation letter A letter designed to create a record or restate the content of the original oral communication.

count The cause of action in the complaint.

counterclaim A claim made by the defendant against the plaintiff—not a defense, but a new claim for damages, as if the defendant were the plaintiff in a separate suit; a countersuit bought by the defendant against the plaintiff

court reporter Individual who transcribes the court proceedings and certifies their authenticity.

cover letter A standard form letter identifying information such as document filings.

cross-claim lawsuit A lawsuit against a party of the same side; plaintiffs or defendants suing each other (defendant versus defendant or plaintiff versus plaintiff).

cumulative sentence A sentence that conveys the information in a comprehensive manner.

D

dash A punctuation mark longer than a hyphen, which is used for limited purposes, such as separating the segments of a two-part sentence.

database A collection of information used in computer systems to provide access to related fields of interest.

de novo Standard appellate review where the appellate court reviews the facts and law independent of the trial court's decision.

deadline date A certain date by which a request or demand should be fulfilled.

defendant/plaintiff table List of the cases alphabetically by the defendant first or a table of cases listing the name of the case both ways.

demand letter A letter requesting action on a legal matter.

deponent The party or witness who is questioned in a deposition.

deposition on written questions A deposition based on written questions submitted in advance to a party; only those questions are answered, with no follow-up questions allowed.

descriptive word index A subject index that provides a researcher with a quick survey of specific key numbers, often from several topics, which apply to a given subject area.

dictum A statement made by the court in a case that is beyond what is necessary to reach the final decision.

digest A collection of all the headnotes from an associated series of volumes, arranged alphabetically by topic and by key number or summary of testimony with indexed references of a deposition.

disclaimer A term which limits claim or denial.

discovery The pretrial investigation process authorized and governed by the rules of civil procedure; the process of investigation and collection of evidence by litigants.

discovery Process in which the opposing parties obtain information about the case from each other; the process of investigation and collection of evidence by litigants.

discussion and analysis The heart of the memorandum, which presents the legal analysis with supporting citations.

disposition Appears at the end of the opinion and tells the reader how the court handled the lower court decision.

dissent Opinion in which a judge disagrees with the result reached by the majority.

dissenting opinion An opinion outlining the reasons for the dissent, which often critiques the majority and any concurring opinions.

docket number The number assigned by the court to the case for its own administrative purposes.

duces tecum A deposition notice requiring the deponent/witness to "bring with him" specified documents or things.

E

editing To delete, eliminate, or change the text of a legal document.

ellipsis A form of punctuation that indicates the elimination of text from an extended quote.

embedded citation A citation placed within a sentence.

en banc decisions Decisions by the court as a whole because of their legal significance.

equitable relief A remedy that is other than money damages, such as refraining from or performing a certain act; nonmonetary remedies fashioned by the court using standards of fairness and justice. Injunction and specific performance are types of equitable relief.

error of fact Legal standard on appeal alleging the facts accepted by the trial court judge are incorrect.

error of law Standard of review on appeal alleging error of the court in applying the standards of the law.

ex parte A communication between one party in a lawsuit and the judge.

exclamation point A form of punctuation used to highlight something extraordinary.

F

fact pleading A style of pleading that requires you to identify all the facts necessary to allege a valid cause of action.

facts Significant objective information in a case.

flow A quality within or characteristic of the text that moves the reader easily through the text from point to point.

form books Publications that contain complete or partial sample documents, often with sample factual situations and various alternative methods of stating that legal document.

forms Documents that set forth standardized language and are used as a drafting guide.

G

general defenses Specific responses by defendant to plaintiff's complaint.

General Demurrer A responsive pleading filed by a party attacking the legal sufficiency of a complaint.

H

harmless error Standard of review that has not caused legal error requiring reversal of the trial court's decision.

header Text that appears at the top left margin of all subsequent pages, and identifies three elements: the person to whom the letter is addressed; the date of the letter; and the page number.

heading A line or more of text that identifies the party for whom the memorandum was prepared; the person by whom it was prepared; the date of preparation; and the subject matter.

headnote A key-numbered paragraph; an editorial feature in unofficial reporters that summarizes a single legal point or issue in the court opinion.

holding That aspect of a court opinion which directly affects the outcome of the case; it is composed of the reasoning necessary and sufficient to reach the disposition.

hornbooks Scholarly texts.

hyphen A form of punctuation used to draw together two or more words to form a single idea.

I

immaterial fact A fact that is unimportant to the case and its holding.

indefinite pronoun A pronoun that does not specify its object.

independent clause A clause that can stand on its own as a complete sentence.

indexing method Referencing method of the record to assist in identifying the important pieces of information, such as the transcript excerpts and pleadings, which will be used in the various parts of the appellate brief.

informative letter A letters that transmits information.

instructions and definitions A section in many forms of discovery requests that defines terms in the document to avoid confusion.

internal memoranda Objective documents that present all aspects of the legal issues involved in the matter.

internal memorandum of law An internal document that analyzes objectively the legal issues in a client's matter.

interrogatories Discovery tool in the form of a series of written questions that are answered by the party in writing.

interrogatory A discovery tool in the form of a series of written questions that are answered by the party in writing, to be answered under oath.

issue The legal problem presented or point of law or fact on which the appeal is based.

issues or questions presented A section that identifies the legal issues presented in the memorandum of law to the trial court.

J

jargon Legalese.

jump cite Same as a pinpoint citation.

jurisdictional statement Section of the brief that identifies the legal authority that grants the appellate court the right to hear the case.

K

Key Number System A detailed system of classification that currently divides the law into more than 400 separate categories or topics.

KeyCite The Westlaw case updating and validation system, which is similar to Shepard's Citations System.

L

law reviews Periodicals edited by the top students at each law school, featuring scholarly articles by leading authorities and notes on various topics written by the law students themselves.

legal encyclopedia A multivolume compilation that provides in-depth coverage of every area of the law.

legal jargon Legalese.

legal remedy The recovery of money damages in a lawsuit; relief provided by the court to a party to redress a wrong perpetrated by another party.

legalese Language that is characterized by the frequent use of Latin, French, and Old English terms unfamiliar to most present-day vocabularies in legal writing.

legally significant facts Facts that are critical to the analysis of a case.

legislative history The transcripts of the legislative debates leading up to the passage of the bill that became the law or statute.

letter bank A depository for firm letters regarding client cases.

letterhead Standard stationery.

local rules Individual rules for a particular court that supplement the other rules of court.

looseleaf service A service that publishes recently decided court decisions in looseleaf binders, such as *U.S. Law Week*.

M

majority opinion An opinion where more than half of the justices agree with the decision. This opinion is precedent.

mandatory authority Authority that is binding upon the court considering the issue—a statute or regulation from the relevant jurisdiction that applies directly; a case from a higher court in the same jurisdiction that is directly on point; or a constitutional provision that is applicable and controlling.

material fact A fact that is essential to the case and its holding.

memorandum at the request of a judge A persuasive memorandum of legal points requested by the trial court judge.

memorandum in regard to a motion A persuasive memorandum supporting the points and authorities in a motion.

memorandum of law to the trial court An adversarial document filed with the trial court and written to persuade the trial court of a party's position on a disputed point of law.

metaphor A figure of speech that links dissimilar objects, but it is more powerful than a simile in that it equates, rather than compares, the objects.

models Copies of actual complaints, obtained from your firm's files, that have a similar factual foundation.

modifiers Words that describe a subject, verb, or object in a sentence.

motion A procedural request or application presented by the attorney in court.

Motion for More Definite Statement A request by a defendant for additional specificity of plaintiff's complaint.

Motion for Protective Order A motion filed by a party upon whom a discovery request has been made to protect the disclosure of information.

Motion for Sanctions A motion filed by any party to counter alleged violations by another party in the case.

Motion to Compel Discovery A motion filed by a party seeking to force compliance with a discovery request.

Motion to Dismiss A motion that dispenses with the lawsuit because of a legal defense.

N

neutral citation Uniform citation system that contains the name of the case, year of decision, court (postal code) abbreviation, opinion number, and paragraph pinpoint for references.

notice pleading A short and plain statement of the allegations in a lawsuit.

nutshell A paperback series of the law.

O

objective documents Documents that convey information and avoid bias.

official reporter Government publications of court decisions.

opinion letter A letter that renders legal advice.

oral deposition A discovery tool in a question-and-answer format in which the attorney verbally questions a party or witness under oath.

Order Nunc Pro Tunc An entry made by a court now of an event that previously happened and made to have the effect of the former date.

outline The skeleton of a legal argument, advancing from the general to the specific.

outlining A preliminary step in writing that provides a framework for the assignment.

P

parallel citation A citation of a case text found in two or more reporters.

parallel construction Repeating usages to make a point, to suggest either a connection or a contrast.

parentheses A form of punctuation that unites cohesive passages.

parenthetical phrase A phrase that supplements or adds information to a complete thought.

passive voice A verb form in which the subject of the sentence is the object of the action.

per curiam decision A decision that reflects agreement of all the judges on the correct disposition of the case.

periodic sentence A sentence that conveys the information at the end of the paragraph.

permissive counterclaim A counterclaim that is not required to be filed with a complaint because the facts do not arise out of the same set of circumstances as the complaint.

persuasive authority All nonmandatory primary authority.

petitioner Name designation of a party filing an appeal.

pincite Same as pinpoint citation.

pinpoint citation (or jump cite) The page reference in a citation that directs the reader to the cited material in the case.

pleadings Formal documents filed with the court that establish the claims and defenses of the parties to the lawsuit; the complaint, answer to complaint, and reply.

pocket parts Annual supplements to digests.

point headings Headings that outline and identify the argument in the section.

prayer for relief A summation at the end of a pleading, which sets forth the demands by a party in the lawsuit.

precedential value The force that a cited authority exerts upon the judge's reasoning.

precise Accuracy of written communication.

precision Legal writing that clearly and definitely conveys the point of the document.

primary authority The original text of the sources of law, such as constitutions, court opinions, statutes, and administrative rules and regulations.

prior proceedings The previous procedural history of a case.

process server A person statutorily authorized to serve legal documents such as complaints.

pronoun ambiguity Lack of clarity that results from an unclear indication about the noun to which the pronoun refers.

Q

query A string of key terms or words used in a computer search.

questions presented Section of the appellate brief that identifies the grounds upon which the decision of the trial court is questioned.

R

reasoning The court's rationale that sets forth the legal principles the court relied upon in reaching its decision.

record Documentation of the trial court, including pleadings, physical evidence, transcript, and decision of the trial court.

recusal Voluntary disqualification by a judge due to a conflict of interest or the appearance of one.

redacted Eliminated information or material from a legal document due to privacy and security matters.

redundancy The repeated use of the same point or concept.

reference line A line of text that appears below the address block, and identifies the subject matter of the letter.

regional reporters Reporters that contain the cases of all the states in a particular geographical area.

relevant fact A fact that is significant to a case and its holding.

remanded Disposition in which the appellate court sends the case back to the lower court for further action.

reply brief Short responsive brief of the appellant to the appellee's brief.

reporters Hardbound volumes containing judicial decisions.

request for admissions A document that provides the drafter with the opportunity to conclusively establish selected facts prior to trial.

request for medical examination Form of discovery that requests a medical examination of an opposing party in a lawsuit.

respondent Name designation of the party responding to an appeal.

restatement A recitation of the common law in a particular legal subject.

restrictive phrase A phrase that specifies or restricts the application of something.

retainer letter A form of correspondence that sets forth the agreement and relationship between the attorney and client.

reversed Disposition in which the appellate court disagrees with trial court.

rhythm A pattern of writing conveyed through word choice and word placement in the sentence.

rule of law Sources of law that control the issue.

rules of court The rules that govern the litigation process in civil and criminal proceedings.

run-on sentence A sentence that contains two independent clauses that are not joined by a conjunction.

S

salutation A greeting that appears below the reference line.

secondary authority Authority that analyzes the law such as a treatise, encyclopedia, or law review article.

semicolon A form of punctuation used to indicate a break in thought, though of a different sort than that indicated by a comma.

sentence fragment A group of words that lacks necessary grammatical information, such as a verb, that would make it a complete sentence.

service of process The procedure by which a defendant is notified by a process server of a lawsuit.

session laws The second format in which new statutes appear as a compilation of the slip laws.

Shepardizing Using Shepard's verification and updating system for cases, statutes, and other legal resources.

short citation form Citation used after the complete citation is used in the legal document.

short summary of the conclusion A summary that provides the reader with a quick answer to the yes or no questions raised by the issues.

signals Words that introduce additional references to the legal authority cited, such as *see* and *accord*.

signature block Section of the brief for attorney's signature that includes the name, address, bar card identification, fax number, and telephone number.

simile A direct comparison of dissimilar objects, for the purpose of emphasizing a common characteristic.

simple sentence A sentence that has a simple format—subject/verb/object.

slang Informal expressions.

slip law The first format in which a newly signed statute appears.

slip opinion The first format in which a judicial opinion appears.

special defenses Affirmative defenses.

standard of review Guideline the court applies in evaluating the errors on appeal.

stare decisis Decisions from a court with substantially the same set of facts should be followed by that court and all lower courts under it; the judicial process of adhering to prior case decisions; the doctrine of precedent whereby once a court has decided a

specific issue one way in the past, it and other courts in the same jurisdiction are obligated to follow that earlier decision in deciding cases with similar issues in the future.

star-paging A practice that enables the reader to identify the page breaks in one reporter by reviewing the decision as reprinted in another reporter.

state supreme court The final and highest court in many states.

statement of facts Section of a brief that sets forth the significant facts and information needed to analyze the issues presented.

statement of the case Section of the appellate brief that sets forth the procedural history of the case.

string citations List of citations in the brief following a point of law cited.

structured enumeration Identification of each point in a sentence sequentially.

subheadings Headings that identify the subpoints in an argument section.

subordinate clause A clause that cannot stand on its own as a complete sentence.

subpoena A document that is served upon an individual under authority of the court, and orders the person to appear at a certain place and certain time for a deposition, or suffer the consequences; an order issued by the court clerk directing a person to appear in court.

subsequent history History of a case on appeal.

summons The notice to appear in court, notifying the defendant of the plaintiff's complaint.

supplemental pleading A pleading that adds to a pleading without deleting prior information.

supplemental response Additional response to previously filed discovery because of newly found information.

supra Above.

syllabus A short paragraph summary in the official reporter identifying issue, procedural history, and ruling of the court; an editorial feature in unofficial reporters that summarizes the court's decision.

synopsis A short paragraph summary prepared by the publisher in unofficial reporters that identifies the issue, the procedural history, and the ruling of the court in the instant case.

T

table of authorities Section of the appellate brief that identifies the cases, statutes, constitutional provisions and all other primary and secondary authority contained within the brief.

table of cases Lists of all the cases whose text appears in the associated volumes.

table of contents Road map of the appellate brief, which includes the section headings and corresponding page numbers in the brief.

terms of art   Words that are commonly used in the legal profession and have an accepted meaning.

texts   One-volume treatises.

title page   Cover page of the brief.

tone   The way a writer communicates a point of view.

topic sentence   The first sentence of the paragraph, which introduces an idea.

transactional documents   Documents that define property rights and performance obligations.

transcript   Written account of a trial court proceeding or deposition.

transition   The writer's ability to move the reader from paragraph to paragraph.

transitional function   Moving the reader though the material they are reading in an orderly progression.

transmittal letter   A type of confirmation letter that accompanies information sent to a designated party.

treatise   A scholarly study of one area of the law.

trial courts   Courts that hear all cases and are courts of general jurisdiction.

U

unpublished case   A case decided by a court that is not published in a reporter because it does not set precedent.

unsolicited memorandum anticipating legal issues   Memorandum of law prepared by one of the parties to the case in support of an anticipated legal issue.

V

vacated   Disposition in which an appellate court voids the decision of the lower court.

verbosity   The use of an excessive number of words, or excessively complicated words, to make a point.

verification   Acknowledgment by a party of the truthfulness of the information contained within a document.

video deposition   Videotaped version of the oral deposition; the videotape serves as an additional method of preserving the testimony, in addition to the transcript.

voice   The sound heard in the mind of the reader, or the impression created by virtue of the words chosen.

W

Westclip   An electronic clipping service used on Westlaw that monitors legal developments.

words and phrases   An index to a digest that construes a judicial term.

writ of *certiorari*   Request for appeal where the Court has the discretion to grant or deny it; granting of petition, by the U.S. Supreme Court, to review a case.

Case Index

A

Ascot v. Wellington Company, 272

B

Bakke v. California Board of Regents, 335
Bradshaw v. Unity Marine Corporation,
    Inc., 142
Brown v. Board of Education, 335
Busch v. Flangas, 96

C

Carlino v. Gloucester City High School, 241
Catellier v. Depco, Inc., 326
Cicio v. City of New York, 6
Clement v. Public Service Electric and Gas
    Co., 118
Crawford v. Dammann, 324

D

Dallas Anesthesiology Associates, P.A. v.
    Texas Anesthesia Group, P.A., 323
DeSilva v. DiLeonardi, 335
Dube v. Eagle Global Logistics, 183
Duran v. St. Luke's Hospital, 70, 72, 74–77,
    78, 89, 90–91, 94

E

Ernst Haas Studio v. Palm Press, Inc., 266

F

Federal Intermediate Credit v. Kentucky Bar
    Association, 158
Frith v. State, 158

G

Gilmore v. Gonzales, 66
Glassalum Engineering Corp. v. 392208
    Ontario Ltd., 55
Gordon v. Green, 155

H

Henderson v. State, 140
Hurlbert v. Gordon, 332

I

In Re Ferguson, 205
In Re Fletcher, 95
In Re Gershater, 220
In Re Hawkins, 142
Independent Towers of Washington v. State
    of Washington, 305
Insulated Panel Company v. The Industrial
    Commission, 299
Iowa Supreme Court Board of Professional
    Ethics and Conduct v. Lane, 162

J

Jacobellis v. Ohio, 122

M

Mendez v. Draham, 122
Miranda v. Arizona, 6
Missouri v. Jenkins, 289

P

Peerless Wall and Window Coverings, Inc. v.
    Synchronics, Inc., 46
PGA Tour, Inc. v. Martin, 183
Philadelphia Gear Corp. v. Swath
    International, Ltd., 200, 268
Politico v. Promus Hotels, Inc., 137
Pony Lake School District 30 v. State
    Committee for the Reorganization of
    School Districts, 324
Precision Specialty Metal, Inc. v. United
    States, 185

R

Roe v. Wade, 335

S

Smith v. United Transportation Union Local
    No. 81, 179
State Ex. Rel. Bar Association v.
    Zakrzewski, 233
Stephens v. Kemp, 54

T

Taylor v. Belger Cartage Service, Inc., 251
Taylor v. Chubb Group of Insurance
    Companies, 289
Toledo v. Ordway, 213
Tory v. Cochran, 9, 78, 83, 95

U

United States v. Booker, 59, 62, 63, 93,
    94, 97
United States v. Dunkel, 305
United States v. Kouri-Perez, 287
United States v. Leahy, 78, 79, 81
United States v. Molina-Tarzon, 322
United States v. Nixon, 335

Y

Yankee Candle Company, Inc. v. Bridgewater
    Candle Company, LLC, 267
Young v. District of Columbia, 39, 44

Subject Index

A

A fortiori, 105
Abuse of discretion, 323
Accord, 182
Active voice, 135–136
Address block, 196–197
Adjectives, 134
Administrative rules and regulations,
    18–23, 26
Advance sheets, 9
Adverbs, 134
Adversarial documents, 106
Advisory letter, 193
affect; effect, 156
Affirmed, 78
Alert, 64
Allegations, 254
A.L.R. Digest, 13
A.L.R. Federal, 12
A.L.R. series, 12–13
ALWD Manual, 6, 170–171, 172
Am. Jur. 2d, 26, 29
Ambiguity, 152–153
Amended pleading, 267
American Jurisprudence, 2d, 26, 29
American Law Reports (A.L.R.), 12–13
Amicus brief, 335
Amicus curiae, 335
and/or, 156
Annotated codes, 17
Annotation, 12–15
Answer, 261–265
Apostrophe, 133
Appellant, 320
Appellant's brief, 335
Appellate brief, 71, 118, 317–349
    amicus brief, 335
    appellant's brief, 335
    appellee's brief, 335
    appendix, 334
    argument, 332–333
    certificate of compliance, 334
    certificate of interested parties, 328
    certificate of service, 334
    citations, 329
    conclusion, 333
    defined, 319
    format requirements, 324–326
    jurisdictional statement, 330
    notice of appeal, 320, 321
    parties, 319–320
    practical considerations, 338
    procedural rules, 318–319, 320
    questions presented, 330
    record, 321–322
    reply brief, 335
    sample brief, 340–346
    signature block, 334
    standard of review, 322–324
    statement of facts, 330–331

statement of the case, 330
summary of argument, 331–332
table of authorities, 328–329
table of contents, 328
title page, 327–328
writing the brief, 336
Appellate courts, 4
Appellate process, 319
Appellate rules, 318, 320
Appellee, 320
Appellee's brief, 335
Appendix, 334
Argument
    appellate brief, 332–333
    trial memorandum, 305–307
Atlantic Reporter, 8
Attorney/client privilege, 225
Audience, 106
Audience analysis, 194–195
Authorization letter, 201

B

Background interrogatory, 276–277
Bar card numbers, 257
bcc, 201
Black letter law, 290
Blind copy (bcc), 201
Block quote, 130, 183
Block style letter format, 201
Bluebook: A Uniform System of Citation,
    The, 6, 169–170, 171, 172
Body
    appellate brief, 332–333
    complaint, 252–255, 256
    letter, 198
    paragraph, 137
    pleading, 250
Boilerplate, 116
Boolean logic, 65
Brackets, 131–132
Brevity, 148
Brief, 118
Brief bank, 228
Brief in support of motion, 296. *See also*
    Trial memorandum
Briefing a case. *See* Case brief

C

California Reporter, 9
Capitalization, 140
Caption, 73
    complaint, 252
    interrogatories, 274
    pleadings, 249
    trial memoranda, 299, 300
Case brief, 89–95
    disposition, 95

facts, 92–94
holding, 94–95
identification of case, 89
issue, 92
parties, 91–92
practical consideration, 96–97
practical tips, 96
prior proceedings, 94
reading the case, 89
reasoning, 95
updating the case, 89
Case law, 26. *See also* Finding case law
Case-specific interrogatories, 277
Catch-all conclusionary interrogatory, 279
cc, 200–201
Cell phones, 241
Certificate of compliance, 334
Certificate of interested parties, 328
Certificate of service
    appellate brief, 334
    interrogations, 279
    pleadings, 250–251
    trial memorandum, 307–309
Certiorari, 105
C.F.R., 23
Chronological development, 162
Citation, 6–8, 168–190
    administrative rules and regulations, 177
    A.L.R. annotations, 178–179
    ALWD Manual, 170–171, 172
    appellate brief, 329
    Attorney General opinions, 178
    basics, 173–174
    Bluebook, 169–170, 171, 172
    constitutions, 177
    court rules, 177
    depublished cases, 185, 186
    electronic sources, 185
    embedded, 180
    federal reporters, 175–176
    id., 180
    incorporating, into legal writing, 179–181
    law reviews, 178
    legal dictionaries, 179
    pinpoint, 186
    practical considerations, 187
    recent case decisions, 174
    restatements, 178
    secondary sources, 178–179
    sentences, in, 179–180
    short citation form, 180–181
    state subsequent history guides, 175
    statutes, 176–177
    string citing, 181
    subsequent history, 174–175
    supra, 180
    uniform citation system, 171–173
    unpublished cases, 185
cite; site, 157
C.J.S., 26, 27–28
Clarity, 104, 148–149

Clause, 134
Cliché, 154–155
Client opinion letter, 217–218
Closing, 199, 200, 221
Closing sentence, 138
Code of Federal Regulations, 23
Codes, 16
Collection letter, 205–207
Colloquialism, 155
Colon, 130
Comma, 127–128
Compare, 182
Complaint, 252–261
    allegations, 254
    body, 252–255, 256
    caption, 252
    checklist, 259, 261
    introductory paragraph, 252, 253
    multiple causes of action, 254
    parties, 253
    prayer for relief, 255
    restatement of allegations, 254, 255
    sample, 259–260
    service of process, 258
    signature block, 256–257
    verification, 257–258
Complex sentence, 134
Complex word, 157
Compound sentence, 129, 134–135
Computer-assisted legal research, 61–66
    Internet. *See* Internet
    Lexis, 64–65
    Westlaw, 64
Conclusion, 108
    appellate brief, 333
    internal memo of law, 234, 237
    trial memorandum, 307
Concur, 78
Concurring opinion, 78, 82
Confirmation letter, 193–194
Constitution, 17, 23, 26, 177
Consumer demand letter, 207–209
Consumer protection letter, 207
Contractions, 152
Copy (cc), 200–201
Corpus Juris Secundum, 26, 27–28
Count, 254
Counterclaim, 247
Court reporter, 322
Court rules, 17–19
Court system
    appellate courts, 4
    federal circuits/district courts, 11
    state supreme court, 4
    trial courts, 4
    U.S. Supreme Court, 9–11
    websites, 32
Cross-claim, 247, 262
Cross-complaint, 262
Cumulative sentence, 159, 160
Cyberspace discovery, 290

D

Dash, 132
Database, 63
De novo, 323
Deadline date, 206
Defendant/plaintiff table, 46, 53
Definite pronoun, 142
Definitions, 275, 276
Definitive approach, 161
Demand letter, 205
Demurrer, 105

Deponent, 283
Deposition, 283–285
    basics, 283–284
    digest, 285
    notice of intention to take oral, 284, 285
    preparation, 285
    subpoena, 284
    summary, 285
Deposition on written questions, 283
Deposition summary, 285
Depublished cases, 185, 186
Descriptive word index, 46, 47–48
Dictum, 82
Digest, 41
Digest system, 38–54
    defendant/plaintiff table, 46, 53
    descriptive word index, 46, 47–48
    digest page, 43
    digest topics, 44
    headnote, 39
    key number system, 38–41, 45
    partial index page, 42
    pocket parts, 54
    table of cases, 46, 52
    words and phrases, 46, 49
Digesting a deposition, 285
Disclaimer, 217
Discovery, 272–293
    defined, 273
    deposition, 283–285
    discoverable information, 273
    electronic data, 290
    interrogatories, 274–281. *See also*
        Interrogatories
    motions, 286–289
    practical considerations, 290
    request for admissions, 281–282
    request for medical examination, 283
    request for production, 282, 283
Discovery documents, 119
Discovery motions, 286–289
Discussion and analysis, 233–234, 235–237
Disposition, 73, 74–77
Dissent, 78, 82
Dissenting opinion, 78, 82
Docket number, 73
Documents, types of, 114–119
Doublets, 157
Duces tecum, 105, 284

E

E-factor
    cell phones, 241
    citing cases from electronic sources, 185
    cyberspace discovery, 290
    e-mail, 163
    electronic filing of briefs, 310
    faxing, 220
    grammar check, 143
    Internet. *See* Internet
    spell check, 122
    text messaging, 163
    word-counting programs, 337, 338
E-filing, 310–311
E-mail, 163
Editing, 120–121
EEOC Decisions, 23
e.g., 156, 181
Electronic data discovery, 290
Electronic document and signature, 308
Ellipsis, 132
Embedded citation, 180
En banc, 78

Equitable relief, 255
Error of fact, 323
Error of law, 323
etc., 156
Ex parte, 105
Exclamation point, 133
Expert witnesses, 277–278

F

Fact pleading, 247
Facts, 92–94
Fair debt collection statutory letter, 206
Faxing, 220
Federal Appendix, 176
Federal Cases, 11
Federal circuits/district courts, 11
Federal court decisions, 11–12
Federal Register, 19
Federal regulations, 19, 23
Federal Reporter, 11, 175
Federal Rules Decisions, 12, 176
Federal Rules of Civil Procedure (FRCP),
    19, 247
Federal Rules of Criminal Procedure, 19
Federal Securities Law Reporter, 16
Federal Supplement, 11, 175–176
Fee splitting, 289
Filing of pleading, 251
Finding administrative regulations and
    decisions, 19–23
Finding case law, 6–16
    A.L.R. series, 12–13
    citations, 6–8
    federal court decisions, 11–12
    looseleaf services, 13, 16
    National Reporter System, 8–9
    official reporters, 8
    unofficial reporters, 8–13
    U.S. Supreme Court decisions, 9–11
Finding statutes and constitutions, 16–19
    annotated codes, 17
    codes, 16
    constitution, 17
    court rules, 17–19
    legislative history, 17
    local ordinances, 17
    session laws, 16
    slip laws, 16
Flow, 149
For your information (FYI) letters, 193
Form books, 255
Forms, 116
FRCP, 19, 247
FYI letters, 193

G

Gender-neutral terminology, 154
General demurrer, 92
Grammar, 140–143
    grammar check feature, 143
    preposition, 142
    pronoun, 141–142
    split infinitive, 143
    subject-verb agreement, 140–141
Grammar check, 143

H

Harmless error, 323
Header, 199

Heading
    internal memo of law, 229–230
    point, 305, 332
    subheading, 162, 305
Headnote, 39
Health Insurance Portability and
    Accountability Act (HIPAA), 215
Hierarchy of the law, 23–26
HIPAA, 215
Holding, 82, 94–95
Hyphen, 132

I

i.e., 156
Immaterial fact, 94
Indefinite pronoun, 141, 142
Independent clause, 134
Index to Annotations, 13
Indexing method, 331
Informative letter, 193
Instructions and definitions, 274, 276
Inter alia, 105
Interior quotation, 130
Internal memo summarizing information,
    225, 226
Internal memorandum of law, 227–228,
    229–241
    conclusion section, 234, 237
    discussion and analysis, 233–234,
        235–237
    heading, 229–230
    IRAC method, 234
    multiple-issue memorandum, 231
    post-writing considerations, 237
    preliminary considerations, 228–229
    sample memorandum, 237–241
    short summary of the conclusion,
        231, 232
    statement of facts, 232–233
    statement of issues presented, 230
Internal office memorandum, 115, 224–245
    internal memo summarizing information,
        225, 226
    internal memorandum of law, 227–228.
        See also Internal memorandum of law
    interoffice memo, 228
    memorandum documenting
        information, 227
    post-writing considerations, 237
    practical considerations, 242
    preliminary considerations, 228–229
Internet
    Boolean logic, 65
    court websites, 32
    limitations/constraints, 33
    online updating, 57–61
    research, 65–66
Interoffice memo, 228
Interrogatories, 274–281
    background information, 276
    caption, 274
    catch-all conclusionary interrogatory, 279
    certificate of service, 279
    content of pleadings, 278–279
    defined, 274
    definitions, 276
    expert witnesses, 277–278
    instructions, 276
    introductory paragraphs, 275
    responses to, 279–281
    signature block, 279
    specific case information, 277
    title, 275

Introduction, 159–160
IRAC method, 107–108, 161, 234
Irregardless, 157
Issue, 92, 108
Issues or questions presented, 299, 301

J

Jargon, 104, 155
Jump cite, 186
Jurisdictional statement, 330

K

Key number system, 38–41, 45
KeyCite, 59, 61

L

Laches, 105
Law reviews, 30
Lawyers' Edition, 9
Legal correspondence, 192–223
    advisory letter, 193
    audience analysis, 194–195
    authorization letter, 201
    client, to, 194
    client opinion letter, 217–218
    collection letter, 205–207
    confirmation letter, 193–194
    consumer demand letter, 207–209
    consumer protection letter, 207
    court, to, 195
    demand letter, 205
    informative letter, 193
    letter. *See* Letter
    letter notifying of intention to litigate,
        207–210
    letter requesting information, 201, 203
    medical information, 215–216
    medical malpractice cases, 211–216
    opinion letter, 216–220
    opposing counsel, to, 194–195
    practical considerations, 220–221
    response to demand letter, 210–211
    response to notice of litigation, 211
    retainer letter, 201, 204
    third-party opinion letter, 218, 219
    transmittal letter, 201, 202
Legal encyclopedia, 26
Legal jargon, 155
Legal periodicals, 31
Legal publishers, 7
Legal remedy, 255
Legal research
    computer-assisted research, 61–66. *See*
        also Computer-assisted research
    digest system. *See* Digest system
    finding administrative regulations and
        decisions, 19–23
    finding case law. *See* Finding
        case law
    finding statutes and constitutions. *See*
        Finding statutes and constitutions
    hierarchy of the law, 23–26
    how to begin, 66
    Internet, 65
    overview, 3–4
    secondary sources, 26–31. *See also*
        Secondary sources
    updating the law, 54–61

when to stop, 66–67
Legal writing, 103–125
    ambiguity, 152–153
    brevity, 148
    clarity, 148–149
    cliché, 154–155
    colloquialism, 155
    contractions, 152
    defining/researching issues, 107–108
    definitive approach, 161
    document length, 109
    documents, types of, 114–119
    editing, 120–121
    format style, 109
    identifying the purpose, 106–107
    informal organization, 114
    introduction, 159–160
    IRAC method, 107–108
    jargon, 155
    logical development, 161–162
    mechanics of construction. *See*
        Mechanics of construction
    metaphor, 152
    misconceptions about, 157–158
    misplaced modifiers, 153–154
    misused words, 156–157
    outline, 109, 114, 115
    parallel construction, 150–151
    plagiarism, 158
    plain English, 105
    politically correct terminology, 154
    positive statements, 160–161
    post-writing considerations, 119
    practical considerations, 122–123, 163
    precision, 149
    prewriting considerations, 106–108
    proofreading, 121
    quotation, 182–187
    redundancy, 155
    revising, 119–120
    rhythm, 149–150
    sexism, 154
    signals, 181–182
    simile, 152
    slang, 155
    structural enumeration, 160
    terms of art, 105
    time constraints, 109
    tone, 151–152
    topic sentence, 159
    verbosity, 155–156
    voice, 149–151
    word choice (thesaurus), 156
    write in third person, 158
Legalese, 104, 105, 155
Legally significant facts, 233
Legislative history, 17
Letter, 15, 195. *See also* Legal
    correspondence
    address block, 196–197
    blind copy (bcc), 201
    body, 198
    closing, 199, 200, 221
    copy (cc), 200–201
    date, 196
    formatting, 201
    header, 199
    letterhead, 195
    reference line, 197, 198
    referencing initials, 199–200
    salutation, 197–198
    signature block, 199, 200
Letter bank, 205
Letter notifying of intention to litigate,
    207–210